PATRIOTS

PATRIOTS

THE VIETNAM WAR
REMEMBERED FROM ALL SIDES

Christian G. Appy

Viking

VIKING

Published by the Penguin Group
Penguin Group (USA) Inc., 375 Hudson Street,
New York, New York 10014, U.S.A.
Penguin Books Ltd, 80 Strand,
London WC2R 0RL, England
Penguin Books Australia Ltd, 250 Camberwell Road, Camberwell,
Victoria 3124, Australia
Penguin Books Canada Ltd, 10 Alcorn Avenue,
Toronto, Ontario, Canada M4V 3B2
Penguin Books India (P) Ltd, 11 Community Centre, Panchsheel Park, New Delhi—110 017, India
Penguin Books (N.Z.) Ltd, Cnr Rosedale and Airborne Roads, Albany, Auckland, New Zealand
Penguin Books (South Africa) (Pty) Ltd, 24 Sturdee Avenue,
Rosebank, Johannesburg 2196, South Africa

Penguin Books Ltd, Registered Offices:
Harmondsworth, Middlesex, England

First published in 2003 by Viking Penguin,
a member of Penguin Group (USA) Inc.

Grateful acknowledgment is made for permission to reprint excerpts from the following copyrighted works:
"I-Feel-Like-I'm-Fixin'-to-Die-Rag," lyrics by Joe McDonald. ©1965, renewed 1993 by Alkatraz Corner Music Co. (BMI). Used by permission.
"Ohio" by Neil Young. ©1970 (renewed) Cotillion Music, Inc., and Broken Arrow Music. All rights reserved. Used by permission of Warner Bros. Publications U.S. Inc., Miami, Florida.

Library of Congress Cataloging-in-Publication Data

Appy, Christian G.
Patriots : the Vietnam War remembered from all sides / Christian G. Appy.
p. cm.
Includes index.
ISBN 0-670-03214-X (alk. paper)
1. Vietnamese Conflict, 1961–1975—Personal narratives. I. Title.

DS559.5 .A66 2003
959.704'3'0922—dc21
2002034882

This book is printed on acid-free paper.

Printed in the United States of America

Designed by Jaye Zimet

1 3 5 7 9 10 8 6 4 2

For Shirley K. Appy

CONTENTS

PART FOUR: THE TURNING POINT (1968–70)

PREFACE

Five years ago I began traveling the United States and Vietnam to interview people from all sides of a war that pitted the two nations against each other, created bitter hostilities within both, aroused global alarm, and unleashed the most costly and ruinous destruction of any conflict since World War II. I wanted to explore the vast range of war-related memories that rarely appear together between the covers of a single book.

In the United States today, "Vietnam" is shorthand for our longest and most divisive foreign war, and it is often evoked as little more than a political or media cliché, a glib reference to a controversial war that ended badly, a time of domestic turmoil, a history to be avoided in the future. For many Americans, the war's meaning has been winnowed down to the Vietnam Veterans Memorial in Washington, D.C., where we stand in silence, filled with emotion, but unsure how to move beyond our private reflections to a broader engagement with this daunting subject. And now that two of every five Americans were born after the fighting ended, a growing number of our citizens draw most of their reflections from Hollywood movies about U.S. combat soldiers that tell us almost nothing of how the war began, why it bred so much dissent, or why it lasted so long.

What might happen to our conception of the Vietnam War if we simply began to hear the accounts of American veterans alongside the memories of Vietnamese who fought with and against them? What if we witnessed those distant jungle firefights through the eyes of people who regarded the battlefield as home and called this epic struggle "The American War"? How might understanding be further enlarged if we listened to former policy makers who participated in the decision making that expanded and prolonged the war, and the generals charged with executing those policies? And what if we took into account the journalists who covered the war, the antiwar activists who tried to stop it, the nurses, medics, and doctors who treated its casualties, and the almost unlimited variety of people whose lives were swept up in this complex, enormous cataclysm that killed some three million people?

These questions took me on a journey through twenty-five American states and the length and breadth of Vietnam—from a Boston suburb to a trailer park in Montana, a hamlet in Cu Chi to a Senate office in Washington, a small mining town in Appalachia to the Presidential Palace in Hanoi, "Little Saigon" in Westminster, California, to the old Saigon now called Ho Chi Minh City.

By the end I had interviewed 350 people. Some are prominent—the four-star generals William Westmoreland and Vo Nguyen Giap; President Lyndon Johnson's national security adviser Walt Rostow; diplomat Nguyen Thi Binh; Pentagon analyst turned antiwar activist Daniel Ellsberg; Nixon chief of staff Alexander Haig; senator and former POW John McCain; filmmaker Oliver Stone; and writers Tim O'Brien and Le Minh Khue. But most of the people in this book are less well known. We meet, for example, Henry Prunier, an American who parachuted into Vietnam in 1945 to train Ho Chi Minh's guerrilla fighters; Luyen Nguyen, a South Vietnamese "lost commando" imprisoned in Hanoi for twenty-one years; Roger Donlon, a Green Beret captain who received the war's first Medal of Honor; Sylvia Lutz Holland, a nurse who treated hundreds of casualties including a mortally wounded colleague; Le Cao Dai, a North Vietnamese doctor who operated on patients in a jungle hospital under a small light powered by a bicycle generator; Anne Morrison Welsh, whose husband burned himself to death to protest the war; Barry Zorthian, a public affairs officer who conducted daily press briefings in Saigon; and Luu Huy Chao, a MiG pilot who flew dogfights against American jets in the skies over North Vietnam.

Since the 1960s, thousands of books have been published about the war. Important as many of them are, most focus on a particular topic or group of historical actors. We have memoirs and novels by American veterans, studies of U.S. policy makers, military histories, chronicles of the antiwar movement, and a variety of Vietnamese accounts. Although we almost instinctively divide the war into separate categories, each individual's experience was, in fact, inextricably connected to those of many others about which he or she knew little if anything. Bringing them together allows us to envision the war's full scale and significance.

It is not, however, an easy stretch to make. Even in Vietnam, where the war's history is more evident, it has largely been relegated to museums, memorials, tourist sites, and souvenir shops. On street corners in Hanoi and Ho Chi Minh City, children selling postcards also hawk two superb novels about the war—Bao Ninh's *The Sorrow of War* and Graham Greene's *The Quiet American*—but virtually all copies are in English and meant for tourists. Within an hour of Ho Chi Minh City you can visit the famous Cu Chi tunnels where Viet Cong guerrillas once ate, slept, took care of their wounded, planned attacks, and hid from American bombs. You are invited to scramble through underground chambers specially enlarged to accommodate Western physiques.

Many American tourists I met in Vietnam reported with amazement on the friendliness of the Vietnamese, how apparently lacking in war-related bitterness they are, how successfully they seem to have put the war behind them. These are important, if partial, observations. After all, almost two-thirds of Vietnam's population was born after the Communist victory of 1975. Some Vietnamese worry that younger generations lack sufficient respect for the wartime sacrifices of their elders. A Vietnamese friend told me, with a note of bemused dismay, that *Tuoi Tre (Youth)* newspaper conducted a survey in 2001 asking young people to name their idols, and Bill Gates, the head of Microsoft, nearly outpolled Ho Chi Minh, the founder of the Indochinese Communist Party and virtual father of modern Vietnam.

Stories like that are indicative of the power of the global economy, and in Vietnam's cities it is easy to find other kinds of evidence—four-star hotels, Western fashions, cell phones, and young Vietnamese entrepreneurs, to name but a few. At bottom, however, Vietnam retains a deeply rooted culture with a strong historical consciousness. The great majority of Vietnamese still depend on the land and their families to make a living, and rice farming remains their primary activity. The average monthly income is thirty dollars. Even in the cities family life remains so strong that almost no one lives alone. Family tradition itself is perhaps the most potent carrier of historical consciousness. Every household maintains an ancestral shrine with photographs of parents and grandparents who have died. Because nearly all the men and women in those pictures endured years of war, these shrines are, in effect, family war memorials, constant reminders of Vietnam's embattled past.

Not far from the Cu Chi tunnels tourist attraction is a large war memorial that lists the names of Vietnamese who died only in that relatively small region—about six hundred square miles—while fighting the Americans and their South Vietnamese allies. It contains roughly the same number of names as appear on the Vietnam Veterans Memorial. Had the United States lost the same proportion of its population as Vietnam, the Wall in Washington would include not 58,193 names, but at least twelve million. Almost every Vietnamese family continues to feel the weight of the war's history.

The complex relationship between present-day Vietnam and its history struck me one day while on my way to an appointment with Vietnamese veterans of the American War, where I would ask questions and my companion, Hoang Cong Thuy, would translate. The streets of Ho Chi Minh City were jammed with every conceivable vehicle—motor scooters, cars, buses, trucks, bicycles, and cyclos, all jockeying for position in the morning traffic. With countless horns blaring I had to lean close to catch Thuy's words. We had just turned onto Tran Hung Dao Street, named after a famed thirteenth-century Vietnamese commander. In 1284, three hundred thousand Mongols had stormed down from China to conquer Vietnam. Badly outnumbered, Dao's army had lost several battles. The Vietnamese emperor asked his general if perhaps it would be wiser to capitulate. Dao's response is still well known in Vietnam. "Your Majesty," he said, "if you want to surrender, please have my head cut off first." And so he fought on, leading his troops to victory with a tactic used successfully three centuries earlier by another revered Vietnamese general, Ngo Quyen, against the Chinese. He had his men drive iron-tipped spikes into the Bach Dang River, a tidal waterway near the modern-day city of Haiphong. At high tide, with the spikes submerged, the Vietnamese retreated up river, luring the Mongol boats over the spikes. As the tide began to ebb, the Vietnamese forced the Mongol fleet back onto the exposed spikes, sinking their ships. The enemy was then routed and driven from the country.

Suddenly, the taxi driver slammed on his brakes and a young couple on a motor scooter crashed into our rear. No one was hurt, but a brake light cracked and our driver insisted on immediate compensation. Thuy helped negotiate a settlement and we moved on, looking for topics to lighten the mood. That wasn't hard because, like many Vietnamese, he seemed to prefer talking about the present. We had been together many days before I learned that he had lost two relatives in President Richard Nixon's 1972 "Christmas bombing" of the North Vietnamese capital of Hanoi and its principal port, Haiphong.

So I was somewhat taken aback when, seemingly out of the blue, Thuy turned to me in the taxi and said, "Do you realize we are the only nation on earth that's defeated three out of the five permanent members of the United Nations Security Council?" No, I conceded, it had never occurred to me, but the Vietnamese had indeed driven China, France, and the United States from their land. Thuy's question was a spare and striking evocation of Vietnam's remarkable history and one that made me feel for the first time that I was not in a small, faraway country on the other side of the world, but at an epicenter of global conflict, among a people whose history stretches back two millennia and intersects with that of every great power.

For many Vietnamese, the "Vietnam War" is not a single event, but a long chain of wars for independence against foreign enemies that began in the year 40 when the Trung sisters led the first insurrection against Chinese rule. Not until 1428, after dozens of wars, did Vietnam permanently establish its independence from China. French missionaries began arriving in the seventeenth century, and two centuries later, in 1883, France took formal possession of Vietnam, abolished its name, and divided the nation into three parts. Resistance to French rule grew over the next century and culminated in a brutal eight-year war (1946–54). After a major Vietnamese victory at Dien Bien Phu, it ended with a peace settlement in Geneva. The anti-French war had been led by the Indochinese Communist Party but included many non-Communist nationalists. In the final years of that war, the United States provided massive military aid to the French. From that point on, many Vietnamese viewed the United States as an enemy in their quest for independence and the American War as a direct outgrowth of the war with France.

In 1954 at Geneva, the great powers agreed to divide Vietnam temporarily at the seventeenth parallel. The idea was not to create two separate Vietnams, North and South, but to establish the peaceful conditions that would allow for a nationwide reunification election in 1956. However, those elections were never held as the United States stepped in to build and bolster what it hoped would be a permanent, non-Communist South Vietnam. The Communists retained significant support throughout Vietnam, however, and set their sights on an eventual overthrow of the American-backed regime in Saigon, the capital of the newly created country.

For most Americans, Vietnam was not even a familiar name until the mid-1960s when their nation dramatically escalated its military intervention. Few realized the United States had been involved in Vietnam since the 1940s or that it had presided over the creation of South Vietnam. Instead, they believed their country had entered a war already in progress whose origins were mysterious. American leaders claimed that our troops were needed to help a small, struggling democracy in South Vietnam to maintain its independence from external Communist aggression launched from North Vietnam and engineered by the Soviet Union and Communist China, and that if the United States failed to prevent a Communist takeover of South Vietnam, one country after another would fall under the control of America's Cold War enemies. These arguments had great resonance in American political culture in the 1950s and early '60s, and there was widespread public support for intervention in Vietnam that lasted through years of mounting escalation.

Over time, however, ever more Americans came to believe their leaders had misled and even lied to them about the realities of the war. Many concluded that South Vietnam was neither a democratic nor an independent nation, but a corrupt and unpopular regime entirely dependent on U.S. support; that preserving it was not vital to national security and that the United States was itself acting as an aggressor. Even many who supported the objectives of U.S. policy came to doubt whether they were achievable or worthy of the cost. By the end of the 1960s, the war had become the most unpopular in our history, producing an antiwar movement of unprecedented size.

· SOUTHEAST ASIA *1954–75* ·

Even so, there was no predicting when the war might end. Although American presidents regularly announced steady progress, the fighting only continued, often on the same ground as previous battles, and spread to battlefields in neighboring Cambodia and Laos. Ho Chi Minh often said that the Vietnamese were willing to fight for ten, twenty, even a hundred years, to drive out the Americans and overthrow the U.S.-backed government in Saigon. Such claims were not taken seriously by American leaders who persuaded themselves that eventually they could break the will of the Vietnamese. They never could. Nor did they persuade the American people that they should be willing to wage another ten or twenty years of war in Vietnam.

The South Vietnamese who supported the Saigon government were engaged in a civil war against their own countrymen. A considerable portion of them had allied themselves with the French in the previous war and many were Catholic in a predominantly Buddhist land. Their struggle to build a separate, non-Communist Vietnam cost them more than two hundred thousand lives, but their cause failed to gain widespread allegiance throughout the South. Among those who regarded American support as necessary, few anticipated how massively the United States would intervene, how deeply its presence would antagonize other southerners, and how dependent their own lives would ultimately become on a foreign ally. When the Communists took over in 1975, many who had linked their fates to the United States were not only defeated but abandoned. Eventually, more than seven hundred and fifty thousand Vietnamese made their way to the United States. For those who fled, Vietnam is not just a lost war, but a lost homeland.

Vietnamese sometimes liken the shape of their country to a long carrying pole with baskets of rice attached at each end. The carrying pole, placed across a shoulder, has been used for centuries to haul heavy loads. The two "baskets" of Vietnam—the Red River Delta in the north and the Mekong Delta in the south—are quite literally filled with rice. Joining these low-lying deltas is a long "pole," the narrow curving stretch of mountains and plateaus that extends for almost eight hundred miles between north and south.

The length and thinness of central Vietnam (in one place only forty-five miles across) has posed a formidable challenge to Vietnamese nationalists over the centuries. Foreign rulers had long used the geography of the land to divide and conquer. When the country was divided in 1954, many felt as if the carrying pole had been snapped in two. North Vietnam and its southern allies—the Viet Cong—waged a twenty-one-year campaign to repair the break and reunify the nation.

· SOUTH VIETNAM *1954–75* ·

Most of the fighting took place below the seventeenth parallel in South Vietnam, a war zone of extraordinary geographic and political complexity. On the smallest scale, a great deal of the war can be understood by imagining a few dozen heavily armed men trudging through small Vietnamese hamlets, across muddy rice paddies, over dikes, through tall, sharp elephant grass, into thick jungle, and up into the highlands. These American or South Vietnamese soldiers are patrolling the countryside, hour after hour, in search of the southern guerrillas they call Viet Cong and troops from the North they call NVA (North Vietnamese Army). Days, even weeks, might pass before combat erupts. Most of the time the infantrymen are simply looking and waiting. In the hamlets you might see them interrogating villagers or poking into thatched houses looking for any signs of an enemy presence. Since it is rare to find young men in the villages, they look for weapons or large supplies of rice or documents. Whether they find anything or not, the villagers are unlikely to offer information about the whereabouts of the Communist forces. The villagers could themselves be Viet Cong. (It is almost impossible for the Americans to tell.) If so, late at night some of them might make booby traps or land mines to be placed on the trails near their homes. Perhaps they will use materiel from a few unexploded American bombs and artillery shells that fell in a recent attack, a strike that further fueled their hatred of the South Vietnamese government they call the "puppet" of "American imperialists."

As the patrol moves off into the jungle, the silence is shattered by small arms fire. The platoon has walked into a Viet Cong ambush. As was so often the case, the Americans did not find the enemy until the enemy found them and decided to initiate combat. Twenty miles away at an airbase in Danang or offshore on an aircraft carrier in the South China Sea, word arrives that an American unit has made contact. Several F-4 Phantom jets are scrambled. Within minutes they catch sight of a small forward observation plane marking a spot in the jungle with a flare. There is a deafening roar as the jets sweep in and drop napalm and bombs on the target.

The guerrillas have learned to anticipate the likelihood of an air strike and may have disengaged quickly to scurry deeper into the jungle or into an underground bunker. Or perhaps they continue to "cling to the belt" of their enemy, a common guerrilla tactic. Occasionally, combatants on both sides are caught in the destruction that rains down from above, their fates entangled by forces beyond their control. Survivors are left to evacuate their wounded, the guerrillas to the nearest jungle hospitals, the Americans onto medical evacuation helicopters that often put casualties into field hospitals in a matter of minutes.

This small scene only begins to suggest the range of combat-related experiences the war encompassed. For every U.S. infantryman or "grunt" in the field, there were seven or eight Americans playing different roles, some of them in quite distant locations. From an air base as far away as Guam, B-52 pilots flew twelve-hour, round-trip missions to bomb targets in South Vietnam. From bases in Thailand, U.S. jets bombed North Vietnam, Laos, and Cambodia. The offshore destroyers and aircraft carriers used Subic Bay in the Philippines as their home port. From bases in Japan and Okinawa, hundreds of thousands of U.S. troops were channeled into the war zone. For one-week R and Rs—rest and recuperation breaks—American servicemen were flown to cities like Hong Kong, Taipei, Bangkok, and Sydney. Some of these cities provided much more than entertainment. The United States persuaded, and in several cases paid for, a handful of nations to enter the war on behalf of the South Vietnamese government. South Korea, Thailand, Australia, New Zealand, and the Philippines supplied a total of more than three hundred thousand troops who fought in Vietnam.

Of course, the Communist forces had their own vital supply lines, sanctuaries, and foreign allies. In the early years of the war, the Viet Cong acquired many of their weapons by raiding South Vietnamese military posts or taking them from enemy dead on the battlefield. They also relied on local villagers for food and cover. As the war escalated, however, they became increasingly dependent on weapons and supplies carried on bikes and trucks from North Vietnam. This materiel flowed south on an elaborate network of footpaths and roads that became familiar to Americans as the Ho Chi Minh Trail. Winding down from North Vietnam through the mountains of Laos and Cambodia into various parts of South Vietnam, the Ho Chi Minh Trail not only supplied the southern guerrillas, but also provided the route to war for hundreds of thousands of regular North Vietnamese troops. By war's end, large sections of the trail were paved and an oil pipeline stretched from North Vietnam to within eighty miles of Saigon. North Vietnamese and Viet Cong troops also relied on the jungle areas of Laos and Cambodia near the trails to hide, rest, regroup, and stage operations into South Vietnam. In 1964, the United States began bombing Laos in an effort to thwart the North Vietnamese war effort as well as to destroy the Pathet Lao, a group of Communist-controlled Laotian revolutionaries. The war also expanded into Cambodia, which the United States bombed from 1969 to 1973 and invaded in 1970.

North Vietnam received enormous amounts of military aid from its Communist allies, China and the Soviet Union, with some support as well from Eastern European nations—not only small arms, but mortars, artillery, tanks, surface-to-air missiles, and MiG fighter jets (the latter two used almost exclusively for the air defense of North Vietnam). In addition to war materiel, China and the Soviet Union provided personnel ranging from ordinary laborers who helped build and maintain the Ho Chi Minh Trail to soldiers who helped man and maintain antiaircraft sites. Some three hundred thousand Chinese and several thousand Russians served in North Vietnam.

The war produced such a tremendous range of experiences only a modest portion of them can be included even in a large book. As it was, I had to limit the book to fewer than half the interviews I conducted. Consolation lies in knowing that every individual I was able to include makes us aware of other experiences we might not have imagined and shows how the war's impact rippled from one person and event to another, all worthy of attention.

While gathering these interviews, I sometimes felt the project was a race against time, the last possible moment to do an oral history that included the memories of people whose experiences go back to the early years of the war or who held senior wartime positions. On several occasions interviews had to be canceled because of terminal illness. Other times I called a year or two after an interview to ask some follow-up questions and found myself speaking with grieving relatives.

However, most of the people I interviewed were middle-aged and had remarkably vivid memories of the war. Some recalled those years more clearly than any historical moment since. Even so, a surprising number had never fully shared their experiences. Quite often it proved emotionally wrenching. People would launch into their accounts in full control only to reach some unexpected roadblock. Voices would suddenly stop, or crack, or dissolve as powerful feelings shot to the surface. Along with tears came countless other emotions not always predictable—flashes of delight, anger, nostalgia, regret, relief, guilt, and pride. There were, as well, special moments when people stumbled upon a valuable but long-forgotten memory or a previously unconsidered insight. Those of us who have not experienced war directly sometimes assume that its memory holds nothing but misery. The more complicated reality is that, like all extreme, life-threatening experiences, war magnifies the full range of human emotions. It is not unusual to meet people who hated the war but also miss it, or miss the best of what it brought out in them and their friends—the feeling of being fully alive, of having others depend on you, of making history.

Although most people readily agreed to be interviewed, there were notable exceptions. Robert McNamara (secretary of defense under Presidents Kennedy and Johnson), Henry Kissinger (President Richard Nixon's national security adviser and Gerald Ford's secretary of state), and Nguyen Van Thieu (president of South Vietnam from 1966 to 1975) all declined my repeated requests. At one point McNamara finally agreed, but changed his mind the next day. "I suspect you're interested in feelings," he said, "and I don't want to talk about that."

There are silences to be considered beyond those of people unwilling to talk. The most obvious, but rarely considered, is the silence of the dead, the millions whose stories will never be heard. However close the living can bring us to the heart of the war, they cannot speak for the dead. It is possible that even the grimmest survivors' tales do not convey the worst of it. And there are things some people will not share. There was the former marine whose wife begged him to tell me the story she knew was plaguing him. She had never heard it herself, but thought telling me would do him good. He never did. There was the pilot shot down in the A Shau Valley who found himself surrounded by enemy soldiers. He wouldn't say what happened before the rescue helicopter arrived. "If I tell you, I won't sleep." And in some cases people tried to talk but couldn't find the words.

In Vietnam there were additional forms of silence. Like all foreign writers, I had to receive government permission to conduct interviews. Most were arranged by the Vietnam-America Friendship Association (Viet-My). While the Viet-My staff did their best to honor my interview requests, there were certainly limitations on my ability to work as freely or independently as desired. And because Vietnam remains a one-party state that does not allow full freedom of speech, I was concerned that my questions might not be answered with complete candor. There were linguistic barriers as well. Lacking Vietnamese, I had to rely on interpreters to translate on the spot between two radically different languages. Then I brought the tapes home and worked with a Vietnamese scholar to make a complete translation of the Vietnamese responses. Despite such obstacles, I was often amazed by how forthcoming the Vietnamese were, how much of their lives they were willing to offer.

One of the virtues of oral history is its capacity to encompass a wide range of individual experiences and viewpoints. In these accounts people are, in the best sense, speaking for themselves, making vivid the lived experience of the past, what it felt like to be them at an important moment in history. While this is not a conventional historical narrative of the war, I have tried to organize and introduce the interviews in a way that provides readers with sufficient historical context to be able to make each account as meaningful as possible. Of course, everyone's memory is partial, selective, and sometimes faulty. While it is impossible to verify all that anyone says, wherever possible I have tried to ensure that people participated in the events they describe. Some have careers that have been amply documented. Others shared official records, award citations, photographs, or letters. When I had serious doubts about the accuracy or plausibility of an account, I did not include it. Moreover, everyone in the book agreed to the use of his or her real name.

In the course of doing this work, people sometimes expressed concern about my psychological well-being. Wasn't it difficult, they wondered, listening to so many war stories? Didn't it cause nightmares or depression? In truth, any distress was almost always exceeded by gratitude for the efforts people made to communicate their experience. The struggle to make meaning of the past is one of the greatest gifts anyone can offer the future. And in some cases it came at a cost, not only in time but in emotional turmoil. Quite often it occurred to me that I was not only the recipient of valuable historical contributions, but also a witness to genuine acts of courage.

A word about the title. I was repeatedly struck by how forcefully patriotism shaped the lives of people on all sides of the war. I do not mean to suggest by this that everyone viewed patriotism in the same way. Indeed, debates about the meaning and value of patriotism were as contentious as the war itself. Many of the people I interviewed have wrestled with patriotism's hardest questions: Should love of country be unqualified or conditional? Should it require loyalty to a government's policies whatever they are, or welcome dissent based on allegiance to a nation's highest principles? Or is it enough to be faithful to individual or universal values? In what ways might patriotism be a force for good or inspire noble sacrifice, and when does it become a club for stifling dissent and a rallying cry for unjustifiable destruction? Such questions remain as critical now as ever. One of the legacies of the Vietnam War is to offer us ways to reengage them.

We turn now to the voices that illuminate this vast, sprawling, and complicated history, beginning with an American general who recalls with great insight his two tours of duty in Vietnam but cannot yet bring himself to visit the Vietnam Veterans Memorial and face the loss of life it represents. The book ends with a poem left at the Wall by a visitor from Hanoi who came to pay his respects to the Americans he had long ago opposed. In part, each of the many accounts represents its own historical memorial. For all their differences, none encourage us to forget or romanticize or evade the past. Together, they challenge us to remember more than we ever knew.

PATRIOTS

PART ONE

INTRODUCTIONS

COMMANDERS

BERNARD TRAINOR

"It turned out the mayor of Danang was a double agent."

It's a radiant spring morning in Lexington, Massachusetts, birthplace of the American Revolution. In this prosperous suburb with many grand homes, he and Peggy, his wife of forty years, live in a relatively modest duplex. They have four adult daughters. The seventy-year-old retired lieutenant general, wearing a maroon running suit, lights a cigar and settles into his armchair. His friends call him "Mick."

Though it has been thirty-two years since he commanded troops in Vietnam and seventeen years since he retired from the Marine Corps, General Trainor has remained fully engaged with the political and military crises of our times. In the 1980s he was a military correspondent for The New York Times, *and in the 1990s he taught at the Kennedy School of Government where he also wrote a book about the Persian Gulf War. He still appears occasionally on television as a military analyst. Yet, for all that has unfolded in his life and elsewhere since the 1960s, his mind and emotions are still powerfully drawn back to Vietnam, where he served two tours.*

In 1965, as the number of American troops in Vietnam rose from twenty-three thousand to almost two hundred thousand, Trainor was assigned to a small, top-secret program directing covert South Vietnamese attacks against the coast of North Vietnam, part of a clandestine war that had been going on since 1961. In 1970, he returned to the war in a more conventional role as an infantry battalion commander. By the following year most of the U.S. Marines had been withdrawn from Vietnam.

I grew up in the South Bronx just above Yankee Stadium and across the river from the Polo Grounds. When I was in high school I was probably one of the few people sorry to see World War II end. I was dying to get into the military, so when I graduated in 1946 I enlisted in the marines. Coming from a Catholic education and an Irish Catholic family in a working-class section of the Bronx, going into the Marine Corps with its strict regimen wasn't that much of a shock.

The Marine Corps sent me to Holy Cross for college. I'll never forget the first week of classes. I answered a question and Father Joe Curran, the Jesuit professor, said, "Why?" I'd been brought up in a world where you learned what you were supposed to do and not to question. Nobody had ever asked me why before. I credit the Jesuits for whatever intellectual progress I was able to make after that.

Even before I went to Korea, I was reading about the French fighting in Indochina and in the early sixties one of my jobs was to develop reconnaissance tactics specifically for Southeast Asia. There was an awareness that we might end up there and we all thought we were doing the right thing. We were inflamed by Kennedy's rhetoric to bear any burden, pay any price for liberty. We viewed Communism as a monolithic dragon which controlled all of the Eurasian land mass. We didn't see any distinction between Chinese and Soviet Communism. We had seen the Communist attempt to take over Korea, we had seen what they tried to do in the Philippines with the Huks, a Communist-led insurgency, we saw what they were trying to do in Indonesia with the PKI [the Indonesian Communist Party], and we now saw their attempt to take over Indochina. We didn't identify it as a nationalistic or patriotic war; it was Communist expansion. We were on a holy crusade to stop the spread of godless Communism and to give the budding democracy in South Vietnam an opportunity to take root.

By 1965 I had been earmarked to go out to Vietnam as an adviser with the Studies and Observation Group. That was the cover name for a covert operation aimed at North Vietnam that had been started by the CIA. We operated out of a secret base at the end of Monkey Mountain near Danang. We wore civilian clothes without rank or insignia. Serial numbers were filed off our weapons, most of which were foreign—Swedish K submachine guns and that sort of thing. We had these Norwegian PT boats with enormous Rolls Royce engines—just fantastic—and we would go north in these boats.

The skippers and the crews were Vietnamese. Most of them were northerners and Catholics who had come south, dissatisfied with the Communist regime. We had special teams of these South Vietnamese for raiding parties. Usually they'd be discovered because the North Vietnamese had pretty tight control along the coast and our guys wanted to draw their rice and their pay but were not overly interested in getting shot at.

Because Americans were not supposed to accompany the teams—I'm not going to say the rule wasn't occasionally violated—they didn't have the hard hand behind them to make them more aggressive. One thing I learned about the South Vietnamese was that they always left their enemy an opportunity to escape. When Americans get into an action, you aim to "kill 'em all." But the idea of a battle of annihilation was not part of their culture and I had to accommodate my plans to take this into account.

One coastal target in the north was identified by Saigon intelligence as a rest and recuperation center for Viet Cong cadre, but the Vietnamese PT skipper said, "No, that's a leper hospital." My intelligence said it was a communist R and R center so that was that. We sent a team in there firing as they went, and they killed a lot of people. It turned out to be a leper hospital just as the Vietnamese officer had predicted.

When the team got back I'll never forget the look the skipper gave me. His eyes said everything. He pointed at me and said, "Hospital." That really did a great deal of damage to our credibility. These people were going up north based on their trust in the accuracy and dependability of American intelligence. Needless to say, after that some of the teams we sent north never went ashore. They always found a reason not to do so—the dogs were barking, or the geese were honking, or the beach was being patrolled, or something. They had lost confidence in us.

Despite setbacks like that, I thought our operations were doing pretty well. It was primarily a psychological operation against the North and we may have given them far more trouble than we gave ourselves credit for. I left Vietnam in 1966 as totally convinced of the nobility of our cause as I was when I arrived. Although it was a tougher war than I had anticipated, I was sure we would succeed.

When I went back for my second tour in 1970, I was disabused of all that because in the intervening years we saw that South Vietnam's "budding democracy" was corrupt and venal. There was also the realization that our enemy's cause was partially nationalistic and anticolonial as well as Communist. And, of course, we realized that Communism wasn't the monolith we thought it was.

Between my two tours I taught at the Command and Staff College. You could see the disillusionment and unhappiness that officers returning from Vietnam had toward Westmoreland's strategy of search-and-destroy.* We were destroying the North Vietnamese, but we were also destroying innocent civilians and destroying ourselves.

In 1970, I took over the 1st Battalion, 5th Marine Regiment. We ran quick reaction operations out of Hill 34 near Danang. We would get a package of helicopters each day and, on the basis of intelligence reports, go after known or suspected enemy locations. My philosophy was that if we didn't make contact

*General William C. Westmoreland was the commander of U.S. forces in Vietnam from 1964 to 1968.

when we landed at our target we would just pull out and fly to an alternative site. I didn't want people beating the bush in areas loaded with booby traps and mines. The only thing you do by blundering along in the rice paddies or up in the hills is get people blown up. There had to be a better way.

I wanted to do my job professionally with a minimum of casualties. Clark Judge, the commander of the 5th Marines, said to me, "You know, we're not out here fighting a war; we're out here campaigning." If you're fighting a war you do what's necessary to win. What Judge meant by campaigning was that it was like the British nineteenth-century colonial army up in the northwestern frontier of India where they were just trying to manage the unwinnable. In a sense, we were only biding time until we were pulled out of Vietnam.

The assistant division commander did not like the way I was operating. He felt I wasn't being aggressive enough. So he put a bug in the ear of the division commander, General Widdecke, who interrogated me. He said, "You explain to me exactly what it is that you are doing." There was the clear implication that I could be relieved of my command if he didn't like my answers. I would have been put in a staff job in the rear and never have made general. Everyone would have interpreted it as, "Trainor's afraid to mix it up with the enemy. He gets in there and then runs away." It would have been the end of my career.

Fortunately, in the middle of this interrogation a radioman came in and said, "Excuse me, gentlemen. Colonel Trainor, your unit's in contact." So I looked at General Widdecke and he said, "Go with your unit." Out I went and our contact led to a spectacular success which completely eliminated any danger of my being relieved of my command.

The firefight was in a remote jungle draw in the Que Son Mountains. It lasted throughout the day and into the night and we employed both the new Cobra gunships and snake and nape [250-pound bombs and napalm] from A-4s. Eventually the firing stopped and I set the troops to beating the bushes in search of a cave entrance. We had captured a high-ranking Viet Cong intelligence officer who had fingered this general vicinity as the location of a major underground Viet Cong headquarters.

A day or two later, two snuffies [marine infantrymen], out of sight of their masters and bored to death with this senseless exercise, decided to entertain themselves with a Frisbee. They tossed it back and forth until it went over one kid's head and landed in a clump of bushes. When he went to retrieve it, lo and behold he spotted a hole. He enlarged it with his K-Bar and sure enough it opened into a tunnel. It turned out to be one of the many entrances to a cave that was the Quang Da Special Zone headquarters for the Hue-Danang–Chu Lai area.

We got into the thing and I have never seen anything like this. They must have worked with coolie labor for years. It was a big, big cavern. They had bunks made of bamboo and wire that could sleep two hundred troops. They had running water through bamboo pipes. They had bamboo baffles to dissipate smoke in various locations so you wouldn't be able to see when they cooked. They even had a special room for the commanding officer. But the big find was in these five-pound cans that GI coffee used to come in. They contained the dossiers and personal records of all the Viet Cong double agents in the Quang Da Special Zone. It turned out the mayor of Danang was a double agent. So, this was my proudest moment. From what I heard, it was the biggest intelligence find they had in I Corps* during the war.

A lot of people said we should have bombed the North back into the Stone Age. To a certain extent we tried that, but they continued to fight. More bombing wouldn't have worked. I think the parallel is with our own American Revolution. Like the American revolutionaries, the Vietnamese would go on fighting forever. The American colonists, an agrarian people, had come to the conclusion that independence was an absolute necessity. They pledged their treasures and their lives to achieve it and by God they were not going to put up with the depredations and humiliations imposed on them by the British Crown. So it was a war to the death. The colonial army could lose battle after battle after battle, as they did, but just by maintaining a force in the field eventually they were able to wear down and defeat the British. For the British, on the other hand, it was a kind of peripheral exercise. There wasn't any national sentiment on the part of their soldiers and least of all among their mercenaries. By the time of Yorktown, they'd become pretty disenchanted with the whole operation and there was a great movement in Britain to bring the thing to an end. In the long run, the strategy of the American revolutionaries worked. Washington was assiduous in making sure that no matter what happened he maintained an army in the field. He could not afford to have some sort of climactic battle in which his field army got destroyed. He pecked away at the British until he wore them down. That's pretty much what the North Vietnamese were able to do to us.

Our hope early on in Vietnam was to win the hearts and minds of the people, but that hope was destroyed by the South Vietnamese government's failure to gain the people's allegiance and by Westmoreland's strategy of search-and-destroy. It was basically a strategy of attrition and it went back to our Civil War when Ulysses S. Grant finally found the key to victory against the South by making use of his enormous personnel and industrial resources just to grind

*The U.S. military divided South Vietnam into four military regions. I Corps (pronounced "eye core") consisted of the five northernmost provinces.

the Confederates down. You simply pile on and crush 'em. That was Westmoreland's approach in Vietnam. There was no subtlety. His idea was to go after people and kill them in great number. That's why the body count became such an important standard for evaluating success in the war. It was based on the faith that if you kill more of them than they do of you, in the end you have beaten them. However, one of the basic problems was that the North Vietnamese had an almost bottomless pit of people with the determination to outlast the Americans. And they were able to engage us on terms favorable to themselves. They would inflict casualties and then disappear. In a sense, the North Vietnamese turned the philosophy of attrition warfare against Westmoreland. Their strategic aim was to wear us down until the American public turned against the war. It worked. People thought, we keep taking terrible casualties and we're not seeing any benefit. Where are we going with this?

In the Marine Corps we thought Westmoreland's strategy of attrition was the dumbest thing to do. We felt the solution was to put marines or soldiers into the villages and stay there in small teams to protect the people and gain their trust, to respect their culture and generate a legitimate government that they could support. The idea was to deprive the North Vietnamese and Viet Cong of the support they depended on. The marines tried to do this with what we called the Civil Action Program. We sent small teams into various villages to live with the people and didn't retreat during the night. It was a very successful program, but Westmoreland rejected that approach. Whether it would have worked in the long run is doubtful, though, because the Saigon regime showed no inclination to improve its deportment. In the absence of decent government and protection of the people, the U.S. effort was doomed. Then your only alternative was the heavy club, which was what Westmoreland tried, and it was totally self-defeating.

Trainor once wrote that the Vietnam War produced a "genie of anguish" that he had bottled up inside. Asked to elaborate he says, "Well, I still can't go to the Vietnam Veterans Memorial." With these words he suddenly chokes up. A dam of emotion seems about to break, but within seconds he regains control. "The genie's still there. I don't know. And I'm not alone. I guess it was the waste and the frustration, both seen and what you knew about. You say, 'Jesus Christ, fifty-eight thousand people—good kids.' That's about all I can say. Deep down there's a hurt and I don't know what it is. I can't control it. It's always there and I think I'll just live with it for the rest of my life."

DANG VU HIEP

"With all those choppers they seemed terribly strong."

As the retired general speaks, he flips through a small notebook bursting with inserted pages and note cards, full to the margins with his jottings—tactical principles, statistics, key events, reminders of a history that consumed thirty years of his life. A stocky man with a stiff, salty brush cut, he fought against American forces in the Central Highlands of South Vietnam.

A northerner, Hiep joined the Viet Minh revolution against the French in 1945 and served as a battalion political officer in the eight-year war that followed. Between the French and American wars he studied for five years in the Soviet Union. In September 1964, as a lieutenant colonel, he left his wife and three children and made the three-month trip down the Ho Chi Minh Trail to South Vietnam. He was part of the command group that led North Vietnamese troops in their first major engagements against American troops in 1965. He returned home a general in 1975.

I spent ten years in the Central Highlands. All the military strategists considered it a crucial region. Whoever controls the Central Highlands can control all of Vietnam. The Americans saw that as well, so in 1965, even though their troops were still relatively few, they sent two divisions there. We began with only three regiments in the Highlands. By 1975, we had three divisions.

Many Americans ask about the attack against U.S. troops at Pleiku on February 7, 1965, because after that attack Johnson ordered air strikes on the North and sent in combat troops.* Some Americans claim that Hanoi ordered the attack to provoke the United States into these actions; that we did it specifically to kill Americans and planned to do so on a day when [U.S. National Security Adviser] McGeorge Bundy was in Saigon and [Soviet Premier] Alexei Kosygin was in Hanoi.

I have never understood why the U.S. government regarded this attack as provocative. It was just a normal battle, part of a long-term dry-season offensive in the Highlands. We were achieving major victories against the Saigon regime, liberating most of the rural areas of Kontum Province and half of Binh

*With mortars and satchel charges, Viet Cong guerrillas attacked Camp Holloway, a U.S. advisory compound and airstrip, near the city of Pleiku, killing nine Americans, wounding 126, and destroying ten U.S. aircraft. It was, to date, the most costly assault on a U.S. position in Vietnam. In response, Lyndon Johnson ordered Operation Flaming Dart, a bombing strike against North Vietnam. Some key American policy makers regarded the Viet Cong attack as a pretext for the more systematic bombing of North Vietnam. As McGeorge Bundy put it, "Pleikus are like streetcars"—if you miss one, another will come along shortly.

Dinh Province. Because of our successes, the Saigon regime sent their forces against us. In response, our small commando units attacked their military headquarters. Pleiku was the headquarters for Saigon's 23rd Division so it was an obvious target. We used just thirty people and it didn't require a lot of preparation either. In fact, it was planned and ordered by the commanders in the field, not by Hanoi. I learned later that we killed nine Americans and wounded about eighty, but at the time we didn't even know for sure whether Americans were stationed at Pleiku. In any case, our main objective was to destroy the enemy and we made no distinction between South Vietnamese and U.S. troops. We considered them both enemies. As for Bundy and Kosygin, I didn't realize they were in the country until years later when I read about it in books by General Westmoreland and [Secretary of Defense] Robert McNamara.

In recent years we have met with Robert McNamara and he says that if we hadn't attacked at Pleiku, American air strikes wouldn't have begun. But we consider that a groundless claim. We believe the U.S. used Pleiku as a pretext for launching long-planned bombing strikes. The air raids occurred just hours after the commando attack. How could that happen without preparation? In Westmoreland's memoir he writes that Johnson ordered planning for bombing back in April 1964. It was called OPLAN 37. So the bombing plans existed long before the attack on Pleiku.

The Americans introduced combat troops in 1965 to forestall Saigon's defeat. That was probably the time of our greatest difficulties. We had very little understanding of the U.S. army. Many things were new to us. Sometimes we had to fight against airborne units with four hundred helicopters. With all those choppers they seemed terribly strong. How could we manage it? We had such heated discussions about how to fight. Should we be on the offensive or defensive? It was a very hard question.

Fighting the U.S. wasn't easy. We had to rely on our creativity. As time went on we found a way to deal with their airborne units. In order to engage us, they had to find landing zones for their helicopters, so we began to set ambushes where we guessed they would land. And in the Ia Drang battle* we discovered that we couldn't destroy a whole battalion at one go, but had to do it one company at a time. We also learned that wherever we attacked the enemy, their airborne units would bring in more troops at our back, a tactic they called leapfrogging. Once we figured that out we began to lay ambushes in our rear to hit the American reinforcements. Then we began to see the advantage of

*Fought in November 1965, it was the first major battle between American and North Vietnamese forces.

stretching out enemy forces by luring them away from their large bases. Once their troops were all strung out we could attack where they were least powerful.

We couldn't have overcome all our hardships without help from the people. I still remember one time when we didn't have any medicine and one of our soldiers was wounded. A young woman from the Benai ethnic minority wounded herself so that she could go to the enemy post and ask for medicine, which she brought back to treat the wounded soldier.

In the North, because of wartime food shortages, people had to mix cassava into their rice. In the Central Highlands there was so little rice we used to say that our cassava carried rice on its back. Whenever possible we caught fish and killed animals for which we could now be put in prison, including tigers, monkeys, and bears. But every soldier had to care for five hundred cassava plants so we could continue fighting even when we couldn't kill enough game or didn't get rice from the North. From commanders down to ordinary soldiers, we all grew cassava. Every year we grew it closer to our objective. When we wanted to lay an attack on Highway 14, for example, we started very far away, but each year we planted closer and closer.

Once when we were feeling very optimistic we composed a song we called "The Cassava Offensive." I apologize for recalling it, but it goes something like this: [He sings] "For every cassava grown, one American GI is killed / A thousand cassavas raised, blood from a thousand GIs is spilled / We enjoy it, enjoy it, enjoy it so / I love the cassava plants I grow." There were lots of ups and downs, many hardships but a lot of joy. I'm seventy-two now, but I think those years in the Central Highlands were the high point of my life.

WAR HEROES

ROGER DONLON

"We were babes in arms in every way."

He was the first American in the Vietnam War to receive the Medal of Honor, the highest military decoration the United States can confer. A Green Beret captain, he commanded the Nam Dong Special Forces camp in the mountains of northern South Vietnam near the Laotian border. It was that time in the war just before the full-scale buildup of U.S. forces, when small teams of Americans worked with much larger South Vietnamese military units. About two-thirty in the morning on July 6, 1964, the Nam Dong camp was attacked by a reinforced Viet Cong battalion. The battle lasted five hours. According to his Medal of Honor citation, Donlon "dashed through a hail of small arms and exploding hand grenades," "completely disregarded" serious shrapnel wounds to his stomach, shoulder, leg, and face, "marshaled his forces," personally "annihilated" an enemy demolition team, dragged wounded men to safety, carried weapons from one position to another, administered first aid, directed mortar fire, all the while crawling and scrambling back and forth across the camp. "His dynamic leadership, fortitude, and valiant efforts inspired not only the American personnel but the friendly Vietnamese as well and resulted in the successful defense of the camp."

With broad shoulders and firm jaw, he looks like he could be an aging star of movie Westerns. Speaking in a calm, even-paced voice, he takes time-outs to entertain his baby granddaughter and to point out the red, white, and blue birdhouse in the yard of his Leavenworth, Kansas, home.

Our mission was to advise, assist, and train the Vietnamese. The central government was trying to do some things to give the impression that it was in control of all the country, including the countryside. They had set up "strategic hamlets" to give the people a sense of belonging to a program that came from the central government. Our job was to make sure these people could defend these outposts of freedom scattered throughout the whole country.

We trained a Vietnamese Strike Force of about three hundred men—a Civilian Irregular Defense Group. Some of them were coastal folks. Their families had been fishermen for generations and they were relocated as part of the strategic hamlet program and told to make their new homes there in the mountains. But when you start to move populations, the enemy knows what's going on and will put in infiltrators. Whenever you have population relocation it's bound to happen. Of the three hundred members of our Strike Force it turned out that about a hundred sympathized with the enemy. We never had a sense of the magnitude of the problem because we never had any real outside intelligence from higher headquarters. We were babes in arms in every way. We were working with and against cultures that were two thousand years old. They could manipulate us.

On the inner perimeter of the camp we had a Special Forces team of twelve Americans. That was our nucleus. We also had six Vietnamese Special Forces. They had airborne training but were political appointees and so they lacked the same commitment we found among ourselves. Then I had my sixty Nung mercenaries. We inherited them from the CIA who had used them for years. We hoped we could trust the Vietnamese, but we knew we could trust our Nungs. They were a Chinese ethnic minority that came out of mainland China after World War II and had stayed one step ahead of Communism when Mao took over. When North Vietnam fell in '54, the Nungs came south. They were very, very dedicated anti-Communists. We were being placed in isolated situations and we needed dependable security. We paid them more than the Vietnamese.

On the outer perimeter of the camp we had our Vietnamese Strike Force. The day before we were attacked, there was a fight between some of the Vietnamese and the Nungs. The Vietnamese were milling around the inner perimeter fence and started pummeling the Nungs with rocks. That sent the Nungs running toward their mortars and machine guns. The Vietnamese peppered the inner perimeter with their carbines. Sergeant Alamo got up between the two sides and the firing stopped. We estimated that about five hundred rounds were fired, but somehow no one was killed.

About two-thirty in the morning I had just finished making my rounds of the inner perimeter and gotten back to the mess hall when it was hit by a white phosphorous mortar shell. I was knocked back through the door. My first thought was that the Vietnamese Strike Force was back in action against the Nungs, but we were under heavy attack by the Viet Cong. My communications sergeant got on the transmitter. There was no time for code so he said in plain English: "Hello Danang . . . Nam Dong calling . . . We are under heavy mortar fire . . . Request flare ship and air strike." He fled the communications room just before it went up in a fireball. So with the first mortar rounds all our communications were eliminated. The enemy knew us so well, they knew exactly what to hit and where it was. And all our buildings were thatch and rattan, so the white phosphorous not only set everything on fire, but silhouetted us when we tried to move.

Higher headquarters knew we were under attack but it was Fourth of July weekend and everybody was celebrating. When they went to scramble a plane, the hangar was locked and the plane wasn't fueled. So what could have been a twenty-minute response took several hours.

As commander, my job was not only to lead but to communicate, and the only way to do it was to move from point A to B to C. I just had to take my time and pray I could survive. I'd say a third of our Vietnamese forces on the outer perimeter fought for the other side. The first thing each of the traitors did when the attack started—and they knew it was coming—was to slit the throat or break the neck of the person next to them. So right off the bat our Strike Force went from three hundred down to two hundred, and possibly closer to a hundred. And the people we thought would be shooting outward were now shooting inward. It got pretty spicy very rapidly. We didn't have much help on the outer perimeter so we just had to hang on.

The VC used the veil of darkness to their advantage. Our job was to strip that veil as best we could. Just a few days before, we had received a high-tech, handheld flare. You just took off the top, slapped it on something hard, and it'd shoot. You'd get about twenty or thirty seconds of illumination. It was just pure luck that we had fifty or sixty of them in each of our five mortar pits.

The enemy came over the wire. They were gallant and brave and they thought by being numerically superior they could easily overrun us. We found out after the fact that a similar force had attacked another Special Forces camp the night before and overrun it. We didn't even get word of it. That shows you how bad our communications were with higher headquarters.

Early in the attack George Tuan, one of our Vietnamese interpreters, was running like mad to his assigned mortar pit. Partway there a 57-millimeter round caught him right at the knees and took his legs off. He just kept running on the stumps. Within about thirty seconds he was dead. That's one of the things you'd like to forget.

Primarily my job was to make sure we got our mortars firing in the key areas. Our guys were pretty good—they practically had the mortars vertical. It was pretty dangerous. Some of our mortars were going up a thousand feet and coming down within twenty-five yards of us.

You try to keep a cool head, but emotions would get in there. When John Houston died I knew he had just received a letter from his wife, Alice, informing him that they were going to be the proud parents of twins. Alice later gave premature birth to those twins. One of them died and is interred with his father in Arlington. The casualties of war go far beyond the immediate battlefield.

What I remember most was my effort to rescue Pop Alamo, a forty-six-year-old veteran of World War II and Korea who was our senior noncommissioned officer. He was pretty severely wounded and I tried to get him out of a mortar pit. As I carried him out we were blasted back into the pit. I thought that was the end. I don't know how long I was unconscious but when I came to, I found that Pop had died in my arms. What keeps you going at times like that is the love you feel for your fellow teammates. At the time you called it respect, but as the years go on you realize it was really a deep, deep love.

I just kind of ran out of fuel about eight o'clock in the morning. I got it in the shoulder and the arm and the gut and the leg and a few other places. Even breathing was excruciating and by the time they evacuated me I was unconscious. As they unloaded the chopper I regained consciousness. They were putting the dead in body bags and I heard somebody say, "Put that guy in a bag." He thought I was gone.

When I got out of the hospital I took some visits to the beach where I saw a navy ship that had Old Glory flying. It was beautiful and healing in a lot of ways. Since we were in Vietnam as guests just to advise and assist, the only place the American flag flew in-country was at the U.S. Embassy. We had to do what we could to help the Vietnamese develop a sense of pride in their own flag, so we used to have a flag ceremony every morning in the center of the camp. We always wished we could put our flag up at the camp too, but that wasn't permitted. Not seeing it made us all a little more lonely.

TRAN THI GUNG

"I was stuck in a tunnel for seven days."

The petite woman, whose given name means "ginger," fills little more than half a chair and her toes barely reach the floor. Opening a stylish beige handbag, she removes a photograph from 1966 taken by the combat photographer Duong Thanh Phong. It shows her at age twenty, lying on her stomach in a sun-drenched field, perched on an elbow. A braid of waist-length, jet-black hair falls across her shoulder. She's aiming a*

**Duong Thanh Phong's account is on pp. 247–50.*

rifle, the butt of the weapon against her cheek, the barrel resting on a decaying log, and her right finger on the trigger. Around her waist, a thick belt holds cartridges of ammunition and grenades. "I was a member of the guerrilla force of Trung Lap Ha Hamlet near Cu Chi. I was in so many fights for so many years, I can't possibly remember them all."

Her village, only twenty-five miles northwest of Saigon, the capital of South Vietnam, had been a center of resistance against French colonial rule back in the early 1950s. To fight the French, villagers began to build a network of underground tunnels to use for hiding, quick escapes, and the storage of food and weapons. By the mid-1960s these had been expanded into hundreds of miles of tunnels, some going down three levels with kitchens, living quarters, hospitals, and storage chambers.

The revolutionaries of Cu Chi were southern guerrillas, Viet Cong, who regarded the Saigon government and its soldiers as mere "puppets" of the United States. They looked to Ho Chi Minh ("Uncle Ho") and the Communist North to support their struggle to drive out the Americans and overthrow the government.

Tran Thi Gung was the only woman in her unit, a detail that comes up in passing, as if hardly worthy of mention.

When the revolution broke out I was just a kid. In 1962, the puppet soldiers came to my house and said, "Your father was a Viet Cong so we killed him. Go fetch his body." He had gone to a meeting with his comrades. The southern soldiers surrounded the building and killed everyone. From then on, I decided to take revenge for my father's death.

Also, the people in my neighborhood suffered from poverty and deprivation and were always brutalized by the police and puppet soldiers. I wanted to do something to liberate my country and help people get enough food and clothing. I believed my mission in life was to continue my father's cause, so in 1963, when I was seventeen, I joined the guerrillas.

My first battle with the Americans was in late 1965 or early 1966, near the Dong Du outpost where some Americans were based. Our commanders informed us that we were going to engage them in battle at Xom Moi hamlet. In preparation for such attacks the people had dug trenches around many hamlets. "Anti-American belts," we called them. Of course there were also underground tunnels everywhere around Cu Chi. We arrived in Xom Moi about four in the morning to wait for the Americans. Just before dawn they started shelling us but we hid in our tunnels. As soon as the shelling stopped we moved into our fighting trenches.

We knew the Americans were unfamiliar with the area, but I felt very scared and very nervous because I was just a small girl and the Americans were so big. When I was a young guerrilla fighter I was smaller than I am today. We knew we couldn't shoot them from a distance. We had to wait for them to come very close. As soon as I started to fire, I killed an American. After he fell, some of his friends came rushing to his aid. They held his body and cried. They cried a lot. This made them sitting ducks. Very easy to shoot. From then on we knew that if we just shot one American soldier others would rush to him and then we could shoot many more.

After a few minutes they pulled back, taking the bodies of their friends with them. But they didn't pick up all their rifles so I crawled out and grabbed five or six AR-15s. I learned to use an AR-15 right on that battlefield. In time I could use just about any weapon, including B-40 rockets.

When the Americans pulled back we knew they would call in artillery fire, maybe even air strikes. So we grabbed their rifles and ran for the tunnels. There we took a short break and reloaded. As soon as it was quiet we returned to the trenches. The second time they advanced they took more casualties. They were such big targets, so easy to hit, I was no longer scared. They retreated again and once more the shelling began. They did this all day, from six in the morning till six at night. Every time they pulled back I crawled out of my hole to seize more weapons. In that first battle against the Americans I shot so many GIs I was awarded a decoration with the title "Valiant Destroyer of American Infantrymen."

I think the Americans lost many people because they were applying conventional tactics against our ambushes and tunnels. Their shells and bombs were extremely powerful and sometimes they killed people in the tunnels, but it didn't happen as often as you might think. The Cu Chi tunnels had such small openings it was very rare for a shell or bomb to land right in a tunnel. As Uncle Ho said, "A stork can't shit into a bottle, so with our tunnels we shouldn't be scared of American bombers."

When GIs discovered tunnel openings they dynamited them, but the tunnels were so deep and had so many twists and turns, they couldn't do too much damage. It was like an underground maze. Most of the tunnels were just wide enough to crawl through and so cramped. There were only some places where you could sit up, never mind stand. Most of the time we lived in the dark. We used kerosene lamps for meetings but never candles. There wasn't enough oxygen so they went out very easily.

Usually we didn't have to stay underground for more than a few hours at a time. After all, we had to be aboveground to fight, right? But one time I was stuck in a tunnel for seven days and seven nights while the Americans were constantly bombing us. After several days our food supply ran short, so even though we were terribly hungry and thirsty, we just ate a few specks of dried rice and drank a few drops of water. When the bombing ended, American tanks rumbled through the area and accidentally buried the tunnel exits. Lots of times the Americans were able to block one or two exits, but there was always some way out. This time every single one was closed. Luckily we had American bayonets taken from the battlefield and we used them to dig ourselves out.

In addition to laying ambushes we guerrillas attacked enemy outposts. I always volunteered to sneak onto the bases at night to reconnoiter and draw maps so we could plan our attacks. Once we launched an assault on an outpost of the southern army—the training center of Trung Hoa. It was such a dangerous mission the commander feared I might be killed, so my unit conducted a death ceremony for me before I left. It was called a "funeral mass for the living," but was exactly like a funeral mass for the dead. They read the entire funeral oration in my presence. I just listened. They recited my full name, my birth date, and recounted my achievements in the war—she got such-and-such medal for this, a citation for that, a decoration for something else. They talked about how sad they were that I had been killed in action. They spoke exactly as if I were already dead.

To collect all the information we needed, I had to sneak into the training center five times. By then I knew the post so well, I guided our forces in. And because I was a sharpshooter I began the attack by picking off a few of the men on guard.

Fighting the southern soldiers could be a tough job. We had to be extra careful because they were Vietnamese and understood the way we thought. But when we attacked the Trung Hoa training center, after a brief exchange of gunfire all the southern soldiers scrambled for their lives. One guy I chased suddenly stopped and turned around. "Big sister," he pleaded, "please don't shoot me." I realized he knew me. Since I grew up in the area, I knew many of those guys personally. I shouted, "Hey, where's your weapon?" He pointed to the riverbank. Of course I didn't shoot him since he'd already surrendered.

One time I even captured an American. Actually, three of us captured him but I was responsible for leading him back to camp. Before I met a GI in person, I called them all "American errand boys." But this man was so big and tall I didn't dare call him that and when I led him into camp our leaders were upset with me for not blindfolding him. They said, "Why didn't you do that?" I didn't know how to answer. I hated the enemy but when I captured that American, I felt sorry for him. They told me to blindfold him right away so I used my checkered scarf. We sent him on to district headquarters right away.

I had many close calls but was only badly wounded once. Shrapnel from an M-79 [grenade launcher] hit me in the head. I didn't even realize it until I felt my face covered with blood. In battle your comrades know when you're hit or killed if your rifle is silenced. When they realized I'd stopped firing they came to my rescue. I'd already passed out. They carried me to a jungle hospital and my wound healed quickly. I was only there for two or three weeks.

During the war I witnessed a lot of killing and suffering. I can't imagine how many GIs I killed. After all, I detonated land mines and threw grenades, both of which could kill many men at a time. I was also an excellent sniper and involved in countless firefights. And, of course, I saw many Vietnamese killed in the war, some right next to me.

Whenever anyone asks me about the suffering of the war, I have a terrible nightmare that very night in which I relive these experiences. I miss my comrades very much and often see them again in my dreams. But I never felt guilty about the killing I did. It was war. Wouldn't you shoot me if you saw me holding a weapon and pointing it at you? I think it was justified. But if I went to America and killed people there, I would feel very sorry and guilty. Since the Americans came to my country, I don't feel guilty.

PAYING THE PRICE

TA QUANG THINH

"They carried me the whole way back to the North."

A broad-shouldered man with silver hair wearing a white pullover jersey, he sits with three companions in the courtyard of a convalescent home for war invalids about twenty kilometers outside Hanoi. The veterans have parked in a cluster to chat. Their wheelchairs, which look like straight-backed lounge chairs atop three wheels, allow the men to rest their paralyzed legs straight out in front of them. Thinh went south in 1965 as a nurse. At the front he received the additional training necessary to become a doctor's aide and perform minor surgery. "Most of the wounds I treated were caused by artillery shells. Bombing also caused many shrapnel wounds and concussions." He was himself wounded in Tay Ninh Province in 1967. "I spent a lot of time in that violent place."

I was asleep in the jungle hospital when a male nurse woke me to tell me that Hue's blood pressure had gone down. Hue was one of our patients recovering from serious wounds in a postoperative care unit, a makeshift underground room with an A-frame roof made of logs and covered with a tarpaulin. So I got out of my hammock to go see him. I remember putting the stethoscope in my ears to listen to his pulse. I glanced at my watch and it was almost eleven o'clock. That's all I can remember.

Later my friends told me that we were hit by a bomb from a B-52. There were six of us in that room—myself, two male nurses, and three patients. I was crouched over Hue when the roof collapsed. It broke my spine and paralyzed me from the middle of my back down. They dug me out of the rubble the following morning. I was the only survivor. Somehow there was enough air to breath and I was closer to the surface than the others, easier to dig out.

I stayed in the South another four years, treated that whole time in a jungle hospital, just wishing the war would end quickly. I couldn't communicate with my family for six years. Even if they had carried letters south, how would they have found us? We moved all the time.

In 1971, they were finally able to take me home. I was flat on my back in a hammock, two people at a time carrying me. They carried me the whole way back to the North. A third porter went along to relieve the other two. There were many stations along the way and I was relayed from one group of porters to another. It took us seven months. Of course it was very painful to be carried like that. I took painkillers but they didn't help much.

When I got home, I think everybody, including myself, was sick of the war. We abhorred it. It was not only cruel, it was absurd. Foreigners came to our country from out of the blue and forced us to take up arms. Don't you think that's absurd? We just wanted to be prosperous and live like other people. Of course we had to fight to protect our country but we were really sick of the war. Deep down we didn't like it. Casualties were enormous. And not just that—our savings, our houses, our plants and animals, everything was wasted by that war. I have many memories but I don't want to remember them. It sounds like a paradox to say that, but it's because I don't like war. I don't think anyone liked the war.

"I got married before going south. After I had been hospitalized in Hanoi for a few months, my wife came to see me." He is reluctant to say more, just that "she was very sad when she saw me" and that she visits him once a year.

GEORGE WATKINS

"That sand was probably the only thing that saved me."

He was a grunt with the 196th Light Infantry Brigade. In April 1968, near Camp Evans in Quang Tri Province, he stepped on a land mine. He lost both legs and both eyes. His legs were amputated just a few inches below his pelvis. He lives with his sister in the Appalachian town of Big Stone Gap, Virginia. "She cooks and cleans the house, but I take care of all my personal needs—getting on and off the couch, into bed, going to the bathroom."

Sitting sideways at one end of the couch, he carefully lights a cigarette. His empty wheelchair is next to him, an ashtray attached to one of its arms. He taps an ash into the familiar spot and asks about my minidisc recorder, wants to know how it compares to the cassette player he uses for books-on-tape. Looking into his bright blue artificial eyes, I have to remind myself that he cannot see the machine; that I need to slide it over to his hand.

My daddy built this house. He built it from the ground up, a piece at a time. We moved down here when I was three years old. He wanted to get all us kids out of the coal camps. He was a coal miner for thirty-six years and he did not want us in the mines, period. That's one thing Daddy would not let. He told the man who run his division of Westmoreland Coal that if he hired any one of his sons, that'd be the day he'd walk out of the mines. I have a brother in the railroad, and one that makes mining equipment, and one that just retired from the highway department. So we all stayed out of the mines.

I was drafted on June 19, 1967. I knowed it was coming. Just a matter of time. Come close to not getting drafted. Had high blood—borderline. They kept me three days at Roanoke to watch my blood pressure. I think the three days just laying around doing nothing brought it down.

I knowed very little about Vietnam. I mean what I know now about it and what I knowed then is just from scary. I didn't really pay a whole lot of mind to it. I just knowed that we was fighting over there against Communism, so-called. I started doing more thinking about it after I got drafted, in basic training, trying to find out more, but in there it was hard to find out anything.

I went to Fort Bragg and then to Fort Leonard Wood. Spent two months training as a combat engineer. That's what my MOS [military occupational specialty] was. I was told when I left I would be with an engineer battalion at Pleiku—that's where I thought I was going. But when I got to Vietnam, I reckon they needed infantry and I reckon they just drawed the line somewhere on the list and I went to infantry and the rest of them went over to what they's supposed to. In Cam Ranh Bay they said I was going to Chu Lai to the 196th and I hadn't had one bit of infantry training. The first night I was out there, they put me behind an M-60 machine gun and I had about a two-minute lesson. "Here's the safety, here's the trigger, and here's the bolt."

Our worst time was about the entire month of December 1967. We stayed in the field. Everything we had, we had on our back. Where we stopped, that's where we slept. It was just a continuous patrol and ambush at night. Search-and-destroy in the day, and every third night you was on an ambush. You was lucky to get four hours' sleep. It was nothing to go thirty to forty hours with no sleep. As a matter of fact, the longest we ever went was seventy-one hours. We lost quite a few people that time. Seemed like everywhere we moved, they was right behind us. Seemed like we couldn't get away from them. We went from ninety-three men down to forty. They brought one Chinook in and took us all out. One Chinook. As they say in the army, we was no longer an effective fighting force.

Then we was in one valley, called the Que Son Valley, two miles wide and ten, twelve miles long. We cleaned out every living thing in that valley—people and animals—and destroyed everything else. We just rounded them all up—four to five hundred people—and started moving them eleven klicks [kilometers] to some type of a camp. All their animals was killed. Then we made the valley a free-fire zone. After we cleaned it out, anything you saw was a legitimate target. Two days later, half the people were right back in it. They went back to nothing because we burned and destroyed everything.

They had to be some good people to withstand all that. They come right back to nothing and start over. Go out and get some thatch or find some that wasn't burnt, tie it together with a couple branches over some poles, and sit up under it with their little beat-up aluminum pots. They's some of the most determined people I've ever run into. I don't hate them. They did what they had to do. It's the politicians that put everybody in that place. Although I would like to get ahold of that one that set the booby trap. [Laughs.]

They moved us up to Camp Evans right after the big push into Hue during the Tet Offensive. That's where I got hit. We was doing a road sweep. We had about a five-mile stretch of road and we had to sweep it every day for mines. All that area is flat and sandy—real sandy country. There just about wasn't any cover. Just dirty white sand. Over the years it had blackened like soot. I've still got some of it in me. The doctors say that sand was probably the only thing that saved me. Instead of coming straight up, it spread the explosion out real big.

It was real early, just after daybreak on a Sunday morning. We moved out in two platoons to that road we were supposed to sweep. My platoon was last and I was second or third from the very last man. We had just moved about a hundred feet when I hit it. Seems like I remember looking at my watch and seeing seven-thirty. Sometimes I think that's why I was looking down—why it got in my eyes. I was unconscious for just a couple minutes. I come around and I was laying in a hot hole with my arms up on the side. There was absolutely no pain, just numbness—total numbness. It was hot from the blast. That's the only thing I remember. I told them to get me out of that hole because it was hot. I got some burns on my back from that.

They tell me I hit a pressure-detonated mine—one of our duds, a 105-millimeter round that had been booby-trapped. Its about twenty inches long and 105 millimeters in diameter. Roughly forty people walked by it before I hit it. It also hit a boy in front of me and one to my immediate right. That boy lost a left eye, his left ear, and I think some movement. And I had just mentioned to him to move because he was way too close, just about shoulder to shoulder. I met him later at the hospital in San Antonio and he thanked me. He thinks it would have got him worse if he hadn't moved. And the boy in front, the radio saved his life. He was carrying the radio on his back. Our platoon leader wrote me a letter while I was in the hospital saying they found a piece of shrapnel the size of your hand embedded in the radio.

Doc patched me up and the helicopter sent me to an aid station at Camp Evans. A doctor did something and I was right back on the helicopter and they took me out to the SS *Sanctuary* hospital ship. That's when the pain really started hitting me and then it was just unbearable. They pushed me over to the side and was taking people over me. I think it was a triage decision, probably taking the ones that was worse. I can remember laying on that stretcher and it seemed like a long time, but they say in circumstances like that sometimes you don't lose a lot of blood. A lot of times the force of the explosion will seal the ends of the arteries and veins.

I knowed something was wrong with my eyes, but I was telling myself that my sight wasn't gone, that it was just sand or powder burn. When I come to after surgery my whole head and face was wrapped in bandages and I just kept telling myself I could still see. Nobody did tell me, but the more the days went, I finally began to tell myself, "No, you're going to be blind." A few days later a doctor says my eyes were just like you took and scrambled an egg. Like you took an egg and you just scrambled it. He said that was the shape my eyes was in.

I'll tell you what's surprising. I didn't think about my legs. Legs was a second thought. For some reason my sight meant a lot more than my legs. That's all I can say. All my thoughts and worry was on my eyes.

I still had my right leg for seven days. The doctors told me there's four inches of bone missing, but there was a little bit of tissue still holding it together. They tried to save it, but after seven days gangrene set in and my temperature got up to a hundred and six. I was plum out of it. The next thing I remember is running my hand down to my leg and feeling with my fingers. I just said, "It's gone."

I don't have much bitterness. Well, I don't think I do. I just wish that none of it ever happened—for everybody's sake. It was a bad political mistake. Have you been to the Wall? I was there in '85. I guess that made me feel the worst that I had felt since I'd been home. I sat right in the middle of it, right at the "V" of it, and run my hands up a ways on it. All those names. And then we went from end to end and picked out some that got killed in our outfit. I felt them. Spelled them out even. Each letter. I sat right there and just tried to think, "Why did all these people die?" The majority were my age. Their lives and their families all messed up. What was gained from it?

At the end of the interview, he worries about how the published version will turn out. "I say things that don't look good in print." He cannot be convinced otherwise. On my way out, he makes a request I do not know how to honor: "Fancy it up," he says.

PHAN XUAN SINH

"All my ancestors are buried here."

In 1969, he was drafted by the Army of the Republic of Vietnam (ARVN), the largest branch of the South Vietnamese military. After graduation from Thu Duc Military Academy in 1971, he was assigned as a platoon leader to a scout company of the 51st Regiment. In 1972, on a narrow footpath, one of the men in his small reconnaissance team stepped on a land mine. The explosion killed the soldier and badly wounded Sinh. "I lost my right foot. It happened very near to where I was born, about eight kilometers from Danang. Had I not been wearing a helmet I would certainly have died. A piece of shrapnel penetrated the helmet and lodged right next to my temple." He came to the United States in 1990 and now owns a convenience store in Massachusetts. He prefers to tell his story in Vietnamese. Some of his memories bring him—and our translator—to tears.

It was a war with countless heartbreaking experiences. One time intelligence told us a company of Viet Cong would be landing by boat at Cam Hai, a small coastal village six kilometers south of Danang. We were ordered to set up an ambush near the beach. My recon unit served as an advance party. We got as close as possible to the inlet so we could radio back to the other men in our company as soon as we saw the Viet Cong boats come in. It was one or two in the morning and very dark. We could hardly see a thing, but pretty soon we heard boats approaching. As they got closer we saw one boat after another and many rifles silhouetted against the sky. It looked like a full company of Viet Cong.

We notified our commander and opened up with all our firepower—rifles, machine guns, everything. We kept firing until I realized that there was no return fire. I got on the radio and asked a nearby artillery unit to fire some flares over the beach so we could see. When the flares went off I knew instantly that we had made an awful mistake. We had fired on a large group of fishermen. What we thought were rifles were only fishing poles. In Vietnam, it's not uncommon for fishermen to go out whenever they believe the fish will be biting, even in the middle of the night. I was completely stunned. Among the dead were many old people and women. Even children. Up to twenty of them died and about forty were wounded. I helped evacuate some of the wounded children by helicopter and as we flew away I was in tears. It's clear that common people on all sides bore the brunt of the killing and suffering.

In South Vietnam there were many areas that had been occupied by the other side for a long time. We declared those regions "free-fire zones" and anything that moved there could be fired upon. At night we often shelled free-fire zones indiscriminately. One day I was flying over a free-fire zone and saw a thatched house. I asked the American pilot to land the helicopter. We checked it out and found an old man and woman still living inside. I tried to explain that it was an extremely dangerous place and they had to move. We packed a few of their belongings into knapsacks and helped them onto the helicopter to move them to a refugee camp where they would be safe. Before taking off, we burned down their house to make sure they wouldn't come back.

About two or three weeks later, on another mission, I happened to fly over the area again and was surprised to see a new thatched house in the very same spot. Again we went down and found the same old couple living there. I said, "Uncle, I told you before, this place is too dangerous to live in. Why in the world did you come back?" He said, "All my ancestors are buried here and this is our land. We're not going to leave." At the time I didn't fully understand, but of course the land was unimaginably important to Vietnamese peasants. They were extremely poor and the land was all they had, all they loved.

With so many experiences like that, our overwhelming hope was simply that the war would end. In general, my generation hated the war, but we had no choice. We were drafted. Only those who gained power or wealth from the war had a vested interest in prolonging it, and they didn't have to fight. They remained in the rear with all their privileges. Those of us in the South Vietnamese military saw the injustices so clearly. That's why many of us thought that even living under the other side's authority would be preferable to continuing the war. People like me didn't hate the other side. We were forced to bear arms and saw no compelling reason to fight. We just hoped to find a way to live together with our brothers.

What I didn't realize was how deeply the Communist side hated us. It became clear to me one day when we found an underground tunnel. As usual, before searching it, we dropped explosives inside. We discovered that we had killed a man who delivered mail. He had a big bag of letters with him. As I carried them back to G-2 [intelligence] I was very curious and couldn't resist opening a few. I was amazed by the intensity of feelings they expressed. They had such a deep commitment to the war and so much hatred for us, the enemy. They said things like, "Don't worry about us. We'll survive. Just do your best to destroy the enemy." One letter after another conveyed this basic spirit. We never had such strong feelings about the war. I think that's why they were able to prevail.

Unfortunately their hatred didn't end in 1975. I never expected them to treat us so harshly, to have such a strong desire to seek revenge.

WHERE IS VIETNAM?

JO COLLINS

"I just thought I was going to Europe."

She was Playboy's *"Playmate of the Year." "Everything was Playmate pink. I received a pink car, pink furs, pink clothes, pink champagne glasses, and a pink pool table which I gave to my hairdresser who loved it." It was 1965, the year the magazine introduced an intriguing promotional offer. Anyone who bought a lifetime subscription would have his first issue delivered in person by a* Playboy *playmate. Over in Vietnam, Lieutenant John Price gathered his platoon from the 173rd Airborne Brigade and together they came up with the $150 subscription.*

I was in Oregon visiting my family and got a call from *Playboy* saying they wanted me to fly to Vietnam to visit the troops. A lieutenant had sent a letter to *The New York Times* and the *Chicago Tribune* saying that if Hugh Hefner [*Playboy*'s publisher] didn't see fit to have me deliver their lifetime subscription they would just fade off into the jungle never to be heard from again—one of those sad stories. And so, of course, since they had put it in the paper, Hefner said, "Well, you know what? This would be a great opportunity!"

I was nineteen years old. I had no clue where Vietnam was or what I would find there. I mean, I just thought I was going to Europe. Everything happened so fast I didn't even have time to shop. This was December. I had no idea what to take with me. I just packed what I had in Oregon—wool skirts and sweaters. I didn't realize how hot it was in Vietnam.

I flew over on a commerical airliner, a huge jumbo jet, and it was just myself, my chaperone, a photographer, and Admiral Rickover.* What a delight he

*Admiral Hyman Rickover became well known in the 1950s for his advocacy of nuclear-powered, nuclear-armed submarines.

was, a little old grouchy man. He was doing paperwork and I was talking to my chaperone and the photographer was taking pictures.

When we got off the plane in Vietnam there were five thousand GIs at the airport. It had been in the *Stars and Stripes* [the army newspaper] that I was coming, and there was ABC and NBC and CBS. Oh my God! They asked me, "So, Miss Collins, tell us why you are here." You have to remember I'm getting off a twenty-one-hour flight and I'm just exhausted. So I said, "Well, I'm here to deliver a lifetime prescription." [Laughs.] They were all, like, "Well, honey, we know you're just what the doctor ordered, but now tell us, why are you here?" It got on *Huntley-Brinkley* [NBC's evening news show]. It was like, "Oh my God, I meant *sub*scription."

So I was fitted immediately for my own fatigues—that's what I wore the whole time, fatigues and a black beret. I also became a "sergeant" right away. There wasn't any way to be glamorous, trust me. By the time you got on and off the helicopters with the propellers blowing dust in your face, oh brother.

They took me to see Jack Price, the lieutenant whose platoon bought the *Playboy* subscription. He'd been shot in the shoulder and was in the hospital. He knew I was coming to see him so he refused to be sent home until I came. When I met him he just had the biggest smile. What a wonderful guy. After he saw me, he went home a happy camper. We still see each other every once in a while.

Of course, I wasn't there just to see Jack Price. For two weeks I visited troops everywhere. We really flew into remote areas. I saw guys that never got into a base. That's what made it so special. The danger really started hitting me when we flew a helicopter to the top of Black Virgin Mountain. That was the only way we could get in. It was totally surrounded by Viet Cong. We landed and were shot at by mortars.

We'd go to the field hospitals and talk to the guys. My chaperone and photographer had boxes of autographed pictures. Everybody got one. In one hospital we were exhausted and lying down on cots to rest. A nurse came in and said helicopters were bringing in guys that had just been blown up and someone was asking for me. So I ran out and they had this guy on a stretcher. He had stepped on a land mine and he was so charred all I could see were the whites of his eyes. He looked at me and said, "Hi sweetheart. I'm so glad you made it. I've been waiting for you." They rushed him away to try to save him. They told me later he died.

Nobody wants to go to war, but if our men are directly involved, how can we not be behind them, right, wrong, or indifferent? When I see people who were against the war, fled the war, didn't want to go, it just irks me to death.

Because here were these boys that had to go and they were like myself—they didn't know where Vietnam was. They were going because they were fighting for their country.

"When I decided to pose for Playboy *I didn't tell anybody. They changed my name to Jo Collins, so who would know? But my cousin, bigmouth of the world, called my mother and said, 'Aunt Lorraine, I think that's Janet in* Playboy *magazine.' My mother said, 'No way,' but she sent one of my other cousins to the store to get a* Playboy *in a brown paper wrapper. She about had a heart attack. All my relatives got together and you would think I had disgraced the whole family. But when I came back from Vietnam, and especially after I was a guest of honor of the 173rd Airborne at the White House, then, my gosh, it was a whole different story. Then they decided I had done something for God and my country."*

DEIRDRE ENGLISH

"How can my country be at war and I don't know about it?"

In the late sixties and early seventies, she was among the millions of Americans who participated in the largest antiwar movement in U.S. history. A decade later she was the editor of Mother Jones *magazine, a journal of investigative reporting. Though she has written on many topics, especially women's history, the Vietnam War was a central event in forming her social and political values.*

One day in 1966, when I was a senior in high school, I went to the Museum of Science and Industry in Chicago near my home in Hyde Park. They had an exhibit of helicopters sponsored by the Defense Department, parading their latest war technology. You could actually get inside these helicopters and pretend to train weapons at moving images. What you saw out the doors and windshield were Vietnamese villages and people in conical hats.

I remember being incredibly shocked by this game-like display of dominance, but I had never heard of Vietnam. As I walked out of the museum, there was a very small demonstration put together by University of Chicago students. It was obviously connected to the exhibit. There were posters that said "U.S. out of Vietnam," and I'm thinking, where's Vietnam? I stood at the edge of the crowd and the speaker was saying, "Most Americans don't even know that we're at war in a little Southeast Asian nation called Vietnam." And I thought, yeah, I'm most Americans.

Seeing this demonstration raised a throng of questions. How can my country be at war and I don't know about it, and my teachers don't talk about it? Why is this museum showing military technology that seems to be oriented towards killing Asian people in little villages? And why would our army be targeting peasants? Eventually, the war in Vietnam made people start to question everything. Once you ask whether a war is legitimate, you start to question the way all decisions are being made.

After Nixon invaded Cambodia in the spring of 1970, a national student strike was called. I was at Wesleyan College that year, one of the first women students there. I remember our going around to different classes, just barging in and saying, "Professor, we're from the National Student Strike Organizing Committee and we'd like to talk to you and your class right now." I don't remember anybody saying, "No, you can't." We'd come in and say, "The campus is on strike. We're asking everybody who is against the war in Vietnam to leave class right now and go out to the green for an all-campus meeting." Most students and quite a few professors followed us out the door.

We were jumping in cars and driving to every campus we could find. We felt like Paul Revere. "National student strike. Spread the word!" And we didn't have the Internet. We didn't have e-mail. In those days we didn't even have phones in our dorm rooms. We just piled into borrowed cars and drove. It was great fun.

Then, a day or so later, on May 4, 1970, Kent State happened, and a whole new atmosphere of seriousness took hold. We began to wonder if the government was not only at war with the Vietnamese, but would go to war with America's own youth. We became more determined to raise the social stakes of the war to an intolerable level, defying Nixon to sacrifice us protesters along with the draftees being sent as cannon fodder to Vietnam.

PART TWO

BEGINNINGS (1945–64)

"HISTORY IS NOT MADE WITH IFS"

In 1965, millions of Americans like George Watkins, Jo Collins, and Deirdre English were just starting to wonder where Vietnam was and what the United States was doing there. They found themselves drawn into a war-in-progress, the origins of which seemed distressingly vague and confusing. Even people who understood that the roots of American intervention in Vietnam stretched back at least as far as the early 1950s were unable to identify, or agree upon, a decisive starting point for this complex, blood-soaked, still unfolding experience. There was no initial invasion or battle to mark the outbreak of hostilities, no home-front mobilization, no presidential announcement that war had officially begun, and, of course, no congressional declaration of war. Americans entered Vietnam, both literally and psychologically, at different points in time, swept along by a history they could neither fully fathom nor control. When most people finally became aware of the war, it had been going on long enough to seem almost inevitable, if not unstoppable. Grasping when and how it all began was almost as elusive as predicting when and how it would end.

Five American presidents might have ended U.S. intervention in Vietnam, but all of them acted as if they were trapped by the history they inherited. All pledged to honor past "commitments" even when they poorly understood the history they held responsible for limiting their options. All promised new plans to bring the war to a successful conclusion, but only succeeded in expanding and prolonging it before passing it on. Even when President Nixon finally extracted the last U.S. combat troops from Vietnam in 1973, the war still continued for two more years with American aid.

History is a product of human agency, not blind fate. Vietnam War policies were shaped by powerful political, social, cultural, economic, and ideological forces, but alternative choices were always possible and might have fundamentally changed the course of history. The first decisive American step toward war in Vietnam came shortly after World War II with President Harry Truman's decision to support France's efforts to reclaim its Indochinese colony. While it proved a momentous commitment, it was neither inevitable nor irreversible.

One of this history's most arresting "what-ifs" lies here, at the very beginning of U.S. involvement in Vietnam.

In the early days of World War II, American President Franklin Roosevelt and British Prime Minister Winston Churchill inspired high hopes throughout the world that an Allied victory might bring an end to colonial domination. In 1941, they met off the coast of Newfoundland and drafted the "Atlantic Charter," a vision of the postwar world in which all nations, rich and poor alike, could enjoy the blessings of self-determination and independence.

That was precisely what millions of Vietnamese were seeking. At the outset of World War II, after decades of French colonial rule, Vietnam had been occupied by Japan. The Japanese claimed to be liberating the Indochinese from European colonialism under the motto "Asia for Asians." In truth, their rule would be as harsh as that of any prior colonial master. Exercising control through French collaborators for most of the war, Japanese policies brought economic catastrophe upon the country and, in 1944–45, a famine that may have killed as many as two million Vietnamese.

Rising in opposition to the Japanese occupation was a Communist-led coalition of Vietnamese nationalists called the Viet Minh, the League for Vietnamese Independence. Founded in 1941, the Viet Minh effectively began to organize peasant resistance to the Japanese. Their efforts were noticed by America's Office of Strategic Services (OSS), predecessor to the Central Intelligence Agency, and a working alliance was established. The Viet Minh provided intelligence to the OSS and helped rescue downed U.S. airmen. In turn, the OSS parachuted a small team of Americans into the jungles of Vietnam to provide the Viet Minh with arms and military training.

This tenuous association was in its infancy when the war ended and the Viet Minh entered the Vietnamese capital of Hanoi to declare themselves the rightful leaders of an independent Vietnam. On September 2, 1945, some four hundred thousand Vietnamese gathered in Hanoi's Ba Dinh Square. Entire communities walked in from the countryside to join the festivities, many dressed in their best clothes, some carrying ancient scimitars and bronze clubs—symbols of historic campaigns against foreign domination. American members of the OSS joined the crowd. Signs in Vietnamese, French, and English read, "Viet Nam to the Vietnamese," "Independence or Death," and "Welcome American Delegation."

The crowd was addressed by a small man with a wispy goatee wearing a high-collared khaki jacket and white rubber sandals. The fifty-six-year-old revolutionary had lived in exile most of his life under the name Nguyen Ai Quoc—Nguyen the Patriot. While living in France, the Soviet Union, and

China, Quoc had immersed himself in Marxist and Leninist theory and was a principal founder of the Indochinese Communist Party in 1929. A revolutionary nationalist and a committed Communist, he viewed both causes as inseparable. Yet he was also a shrewd pragmatist willing to entertain the support of any great power that might aid his most cherished goal of Vietnamese independence. At the beginning of World War II, to protect his identity, Quoc changed his alias to Ho Chi Minh—Ho the Bringer of Light.

In 1945, Ho was optimistic about American help. As he stepped to the podium in Ba Dinh Square his first words were these: "All men are created equal. The Creator has given us certain inviolable rights: the right to life, the right to be free, and the right to achieve happiness." Then he paused and said, "Fellow countrymen, can you hear me clearly?" "YES!" they roared back. "These immortal words were taken from the Declaration of Independence of the United States of America." At one point two American P-38 Lightnings swooped over the crowd. It was probably a random flyby, but the crowd took it as a dramatic signal of American support.

The wartime help of the OSS, along with President Roosevelt's public endorsements of self-determination for all nations, fueled Vietnamese hopes that the United States would oppose any French effort to reconquer Indochina. In declaring their Vietnamese independence, Ho Chi Minh announced the formation of a new state, the Democratic Republic of Vietnam (DRV), and sought international recognition. But he had not counted on the coming of a new war, the Cold War. The new American president, Harry Truman, was determined to build a strong European alliance against the Soviet Union. To secure French support in that coalition, he was prepared to help them regain their Indochinese colony.

And so, just a few months after World War II ended, U.S. merchant marine ships that had been bringing American troops home from the war received new orders. They were to transport thirteen thousand French soldiers from Europe to Vietnam. Many of the American seamen opposed the assignment. Crew members of the *Winchester Victory* cabled Washington to "vigorously protest the use of this and other American vessels for carrying foreign combat troops . . . to further the imperialist policies of foreign governments when there are American soldiers waiting to come home." That cable marked the beginning of what would be a long history of American opposition to involvement in Vietnam. In the first few years after World War II, Washington also received at least seven cables and letters from Ho Chi Minh. Each time, he urged the United States to recognize Vietnam's right to self-determination and independence. His communications were not even acknowledged.

Truman's crucial decision, like so many that would determine America's actions in Vietnam over the next three decades, had very little to do with Vietnam itself, but with U.S. priorities on the world stage. Given Washington's preoccupation with maintaining its superpower status in the postwar era, it is not surprising that policy makers gave virtually no attention to a few OSS officers on the ground in Vietnam or to Ho Chi Minh, someone most people in the State Department had never heard of, much less that they would be emboldened to honor the principles of the Atlantic Charter and defy a European ally they deemed essential to world order.

Thus, American recognition of Vietnamese independence would have required bold and unconventional leadership. How that might have changed history is, of course, unknowable. There is no compelling evidence that Ho Chi Minh would have allied himself with the United States in the Cold War, nor great reason to assume that Vietnam would have taken a non-Communist road into the future. However, it does seem certain that American support for Vietnamese independence would have averted decades of warfare and the loss of millions of lives.

HENRY PRUNIER

"These were not ragtag farmers."

At first glance, his living room looks like many others in New England—a fireplace, some family photographs, a tidy arrangement of furniture. But he points with pride to a silk-embroidered tapestry depicting a menacing Mongol invader aiming a bow and arrow at a defenseless Vietnamese couple. "This," he says, "was a gift from Ho Chi Minh."

Henry Prunier is a retired brick and masonry contractor. Yet for a few weeks in 1945 he was an ally of Ho Chi Minh, the leader of Vietnam's wars against France and the United States, a man regarded by five American presidents as a dangerous enemy, and arguably the most important figure in Vietnamese history.

Just as World War II was ending, in July 1945, Prunier parachuted into the jungles of northern Indochina as part of a seven-man "Deer Team" organized by the Office of Strategic Services. Their mission was to support an anti-Japanese resistance movement called the Viet Minh led by a "Mr. Hoo." Prunier was a twenty-three-year-old private who had received a year's instruction in Vietnamese.

I landed beside a rice paddy and I was really scared. These Orientals came up. I didn't know whether they were Japanese or Vietnamese. I was so flabbergasted I couldn't even speak English, never mind Vietnamese. But they brought us into a village and there was a big decorated archway that said, "Welcome to Our American Friends." That same evening they had a big feast for us. They slaughtered a calf and served us beer.

All we knew is that we were supposed to make contact with a resistance group headed by a "Mr. Hoo" and a "Mr. Van" [the alias of Vo Nguyen Giap, the military commander of the Viet Minh and later the commander of North Vietnam's People's Army] who were going to help us organize a guerrilla group to harass the Japanese. That was our mission. A few days after we arrived they took us to a hut, about a half mile from our camp, to meet Ho Chi Minh. He had just walked all the way down from the Chinese border and he looked like a bag of bones. He was just decimated. His cheeks were all sunken in and his color was awful. He was dying from malaria, dengue fever, dysentery—whatever tropical disease you can think of. He couldn't even stand up. But even in his sickness his eyes were very bright. He had the brightest eyes you could possibly imagine. Our medic gave him quinine and sulpha drugs, although the traditional Vietnamese medicines he was taking may have done just as much to save his life.

After some days setting up our camp, we started working with the Viet Minh. There were about two hundred of them, but we only had enough weapons to train about eighty-five. They were very ill-armed. They just had some old flintlock rifles and a few confiscated French rifles. We had carbines, M-1 rifles, machine guns, grenades, bazookas, and mortars dropped in by parachute.

Vo Nguyen Giap was with us almost constantly. He was never in military uniform. He always wore a white linen suit, black shoes, and a black fedora. He was a ball of fire and into everything. In fact, when I was teaching the 60-millimeter mortar, Giap came over to watch and he was wondering what actuated the shell. He couldn't understand what made it fire off so he came over and looked right down the barrel. Can you imagine that? Fortunately there was no shell in it and they pulled him away.

But don't get the wrong impression—this was an elite group that we trained. They were all hand-picked and came from all over Vietnam. They were really sharp. When I learned the M-1 rifle in basic training it took me about three or four days before I could take it apart and put it back together without thinking about it. After teaching them one time, they could almost do it blindfolded. These were not ragtag farmers, and it would be ridiculous to assume that our training and weapons had anything to do with their eventual victories over the French and then the United States. Whatever the Viet Minh learned about guerrilla war, they learned on their own. After all, we only worked with them for about two and a half weeks before World War II ended.

Ho Chi Minh was happy to have our military training and weapons, but I think what he really wanted was America's political support. He hoped our being there would help convince the American government to support Vietnamese independence after World War II was over. I also think he felt our presence would help him solidify his support in Vietnam. He could tell various political factions that the United States was behind the Viet Minh and that might give him some added credibility.

It is not an exaggeration to say that Ho's troops loved him like a father. Their respect was obvious. And when you saw him with his men he really did come across as a man of the people. He mingled with them much more than Giap. One time I saw Ho fooling around with a group of his troops doing jujitsu moves. But mostly he just went around talking with people. He was the type of person who would draw you out, a soft-spoken, really meek-looking individual. He didn't seem like the type who would take up a gun or kill people, but I guess he could be ruthless in his mind, even though we didn't get that impression. He just didn't seem like a military type.

When World War II ended it took us about two weeks to walk out of the jungle. At the town of Thai Nguyen the Japanese refused to surrender and the Viet Minh engaged them in skirmishes that lasted almost a week. Unfortunately, we missed Ho Chi Minh's Declaration of Independence on September 2.* But when we did get to Hanoi we were treated like heroes. We were invited to the Governor's Palace and Ho gave each one of us a gift in recognition of our contribution toward defeating the Japanese and toward Vietnam's independence. He said we'd be welcome to come back and see him any time. At one point someone asked him directly if he was a Communist and he said, "Yes, I'm a Communist, but there's no reason why we can't be friends, why we can't live together."

I'm sure Ho did not foresee the struggle between the United States and his people. After all, we were there in the jungle as representatives of the American government and supporting him. One of the greatest disappointments in his life must have been that the United States sided with the French, and then Diem [president of South Vietnam from 1954–63], against him. It should never have happened.

I was sort of a silent antiwar person. For a while in the sixties I made talks about my experience in the OSS at the Rotary Club and an article was published in the local paper. In the article I said that I thought Ho had the genuine support of the Vietnamese people. I had three daughters in high school at the

*While the Deer Team was not yet in Hanoi, several other Americans, including Major Archimedes Patti, did attend the ceremonies in Ba Dinh Square on September 2.

time and some of their classmates said, "Oh, your father's a Communist." I was by no means a Communist, but I knew that the patriotism of the Vietnamese was going to far outdo anything we could throw at them, and it did. But I didn't want my daughters to be persecuted by something I was saying, so I stopped talking about it and I never got involved with any demonstrations.

In 1995, a delegation of OSS veterans went back to Vietnam for a reunion. "At one of our meetings General Giap was staring at me, apparently trying to recall whether he remembered me or not. Then he grabbed an orange out of a dish and made a motion like he was lobbing a hand grenade. Isn't that amazing? I actually did teach them how to toss hand grenades."

VO NGUYEN GIAP

"The most atrocious conflict in human history."

"When people ask me where I received my military training, I say, 'Nowhere.' I learned from books and my own experiences." At eighty-eight he does not always feel up to an interview, but after one postponement he appears in the reception room of his substantial compound in downtown Hanoi wearing his military uniform, four stars gleaming from each shoulder and his skin surprisingly smooth.

In 1929, when he was just eighteen, Giap was sentenced to three years in a French prison for his anticolonial activism. He married a woman who shared his revolutionary Communist convictions and years later, during World War II, she died in a French prison. Giap was a scholar and a political theorist long before he became a military commander. One of his first books, published in 1938, was called The Question of National Liberation in Indochina. *In 1944, Giap began to recruit and train an anticolonial army—thirty-four men in the beginning. In 1954, he led an army of more than three hundred thousand to victory against the French.*

In the American War his power was contested and at several crucial moments outmatched by equally powerful members of the Communist Party, especially Le Duan, the secretary-general. Nonetheless, he remained a formidable architect of North Vietnamese military policy until his retirement in 1973. He is the most prominent surviving member of the revolutionary generation.

Journalists and scholars all ask me the same question: "How did we win?" There are many books on the subject, but people are still not clear about it. One American professor said, in effect, that the Vietnamese people won because we know how to use our intelligence against the power of steel. Well, that's right, but intelligence alone is not enough. We won the war because we would rather die than live in slavery. Our history proves this. Our deepest aspiration has always been self-determination. That spirit provided us with stamina, courage, and creativity in the face of a powerful enemy.

Militarily, the Americans were much more powerful than we were. But they made the same mistake as the French—they underestimated Vietnamese forces of resistance. When the Americans started their air raids, Uncle Ho said, "The Americans can send hundreds of thousands, even millions of soldiers; the war can last ten years, twenty years, maybe more, but our people will keep fighting until they win. Houses, villages, cities may be destroyed, but we won't be intimidated. And after we've regained our independence, we will rebuild our country from the ground up, even more beautifully."

History is not made with "ifs," but if American leaders had been wiser I think we could have been spared the war. In my opinion, the Vietnam War was not in the American interest. It was a big mistake. U.S. expenditures were vast, and for the Vietnamese people, casualties were enormous. The American War can be described as the most atrocious conflict in human history. The Americans inflicted insane atrocities. The My Lai massacre was just an example. And in December 1972, they bombed Bach Mai hospital in Hanoi. Perhaps the American people know this already, but they need to be told again and understand more.

All his life Uncle Ho devoted his love and energy to the country and the people. A few days before he died in 1969, he wanted to talk with me and other leaders. He was rather sick and we said we would come to see him. But he insisted on coming to see us instead. We gathered at a house close to Ho Tay Lake. It was raining cats and dogs, so when he arrived he was soaking wet. I said, "Take a rest, Mr. President." In his final days he was still thinking hard about how to win the American War. He asked many questions about the situation at the front. He had always longed to visit the South. I said, "Everything is okay. The army is fighting well. We will certainly win and you will have your chance to see the South."

From the first day to the last, memories of working with him are always with me. We first met in Pac Bo cave with Pham Van Dong [future prime minister of the Democractic Republic of Vietnam]. A few years ago I showed the American senator John Kerry that cave and he asked, "How did you plan to win a revolutionary war from such a dark cave?"

I remember one meeting in that cave in the 1940s. We were sitting near a fire at night and I said, "We talk about a general uprising, but we don't even have any weapons." Uncle Ho calmly replied, "Don't worry, if we have the people, we have the weapons." So we started mobilizing the people to help us. I went into the mountains to live with the ethnic minority people—the Tho, the Thai, the Man, the Dao, and the Hmong. I learned to speak three ethnic minority languages. We formed self-defense units in the hamlets and we formed an army. At first there were only thirty-four soldiers, thirty-four strong men. But after a few years everybody in those mountains followed the Viet Minh.

At the end of World War II, I worked closely with American OSS officers in Tan Trao, Thai Nguyen, and Hanoi. The OSS commander was Major [Allison] Thomas and we still keep in touch. In one letter he wrote, "Yesterday you were in the jungle. Today you're running an independent country. Isn't that wonderful? The history of your nation is like a novel. I hope we can have good relations." Me too. But to do so Americans should understand more about Vietnamese history and culture. We cannot be compared to the United States in wealth, science, or technology, but a good relationship should be built on an equality of respect.

In the midnineties Giap participated in discussions held in Hanoi between an American delegation led by wartime U.S. Secretary of Defense Robert McNamara and a group of Vietnamese historians, retired generals, and former diplomats. McNamara hoped to examine wartime "misunderstandings" between the two countries and identify possible "missed opportunities" for negotiating an earlier end to the war. An initial exchange between McNamara and Giap revealed a fundamental difference in their historical views of the war:

McNamara: "We need to draw lessons which will allow us to avoid such tragedies in the future."

Giap: "Lessons are important. I agree. However, you are wrong to call the war a 'tragedy.' Maybe it was a tragedy for you, but for us the war was a noble sacrifice. We did not want to fight the United States, but you gave us no choice."

"DELIVER US FROM EVIL"

In the late 1940s, Washington recognized French sovereignty in Indochina but was reluctant to offer direct military aid to France for its war against the Viet Minh. In 1949, however, France recast that war as an anti-Communist crusade on behalf of the "State of Vietnam," offering vague promises of future independence. Since France retained complete control over the Vietnamese government it had installed, the change was essentially window dressing that allowed Washington to describe the war as part of a global campaign to contain Communism, not as an effort to suppress an anticolonial war for independence. By 1950, American aid had begun to flow directly to French forces.

In 1949, the Chinese Communists under Mao Zedong won a stunning revolution over the American-backed government of Chiang Kai-shek, creating an acrimonious political backlash in the United States over the question "Who Lost China?" That debate taught a whole generation of American leaders a fundamental Cold War lesson: If Communists achieved victory anywhere in the world on your watch, you would be held personally responsible. The outbreak of the Korean War a year later only intensified Washington's concern about the spread of Communism in Asia and fueled rapid increases in U.S. support for the French-Indochina war. By 1954, America was paying almost 80 percent of its ally's war expenses. As France grew ever more dependent on American aid, increasing numbers of Vietnamese came to regard the United States as an enemy. For all but a few Americans, however, the war in Indochina was at most a remote story on the back pages of the newspapers.

Eight years of bitter warfare, almost half a million troops, and $3.5 billion in U.S. aid led only to a precarious stalemate, while the war was becoming so unpopular in France that it had to rely almost wholly on Vietnamese conscripts, soldiers from its other colonies, and its foreign legion, to continue the fighting. In 1953, the French commander Henri Navarre deployed fifteen thousand troops to Dien Bien Phu, a small outpost in a remote river valley of northwestern Vietnam. He regarded it as an unassailable position from which to launch attacks on the Viet Minh's rear bases. It proved a colossal blunder. General Vo Nguyen Giap surrounded the isolated French garrison with fifty-five thousand Viet Minh soldiers. An even greater number of peasants helped drag heavy howitzers and antiaircraft guns through impossibly rugged terrain. For two months in the spring of 1954, Dien Bien Phu was under siege.

A French request for U.S. military intervention received serious consideration by the Eisenhower administration. The Pentagon even prepared studies on "the feasibility of successfully employing atomic weapons in Indochina." Ultimately President Eisenhower decided that he did not have enough congressional and international support to go to war. Among the critics of possible military intervention was Massachusetts Senator John Kennedy. "I am frankly of the belief," he said, "that no amount of American military assistance in Indo-China can conquer an enemy which is everywhere, and at the same time nowhere, [and which] has the sympathy and covert support of the people." In Korea, thirty-four thousand Americans had died fighting North Korean and Chinese troops without changing the status quo antebellum. In the wake of that anguishing stalemate, there was little enthusiasm for direct participation in another Asian war.

France surrendered at Dien Bien Phu on May 7, 1954, and the next day representatives of nine countries gathered in Geneva, Switzerland, to settle the war. Having defeated the French, Ho Chi Minh's Democratic Republic of Vietnam (DRV) believed it had a legitimate claim to govern all of Vietnam. However, the major powers at Geneva backed France's desire for a face-saving exit that would temporarily divide Vietnam at the seventeenth parallel, with the DRV controlling only the North. Even the two Communist powers, the Soviet Union and China, fearing that full Communist control of Vietnam might draw the United States into war, pushed the DRV to accept the compromise.

Viet Minh loyalists were deeply disappointed by the outcome, but heartened by the agreement's promise of a nationwide election in 1956, confident that Ho Chi Minh would win it. Washington was upset that any territory had been granted to the Communists. Secretary of State John Foster Dulles refused to sign the agreements, but did pledge to honor its terms.

The accords allowed former combatants and civilians to "regroup" north or south of the seventeenth parallel. In 1954, roughly nine hundred thousand northerners, most of them Catholics who feared Communist reprisals, headed south, largely transported by the U.S. Navy. Roughly two hundred thousand southerners, mostly Viet Minh soldiers, moved north, assured that they would rejoin their families in the south in two years when the nation was reunified.

However, American intelligence operatives were already in the south laying the groundwork for a permanent non-Communist nation. Where France had failed, Washington believed it could succeed. After all, as Dulles put it, "We have a clean base there now without a taint of colonialism." Not just Vietnam was at stake, he argued. Should all of Vietnam "fall" to Communism, other nations throughout Southeast Asia would follow suit. This staple of Washington's Cold War thinking since the late 1940s gradually came to be known as the "domino theory." In 1954, President Eisenhower was among the first to articulate this metaphorical image of Communism's danger. "You have a row of dominoes set up," he said. "You knock over the first one, and what will happen to the last one is the certainty that it will go over very quickly." In Washington's view, no nation could "fall" to Communism due to eternal causes. A domino would only topple if pushed from the outside by China or, especially, the Soviet Union. And once a single country toppled there would be no chance to uphold the others. Preventing a Communist victory in Vietnam was not itself Washington's foremost concern. Rather, it cared about Vietnam because of the chain reaction it might trigger elsewhere.

To keep the first domino from falling, the United States gave its support to Ngo Dinh Diem, a Catholic aristocrat from central Vietnam who had spent the previous four years in exile, partly at a Maryknoll seminary in Lakewood, New Jersey. In 1954, he returned to Saigon, the new southern capital city, where the United States was instrumental in securing his appointment as premier of a South Vietnam. To the surprise of some in Washington who doubted his ability to prevail against multiple rivals, Diem successfully used his first $12 million in covert aid from the CIA to buy off and crush several powerful sects in the South. He also launched a massive campaign of repression against former members of the Viet Minh who had not regrouped to the North. Suspected Communists were interrogated, tortured, imprisoned, and, in thousands of cases, executed.

As Washington gained confidence in Diem's ability to rule a non-Communist south, aid poured in. By 1956, his government was receiving $270 million annually. That same year Diem, with American approval, refused to hold the Geneva-mandated nationwide elections. American intelligence reports indicated that Ho Chi Minh would have won overwhelmingly. Instead, while claiming that Communists could not be trusted to participate in fair elections, Diem held his own rigged vote and made himself the president of the Republic of Vietnam (South Vietnam).

In the North, the Communist Party that ran the Democratic Republic of Vietnam used the time to consolidate its rule and build a socialist state. At the heart of that effort was a radical land reform campaign. In the name of equality, land was confiscated not only from large landholders but also from many modest property owners and those deemed enemies of the revolution. "Reactionary" targets of the campaign were not only stripped of their property and vilified in public denunciations, but an estimated eight thousand were executed. In 1956, Hanoi's Communist Party leaders admitted that the program had produced many "excesses" and a considerable amount of land was restored to the original owners, but much of the damage could not be rectified and it proved a severe blow to political unity in the North.

Despite their disappointment over the cancellation of a nationwide election, Hanoi's leaders still hoped for a political road to unification and did not believe it feasible to launch an immediate war on behalf of southern comrades who sought to overthrow Ngo Dinh Diem. They had their own rebuilding to do after the French war. Their allies, the Soviet Union and China, agreed, and for the remainder of the 1950s, Hanoi told southern Communists and supporters to focus entirely on political efforts to build a revolutionary base in the South. Armed resistance would have to wait.

DANIEL REDMOND

"The doctor who won the war in Indochina."

At age seventy, the lean, semiretired lawyer still takes seven-mile walks around his Arlington, Virginia, neighborhood. He credits his early career in the navy for most of what was best in his life. In 1954, he was sent to Vietnam as a twenty-four-year-old ensign to assist in Operation Passage to Freedom, the transportation of almost a million North Vietnamese, most of them Catholics, to South Vietnam. It was one of the largest short-term migrations in history and was promoted by the CIA in hopes of providing a political base for the new Catholic ruler Ngo Dinh Diem. Under the leadership of Edward Lansdale, CIA operatives flooded northern Catholic villages with leaflets saying that Jesus and the Virgin Mary had moved south and it was the duty and salvation of all Vietnamese Catholics to do so as well.

While in Vietnam, Redmond met Thomas A. Dooley, a navy doctor who wrote a best-selling book about the Vietnamese refugees called Deliver Us from Evil. *Dooley's book, along with his many public speeches and television appearances, cast America's involvement in Vietnam as a moral obligation on behalf of suffering peasants fleeing Communist persecution. He inspired many young Americans to dedicate their lives to foreign service, and when John Kennedy announced the formation of the Peace Corps in 1961, he invoked the name of Tom Dooley as a model of patriotism and self-sacrifice.*

Sitting at a table in his downstairs office, Redmond takes out a photograph of Vietnamese refugees gathered in front of a transport ship, loaded down with belongings.

It turned out to be a really monstrous job. The people were terrified, absolutely terrified. Your heart just broke when you saw them. They had come from these little villages where they had never traveled farther than a mile or two from home. They had never been on a ship. Everything they owned they carried on balance sticks over their shoulders. The smell was so awful it almost made you gag. They had never used bathrooms before. I remember one mother gave birth, refused our help, bit off the umbilical cord, took the baby into the dirty river, and washed it off.

Almost a million people were evacuated. It started in August 1954 and ended in May 1955. I was the embarkation officer. We'd go up the river in LSTs [landing ship tanks]—fairly large amphibious crafts—take on refugees and bring them down to Haiphong where we'd offload them onto ships that would transport them the rest of the way down to South Vietnam. While they were waiting for the boats, our guys would be busy spraying them with DDT to kill the lice. These were pre–Rachel Carson days.*

One day I loaded three thousand people onto one LST. These goddamn French legionnaires were shoving people on like they were cattle. I felt like a war criminal, but at least I got them out of there. Personally, I felt very good about the operation and I'm proud to have been involved with it. It was primarily a humanitarian operation. I developed a tremendous liking for the Vietnamese, and since I'm Catholic I felt a religious affiliation with the refugees. The Communist propaganda on the radio was that we were going to throw them all overboard and sell their women to brothels in the South. I just despised the Viet Minh. They were a bunch of murderers. At the same time, I didn't see our operation as some kind of golden mission, some big crusade to save these people from the Commies. They were victims more of the French than the Communists. I was as pissed off at the French as I was at the Viet Minh.

And I knew our operation was political, that we were underwriting Ngo Dinh Diem. These people became his base down south because most of them were Catholic like him, whereas most Vietnamese were Buddhist. I always laughed when I saw the big sign in the LSTs—"This Is Your Passage to Freedom." It was written in both Vietnamese and English, but most of the peasants couldn't read. It seemed to me typical American public relations, directed more at the U.S. home front than at the Vietnamese.

I do think it was right for us to take the people down there, but it was our first commitment to the disaster that happened in the sixties. I never had any idea we'd be involved in a war out there ten years later. The situation was such

*Carson was the author of *Silent Spring*, an influential attack on the use of pesticides such as DDT, published in 1962.

a debacle for the French, I couldn't believe the United States would willingly get involved in a similar thing. We should have just supported the South Vietnamese financially and stayed the hell out of there.

Of course I worked with Tom Dooley, the guy who became very famous for his book about the operation called *Deliver Us from Evil*. I admired him for his religious practices, but he was a mystery to me, probably the most complex man I ever met. Sometimes I liked him and sometimes I thought he was a pain in the ass.

Dooley was from a prominent St. Louis family, and the chief of naval medicine was a family friend, so Dooley was always writing this admiral about what he was doing in Vietnam. The letters were boastful and self-promoting, but the admiral was totally taken with Dooley and put excerpts of them into the bulletin that went out all over the world to navy doctors. We started calling Dooley "the doctor who won the war in Indochina." And when his book came out I can remember people, particularly Catholic women, just about swooning. All of a sudden, from an obscure lieutenant junior grade, he became an idol! Every time you turned around you heard about Tom Dooley.

I didn't know it at the time, but Tom was a homosexual. He went out of his way to be macho. Of course he had to hide his sexuality and had the tremendous dilemma of justifying it with the demands of his religion. Eventually he was caught and the navy got rid of him.*

Though I found his self-promotion aggravating, he always surprised me with his kindness. Occasionally he'd suggest that we go up to a field hospital and visit the French survivors of Dien Bien Phu. He was genuinely concerned about those people. And he could be extremely charming and gregarious, especially with enlisted men and the Vietnamese. He gave hilarious lectures on VD to the crew that had them rolling on the deck. He was very much a showman—played the piano, spoke French, sang songs. He also had a real facility for language and picked up Vietnamese very fast. The Vietnamese loved him.

But frankly, I thought *Deliver Us from Evil* was a piece of shit. When I read it I almost threw it across the room I was so mad. I kept finding inaccuracies and he really laid on that Communist stuff. Tom was given to exaggeration and to me it was symbolized by a picture in that book of a young Vietnamese guy on the street in Haiphong who was very deformed. The caption said he was the victim of Ho Chi Minh's torturers. I used to see that guy every day. He was no more a victim of Communist torture than I was. He was a simple beggar

**Dooley was investigated by the navy for homosexuality and discharged in 1956. However, his promotion of the American mission in Vietnam had been so successful that the CIA helped to support Dooley's return to the region as a civilian. Under the auspices of the International Rescue Committee, Dooley set up medical clinics in Laos. He died in 1961 of cancer.*

who probably was born that way. Never once did he ever hint that the Viet Minh had tortured him. Hell, in that strange place he may even have worked for the Viet Minh.

I shared Dooley's anti-Communism, but not the way it was put in that book.

He reads from a long letter he wrote to a friend in 1955. "We sometimes wonder if people at home are conscious of the fact that the Orient is, and will be, the scene of the final struggle between human dignity and undisguised barbarism." With this line he stops and laughs at the fervor with which he, too, like so many Americans, had divided the world into good and evil. "I was really into it I guess. I wouldn't say that now." He continues reading the letter: "I have seen some of the harsh realities of Communism, Joe, and I am concerned for our country's future. If the Communists have their way out here, we will have lost the Far East. But my work has taught me one fact—the problems are too complex for canned thought. A preventive war is no solution. I pray God we find one."

Dan Redmond died in 2001.

RUFUS PHILLIPS

"Tell 'em I'm not French before they lynch me."

In 1951, the strapping football player from rural Virginia graduated from Yale and joined the CIA. Three years later, as an army lieutenant stationed in Korea, he was ordered to report to Vietnam and assigned to the Saigon Military Mission, a semicovert team of operatives directed by the already legendary Edward G. Lansdale. A former advertising man, now a charismatic air force colonel attached to the CIA, Lansdale was regarded by Washington as a master of psychological warfare. He was considered responsible for almost single-handedly suppressing a left-wing insurgency in the Philippines by building support for Philippine president Ramon Magsaysay. He was sent to Vietnam in June 1954 to produce a similar feat.

"Rufe" Phillips worked on Lansdale's team from 1954 to 1955, went to Laos for the CIA in the late fifties, returned to Vietnam in 1962 with the Agency for International Development, and made several more trips to Vietnam from 1965 to 1968 as a consultant.

Lansdale was sent out there by Allen Dulles, head of the CIA, with a very brief message. It literally said, "Save South Vietnam. God bless you." He scoured Asia to see who might help him, and because I had been in the CIA earlier and had some French language I got tagged. I had never heard of Lansdale. Shortly after I arrived in August 1954, he came to speak to all of us at the Majestic Hotel. He was forty-six years old, had a high forehead, a clipped mustache, and was dressed in khaki shorts, knee socks, a short-sleeved shirt, and an air force officer's hat worn at a slightly rackish angle. He said he didn't have a clear idea yet of what we were going to do but he had been sent there to help South Vietnam defend itself and avoid a Communist takeover. When one team member later asked him to clarify our mission, his reply was deceptively simple: "Find out what the Vietnamese people want and then help them get it."

The next meeting I had with Lansdale he asked me what I knew about psychological warfare. I said, "Nothing." He tossed me a book called *Psychological Warfare* and said, "Well, read this." Then I went to the USIS [United States Information Service] library and read a number of books about Vietnamese culture and history. But it was very confusing because there were all these refugees coming down from the North, there were still French there, and then you had the Binh Xuyen, a gangster sect that ran the police and had their own private army riding around in blue helmets. You had the foreign legion, you had Senegalese, you had the Vietnamese army, you had people carrying bamboo poles of food up and down the street, women in conical hats, and there were still remnants from the war against the French. At the old Continental Hotel they had a steel screen in a curve going outward to make sure you couldn't throw grenades in. I thought, my God, will I ever understand anything about this place? It really did seem to me to be the mysterious Orient.

In this chaotic snake pit we began our work with Colonel Lansdale. There were about fifteen of us, nearly all with military or paramilitary backgrounds, but only one who had any previous experience in Vietnam. The month before I arrived, Ngo Dinh Diem had been appointed prime minister. He came from a prominent central Vietnamese mandarin family. Since he was the only non-Communist leader left who had never cooperated with the French, he had impeccable credentials as a nationalist. But initially he really didn't have any authority.

The South Vietnamese government existed in name only, a collection of French-trained civil servants who didn't have a clue what to do without the French giving them orders. We didn't know if Diem would survive or even if South Vietnam would survive. I think most Americans on the spot had pretty well written it off. They were extremely pessimistic. One of my first assignments was to go out to the U.S. economic aid mission to ask for some medical kits for a Vietnamese psychological-warfare company that was going to distribute them in the countryside. This American official refused. He said, "They'll only be turned over to the Viet Minh." His attitude was that the place was already lost, so why the hell should we equip the Viet Minh with our medical kits?

But the immediate threat wasn't the Viet Minh. It was all the various sects that opposed Diem—the Binh Xuyen, the Cao Dai, and the Hoa Hao. There was a question whether the Vietnamese army would fight them. The Binh Xuyen not only ran the police, but ran gambling, opium, and prostitution in Saigon. They even had a ring of car thieves. In fact, initially Diem's own palace guard were Binh Xuyen. Eventually the Binh Xuyen launched a war against the army in the streets of Saigon with help from some elements of the Hoa Hao and the Cao Dai general, Trinh Minh The, who had his own army. Lansdale established contact between Diem and The. Diem agreed to pay The's army and they merged forces. That was the key factor in weakening the sects and clearing the Binh Xuyen out of Saigon.

Lansdale had a bunch of ideas for pulling the country together. He would take some of Diem's ideas, mingle 'em with his own, and feed 'em back in a way that Diem thought they were all his own. One idea was to give the armed forces a more positive role. Lansdale assigned me initially as an adviser to a Vietnamese psy-war [psychological warfare] company. We were using the army to reoccupy large areas of South Vietnam that were being evacuated by the Viet Minh according to the terms of the Geneva Accords. The Viet Minh occupied about as much territory in the South as they did in the North, especially down in the Ca Mau Peninsula and in the central provinces of Quang Ngai and Binh Dinh. One of the problems facing Diem was how to reestablish government in those areas.

The first operation was down in Ca Mau. I used French to communicate because only a few Vietnamese spoke passable English. I didn't know what to expect. We arrived at dusk when clouds of mosquitoes came out of the mangrove trees. I thought it was some kind of fog. They led us over to this very primitive outdoor cafe and put smoke pots under the tables. We had tea and a crowd of people gathered around. They started murmuring under their breath and it got louder and louder, so I asked one Vietnamese, "What's going on?" He said, "They think you're French." I said, "Tell 'em I'm not French before they lynch me." The French had bombed that place repeatedly.

But it was very obvious to the Vietnamese after a while that we were there to help them. It wasn't an ego trip. We had no ulterior motive. We were not trying to do something purely in the interest of the United States. When we'd have Vietnamese come in and say, "I want to work for you," Lansdale would say, "Well, I don't want you to work for us. You should be working to help your government." Then the guy would say, "There's nobody in the government to hire me."

"Well, we'll help you for a while," Lansdale would say, "but then you get a job with the government. We're not signing you up on some dotted line. You aren't an agent of the United States." So that established a bond of trust with the Vietnamese. Lansdale could establish trust with Asians very, very quickly. He had a way of communicating even though he didn't speak either French or Vietnamese.

At first the Vietnamese had very little self-confidence. The French had put them down so much and never really let them get into decision-making positions. All the military operations were run by French officers. The Vietnamese were told where to go and what to do. So a big part of our job was to help them build up confidence.

In April and May 1955, the Vietnamese army conducted a two-division reoccupation up in central Vietnam that was executed extremely well. I was kind of a facilitator and on-the-spot adviser. The troops had been indoctrinated in proper behavior and civic action, the concept of helping the people. So despite Viet Minh propaganda that the government troops were going to come in and rape and pillage, during the whole reoccupation we had not one single incident between the army and civilians. By the time we got to the end people were coming out with bowls of water and greeting the troops. It was quite moving and effective.

Of course the Viet Minh did leave behind an underground network obviously laying the groundwork for their return. And in those areas there was a problem trying to change the village leadership because they had been under the Communists. I think the South Vietnamese made a mistake just canceling all of the village leadership without coming up with a logical program for replacing them.

When I was in Laos [in the late 1950s] I knew the Diem government was beginning to go off the rails. There was a real opening in 1955 and '56 for the establishment of democratic institutions in South Vietnam. That was Lansdale's principal thesis. He believed the only way Communism could be defeated was by offering the Vietnamese people something better. He wanted to put Diem within a constitutional framework that would oblige him to learn how to govern democratically. But Washington refused to support Lansdale. They thought constitutional checks and balances would make Diem too weak to govern effectively.

Instead of insisting on democracy when Diem was still open to advice, the U.S. supported the creation and development of a secret, elite political party called the Can Lao. It was controlled by Diem's brother, Ngo Dinh Nhu. It was almost a carbon copy of the Communist party as an organizational weapon. The idea was to build a kind of personality cult around Diem and to have one party that would, in effect, swear people to loyalty. When Lansdale argued against it with Allen and Foster Dulles, he was told he was being naive. So we aided and abetted the worst side, not just of Diem but of the Vietnamese who had no experience in democratic politics.

But I don't think we should have pulled out of Vietnam. I mean, there was something to the domino theory because there was a political vacuum in the rest of Southeast Asia. You could have marched through Laos with an army of five hundred men and taken the place. Cambodia was the same way. One of the things that happened as a result of our intervention in Vietnam is that the rest of Southeast Asia wound up being so strong the Communists were really only able to take over the remainder of Indochina, but not Thailand, not Malaysia, not Indonesia, and not Singapore.

NGO VINH LONG

"If they're making maps, they're preparing for war."

In 1964, the twenty-year-old South Vietnamese student arrived at Harvard and added his quiet but forceful voice to what was then a small movement in opposition to American policy in Vietnam. He spoke and wrote against the war at a time when few Vietnamese even lived in the United States. Raised in the Mekong Delta, he was, as a teenager, an enthusiastic proponent of U.S. support for Ngo Dinh Diem's government. At age sixteen he was hired to travel the length and breadth of South Vietnam making maps for the military. It was that experience, from 1959 to 1962, which fundamentally transformed his view of American policy.

After war's end in 1975, when hundreds of thousands of Vietnamese refugees came to the United States, Long became a target of criticism and abuse from some of the new emigrants. They were enraged by his participation in the antiwar movement and convinced that he was an apologist for the Communist government of Vietnam. In 1981, several hundred Vietnamese Americans gathered at a Harvard lecture hall to denounce him as he gave a talk on postwar Vietnam. Several in the audience threw Molotov cocktails at him. Fortunately, the gas bottles failed to explode. However, threats against his life continued and during the following year he changed his residence eight times.

Today he is a college professor in Maine. At age fifty-eight, he is the father of a two-year-old child.

Throughout my childhood, the French made routine patrols and killed a lot of Vietnamese. They dumped the bodies into the river and the currents carried them into lakes and ponds. Every time I went down to the pond I would see floating corpses. I hated the French. My father said we shouldn't hate the French people, only French colonial policy.

He also talked to me about the United States. The Vietnamese have two names for the United States—*my quoc*, which means "beautiful country," and *hiep chung quoc hoa ky*, which means "racially harmonious country." Having grown up with the French, who treated the Vietnamese like dirt, I was extremely impressed by these images of the United States. I always thought of it as the ideal place. When my father first tried to teach me French, I refused. I said I wanted to study the language of that beautiful country, the United States. So in 1949, when I was just six, my father and I walked all the way from Vinh Long province to Saigon to find some books in English. It was a journey of a hundred miles. There were no English-Vietnamese dictionaries so we bought an English-French dictionary and a number of Charles Dickens novels. My father and I went home and started with *Great Expectations*. We memorized it word by word, sentence by sentence, page by page. That's how I learned English.

My father was very idealistic. He considered himself a Christian and joined the revolution against the French because the Bible says it is more difficult for a rich man to enter heaven than it is for a camel to pass through the eye of a needle. He gave most of his land to the peasants in his village in the North and moved to the Mekong Delta to organize for the Viet Minh as a schoolteacher. In 1951, he was horribly tortured by the French. They bashed his head and broke his ribs, puncturing his lungs. Doctors said he had only a week to live, but he refused to die. He died only five years ago.

As early as 1953 my father told me that the Americans were supporting the French and would replace the French. He was worried about that. I said, "Dad? You've been telling me that America is this beautiful, wonderful country where there is racial harmony. Why are you bad-mouthing them now?" He said, "Well, it's not the American people, it's the policy of the American government." I didn't understand any of it.

My father taught me everything I knew—Chinese, French, mathematics, chemistry, physics. Because I was homeschooled I had to get special permission in 1959 to take the high school graduation exam. Only about five percent passed it. I had the highest score in South Vietnam, so at age sixteen I became quite well known. Very wealthy people in Saigon asked me to tutor their sons and daughters. I got invitations to tea at the U.S. Embassy and to the Cercle Sportif, the most exclusive country club. It felt like one big party. Whenever I was invited to the Cercle Sportif I was given free Coca-Cola and to me that was like a symbol of civilization. People were dressed in white suits and white tennis outfits. I danced with the daughter of Mrs. Ngo Dinh Nhu [sister-in-law of President Ngo Dinh Diem], met generals and ambassadors, and young American girls talked with me about dating in the United States. They asked me whether I went "parking" and I didn't know what the hell that was. I said, "Well, first of all, I don't have a car, so what's parking?" They thought I was cute.

People kind of liked me. I had a pleasant personality then. I'm a lot grouchier now. [Laughs.] And I liked the American presence. I used to get my news from *Time, Newsweek, Life,* and *Look,* and the American generals gave me *Stars and Stripes*. I liked *Stars and Stripes* because of the cartoons. I had stacks and stacks of them. I knew that America was behind the war but I didn't believe my father. I thought the United States was doing this for the good of Vietnam, that the U.S. stood for freedom and democracy.

One day an American general happened to mention that they had hired a Filipino company called Vera Cruz to make maps of South Vietnam for the Vietnamese government. I said that the Filipinos were foreigners who didn't know how to operate in Vietnam and that they might get killed because the revolution was beginning again. I was just blabbering some things I'd learned from my father. I said that eighty years of French exploitation had made many Vietnamese xenophobic and if you want to make maps you have to know how to deal with the people. I suggested that if they hired me I could show them how to do it. Two months later, after two Filipinos were killed in the Mekong Delta while making maps, they hired me to be the public relations person for one of the five mapping teams.

Wherever we went people were suspicious. Some of them said, "If they're making maps, they're preparing for war." I said, "Well, maybe, but if they have good, detailed maps then they're not going to bomb or shell innocent civilians, so what's wrong with that?" People usually left us alone but by 1962, at least in provinces like Quang Ngai, we had to have a couple regiments in the area to protect us before we could go in and measure.

One time, way up in the Central Highlands, some Montagnards* fired at us with their crossbows. They hit me with an arrow that went right into my shin. Diem had stolen a lot of land from the Montagnards and they thought we were surveying their land in order to take it away. But I talked with a lot of Montagnard leaders and they stopped doing that.

We worked with old French maps made in 1910, but we also had current U-2 reconnaissance photographs to help. Since we were making military maps,

*Meaning "mountain people," Montagnards was a French term for the dozens of Vietnamese ethnic minorities, most of whom lived in the Highlands.

they had to be extremely detailed. You had to know the exact altitude of places so if they placed artillery somewhere they could shell another location exactly. We even had to measure barometric pressure during different months, and the tides. We measured everything. These were the maps the U.S. military used in Vietnam.

By traveling all around Vietnam, I witnessed what was happening. When I saw for myself, I became convinced that U.S. policies in Vietnam were wrong. Starting in 1959 the Diem government began creating "agrovilles." The basic idea was to control people by rounding them up and herding them together in newly constructed villages—or, in some places, they just put fences around old villages. The British used a similar thing in Malaysia against the revolution there and they succeeded, so the United States wanted to transplant that program to Vietnam. Within the agrovilles people were divided into groups of five families that were mutually responsible for each other's activities. So if one family had a son or daughter who joined the National Liberation Front, then the rest of the families would all be punished with fines or imprisonment. By 1959 there were already about a hundred thousand political prisoners in the South.

In 1961, the agrovilles were renamed "strategic hamlets," but it was basically the same program. It created tremendous destruction to peasant life, especially in central Vietnam. People were sometimes moved great distances from their land and put in villages behind barbed-wire fences, moats, and spikes. Their old rice fields were often burned down so the NLF wouldn't be able to make use of the crops, and in 1960 the U.S. started to use defoliants to destroy those crops. With their old fields destroyed, peasants had to start over.

It caused tremendous dislocation, even starvation. One day I entered a village by the name of Ka Rom where highlanders had been regrouped into a strategic hamlet. They said that two hundred people had starved to death in the past month. I knew they were telling the truth just by looking at them. Their hair was crinkled and brown, their skin was dark and flaky, and they smelled horrible. It was just what my father said people had looked like during the famine of 1944–45 in the North.

People in Saigon didn't believe it was starvation. They finally sent out some doctors, but they said it was just dysentery or a "sickness from heaven" and left. So I refused to move on with my mapmaking team. We stayed in the village, cooked rice with a lot of water, added some sugar, and fed the people this gruel. After three weeks most people were healthy again. I wrote to the U.S. Embassy and the Saigon government to say that people were starving in many places and we should stop these policies. They said, "Long, this is how we are going to defeat the Communists." I said, "No, this is not how you defeat the

Communists, this is how you make more Communists." They refused to do anything.

We grew up with Diem. He was made president when I was just eleven. Every time we went to the movies there was Diem's picture and we had to stand up and sing. [He sings in Vietnamese.] "Who's the person who traveled the world to find a way to save Vietnam?" The answer of course was Ngo Dinh Diem. I thought he was a good guy. But traveling around the country was a real eye-opener. I saw the callousness of Diem's officials, his police and army.

The Diem government had many public executions. A lot of people in the West denied that it happened but Diem made no bones about it. They advertised the executions and there were pictures in the paper of people getting their heads chopped off by a guillotine. Officials read a list of crimes the person was supposed to have committed, the blade came down, the head rolled into a box full of sawdust, and that was that. The whole thing was meant to intimidate the population not to join the revolution against Diem. In 1959, when I went around with the map teams there were many military outposts where they summarily chopped off the heads of people they thought were Communists. They put the heads on stakes right in front of their outposts, sometimes with two cigarettes up the nostrils. They even invited people to take pictures of it. They were very proud of themselves. It was a really savage time. It was like back to the Middle Ages.

In 1962, I resigned in disgust and became involved in the Saigon Student Union. We began protesting against the U.S. intervention and the Saigon government. One of our demonstrations in 1964 was against the constitution that the United States had written for Vietnam. It was actually written by a team of American professors. It said that in case of war the population of Vietnam had to quarter troops and turn their property over to the army for its use. We thought that was extremely undemocratic and burned copies of the constitution in the streets of Saigon. Many of my American friends, some of whom worked for the CIA, said, "Long, you should get the hell out of here because if you don't, one of these days you'll be arrested." So I applied to Harvard University and was accepted. But I had a hard time getting my passport and visa because I had made myself such a nuisance to the government. One day when I was being chased by the police I ran to the home of a U.S. general I knew. His wife called the U.S. Embassy and seven hours later I had my passport, visa, and a one-way ticket to Boston.

When I arrived some reporters and photographers were waiting to interview me. I said I thought the United States would invade Vietnam very soon. People were very surprised I used the word *invasion*. Then I said, if that happens there will be a long war, perhaps as long as the American Civil War, and with an impact as great as the French Revolution.

At Harvard he became involved in the antiwar movement but also studied with professors who came to play important roles in the formulation of U.S. policy in Vietnam. He had individual tutorials with both Samuel Huntington and Henry Kissinger. Huntington consulted for the government on Vietnam and Kissinger would become Nixon's national security adviser. "I tried to prove to them that the United States could only win the war by destroying the country, and they shouldn't do it. Both Huntington and Kissinger said, 'Long, you are really naive. Every country, like every human, has a breaking point, Vietnam included.' "

"KICK THE TIRES AND LIGHT THE FIRES"

From 1954 to 1960, Viet Minh veterans of the war against the French organized in the South Vietnamese countryside to build political opposition to the government of Ngo Dinh Diem. Much of Diem's campaign to root out antigovernment dissent was directed at the Viet Minh. Because many southerners admired the Viet Minh as patriots, the United States Information Services suggested in 1956 that the government and the Saigon newspapers begin calling them "Viet Cong," short for Vietnamese Communists, hoping the new appellation would be taken as a pejorative label and diminish the movement's considerable popular appeal. It took several years for the name to catch on in Saigon and did nothing to dampen the respect many peasants had for the cause of national liberation.

What did damage the movement were government policies like Law 10/59, a draconian decree passed in 1959. Under the new law, anyone suspected of threatening the security of the state could be sentenced to death by a military tribunal with no right of appeal. Roving tribunals scoured the countryside rounding up suspects and staging public executions, often by guillotine. Over time, Diem's repression created more opposition than it eliminated, fueling widespread hostility in the South toward the Saigon regime. In the short term, however, it devastated the ranks of the southern Communist Party.

Those southern revolutionaries who had not been jailed or executed were clamoring to fight back with arms, but their comrades in Hanoi repeatedly counseled patience and restricted them to political organizing. According to the party, armed struggle might eventually be required, but was still premature. Some southerners were not content to wait for a green light from Hanoi and launched unauthorized attacks on government troops and officials. While Hanoi clung to hopes that the Diem regime might collapse through political upheaval alone, at the 15th Party Plenum in 1959 Communist leaders agreed that Diem's repression and growing U.S. aid was putting such pressure on the party's southern branch that it was threatened with extinction if not given some support for armed struggle.

Over the next two years Hanoi authorized a growing number of violent actions in the South, including the assassination of Diem-appointed officials, ambushes of government patrols, and attacks on military outposts. To oversee and coordinate the political and military aspects of this new phase of the war, the party established a revolutionary umbrella organization in 1960 called the National Liberation Front of South Vietnam (NLF). Though Communist-led, it was charged with recruiting a broad spectrum of southern dissidents.

When President John F. Kennedy came to office in 1961, the United States had already bankrolled Diem for six years to sustain a non-Communist South Vietnam. The conventional Washington wisdom was "sink or swim with Ngo Dinh Diem." When departing president Dwight D. Eisenhower briefed the new president, however, he did not even mention Vietnam and in Kennedy's first months in office it would rank well down his list of foreign policy priorities. Cold War crises in Berlin, Cuba, and Laos all received more attention.

In the fall of 1961, however, Kennedy began receiving reports that the Diem regime was in serious trouble. Without the direct intervention of American combat soldiers, his advisers warned, the government might fall to the Viet Cong. Kennedy was not eager to escalate U.S. involvement, nor especially confident in its success. But as a hard-nosed cold warrior, he considered Communist victory in South Vietnam an intolerable prospect, a blow to American power and prestige that would almost certainly lead to further Communist victories throughout Southeast Asia. By the end of 1961 he had increased the number of U.S. military personnel in Vietnam from eight hundred to three thousand. Though termed *advisers,* they included fighter pilots, helicopter companies, Special Forces teams, and regular army officers and enlisted men. The administration denied any of them were engaging directly in combat, though in many instances they were. By the end of 1962 their number had increased to eleven thousand, a year later to sixteen thousand, by which time more than a hundred had died.

In the months before his own death, Kennedy began to doubt the capacity of the Diem regime to defeat the Communist insurgency and govern South Vietnam effectively. Diem's popular support was thin, his military largely inept, his government riddled with corruption. In addition to the guerrillas threatening Diem's rule in the countryside, Buddhists were marching through the cities to protest the government's favoritism toward Catholics and its anti-Buddhist policies. Many Americans became conscious of the crisis in June 1963 when a Buddhist monk burned himself to death as a protest against the Diem regime. In the months that followed, the Kennedy administration secretly threw its support behind a group of Diem's generals who were plotting a coup. On November 1,

1963, Diem was assassinated. Three weeks later, Kennedy was himself assassinated. While his death has fueled an irresolvable debate about whether he would have withdrawn from Vietnam or expanded U.S. involvement, it is clear that his policies established the pattern for blunt intervention and further escalation.

RICHARD OLSEN

"It was like 'Terry and the Pirates.'"

A painter who recently retired from the art department at the University of Georgia, he bubbles over with enthusiasm. In 1962, he and his twin brother went to Vietnam as pilots in the same flight company. They were among the thousands of U.S. servicemen sent to Vietnam as "advisers" in the Kennedy era. Their job was to fly South Vietnamese combat troops into the field on H-21 twin-rotored helicopters—huge, lumbering choppers with long curving tails. To preserve the fiction that the United States was not directly involved in the war, American pilots were officially forbidden to fire their weapons unless fired upon.

The H-21 "Banana" was a romantic aircraft. Everyone who flew it knew how hard it was to fly. It was eighty-seven feet long and could seat twenty people, but it didn't have enough power to fly 'em all up in the hot air so we only carried about nine or ten troops. It was designed in the late forties for the Arctic when the Russians were a threat to come over the North Pole. We were stuck with the Banana in the tropics.

My brother Don and I became officers at the tail end of the old army. We got to fly with the world's greatest aviators. I was a twenty-seven-year-old lieutenant flying with pilots who were thirty-five, forty, forty-five years old, guys who had flown in World War II and Korea and were still rounding out their careers. Most of them were warrant officers, so I actually outranked them, but they had much more experience and I was lucky to be with them. Even nineteen-year-old door-gunners were groomed by these older guys and picked up their spirit. Our rule was, the guy with the most experience worked with the person with the least time. I was just trying to be good enough so that these great men didn't frown on me. That's the only worry I had.

So I'm not one of those veterans who's embittered with a whole host of grievances. I have nostalgia and enormous reverence for my experience. I felt like I was in the middle of world history, part of a world process, not a local insurrection. I wanted Communism and totalitarianism to be ruled over by a

Free World spirit. This was the early phase of U.S. involvement and we had the collective idealism of the Kennedy years. We were enthusiastic about nation-building. I celebrated being able to stay alive and manipulate that aircraft into very interesting, difficult, and dangerous places.

I was in a romantic mode in that part of my life. I was with the best men in the world flying over rice paddies, canals, serpentine rivers, and savannas of elephant grass. It was similar to my concept of old African hunting trips with Teddy Roosevelt. All of my daydreams from when I was ten or fifteen years old were coming true right in front of me. In my mind, I was in Hemingway's world. It was all exciting, a rite of passage into manhood.

Vietnam was all about cool pilots. Kick the tires and light the fires. We had an officers club called the Thunderbird Lounge. It was named after our commander's favorite place in Las Vegas. We would fly right over the Thunderbird Lounge at low level to let everyone know we were coming home. It was like "Terry and the Pirates."* You'd put in your reports, go take a shower, get some mess, go to the club, and tell some stories. A drink chit was twenty-five cents. The drinking ceremonies of pilots are legendary and in those days no one thought of booze as a thing that ruins your lifestyle. The whole temperament of the times was to drink as much as you could.

Our main job was to fly South Vietnamese troops into the field. We sometimes fired at targets from the air, but it was absurd because we were not allowed to shoot unless we were shot at. We followed that order. One time an ARVN [Army of the Republic of Vietnam] general ordered me to circle an area and have my door gunner shoot into this vast empty "war zone," as he called it, but that was the only exception. And I had to explain what happened in my after-action report because we were responsible for abiding by the U.S. rules of engagement. We were "flying ducks" in a gallery—with flak jackets and seat padding. Ironically, on the mission when I was shot through the thigh, I didn't wear my seat pad.

On the whole, Vietnamese culture is tougher than ours. I saw Vietnamese kids with bullet holes in their legs who didn't complain. But the South had a softer culture than the North. In the North they had songs that were about sustaining for the future. They were like our songs from the 1930s—"Somewhere Over the Rainbow." In the South it was more like the sixties, the Beatles. They tended to have songs that said "kiss me now."

Their armies were the same way. The army in the South would have siesta from twelve to three. If you dropped them into an area at nine in the morning you couldn't come out to get them between twelve and three because they'd be

*A war and adventure comic strip originated in 1934 by Milton Caniff that ran until 1973.

sleeping in their hammocks. If you came in then, you'd get ambushed by the wide-awake Viet Cong. The South Vietnamese would call us in to get a dead body and ten guys would want to jump on the chopper to get the hell out of there. Their excuse was to go back for their dead comrade's funeral. I thought, stay out there and fight your own war. One time my door gunner asked, "Can I shoot these guys?" I said, "Cool it, cool it." I had the thought that we needed Americans in there to show them how to do it.

When you look at his war paintings from the sixties you can hardly believe they were produced by the same outwardly positive, upbeat man. They include gruesome and haunting images with titles like "Cong: Kill 'Em," "Enemy's Grave," and "Early Morning Visitation, Compliments of the Viet Cong." "I have painted abstractions since the seventies, but I can't get Vietnam out of my system. My paintings would have something of the war in them even if I painted flowers."

In 1994, some of his work was part of an exhibit called "As Seen from Both Sides," war-related art done by Vietnamese and American veterans. He went to Vietnam for the opening. One day, while visiting China Beach near Danang, he took a sunset swim and was caught in a riptide.

"I thought, how absurd. I survived the war and here I am getting drowned as a tourist! I was gagging on water and in serious trouble. All of a sudden a ninety-pound man came up to my face like a dart. We were face to face. The first thing I thought was, Viet Cong! Here he was, rescuing me, eyeball to eyeball. We looked into each other's soul and he was brilliant. This young Vietnamese lifeguard pulled me up and tugged me in."

MALCOLM BROWNE

"You could smell the burning flesh."

"When I got out of the army in 1958 it was a question of returning to my former vocation as a laboratory chemist or changing things altogether and doing what seemed fun." He became a reporter and went to Vietnam in 1961 to cover the war for the Associated Press (AP).

In 1963, he was the only journalist on the scene when a sixty-seven-year-old Buddhist monk, Thich Quang Duc, burned himself to death in protest against the anti-Buddhist policies of South Vietnam's Catholic President Ngo Dinh Diem. A photograph Browne took of the immolation was seen on the front pages of newspapers all around the world. This horrifying picture became one of the two or three most famil-

iar images from the Vietnam War—a robed monk, head shaved, sitting perfectly upright in the middle of a city street, engulfed in flames.

Early on in Vietnam, Browne fell in love with a Vietnamese woman named Huynh thi Le Lieu. They eventually married and moved to the United States in 1966. Browne returned to Vietnam many times thereafter to cover the war for The New York Times.

Saigon was everything I had hoped for. There was the smell of cassia in the air and there were towering tamarind trees all along Rue Pasteur where the AP had its office. The heat was oppressive, but I was much younger, much thinner, and I smoked about three packs of cigarettes a day to fend it off. I was delighted by the setting and fascinated by the undertone of violent romance. Life was really this odd split. In the evenings you might dress up in black tie and tuxedo for some diplomatic function, and every week you could hear some new chanteuse from Paris like Jacqueline Françoise entertaining at the Caravelle Hotel or one of the other night spots. They were wonderful. And yet one would still have to get up at three-thirty in the morning for a helicopter operation and sometimes you got nicked. An impressive number of journalists were killed or wounded and the danger added a certain spice to life.

During my first month in Saigon a British intelligence officer said I couldn't really understand what was happening without reading Vo Nguyen Giap's *People's War, People's Army*. Giap was the victorious commander of Vietnamese forces against the French during the first Indochina war. He was a boring, turgid writer, concerned mainly with the propaganda content of his words, but he was truly wise when it came to guerrilla warfare. I was duly impressed by this brilliant tactician.

Initially, I spent more time with South Vietnamese troops than with Americans. American officials tended to portray Vietnamese communities as Potemkin villages.* But when anyone took the trouble to spend a couple of tiresome, dark nights in a government militia watchtower or strategic hamlet, one came to the conclusion that the other side controlled the countryside. That was particularly true in the Mekong Delta, the most populous part of the country. A few dozen miles south of Saigon, the entire province of Long An was controlled by the Viet Cong at night. When there was fighting, the guerrillas would often overrun posts, get through the minefields and barbed wire, and kill all the defenders.

*Phony evidence of nonexistent prosperity. The term derives from eighteenth-century Russian history when Prince Grigori Potemkin constructed artificial one-street villages and produced cheering throngs to impress Czarina Catherine II.

For me, one of the most depressing series of stories I did had to do with a hamlet called Dam Doi in the extreme southern part of the country, about thirteen miles from Ca Mau. Dam Doi was constantly being overrun by a large Viet Cong unit called the U Minh battalion that operated out of the U Minh forest to the west of Ca Mau. They were very powerful and could really raise hell. Every now and then they seemed to practice on Dam Doi. They'd come in, burn down all the buildings, and go after any local forces who opposed them.

The first time I went to Dam Doi the town's radio link to the outer world had been cut, and I joined a detachment of Vietnamese marines to find out what had happened. We went through jungle and mangrove swamps—a really lousy place to walk. That's where I got a bamboo punji stake in my foot, which caused tremendous pain for a while. When we got to Dam Doi it was just ghastly. The Viet Cong had taken twelve or thirteen of the people they'd executed and laid them out like the spokes of a wheel around a flagpole and on the flagpole they had raised the red, yellow, and blue Viet Cong flag. Naturally they had booby-trapped the flagpole too. At least half of the bodies had their arms tied behind their backs. The slaughter had happened about three days earlier so the whole village was just one great mass of bluebottle flies and the stench was unbearable. By that time all the bodies were bloated like balloons because of the gas and decomposition—really disgusting. But the Viet Cong kept coming back to Dam Doi about once a year and that was one of the regular things I had to do—fly down to Ca Mau, get some sort of transport out to Dam Doi, and see the horrors. I went four times, each time after a massacre of some kind. The government kept trying to reinforce it, but always the U Minh battalion outnumbered them, outmaneuvered them, and outdid them in every way.

Early on I realized it was a rough war and there were no nice guys in Vietnam. Although Americans were not slaughtering prisoners that I was aware of, Americans certainly knew that their Vietnamese counterparts sometimes resorted to torture. The "ding-a-ling" torture was common. It was done with a hand-cranked generator used to produce electricity for radios. The interrogator hooked electrodes to the genitals of prisoners and turned the crank, causing agonizing pain.

In the early sixties the Americans were really waging a secret war, or at least a shadow war. The official line was that Americans were serving purely as advisers and only shooting at the Viet Cong in self-defense. The air force had a fair-sized contingent purportedly there to train South Vietnamese pilots to fly T-28s and AD-6s. I'd heard stories that U.S pilots were actually dropping bombs, so one day early in '61 I went out to Bien Hoa, the biggest military airfield in South Vietnam, to have a look. I was barred from entering but I watched from outside the perimeter fence and saw two-seat T-28s taking off with racks full of bombs. When they returned, I could see that their racks were empty and there were smoke stains behind their guns. As often as not, a Vietnamese was sitting in the back and the actual pilot was blond and blue-eyed and obviously not from Vietnam. By reporting that, I was threatened with expulsion. The official American line was that the U.S. role in Vietnam was subordinate to that of our Vietnamese ally.

The Special Forces were also a prominent component of the American presence in the early days. At that time the Special Forces wore army uniforms and green berets but they were actually part of the CIA working outside the U.S. Army chain of command. This was very much in keeping with Kennedy's view that the right way to wage wars against Communist forces was by indirect action and stealth. The Kennedy administration even enlisted Mafia help in trying to kill Cuba's Castro. Kennedy was very impressed by the Special Forces. He loved to watch their combat exercises as they traversed gorges on ropes and rappelled down walls. Some called these shows "Kennedy's Disneyland."

Just a month or so after I got to Vietnam in 1961 I spent Christmas Eve at Trung Lap, a Vietnamese Ranger camp run by a half dozen American Special Forces advisers. It was very close to one of the main headquarters of the Viet Cong consisting mainly of an underground system of tunnels. It being Christmas Eve, by about eight o'clock the whole camp was roaring drunk, passing around rice liquor and aluminum wash basins filled with beer. At one point, the Special Forces troops broke out sixty-millimeter mortars and fired into the sky, creating a warlike star in the east. To their surprise, firing began from the direction of the Viet Cong tunnel complex, but the guerrillas weren't aiming at the Special Forces camp. They were shooting tracers up at the star shells as if to participate in the celebration. For that one night of the Christmas season there was no fighting—a rare respite.

In 1963, the Buddhist insurrection came like a bolt out of the blue. I don't think the intelligence services or the South Vietnamese government or any outsiders really understood the depth of anti-Diem sentiment throughout the South and not just among the Viet Cong. There was a broad feeling that the government and all the positions of power were under the control of Diem's Catholic family. On May 8, Buddha's birthday, there was a mass demonstration in Hue protesting Diem's prohibition against flying the Buddhist flag. A number of Buddhists were killed and in the weeks and months that followed there were Buddhist demonstrations almost all the time—processions of two or three hundred monks in their saffron yellow robes. Initially, a couple dozen news correspondents would troop along to cover the story. I had Buddhist friends at several pagodas who told the newsmen that they intended to demonstrate with more than just marching; that a ritual suicide was contemplated. But as the weeks passed and nothing happened, my colleagues sort of decided, to hell with it. Then, one evening, June 10, a spokesman for the monks phoned me to say that I really should come to a certain pagoda the following morning at about seven-thirty.

When I got to the pagoda the next day it was obvious that something really unusual was happening. For one thing, there were many more monks and nuns than I had ever seen in one place before. I also noticed that a group of women preparing tea were wearing white mourning dresses. One of them brought me a cup and there were tears streaming down her face. Then they began a chant I had never heard before. It was hypnotic. It began quietly but got louder and louder and the tempo increased. Joss sticks were burning everywhere.

Abruptly at nine o'clock the chanting stopped and everyone rose and trooped out into the street. In three or four files, the procession began. It was by far the biggest Buddhist procession in Saigon up to that point. We walked quite a distance, all the way to the intersection of Phan Dinh Phung and Le Van Duyet. There was a car with us. In the car, besides the driver, were two young monks and an old monk. Quite quickly the monks in the procession formed a circle around this intersection, blocking all traffic.

The two young monks in the car brought out a cushion, placed it in the center of the intersection, and guided the old monk out. It was Thich Quang Duc. He sat down on the cushion and crossed his legs in the traditional lotus position of Buddhist meditation. Then the young monks got out a big plastic can of pink gasoline, brought it over to Quang Duc, and poured it over him.

They stepped back and he took out a box or packet of matches—I couldn't see which. He struck a match, dropped it in his lap, and the flames went up. You could see the agony in his expression, but he never cried out. His eyes closed, his lips tightened, and the flames enveloped him. You could smell the burning flesh. And there was wailing from the nuns. I just took photographs as fast as I could. It was not so much out of an urge to take pictures. As much as anything else it was to have something useful to do to keep my mind off this horrible spectacle. I'd never seen a man burn to death before.

I would guess he stayed in the lotus position for at least three minutes. Maybe five. He was still sitting upright when the police and fire department arrived. A fire truck tried to break through the line and a half dozen of the younger monks just lay down in front of the wheels so it couldn't move without crushing them.

The monks told me later that they had prepared, after experimenting, a special mixture of about two-thirds gasoline and one-third diesel fuel to make it burn longer and hotter. But it took him quite a while to die. Finally, when he pitched over, his arms were extended and he was in a state of total rigor, completely burned but intact.

Because his arms were splayed out, they couldn't get him into the coffin they had brought along. So they just put him on top of it and paraded the coffin into the Xa-Loi pagoda where the old monk lay in state for a few hours. Then they removed his heart and sent the rest of his body to be cremated. They kept the heart in the pagoda where it became a kind of icon of the Buddhist insurrection.

I was numb. But at the same time I realized that this was something of great, great importance, so the immediate task was getting the film sent by air freight to our bureau in Manila. I sent out the raw film. A little later, the South Vietnamese authorities insisted on developing all film before it left Saigon. They developed an informal, but effective, form of censorship.

Diem's sister-in-law, Madame Nhu, suggested that I had bribed the monks to produce a martyr. That was just silly, of course. But I was friendly with many monks. Occasionally I stopped by the pagodas to have lunch with them. They were all wonderful cooks. You can't help liking even sometimes naive Buddhist monks and hating secret police sadists. For the most part I found the Buddhists kindly people representing a faith that was intrinsically nonviolent.

Of course I came in for problems from the police from that moment on. At a subsequent demonstration, plainclothes police sailed into me and my colleague Peter Arnett with bricks to smash our cameras and beat us up. Then they charged us with having attacked the police.

In spite of all this civil turmoil, the war itself exerted a powerful attraction for many Americans through the midsixties. Some of it was because of the image created by the Special Forces. They were America's glamour boys. Many were serving long series of enlistments and felt very much at home in Vietnam. I remember one guy named Al Combs who was very enthusiastic about the war and very fond of Vietnam. Like so many of the early people there, he was enraptured by his Vietnamese girlfriend who eventually became his common-law wife. He managed to keep getting reassigned to Vietnam, and by 1965 they had two children and she was pregnant with a third. In June that year the whole family was dining at the My Canh restaurant in Saigon—a floating restaurant on the Saigon River. That was the night the Viet Cong attacked it. They fired a rocket causing everyone to panic and run for the gangplank. But the Viet Cong had planted mines aimed up the plank and detonated them as people came out. Combs and his wife were killed. That sort of thing happened fairly often to the very early lifers.

But somehow the danger only added to the mystique of the Green Berets.

In 1965 a Special Forces sergeant named Barry Sadler wrote an extremely popular song called "The Ballad of the Green Berets." In those days Vietnam was a magnet for Hollywood celebrities who would come out to add some luster to their names by association with U.S. troops. This included not only the Bob Hope troupe and the glamour girls of the period, but people like John Wayne and Van Heflin. Wayne was a legend and tremendously admired. I have a cousin who was a marine officer and he practically worshipped the Duke.

In my mind, Wayne was one of the people who did much harm by misleading the American public as to what the war in Vietnam was all about. It happened that he and I were in Danang at the same time at a marine officers club. I'd seen him somewhere else along the line and he recognized me when I walked in. He was dressed in battle fatigues and kind of drunk. The marines were eagerly showing him a new pistol that fired little rockets instead of conventional bullets and he was blasting them into the wall, really enjoying shooting up the officers club. Things were getting pretty rowdy and Wayne was saying what a great job the marines were doing, how the whole country was grateful, and if it weren't for these pantywaist liberals, things would go much more smoothly. At that point he looked right at me and said, "and here's another pantywaisted liberal walking into this den of heroes." I was really pissed off. I must have said something like, "How come we're still fighting if the other side are such lousy soldiers?" He kept repeating nasty remarks about liberals and it became a shouting match. A colonel came in and said, "Okay, let's all have some more drinks and forget about it."

That fancy pistol Wayne was playing with was typical of what the war was all about. Vietnam was probably the most technologically oriented war the Americans had ever waged. All kinds of wild ideas were tried even though they were known to be expensive and likely to fail. I remember the great bedbug detector. It was a gadget that was carried like a mine detector by troops. At the end of a carrying pole there was a little capsule holding a bunch of bedbugs. Sticking out the front of this capsule was an air sniffer. You could push it into a bush or a hole and the idea was that when the bedbugs smelled a human being they would become very agitated. There was an instrument inside the capsule to measure the activity of the bedbugs. A huge amount of money was spent on this and as far as I know it only succeeded in producing some laughs.

Another failure was the M113 Amphibious Personnel Carrier. They were lousy in Vietnam combat because they'd get stuck in mud puddles and canals and couldn't crawl their way out. On the other hand, South Vietnamese generals found them of great use in making coups. They were ideal for attacking a radio station or a palace in Saigon.

Of course, the quintessential weapon of the Vietnam War on the American side was the helicopter. Typically you'd be up at three-thirty in morning to get out to the airfield and you'd get ready to board the helicopters—a whole fleet of them. Then word would come that fog had blanketed the area and it would be impossible to take off. So you'd wait until eleven or twelve in the morning. There'd be all sorts of mishaps along the way and by the time you'd finally stagger into the air, chances were that word had filtered back to the opposition that you were on the way. Often as not these great masses of helicopters would land along the edge of a rice paddy and everybody would go charging into a tree line, blazing away like crazy. And there would be nothing there. Maybe some dead civilians but no sign of opposition. That was a typical helicopter mission. On much rarer occasions there would be very strong opposition, but by and large war is boring and in Vietnam waiting for transportation was particularly boring—not just for journalists, but for the troops. The heat was so oppressive after waiting five or six hours to get on a helicopter, mental exhaustion would set in and, of course, this was one of the things the other side relied on.

While the Viet Cong got better and better at negating the American technological advantage, the Americans never really grasped that the war was not about who had the most firepower. To the very end Nixon believed the bombs would prevail or at least forestall defeat. Even John Paul Vann, who was celebrated as a maverick for his disavowal of U.S. military tactics in the early years of the war, became a great believer in air power.* Toward the end of his life in 1972 he frequently called for B-52 strikes. He had once criticized the American approach to guerrilla war as comparable to trying to sink a cork with a sledgehammer. It was astonishing how he had changed. I was with him practically every day in the final weeks of his life. In an earlier phase of the war he had condemned saturation bombing, but now he was calling almost daily for B-52 strikes known as "arclights."

B-52 attacks often consisted of three bombers each loaded with thirty five-hundred-pound bombs. They dropped them in a rectangle and this saturation bombing was designed to blast everything out of existence. One time I was about a mile from a B-52 attack. Even from a mile away you could feel your

*Vann was first in Vietnam from 1962 to 1965 as a lieutenant colonel and senior adviser to an ARVN division in the Mekong Delta. Always a believer in the American cause, he became famous among journalists, policy makers, and the military command as a trenchant critic of American military strategy, including the indiscriminate use of massive firepower. He retired from the military but returned to Vietnam in 1965 as a civilian to work on pacification programs. In 1971, as a civilian, he was given command of military operations in the Central Highlands with a rank equivalent to that of an army major general. He died in a helicopter crash in 1972 and became the subject of Neil Sheehan's best-selling book *A Bright Shining Lie*.

clothing slapping against your skin from the concussions. It just seemed inconceivable to me that anything—even earthworms—could survive such a devastating attack. And yet about ten minutes after this raid the unit I was accompanying began to draw fairly heavy and effective fire from the people who had been underground during the attack. Of course maybe forty percent had been killed and many others had their eardrums shattered, but they were still an effective fighting force.

In 1994, Browne and his wife, Le Lieu, went to Vietnam once again. They were eager to visit some of their old Buddhist friends, especially Thich Tri Quang, a leading Vietnamese monk who had been a key figure in the anti-Diem protests that Browne had covered so long ago. They were told that Quang was unavailable. One monk whispered that the pagoda was full of secret police. Then, out of the blue, another monk said, "If you have to use the bathroom you know where it is." Browne took the hint and he and Le Lieu went to the bathroom. "We found Thich Tri Quang swabbing the floor. He was reluctant to say anything, but he let us know that he was under house arrest and that the human rights problems under the Communists were as bad as they had been under Diem."

LE LIEU BROWNE

"There was one coup after another."

In 1945, when she was nine, her father disappeared, the probable victim of Viet Minh attacks against Vietnamese who worked for the French. She spent most of the 1950s studying in France and London. When she returned to Saigon in 1959, she worked as a censor for President Diem's Ministry of Information. In that post, she met her future husband, Malcolm Browne. The two of them recalled their first encounters from the living room of their summer home in Vermont. He smiled and said, "When anything I wrote offended the government, it was her job to call me in for a chewing out." Thus began an unlikely romance between an inquisitive foreign journalist and the woman who was supposed to keep him in line.

I grew up in Ben Tre in the Mekong Delta, which was reputed to be a stronghold of Communist sympathizers. The French controlled big towns while the Viet Minh controlled the countryside. When the French tried to occupy Ben Tre with their legionnaires and Morroccans and Nigerans they were brutal. But so were the Viet Minh. If they found civil servants or "progovernment elements" they took them away and we never heard from them again. That happened all the time.

My father worked for the Land Development Ministry. The boss was always French and a Vietnamese could never be the head of any department. My father always said that he was a nationalist and he had enthusiastically welcomed the country's independence when the Japanese troops withdrew. But one night in 1945 the Viet Minh came and took him away. He just disappeared and we never knew what happened to him.

About half the students in my high school were pro–Viet Minh. They organized demonstrations and strikes which constantly closed down the school. My mother worried about our education and decided to send me, along with my twin brothers, to France. In the fifties a great number of Vietnamese youth lived in France, either with their families, or alone as we did. Young men went to avoid being drafted into the military. Others were there for a better education and professional training. Most of us contemplated returning to Vietnam to help our country. I had friends who leaned toward Socialism or Communism and they often spoke to me about North Vietnam. In casual conversations they invited me to go live with them there. They said, "You speak French and English. The North Vietnamese government badly needs people like you and you'll be received with open arms." For me, it was a preposterous idea. I was ready to go back to serve my country under Diem. I had heard that the South was peaceful and free.

When I returned in 1959 I worked for the Ministry of Information. All foreign press dispatches had to go through the Post Office where they were read by security officers. If they found something that was politically sensitive they alerted the Ministry of Information. In turn, if the minister found the wording too strong or unfair he asked me to try persuading the correspondent to change it. Sometimes I had to call up Malcolm and say, "Listen, they felt your work wasn't quite right. Would you like to soften it a little bit?" If his article was too critical of the government, the minister was forced to call Malcolm in to give him hell. They had some big arguments and I had to do the translating. That often upset Malcolm and our relationship would turn sour for a few days. Before Malcolm arrived, one of the AP reporters had been expelled, so he knew if he wasn't careful he too might become a persona non grata and be expelled.

I also censored books and magazines, publications written in French and English from foreign countries. Mostly I read novels to see if they had anything in them that was pro-Communist. If so, we'd cross off the names of those books from the list of titles submitted to the ministry prior to shipment. One time an English-French dictionary came to my office and I said, well it's just a dictionary. But I was called by the minister and he said, "Yes, it's just a dictionary but we shouldn't allow it to be displayed in the front window of stores. It should be put discreetly in the back because it includes the word *Communism*."

I worked there for three years but I wasn't happy and wanted to get out. It was a propaganda ministry and I didn't like the politics. Every week we had to attend a political education meeting. We had to study the government's rules and were forced to listen to their lectures on Personalism.* To tell you the truth, I didn't understand it and didn't listen. Most of the high-ranking South Vietnamese officials came from the North and had a very heavy northern accent. Sometimes I literally couldn't understand them, but I also didn't make any effort. I thought it was all nonsense. I strongly believed in freedom and suddenly we were ordered to wear uniforms to work and go to political meetings. It sounded to me more like Communism than democracy.

I also wanted to advance my career and my family was Buddhist. To be the manager or director of my office I would have had to convert to Catholicism. That was the rule. I had many friends who willingly converted in order to be promoted. My job was already very sensitive, and being a woman in a man's world I felt very uncomfortable and even threatened because the political situation sometimes got dicey.

By the time of the Buddhist crisis in 1963 I had left the government and was living with Malcolm. The police got more and more aggressive. One night, they came to our apartment under the pretext of checking our identity cards. Malcolm was already a target for harassment as the Buddhist demonstrations intensified. I was still a Vietnamese citizen and it was illegal for me to live with him so the government might cause us some embarrassment.

The Buddhist crisis went from bad to worse. The Diem government kept harassing the demonstrators and arresting monks. The American press continued to cover the situation and Malcolm took the picture of the burning monk. Diem's sister-in-law, Madame Nhu, was sent to the States to explain and defend the Vietnamese government's actions. Unfortunately, she called the immolated monk a "barbecued monk." That infuriated the Buddhist population and caused Diem and Nhu's downfall.

At the time, I couldn't believe she was so callous and insensitive. But I believe she was the victim of her own ignorance. She was constantly besieged by the American media. Her pictures were in foreign publications all over the

*The Ngo family's espousal of "personalism" took the form of a political party called the Can Lao (the Revolutionary Personalist Labor Party). Run by Diem's brother Nhu, it had a peak membership of fifty thousand, most of them Catholic military officers and state employees. It controlled an extensive intelligence apparatus and secret police force that were used to intimidate and terrorize opponents.

world, showing a beautiful and powerful "First Lady." She was surrounded by people who gave bad advice. Being a southerner, she was frank and naive. And her English wasn't very good, so some of the offensive things she said may have been because she didn't know the proper English word to use. In Vietnamese she never would have referred to the Buddhist immolation as a "barbecue." She didn't understand that Americans could not stomach such blunt language. On the other hand, the Americans never tried to understand our culture, customs, and sensitivity. We had been dominated by foreign powers before and distrusted any foreign intervention.

Despite all that, I admired Madame Nhu for what she did for Vietnamese women. She was a role model in the sense that she promoted the idea that Vietnamese women were as good as men. For almost a century we Vietnamese women had worked side by side with Vietnamese men, holding responsible jobs. We had women doctors, lawyers, politicians, educators, and businesspeople, yet we didn't really feel we had to demonstrate that we were liberated until Madame Nhu came along. She empowered us and politically reinvigorated us to fight for recognition.

As for Diem, he was once a good man. But he was considered too traditional and too aloof. I was often told that people were so afraid of him that after a meeting they avoided turning their back to him on the way out for fear of being accused of disrespect to our "royalty." I met him on many occasions, either during diplomatic functions or during trips to strategic hamlets, which were regarded at that time as Diem and Nhu's proud achievements. He was always reserved and courteous. He spoke very little and smoked a lot. He was often accused of behaving as a mandarin toward his subjects. That was certainly visible as he traveled in rural areas and peasants lined up to greet him. I found him distasteful.

After the coup against Diem, the military generals competed with one another to take power and there was one coup after another. These Vietnamese generals had no experience in administration. They were even more corrupt than Diem and Nhu. It wasn't good to have generals as presidents. They gave me no hope. But the American buildup also left me skeptical. If the French who colonized our country for a century could not win our support, how could the Americans, the newcomers with a different culture and language, hope to win the war against the Communists? We seemed to return to the situation in the fifties in which the government controlled the cities and the Viet Cong controlled the countryside. Corruption and police harassment made people distrust the government and sympathize more with the Viet Cong. But still I didn't think the Viet Cong would win. I just thought the war would go on forever.

PAUL HARE

"My cock lost the fight."

The "mostly retired" diplomat now directs the U.S.-Angola Chamber of Commerce. A well-built man of sixty, he arrives at his office in a salmon-colored polo shirt and pauses to confirm an afternoon golf date. In 1964, at age twenty-three, he was stationed in Tunisia. One day the American ambassador called him into his office. A cable had just come from Washington ordering the young foreign service officer to Vietnam "without passing GO." "I think the only criteria used in selecting me was that I was single and spoke French." He would be posted in four different provinces and stay in Vietnam until early 1969.

In the 1980s he became the U.S. ambassador to Zambia. Struck by his friendliness, I was curious to know if he had made any lasting friendships among the Vietnamese. "Not really," he responded. "Not like in other parts of the world."

I picked up a *Time* magazine to read en route, hoping to learn something about Vietnam. I knew virtually nothing. I spent four or five days in Saigon and then was told to go to Can Tho to get my assignment. So I flew down and saw the local coordinator of the Agency for International Development. We were drinking that night and I asked, "Well, what am I supposed to do?"

He said, "Your mission is to make pacification work."*

Since I really didn't know what pacification was all about, I was too embarrassed to pursue it any further. Then he said, "Well, I'm going to put you down in Ba Xuyen Province, the capital of which is Soc Trang. You can drive down there tomorrow. It's a little bit risky, but you'll get a good sense of the countryside."

So I drove a Scout down to Soc Trang. One of the first things I did was to meet the district chief—a Vietnamese captain who had fought with the French against the Viet Minh. We sort of got along all right and he said, "I'd like for you to go out to some villages with me tomorrow morning very early."

So about four A.M. we packed up. We had a little ragtag military unit with us—some regional forces. You could not have told them from the Viet Cong. They all were dressed in various shades of black. We went off along the canals and finally about nine o'clock in the morning you could see a vast delta of rice

*Pacification was a catch-all term used by U.S. and South Vietnamese forces that referred to virtually all efforts to establish political control in the countryside and to counter the influence of the Viet Cong. Originally it pertained to non-military aid projects and the formation of local security forces, but it came to refer as well to lethal counter-insurgency initiatives such as the Phoenix program.

fields and clumps of villages way off in the distance. About a half kilometer away, underneath a tree, were two men in black. Our little military group became very excited and got their guns ready. It turned out the two were elderly gentlemen with little wispy beards drinking rice wine and fishing. They sort of looked like Ho Chi Minh.

One of them didn't pay any attention to the Vietnamese captain and came up to me. He started speaking in broken French, telling me about how he had fought with the Viet Minh against the French and recounting his life history. Then he ended triumphantly with a great smile on his face, saying, "*Et même, monsieur, j'ai vu Paris*" (and even, sir, I have seen Paris). At that moment I looked around. Here I was in the middle of this vast unending landscape of rice fields wondering, what the hell am I doing here? I really felt a total sense of dislocation, but I was savvy enough to know that these two guys were probably going to go tell the local Viet Cong chief about their encounter that morning on the side of the canal. And, indeed, we were attacked that night. I think it was designed to scare us more than anything else. It was a small attack and no one got hurt, but I was scared.

I mention this story because that sense of dislocation, that uncertainty, never left me. I spent four and a half years in Vietnam and I never felt sure about my understanding of the Vietnamese or where they stood with respect to this conflict. One thing I realized very quickly was that these guys had been at it for a long, long time. They had seen battles come and go, they'd seen their friends and family members killed, and here we were, the Americans, coming in to try to put the whole thing right. I always was of the belief that whatever we were trying to do should be through the Vietnamese.

We were supposed to be helping rebuild schools and clinics, improve seeds and fertilizers, to make village life better. One of the projects that was probably more successful was repairing the temples which, more often than not, had been destroyed by the Viet Cong. If the Vietnamese were willing to put in the labor we were willing to provide the supplies. These self-help programs had a particular resonance with the local people.

We had a helicopter base in Soc Trang which was both a blessing and a curse. Sometimes they would shoot up the wrong territory. We had some incidents of that sort and then we'd have to go rushing out to take care of the local damage by quite frankly offering them money. And in 1965 or early '66 our air force bombed Ben Tre by accident. Apparently they got the wrong grid coordinates. They hit a hospital. Needless to say, that caused problems, but we did get air force generals down there apologizing and providing reparations. There were, as I recall, probably ten or fifteen people killed.

I wasn't a strategist. I'd just been plucked out of Tunis and plunked into this province in Vietnam. But I was always skeptical about the Americanization of the war. If I were a Vietnamese and the Americans wanted to come in and do this job after I'd been struggling with it, I'd say go ahead. In 1964 I was the only American civilian in Ba Xuyen province and I sometimes think that was a more effective presence. When I finished my last assignment in Ninh Thuan Province in 1969 there were probably a hundred and fifty Americans in the advisory group, and it was not a big province.

One little hobby that I picked up while I was there was cockfighting. It was very popular. There was a Vietnamese fellow who had a little cock-ring and on the weekends he would fight cocks and sell food and beverages. People came from all around, including, you can be sure, from the Viet Cong–controlled areas. There was a lot of rubbing of shoulders and I was the only American. Occasionally American visitors would come and I'd take them—show them a little bit of the local life.

The province chief had given me a champion cock, a real beauty. One weekend a group from the province to the north came down with their champion cock. That was a big day. There was a lot of betting, a lot of money. I probably had five hundred dollars on my cock—the highest I'd ever bet. It was the big fight of the year, like the championship fight of the Delta. But that was the end of my cockfighting days because my cock lost the fight.

Subsequently someone showed me this memo that Edward Lansdale had prepared for Ambassador Lodge describing my cockfighting exploits. It was the sort of thing Lansdale liked. The memo said something like, "This is what we need—Americans who are really out there rubbing elbows with the Vietnamese."

"THE EMPEROR HAS NO CLOTHES"

Robert McNamara, secretary of defense from 1961 to early 1968, was such a key architect of American policy in Vietnam that many people called it "McNamara's War." In 1995, he published a memoir declaring that the United States had been "terribly wrong" to intervene. More than that, he revealed that as early as 1965 he had privately concluded that the war could not be won. Publicly, however, McNamara had never been so candid. Long after his secret doubts began, he often expressed unqualified optimism about "progress" in Vietnam and he firmly defended a policy of massive military escalation. In 1966, for example, he returned from a two-day visit to Saigon. Just before the plane touched down in Washington, he commented to an aide: "I say things are worse than they were a year ago." When the plane landed, he walked briskly to a group of reporters and announced: "Gentlemen, I've just come back from Vietnam and I'm glad to be able to tell you that we're showing great progress in every dimension of our effort."

In countless ways, wartime policy makers hid their private misgivings about the war. A surprising number harbored reservations about the capacity of Americans to sustain a permanent non-Communist regime in South Vietnam. In front of microphones, however, they sought to project an image of steely determination, unyielding confidence, and unmatched intelligence. Even among themselves, policy makers tried to bolster each other's will to carry on, scorning fundamental criticism as a sign of weakness, defeatism, disloyalty, or ignorance.

In his memoir, McNamara attributed much of America's failure in Vietnam to a lack of intelligence. "I had never visited Indochina, nor did I understand or appreciate its history, language, culture, or values. . . . When it came to Vietnam, we found ourselves setting policy for a region that was terra incognita." It is certainly true that American policy makers lacked knowledge about Vietnam, but mere ignorance does not adequately explain why the United States intervened, fought so long, and lost. A better explanation is that policy makers were wedded to a Cold War orthodoxy that made detailed knowledge of Vietnam virtually irrelevant to them. At the heart of that orthodoxy was the view that Communism was an international movement controlled by the Soviet Union and China.

The major Communist powers did indeed provide substantial military and economic aid to North Vietnam, especially from 1965 to 1975. During that decade the Soviet Union provided at least $5 billion worth of surface-to-air missiles, artillery weapons, planes, tanks, and ammunition, along with some three thousand military advisers and technicians who trained North Vietnamese personnel and maintained advanced equipment. Chinese aid was at least as important. Surpassing in quantity that of the Soviet Union, Chinese aid was especially critical in the early 1960s when Soviet support was relatively minimal. In addition, from 1965 to 1970, more than three hundred thousand Chinese support troops went to North Vietnam to help with air defense, rail and road construction, and military training.

Crucial as their support was to the Communist cause in Vietnam, Moscow and Beijing never had the control over Hanoi that leaders in Washington imagined. Nor were they part of an ironclad, monolithic Communist alliance. The Sino-Soviet alliance began fraying in the 1950s and they watched each other's actions in Vietnam very closely, neither one wanting the other to have greater influence. Ultimately, the forces driving the National Liberation Front and the Democratic Republic of Vietnam to overthrow the American-backed government in Saigon were almost wholly Vietnamese in origin and substance.

Yet to American policy makers, the revolutionary guerrillas in South Vietnam were merely the pawns of the Communist leaders in Hanoi who were in turn pawns of Beijing and Moscow. Since the main enemy was always thought to be located somewhere other than the battlefields of South Vietnam, Washington never regarded it as a top priority to understand the particular cultural, political, and economic realities of the Vietnamese.

The almost willful ignorance about Vietnam among top policy makers does not mean they lacked access to an abundance of information that might have led them to other courses of action. One of the most powerful myths of the war is the notion that the United States intervened in Vietnam with naive optimism that it could easily prevail, only to find itself sucked deeper and deeper into a quagmire. In fact, policy makers continued to expand U.S. commitments in Vietnam in spite of ample evidence that their objectives were not being met and in spite of pessimistic appraisals of future prospects of success. They expanded the war not out of confidence of ultimate victory, but out of fear of defeat. According to the contemporary documents that circulated in secret among top leaders, the best that was usually said about each new escalation was that it would probably forestall a Communist victory.

For example, in 1965 when National Security Adviser McGeorge Bundy recommended the continuous bombing of North Vietnam (he called it "sustained reprisal"), his memo to President Johnson said, "We cannot assert that a policy of sustained reprisal will succeed in changing the course of the contest in Vietnam. It may fail and we cannot estimate the odds of success with any accuracy. . . . What we can say is that even if it fails, the policy will be worth it. At a minimum it will damp down the charge that we did not do all that we could have done."

Driving Washington forward, then, was the fear that a Communist victory in Vietnam would be an intolerable blow to American power and prestige, and, of course, to their own as well. America's leaders wanted to believe the rosy reports of progress the government routinely issued in public. In the face of negative news, they sought comfort in the bottom line of American power. How, they wondered over and over again, could a small, largely peasant country, even with massive military aid from larger Communist nations, resist America's overwhelming military and technological superiority? Surely, steady increases in U.S. firepower would ultimately break its will to fight on, or at least force the Vietnamese enemy to accept a negotiated settlement favorable to American objectives. After all, as Lyndon Johnson put it, Vietnam was just a "raggedy-ass, little fourth-rate country."

PAUL KATTENBURG

"What's good for Peru is good for Vietnam."

He was a Vietnam specialist long before most Americans had ever heard of Vietnam, and in the 1950s, an enthusiastic supporter of Ngo Dinh Diem. "When I was in Vietnam in 1952, I heard that Diem was well known and very popular. I wrote a memorandum recommending that we look at him as a genuine nationalist who was possibly qualified to lead an independent Vietnam. But I was only able to communicate in French with Vietnamese elites. To get Vietnamese mass opinion was virtually impossible unless you knew the language fluently and really lived with them."

In 1963, as head of the State Department's Vietnam Task Force, Kattenburg returned to Vietnam for the first time since the midfifties. "It didn't take me very long in Saigon to come to the conclusion that we were dealing with an absolutely sinking ship. I saw Diem on the last day of my visit. He appeared to be off his rocker. He went on for hours in an impossible-to-follow monologue about Communist infiltration."

On August 31, 1963, just back from Vietnam, Kattenburg was ushered into a meeting of the National Security Council (NSC). Formed in the early years of the

Cold War, the NSC offered policy recommendations directly to the president. The August 31 meeting focused on whether the United States should continue to support Diem or encourage a group of rebellious generals to launch a coup to overthrow him. The latter option was eventually chosen and it prolonged American intervention by throwing U.S. power behind a new set of South Vietnamese rulers with little popular support. Kattenburg was the first person at any high-level Washington meeting to suggest a more fundamental alternative—withdrawal. He said the situation was deteriorating; that he had known Ngo Dinh Diem for ten years and there was no reason to believe that Diem would reform his own repressive and corrupt regime. It would be better, he said, "to get out while the getting is good."

It was very imprudent really. This was the first time I was in a National Security Council Executive Committee meeting and normally junior people don't speak. But what struck me more than anything else was just the abysmal ignorance around the table of the particular facts of Vietnam, their ignorance of the actual place. They didn't know what they were talking about. It was robot thinking about Communism and no distinctions were being made. It was technocratic talk. They were talking in a vacuum on the basis of experience gained largely in other crisis situations.

Walt Rostow in particular was completely impervious to area knowledge.* It didn't make any difference to him. He'd figured out how to build nations, you know, so what's good for Peru is good for Vietnam. I mean they made absolutely no distinctions between countries with completely different historical experiences. Those of us who had been there in the fifties knew that this was a very, very difficult area. We knew that the French had put everything they possibly could into Indochina and they'd been *defeated*. But when the New Frontier came in under Kennedy they paid no attention whatsoever to what went on before. They came in with this nutty idea that we could manipulate other states and build nations; that we knew all the answers.

So I said that I thought it would be better if we just left with honor. I hadn't thought about it in advance. I just blurted it out. [Secretary of State] Rusk said there was no evidence for what I was saying, but of course he had been getting all my reports. And [Vice President] Johnson said something like, "We haven't gone this far with this whole thing to give it up now."

Later in 1963, after another two months in Vietnam, I came back even

*Rostow was deputy special assistant for national security affairs and later became President Johnson's national security adviser. He came to the attention of the Kennedy administration for his work as an MIT economist in the 1950s where he was best known for advocating the rapid capitalist development of the Third World as a means to build nations that could withstand the threat of Communist insurrection. Rostow's account is on pp. 124–27.

more pessimistic. I wrote a report saying the South Vietnamese were going to lose the war within the next year or two. It was going down the drain. The real weakness was the Vietnamese didn't want to fight. I mean they never did, at any time. They had chosen comfort and easy living over the miserable existence of the Viet Minh and the Viet Cong.

My first day back on the job Roger Hilsman [assistant secretary of state for Far Eastern affairs] had read the report and he said, "You know, President Kennedy has this saying—'When it's too hot in the kitchen, get out of the kitchen.' Do you want out? I think you ought to get out of this." I said, "Well, I think I better pull out. I'm not going to be any good because I don't believe in it anymore." So I was kicked out of the Bureau of East Asian Affairs and sent up to Policy Planning, which is where you put people who are really off base.

When the bombing started in 1965, I thought it was probably time to resign and make a statement about Vietnam. I still wish I'd done it, but it wouldn't have done any good. It would have hit page eighteen of the *Washington Post.* Nobody would have taken any notice. In order to do dissent significantly and change policy around you have to be a large group of people in many agencies.

After his recommendation of withdrawal, Kattenburg was excluded from all top-level discussions of Vietnam policy and was eventually transferred to a diplomatic post in Guyana.

EVELYN COLBERT

"Dissent which contradicted the public optimism was ignored."

From 1962 to 1974 she worked for the Southeast Asia Division of the Bureau of Intelligence Research at the State Department. She is eighty-two.

McNamara now says we didn't know anything about Vietnam and what was really happening was not understood. That's a lot of garbage. We would come out with papers showing that things were going very badly indeed. I would say that the great bulk of the work produced in my office and in the intelligence community in general having to do with the impact of what we were doing in Vietnam was somewhat pessimistic. But the record shows that dissent which contradicted the public optimism was ignored. My conclusion about this whole period is that we were saying to our masters, "The emperor has no clothes," and they were saying, "Yes, you're right, but doesn't he look beautiful that way."

In 1963, during the Buddhist crisis, my shop wrote a paper which took the statistics that were being produced by the military and made the case that these very statistics showed that the Viet Cong were doing very well. Naturally, the military got annoyed. Secretary of Defense McNamara wrote a note to Secretary of State Dean Rusk saying the State Department has no business producing papers on military subjects that have not been cleared with the Defense Department.* Rusk made a conciliatory reply.

CHESTER COOPER

"Boy, you speak just like an American."

"As you may have gathered, I'm a pain in the ass." Short, crusty, and barrel-chested, he worked on U.S. policy in Vietnam from 1953 to 1968. He was a CIA intelligence analyst for Southeast Asia from 1953 to 1963. Then he served for three years as McGeorge Bundy's deputy on the National Security Council. From 1966 to 1968 he worked for a negotiated settlement of the war as a special assistant to Averell Harriman. Now eighty-three, he tells a few "revelatory" anecdotes.

I was sent to Geneva in 1954 as the intelligence analyst on the American delegation. Our ignorance about Indochina was pervasive. My first assignment at Geneva was to find out if there really was such a person as Ho Chi Minh or whether he had died many years before and somehow the Vietnamese were just keeping his image alive. We had no idea. So I went down to the UN secretariat and asked if I could see the invitation extended to the Vietnamese and their acceptance. They showed it to me and it was signed by Ho Chi Minh. So it seemed to me, in my young innocence, that there was such a person. [Ho Chi Minh lived until 1969.]

When we started the war there was no American in the embassy in Saigon who could speak Vietnamese. There wasn't even anybody who knew anything about Buddhism. We finally located a foreign service officer who was an American Buddhist. Until the late fifties, if you wanted to find out anything about Vietnam you went to the French desk at the State Department. And the focus

*The exact wording of McNamara's note was: "Dean: If you promise me that the Department of State will not issue any more military appraisals without getting the approval of the Joint Chiefs, we will let this matter die. Bob."

of most of Kennedy's team was on Western Europe. They were very smart guys, I promise you, but they also had a great deal of hubris. One of the problems was that they didn't know that they didn't know anything. Most of them couldn't find Vietnam on an outline map of Asia. [National Security Adviser] Mac Bundy had never been to Asia until 1965. There was this appalling ignorance.

In the midsixties I was making almost monthly commutes back and forth to Vietnam. One time in 1965 I was talking to an economic warfare specialist named Mike Deutch, father of the future CIA director. He told me that two-thirds of all the stuff we were sending to the South Vietnamese army was being stolen. I said that sounds like a lot so he said he'd pick me up at one in the morning and we'd go to the Saigon docks. Off we went and it was pretty scary. It was pitch black and the smell was awful. We hid behind one of the big piles of crates. Sure enough these little flashlights appeared and what was once a pile of materiel intended for the ARVN went in two hours from eight feet to three feet. So he was right. Could we stop it? No.

Going to Vietnam with McNamara was no picnic because he insisted on flying in a converted tanker to demonstrate that he could rough it and save money. You flew until you were exhausted and then had fifteen minutes to wash up and attend a three-hour briefing. After a couple of those trips I decided that maybe I could be of better service to McNamara if I went a couple days ahead of time by Pan Am. [Laughs.] I'd stop off in Honolulu and spend the night briefing people there. Those stops convinced me we weren't gonna do it in Vietnam. I'd have breakfast on a porch of the Bachelor Officers Quarters overlooking the harbor and between orange juice and coffee, my god, I'd see three tremendous battleships, five cruisers, and ten nuclear-powered submarines. Then eight or ten hours later I was in Saigon and here are these guys fighting us with antiquated weapons and pointy sticks and black pajamas and none of that U.S. power that could have blown up the world in an hour could be brought to bear. People thought we were going to go to war with this stinking little country and it would be a shoo-in, a piece of cake. But they knew how to do it and we didn't.

In February 1966, [President] Johnson made yet another one of his impulsive decisions. I got a phone call from somebody in his office who said, "Look, we've decided to have a meeting with the Saigon government next week in Honolulu.* I want you to call the Royal Hawaiian and reserve the hotel." A week's notice. I had a long argument with the manager of the hotel. I didn't

*Johnson called the conference to divert media attention from televised hearings on the Vietnam War to be held at the same time by the Senate Foreign Relations Committee under Senator William Fulbright.

care if people had made reservations twenty years before, we needed the whole hotel. I went back there a few years ago and the new manager had heard about it. It was still part of hotel lore.

LBJ was not terribly good at interacting with anybody who didn't come from Texas, let alone somebody who came from another country and was half his size. And [South Vietnamese Prime Minister Nguyen Cao] Ky and [Chief of State Nguyen Van] Thieu were really unremarkable-looking people. When I first met Ky he came to the embassy in Saigon dressed in a tight little white jacket and a little bow tie and pointy shoes, looking like a saxophone player in a second-rate Filipino band.

But the meeting accomplished its purpose. Johnson could demonstrate that he and the Vietnamese government were operating together. There were lots of photographs and anodyne statements. Ky was the star performer of the entire show. He sold himself as a progressive and farsighted statesman determined to proceed with a non-Communist economic and social revolution. He talked about everything from rural electrification to low-cost housing. Then he closed by expressing gratitude for American support. At that point, Johnson leaned across the table and said, "Boy, you speak just like an American." The man who wrote Ky's speech was, of course, an American, an old friend of mine, and it was based largely on the texts of President Johnson's own speeches.

Averell Harriman, who became my boss in 1967, was one hundred and one percent committed to negotiations with the Vietnamese Communists. And I, who had been involved in this since 1954, was desperate to see it end. I saw nothing but bad things happening, so I, too, became preoccupied with negotiations. There was very little public interest in negotiations because virtually all of them were secret and nothing ever happened. But I traveled all over the world chasing every possibility, fighting for every extra day of a bombing halt, and looking for every indication of a diplomatic opening. For example, there was the case of a Norwegian ambassador to Beijing. He was home on medical leave and I met him in Oslo. He agreed to go to Hanoi where he was known and deliver whatever message we wanted. We had a formula we thought might work. The only condition he made was that we not bomb the airport the day he was coming into Hanoi. I thought that was a reasonable request and promised him everything would be okay. When I got back to Washington I discovered that we were going to bomb the airport on the very day he was going to arrive. I went to [National Security Adviser Walt] Rostow, but had no luck in persuading him that this was a stupid thing to do and that I had made a commitment. As a consequence of the bombing, the Norwegian ambassador's mission was aborted.

SERGEI KHRUSHCHEV

"The Vietnamese had their own ideas."

The resemblance is close enough to remind you of old black-and-white images of his father, Nikita Khrushchev, the bald, portly man who presided over the Soviet Union from 1953 to 1964. At sixty-seven, the son is now the same age his father was in 1961 when, just two weeks before Kennedy's inaugural, he proclaimed enthusiastic support for "just wars of liberation and popular uprisings." The statement was interpreted by the new president's advisers as an ominous escalation of the Cold War.

Since 1991, Sergei Khrushchev has lived in the United States and has written several books, including Khrushchev on Khrushchev, *about his father's years as premier of the Soviet Union. We talk in his office at Brown University where he is a senior fellow at the Thomas Watson Institute for International Studies.*

He views his father as the greatest Soviet reformer prior to Gorbachev, a man more concerned with domestic development than foreign intervention. While Nikita Khrushchev offered strident rhetorical support to Third World revolutions, his concrete aid to Communist insurgencies was far less than that of his more hard-line successors, Alexei Kosygin and Leonid Brezhnev. Toward the end of his tenure Khrushchev grew increasingly disenchanted with the Vietnamese Communist leadership and significantly reduced Soviet aid to the Democratic Republic of Vietnam. Had he not been ousted in October 1964, some Soviet scholars believe he would have totally disengaged from Vietnam (just as some American scholars believe that had John Kennedy not been assassinated he would have pulled out of Vietnam).

In 1964, I remember asking my father, "What will you do if Vietnam is attacked by the Americans? Will you support Vietnam?" He said he didn't think so because at that time it was unclear whether the Vietnamese [Communists] stood with the Soviet Union or China. That was in the last year of my father's time and Soviet-Chinese relations were at a very low point. He thought Ho Chi Minh was pro-Chinese so why should we go to war for him? The Soviets thought Hanoi was controlled by Beijing and the Americans thought Hanoi was controlled by Moscow. In reality, the Vietnamese had their own ideas. They played their own game. The winner would not be the Soviet Union or China or the United States, it would be the Vietnamese.

Even if my father wanted to intervene in Vietnam it was very difficult, practically speaking, because the Chinese would not even let us move through their territory to get to Vietnam. We would have had to bring everything by sea and the Soviet Navy could not compete with the U.S. Navy. It would be the same as in Cuba during the Cuban Missile Crisis when everything was very vulnerable. There might be an American blockade and that would bring us once again to the brink of nuclear war, so my father didn't want to try this.

Of course he thought we had to support colonial countries who were fighting for their freedom and independence. At the United Nations in 1961 he proclaimed support for wars of national liberation, but his first concern was with our own country's development. We couldn't just spend our resources here and there. Yes he wanted to support all revolutions, but not on a large scale. His understanding was that if a revolution was being fought by real freedom fighters who had the support of the people, they wouldn't need much Soviet involvement.

Of course the Soviet Union did everything it could to make America's life in Vietnam worse. It was the simple rule of the Cold War. If you could do something bad to the opposite side you had to do it. Americans did the same to us in Afghanistan.

In the 1960s, I was one hundred percent an engineer. I was designing cruise and ballistic missiles so I was very interested in the success of our antiaircraft missiles in Vietnam. I remember there was a big scandal during the first large-scale U.S. air attacks in 1965. The guidance systems of our surface-to-air missiles didn't work as well as we expected and the Americans were able to jam some of them. As a result of those failures the Soviets fired the deputy minister in charge of the production of those guidance systems. He was a good man who was just a scapegoat.

Soviet propaganda presented the war as an example of American imperialists battling against brave freedom fighters, but the war wasn't then considered a big threat to the Soviet Union. For example, when I worked with the Soviet Navy a captain told me that, yes, we are patrolling the Vietnamese coasts alongside the Americans but there is no fear. In fact, he said that for many days his submarine cruised on the surface only a short distance away from an American destroyer. After a while they even started to visit each other. I don't know if it's a true story, but I think it is. He told me they exchanged gifts and the Americans gave them fresh fruit—bananas and apples—which they didn't have on the submarine. However, when the Americans started supplying them with magazines and other literature the exchanges were ended. The Soviets said fruit's okay, but no magazines.

The Russian people always wanted improved relations with the United States. They never believed that the American government was against them. I think ordinary Americans were far more affected by Cold War propaganda, much more hostile to Russians, and much more fearful. In the Free World you could have open discussions, but Americans tended to believe what they read and saw on television. In Russian culture, all the way back to Czarist times, our first reaction has been to distrust what we read, so we're much less affected by the media.

We always tried to listen to other radio stations, especially the BBC [British Broadcasting Company] or even the Voice of America, though we didn't trust it as much. When you saw friends you'd ask, "Did you listen to the enemy's voice?" That was our nickname for the Western stations. Even my father listened when he was out of power.

There are many parallels between the Vietnam War and the Soviet war in Afghanistan. In the beginning we never expected to have a massive presence there. After all, the fighting was between Afghanis. And then it seemed so simple. We were so much more powerful. Such wars are like gambling. Each time you take one more step, you think you'll win. My feeling was that sooner or later we would, and of course if we had put in two million soldiers and thirty thousand tanks we could have won, but what would that mean? You could kill all the Afghans, but what would you have won?

During the Vietnam War I thought the U.S. antiwar movement was a sign that America was awakening. I still have that opinion. That was when Americans started to understand that not everything depended on the will of their government, that the world was not so simple. But now they have forgotten. With all this fighting terrorism since the 9/11 attack they are making the same mistakes, oversimplifying and creating more enemies than friends. As the leading power in the world, America cannot behave like the elephant in the china shop.

"PARADISE ISLAND"

JOHN SINGLAUB

"We sent them all back with a generous gift package."

From 1966 to 1968, he ran the secret war against North Vietnam. He was the commander of SOG, America's largest clandestine military unit. SOG originally stood for Special Operations Group, but was soon given an academic sounding cover name—"Studies and Observation Group."

For eight years, from 1961 to 1968, first the CIA and then SOG kidnapped and indoctrinated more than a thousand North Vietnamese civilians, ran "black" and "gray" radio stations, inserted spies into North Vietnam and Laos, attacked military and civilian installations along the northern coast, planted booby-trapped weapons behind the lines, and more.

From a window of his seventh-floor condominium in Arlington, Virginia, you can glimpse a corner of the Pentagon. He's a short man with a gray crew cut, large ears, and a charming smile.

Our psychological operations group created an elaborate sham resistance movement known as the "Sacred Sword of the Patriot League." We didn't have a viable resistance movement in the North, so we tried to create one with our Sacred Sword deception. We put Vietnamese commandos on fast patrol boats and they would go up the North Vietnamese coast to snatch prisoners. They would capture fishermen or peasants from coastal villages, blindfold them, put them on the boats, and bring them to "Paradise Island" [Cu Lao Cham Island] near Danang.

On the island we had constructed a fortified hamlet facing the sea with no view of the mainland. It was designed to look like a northern coastal village and the prisoners were told that they were in a "Liberated Zone" held by the "Sacred Sword of the Patriot League," that it was a base for guerrilla operations against the Communist government. The Sacred Sword had its own blue-and-white flag that flew above the bamboo stockade.

All the personnel on the island were South Vietnamese who spoke with a Northern dialect. We would keep the captives for at least a month and take care of all their physical problems. Usually they were suffering from malnutrition or they had skin diseases, malaria, or worms. We'd clean them up and fatten them up and make them healthy again. They were also gently indoctrinated in the beliefs of the sham resistance. We'd get into the philosophy that people should be able to receive pay equal to their contribution and equal to their ability—concepts that had been stifled by the Communists. That very practical type of comparison would get these people very slowly indoctrinated in the concept of freedom.

Eventually, we sent them all back with a generous gift package—things we knew were in short supply up north; simple things like fishhooks, sewing supplies, and medicine. We fully expected that the Communist security forces would confiscate these gift packages, but at least the villagers would spread the word about this liberated zone Shangri-la. Later we started giving out two gift packages, one for the Communist cadre to confiscate, and the other for them to hide and get later. It was a good psychological program. We were constantly putting missionaries back into the North who had tasted something besides what the Communists were putting out.

We also gave them a transistor radio pretuned to the Patriot radio frequency, a black propaganda station that pounded relentlessly at venal and corrupt Communist officials in the North. These radios were not tunable—they couldn't be used to listen to Radio Hanoi. With black propaganda you deliberately give a false identity. Periodically the Patriot Voice of Resistance would announce that it had to go off the air for a while because it was being attacked by government forces and would have to change its location.

With gray propaganda you do not tell the source of the deception—you let the receiver imagine it. We had a gray radio station called the Voice of Freedom. It was an enormous, very high-powered station. It was up near Hue. Eventually that station went from two hundred and fifty thousand watts to one million. It was only the second station in the world with that much power. But some of the equipment was damaged during the Tet Offensive so it never got into full operation. We broadcast news and entertainment—good, classical Vietnamese entertainment but primarily news. We learned later that it had a big audience. We dropped thousands of small, inexpensive radios into North Vietnam. They had two channels—they could pick up the Voice of Freedom or the Patriot Voice of Resistance.

In addition to sending South Vietnamese commandos to snatch prisoners in the North and bring them south, we also dropped commandos into enemy territory to gather intelligence and carry out resistance activities up there. Some of them were dropped by parachute, some were infiltrated from Laos by helicopter, and some were put ashore by patrol boats. We sent in more than we could support adequately and they became less effective as time went on.

Unfortunately, the resistance potential in North Vietnam was dismal because practically everyone who was anti-Communist had been removed from North Vietnam in 1954 as an act of compassion on the part of Americans. It's very difficult to run a resistance operation if you strip the area of all the friendly people. In World War II, if all the anti-Germans had been allowed to escape France, we would have had a lousy resistance movement in France. In Vietnam we said all the people who want to leave the North can move and the Americans will provide a ship to take you south. Well, the Catholic Church realized how they were being persecuted so they would take whole congregations and trek down to Haiphong and get on a ship.

When I became commander of SOG, I made a very detailed survey of every team of South Vietnamese commandos we had sent north. My conclusion was that the program did produce some good intelligence at times, but most of the agents were either captured, killed, or doubled [became "double agents" who worked for the North Vietnamese]. After the teams were captured they would force the radio operator to send back signals to us that everything was okay. You could tell they were doubled by the kinds of reports they sent back and the orders they would not carry out. We also discovered that our organization had been penetrated by an enemy agent who had signaled the North when and where we were going to put in a new team of commandos. I asked for permission to drop the program, but Secretary of Defense McNamara did not want that. There was great pressure from McNamara to increase the number of forces operating in the North. It's hard to say why. Maybe he had a map with pins in it and he wanted to increase the number of pins in the North. I can't explain why they wanted to do this except that it may have been good conversation at the cocktail parties in Washington.

Another major part of our activities were cross-border operations in Laos and Cambodia. Americans were on those teams and we captured a lot of important people and critical documents along the Ho Chi Minh Trail. I was always telling the guys back at MAC-V [Military Assistance Command, Vietnam—U.S. military headquarters] that we had no problem locating the enemy, but we weren't hitting him effectively enough. We weren't using the kind of aircraft that can kill people in triple-canopy jungle. When you're trying to hit a truck that's on a trail you can't do it with a jet that's traveling five hundred miles an hour. The slow, propeller-driven airplanes, the World War II aircraft like the A-ls, were doing a much better job, whether you measured their efficiency by kills per sortie, kills per hour, kills per mission. But the air force didn't want that. They wanted to have an all-jet air force.

There are so many decisions that had little logic. But the one that made the biggest difference was the refusal of our administration to close the port of Haiphong. Haiphong was the key logistical entry point for all Communist forces. Without those supplies there would have been no chance that the North Vietnamese could have conducted offensive operations. When the air force started knocking out some of the supplies coming down the Ho Chi Minh Trail, they would just bring in more supplies through Haiphong from the whole Communist-Socialist world. If they needed ten truckloads in the South every day, they'd send down twenty and ten would get through. And even if we knocked out ninety percent of the trucks, they would put a hundred in and ten would still get through. If we had bombed and mined the port of Haiphong from the start, we could have shut them down.

What gave great encouragement to Ho Chi Minh and his people were the traitors like [actress] Jane Fonda and [former Attorney General] Ramsey Clark and [antiwar activist] Tom Hayden who went over there and said, "Just hold on, hold on. We're winning it at home. We're destroying the morale of the people at home." And they did. The antiwar movement was an essential part of the Communist strategy to destroy American morale.

We had guys whose morale was so damaged as a result of returning to the States after their first tour that they volunteered to come back. They could simply not stand to read the paper or watch the television. I couldn't believe the newspaper clippings my family was sending me after the Tet Offensive [a coordinated attack by North Vietnamese and Viet Cong units throughout South Vietnam in early 1968]. Here in the United States, people thought it had been a great victory for the Communists and a terrible defeat for us. Well, we didn't feel that way. We had been trying for years to get them to come out in the open so we could slaughter them, and we slaughtered them. Man, we just cleaned their clocks. In all the wars I've been in I've never seen so many dead people stacked up. It was an enormous victory for us and we should have really pressed on.

The media was so biased. All of the great work American advisers were doing out in the countryside to benefit these people—agricultural work, building bridges, digging wells—all that was totally ignored. Out of half a million Americans who were largely involved in constructive or worthwhile efforts, maybe thirty of them were ambushed and so the press corps would all go up there and photograph the dead and interview the survivors with their own editorial comments on how horrible it was.

Those of us who were there had a good feeling, especially the advisers. We were a cross between a missionary among heathen and a frontiersman who was building in the face of enemy attacks. This was Viet Cong as opposed to the Indians who were attacking our forefathers as they went westward. We established a rapport with the Montagnards [ethnic minority mountain people] that was very, very good. We were teaching their villages sanitation and helping them. We'd have our medics rotate through the various villages and do civic action types of things. That gave us the feeling of being missionaries.

In 1976, he became chief of staff of the United Nations Command and U.S. Forces, Korea. In 1977, after he criticized President Jimmy Carter's plans to remove American combat troops from South Korea, Carter had him relieved from his command and reassigned. Several months later, he resigned from the military.

In the 1980s he became chairman of the World Anti-Communist League. Founded in 1966, the WACL received most of its backing from South Korea and Taiwan. Singlaub's name returned to prominence during the Reagan administration when the Iran-Contra hearings revealed that he had worked closely with Oliver North to raise millions of dollars around the world—much of it from the WACL—to support the Contra war in Nicaragua.

LUYEN NGUYEN

"She divorced her second husband and waited for me."

He was a "lost commando," one of about five hundred South Vietnamese soldiers the United States sent into North Vietnam on top-secret, small-team infiltration missions almost guaranteed to fail. Dropped into a politically and militarily unified society, virtually all of the commandos were captured, killed, or turned into double agents. Not one commando returned to the South before the end of the war. Despite the program's utter failure, it ran from 1961 to 1968.

Captured by North Vietnamese soldiers in 1966 at the age of thirty-three, Luyen Nguyen was imprisoned for twenty-one years, eleven of them in solitary confinement. In response to my confusion about how his feet had been shackled during imprisonment, he leaves the room and returns with a rod to demonstrate. He places his heel on top of the bar. "Just like this." Then he turns his ankle to show the scar produced by the shackling. Later, perhaps a bit astonished by all he has revealed, he says simply, "I have never told my wife or children about these experiences."

In 1964, I was assigned to recruit and train commandos to be dropped behind enemy lines. These guys were dissatisfied with their lives and seduced by the benefits. A commando recruit was paid as much as a major in the army. I was a captain and my salary was lower than the men I recruited. They had a daily rice ration triple the size of the officers. And they lived above the law. They could do anything and the military police had no right to arrest them.

The student commandos had way too much freedom. When I suggested that we put the recruits under stricter discipline, the U.S. captain told me, "I've been here long before you. I know how to do my duty. You know nothing." The U.S. advisers in this operation were very arrogant. One time, a U.S. lieutenant colonel disagreed with one of my decisions and criticized me in front of my men. It was a serious mistake for a military man.

I often told my men, you are fighting for your country, not the Americans, but the U.S. advisers told the commandos—we hired you, we pay you, you should obey us and ignore the Vietnamese. One time a team was training near lunchtime. The American adviser returned to the U.S. mess to take his lunch and the Vietnamese instructor was still standing behind the microphone. He tried to complete the lesson but the team got up and went back to camp. I was so angry I rushed after them. I intended to take them back to finish the lesson. But one of these guys opened the safety on his machine gun. He was ready to shoot me if I insisted they go back.

When the training was over and we prepared to drop a team behind enemy lines we moved them into a restricted area where they were not allowed to contact anyone. Half of them had already deserted. Many recruits planned to desert after receiving a few months of benefits. The day before we moved them to the restricted area the team invited me to eat. The atmosphere was very solemn. They told me that if I didn't go with them on the mission, all of them would desert. At my rank I had no duty to go to the North. No one at my rank went north. I knew all the previous teams had not returned, but I absolutely believed in my ability to take them behind enemy lines and get them back, so I promised to go with them.

We took off from Thailand in a helicopter and infiltrated from the west of North Vietnam close to the border between Vietnam and Laos. Fourteen men and myself. During the flight the men joked with each other as if they were on their way to school. I didn't see any sign of fear in their faces. It was like they thought they were at a school playground. They had no idea of the danger.

They were incapable of doing their duty even though this team had the highest results in training. They had no experience of combat. When they didn't see the enemy they thought they were completely safe. They could not imagine that the enemy might have observed the helicopter landing. At night they fell asleep while on guard. And when they knew the enemy was close, they lost their spirit and became passive. It's like they lost their souls.

The basic mission was to get information and recruit local people in the North. But this was only a general notion. The only specific order was to establish a safe area, report to headquarters, and wait for further orders. I was their commander but even I knew nothing about the plan and process of the missions.

I believe this was a planned failure.* There's no way the CIA could be so stupid. For example, from the first team to the last team, they dropped us in wearing black berets, black clothes, black boots. But they knew that in the North they use brown cloth in the jungle areas. In the North, a man dressed in black from head to toe looks like a monster who dropped down from another planet.

We survived for a month before being detected. Our position was five miles from the Ho Chi Minh Trail and several times we moved close to the trail to do reconnaissance. We moved from one safe area to another. But a few days before we were captured we heard gunshots near one of our old positions. The enemy hoped we'd answer their shots. The kids knew they had been discovered and became afraid. I tried to assure them that I would find a way out, but it was too late. We were soon captured and put in prison.

During the first eleven years in prison they kept me in a dark cell and shackled me all the time. I had to lie down on a plank. There was a steel bar at the end of the plank and I had to put my ankles on top of the bar. They used a shackle to lock my feet above the bar. They also used a very small shackle that blocked the vein over here. Your feet swell and after about thirty minutes half your body goes numb and you fall into a trance. If they keep that small shackle on for at least six hours you die. They used it on me again and again, but never for more than three hours.

When I was completely exhausted and they saw I was going to die, they brought me out of the dark cell, took me to another room with an open window, and gave me a little bit more food. During the daytime they did not

*Support for this idea comes from Clyde Russell, chief of Studies and Observation Group from 1964 to 1965, who expected the missions to fail but didn't want to stop the missions for fear that commando recruits would reveal information in South Vietnam about the secret war against the North. "We had to get rid of them. . . . Our solution was to put them up North." See Richard H. Shultz Jr., *The Secret War Against Hanoi* (New York: HarperCollins, 1999), p. 105.

shackle me. They gave me two or three months to recover my health, then took me back to the dark cell.

For a short time at the end of 1966 I was in a prison camp with some U.S. pilots. At dinnertime I saw the guards bring trays of food for the Americans and I knew it was a U.S. ration because it was much better than what we had. They had rice, a little bit of vegetable, a banana, a cigarette. Usually the U.S. POWs threw some of their food to the Vietnamese commandos who lived next to them.

When I was called for indoctrination they wanted me to declare that I was a puppet of the United States, a henchman, and that the U.S. invaded Vietnam to dominate our country. They repeated these things over and over for the first eleven years. But I refused to acknowledge these things. I tried to keep my loyalty to the army. If I had acknowledged that I was a U.S. henchman, they would've let me out of the dark cell to do forced labor. The commandos who did forced labor lived almost like workers in a special area and after the war they got permission to go south to see their families every year. But I did not want to do forced labor. A lot of my comrades-in-arms died of exhaustion due to forced labor.

Many commandos were affected by Communist propaganda. When they were captured they acknowledged that they had fought because they needed the money and they agreed that the Americans were invaders who came to dominate our country. They remembered the U.S. officers who had told them that they were working for the Americans. If the commandos had been told that they were fighting for their own country and their own people, then they might have stayed loyal when they were in the hands of the enemy. But the U.S. destroyed their patriotism, turning them into disloyal people, disloyal even to the Americans.

When I left the South, my family lived in Saigon. Three months later my wife was informed that I was missing. She collected the death benefits and moved our seven children to Can Tho where her parents lived. She took the day I left as my death day and every year, in the Vietnamese tradition, she had a death anniversary for me and evoked my soul. In prison, I had no contact with my wife. Several times they called me to the office, offered me envelopes, paper, and stamps, and urged me to write. I refused. When they asked me why I refused such a humanitarian policy, I told them, "I don't want to disturb the peaceful life of my wife and children. All of them believe I'm dead and their tears are dry. I don't want to make them cry again."

In 1974, my wife was so depressed and so poor she married again and gave birth to a daughter. In 1982 or 1983, the first of us commandos was released and because of his kindness he found my family to tell them I was still alive.

When my wife heard the news, she divorced her second husband and waited for me to return. I didn't blame her for remarrying, but it was a very hard blow. You can't imagine what I had to suffer in my heart. In Vietnamese culture it was intolerable. I was dumbfounded and mortified at first, but in a society at war it is a common misfortune. A lot of my comrades suffered such things.

When I left home in 1966 my eldest son was ten years old and when I returned home he introduced me to his son, my eleven-year-old grandson. My youngest daughter was in her mother's womb when I left home. When I returned she was twenty-one and married.

Luyen Nuyen and his wife moved to the United States in 1990. In 1999, the U.S. Congress voted $42,500 in compensation to the surviving lost commandos. After paying his lawyer, Luyen sent the remainder of his check to his children, all of whom stayed in Vietnam. In 2000, at age sixty-seven, he completed a master's degree in American Studies at the University of Massachusetts, Boston. He works now as a student counselor.

PART THREE

ESCALATIONS (1964–67)

TRAILS TO WAR

Even today, flying from the United States to Vietnam is exhausting. Leaving New York, a typical route takes you to Hanoi via Anchorage, Seoul, and Hong Kong. The trip of well over thirty hours, including plane changes and layovers, makes it hard to believe that the United States could have fought in a land so far way with no prior claims on American consciousness.

What, then, must it have been like for the three million American troops who went to Vietnam between 1961 and 1972? In the early years most arrived via troop ship or military aircraft, but by 1966 the vast majority traveled to Vietnam on commercial airliners not so different from the ones we fly today. Most went not as units but as individual replacements, completely unaware of where in Vietnam they would be fighting, with whom, and, in many cases, why. Of the Vietnamese they knew nothing. They sat next to strangers on an air-conditioned ride to a war half a globe away. You can't help but wonder how many had ever been to a foreign country, much less a Third World nation about as different from the United States as any in the world and in which they arrived as soldiers.

In the early 1960s, American policy makers had cloaked U.S. war making by calling it "advisory." In the late sixties, when combat was too heavy and the killing too pervasive to conceal, combat soldiers nonetheless flew to war as if they were headed for a tropical vacation. They didn't even carry weapons. Though there is no evidence that commercial jets were used to disguise the scale of American intervention, a fleet of troop-carrying transports continually crossing the Pacific would certainly have been a more concrete signal of the massive movement of soldiers in and out of the war.

There was, of course, no hiding the colossal logistical effort required to clothe, feed, and arm U.S. and South Vietnamese troops, and to transport them within Vietnam. During the peak years of escalation, beginning in 1965, more than one hundred U.S. ships often waited for weeks off the shore of South Vietnam for a berth to unload their supplies. Eventually, the United States built six seaports in South Vietnam, dozens of major bases and airfields, and hundreds of helicopter landing zones and artillery firebases. The amount of materiel the

United States sent to Vietnam was so staggering that in September 1968 the surplus alone was estimated at more than two million tons.

For the Vietnamese, by contrast, their homeland was a warland. This was especially true in the South, the site of almost all ground combat, where every province endured firefights, bombing, and military occupation, where at least half of all the hamlets were destroyed by war's end. A considerable number of South Vietnamese on both sides of the war fought in and around their own villages, sometimes quite literally in their own backyards. A greater number were sent to fight in other parts of South Vietnam far away from home. And millions of civilians saw their homes razed or burned and were forced into the cities or refugee camps. The war profoundly uprooted Vietnamese society, separating countless people from their ancestral land and their families.

In the North, war came mostly from the air, in the form of American bombing. The whole society was mobilized to defend against those attacks and to support the ground war in the South. All major North Vietnamese resources—factories, armories, troops, medical care—were decentralized throughout the countryside to reduce the impact of bombing. Children were evacuated from cities. Villages organized self-defense forces and antiaircraft units. Of course, those in the North understood that the ultimate goal of national unification required a victory in the South, and it was the South that was commonly referred to as the "front."

Hundreds of thousands of northerners were exposed to some of the war's most dangerous and debilitating experiences just traveling to the front, or helping others to get there by building and repairing roads and bridges leading south. Among them were the teenage volunteers who went to the mountain jungles to carve out the Ho Chi Minh Trail. For years they were threatened by bomb strikes, malaria, and malnutrition. And the troops that moved down the trails went mostly on foot, a grueling and perilous journey requiring three to six months. We don't know precisely how many died en route, but estimates suggest that the total exceeded the number of Americans who died in the war.

Construction of the Ho Chi Minh Trail began in the mid-1950s. Never a single route, from the beginning it was a network of footpaths and roads weaving through the Truong Son Mountains that form the north to south border between Vietnam and Laos. Small numbers of North Vietnamese troops began moving south in 1959. As the number of U.S. forces in South Vietnam began to escalate, Hanoi responded in kind. In 1964, 12,000 Northern troops reached the front, and 33,000 a year later. From 1966 to 1971, some 600,000 North Vietnamese Army (NVA) troops came down the trail. By the early 1970s their numbers far exceeded those of the U.S. military. In the major years of escalation, however, the intervention of American troops significantly outpaced

North Vietnam's, rising from about 23,000 at the end of 1964, to 185,000 in 1965, 385,000 in 1966, 465,000 in 1967, and 536,000 in 1968.

The rapid influx of North Vietnamese troops was made possible by a massive program to improve and expand the trails launched in 1965. In addition to the tens of thousands of North Vietnamese who worked on the trails, Hanoi relied on Laotian laborers and Russian, Chinese, and North Korean engineers. The system continued to grow despite systematic American bombing. In the final years of the war North Vietnam widened and surfaced many stretches of road and ran an oil pipeline all the way down from North Vietnam to Loc Ninh, a village about eighty miles north of Saigon. Ultimately, the entire network included more than ten thousand miles of trails.

Heavy materiel was also transported by ship to Sihanoukville, Cambodia, and then by ground into South Vietnam (although this traffic was halted in 1970 when Cambodia's Prince Sihanouk was overthrown by American-backed General Lon Nol). There were crucial supply lines into North Vietnam itself from the Soviet Union, China, and Eastern Europe. Most of the Soviet and Eastern European materiel came into Vietnam by ship into the port city of Haiphong. Supplies from China came primarily overland via road and rail lines.

While our most familiar images of the war feature isolated jungle patrols and ambushes, it was, in fact, a war that was largely supplied and sustained by a nexus of global operations.

VU THI VINH

"The Truong Son jungle gave us life."

Along with tens of thousands of North Vietnamese girls, she volunteered to work on the "Truong Son," the dozens of footpaths and roads known to Americans as the "Ho Chi Minh Trail." The Volunteer Youth Corps was formed in 1965 as part of the massive effort to expand and improve the transportation network. These teenage boys and girls cut down trees, cleared and leveled trails, filled in bomb craters, and defused unexploded bombs.

Discussing that experience with five women veterans of the Volunteer Youth Corps, one thought the minimum age to volunteer was sixteen, another seventeen, and another eighteen. Then one said, "If you insisted, they would let you go whatever your age." Vu Thi Vinh lied about her age and volunteered to work on the trails at age fifteen despite her parents' opposition. "We were so young we didn't know anything, but our patriotism was very high. We went to war willingly."

At first there were no trails, just mountains. Cutting the roads was a superhuman task. Our only tools were picks, shovels, and saws. When trees were too big to cut down by hand we blew them down with dynamite. It took at least twenty people to roll the big trees aside. We also had to dam up streams with rocks to keep them from swamping the trails. Sometimes we had to stand forever in water up to our chests. During the rainy season, it was almost impossible to get dry.

Most of the time we worked only at night because that's when the trucks and soldiers came and we needed to be ready to help if they got stuck. Usually we slept from about seven-thirty to eleven in the morning. Then we had lunch and took classes to continue our education. After that we slept again until four-thirty. Supper was at five o'clock and then we were off to work again. Of course, in emergency situations we worked day and night. If the trail was blocked for just one hour there'd be a terrible traffic jam and that was an invitation to American bombers. Anytime bombs hit the trail, we had to rush out and fill in the craters immediately.

After one bombing strike we discovered a big bomb lying unexploded in a small stream next to a bridge. There was a danger that a truck passing over the bridge might set it off so our leader selected a "dare to die" team to defuse the bomb. Everyone wanted to be on the team so we had to write a short essay to apply. The only safe way to defuse the bomb was to explode it, even though that meant destroying part of the bridge we'd built. But we managed to explode the bomb and repair the bridge before the trucks came that night.

Needless to say, life in the jungle was extremely hard. When we weren't supplied with rice we ate whatever we could find. We searched for crabs under rocks in the streams and occasionally we were lucky enough to come up with some cassava. Sometimes we had to scrape fungus and moss off rocks. "Aircraft 'vegetables'" we called them because they were the only edible things left after all the bombing. We were so hungry everything tasted good. The mountains were filled with red ginseng trees. We'd boil the leaves and stems and then throw them away and drink the broth. It was very sweet and nutritious. The Truong Son jungle gave us life.

After our exhausting labor we'd go back to our camps and sing songs or perform plays. We sang all the time to keep our spirits up. We used to joke that you couldn't hear the bombs over our singing.

NGUYEN THI KIM CHUY

"We came home hairless with ghostly white eyes."

She worked in the jungles of the Truong Son as a Youth Volunteer for four years. Today she lives on the outskirts of Hanoi where she grows and sells flowers.

I was sent to the Truong Son to help make three new trails—Number Fifteen, Number Twenty-One, and Number Twenty-Two. That was my contribution to the war against the Americans. We worked in Quang Binh Province, the gateway to the Truong Son, where the United States dropped so many bombs that we called it the "bombing capital." We could distinguish every kind of bomb by its sound. For example, a cluster bomb lands with a thud. That's because its a "mother bomb" and doesn't itself cause the destruction. It just opens and out fly the "baby bombs." Those small baby bombs are lethal.

One day we had to withstand seven bombing attacks, while working day and night to fill the craters. At one point my commander asked me to go check on a group of girls about a hundred meters away. As I was walking in their direction, I saw with my own eyes a bomb drop into a shelter hole. Everyone stopped working and rushed there, screaming and crying. We were on our hands and knees clawing at the dirt. Our arms were smeared with blood. There were five people in that shelter. Four of them just turned to porridge. We couldn't tell them apart. We just divided the parts arbitrarily into four small mounds, gave each one a name, and buried them. Only one body was recognizable—a local woman who was visiting us. An official of the Communist Party, I think. She had her two-year-old child with her. That woman was holding her child so tightly we couldn't separate them. We buried them together. After that terrible experience we still had two craters to fill. So we went on with our work as if it hadn't happened.

If we had to travel from one part of the Truong Son to another we always moved in the middle of the night to reduce the risk of being bombed. When I was a young child I never had a sleepless night. I couldn't get used to losing so much sleep. Sometimes, I actually slept a little as I walked. One night I sleepwalked right off the trail into a thicket and they had to pull me out. From then on we tied ourselves together with a long rope looped around each of our waists. So a few nights later I took the lead on a small footpath. Once again I fell asleep, only this time I pulled everybody into the woods. [Laughs.]

We saw many soldiers traveling down the Truong Son. They loved us because we were courageous girls and worked so hard. When the Americans came to bomb us our boyfriends were very eager to protect us, but it was just innocent romance. No babies were born. Even if we wanted to do more, how could we? We lived apart from the boy volunteers and most of the soldiers moved on so quickly to the South. We didn't have much time together.

Almost everyone got malaria and quite a few died from it. When I had it, I was told that eating a worm was a good folk remedy. They gave me a worm that was dirty, disgusting, and black, but I felt so sick I was willing to do anything to get better and I ate it without hesitation. I don't think it helped. Many of us temporily lost our hair from malaria and living in the jungle for so many years made us look terrible. After the war we came home hairless with ghostly white eyes, pale skin, and purple lips. Some girls lost their ability to have children. I developed terrible arthritis. When my old boyfriend came back from the war, I didn't think my health was good enough to have a family so I said good-bye to him. It was a very painful parting since his house was just around the corner in our village. Even after my family nourished me and gave me medicine, I weighed only thirty-seven kilos [eighty-two pounds]. Though I never married, I did adopt my older sister's daughter.

"Children always beg me to tell them stories about the Truong Son trail. They listen to my stories as if they were fairy tales. It's hard to imagine how we could have endured such hardship."

HELEN TENNANT HEGELHEIMER

"I was their wife, their sister, their girlfriend."

In 1966 and '67 she was a flight attendant for World Airways, one of the civilian airliners that had a government contract to ferry U.S. troops in and out of the war zone. An old photograph shows her standing on the tarmac smiling from beneath a hat that resembles a billed pumpkin. "Go ahead and laugh, but back in '66 that outfit was the cat's meow. Stews from other airlines would come up and say, 'What a wonderful uniform!' "

When I was a young gal I watched *The Mickey Mouse Club* and they did a program on what it was like to be a stewardess. I was absolutely glued to the TV set. After that, I cannot remember a time I didn't want to be a stewardess.

We had extremely strict rules about our appearance. Everybody had to look exactly the same. We even had to wear the same fingernail polish and the same kind of perfume. We weren't allowed to wear earrings and our hair had to be short or at least worn up. You couldn't look provocative in our uniforms. They were very tailored, sort of Jackie Kennedy–like camel-hair suits. The skirts were midknee even though it was the sixties. The most distinctive thing was our polo hat with this huge crown on it.

Of course there was a lot of sexism in those days but I don't remember any of the guys on the Vietnam flights ever giving me a bad time. They were very respectful. Our real job was to distract them at all costs, to get their mind away from where they were going. If that meant flirting with them a little bit, so what? It never did go over the line. But the captain could get away with just about anything. For instance, we were required to wear girdles, so if the captain came up behind me and slapped me on the butt he'd say, "Girdle check." Most of the pilots were World War II or Korean War veterans. I thought they were ancient and didn't want anything to do with them.

Going over, there were usually two legs—Travis Air Force Base to Japan, and Japan to Vietnam. From California to Japan the troops did a lot of letter writing. Guys would ask me, "Is this a good letter? If you received this, would you wait for me?" At first I read the letters, but they really pulled at your heart, so after a while I would just pretend to read them and say they were perfect.

There were always some chatty guys who wanted to talk and if we had any special unit guys—Green Berets or Airborne Rangers—there was a lot of bravado. They spoke proudly of their training, how difficult it was for them not to get "washed out." Over time I realized they weren't really trying to impress me as much as they were trying to convince themselves their training would help them. These were boys destined for combat and they had been told in training what their expected mortality rate was. I remember an air force Blue Beret actually told me they were trained to die. He didn't expect to ever go home.

But most of the guys were really pretty quiet. They asked us for alcohol and we said, "If the military wanted you to have that they would have put it in the contract." Since the war I've had a lot of vets tell me they were served alcohol, but I don't think so. Maybe the policy changed later in the war, but sometimes people's memories do strange things.

When we got to Yokota Air Force Base in Japan we had a crew change. So after a layover, I'd get on another plane with a group of guys I hadn't met who had already been on the plane for twelve hours. We had to kind of feel out the mood. By then they were usually very quiet. It was five hours to Vietnam and five hours back. We called this the Vietnam turnaround. We'd go in and out with minimal ground time.

Sometimes we had F-4 Phantoms escort us in. All of a sudden they'd just appear, right on our wingtips, and come all the way down with us. It was an absolutely gorgeous sight. We'd touch down and they'd pull up. But they didn't escort us every time so you wondered what was going on down there to make them appear. The guys would always ask and we'd just tell them the F-4 pilots wanted to show off.

I especially remember when we came in at night. That's when you saw the tracer rounds [chemically treated to emit a bright color when fired]. I was so naive I didn't realize tracers were live rounds. I don't know what I thought I was seeing—maybe target practice or fireworks. Who knows? Only years later did some veteran tell me I'd been witnessing actual firefights, that the red tracers were ours and the green tracers were theirs. I said, "Who in this world sits down and says, you're going to have this color and you're going to have that color?"

Sometimes the senior stew would come around and ask for another pair of eyes and ears in the cockpit. I did that several times. There's a jump seat right behind the captain with earphones. On my first flights into Tan Son Nhut, the tower was still run by Vietnamese and the pilot couldn't always understand their English. I'll never forget the captain turning around and saying, "Did anybody understand what that guy just said?" And we were on final approach. One time I was sitting in the jump seat when an ammo depot blew up right in front of us. The guys on the ground thought it was us that blew up.

It was the senior stew's position to be at the top of the ramp when the men got off in Vietnam. But when we were about two hours out she would usually ask for a volunteer to take the forward door. All you had to do is stand at the door and say good-bye, but nobody wanted that job. It's nothing disparaging about the other gals, but many just couldn't do it. I'd always take the forward door and I was good at it.

I never said "good-bye" or "good luck." I would shake their hand, look them in the eye, smile, and say, "See you later." Sometimes I'd say, "See you in twelve months." They really wanted somebody to look at them. At the top of the ramp was the world, at the bottom of the ramp was the war. I saw eyes full of fear, some with real terror. And maybe this sounds crazy, but I saw death in some of those eyes. At that moment, at the top of the ramp, I was their wife, their sister, their girlfriend, and for those troops who had no one else—and there were many—I was their mother. That was the most important thing I've ever done. I can't imagine doing anything more important than to nudge a troop into war. If he wasn't lucky, I was nudging him to his death with the best "It will be okay" smile I could conjure up.

I don't think there was one of us who did not want to keep them on the plane. That's why some of the girls were back in the bathrooms crying. They couldn't stand to watch them leave. We were very aware we were sending them to war and that some would never come back. Therein lies the guilt. I've spent a lot of time wondering if instead of distracting them I should have warned them. I've been assured by veterans that there was nothing I could have said. I mean, imagine some stewardess saying, "Hey you guys, listen, this is really going to be rough." For a long time I felt guilty, but I still think it's the best thing I've every done, the most unselfish. I just thought they deserved to have someone from home stand there and be as strong as they were.

We never showed any emotion in front of the troops but we sure drank a lot when we got back to Japan. We substituted booze for crying. There were an awful lot of guys who said, "I don't have anybody to write to. Will you write to me?" You could pretty much tell whether they were pulling your leg or not, so my roommate and I wrote to a lot of them. We'd also go to the local liquor store when the new issue of *Playboy* arrived and buy up the entire supply. Then we'd have this mass mailing night sending *Playboy* magazines to these guys in Vietnam.

The first thing we'd ask when we arrived in Vietnam is, "Are we taking troops out?" If you took a hundred and sixty-five men in and a hundred and sixty-five out, you really could fool yourself into believing that they were all coming home. But in '66 and '67 the war was escalating so we often left Vietnam with an empty plane. There was nothing else to say other than, "They're not all coming home." It would just slam you right in the face. You did not want to be on that airplane if we flew back empty. There were five stewardesses and we didn't even sit with each other. And when we got back to Japan we drank even heavier.

I've heard stories about guys cheering when the plane took off from Vietnam, but I don't remember any cheering. When the plane lifted off, I could see right down the aisle from a seat in the back. There might be one or two hands that reached across the aisle to shake hands. But it was quiet. Pretty soon the captain came on and said, "Gentlemen, we've just cleared Vietnam airspace." [Her voice catches.] It still gets to me. So then it was as if everyone on the plane exhaled. But they still didn't cheer.

On the way back we walked down the aisle looking to see which ones might want to talk and which ones you ought to leave alone. You'd just started by asking, "Where you from?" But we never asked them anything about what they did in Vietnam and I don't remember anybody ever saying anything to me about it. I clearly remember thinking, these guys are not going home to their girlfriend and that '55 Chevy they had been working on. Their youth was gone and it showed. You absolutely saw a different look in their eyes on the way home.

There were guys who came up to me and said, "I need to talk because I want to practice. I'm afraid I'm going to swear in front of my mother when I get home." So they'd talk and every other word was a swear. I wouldn't flinch. I'd just say, "Don't worry, you'll be okay." "No," they said, "I can just see me sitting down to dinner and the first word out of mouth is fuckin' this or goddamn that." These boys grew up the same way I did in the fifties. We attended church, we understood right from wrong. I believe they did things in Vietnam that were totally against everything they were brought up with and I'm not really talking about the killing. I'm thinking about those other things that happen to young men in a war—drinking, and maybe drugs, and contact with girls. So they weren't just afraid of swearing in front of their mothers; they were afraid their mothers would be able to tell everything they had done in Vietnam. I think this was a big reason why so many veterans just shut down and wouldn't talk about the war to anyone except someone else that had been there.

And they came home to a world that was very different, even just twelve months later. Flying in, some guys asked, "How bad are the antiwar demonstrations?" That's the hardest question I've had to answer in my life. I'd say, "They're bad." There were often protesters at the gates outside Travis. I had to tell these boys that had just served their country to get out of their country's uniform as soon as they could. If they weren't wearing their uniform then maybe they wouldn't be targeted by the protesters. I didn't like the antiwar movement then and I haven't changed my mind today. It just seemed like the protest movement targeted the soldiers more than they did the policy makers—making it seem as if all the soldiers had gotten together one afternoon in a bar and decided to go commit some sort of crime against the people of Vietnam.

They came home so quickly, they had no time to adjust. Some men had just gotten out of combat a few hours before they got on the plane. Before a meal service, we'd make sure everyone was awake. We always had to be very careful about waking these guys. If you touched them, they'd wake up defending themselves—arms flying all over the place. We managed to hold them down until they realized where they were. It only took a second and we always smiled. They always apologized. "Oh ma'am, I'm sorry, I didn't hurt you, did I?" We'd try not to make a big deal out of it.

Every time we arrived at Travis Air Force Base I was disappointed. I had grown up with World War II movies and everybody had a band or something to welcome them home. At Travis there was absolutely nothing. It was just me at the bottom of the ramp. An ungrateful nation let some twenty-three-year-old stewardess welcome these guys home. That was their only greeting.

In the nineties she started going to Washington, D.C., for Veterans Day. A highlight of the trip is the "DMZ to Delta Dance" sponsored by a chapter of Vietnam Veterans of America. "It's a bunch of old people dancing to great rock 'n' roll. The theme song of the dance, of course, is 'We Got to Get Out of This Place.' It's always the last song of the evening."

"YOU WANT ME TO START WORLD WAR III?"

On the night of August 4, 1964, President Lyndon Johnson went on television with an ominous announcement: "Aggression by terror against peaceful villages of South Vietnam has now been joined by open aggression on the high seas against the United States of America." Without provocation, North Vietnamese patrol boats, he explained, had launched torpedoes at two American destroyers, the *Maddox* and the *Turner Joy,* in the Gulf of Tonkin off the coast of North Vietnam. U.S. bombers were already making retaliatory strikes against North Vietnamese targets. A few days later Johnson asked Congress to pass a resolution giving him the power "to take all necessary measures to repel any armed attack against the forces of the United States." The Gulf of Tonkin Resolution passed overwhelmingly with only Senators Wayne Morse and Ernest Gruening dissenting. Though it was not a declaration of war, LBJ used the resolution as a blank check to initiate massive increases in America's military commitment to Vietnam. Many congressmen later regretted their support of the resolution, including William Fulbright, the chairman of the Senate Foreign Relations Committee, who would become a leading critic of the war.

What virtually no Americans knew at the time, including Congress, is that the Johnson administration lied about the Gulf of Tonkin incident. Hardly unprovoked, North Vietnam had been the target of secret U.S. military operations since 1961. The *Maddox* and *Turner Joy* were not sailing innocently in the Gulf of Tonkin, as LBJ implied, but were gathering electronic intelligence in conjunction with Operation Plan 34A (OPLAN 34A), a series of covert commando raids on North Vietnamese islands and coastal villages. Johnson also distorted the truth when he claimed there were two separate attacks on U.S. ships in the Gulf. The second alleged attack was unconfirmed and soon proved not to have occurred. Finally, the White House did not formulate the Gulf of Tonkin Resolution in response to the events Johnson described on television but had written it two months beforehand in anticipation of an event that would rally support for its passage. LBJ wanted to avert the necessity of a formal declaration of war and the intense debate it would produce.

The presidential election of 1964 was a crucial part of the context in which these momentous decisions were made. Republican candidate Barry Goldwater had accused LBJ of cringing in the face of Communist bullying and promised, if elected, to fight in Vietnam with a force and resolve Johnson lacked. The president's response to the Gulf of Tonkin incident spiked his poll ratings and he no longer felt so vulnerable to Goldwater's attacks. Instead, he painted Goldwater as a dangerous extremist who might lead the United States into World War III and presented himself as a man of peace. "We are not about to send American boys nine or ten thousand miles away from home to do what Asian boys ought to be doing for themselves," Johnson pledged.

The "peace" candidate of 1964 had been a war president since November 1963, when he was thrust into office by the assassination of John Kennedy. In early 1965, just months after his landslide victory over Goldwater, LBJ launched Operation Rolling Thunder, the sustained bombing of North Vietnam. He also deployed two marine combat battalions to Danang, South Vietnam, the first major American infantry units to enter the war. Like the Tonkin Resolution, these major escalations of the war had been secretly planned long in advance of their announcement. And with the resolution safely in hand, Johnson did not feel obliged to have his new war policies debated and approved by Congress.

Saigon, meanwhile, was reeling from one coup to another. Since the assassination of Ngo Dinh Diem in 1963, the government had changed five times in little more than a year. At one point in early 1965, an exasperated U.S. ambassador, Maxwell Taylor, called a handful of South Vietnamese leaders together and dressed them down like schoolboys. "Do all of you understand English?" he asked. "I told you all clearly . . . we Americans were tired of coups . . . now you have made a real mess. We cannot carry you forever if you do things like this."

But such threats proved idle as the United States continued to intensify its warfare. In June, huge American B-52 stratofortresses began bombing targets in South Vietnam, each plane dropping up to twenty-seven tons of explosives per mission. In July, Johnson announced that he was sending another fifty thousand troops to Vietnam. What he didn't say is that he had privately authorized an additional one hundred thousand by the end of 1965, raising the total to almost two hundred thousand. He had also left the door open for further escalations to come.

Despite the obvious buildup, Johnson, like all our Vietnam-era presidents, often spoke of the war as if it represented some other activity altogether—an exercise in "nation building," or "support" for an ally, or the fulfillment of a "commitment," or the pursuit of "peace." In April 1965, with major escalations under way, Johnson said: "Now there must be a much more massive effort to improve the life of man in that conflict-torn corner of our world." Food, medicine, rural electrification—all, he claimed, should come to Southeast Asia.

Part of Johnson's rhetoric was designed to persuade Americans that his aims were peaceful even as he presided over an ever-enlarging war. Yet he was also genuinely worried that U.S. actions in Vietnam might lead to a larger showdown with the Soviet Union or China. That was his primary reason for rejecting proposals by his top military commanders to launch an all-out air attack on North Vietnam and to mobilize the reserves. He did approve a gradual increase in the number of bombing missions in the North but restricted them, in 1965, to targets south of the twentieth parallel below the major cities. Johnson well remembered when American troops advanced to the northern border of North Korea in 1950 and three hundred thousand Chinese combat troops intervened in the Korean War.

Over the next three years Johnson raised the U.S. troop commitment in South Vietnam to more than five hundred thousand and intensified the air war over North and South Vietnam, as well as on targets in Laos where he sought to prevent North Vietnamese troops and supplies from moving down the Ho Chi Minh Trail.

Throughout those years, the Johnson administration routinely expressed optimism about American success in Vietnam. Privately, however, LBJ was full of more doubts than any citizen might have imagined. As early as March 6, 1965, having just ordered marine combat units to Vietnam, he confided to Senator Richard Russell, "I guess we've got no choice, but it scares the hell out of me . . . [the Viet Cong are] not going to run. Then you're tied down. . . . And we're losing more every day. . . . We're getting in worse."

Johnson genuinely hated the war, which was taking money and support from the social and economic reforms of his beloved Great Society. The cost was also personal. Student antiwar activists were already shouting, "Hey, hey, LBJ, how many kids did you kill today?" But the president believed he had to fight the war even if, as he feared, it could not be won. Withdrawal or compromise, he felt certain, would be perceived throughout the world as a sign of weakness and cowardice.

Johnson's heart belonged in domestic politics and the nitty-gritty of passing legislation on behalf of civil rights and the "war on poverty." Try as he might, he could not convince the world, or perhaps even himself, that his "bitch of a war" in Vietnam was an extension of the Great Society, an opportunity to bring prosperity and promise to faraway hamlets and villages. But he escalated it nonetheless, however reluctantly, until it finally drove him from office.

JAMES THOMSON

"This was crazy and deceitful policy making."

As a young boy he lived in Nanking, China, the son of missionary educators. After launching an academic career in Asian history and politics, he was drawn to Washington in 1961, inspired by President Kennedy. He was hired as an aide to Undersecretary of State Chester Bowles and was later made special assistant to McGeorge Bundy, President Lyndon Johnson's first national security adviser. In that capacity, from 1964 to '66, he spent most of his time on Vietnam policy.

In an upstairs room of his Cambridge, Massachusetts, house, Thomson moves piles of books and clutter to clear space for a conversation. A rumpled man, with an air of sadness buoyed by an irrepressible sense of irony, he lights a cigarette. His gravelly voice cuts through the fog of smoke.

Early in my tenure with McGeorge Bundy—the summer of 1964—my secretary announced that Colonel so-and-so was here with "the book." I said, "Okay, let him in." So the colonel comes in, salutes, and says, "Sir, we have the schedule for the next seven days, weather permitting, and we need your White House clearance on this."

I open it up. It's a map of Indochina—Laos, North Vietnam, South Vietnam, and part of Cambodia. And there's dot, dot, dot, dot, dot, dot, dot—a track of little dots indicating a path that something or someone was going to take.

And I said, "This is?"

He said, "The usual."

I said, "You mean?"

He said, "Oh, armed recce," r-e-c-c-e [pronounced "wrecky"].

"Mm-hmmm," I said. "Oh, yes. I see. It says 'armed recce' right here."

"And this," he said, "is the path that the planes will take."

So I said, "Would you mind leaving the room for a minute, Colonel?" I call Bromley Smith, who was the perennial executive secretary there. "Bromley, the colonel has come in here with something he says he does weekly, to get White House clearance on armed recce. What do I do?"

Smith said, "Well, if it looks right to you, sign it. Just sign off for Mac [Bundy]." Gulp. So the colonel came back in. I signed off and as soon as he left I asked Bob Komer [Bundy's senior aide] what armed recce was. He goes "armed reconnaissance." And I thought, Oh, reconnaissance. Yes. You mean taking pictures. The armed part, I assumed, meant that if people fire at you, you can fire back. The colonel came back every week and I got accustomed to saying,

"Oh, it looks fine to me—good flight plan." I still thought it was about taking pictures and fire if fired upon.

It took quite a while to learn that armed recce meant not only taking pictures, but shooting at anything that looks suspicious. Armed reconnaissance planes basically flew up and down both halves of Vietnam and over Laos, taking pictures and shooting at anything they wanted to. Many months later I realized I was authorizing quite a bit of killing with no knowledge of what it was all about and it staggered me.

Years later a ferociously antiwar friend of mine, Jonathan Mirsky, was teaching at Dartmouth and he and a group of faculty and students were arrested for blocking a bus of draftees. The defense argued the case on the basis of the illegality of our war efforts. According to my lawyer friends, it was the one and only time in the history of the Vietnam War that a judge allowed this kind of testimony. I testified that I did in fact approve all those flight plans and was party to a criminal action and therefore people like Mirsky had a right to commit civil disobedience. After all, we were not at war at the time of those missions.

In August 1964, I had been on the National Security Council staff only a month when a message arrives saying: "Am under fire from Vietnamese torpedo boats." It was from the [destroyer] *Maddox*. So I run across the hall to Bob Komer and I say, "Bob, what do we do?" It's around noon and he says, "Jimmy, when this kind of thing comes through, the big boys take over. You and I go have lunch."

Two days later, during the second so-called Gulf of Tonkin incident, I'm suddenly told to go to a policy planning meeting chaired by Walt Rostow over at State. Normally Komer goes, but he couldn't make it. So I was the National Security Council representative. I go to this long dining room on the seventh floor and there is a crowd of people presided over by Rostow. They're having sherry or something nonlethal. As I enter, I hear Rostow saying, "You know, the wonderful thing is, we don't even know if this thing happened at all. Boy, it gives us the chance really to go for broke on the bombing. The evidence is unclear, but our golden opportunity is at hand."

I was a little taken aback. I sit like a new boy through this meeting. Then I come running back to Komer and he said, "How did it go, Jim?" So I describe it. He said, "Jesus Christ. You've got to get on the horn and tell Walt to button his lip about that evidence thing."

I said, "Excuse me, Robert? I am a little kid over here. I just turned thirty and this is the first time I've been in a Rostow meeting. Who am I to tell Walt to button his lip?"

"Well," he said, "I'll call Mac [Bundy]." And the next thing I know, Mac has called Walt to tell him to button his lip. An act of violence on our part was going to be undertaken in response to something that had not happened or was not proved. This was crazy and deceitful policy making.

Immediately after the Johnson landslide of 1964 I'm thrust into the later stages of planning policy options for postelection action on Vietnam. I was increasingly surprised and shocked by what I heard. They seemed to be ruling out any kind of negotiations, any kind of gradual withdrawal option, any kind of neutralization, any kind of international conference, all these other possibilities. Instead they were going for slow-motion but systematic escalation and the aerial bombardment of enemy positions north and south.

The first week in December 1964, Mac Bundy calls me into his office. He says, "James, I want you to sit down on that sofa and I want you to take this folder and read it. Take your time. Read it slowly and tell me what you think." It was a statement of the chosen option—the slow-motion escalation through systematic aerial bombardment to bring the enemy to his knees.

I said, "Look, I know very little about the weaponry of war. The last airplane I could recognize was the P-38 in World War II. But I do know one thing. No matter what we do—even if we bomb them back to the Stone Age, push them back into the bush, and destroy everything they've built—they know that someday we will leave. And they're willing to wait. And they know that we know that someday we'll leave. So given my lack of qualifications, I nonetheless think that this is a road to folly at a time when we have the greatest opportunity imaginable to discretely disengage."

After a long pause, Mac finally says, "Well, James, you very well may be right. Thank you for looking at it." Those words of his, for better or worse, kept me working for him. He could hear dissent as long as you didn't shout it from the rooftops or pass it around. But Johnson made only one option possible—this "reasonable" middle course. It seemed to me a fraud. And more and more of what I read makes me think that the president was the problem. I used to think it was the advisers. But that intimidating guy who could not ever be the president who had lost a war was the key figure and he was unpersuadable. And he was surrounded by people who found it almost intolerable to stand up to him.

SETH TILLMAN

"We could stop this war tomorrow."

In 1961, as a twenty-nine-year-old Ph.D. from the Fletcher School of Law and Diplomacy, he was hired by Senator J. William Fulbright, the Arkansas Democrat who was chairman of the Senate Foreign Relations Committee. He remained a committee staff member until 1977. In that role he drafted many of Fulbright's speeches and helped him write several books, including The Arrogance of Power.

"Fulbright was fundamentally a conservative but I was attracted to him because he had a free-ranging mind and the kind of curiosity that entertained ideas whether they were familiar or unfamiliar, conventional or unconventional, or even outrageous." By the midsixties, Fulbright had become one of the Senate's leading critics of the Vietnam War. He held several televised hearings on the war, beginning in January 1966. Angered by Fulbright's dissent, President Johnson began referring to him as "Senator Halfbright," and "a frustrated old woman."

In 1964, Fulbright had a pretty conventional perspective on Vietnam. He was much more engaged with other matters. The Gulf of Tonkin Resolution was a crucial watershed. As chairman of the Foreign Relations Committee, Fulbright was asked to get the resolution through the committee and the Senate, which he did readily, almost enthusiastically. I remember Secretary of State Dean Rusk and Secretary of Defense Robert McNamara offering testimony before the Foreign Relations Committee. They laid out the Gulf of Tonkin incident as a clear, unmistakable, and unprovoked attack by North Vietnamese PT boats on the *Maddox* and the *Turner Joy*. There was no inclination whatsoever to doubt or question them. The atmosphere of trust and confidence was such that if the Johnson administration and its leading representatives said it happened that way, you accepted it.

Fulbright quite readily admitted many times afterwards that he didn't want to give [Republican presidential candidate Barry] Goldwater any political ammunition to use against Johnson. He was worried to death that Goldwater might actually have a shot at defeating Johnson in the 1964 election. Fulbright thought Goldwater was dangerously irresponsible, making draconian threats about defoliating the jungle in Vietnam and bombing and launching a major war—all the things Johnson eventually did himself. Fulbright thought the resolution would help Johnson establish his credentials as sufficiently tough on Communist aggression. And none of us, certainly not I, who wrote his floor speech endorsing the Tonkin Resolution, advised otherwise.

To his subsequent great regret he declined to accept an amendment offered by Senator Gaylord Nelson, a Democrat from Wisconsin, that the resolution not be understood as authorization for war. Fulbright didn't want to clutter up the resolution and wanted a strong statement of unified support for the president in the wake of these alleged provocations.

Later on, when the evidence became persuasive that we had been duped, Fulbright felt very badly burned. He became intensely skeptical. For the rest of his life his attitude was, I don't know whether they're lying to me or not. I have to have evidence.

The year and a half that followed the Gulf of Tonkin was decisive in committing Fulbright to open and public dissent, which was not his first inclination. He was trying privately and confidentially to influence Johnson against escalating the war. Johnson, in his style, went through the motions of being very receptive. The arm on the shoulder stuff and, "I value your advice, Bill." But Fulbright caught on that nobody was taking his advice. He wrote Johnson a memorandum on April 5, 1965, stating flatly not only that we ought to disengage from Vietnam, but that there was no fundamental reason in his judgment why we could not accommodate ourselves to a unified Communist Vietnam, with the expectation of encouraging an essentially Titoist government [a reference to the Communist government of Yugoslavia under Josip Tito which remained independent of Soviet control].

I heard that Johnson was ridiculing this memorandum but I never passed along that nasty gossip to Fulbright. I didn't want to poison the well. But Fulbright and those of us around him were in over our heads when it came to political manipulation. We were dealing with Johnson, the all-time champion political operator.

I think there was a lot of apprehension in Congress about the war and it was mounting, but the prevailing wisdom was that you had to walk very carefully in dealing with Lyndon Johnson; that overt criticism infuriated him and could have the opposite result of what you hoped and intended. Fulbright frequently noted the fact that members of the Senate and House who might be quite critical of the president at a distance were utterly deferential to him in his presence. And when Fulbright went into open opposition, he became worse than an enemy. In Johnson's perception, he was a traitor, a friend who had betrayed him.

What really led Fulbright to public dissent over the Vietnam War was the United States intervention in the Dominican Republic in April 1965. That intervention gave rise to closed-session hearings and they showed to the satisfaction of Fulbright and many members of the Foreign Relations Committee that the Johnson administration had drastically misrepresented the facts and the reason for the intervention. The claim that we went in to save American lives was phony. No American lives were at risk until we sent in the marines. It was panic-stricken fear of another Castro. The committee staff produced a very severe indictment of the Dominican intervention but the committee members were disinclined to do anything about it. They were not looking for a direct confrontation with Lyndon Johnson. So the question became, "What should Fulbright, the chairman, do? Do you write another confidential memorandum to the president or do you go public?" The staff split. The principal advocate of staying private was Lee Williams, one of only two administrative assistants Fulbright had in thirty-two years. Lee was passionate against going public. I can almost hear his words, "Don't do this. I understand Johnson. He'll never forgive you. You will shatter any semblance of influence you might ever hope to have." On the other side two of us were saying, "We think you have a responsibility as chairman to go public." Well, he decided to go public and made a speech on September 15, 1965, and it had all the consequences Lee predicted. Johnson was enraged. That was the end of Fulbright's influence with Johnson. He struck him from the White House invitation list. They never had a personal relationship again. Johnson never forgave him. He took everything so personally. There was almost a kind of naïveté on Fulbright's part. He thought Johnson had made a mistake and should correct it, that it's useful to have mistakes called to your attention. He didn't understand why Johnson would take it personally since he was not personally hostile to Johnson. Fulbright was a much more secure man and could withstand criticism.

After the Dominican intervention private persuasion was no longer an option so Fulbright decided to begin public hearings about the Vietnam War in January 1966. He had a kind of visceral distaste for the military and military thinking and the use of force. His greatest enthusiasm and affection was for the Fulbright scholarships. He loved that program and took it very seriously. I was with him on a trip to Europe with a sizable group of congressmen and senators. A number of them were going out into the Bay of Naples to visit the *Forrestal,* a big American aircraft carrier. It was all lit up like the Brooklyn Bridge. I asked if he wanted to go, partly because I wanted to go. He said, "No, I'd rather go to the binational center and visit with some students." That was real Fulbright. He said, "Those fellas on the *Forrestal* don't know where the real power is." You can call it naive, but you can't call it phony.

Congress could have stopped the war. As Fulbright himself said on a number of occasions, "If we were willing to take the responsibility, we could stop this war tomorrow." He even said, "I don't know why we complain about the president so much. We could do it." But he knew he could never get a majority. He was pretty persuasive within the Foreign Relations Committee, but he didn't know how to twist arms and didn't like it. He didn't lobby his colleagues and he resented it when anybody did that to him. He didn't have any particular skill about getting things through the Senate. His notion of how you get something through is that you make a speech, spell out your proposals as clearly and logically as possible, and hope somebody will pay attention.

He was profoundly engaged with Vietnam. He sat through those hearings on the war hour after hour after hour. He never got up. He never interrupted. He was relentless. I don't know any other senator who was involved with that kind of intensity. And he was sympathetic to the antiwar movement. He would receive protesting students and speak very respectfully to them about what they were doing. When John Kerry, now a senator from Massachusetts, was leading the Vietnam Veterans Against the War, they were camped out on the Mall. Fulbright had one of us go down and invite Kerry up to testify before the committee, which he did. But he never got directly involved. I once tried to persuade him to accept an invitation to talk at some big rally in Madison Square Garden. That wasn't his style.

CHARLES COOPER (I)

"He used the f-word more freely than a marine in boot camp."

Raised in the Mississippi Delta, he was a 190-pound tackle on the Ole Miss football team. In 1946, he transferred to the Naval Academy. "I never one day regretted becoming a marine. I found something I was good at. I could kick tail and take names without making people mad. That's the secret to leadership." When he retired in 1985 as a lieutenant general he was the third-highest-ranking marine in the nation.

In 1965, the thirty-seven-year-old major was aide to Admiral David L. McDonald, a member of the Joint Chiefs of Staff. The JCS asked him to prepare a map to be used in a briefing of President Johnson. In early November he found himself in the Oval Office. "I was an easel with ears."

I went down to a little shop in the basement of the Pentagon and made this map out of three-quarter-inch plywood. I put acetone on it and a little tray down at the bottom for grease pencils. I called over to the White House and said, "Hey, we're coming over with this thing, can you have an easel ready?" Oh yeah, no problem.

We were ushered into a room right across the hall from the Oval Office. The admiral asked me to wait out in the hall. Right at two o'clock the Oval Office opened, and there's Lyndon Baines Johnson. So he ushered the chiefs in and I'm kind of looking over the president's shoulder to see where the easel is. But I didn't see one. As I'm looking, Johnson says, "Come on in, Major. You can stand right over there." So I'm standing there with this heavy damn map. If I'd known I was going to have to hold the damn thing, I would have used thin plywood.

Johnson didn't invite the chiefs to sit down. Instead he took us over near some big picture windows and started lining us up. He had me stand in the middle with the map. Then he said, "Well, it's really nice to have you people over here. You're so kind to come over and brief me." I was thinking to myself, he's kind of greasy. That's the term we used in the Naval Academy when some guy was overly solicitous. So then he says, "Well what have you got?"

General Wheeler, the chairman, said, "Well, Mr. President, we fully realize that what we're going to present to you today requires a very difficult decision on your part." The essence of what he said was, "We all have very serious misgivings about the direction of the war. We don't want to be piling up American boys like cordwood fighting endless Asian troops. We feel that we can bring this war to a quick conclusion by using overwhelming naval and air power." The basic idea was that we had to use our principal strengths to punish the North Vietnamese or we would risk becoming involved in another protracted Asian ground war with no definitive solution. Wheeler proposed mining Haiphong harbor, blockading the rest of the North Vietnamese coastline, and simultaneously beginning a B-52 bombing offensive on Hanoi. The assumption was that the North Vietnamese would sue for peace if we increased the level of punishment.

At one point Johnson interrupted to say, "So you're going to cut them off, keep them from being reinforced, and then you're going to bomb them into the Stone Age."

Air force chief McConnell said, "Well, that's not exactly it, but you've got to punish them." When the briefing was over Johnson turned to the army and marine chiefs who had remained silent and asked, "Do you fully support these ideas?" Both generals said they totally agreed.

At that moment, Johnson exploded. I almost dropped the map. He just started screaming these obscenities. They were just filthy. It was something like: "You goddamn fucking assholes. You're trying to get me to start World War III with your idiotic bullshit—your 'military wisdom.'" He insulted each of them individually. "You dumb shit. Do you expect me to believe that kind of crap? I've got the weight of the Free World on my shoulders and you want me to start World War III?"

He called them shitheads and pompous assholes and used the f-word more freely than a marine in boot camp. He really degraded them and cursed at them. Then he stopped and went back to a calm voice, as if he'd finished playing his little role, and said:

"I'm going to ask you a question and I want you to give me an answer. Imagine that you're me—that you're the president of the United States—and five incompetents come into your office and try to talk you into starting World War III. Then let's see what kind of guts you have with the whole damn world to worry about. What would you do?" The silence was overpowering. Finally he turned to Earl Wheeler and demanded an answer.

General Wheeler said, "Mr. President, we've obviously upset you." The understatement of the year. Then he said something very close to this: "There are many things about the presidency only one human being can understand. You, Mr. President, are that human being. With that thought in mind, I cannot take your place, think your thoughts, know all you know, and tell you what I would do if I were you. I can't do it, Mr. President. No man can honestly do it. It's got to be your decision and yours alone."

So then Johnson went down the line and they just kind of agreed with Wheeler. Then Johnson erupted again. "The risk is just too high. How can you fucking assholes ignore what China might do? You have just contaminated my office, you filthy shitheads. Get the hell out of here right now." I know memories are normally dimmed by time, but not this one. My memory of Lyndon Johnson on that day is crystal clear.

The chiefs really thought they could sell their plan to the president. They had really built up a head of steam going into that meeting. I think Johnson had already made up his mind long before they got there and was using his most forceful way to kill the plan. When I got back into the car with Admiral McDonald, he said, "Never in my entire life did I ever expect to be put through something as horrible as what you just watched from the president of the United States to his five senior military advisers." He was just destroyed.

For three or four days they seriously considered a mass resignation—all of them. I think the reason they didn't was that we were at war and they did not want to be labeled traitors who quit in the face of the enemy. Well, I've been in positions damn near this tough and I wouldn't have done what they did.

WALT WHITMAN ROSTOW

"Take the North Vietnamese city of Vinh hostage."

He was one of the leading "hawks" in the Kennedy and Johnson administrations, an enthusiastic and persistent advocate of American military escalation. As a young officer during World War II he had selected bombing targets in Europe, an experience that gave him great confidence in the effectiveness of airpower. In the 1950s, as an economist at the Massachusetts Institute of Technology, he was even more effusive about the ability of the United States to defeat Communism by sponsoring capitalist "modernization" in Third World countries. It was his promotion of this idea that brought him to the attention of Senator John Kennedy and later helped win him a place in Kennedy's State Department. From 1966 to '68 he was President Johnson's national security adviser.

As many of his colleagues grew ever more pessimistic about American prospects in Vietnam, Rostow remained resolutely optimistic. In 1967, the Atlantic Monthly *published a wicked satire about Rostow written by former colleague James Thomson* *(see pp. 115–17).* *When the Rostow character—"Herman Melville Breslau"—receives word that Saigon has fallen to the Viet Cong he insists that the horrible news is, in fact, "a wholesome and not unexpected phase in South Vietnam's growth toward political maturity and economic viability." Rostow's ardent conviction that the Communists had negligible support in South Vietnam was expressed most memorably in Peter Davis's documentary* Hearts and Minds *(1974) when he said, "I don't think [Ho Chi Minh] could have got elected dogcatcher in South Vietnam."*

In 1969, Rostow returned to academic life at the University of Texas where, at age eighty-four, he still teaches some classes. "I'm not haunted by Vietnam, although I've had to answer many questions about it in my time. I've written a lot of books on other subjects."

Except for people who think the greatest thing that ever happened was the march on the Pentagon in 1967, the conventional view of the American people is now: Well, the Vietnam War was an awful mess, but it was part of deterring the spread of Communism.

My wife recently heard [retired Harvard economist] Ken Galbraith say that Lyndon Johnson was a much more important president than people thought, except for Vietnam. She disagreed and said, essentially, look, we entered this effort for the independence of South Vietnam with exactly the same spirit as the New Frontier and the Great Society. Which is true. We looked at the South Vietnamese as trying to make a democracy in their country. We wanted to help them and we did help them. We even brought people in and taught them how to make a modern chicken farm.

I had great human sympathy for them and that was very much the view of LBJ. He felt they were the underdogs and they were being attacked by the Russians and the Chinese. So it was partly an idealistic crusade combined with the feeling that we had to have the same deterrence in Southeast Asia as we'd had in the Korean War for Northeast Asia. It was part of a global strategy of deterrence and holding the line.

I had the view that we'd never win the war unless we cut the Ho Chi Minh Trail. It would have played to our strength. Instead of fighting a war of attrition in South Vietnam, we should have moved into Laos to block the crucial supplies coming down the Ho Chi Minh Trail. That would have forced the Vietnamese to put their troops right up against our organized main strength instead of dodging us with hit-and-run tactics. The logic of my position was to force them to fight our kind of war.

It would have been easy for us to do. I figured we'd need two divisions reinforced with heavy artillery and concentrated bombing. The Ho Chi Minh Trail had multiple entry points, but they were in a certain area. U.S. forces would go into Laos at the eighteenth parallel. No one lived there so you wouldn't kill any civilians. That whole area could be subjected to bombing. We could go back and back and back with air strikes just as we did in World War II when we took out the German aircraft industry and oil production with strategic bombing.

If we had cut the trail, it wouldn't have taken very long to win the war because all the supplies came from the North. The Viet Cong didn't produce anything by themselves—not even a Saturday Night Special. All their supplies had to be brought in and all their men had to be brought in. Had we done this, it would have shriveled the Communists out of Cambodia, Laos, and South Vietnam. The antigovernment resistance in the South was thoroughly capable of being handled if cut off from the North.

In addition to blocking the trail, I also wanted to take the North Vietnamese city of Vinh hostage. We could have taken it by an amphibious attack from the coast. Then we'd tell Ho Chi Minh, "Get the hell out of Cambodia and South Vietnam or we're going to stay in Vinh until you do."

I made these recommendations formally at a meeting with the president, the Joint Chiefs of Staff, and Secretaries Rusk and McNamara on April 27, 1967. It was only the second time I spoke up at a meeting with cabinet members. I usually presented my views to Johnson in private. But I felt strongly about this. I went up to the map and I showed exactly where we should cut the trail and how to take Vinh hostage.

LBJ rejected my recommendation. He felt the rules of engagement should remain: that no Americans should cross the South Vietnamese border on the ground. He and Secretary of State Rusk were much influenced by the entrance of the Chinese into the Korean War. They were afraid that sending ground troops into North Vietnam or Laos would draw China directly into the war. In my view it was a false analogy. In Korea, the U.S. went right up against Manchuria, which was an exceedingly sensitive point. I didn't want to go any closer than two or three hundred miles from the Chinese border. Besides, the Vietnamese didn't want the Chinese to get overly involved. They had a long history of hostility with the Chinese, which was soon evident.

A rational view would say the North Vietnamese couldn't beat us if we cut the Ho Chi Minh Trail. But you've got to understand that at the time the whole question of nuclear war was an enormous burden, more than any mortal man should have had to carry. Johnson figured he was up against two nuclear powers—China and the Soviet Union. He said over and over again that the alternative to doing what he was doing was a larger war and quite possibly a nuclear war. He felt for America and the human race he had no right to start such a war and that accounted for his rules of engagement being what they were.

I disagreed with him, but I wasn't elected by the American people. Attrition was a lousy way to fight a war, but I still thought maybe we'd luck out and win. We gradually improved from 1965 to 1967. Nineteen sixty-six was a year of distinct progress for us. But the country became restive and impatient.

The hawks were the majority of the American people before the Tet Offensive of 1968. They were all for using full force against North Vietnam. It wasn't until after Tet that the hawks said, "Ah, to hell with it." What turned them off was that we didn't react to Tet; that we didn't capitalize on our victory. It was a tremendous debacle for the North Vietnamese militarily, and for the recently elected South Vietnamese it constituted a great boost of confidence. But we stuck to the rules of engagement and only reacted in the South.

And then when Nixon went to China in 1972 the view of the hawks was, "Well, if they're making friends with the Chinese, why the hell are we taking this misery in Vietnam?" Because that was exactly why many of them believed we were there—to keep the Chinese out.

Just before he died in 1973, Johnson called me up on the phone and said, "Historians will argue whether I used too much strength against the North, or too little strength. I have come to the conclusion that I used too little." He told the same thing to Colonel Jim Cross, who flew *Air Force 1*. Before he died I think he wanted to tell this to two hawks in his family.

What Lyndon Johnson did was more costly perhaps than it had to be, but he saved Southeast Asia and we hold the balance of power in Asia today. The

Vietnam War was part of the long, hard process which led the Russians to throw in their hand.

In 1971, Nixon did something close to what Rostow had recommended in 1967. He sent two South Vietnamese divisions into Laos to cut the Ho Chi Minh Trail. They were routed. "It was a caricature of what I wanted to do. The South Vietnamese divisions were smaller than our divisions, for one thing, and they didn't have the full backing of American artillery and airpower. They were put in an impossible position. The North Vietnamese reacted just as I thought they would. They threw all their divisions in there and mopped up."

CENTRAL HIGHLANDS

Inside Vietnam, the war had to be won politically in order to be won militarily. The truest measure of success in the Vietnam War was not who killed the most enemy combatants, or who controlled the most territory, but who had the greatest political and moral legitimacy in the eyes of ordinary Vietnamese citizens. At root, the Communists won the war because they marshaled a greater number of devout partisans than the American-backed regime in Saigon.

That said, the land and geography of Vietnam was vital to the survival and military effectiveness of the Viet Cong and the North Vietnamese Army. The vast tracts of dense jungle, formidable mountains, and lush watery lowlands provided as much protection as land could offer from the vast arsenal of American firepower and the airborne mobility of U.S. troops. From remote and nearly invisible natural redoubts, Communist forces could rest, regroup, care for their wounded, and launch military operations.

Some of South Vietnam's most demanding wartime terrain was located in the Central Highlands. Beginning about a hundred miles northeast of Saigon below the town of Ban Me Thuot, it stretches north through Pleiku, Kontum, and Dak To, where it merges with the Truong Son Mountains that run through Laos all the way into North Vietnam. Comprised of rugged mist-enshrouded mountains, steep twisting ravines, hidden plateaus, and triple-canopy jungle, it was home to only 5 percent of the South's seventeen million people. But by the mid-1960s it also became home to thousands of North Vietnamese troops who had walked down the Ho Chi Minh Trail and had taken one of the many spurs that emptied into the Highlands.

It was a North Vietnamese military axiom that control of the Central Highlands was a prerequisite to nationwide control. In 1964, North Vietnamese commanders began to plan an offensive in the Highlands for October 1965 designed to cut South Vietnam in two and crush the Army of the Republic of Vietnam (ARVN). As the date neared, and they realized that the United States had deployed two divisions in the Highlands—the 173rd Airborne and the 1st Cavalry—the North Vietnamese decided to launch the offensive anyway and test themselves against the Americans.

When the 1st Cavalry Division arrived in the Highlands there was great fanfare in the American press over their hundreds of sleek new helicopters. It was a cavalry not of horses but of flying "birds." "Freed by their choppers from the tyranny of terrain," *Time* magazine crowed, "the First Team can roam at will over blasted bridges, roadblocks, swollen rivers, and jungle mountains to hit the VC from the northern tip of the nation to the delta."

In November 1965, General William Westmoreland, the commander of U.S. forces in Vietnam, ordered the 1st Cav to seek and destroy three regiments of North Vietnamese troops in the Ia Drang river valley west of Pleiku. What followed was a month of intense combat, the first time in the war U.S. forces clashed with major units of northern troops—the People's Army of Vietnam. In scale and duration it was one of the largest and most conventional campaigns of the war. While helicopters played a crucial role in moving infantrymen into the field, extracting wounded, and bringing in replacements, they did not render the terrain irrelevant. Nor could they prevent American infantry units from getting pinned down in long and devastating ambushes.

Perhaps the most surprising aspect of the Ia Drang battle from the perspective of the American command was the willingness of enemy troops to fight in force and sustain contact for days at a time. Most previous combat had involved brief firefights between small units. It had been largely a guerrilla war of snipers and hit-and-run ambushes. American commanders were preoccupied with the challenge of finding an enemy to engage. Most patrols came up empty. Thus, when hundreds of North Vietnamese troops massed themselves in the field to fight the Americans, Westmoreland saw it as a welcome opportunity. Finally, it seemed, the enemy had decided to fight it out on terms favorable to the Americans. At last the United States could bring to bear the full force of its colossal power—including fighter jets, artillery, gunships, and B-52 bombers.

After a month of combat in the Ia Drang, the Americans had taken their worst casualties of the war to date, with more than three hundred dead. Yet, the U.S. command claimed to have killed more than three thousand enemy soldiers. General Westmoreland declared the battle a victory and took it as confirmation that he could win the war by grinding down the Communists through a war of attrition. It reinforced the American tendency to look for a purely military solution to the war, to believe that killing large numbers of enemy forces was itself a prescription for victory. Westmoreland's goal was not to seize and secure territory but to kill on such a scale that Hanoi would either lose its will to continue fighting or be unable to replace its losses. To achieve that end, he sent U.S. units on countless "search-and-destroy" operations throughout the Vietnamese countryside. Their mission was to "make contact" with enemy forces, engage them in firefights, and make full use of air support and artillery.

After combat, the Americans would count or estimate the number of Vietnamese they had killed and continue the hunt somewhere else. Much of the war for American soldiers consisted of "humping the boonies," trudging day after day, with heavy packs, from one spot on a map to another looking in vain for an elusive enemy.

For the North Vietnamese command, the lesson of Ia Drang was that big-unit battles of long duration should be launched only sparingly. Mostly the Americans should be fought in quick-striking close combat, a tactic the Viet Cong and NVA called "grabbing onto the enemy's belt buckle." By getting close, fighting quickly, and withdrawing, they were less likely to be decimated by U.S. air strikes and artillery. The tactic also allowed them to determine the time, place, and duration of the vast majority of firefights.

Though there would be major Communist offensives periodically, especially during the Tet holiday in 1968, and again in 1972 and 1975, much of the war's fighting remained on a smaller scale. The big unit engagements in the Ia Drang proved an exception, and as Washington continued to pursue an essentially military solution to the war, Hanoi was as determined as ever to secure the political support of South Vietnamese villagers.

DENNIS DEAL

"Man, if we're up against this, it's gonna be a long-ass year."

After ranger and airborne school, "I thought I was really a bad ass, and what five-foot, one-hundred-pound little Asian punk was gonna hurt me? I soon found out." It was November 14, 1965, and his first combat mission as a young lieutenant put him in the middle of the largest battle the Vietnam War had yet produced. In the Ia Drang Valley of the Central Highlands, a battalion of the 1st Cavalry Division—some 450 Americans—were surrounded and attacked by three North Vietnamese regiments—a force of more than two thousand. This battle is the subject of We Were Soldiers, *a Hollywood film based on a book by Lieutenant General Harold G. Moore and Joseph L. Galloway.*

We landed and it was almost bucolic. It was just so beautiful out. It was like a national park—really, really peaceful. We were at the base of a nine-hundred-foot mountain that overlooked this river valley. All of a sudden our sister platoon captured a North Vietnamese soldier. There was some question as to whether he was a deserter, a decoy, or what. He had no weapon, no equipment, no canteen, no food, just a set of fatigues on. The guy told our Vietnamese interpreter, "There are a lot of us in the hills and all we've had to eat for five days are bananas. And we all very much want to kill Americans." Well that kinda made us all pucker up a little.

Colonel Moore, the battalion commander, ordered our company to move up the mountain. We started up a ravine with my platoon bringing up the rear. Just a few minutes later we could hear firing up front. Henry Herrick's platoon had come under heavy fire, and it started to work its way down the ravine toward us. I'm telling you without exaggeration that at any given second there were a thousand bullets coursing through that small area looking for a target—a thousand bullets a second. Henry saw a few North Vietnamese standing up and shaking bushes. I saw it too. It was movement designed to attract attention.

Henry immediately held his rifle up in the air, like the classic pose of a leader in combat and yelled, "Follow me." His whole platoon broke ranks and followed Henry to where those three North Vietnamese were. That's the last I saw of any of them. They were swallowed up in the vegetation. One of his sergeants told me later that he knew Henry had made a mistake the very moment he said, "Follow me." Sure enough, the North Vietnamese had rigged an ambush and within seconds eight Americans were killed, twelve were critically wounded, and only seven were what we call "effectives" and could fight on. It was a fourth-grade playground trick that Henry fell for. That's no disrespect to Henry—he gave his life for his country and he was happy to do so. Those were his dying words: "I'm glad I could die for my country." He was aggressive to a fault and he got a silver star for his actions.

We moved up to try to help. We desperately wanted to get to these guys. As we advanced, some Vietnamese were even firing at us from up in the trees where they had tied themselves in with ropes. And the noise was deafening. We had every fighter bomber in Vietnam in direct support. They were stacked at one-thousand-foot intervals: navy, marine, and air force all waiting to deliver their ordnance. Well, one of them was hit with ground fire directly above my position, probably just three hundred feet above us. Now here was a jet engine screeching and falling apart, shot to hell, and we did not hear it. That's how loud the battlefield was. That's how much ground fire there was. And there was a napalm strike three hundred meters to our rear and we didn't hear that either.

It was terrifying. I was terrified almost to the point of insanity. But what you have to do when you're a leader and everybody's looking at you is to figure out a way to pull out that extra millimeter of courage. All you need is one more millimeter than the guys around you and they're okay. But if you show failure, they're going to stampede.

We managed to get a hundred yards from Henry's platoon. I radioed them and said, "Shoot one round off, then stop and shoot two more so I can pinpoint where you are." They did it perfect and I got all my guys together and said, "Let's go." But between us and Henry's platoon there was a gully and North Vietnamese were in it shoulder to shoulder with a machine gun on each flank. When we stood up they just mowed us down. Just like they were in the Ia Drang bowling alley—just blew us away.

The first guy I lost was the most valuable man in my platoon, Sergeant Wilbur Curry. He was my weapons-squad leader and the best machine gunner in the division, a full-blooded Seneca Indian and a nineteen-month veteran of the Korean War. He was standing right next to me when he got shot. I got down, kneeled next to him, and I held his head in my hands. I focused on him as hard as I knew how because I never wanted to forget what this wonderful man looked like. Within a matter of minutes at least fifteen of our men were wounded or dead. Our medic, Calvin Bouknight, ran over and succeeded in treating four or five of them, always by placing his body between the continuous sheets of heavy fire and the man he was treating. Bouknight was mortally wounded less than five minutes after he began performing his stunningly heroic acts.

Every time we tried to advance they'd just blow us right back down and every time this happened we had fewer and fewer effectives to carry casualties. I was doing mental arithmetic the whole time. Once in ranger training we were on a patrol with about twenty-four guys and our instructor made us carry one man as a "casualty," and I'm here to tell you that just one man wore out a whole rifle platoon to the point of almost hallucinogenic exhaustion. So I'm figuring that we've got only four men per nonambulatory casualty. Then we lost others and I thought, well now we got three, okay we'll go with three. And then, when I started thinking in terms of two effectives for every casualty, I knew I had to get out of there. Otherwise, I was going to have to leave people behind, which is not an option. At first I was attacking to get to Henry. Then it changed and I was suddenly more concerned with getting my own people out of there.

As we moved back toward the landing zone one of the things I most regret occurred. I saw a line of men, probably about two hundred, moving on our right flank. The light from the sun shown through a large opening in the canopy and it highlighted them just like a backdrop of lighting would in the scene of a movie. I could see bodies and weapons, but I couldn't see nuances of color and height and I could not positively identify them. I told the few men around me who weren't busy carrying casualties to get their weapons up, but I was not going to be stupid and just start shooting because I saw a target. I required myself to be a hundred percent sure these were the bad guys. I was willing to blow away as many of them as I could, but I was not going to be shooting any more Americans—too many had already died. Unfortunately, they proved to be the Vietnamese we had to fight later that day. That's something I've had to live with.

We finally got back to a dry creek bed, which was very comforting because it was about four feet high. It was very nice to be at the bottom of that. That afternoon at about five o'clock Colonel Moore told us to saddle up to make another assault to go get Henry. We were given the word to go, went about three steps out of the dry creek bed, and the whole world just exploded. The North Vietnamese had gotten between us and the lost platoon again, shoulder to shoulder, and just shot the living heck out of us. My platoon was on the right flank and I was right man. Nobody was to my right—I was alone. If anybody was going to get flanked, they were going to flank around me. These people had blown us so badly to bits we went down first to our knees and then we went down to the low crawl. So I'm crawling forward trying to assault like everybody else and all of a sudden I had this Darwinian type feeling—a survival-of-the-fittest type thing—which said, if you don't turn around this second, you are going to be dead. I turned around and my whole field of vision was filled with mustard khaki. They'd flanked me and I hadn't seen 'em. There were four to six of them and one of me. I stood up and they just stood there without hitting the ground or taking any cover and we just shot it out with each other. Every one of them went down. I was untouched. My company commander witnessed this and after the battle he came over to me and said, "That was some pretty good shooting, Denny." Hell, if I'd a told that story to anyone who knew what it's like to be outnumbered and how you never win in a situation like that, they would have called me a liar.

The others, not aware of my trials and tribulations, had continued moving so I had to run to catch up to the assault line. As I did, a North Vietnamese machine gunner started shooting at me and he wouldn't let up. Everybody else was pretty much down in the grass but he had me bracketed. He just kept shooting and shooting and I was rolling and jumping. Picture a fish that you've just brought on the deck of a boat, flopping and flipping. That was me on the ground trying to avoid those bullets. Twigs were kicking up, grass, dirt, everything. I mean I was dead.

Well, I just happened to look to my left front and an American soldier got up amidst all this fire, with this horrendous amount of lead coursing through the battle area. I couldn't see who it was through all the battlefield haze and smoke, but I later learned it was Joe Marm. Joe got up and ran straight forward around an anthill. These anthills were huge. You could put a small pickup behind one. Joe had already fired a light antitank weapon at it and it did nothing but make a big bang. Those hills were like concrete. So Joe took out a hand grenade, ran around the left of the anthill, threw the grenade, and came back around to the front until it went off. Then he went around again and just sprayed everybody behind that anthill—there were eleven of 'em. Not only did that earn him a Medal of Honor, it saved my life. His men saw what he did and it just ignited them. They suddenly became tigers and charged forward. They were going to get Joe, their platoon leader, who had been shot in the jaw, and they were going to kill some more bad guys. Surging, yelling—even over the fire you could hear them screaming. It was incredible. But they didn't go much farther than the anthill. We were not getting anywhere so we were called back. I mean, when you're assaulting on your stomachs you're not being very productive.

That first night when we buttoned in, Sergeant Williams walked over to me and kind of kicked at the mud. He had been a two-year combat infantry soldier in Korea. Highly decorated. A real tough guy. He stood there a minute and then said, "Sir, I gotta tell you something. I been in Korea and I can't count how many times I've been in defensive fights, but this beats anything I ever saw in Korea."

The next morning—the 15th of November—at six o'clock, an outpost from Charlie Company saw some North Vietnamese and ran back and said, "They're coming." Charlie Company was decimated—one platoon KIA [killed in action]. It was horrendous. I was less than a hundred yards away.

There wasn't good visibility so no airplanes could come in for support. After that platoon got wiped out, I got my platoon shoulder to shoulder on the northern side of the perimeter in a military assault formation and prepared for the worst. I thought I was gonna die. Every time we encountered an anthill I threw a hand grenade behind it. It was to give us confidence as much as it was to kill them, cause we were scared to death this whole thing was gonna blow up on us again. But this time, finally, there was no resistance.

All of a sudden we got to Henry Herrick's platoon. There was Sergeant Ernie Savage. He looked like he was a piece of the earth. These guys, along with air strikes and artillery, had held off countless attacks for thirty hours. There were dead enemy bodies all over the place, somewhere between one and three hundred North Vietnamese.

None of the people who were in the lost platoon were standing, not a one of 'em. They were laying down and looking at us like we had totally taken leave of our senses. They were still in a state of shock. They didn't want to get up. Even the men who *could* stand up were so traumatized by what had happened to them they preferred to lay down and be as safe as possible. And we didn't push 'em. We let 'em lay for a while but then finally we had to say, "Look, we gotta get outta here. We don't know what's coming next." Then one of the guys who was still laying down said, "Sir, there's something over there that's red and it's bothering me. Will you go get it?" So I went over and picked it up. It was a diary next to a dead Vietnamese soldier. I looked through it and it was a bunch of beautiful script writing in different colored pencils. We had it translated later. It had a note to his wife that said: "Oh, my dear. When the troops come home after the victory and you do not see me, please look at the proud colors. You will see me there and you will feel warm under the shadow of the bamboo tree." So I took it over to the guy and said, "Look, there's nothing to worry about, this is just a diary. It isn't going to hurt you. Why don't you get up and walk with me. I'll be your security guard."

As we prepared to leave, I noticed one of the North Vietnamese bodies had literally had his buttocks shot off and his insides were leaking out a large hole—a very ugly sight. But what this guy did is an amazing story of human endurance. As he was lying there, wounded about as bad as you can be, he had taken a hand grenade, armed it, and wrapped it around the upper hand guard of his rifle stock. He had booby-trapped himself. I thought, "Man, if we're up against this, it's gonna be a long-ass year."

"Vietnam polarized me," he says from his home in Oklahoma City. "It made me extremely conservative, extremely right wing." But his evaluation of the war does not follow any party line. "I have trouble saying this because I hold in such reverence my comrades-in-arms who were killed and maimed, but I think we should never have been there without a national policy supporting the necessity of being there." And if we did have that "national resolve," "we should have let the generals run the war."

When asked about the significance of the Ia Drang battle, his first inclination is to emphasize the positive. "It was a tremendous success." But he immediately says the opposite, as if his first statement had been a slip of tongue. "It was not *a tremendous success. The generals who were running this show tried to cover up the fact that we all felt we'd been beaten. We vowed never to forget the people who denigrated this battle by calling our casualties light to moderate. That enraged us. Westmoreland would have sacrificed you in a minute. He didn't care what kind of danger he sent you into."*

WARD JUST

"It approached the vicinity of the spiritual."

He covered the war for The Washington Post. *On June 8, 1966, he went on a reconnaissance patrol with the "Tiger Force" of the 101st Airborne Division. This forty-*

two-man platoon was "a rugged and motley lot," he wrote, "unshaven, dirty, unlettered, mean, nervous."

In the dense jungle of the Central Highlands north of Dak To, they went searching for the enemy, but the enemy found them. Surrounded by North Vietnamese forces, they were pinned down for six hours by small-arms fire and grenades. Twelve of the Americans were killed and nineteen wounded.

Grenade shrapnel also wounded Just. When a medevac chopper finally arrived, the thick foliage and hilly terrain made it impossible to land. A T-bar was dropped from one hundred feet. The wounded were strapped into a harness and winched to safety one at a time. Though civilians had priority in medical evacuations, Just insisted on being the last of the wounded to be rescued, a fact he never reported.

I had a lot of holes in me and was sort of groggy, but I knew damn well that I wasn't going to die. And there were people on the ground that were just a hell of a lot worse off than I was. There was an army sergeant there named Pellum Bryant who really saved us that day. If it hadn't been for him, the whole thing would have been gone in fifteen minutes. By all reckoning we should have been wiped out—the whole platoon should have been killed. But watching him maneuver, I swear to Christ, it was almost like watching a ballet dancer move back and forth. All of us are strung out on this trail, some at the high end, some at the low end, and I'm in the middle with the command post. Bryant is moving back and forth, left and right, firing as he goes. And not firing blindly—firing with purpose.

It was somebody with superb confidence in himself and what he was doing. Just as a great musician must understand the importance of what he's playing, Pellum Bryant must have had an understanding in the back of his mind that his actions were going to save a lot of people. And all the time he was doing this kind of dance, back and forth, he did not speak a single word.

All of this stands totally separate from whether you like the Vietnam War or don't like it. This is not a word I toss around lightly, but it was *inspiring* to see him in the middle of this stupid damn war. Not to get too elaborate, but it approached the vicinity of the spiritual. I'll tell you truly, none of the things I saw in Vietnam had an effect on me like Pellum Bryant. A few weeks later he was blown up by a mine.

At that time, in 1966, among those of us who were out there, there was no interest whatsoever in the justice of the war. I cannot remember a single conversation about the justice of the war—among colleagues, diplomats, soldiers, whatever. The focus was absolutely on the situation and the estimate of the situation. How were things in Tay Ninh Province? And what was going on in

I Corps? And how many more divisions do we need? It was a one hundred percent focus on the realities on the ground at the time.

There were many facts that could be looked at in absolutely opposite ways. When you got out there in the beginning, you were pretty much inclined to give American officials the benefit of the doubt. Some army colonel tells you blah, blah, blah, and it seems plausible. But the longer you were there, and as things simply weren't turning out well, you'd look for the second interpretation in almost everything you heard.

One fact given to me as evidence of progress was that all of a sudden the VC were leaving weapons on the battlefield. This had never happened before. I went to the CIA station chief and said, "They're telling me that this is evidence that morale is beginning to collapse among the Reds."

He said, "That's possible. But of course there is another analysis of that."

And I said, "What would that be?"

He said, "That they have got so many weapons coming down the Ho Chi Minh Trail they no longer need to risk their troops to go out and police the battlefield for a few beaten up AK-47s." It struck me that the CIA guy was absolutely on the money.

After I'd been in Vietnam about a year I came back to Washington to see my children and I was invited to Robert McNamara's house for dinner. I think this was at the instigation of Joe Alsop [a syndicated columnist who supported the war]. Alsop was there and Bobby and Ethel Kennedy, McNamara and his wife, a few senators—a party of maybe twelve. As we moved from drinks to the first course it became perfectly plain that this whole thing was being done to give me a briefing on what I had failed to see during my year in the war zone. The whole talk at the table was the war.

After the meal the men and women separate, as they did at that time in Washington, and all the men repair to McNamara's study. The brandy is poured and the cigars are gotten out. And then they really get down in earnest. Essentially their message is: You're too close to it. You can't see the forest for the trees. And then somebody, I'm almost certain it was McNamara, announces that he's got a number of documents that he would be happy to let me see so I could see the error of my ways. And during all this time, I'm saying almost nothing because it's plain they're not interested in anything I might add. They are trying to convince me that there is a whole hell of a lot more progress than I can see. I believe McNamara was really quite sincere in believing that not only did I not see the truth, but that the "falsehood" I was reporting was having a terrible, terrible effect in Congress. If I would only read these documents carefully I would see the big picture as they saw it.

After reporting on the war, he quit journalism to become a novelist. The Vietnam War figures in many of his books, most notably in A Dangerous Friend *(1999).*

LE CAO DAI

"Sometimes I operated all night while the staff took turns pedaling the bicycle."

Looking slightly disheveled and distracted, the round-faced doctor greets his visitors at the Hanoi office of the Red Cross where he runs the Agent Orange Victims Fund. Agent Orange was the primary chemical defoliant sprayed by the U.S. military on South Vietnam in an effort to kill the plant life that provided cover for the enemy and to destroy crops that might be used to feed enemy troops. Dr. Dai conducts research on the medical effects of exposure to Agent Orange in the Vietnamese population.

His medical experience goes back to the French War. From 1966 to 1974 he directed the largest jungle hospital in the Central Highlands. His staff of four hundred routinely cared for more than a thousand patients. Every few months they had to move all patients and supplies and rebuild in a new location to avoid detection by American and South Vietnamese forces.

The jungle "hospital" was actually a scattering of some 250 small, half-buried bunkers topped with thatched roofs. Each bunker accommodated four or five patients and a bomb shelter was dug into the side of every one at a depth of two meters. The bunkers were located at least thirty meters apart to prevent a single bombing strike from destroying the entire hospital. "We dispersed our hospital over such a large area that I had to walk for hours to get from one side to the other."

When we were called to the southern battlefield one of my friends came by with his wife. She asked, "How long do you think you'll be in the South?" I said, "Oh, about six months." She started to cry. "My husband said he will be there for a year!" As it turned out, I stayed for eight years. My friend stayed forever. He died in the South.

Initially, we set up our hospital close to the place where the borders of Vietnam, Cambodia, and Laos meet. But it was too far from the front lines so after about six months we had to move closer. It was the first of many moves during the war. We always sought a location that was in triple-canopy jungle—where there were three layers of leaves. Even in the middle of the day the sun couldn't shine through. But the Americans launched innumerable chemical spraying operations to defoliate the jungle. As soon as they sprayed nearby I'd give the order to begin moving the hospital. Even so, we were sometimes spotted by U.S. helicopters or observation planes and then the B-52s would inevitably attack that very night.

There was a shortage of everything. Most of our equipment had been destroyed, lost, or damaged on our journey south. Probably only ten percent arrived and some of that was defective or incomplete. For example, the X-ray equipment arrived safely but we lost the protective lead apron. We didn't even have scalpels or other surgical instruments. We fashioned our own out of used scrap metal from unexploded American bombs and shell casings or pieces of aluminum from planes that had been shot down. We even made intravenous tubes from the rubber insulation we found around electrical wires on American aircraft. So the Americans provided us with many of our supplies.

At first I tried to set up a small hydroelectric system to provide power for the hospital but it got washed away during flooding. Our most reliable source of power was a bicycle-powered generator. Someone had to keep pedaling so I could have light for my operating table. Sometimes I operated all night while the staff took turns pedaling the bicycle.

About seventy percent of our patients were in the hospital for noncombat-related diseases. The most common, by far, was malaria. Almost everyone got it, including the doctors and staff. I was no exception. Three to six months of sickness. The Highlands were extremely malarial. Oddly enough, in 1964 and '65, before I arrived, I heard it wasn't such a serious problem. But in 1966, it just soared. I couldn't explain it at the time. Now I suspect it may be linked to some weakening of our immune systems caused by exposure to Agent Orange. In any case, there was a much higher incidence of malaria after the heavy spraying of chemical defoliants. Many people died, especially those who contracted an especially severe type of malaria that makes you urinate blood and vomit bile in addition to the usual terrible fevers and other symptoms. The only effective treatment would be to relieve the kidney function through dialysis. Of course there was no way to do that in the jungle.

In addition to malaria we saw all kinds of diseases—diabetes, lung cancer, tuberculosis, a very high rate of dysentery. Many people died from acute diarrhea. It was terrible. When I did autopsies on them I found their intestines were as thin as paper. We also had patients with basic nutritional problems. They simply were not getting enough food.

Fortunately, the army supplied rice for all the patients, but the hospital staff was responsible for providing almost all of its own food. We spent endless hours growing cassava but that was hardly sufficient. I also had to organize a team of hunters and fisherman. We hunted monkeys, wild pigs, deer, and elephants. My first year in the Highlands we killed eighteen elephants. An elephant's hide is so thick it's almost impossible to cut. One of our surgeons suggested it might work better to slice open its belly, step inside, and cut the meat from the inside out. He actually stood inside the elephant with blood up to his ankles, hacking away. An elephant could feed our staff for several weeks, but the meat spoiled quickly and tasted pretty awful.

Only about thirty percent of our patients were actually wounded by hostile fire. Among those, the most common wounds weren't caused by bullets but by small fragments from cluster bombs and a wide variety of land mines. There was a mine that exploded whenever something metallic came near it and several that jumped in the air when you stepped on them. When I arrived in the Highlands they told me, "If you step on a land mine, keep your foot in place or the mine might pop into the air and cut you in half. Better to lose your foot than your life." The Americans even had "leaf mines," little explosives that looked so much like actual leaves they were nearly impossible to detect. And they dropped mines from the air that landed without exploding only to shoot out nearly invisible trip wires in every direction.

Believe it or not, our mortality rate for wounded patients was lower than it was at hospitals in Hanoi. The only way to account for this is to assume that most of our severely wounded people died at the front before they could be carried to our field hospital. One of our biggest problems was postoperative infection. At first we closed all wounds after surgery, but we found they frequently got infected. We had better results leaving wounds open. The same for arterial wounds. When we tried to sew the artery it invariably got infected. We found it better to close both ends of the damaged artery and leave the wound open. Trying this led to a very interesting discovery. We found that our soldiers had done so much walking and gotten so much exercise they had developed new arteries known as "collaterals." So when we closed off a main artery these new arteries still provided enough blood to the wounded area to ward off infection.

In 1970, I was allowed to return to the North for a medical meeting—a two-month trek from the Highlands. One of my former professors invited me to lunch and told me about dioxyn [the toxic substance in the chemical defoliant Agent Orange]. At the time, those of us at the front had no idea what kind of chemicals the Americans were spraying. We just knew that a few days later all the leaves died. They'd spray over and over from C-123s that came in very low, almost at treetop level. All we could do was cover ourselves with plastic. The professor asked me if I'd ever seen cases of cancer. "Yes, of course," I said. He asked me for a piece of liver from someone who had died to test for dioxyn. I told him that was impossible. It would take two months to get it back, and even if you had some solution to preserve it in you couldn't count on every porter to take proper care of it as it moved from post to post. It would almost certainly get lost or damaged.

But he was certainly on the right track. During the war, our soil, water, and food were all highly contaminated with dioxyn. In 1973, a Harvard study measured the dioxyn levels in our food. Fifty parts per trillion is considered the upper limit for safe food. That study found eight hundred parts per trillion in some places and a mean of two hundred. Now the food is much better and the soil is okay in most places except former U.S. air bases. Those places were heavily contaminated from storing the chemicals there, pumping them into the planes, and cleaning them out after spraying operations.

No one knows how many Vietnamese have died from diseases caused by Agent Orange, but according to our studies, one million people still suffer from cancers linked to Agent Orange exposure and there are about one hundred thousand people still alive with birth defects that we believe were caused by dioxyn poisoning. We've seen many kinds of birth defects. The American Academy of Science recognizes only spina bifida, but we've seen cleft palate much more frequently among the children of veterans with heavy exposure to Agent Orange. In one study I did after the war, among veterans who had stayed in North Vietnam, about one percent of their children had birth defects. [The United States did not spray Agent Orange over most of the North.] Among veterans who had been in the South the longest, the figure was about five percent. We have also found much higher rates of cerebral palsy among people exposed to dioxyn.

We recognize, however, that our studies are not as strictly scientific as they should be. We rely primarily on broad comparisons of different categories of people. More specific blood sampling would be preferable but we haven't been able to do much of that. It's just too expensive. It costs between one and three thousand dollars for each person tested in such a study.

But even the anecdotal evidence is striking. Ten years after the war the chief of staff of the army, a three-star general named Cao Vinh Thang, died of liver cancer. During the war he and three other men had to go on a mission through a valley that was very heavily damaged by chemicals. It turned out that two of the other men also died of cancer. The only survivor went to war leaving behind a healthy, intelligent daughter. After the war his wife gave birth to a deformed daughter with cerebral palsy. She is twenty-seven now and her mother and father have to take care of her.

Dr. Dai passed away in 2002.

FROM CIVIL RIGHTS TO ANTIWAR

Collective efforts to protest America's war in Vietnam had many roots, but perhaps none so important as the civil rights movement of the 1950s and '60s. Thousands of future antiwar activists participated in, or were deeply inspired by, the boycotts, sit-ins, freedom rides, and community organizing that comprised the mass movement to end racial discrimination in the United States. The experience and example of challenging legal, political, economic, and cultural institutions that sustained racial inequality and division provided valuable political training for many who would later oppose America's actions in Vietnam.

Above all, the civil rights movement provided a way of questioning power that was directly transferable to the antiwar movement. For years civil rights activists had measured official claims of justice against the grim racial realities of American life. As the war dragged on, more and more Americans would ask similar questions of official statements about Vietnam. For example, if the war in Vietnam was for freedom and democracy, as U.S. policy makers claimed, why were those blessings still denied to Americans at home? And why were they denied to the people of South Vietnam on whose behalf we claimed to be fighting? And what about the racial views underpinning the war? Was our willingness to destroy so much of Vietnam, including the land of our "allies," animated by racism toward Asians? Would we have initiated such policies in and against a nation of white people?

The relationship between the civil rights and antiwar movements was not always harmonious. Some civil rights advocates argued against outspoken criticism of the war on the grounds that it might divert attention from the struggle against racial equality or antagonize political leaders like Lyndon Johnson, whose support the movement needed to pass crucial civil rights legislation. Some black leaders also believed the military had done more than any other major American institution to desegregate itself and to offer opportunities to young black men—reason enough, they insisted, to temper criticism of the war it was called upon to fight. Over time, however, an increasing number of antiwar voices were heard from within the ranks of the civil rights movement. As it became clear that Johnson's "war on poverty" was being supplanted by the war in Vietnam, Martin Luther King added his voice to other prominent black antiwar critics like Malcolm X, Adam Clayton Powell, Dick Gregory, and Julian Bond. King claimed that the resources for social reform at home were being diverted to an unjustified war abroad. "The promises of the Great Society," he said, "have been shot down on the battlefield of Vietnam." American foreign policy was "devastating the hopes of the poor at home" and sending their children "to fight and die in extraordinarily high proportions relative to the rest of the population." Finally, King could not reconcile the war in Vietnam with his passionate commitment to nonviolence. On April 4, 1967, exactly one year before his assassination, he denounced his country as "the greatest purveyor of violence in the world today."

Many younger black activists, even those who felt the antiwar movement was largely a white phenomenon, had come to King's conclusion much sooner. In 1966, both the Student Nonviolent Coordinating Committee and the Black Panther Party adopted strong antiwar positions. That was also the year the heavyweight boxing champion of the world refused induction to the military. He had recently joined the Nation of Islam and changed his name from Cassius Clay to Muhammad Ali, but his application for conscientious objector status on religious grounds was rejected. For his defiance Ali was not only widely castigated in the media, but stripped of his boxing title, convicted of violating the Selective Service Act, and sentenced to five years in prison. He appealed the conviction and it was finally reversed by the Supreme Court in 1971, by which time many Americans had concluded that Ali's once unpopular view was prescient.

JULIAN BOND

"They said I was guilty of treason and sedition."

At sixty, he still has the elegant good looks and melodious voice that helped make him, in his early twenties, a leading spokesman for the young civil rights activists who formed the Student Nonviolent Coordinating Committee (SNCC), the group that led the sit-in movement, joined the Freedom Rides, and provided the rank-and-file organizers for voter registration drives throughout the South. In 1965, at the age of twenty-five, he was elected to Georgia's House of Representatives. However, many legislators were so opposed to the young man's civil rights and antiwar activism that they voted to deny him his seat. Only a Supreme Court ruling a year later allowed him to take his duly elected post. He now chairs the board of directors for the National Association for the

Advancement of Colored People (NAACP) and teaches at the University of Virginia and American University.

The Vietnam War seemed pretty remote initially. It wasn't something that pressed on me a great deal. I had friends who were drafted and were going away, but there was no chance of my going because I was classified I-Y, which means you're mentally, physically, or morally unfit for service. My draft board found me unfit because I had been arrested at a sit-in demonstration. But I don't think it was common to exempt civil rights activists from the draft. In fact, it seemed as if many southern draft boards were targeting people in the movement. The head of my draft board was later quoted in *Newsweek* as saying, "That nigger Julian Bond, we let him slip through our fingers."

When I ran for the Georgia state legislature in 1965 I talked about local bread-and-butter issues and I don't think I made any connection between those issues and the war. But in late 1965, just after I won the election, this guy Sammy Younge was killed in Tuskegee, Alabama, shot in the back for trying to use a white bathroom at a gas station. He was a navy veteran who had lost the use of a kidney during his service. The irony of this guy having lost his kidney in the military and then not being able to use the bathroom in his own hometown was so stark.

I think initially it wasn't the pacifist notion that turned most of us against the war—though it was for some people—but the assault on black men and the idea that we were spending all these resources on a war that was not our business. That was initially my feeling rather than any question about the rightness or wrongness of war generally. I thought the big fight was here at home.

Sammy getting killed heightened our awareness of the essential wrongness of asking these young men to go defend the country overseas. It prompted SNCC to release an antiwar statement pointing out that black soldiers were being sent to Vietnam in the name of "democracy" and "freedom" while being denied it at home. It also said that the United States government bears the responsibility for both Samuel Younge's death and the deaths of Vietnamese peasants, in Sammy's case because it wasn't enforcing the law, and in the case of Vietnam because the U.S. was acting aggressively in violation of international law.

I endorsed that statement about a week or so before I was to take my seat in the Georgia legislature. White southerners are tremendously patriotic and jingoistic and a firestorm of protest erupted in opposition to my antiwar position. They said I was guilty of treason and sedition. The protest was led largely by Peter Zack Greer, who called himself "the white man's lieutenant governor." So a dozen of us who had been elected in the fall presented ourselves to be sworn in and I was asked to step aside. They swore in the others and then convened a committee of the whole House. They voted a hundred and eighty-five to twelve to throw me out. They declared my seat vacant and called a special election to fill the vacancy. So I ran again, and won. By this time the legislature had adjourned, so they named a special committee to hear my case and they expelled me again. When I filed a lawsuit in federal court the two Democratic judges voted against me and the Republican voted for me. We appealed that to the Supreme Court. In the meantime, I ran a third time and won that election as well. The Supreme Court heard the case and in December of 1966 ruled nine to nothing that I had to be seated.

When SNCC began to speak out against the war our contributions fell off and we began to suffer financially. Many people who supported civil rights generally, didn't want to see the movement linked with antiwar sentiment. The NAACP and the Urban League were opposed to the civil rights movement taking a stand on Vietnam. That was really disingenuous of the NAACP because of course they had long been involved in questions about African policy and if you can take a position on that, why not Vietnam? They thought President Johnson would become alienated from the civil rights movement and the better course was to either be quiet about the war or support him on it, which, of course, didn't make any sense to us. But the NAACP was certainly right in predicting that Johnson would feel bitterly and personally betrayed by civil rights activists who publicly denounced the war. Whitney Young of the Urban League even opposed Dr. King when he finally made his Riverside Church speech against the war. There was also the idea then that if you were a civil rights personage you could have opinions about civil rights, but you couldn't have opinions about anything else. Unfortunately, that is still true today. I'm just amazed at how seldom I am asked my opinion about anything except civil rights.

I think the civil rights movement was responsible for raising the percentage of Americans opposed to the war and for making black Americans particularly more skeptical about the war. And, of course, Muhammad Ali had an enormous impact because he was so well known and he gave up so much. By refusing to fight in Vietnam he gave up his title as Heavyweight Champion of the World. And he stated his opposition to the war so simply: "No Viet Cong never called me nigger." I mean, that was it. You didn't have to say more than that. You didn't have to talk about the Geneva Accords.

GENERAL BAKER JR.

"When the call is made to free the Mississippi Delta . . . I'll be the first one in line."

He's just finished his midnight shift as a "monkey keeper" at one of Ford's blast furnaces in Detroit, Michigan. "When the slag runs down I've got to lift the gate and fill up these big pots. I'm full of slag burns. The furnace is twenty-seven hundred degrees and you've got to wear your long johns to keep the heat off of you. I've been doing that particular job since 1980." The son of Georgia sharecroppers, he's lived in Detroit since his birth in 1941. While working full-time in the auto industry, he has devoted much of his life to the civil rights, antiwar, and union movements. The name "General" comes from his father, General Gordon Baker, who was named after a WWI British general.

Once I started working full-time at Ford Motor Company in 1963 I transferred from Highland Park Community College to Wayne State University as a part-time student. We created a little organization on campus called Uhuru, which is Swahili for freedom. We got active in the struggle for open housing.* I got my first arrest doing that.

During this period my friends would get together in my apartment on Friday nights and we'd listen to Robert Franklin Williams on the radio.** He had a broadcast from Cuba on Radio Free Dixie. He would open up saying, "White man's nigger no more," and then blow on about the struggle of blacks. And they always played the latest songs by groups like the Miracles. I'll never forget the Miracles. [He sings] "I've got a lover way over there on the other side, and I know that's where I should be." It was just a phenomenal thing to listen to that station. We became real Robert Williams fanatics. We would never miss Radio Free Dixie.

The U.S. put a ban on travel to Cuba, so the Cuban Federation of Students began to send students to Cuba in defiance of this new law. In 1964, they wanted to have some participation of black students so they approached our little group and four of us signed up. We were just told to get to the train station in Chicago at a certain time. There were eighty-four of us by the time we all

*Aimed at passing state and federal legislation to outlaw discrimination in the sale or rental of any housing on the basis of race, creed, or national origin.

**In the late 1950s, Williams, a Marine Corps veteran, became notorious for organizing self-defense rifle clubs among blacks in Monroe, North Carolina, where he was president of the local NAACP. In 1961, after repeated threats on his life, a pitched gun battle lasting several days between crowds of whites and blacks, an indictment, and a nationwide manhunt, Williams fled to Cuba.

got to Paris and then we got a flight to Czechoslovakia. From there we got a Cuban plane and flew back to Ireland and Newfoundland and back down to Cuba. We had to go through all them changes to get to Cuba.

Cuba was a lifesaver for me. It was a real awakening. I would never have been the same person without those two and a half months in Cuba. Robert Williams met us at the hotel as soon as we got there. We had a chance to talk with Che Guevara and play baseball with Fidel Castro. And they had us on TV damn near every day. We met revolutionaries from everywhere—the Congo, Rhodesia, South Africa, Vietnam, Cambodia, Laos, Jamaica, Brazil, Peru. You name it, man, they was in Cuba. It was just a revolutionary laboratory.

When we talked to the Vietnamese it was just before the Tonkin Gulf and the question of escalation was on everybody's mind. I remember asking the Vietnamese, "Do you think that if the United States bombs Vietnam, the Chinese are going to help you?" They tell me, "We don't need Chinese help to defeat the Americans." That shit just fucked me up. I just couldn't understand how these little-ass Vietnamese were going to handle an American invasion. But that was the adamant statement they made.

When I got back I started working for Chrysler and in late '64 I got a letter telling me to come down to the draft board for a physical. I wrote a letter to the draft board explaining that I'm not a dodger and I'm not a conscientious objector, but I'm not going. I'm not going because this is an unjust war. I said, I believe in fighting and here's a list of just wars. When you decide to go to battle to free Latin America from the United Fruit Company, or when the call is made to free South Africa, or to free the Middle East from Standard Oil, or when the call is made to free the Mississippi Delta and 12th Street here in Detroit, then call me, because these are just causes, and it would be a duty and honor for me to serve. I'll be the first one in line.

They sent me a letter back drafting me anyway. My induction was scheduled for September 10, 1965, so we built what was called the September 10th movement. In our propaganda and literature we called on fifty thousand angry blacks to protest the draft on my induction day. We had one slogan—"Destroy the Draft." Nothing else. We put this on signs all over the city. The police arrested us while we were posting them. When we got in the back seat we asked what were we arrested for and the officer said, "Criminal anarchy, rebellion against the government." When we got to the police station they gave us a ticket for unauthorized posting.

Between the time I got my draft letter and the time of my draft date the Watts rebellion broke out in L.A. on August the 5th. In Detroit, we had heard that the authorities had canceled all leaves at the army base and sent a special group of riot rangers up from Virginia. So we basically called off the protest.

We put out one last leaflet saying essentially, "We have information that the city fathers plan to attack the leaders of September 10th. Because of that, we're asking all the hard brothers and sisters to stay in standby positions in the neighborhood. If the leaders of the September 10th movement are attacked, you know precisely what to do. Remember Los Angeles."

On induction day when I got to the point where you take the oath, I told them to go and call the police because I'm not going no further. I had my toothbrush in my pocket because I thought I was going to jail. The captain of the induction center took me into his office and asked me a few questions. Then he said, "Well, I'll tell you what. We're going to send you on home as a security risk." But even if they'd put me in jail there probably wouldn't have been a big protest. There wasn't a lot of people into the antidraft stuff yet. But it started coming along and we continued to participate in the antiwar movement as a black contingent.

From then on, when I came out of the house I'd have one police car in front of mine and one in back, following me everywhere. I used to go up to them sometimes and say, "Why don't I just ride with you and save the gas?" It was that bad. When I got my police files it had things in it like, "General Baker seen leaving 1980 West Philadelphia with three bags of dirty clothes. He goes around 12th Street and goes into the Laundromat. He comes out of the Laundromat and goes next door to buy a six-pack of Carling Black Label beer." I'm not doing nothing but living. I go to work every day at the Dodge main plant and the police would follow me to the parking lot. When I get off at night, the police followed me back home.

During the Detroit rebellion in '67* I got arrested the very first day for violation of curfew. I was just trying to get back home but the police line stopped us and one of them recognized me and my friend. He took our car keys, threw the damned things away, handcuffed us, and took us to the police station. I think that's probably the best thing that could have happened because I got arrested before they started giving orders to shoot to kill. They sent me all the way down to the state penitentiary. I was lucky. The people that got arrested later were locked up outdoors on Belle Isle—seven thousand of them laying out there in the dirt. I did fifteen days in the penitentiary. By the time I got back to work, production hadn't started full blast because too many guys were still in prison. My cell block looked like the assembly line.

*On July 23, 1967, Detroit police raided an after-hours social club where about eighty people were celebrating the return of two servicemen from Vietnam. The raid triggered a week of looting and burning that destroyed thirteen hundred buildings and left five thousand homeless. The resultant crackdown, by five thousand National Guardsmen and an almost equal number of army paratroopers, resulted in forty-three deaths and more than seven thousand arrests.

A lot of auto workers had been in the 101st Airborne and came back to occupied Detroit during the '67 rebellion. They were diverted from Vietnam to hold down the East Side. And if you look at the pattern of killing, most of it took place on the West Side where the National Guard was. The guardsmen were mostly white guys who were scared to death. I don't know where the fuck they found them. I remember, man, I'm down in the underground tunnel coming from the courthouse to the jail. We were handcuffed and chained together in rows of eight and this guy is standing there in the tunnel with an M-16 shaking like a leaf. I said, "Goddamn, what the fuck is wrong with him?" We're all handcuffed together and he's shaking.

"THE ULTIMATE PROTEST"

ANNE MORRISON WELSH

"It was like an arrow was shot from Norman's heart."

On a November afternoon in 1965, she went to school to pick up her two oldest children—five-year-old Christina and six-year-old Ben. While she was gone, her husband, Norman Morrison, drove to the Pentagon. He took along their one-year-old daughter, Emily. Around 5:20 that evening, in a small rectangular garden outside the largest military headquarters in the world, Morrison burned himself to death to protest the war in Vietnam. Emily was found near the scene unharmed. The next day's headline in The Baltimore Sun *read, "Baltimore Quaker with Baby Sets Self Afire."*

The immolation occurred within a stone's throw of Robert McNamara's office. The secretary of defense was called to the window by aides. What he witnessed is omitted from his 1995 memoir, In Retrospect. *But he does write this: "Morrison's death was a tragedy not only for his family but also for me and the country . . . I reacted to the horror of his action by bottling up my emotions and avoided talking about them with anyone—even my family. Marg and our three children shared many of Morrison's feelings about the war . . . and I believed I understood and shared some of his thoughts." Morrison was one of eight Americans who burned themselves to death in opposition to the Vietnam War.*

Anne Morrison remarried in 1967 and lives in western North Carolina just a few miles from her daughter Emily, who is now thirty-six. She has just returned from baby-sitting her grandchild, Emily's infant son. She speaks with the warm Southern accent of her native Georgia.

In 1999, she and her two daughters traveled to Vietnam for the first time. At a peace park created by American and Vietnamese veterans of the war, they planted three trees in honor of Norman Morrison.

Emily and Christina were so young when Norman died they don't remember his memorial service. In a way this was their first real funeral for their father. It was a beautiful and healing experience. Something about planting a tree is very right and grounding. For me, it was sort of putting Norman into the soil of Vietnam, through his memory.

After we had planted the trees a Mr. Hung came up to us. He had such an expressive face and his English was impeccable. We were just captivated by him. He said, "I want to tell you how I heard about Norman Morrison's death, your husband's and father's death. I was a member of the National Liberation Front in the South. On November 2, 1965, I was in the jungle when I heard about his death over Liberation Radio. It came over the radio in my bunker where I was hiding. I want you to know that all I could do was cry."

And when he told us that, he cried again. We were very impressed by that because in our country men don't cry easily. In my whole life I only remember seeing my father cry two times. But when we were in Vietnam for those two weeks in 1999 many, many Vietnamese men cried in front of us. And women too, but the men even more. After we left, Christina said, "Mom, it's so strange. In Vietnam it seems like the women are strong and the men cry." [Laughs.]

It was amazing how many people remembered Norman. We met a lot of people and they all wanted to tell us where they were when they heard about Norman's death and how it affected them. It was so vivid in their hearts and in their memories, thirty-four years later.

I know Norman's death was used politically by the government in Hanoi. There's no question. They widely publicized the news of his sacrifice and even printed a postage stamp with his picture on it. But the political uses of Norman's death cannot alone have had the power to move so many people then and especially now, years and years later. It was like an arrow was shot from Norman's heart, which was so broken because of the war, and the arrow sailed all the way across thousands of miles and pierced the heart of these Vietnamese people, in the way that love pierces your heart. One of them said, "We were such a tiny little country. It was like a gnat fighting an elephant. But someone from that huge country cared enough for us that he gave his life for us." They really believed Norman gave his life for them.

Norman did care about the Vietnamese. He wrote a letter to me which I got after he was dead. He mailed it in Washington. Talk about a shock—to get a letter from someone after they've died. For a minute I thought he hadn't died. He ended the letter with, "Know that I love thee, but I must act for the children of the priest's village." He was referring to a Catholic village near Duc Co that had been destroyed by our bombs. The day Norman died he read an article about it in *I. F. Stone's Weekly.*★ We may even have talked about it just

★The article appears in the November 1, 1965, issue of *I. F. Stone's Weekly,* reprinted from *Paris-Match.* The French priest is quoted as saying, "I have seen my faithful burned up in napalm. I have seen the bodies of women and children blown to bits."

before lunch on the day he died, I can't remember. But in his letter he included the article. He had torn it out and circled the story about Duc Co in red crayon.

So he did care immensely about the Vietnamese, but he also wanted to stop the war for America's sake, so that no more of our soldiers would get killed either. And so we wouldn't lose our sense of moral dignity and integrity. He was afraid that if we kept on fighting in Vietnam we would lose some of our conscience. And I think we did.

It took me a long time to really face Norman's death because I was so shocked and horrified. The next morning, I didn't want to get out of bed. But here are three children. They need breakfast. They had to be taken care of. So you just move on.

Also, the war was still going on and I wanted to honor Norman's memory and his sacrifice. I wanted to work to end the war in every way I could. So I didn't give myself the liberty to grieve. Then in 1970, Ben got sick. He was eleven. At first we thought it was just growing pains. But it got worse, so we went to the doctor and found out it was cancer. We went to Sloan Kettering and for almost five years we tried to save his life. We saved his leg but we didn't save his life. He died in 1975.

When Ben was really sick I felt anger toward Norman for the first time. I had remarried and had support from my husband but it was not the same as having Ben's dad present. I thought, "God, Norman, why aren't you here?" There was so much to deal with during those five years. [She begins to cry.] It's still tough. I don't think you ever get over the loss of a child. I haven't. To be honest, that was the worst thing that's ever happened to me. And it certainly contributed to putting on hold my grief for Norman. There was absolutely no way to grieve for him during that time. So, in a way, I froze that grief for twenty-five years.

Around 1990 or '91, I really let my emotions out. Finally my daughters were at an age where we could sit down together and really look at what their dad had done. Christina was so hurt by her father's leaving because she loved and remembered him well and he didn't even tell her good-bye. I had shielded them, and the act itself kept them from wanting to look at it. We just talked about it and expressed our anguish and our grief and our sadness. We were finally able to face what it did to our family.

In 1995, I read Robert McNamara's *In Retrospect* and felt moved to express my appreciation to him for his acknowledgment that the war was wrong and that it was a tragic mistake. I just felt it was unusual for a public official to admit error, even decades later in hindsight. So I wrote him a letter. It obviously moved him, perhaps in part because most of the reactions to his book were negative, even venomous.

A few days later he called to thank me. He said he was gratified and surprised by the forgiveness I had expressed. We had an amazingly relaxed conversation, almost as if we knew each other. He talked about how he hadn't been able to talk to his family about Norman's death even though they were all deeply affected by it and wanted to talk. I said that I hadn't talked enough about it with my children either in those years. So I just felt this little bit of kinship with him as a parent and a human being. It was almost as if we hadn't been on opposite sides of the chasm that had split our country apart. Then he asked me for permission to quote my letter as he went around talking about his book. I said sure.

I just think forgiveness is what we're supposed to do for one another and we all stand in need of it. But I do share some of the feelings of people who can't forgive McNamara. After all, if he knew the war was a mistake, why didn't he do more to stop it? Why did he help to escalate the war after he began to have that awareness? Think of all the American soldiers and Vietnamese who died between the time of his awareness and his resignation. If he'd had the courage to protest, it might have ended the war sooner and lives would have been saved on both sides. But I don't think he was some mad bomber—a Dr. Strangelove. I think he wanted the war to end and genuinely thought his was the best way to bring about that result. But once he saw it would never work, that's when no more lives should have been lost.

I don't know if McNamara witnessed Norman's death from his window in the Pentagon. Nobody knows exactly what happened that day. The eyewitnesses differed. One person said they saw this and another person said they saw that. I don't know if Norman sat Emily down or gave her to someone else. There was no camera rolling. All I can tell you is that I was given his wallet and his Harris tweed coat to identify when I went over to the Pentagon that night. And our daughter was not physically harmed—not a bruise, not a singe, not a scar.

I didn't have any idea that Norman ever would have thought of going to that extreme. I knew that he felt desperate about the war, but I'm not sure if self-immolation was in his head before that day. He did all the routine things a person would do to oppose the war. He wrote letters to the editor, he lobbied congressmen, he went to demonstrations, and teach-ins, and vigils. The only time I remember self-immolation being specifically mentioned in our home was when a very elderly Quaker woman in Detroit named Alice Herz did it earlier in 1965. It didn't get a whole lot of press. The only thing I remember reading in the newspapers was that she said, "I want to do as the Buddhist monks did." I don't remember our having more than one small conversation about it.

From a formal standpoint it was a suicide. But I don't think that begins to touch what it was. In my mind it was the ultimate protest, the ultimate sacrifice, because there are easier ways to commit suicide. A few months after Norman died I read a letter written by the Buddhist monk Thich Nhat Hanh to Martin Luther King that was published in a magazine. He wrote that self-immolation is not suicide. The idea is to suffer—to burn—and to experience the greatest pain one can in order to show how strongly you feel about something, so strongly that you're willing to suffer and ultimately to die.

I think the Vietnamese mistakenly thought that most Americans were just like Norman. But this was 1965 and Norman's act was highly controversial. Even though I received many letters of support, it made many Americans, including many Quakers, extremely uncomfortable. I think it was the act itself—the self-violence—and Emily's presence at the scene, but also the fact that it was a protest of our government's policy. A lot of people felt that anything done in opposition to the war was unpatriotic and worked against our men-in-arms.

Norman and I wanted to see peace talks—broad and deep. We wanted a cease-fire on all sides. We didn't want anybody to win. As a pacifist it grieves me to think that Norman's act encouraged the people in Vietnam to keep fighting, but I understand now how that happened.

On our last day in Vietnam our guide and translator, Bui Van Nghi, said, "Mrs. Anne, you're old enough to be my mother. I want to tell you some things. I want you to know that no family in Vietnam was unaffected by the war. Everybody lost somebody. I lost three uncles." He said that one of his uncles who died was a newlywed when he went into the military. When he learned that his wife was pregnant he was going to desert. He wanted so much to stay home. But his parents said, "You've got to fight for your country." Nghi's grandmother said, "Remember Morrison. Look at what courage he had. Are you going to be a coward?" He returned to the front, and was killed, and never saw his child.

The realization that Norman gave the Vietnamese courage to fight was hard for our family, because we had just wanted an end to the war. The United States could have withdrawn and ended the war at any point and thousands, maybe millions, of lives would have been saved. But I don't sit in judgment of the Vietnamese for continuing to fight under the circumstances. I'm so glad they knew there were people in America who regarded them as fellow human beings and cared about them. All I know is that Norman's act was a desperate attempt to try to end the war. And Norman was a casualty of the war—there's no doubt of that.

Five days after Norman died, the North Vietnamese poet To Huu wrote a poem called "Emily, My Child." He wrote it in the voice of Norman and had him trying to speak to the soul of America. It was an anguished voice, but also a voice full of hope for the future. What I didn't realize until we went to Vietnam was that two or three generations of students have learned that poem by heart.

When we were in Saigon a very handsome young man in his midtwenties was behind the desk at the travel bureau.

He said, "I can't wait to tell my parents that I met you."

I said, "Well, how would you know me?"

He started to recite "Emily, My Child." He said, "I learned it when I was in the fifth grade."

The poem reads in part:

Emily, my child,
it's getting dark
I cannot take you home.
When my body burns on fire tonight
your mother will come to find you.
Please run to her, circle her with your arms and kiss her for me
and help me to tell her
I leave with joy. Please don't be sad.

The time when my heart is most right,
I burn my body
for the fire, I shine
for the truth.

FREE-FIRE ZONE

JIM SOULAR

"A goddamn chopper was worth three times more than David."

We're sitting in his room at one of Hanoi's "mini hotels." He's back in Vietnam for the first time since 1967 when he served with the 1st Cavalry Division (Airmobile). He was a flight engineer on the enormous, double-rotored Chinook helicopter—the CH-47. "I wanted to come back and see the place at peace. I wanted to put a face on the Vietnamese because I damn sure didn't the first time I was here. They were just 'gooks,' 'slopes,' or 'dinks.'" He decided against traveling with a group of American veterans. "A lot of my veteran friends still hang on to the belief that we could have won the war and I didn't want to hear that." Besides, he prefers being by himself. "I've isolated myself in Montana. It's a good place to hide out if that's what you want."

The taxi ride in from the airport almost undid him. The streets were jammed with every imaginable vehicle—motor scooters, cars, trucks, cyclos, bicycles, you name it—all laying on the horn, all crossing intersections at the same time, and all coming within inches of major collisions. "The thought went through my mind that I survived the war, but I'm going to be killed thirty years later in Hanoi traffic."

I've never been a city boy. I grew up in northern Minnesota, up on the Iron Range—the Mesabi Range. All my family were miners. I spent a lot of time alone, exploring the woods, fishing, and hunting. My dad made a living in the mines, but trapping and hunting, that was where his heart really was. He was an expert outdoorsman, an old-time trapper—muskrat, otter, weasel. I have this image of him on his snowshoes going across the lake and disappearing into the distance following his trap line. It was a twenty-mile loop. Some nights he would make it back, and other times he wouldn't get home until the next day. He was one of the most wonderful, compassionate men I've ever met, one of the few in my family who really understood how Vietnam had hurt me. He would never come out and say it, but he would do things like just wrap his arm around my shoulder.

In 1965, I went to Hibbing Junior College for a year, but I didn't know what I wanted to be or do so I quit and went into the mines. They were open pit and dirty. You start out doing all the grunt work, hosing down conveyer belts, with crap from that red iron ore dripping all over you. It was nasty. But the money was good for a kid—three dollars and eighteen cents an hour. Before that I had made seventy-five cents an hour delivering groceries.

I knew when I quit college I'd lose my student deferment and get drafted. I had no problem with that because I was a patriot. I believed in the flag, I believed in serving my country. And I was good at it. I went through three flight schools before going to Vietnam and was an honor graduate in two of those and second in the third. When the rest of the guys would be screwing off, I'd actually be studying. As flight engineer I was in charge of a one-and-a-half-million dollar helicopter. You know, wherever it went, I went. I took care of all the maintenance, all the records. It was my ship. It didn't fly unless I said it was ready to, no matter how much pressure I got. There was something grand about that for a nineteen-year-old specialist E-4.

And I loved war. I can't deny that. I loved it. I hate it now, but at the time, as a kid, I loved it. I mean I just loved flying. Every time those turbines started winding up, I just thought, *yeah!* It sounds crazy but after a few months you really became one with your helicopter. I could tell if things weren't working right just by feeling the hull of the ship or listening to the pitch of the rotors and the transmissions. It was noisy as hell because we tore out all the soundproofing so you could see where the bullets went through and what lines were hit.

Whenever we took some rounds or had an equipment failure it was my job to assess the problem. Sometimes the pilots would freak out. "We're losing it, chief, we're losing it. We've got to land." I'd say, "You just keep this fucker in the air, sir. We're okay. We're okay. We can make it." If it was just some electrical malfunction, I didn't want to set down in the middle of the Bong Son plain, and I developed a pretty good sense of just how much the chopper could take.

Each Chinook had one machine gunner for every mission, but we carried two machine guns—one on each side. The crew chief or the flight engineer would man the extra machine gun. I loved being on an M-60 machine gun banging away with that thing. God, there was nothing like a combat assault when you went in with twenty, thirty, forty choppers. I mean Hueys everywhere and gunships and CH-47s—just that energy! It was an adrenaline rush. There are some veterans who never got over that. They became addicted to it.

Most of the time we supplied firebases or put in troops and took them out.

The Chinooks were so big, we could move a whole platoon. We also moved Vietnamese villagers. A lot of times areas that were considered to be in the hands of the Viet Cong were declared free-fire zones. We would go in and tell the villagers that they've got to get out, that after a certain date they would be considered VC and anybody we see we can kill. On one mission where we were depopulating a village we packed about sixty people into my Chinook. They'd never been near this kind of machine and were really scared, but there were people forcing 'em in with M-16s so they didn't have a choice. We got 'em all in and had 'em squatting. There were only four of us with sixty of them. I was up on one of the front guns and the crew chief was in the back. All you could do was hand signals. You put your hand out palm downward to keep them down. We started lifting off and one of the Vietnamese in the back stood up and freaked out. He was in his thirties or forties, hard to tell. I couldn't get to him because all the people were between me and him. We were probably sixty feet off the ground, maybe more. The crew chief just thought, fuck it, you're out of here, and pitched the man out the back end. I remember looking out the side of the chopper when he hit the ground. He just laid there. I'm sure he was killed but we never heard anything about it. There was never any follow-up. I talked to the crew chief later and asked what happened. He said, "The guy just freaked out. I couldn't control him. I got scared he would cause a riot and crash us. So to make my point I threw his ass out of there." I said I might have done the same thing.

But even at that time in the war I felt within myself that the forced dislocation of these people was a real tragedy. I never flew refugees back in. It was always out. Quite often they would find their own way back into those free-fire zones. We didn't understand that their ancestors were buried there, that it was very important to their culture and religion to be with their ancestors. They didn't understand what the hell was going on and had no say in what was happening. I could see the terror in their faces. They were defecating and urinating and completely freaked out. It was horrible. After we unloaded the people the helicopter stunk so bad we could hardly stand it. After we hosed it down we sprinkled bottles of aftershave all the way down the length of the chopper.

One time we were given a mission to go out and extract some supplies out of the field. We were expecting to go out and pick up empty water blivets or empty fuel containers or maybe sling out some empty brass from artillery shells. When we got to the landing zone back in the boonies west of Bong Son we saw this deuce-and-a-half truck coming. The guy gets out and says the colonel wants to build a hootch back at base camp so we'd like you to fly it back. The colonel's unit had dismantled an entire Vietnamese hootch, probably fourteen feet long and ten feet wide composed of all these reeds and straw, sheaves of this stuff. There were a few supporting poles we loaded in, but basically it was just a bunch of thatch. Even before we fired up the engines there's grass flying all over the place. Apparently it never entered anybody's mind to just say, "No, this is an inappropriate and dangerous use of a government helicopter." Not even our pilots. We fired up those engines and it was like being in a blizzard, all this loose stuff just flying around. By the time we got back to base camp we had that stuff down our pants, and all for this colonel who wanted a hootch back at base camp. Who knows why. He may have thought it would make him unique. And being a colonel he probably had his own hootch mama to go with it. You wonder about the ego of an individual who can conceive of those sorts of things.

We were always on call, always in demand. When we weren't pulling inspections on our helicopters, we were flying, sixteen hours a day, seven days a week. Sometimes we pulled all-nighters to get our ships up and flyable. My whole time in Vietnam, other than my R and R to Japan, I got into An Khe for one day, Pleiku for one day, and Vung Tau for three days.

One of my big regrets is that we didn't know anything about the Vietnamese when we went there and we didn't know anything more when we left. If you had a pass to go down to An Khe next to division headquarters you could go to a place we called Sin City. It was an enclave that was government sanctioned, about three acres of bars and souvenir shops surrounded by concertina barbed wire with a central pavillon. You had to go through a checkpoint gate, but once you were in there you could do anything. There were all kinds of prostitutes and booze. The army was definitely in control of this thing. The bars had little rooms in the back where you could go with the prostitutes. I know they were checked by the doctors once a week for venereal diseases.

I'll tell one story that's always stuck with me. It was up around Kontum. The jungle was just fierce up there, incredibly dense and menacing. We were going in to extract a platoon, about thirty troops. They had to blow a hole in the jungle for us to get in and there was just barely enough room. It was like dropping down a tunnel. It got darker and darker and darker. It was spooky. After that mission, I was never envious of the grunts. They were out there where you can't see five feet in front of you. As we dropped down in there these guys started materializing out of the jungle. They'd been out so long their fatigues were rotting off. I'll never forget this one guy. He came on board and he had about four or five scalps hanging from his belt. You know, every now and then you'd see a guy with a string of ears, but I'd never seen scalps before. That was truly bizarre. These were bad-looking dudes. But I could tell they were just young guys like us.

I didn't sleep much last night. I kept waking up, thinking, God, I'm in Vietnam again, what the hell am I doing here? Then I remembered Joe Talan. He was the first guy I flew with in Vietnam, a thirty-year-old Hawaiian. He taught me the ropes. The First Cav put together several CH-47 helicopter gunships—they called them Chinook A-Go-Gos. Joe volunteered for them, said he wanted to get closer to the action. He got as close as you can get. I flew by just minutes after Joe's chopper crashed and burned. A couple of Huey gunships were pounding the surrounding area. We couldn't get in there for two or three days because the cinders were still cooking off rounds of ammo from the wreck. We finally brought it back in three small sling loads. There was nothing left of the eight crew members. I was told they went down when one of their blades was hit so I always assumed it was enemy fire. But I just learned recently that the official inspection report concluded that the forward mounting pin on one of its twenty-millimeter cannons broke, elevating it so that it was firing up into its own forward rotor system. In other words, it is very likely that Joe's Chinook shot itself down. All the choppers had nicknames stenciled on the sides. Joe's was called "Co$t of Living." There were three Chinook A-Go-Gos in Vietnam when I was there and they all crashed in various ways. One of the others was called "Birth Control."

Last night I also thought about my best friend who was killed in Vietnam. David's death is one of my greatest sorrows. He died right in front of me and it definitely wasn't at the hands of the enemy. He was shot by another GI in an argument. It was stupid. This guy named Harris pulled a gun on me first. He'd been drinking. He was really toasted. He followed us into our barracks and said to David, "You get Stuvick and I'll get Soular." It just seemed like joking around at that point but David said, "Jesus, Bob, put the gun away. It's just not safe. It's not cool." And Harris took offense to that and said something like, "Fuck you, punk, you don't know anything about anything."

Harris was about thirty-five-years-old, a braggart and a jerk. Talked about how he had been in Korea and mowed down thousands of gooks. But David kept telling him, "It just not safe, Bob. We don't need this kind of horseplay." And Bob said, "You punk, you fuck with me, I'll kill you. I know more about wars and guns than you'll ever learn." We still thought the guy was just blowing off steam, and David said again, "Look Bob, put the damn thing away." Just like that Harris pulled the gun up and shot David in the face.

I went out on a mission the next morning and I still had David's blood on my fatigues. For thirty-two years I've wondered if I could have prevented it. David is still nineteen and I'm fifty-five. When we showed up for the court-martial the guy being tried before Harris was charged with crashing a helicopter. Since he was a crew member, not a pilot, he was not authorized to fly. But a lot of crew members could do a little flying and the pilots occasionally let them. That guy was just trying to move a chopper a short distance to protect it during a mortar attack. He risked his life to save that chopper and he was sentenced to fifteen years at hard labor. Then Bob Harris was tried and I was the only person called to testify. I told them exactly the way I saw it. Harris took the defense that he had been drinking and was sentenced to five years of hard labor for murder. So the guy that just killed my best friend without expressing one bit of remorse got five years, and the guy who wrecked a chopper got fifteen years. To the military, a goddamn chopper was worth three times more than David. That's when the war started unraveling for me.

Twenty years after the war I had someone contact David's family to see if they were willing to meet me. I didn't want to intrude. The intermediary found out that David's father had died, but the mother wanted to see me. David was from Minnesota, where I was originally from, and as a soldier you tend to bond with guys from the same state. And he was such a good kid. So I went back to Minnesota and talked to his mother. She said the bullet that killed David killed his father also. He never got over it. David was an only son.

I assumed that she had been told the truth, that she knew David had been murdered by another American. But the military hadn't told her the truth. She was told that he was accidentally killed in the barracks and that was it. It crushed her that the government had lied to her. She was in her sixties and suddenly realizing that everything she believed in was false—that the government had absolutely no compunction about lying to her, just as it had lied to us constantly during the war.

When I was getting ready to leave she gave me this big hug and said she was glad because she had always been afraid that David had died alone, that nobody was with him when he died. So I knew that regardless of what pain I might have inflicted upon her, I'd also given her some comfort.

I've always considered myself a good soldier, whatever that means. I did what I was told to do. But everything I'd been raised to believe in was contrary to what I saw in Vietnam. All kinds of questions went through my mind and there were no answers. About twelve years ago, it was really strange; I was looking in the mirror shaving and I realized that I don't hate the Vietnamese. All I have is this deep, deep sense of sorrow that this whole thing happened. A day doesn't go by that I don't think about Vietnam—not just what happened to Americans, but what we did to Vietnam. If circumstances had been different, we might have learned so much from them instead of learning nothing and doing so much damage. They seem to have moved beyond the war. But it's still painful for so many of us. I think of Sisyphus rolling the rock up the damn hill. Just when you think you've got it, it comes rolling back down and you start the process over.

TRIAGE

In combat medicine, triage is the system of sorting patients for treatment according to the severity of their wounds. Ordinarily, those in the most critical condition receive treatment first. However, when emergency rooms are inundated with badly wounded people, patients who are deemed likely to die in spite of immediate medical attention are sometimes put aside in favor of those with a better chance to survive. At its best, triage does not arbitrarily "play God" with human lives, but represents the fairest possible way to help the greatest number with limited resources.

In warfare, however, there are forms of triage, often informal and unwritten, that clearly value some lives over others. In Vietnam, for example, it was common for American evacuation hospitals to give U.S. soldiers priority not only over enemy soldiers, but over South Vietnamese soldiers and civilians as well.

And long before anyone is wounded in war, many decisions are made that raise or lower your odds of survival. In combat, of course, who gets hurt can be entirely random, a matter of simply being in the wrong place at the wrong time. One person dies, while another, a few inches away, is unscathed. But who gets put in the most dangerous places is the result of many choices, calculated as well as arbitrary: who walks point, which squads go out on night ambush, who advances into enemy fire, and who is sent on nearly impossible rescue missions.

In a general sense, warfare itself is an enormous system of triage in which powerful leaders and institutions greatly affect the odds of who lives and dies. In the United States, the first level of Vietnam War triage was the Selective Service System. Founded in 1948 as the first peacetime draft in U.S. history, the selective service was never intended to provide for either universal military service or a random selection of possible draftees. Early on in the Cold War, military planners recognized that total military mobilization of the kind that had occurred during World War II was no longer necessary for a highly industrialized, nuclear-armed superpower. Nuclear war, of course, would require hardly any soldiers. Limited wars might still call for a significant number of infantrymen, but would increasingly depend on a growing body of highly educated scientists, engineers, and analysts to produce the weaponry, communications, intelligence, and propaganda for technological warfare.

With that in mind, manpower experts designed a draft that would promote the "national interest" by "channeling" some people into the military and others into higher education. Using the club of induction and the carrot of student deferments (along with a host of special exemptions), they hoped to create a system that would efficiently sort millions of young people into activities that would strengthen the nation in a variety of ways. Although the baby boom produced twenty-seven million draft-age men during the Vietnam War, only 10 percent were needed to fight in Vietnam. Another 30 percent served in Korea, Germany, or at other military posts and potential hot spots of the Cold War, but the majority avoided the military by the many avenues the draft system provided.

The overall effect of the draft was to channel primarily working-class men to Vietnam while encouraging more privileged men to continue their education. Economic advantage made it easier not only to get the college deferments offered to full-time students, but many other military exemptions as well, especially medical ones. The white, wealthy, and well connected also had the best chance of avoiding Vietnam by getting assigned to the military reserves. And while armed forces intelligence testing had once kept many poorly educated men out of the military, when draft quotas shot up during the peak years of Vietnam escalation, the military substantially reduced its educational requirements. Moreover, in many working-class communities, military service was regarded as an unavoidable duty, an inevitable rite of passage to adulthood that was anticipated as uncritically as many affluent children anticipated college. At least a third of those who fought in Vietnam were true volunteers. Another third were "draft-induced" volunteers, enlistees who hoped to have more say in the kind of service that awaited them than a draftee might. The final third were draftees.

Of the 58,193 American military fatalities in Vietnam, more than ten thousand were classified as "noncombat deaths." Eighty-nine percent of the dead were enlisted men or warrant officers. Among the enlisted men who died, 70 percent were between eighteen and twenty-one years old. U.S. forces also suffered more than three hundred thousand wounded. Many of the wounded survived life-threatening wounds, including roughly five thousand who lost at least one limb. Without rapid helicopter evacuation to rear-area hospitals many more Americans would have died.

The Republic of Vietnam Armed Forces (the South Vietnamese military) suffered some 224,000 deaths and more than a million wounded, sobering figures indeed for Americans who assume that the United States did virtually all the fighting while their South Vietnamese allies did everything possible to avoid it.

In 1995, the Vietnamese government announced that 1.1 million Communist troops, including both North Vietnamese regulars and Viet Cong guerrillas, were killed and six hundred thousand were wounded during the American War. While there were perhaps far more people whose wounds went unrecorded or untreated, the fact that fatalities were by far the higher figure is indicative of how difficult it was to treat badly wounded soldiers in jungle hospitals with insufficient medical supplies.

The hardest figures to find reliable estimates for are the number of Vietnamese civilians killed during the war. However, since the Vietnamese male population was so fully mobilized into the military of both sides, it is certain that the vast majority of civilian fatalities were women, children, and older men. Most estimates also indicate that civilian deaths exceeded combat deaths. The Vietnamese government estimates that two million Vietnamese civilians died during the American War. In total, the war extinguished some three million lives.

JAMES LAFFERTY

"No draft board ever failed to meet its quotas."

In 1965, his Detroit, Michigan, law firm opened one of the first free draft counseling centers in the nation. "We were willing to help you stay out of the draft whatever your reason and by using whatever means the law provided." He helped establish dozens of draft counseling centers throughout the Midwest. An activist lawyer for almost four decades, he is now the executive director of the National Lawyers Guild in Los Angeles.

Every aspect of the draft had a built-in bias against the poorest young men in the country. The most obvious inequity was the student deferment that allowed people who could afford to go to college to stay out of the military, or at least put it off. But every deferment and exemption was class-skewed, even those that seemed to favor the poor. For example, whenever I'd argue that the draft system favored the rich someone would say, "What about the hardship deferment?"

Well, in order to get a hardship deferment, you had to show that military service would cause a change of circumstance resulting in economic hardship to the member of your family that was dependent on you for support. If you were an unemployed kid in inner-city Detroit and your mom was on welfare, military service might actually improve your economic circumstances and give you more money to send home to your mom, while the wealthy could claim that military service would be an economic crisis if the circumstances were right. For example, George Hamilton was a "B" actor, as famous for his suntan as anything else, and even though he wasn't on the top of the heap, he made a lot of money. But because he supported his mother in his Hollywood mansion, he was able to get a hardship deferment. He was able to show that if he went into the service, instead of averaging seventeen thousand dollars a month, he was going to get $176, resulting in a radical change in the family's economic circumstances.

Class bias was also blatant in the case of medical exemptions. The poor in general have the worst health. They often haven't had treatment for various ailments and illnesses. So you'd think they would have received the greatest portion of medical exemptions. But most poor and working-class kids who had physical problems had to rely on army doctors to pronounce them unfit for military service, and the examining process at the induction stations bore absolutely no resemblance to the Mayo Clinic or any other legitimate health facility. They were cattle calls. Yes, there were doctors there, but their goal was to process as many people as possible. Day in and day out, people who had legitimate ailments under the written regulations put forth by the Selective Service System were approved for military service.

In order to have much chance of getting a physical exemption you had to come to the induction center equipped with your own medical evidence from some private doctor. You couldn't just walk in and say, "My doctor says I have high blood pressure." It had to be a letter saying something like, "I've been treating this young man for the last three years. He's had high blood pressure on twelve of the fourteen occasions I've measured him. It's a chronic condition." Well, to get a letter like that requires money. You have to be able to afford to go to a doctor and come from a family setting that has the habit of going to doctors. I had lots of poor clients who couldn't afford to see a doctor and build up a bad allergy or asthma case the way better-off young men could.

Even though it was far easier for wealthy kids to avoid the draft, it caused real panic in everyone who faced it. Every other day a client would call up and say, "Hi, this is Bill Smith."

"Hi, Bill, what's up?

"I got a letter from the Selective Service System."

"Oh? What's it say?"

"I don't know. I've been afraid to open it."

I'd say, "Well, Bill, you're going to have to open it, otherwise I'm not going to be able to help you. Go ahead. Open it. I'll wait for you while you open it."

And their voices would just be shaking. It's the terror of the draft notice. Many young men had unsympathetic draft boards. Draft board members were volunteers, all of them, and I rarely ever met a draft board member who wasn't a veteran. They had very little sympathy for anybody trying to "avoid their obligation to the country."

As it got harder and harder for draft boards to fill their quotas, it became harder to get deferments to which people were entitled. To my knowledge no draft board ever failed to meet its quotas. And so what that meant was that if I kept somebody out, somebody else was going in his place. That came to trouble me and it came to trouble a lot of people who were doing draft counseling. That's why we set up free counseling centers in the inner city and tried to level the playing field a bit. But you really couldn't level it, which is why in some ways the people I had most regard for were young political activists willing to go into the service and organize against the war from within the military, knowing that they were going to have one rough row to hoe and might get killed.

Living in Detroit, close to Canada, I can't tell you how many clients avoided the draft by their parents establishing businesses in Canada, and putting their kid in charge. But if you were poor you didn't have those options. In fact, if you're just hanging around with no job prospects you might think the military isn't the worst thing that could happen to you. And in the early days, most young men didn't know what the war was about.

You know, during the Second World War, the draft served a very different function. Most people believed in that war and felt a patriotic urge to enlist in the army. So the draft was used mainly to screen out from service those who were too old, or were needed to work in the defense plants, or whose health was so poor they would have been a liability.

During Vietnam, an awful lot of the middle-class kids who came in said, "If I thought my country was really in danger of being attacked, I'd fight," or, "I'm not a pacifist really, but this war is just ridiculous. I'm not going to fight in this war. What do I do?" Their consciences really troubled them and they were intelligent enough to know that poor kids didn't get college deferments or allergy exemptions. Of course not all these guys were tortured souls. Some of them were just spoiled kids who could use the system and didn't give a shit about anybody else. But that wasn't the majority of people I worked with. Many joined the antiwar movement and were paying something back, not simply quietly hiring us to stay out of the draft.

In 1969, my brother-in-law asked if I would speak at his Kiwanis Club in the suburbs of Detroit. So I go give my rap about why the war in Vietnam is wrong and the draft system is unjust. And when I'm done there's a stony silence. Then this one guy with his little American flag button in his lapel raised his hand and said, "If it was up to me, I'd shoot 'em."

I said, "I beg your pardon?"

"Those guys burning their draft cards," he says, "I'd shoot 'em. That's what should happen to them."

I said, "Well, why don't you do that?"

He said, "Yeah, well, that's just the way I feel. They're a bunch of cowards and traitors. They should be lined up and shot."

I said, "No, no. I believe you believe that. My question to you is, why don't you do it?"

He said, "Well, if they wouldn't throw me in jail, I would."

I said, "Well then, with all due respect, I suggest that you're the coward and not them, because they're prepared to go to jail for what they believe in and you're not."

That brought the meeting to an end. Afterward, a couple of people came up to let me know in a very quiet way that maybe they agreed with me, but weren't inclined to say so in front of the rest of the Kiwanis Club in Ferndale, Michigan, in 1969.

DAVID M. SMITH

"The knife man."

He grew up in Fort Valley, Georgia, the son of an undertaker. In 1968 and '69 he was a surgeon at the Naval Support Activity hospital in Danang and offshore on the USS Tripoli. *Occasionally he went with combat units into the field. During Operation Meade River he and two navy corpsmen treated more than one hundred casualties in a single night, for which he was awarded a bronze star. Today he runs the largest orthopedic practice in New Jersey.*

"Do you have a strong stomach?" he asks. He offers to show slides of wounded patients from the war that he's used in formal presentations to medical colleagues.

Click: "This next case involves a rifleman who sustained a single shot from an AK-47 rifle. It entered his right shoulder and traversed his right lung, pericardium, heart, stomach, spleen, pancreas, small intestine, left kidney, left ureter, left femoral artery, and exited just above the left knee. After eight hours of surgery and twenty-eight units of blood, he died." *Click.*

He is six feet, six inches tall. Often he appeared on the deck of the Tripoli *without a hat, a violation of Marine Corps regulations. Once he overheard a grunt ask his buddy: "How come that dude don't have his cover on?"*

The buddy replied, "Hey man, that's the knife man. Don't nobody fuck with the knife man."

My job was triage officer. I separated out the casualties to determine what needed to be done first, in what order of priority. It was usually pretty obvious. After finishing that I would go back in and be part of the surgical team. I did that for a year and it was an absolutely incredible professional experience. I saw an incredible amount of anatomy and a lot of different approaches that I never ever would have seen any other way. Any surgeon would do anything to have this kind of experience. So professionally it was just wonderful. And regardless of how bad it got, I could always feel I was doing something good for somebody.

I went over there as an absolute hawk. I was truly committed to what Lyndon Johnson was saying. Before I went I almost got into a fistfight with a guy in a restaurant because he criticized the war. After about three weeks in Vietnam you really saw what the war was and it made no sense whatsoever. But I never got to the point where I had to spend a lot of my energies in philosophical decision making about supporting the war or not, because I *was* supporting the war. I was supporting these guys who were out there risking their lives.

I had incredible respect for the marines. I saw how these young, uneducated people, who perhaps didn't have a lot of self-confidence before basic training, honest-to-God felt they could do anything, particularly physically. The other thing that marines had was this discipline about the hierarchy of command. One day we were getting all these heat casualties. Nobody was shot up but they were all going into heat exhaustion. After about the fifteenth one I asked this marine, "What the hell is going on out there?"

The guy says, "Doc, we're out there marching on the beach and it's about one hundred and fifteen degrees."

And I said, "Well why are you doing this?"

And he said, "Because the gunney sergeant said to."

I used to watch these young marines prepare to launch missions. I knew that on some operations twenty to thirty percent would be brought back as casualties. They would be sitting around waiting with their bandoleers of ammunition and weapons. They were not thinking great and serious thoughts; they were reading comic books.

Click: "The next case graphically demonstrates why the Vietnam War was different medically. This marine second lieutenant stepped on a booby trap made from the shell of a 105-millimeter howitzer, which is about six inches wide and about two feet long. He sustained a left hip disarticulation, which means his leg was blown away at the hip, a right leg, above the knee, amputation and bilateral hand trauma, to say nothing of his urologic injuries. Within ten to fifteen minutes the medevac helicopters had deposited him in NSA hospital. The helicopters were directly responsible for the increased survival rate in Vietnam as compared to World War II and Korea. This patient was actually conscious when he arrived and there was no active bleeding from either amputation site because of the reflex spasm in the major vessels. With delayed transportation I am sure the spasm would have relaxed and he undoubtedly would have exsanguinated, or bled to death, on the spot."

I would say ninety to ninety-five percent of the people who made it to us within thirty minutes survived. After all, if you got them stabilized, most of these guys were perfect physical specimens. I have never seen a group of people who were in better shape physically than this in my whole life. If they died, it was usually because they had some postoperative complication such as uncontrolled infection.

Would it have been more merciful to allow some of the most horribly wounded to die? Our job, by God, was to fight death and not give in to it. Physicians are always doing battle like Don Quixote with the windmills of death. To watch somebody die absent your best effort is just not what we do.

I never got a follow-up about whether any of the bilateral amputees lived or died. As a matter of fact, I've rarely come across any of the truly injured people from Vietnam in our society. I don't know where they are.

Click: "This ten-year-old Viet Cong died as a result of his efforts to set a booby trap in front of a bus."

I must confess that I had a great difficulty understanding why we had to perform surgery on people who were trying to kill us. I'm a pretty black-and-white kind of guy and if somebody's trying to do me in I don't really feel any necessity to support him. If he's trying to kill me I would have no trouble watching this guy die. So other than the surgical experience of doing something I hadn't done much of, I really didn't like it, and wasn't doing it for an altruistic reason.

[After several dozen photographs of open wounds] Click: "This is a brass vase I keep on my desk."

I was walking down a road outside Danang one day and I came upon a small building in which there was a small furnace, a bellows, and a lathe driven by an ox walking in circles. There was an elderly Vietnamese man working with metal. As I looked closer I saw that he was taking spent 105-millimeter howitzer shells, heating them red hot, reshaping them with his lathe, and fashioning them into these beautiful vases, which he sold for two dollars apiece.

Americans were firing hundreds of thousands of these rounds and discarding the shells. The Viet Cong picked up many and made devastating booby traps out of them. And in the midst of all this insanity this old guy with an entrepreneurial spirit had seen his way to an object of beauty.

"The first time I went to the Vietnam Memorial I went alone because I knew I would cry for hours, and I did." The memory makes his voice catch and his eyes fill with tears. Though he seems surprised by the sudden jolt of emotion, he does not turn away or stop talking. "I've only been to the Wall twice and both times I cried. Other than that, I haven't. Not thinking about it, not talking about it, or anything."

Wiping away the tears with the back of his hand, he regains his normal voice. "Surgeons are very controlled people but it wells up. If you took a hundred of my colleagues and patients they'd just tell you I'm a hard-ass. But they've never talked to me about Vietnam."

SYLVIA LUTZ HOLLAND

"We saved their lives, but what life?"

She enlisted in the Army Nurse Corps and went to Officer Candidate School at Fort Sam Houston. "We'd fall out in the morning and they'd play songs like 'Thank Heaven for Little Girls.'" While advancing their nursing skills by doing intubations and tracheotomies on anesthetized goats, they also "learned how to handle a .45, do the gas mask thing, march and salute, all that good stuff." From 1968 to 1969 she served at the 312th Evacuation Hospital in Chu Lai, Quang Ngai Province, Republic of Vietnam.

You'd see these young wounded men and they'd say, "Boy, you sure look good." You're sweaty and dirty and you're the best thing they'd seen. And how they cared for one another. They sacrificed so much for their friends. They didn't think twice about crawling out on their bellies and dragging someone back. And then the fear. They were men with guns and all that firepower and they'd just say, "Hold my hand. I know I'm dying, please don't leave me."

You took care of people all day. If they went sour you tried to get them back. Some of them made it, some of them didn't. The doctors were really good. They let us do a lot of things I could never do here. In the States you have to ask permission from a doctor to fart, but back there if you could do it you did. It was the only time in my nursing career when I used every bit of knowledge I had and developed a sense of confidence in my judgment as a professional.

The busiest place was the emergency room. The dust-offs [medical evacuation helicopters] would call on the radio to let us know what they were bringing in, like, "Three-Twelve, this is Medic 2, we have four litters—two body bags, a head wound, and a belly." That meant they had two KIA and two wounded. When the chopper landed, the corpsmen would go out and bring 'em in through the double doors. We had sawhorses set up and they put the litters on the sawhorses. Either a nurse or a doctor would decide who needed help first. You did triage all the time. The GIs had first priority, then the ARVN, then Vietnamese civilians, and finally the Viet Cong. You went from one litter to the next. You'd look at the wounds, check the vital signs, and just make a decision—he's a go or he can wait. We had to move fast but we worked on trying to keep a calm voice and always had some kind of physical contact with the patients. A lot of times, as soon as you touched them you could feel the tension drift away. It was a real important part of what we did. When you got to a man who was too far gone, you didn't say anything and moved to the next litter. In the back of your mind you'd say, I hope he's dead when I get back.

We had a lot of men who had stepped on land mines. It was a guerrilla war and the whole idea was not to kill but to maim and injure and decrease morale. The Viet Cong were really good at that. Very few of the wounds we had in Chu Lai were the result of bullets. When the mines exploded people often lost their legs, but the heat of the blast would cauterize all their big vessels so they didn't bleed out. Sometimes they were still conscious and talking. We had two gentlemen who were gone from the waist down and their arms were gone but they still had a bladder and some bowel and they were alert and oriented. They had surgery and lived. I often wondered what kind of life that was. Quality of life isn't supposed to be an issue when you make triage decisions, but you're saying to yourself, if you send a nineteen-year-old home without his arms and legs, who's gonna want him? Or the guy whose face is all disfigured and burned. Is someone going to love him and share their life with him? I thought about that a lot. We saved their lives, but what life?

Some of the doctors had left lucrative professions. The 312th was one of the few reserve units to get called up. Those guys weren't too happy. They'd joined the reserves thinking they wouldn't be activated. But they did their jobs well. The surgeons were miracle workers. They brought one man in with a gunshot wound to his face and half his lower jaw was missing. He just had jagged edges of his mandible and he was choking on his own blood. I grabbed his tongue and pulled it up, but every time he swallowed he pulled my hand down the back of his throat. That's the only time I got sick. I was holding his tongue, turned around, and threw up. They put in a trac [tracheotomy tube] and took him into surgery. He came in with his face laid open, but after surgery he was whole.

When we had "pushes" we might have days and days of casualties coming in, but we weren't busy every day. Sometimes it was quiet and we basically just sat around. Then you were like a sister, mother, grandmother, girlfriend. You had all kinds of roles. The men might start to talk about what they'd experienced and then you'd see this little protective shield come down. I don't know whether they didn't want to talk because they thought it would upset us or if it was just too painful for them. Mostly they'd talk about their girlfriends, or what they were going to do when they got home, what kind of car they were gonna buy. A lot of them talked about getting Dear John letters. Married men would ask you to write letters home. They had a genuine appreciation that American women were there. I don't know how it would work now because of women's lib and everybody being equal. I've heard about sexual harassment in Vietnam, but that was never my experience. We were treated with the utmost regard. It was like being queen-for-a-day every day.

You'd work a twelve-hour shift, shower, and then go to the officers club at night. They'd be playing music and you'd be dancing and playing cards and having cheeseburgers. Then you'd go to bed, wake up, and go back to the insanity. One minute you're confronting death, and the next you're doing the watusi. After a while you couldn't separate one from the other. Near the end of my tour I was crying a lot and couldn't sleep. I wasn't able to function so I took the chief of surgery aside and said, "I'm falling apart here." He prescribed Librium. I didn't drink and I didn't use drugs, but I did take Librium for about three months. It gave me a kind of false calm. It was like watching a movie.

One of the hardest things to accept was that we had a lot of substance abuse. They'd bring some GIs in who were hooked on heroin and they'd just throw 'em in these big metal conex boxes that our supplies came in. Some guys were locked in there for two or three days. Then they'd put 'em in the medical ward, hydrate them with fluid, and just ship them back out to their units. It was like instant detox. There wasn't any bringing them down gently.

Part of my tour I worked in the Vietnamese ward. Mostly we had women and children and elderly men. They were country people—fishermen or rice farmers—who came in with amputations, abdominal wounds, head wounds, pneumonia, infections, everything. Some of the children came in with napalm burns. Most of them were burned pretty badly and when you touched them a white, powdery dust would come off their skin. It was like their skin was evaporating. It had a really pungent odor of burned flesh and chemicals. Their beautiful country and their homes and families were torn apart and yet they managed to survive. They took care of one another and would absorb people from other families who weren't even blood relatives. They were warm and caring. Family members were always in the hospital. They'd sleep under the beds or on the floor.

The Viet Cong would sometimes mortar our compound and one night around three in the morning a mortar hit the Vietnamese ward. By then I was working a rotation in the emergency room having been replaced in the Vietnamese ward by Sharon Lane. I think she'd been in-country just a month. She was asleep on a bed in the ward. If it was quiet on night shifts we would relieve each other so you could lie down for an hour. The mortar hit right in Sharon's area. There was a loud explosion, the lights went out, and the sirens went off. Then the auxiliary lights came on so there was this little glow. A lot of people were hollering. The corpsmen were running and they came back with Sharon on a litter. She had a big hole in her neck. She was pale and her pupils were fixed. The surgeon came in and tried to start an IV but there weren't any veins. Then he was gonna open her chest and massage her heart. I said there was no reason to do it, she's dead. He kept saying, "No she isn't." Then he started crying. One of the corpsmen took her to the corner and put screens around her because we were starting to get other casualties from the Vietnamese ward. For a long time I had survivor guilt because if Sharon had not come I'd have been working in that ward during the attack.

When wounded Viet Cong prisoners were brought in, the MPs would guard them and they were taken care of at the very end if they lived that long. One time after we'd had three or four bad days they brought in a VC. We got his litter up on the sawhorses to check him out and the doctor just took a scalpel and carved VC on his chest. Then he just put the scalpel down and walked away. Everyone has their breaking point and it was just like he was saying, "I've fucking had this." I don't agree with what he did, but there's always a way to rationalize it. Ten minutes later the doctor was talking as if everything was fine.

One time I had a Viet Cong patient in the recovery room. He was waking up from surgery and I was taking his blood pressure. I could see the hate in his eyes. It was the first time in my life I'd experienced that level of animosity. It was chilling. Then he spit at me. It caught the side of my face. A corpsman standing next to me just hauled off and knocked him out. The nursing supervisor walked through afterward and said, "Isn't anesthesia wonderful." I said, "Yes, it certainly is."

Another time they brought a pregnant Vietnamese woman in with frag wounds in her belly. They did surgery and removed the frags. Afterwards she kept yelling, "I hurt, I hurt." At first we thought it was just pain from the surgery but when I checked she had broken her water and was in labor. The head was already visible and she just popped it right out. I held the baby's head down and milked the throat and it started to cry spontaneously. The doctor walked back in, grabbed it, wrapped it in a chuck—a disposable pad—and said, "The baby's dead. It's premature and we can't waste the oxygen." He handed it back to me and I put it in the trash.

The baby was probably premature and would have needed some form of oxygen for several days to make sure its lungs were fully developed. Oxygen was one of those resources that was not scarce, but it was reserved for the American military first and whatever was left went to the Vietnamese. It was the same with blood and IV solutions. It was reserved for special circumstances so they weren't gonna use it for a Vietnamese baby. That's the way I justified it. Compared to my own babies, I'd say that baby was probably seven months. But it could have been full term based on the stature of the Vietnamese people. What really upset me was the baby did cry spontaneously so the lungs did expand. The baby wasn't dead. It cried spontaneously. In my mind I was thinking, well maybe we should just let it set here and see how it does on its own. But that wasn't an option. I mean, it was an option for me and one I didn't take.

Should I have pulled the baby out of the trash? I had every opportunity to, but at that point in time it was not the thing to do. There's a different mind-set in conflict. There's a totally different way of looking at the world when you're in a war. Life has value but only certain types of life. I just think you rely on those people that give orders to give you direction. Had I been in my thirties maybe I would have reacted differently. I think about it. Where do your principles stop and where do your actions begin? You can't go back and change them and you can't second-guess or you drive yourself nuts. You have to accept responsibility for what you did.

During the Persian Gulf War in 1991 she turned to her son Dan, who was a junior in high school, and said, "You're a conscientious objector." He said, "Why, Mom?"

" 'Cause you're not going. If anybody's going it'll be your old mom." Like many Vietnam veterans, she doesn't want her children, or anyone else, "to experience what I experienced." However, she is not about to disavow her own military service or her loyalty to the nation. Critical as she can be of American policy in Vietnam ("You don't win hearts and minds with guns and bullets"), she is also quick to add, "This is my country, right or wrong, and if there was another war and they said we need nurses, I would go. They'd probably tell me I'm too old, but I'd be there."

CHI NGUYEN

> *"Being wounded was not considered the worst thing that could happen."*

From 1965 to 1974 he was an orthopedic surgeon at the largest Vietnamese military hospital in Saigon. With some luck and a well-placed bribe, his family managed to get on one of the final flights out of Vietnam when Saigon fell in April 1975. He recently retired from the medical staff of a Veterans Administration hospital in Boston.

We sometimes had thirty or forty wounded soldiers lying in our big triage room. I can still see and smell it vividly. Once you've smelled the wounded, you never forget it. It's the smell of desiccated tissue. Sometimes we had patients brought to the hospital five or six days after they were wounded. They smelled worse than the dead.

I remember walking around with a clipboard saying, "This one will go first, this one will go next, and then this one." I felt I held their destiny in my hands and it was a very, very painful situation. But you didn't have time to ponder. You just tried to focus on the patient in front of you. Triage made me develop the bad habit of working very quickly. We neglected details. You asked yourself only one question: how critical is the wound?

We saw every imaginable sort of wound. Of course many were very gruesome. However, I remember one guy who died just because he had so many small shrapnel wounds. He did not have any bleeding wounds, only thousands of tiny, tiny spots all over his body. More than the stars in the sky. Possibly he died of shock.

One young man had a grenade thrown at him. He grabbed the grenade and tried to throw it back. It exploded in his hands. He was blinded and lost both hands. Because of his blindness, prosthetic hands wouldn't work for him, so I performed the Krukenberg procedure, splicing his forearms and wrapping the skin around his bones to make two big fingers. That gave him some feeling and permitted him to hold things. The day he could hold a cup of tea with his four "fingers," he cried.

The most vivid memory I have is the time I took a small diary from the pocket of a young soldier who died on his way to the hospital. On the first page he wrote, "Nothing happened." The next day, "Nothing happened." The next day, "Nothing happened." Every day, he wrote "Nothing happened." That's it. The day he received the fatal wound, the page was left blank. When something finally happened, he was not able to record it. It's a kind of black humor, a very sad black humor.

Our people endured so much over the years that being wounded was not considered the worst thing that could happen. We amputated the limbs of some men who even expressed relief. For them the war was finally over.

MORALE BOOSTERS

> "We're so close to the fighting we had to give the Viet Cong half the tickets."
>
> —*Bob Hope, at Cu Chi, Republic of Vietnam, 1966*

William Westmoreland, commander of U.S. forces in Vietnam from 1964 to 1968, routinely assured the media that the morale of his men was outstanding. In his memoir, *A Soldier Reports,* he explains why:

> In keeping with my belief that it was going to be a long war, the one-year tour gave a man a goal. That was good for morale [and] I hoped it would extend the nation's staying power by forestalling public pressure to "bring the boys home."
>
> While PXs, clubs and messes, and recreational facilities primarily helped keep troops out of the cities . . . they were also good for morale. So too was the R&R (rest and recuperation) program, which provided a man an interim goal to break up his one-year tour. . . . These creature comforts, plus other factors such as keeping men busy and informed, having them participate in civic action projects, and keeping the complaint channels open, helped during the period 1964–69 to generate the highest morale I have seen among U.S. soldiers in three wars. It was only after 1969 that the psychological stresses and strains of an apparently endless war began to show.

Westmoreland sounds here like the personnel manager of a very large corporation offering advice on how to keep short-term employees compliant and productive. Especially fascinating is what his analysis of morale omits. Nowhere does he suggest that it has any connection to a goal larger than surviving a one-year tour. Whether the soldiers understood and supported the aims of the war or believed themselves engaged in a just and worthy cause was, it would seem, irrelevant.

And yet the root meaning of *morale* is fundamentally linked to the moral significance of our actions. Perhaps "creature comforts" and staying "busy" allows people to get by from day to day, but they are hardly a measure of our deepest sense of purpose. Westmoreland was certainly right, however, that American soldiers focused great attention on surviving their one-year tour. It was, for many, a nearly obsessive preoccupation. They knew precisely how many days remained in their tours and crossed them off, one at a time, from the calendars they kept on everything from flak jackets to barrack walls. The one-year tour was perhaps the only concrete thing American troops could count on in Vietnam. And since they could not count on surviving, it was a pretty thin straw to grasp.

Of course, the creature comforts for men stationed in large rear-area bases could be quite remarkable, at least in contrast to the deprivations endured by the grunts out "humping the boonies." As the American presence grew, base construction expanded like a boom-time strip mall. Rear-area soldiers could expect warm meals, hot showers, and electric power. They could shop at PXs stocked with everything from cigarettes, magazines, and candy to cameras, stereos, lingerie, and perfume. At enlisted men's clubs they could drink ten-cent beer and play slot machines. By 1970, the clubs at many large bases had televisions where soldiers could watch *Star Trek, Laugh-In, The Mod Squad,* and *The Beverly Hillbillies.*

Life for the North Vietnamese and Viet Cong soldiers could not have been more different. Year after year they lived a jungle existence, exposed to every hardship nature and war could deliver. While veterans of that experience are sometimes hesitant to talk much about the difficulties they faced (after all, didn't everyone face them?), virtually all of their accounts make some reference to the scarcity of food. And it wasn't just soldiers who suffered. In North Vietnam, where food was rationed throughout the war, most people were allotted less than a pound of meat per month.

Given such grim conditions, American commanders and policy makers were astonished by the steely resolve of their enemy. While enemy defectors sometimes indicated signs of exhaustion and disillusionment among the Communist forces, there were even more signs that the enemy was mobilized by a genuine commitment to the cause of expelling the Americans and unifying the nation. Judging by many passages in the speeches and writings of Communist Party and military leaders, you might think they believed that widespread faith in "the sacred war of resistance against the United States aggressors" required little or no political organizing, that it rose like a "tidal wave" from the "spirit of the people." But, in fact, the Communists were genuinely convinced that victory was as much a matter of political organizing as battlefield skill. They also recognized that politics required not just a lot of rah-rah propaganda speeches ("Long live a peaceful, unified, independent, democratic, and prosperous Vietnam!"), but countless face-to-face efforts to recruit southerners to the cause and to shore up the will of comrades.

One element of this commitment was the use of art and culture to bolster morale among the troops. Every major North Vietnamese combat unit included several artists and entertainers. These singers, musicians, painters, writers, and actors traveled south on the Ho Chi Minh Trail not as separate artistic "troupes," but mixed in among the regular troops, with whom they lived and sometimes fought. Their primary duty was to share their cultural talents in order to inspire the combat soldiers.

The most obvious American corollary to these Vietnamese artists were the entertainers like Bob Hope who came (always with a group of young starlets like Joey Heatherton, Jill St. John, and Ann-Margret) for a few weeks of big shows in front of thousands of GIs. Meanwhile, perhaps not too far away, in a jungle clearing or an underground bunker, another group of soldiers might be listening to Vietnamese folk music or checking out the latest sketches of a "soldier artist."

Back in the States, the antiwar movement had its own morale boosters. There were musicians like Joan Baez, Phil Ochs, and Peter, Paul, and Mary, theatrical groups like the San Francisco Mime Troupe, and underground newspapers like the *Berkeley Barb* and the *Chicago Seed.*

BOBBIE KEITH

"I got a butterfly right on the butt. So that's my war story."

"And now, that bubbling bundle of barometric brilliance, Bobbie the Weathergirl!" She was born in South Carolina, but grew up as an army brat in all sorts of places. From 1967 to 1969, she appeared at the end of the nightly news broadcast of Armed Forces Television, Vietnam. On bases big enough to receive a signal, GIs tuned in not for the weather—it was almost always hot and humid—but to see the girl with the long blond hair who wore a miniskirt that rode a full foot above her knees and all the campy hijinks that made the show a kind of war-zone Laugh-In.

"Bobbie the Weathergirl" became a morale-boosting celebrity. The station sent out thousands of pinups that showed her hanging provocatively from jungle vines or lounging in a bikini. In addition to seven broadcasts a week, she agreed to visit troops throughout South Vietnam. For all of that, she never got a dime; the work was strictly

voluntary, an add-on to her full-time job as a secretary for the U.S. Agency for International Development.

On the Internet you can find some grainy, wartime footage of the nineteen-year-old standing in front of a U.S. map that looks like it was made for a junior high science project. With a slight Southern accent, she says, "Dropping in on the Prairie State of Illinois it was a fair, cool day of fifty-five." Then she twirls and kicks her way over to a handmade map of Vietnam: "It's a rather hot, sticky, and humid day in Hue with a high of ninety-nine." Finally she reports the temperatures in those Asian cities where American GIs were sent for R and R. At show's end, rock music swells and she launches into an arm-pumping frug.

One day I happened to be at the American Club in Saigon having lunch with my girlfriend, and Colonel Nash, the director of Armed Forces Television, walked by. He said, "You look like a weathergirl." I go, "Well this is a different pickup line, isn't it?" But he was serious and asked me to come out for an audition. My girlfriend harangued me like I couldn't do it, or it wouldn't be tasteful. I was a little defiant so I decided to go for it.

Every day a car would pick me up after work and take me over to the studio. I pulled the weather reports off the ticker tape and slapped the stickies on the map—the rain, and clouds, and sunshine. Everything was ad-libbed. If I couldn't obtain the temperatures, I made them up. That wasn't hard in Vietnam. It was usually anywhere from eighty-five to ninety-two degrees with about eighty percent humidity. And if it was monsoon season, it was safe to predict rain. I was usually in and out of the studio in thirty minutes.

It was cute because guys would write in and say, "Bobbie, you haven't mentioned my hometown." So every day I'd say something like, "Dropping in on Chattanooga, Tennessee, today for Sergeant Bill Smith of the 101st Airborne, the temperature is a pleasant seventy-two." People liked to hear local references so I was always mentioning things like the House of Seven Gables in Massachusetts or the Okefenokee Swamp in Georgia. You do all these little things 'cause it brings them home. For the close I'd usually send out a special salute—"Tonight I'd like to send a special salute out to the First Cav. Thank you so much for your hospitality during my visit. This is Bobbie saying good night and I hope you all have a pleasant evening weatherwise and otherwise."

At first they had me sitting on a stool like I was frozen. That was weird because they said they chose me because of the way I stood and my "fluidity of motion." Then they let me stand up and gave me a pointer, but I was fooling around with the pointer too much and they thought it wasn't becoming, so they took it away. Eventually I got more comfortable and I had more freedom. Then the staff started doing jokes. It began one night during monsoon season.

I was talking about the rain and they dumped a bucket of water on me. I was scared that the water would hit my mike and electrocute me. The wire went up my skirt and attached to my bra under my clothing. But I think they turned the mike off because I was swearing. It was funny. They would do it every once in a while after that and I never did know when it would happen. We got a lot of letters from guys about how much they liked it.

The staff was always trying to figure out what they could do to liven up the show. I even did the show in a bikini a few times, but I got a call from Ambassador Bunker's secretary saying that it was rude and unbecoming and I shouldn'ta done it. So we nixed the bikini thing. Once for Halloween I dressed up as a witch and they hoisted me up in this harness and I flew around the studio on a broomstick. Another time I rode in and out on a motorcycle. And one Christmas I wore a Santa Clause hat and a bathing suit. They sent that one out as a pinup.

When you're on TV, all of a sudden you're more of a known entity than just a normal girl, so I got invitations to visit troops all over Vietnam. My first invitation came from the Redcatchers, the 199th Light Infantry Brigade. They flew me around on a Loach—a small helicopter that looks like a bug—and we went hopping around to visit small base camps. I wouldn't trade those trips for a million dollars. When I first started those "handshake tours" I had to get over being shy. I'd land and someone might yell something like, "Wow, what is that?" Or, "Do you see what I see?" But really they were very shy and kept their distance so I had to learn to approach them and say, "Well, hi guys, how are you doing?" There weren't many American women over there so you got a lot of attention. It was flattering and I never had any problems, but I've heard of women who weren't so lucky.

Back in Saigon a lot of the bars and restaurants were on rooftops so that's where we partied. The Rex BOQ [Bachelor Officers Quarters] was a favorite watering hole. They would have steak cookouts up on the roof. They even had a swimming pool up there and movie nights. We had popcorn, for crying out loud. But you always had that rather ominous presence of the war around you. Those rooftops gave you a bird's-eye view of helicopter gunships flying around and air strikes in the distance. People were getting killed out there and we were safe on a rooftop sipping gin-and-tonics and listening to music. That's the duplicity of the whole thing. I think a lot of the men in the rear felt guilty having that safety net. I know I did. But then again, we never knew where the rockets would hit in Saigon, or if the Viet Cong might blow up another BOQ.

And our life in Saigon wasn't as cushy as it might sound. I lived for a while at the Oscar hotel and there were no mosquito nets, no air-conditioning, and no hot water. The sheets weren't adequately cleaned so lice spread all over the hotel. And everybody got diarrhea—Ho Chi Minh's revenge. I got it so bad I wound up in the hospital with IVs in my arm.

There was a curfew at night, but some of the nightclubs just closed the curtain and let you stay later. In a lot of these places most of the women were Vietnamese bar girls. I got along very well with most of them. They knew what they were doing might not be too kosher, but they had a sense of their own morality. They usually supported their families and in many cases they were the sole breadwinner. But some bar girls saw me as competition and I did have one crack a glass over my head one time. Another one set my hair on fire. And then there was Dominic's mistress. Dominic ran a French restaurant next door to the Oscar hotel where I used to hang out a lot with my girlfriend Pat. Dominic wanted to make his mistress jealous so one time when she came back from Paris he said, "I didn't miss you because I've been having an affair with Bobbie." I had some guy tell her that there were five hundred thousand guys in this country and I didn't need some old farty French guy. But she didn't believe it and one night she tore into me with her nails. I had scratches all down my arms. Before they broke us up I gave her a bloody nose. After that an American intelligence officer told me she had put a contract out on me and for a while I had to have a bodyguard. I think that probably scared me more than the Viet Cong.

I went on R and R to Taipei and I was the only girl on the plane. When we arrived we got a little briefing about the local VD problem. Then they told us about the strip where you could get a hotel room complete with your own girl for sixteen dollars a day. And the girl would do anything you want, including shine your boots. I died of embarrassment. But it was also cute because the guys I had met on the plane called me up at my tourist hotel and said, "Hey, Bobbie, *Planet of the Apes* is playing, you want to go to the movies?" I met them downtown and they had gotten their package deal with their girlfriends. They were all really cute young girls and real sweet. They took me shopping and we went to a Mongolian barbecue together. Then we got a little piss-eyed drunk and all got tattoos. I got a butterfly right on the butt. So that's my war story.

But imagine sending these poor young men on R and R. They all fall in love, taste a little freedom, have a good time, pick up their souvenirs and then, dammit, they have to go back to the war. How fair is that? I always thought it was cruel. Sometimes Commander Cori [a U.S. Navy officer] would invite some of us girls for a one-day R and R. He'd fly down to the Delta, pick up a dozen or so men from the LST boats, and we'd all get on a C-141 and head for Con Son Island. Con Son Island's like a paradise. It's got a white sandy beach and lush tropical vegetation. I didn't realize until years later that this was the island that had the tiger cages where the government of South Vietnam held prisoners. No one ever talked about the cages, but we flew right over them.

They'd bring steaks, Cokes, and beer for a cookout. We'd have fun and then I'd get back on the plane and realize that while I was going back to the safety of Saigon they were all going back to the war and I'd want to cry.

A lot of people really didn't talk about the war much, especially before the Tet Offensive. During Tet, though, the war literally came to our doorstep. Then you go, "Holy shit, what did I get myself into?" We put together some box lunches to take out to some engineering troops. I thought it would be a neat adventure. At one point we were standing near a huge heap of garbage and a Viet Cong jumped out of the garbage and started shooting at a man working on a telephone pole. Later, during the May Offensive the rockets came in every morning. You didn't even have to set your alarm clock. I used to put the mattress in the bathtub and sleep in there, thinking that would be the best way to survive if the building got hit.

The worst thing was seeing an American blown up right in front of me. I was visiting a unit down in the Delta and going to take a ride on an air-cushioned vehicle. Its like a huge inner tube powered by a turbo prop that rides very fast on shallow water and has guns mounted on it. They had teeth painted on the front and it looked very frightening. I really don't know what happened. They said it was a freak accident. All I remember is that we were walking down a path through a marshy area toward the boats and there were a bunch of guys standing off to the right. All of a sudden some guy was hit by something—I don't know if it was enemy fire or a booby trap or what, but he just blew up. Parts of his body went everywhere. Some of his skin hit my mouth. Then they grabbed me and I was out of there. I just remember my escort saying, "Enough is enough. I'm not going to bring you back here."

"There are two schools of thought on the war. One says it was a waste and one says we succeeded because if we hadn't been in Vietnam the Communists would have taken over other countries. I'd like to think the latter idea is true because I don't want to think it was a waste."

Since the war she has worked at American embassies in Germany, Jordan, France, Colombia, Turkey, and Morocco. She lives now in Florida.

JAMES BROWN

"After they got the funk they went back and reloaded."

The "Godfather of Soul" removes the foil from his lunch in the studio of his Augusta, Georgia, radio station, WAAF—"Classic Soul." While he eats a hot dog, his granddaughter Tanya, the afternoon DJ, cues up an old Wilson Pickett tune. The corner of Broad Street and James Brown Boulevard is visible through big glass windows. Occasionally, a passerby waves at the famous man wearing a three-piece green suit, a crimson shirt, and cowboy boots. At sixty-seven, he still has his familiar hairstyle—the neat, dark, processed hair, combed in a mound to one side. He jumps from topic to topic, peppering his commentary with asides to his granddaughter and anyone else who happens to pop in. At one point, he waves through the window to a scruffy, middle-aged man who appears to be homeless. "That little man right there plays more drums than any drummer I got. He went to Vietnam and look what he had to come back to. Come back and walking the street. Went there and lost his mind. I always look out for him."

In the summer of 1968, Brown went to Vietnam for two weeks to perform before enormous crowds of GIs. Earlier that year, in the wake of Martin Luther King's assassination, he had gone on television and radio in several major cities, including Boston and Washington, to caution against violence. "I know how everybody feels. But you can't accomplish anything by blowing up, burning up, stealing, and looting. Don't terrorize. Organize. The real answer to race problems in this country is education. Be qualified. Own something. Be somebody. That's Black Power."

In 1968, he endorsed Hubert Humphrey for president; in 1972, Richard Nixon.

You have to pick your words when you start talking about the Vietnam War. My Vietnam thing was one strange situation 'cause the biggest boxer in the world wouldn't go—Muhammad Ali. He refused. I don't know if he was scared or what. A lot of blacks thought they didn't have a real reason to go there because they wasn't getting their rights here. They had mixed emotions on the war. Ali wound up being a real hero, but a lot of people didn't agree with him. My dad didn't agree 'cause he went into the service. He thought that by going to fight he had more to complain about. That's what I felt. I went in '68 because if you want to demand a hundred percent of your rights you got to give your country a hundred percent of your support. See, if I don't make the system owe me one, I can't do nothing. Now, we know the United States don't owe me nothing 'cause it's my home, but think of all the billions of dollars I saved for them after the assassination of Dr. King. If I'd just been cool, ain't said nothing, they'd a burned up everything. But I did that from the heart, I didn't do it for publicity. I did it because our country was being torn up.

I heard a statement that black men were fighting over there in Vietnam but black entertainers wouldn't go. So I volunteered but the government didn't want me to go to Vietnam. I just couldn't make heads or tails of it. Mr. Bob Johnson, the publisher of *Jet* magazine, got me in there. He called Vice President Hubert Humphrey. I'd met Humphrey in 1966 when I put out the song "Don't Be a Drop-Out." So Humphrey agreed that yeah, we'd be glad to take James to Vietnam.

We did two, three shows a day. It was harder than any tour I've ever done. Man, you talking about hot. I go over there in a hundred and twenty-six degree weather. I was singing and sweating and there wasn't a dry spot on me nowhere. I'd get a frozen towel out of the refrigerator and before you got it to your face it'd be like this napkin. I was kicking it out, so after almost every show I'd get my intravenous. I had my IV thing set up like I was in the hospital. Between the shows I lay down and they fill my vein back full of water and my face would come back full.

I lay down to sleep in the hotel in Saigon and the Presidential Palace was just around the corner. Would you believe they shot a rocket and it landed about two hundred feet away from the palace? We'd ride from place to place in a Chinook, a big helicopter. I demanded me a gun. I said, "I have to have a gun or I can't ride." I laid on the floor, but I had a gun. When I got that big .45 I felt good. I had an American uniform on—I had the whole thing on. There was no difference between me and the other American soldiers. It takes my mind right back to what it was. You never know who's over there in them bushes. But you know what I had going? When I went over there, are ya'll ready for this? The Viet Cong had a cease-fire and come to see my show. They said, "Let's get some of this funk for us." So after they got the funk they went back and reloaded. [He explodes in laughter.] Them cats went back and reloaded, boy. They were very smart. They were buddies with the fellows during the daytime and shoot at 'em at night.

The GIs treated me like God. It's 'cause I came over there to perform for them and I didn't have to. I was out in the nitty-gritty, right out there in front of the people. I sang "Papa's Got a Brand-New Bag," "Cold Sweat," "Please Please Please," "Try Me." Probably "Bag" and "Cold Sweat" had the biggest impact on the GIs. The shows all kind of ran together, but I'll never forget the one we did at a base called Bear Cat, I believe. They had the place dug out of the side of a hill, like the Hollywood Bowl. There must of been forty thousand people there. Guys went wild. About halfway through the show we heard this ack-ack-ack, boom, boom, BOOM coming from somewhere behind the stage. Turned out Americans were firing at somebody. The guys in front yelled, "Don't worry, we won't let Charlie get you."

I knew better than to give black power salutes to the GIs. That would have been causing a problem. All those soldiers were over there together. But I did go back and talk to General Forbes. He asked me, "What do you think about the race problem?" I said, "You got a bad one." He said, "Well I don't see no problems and blah, blah, blah." I said, "What do you mean? How you gonna see a problem? When you walk up a cat better not move his eyes wrong or he get court-martialed. You can't see nothing 'cause the cats can't talk back to you, sir. But everytime I go to a place they'd tell me about the blacks and the whites and people thinking they were better than the other one." But that didn't happen with all of them. A lot of blacks and whites became better friends than they ever were in their life.

QUACH VAN PHONG

"An artist can be as important in war as a soldier."

He came of age in Saigon. In 1954, his family was among the two hundred thousand southerners who moved to North Vietnam after participating in the war against the French. He returned to the South in 1963 as an artist attached to the North Vietnamese Army. His assignment was to use art to bolster the morale of ordinary soldiers. Today he lives on the outskirts of Ho Chi Minh City in a spacious home full of his paintings. He asks, "Can we do the interview over beer?" His daughter delivers the drinks and a plate of prawns.

I still keep a lot of wartime sketches. From a purely artistic point of view they might be nothing, but they are really my life. I drew my pictures right in the midst of battle. Many times I didn't have any ink, or even a pencil, so I had to spit in my hand, mix my saliva with dirt, and use a twig to draw. There was no time to make a well-planned, well-structured composition. Years later, when I took my wartime sketches to the Fine Arts Association in Hanoi, people there didn't appreciate them because they saw neither composition nor design. I understood what they meant, but a sketch of war must be done on the spot and immediately. If it's done weeks or months later, it might be a good painting, but it can't be an authentic combat drawing. People who've experienced war know what I mean. For example, when I had an exhibition of my old sketches in Thailand, some former war reporters begged me to sell them the pictures even though they were not for sale. I asked them why they wanted them. They said they could see in them the living details of war as vividly as they had seen them before.

In our jungle camps, I hung my sketches on trees or ropes—wherever possible—so the soldiers could see them. Many of my drawings were portraits. After everyone had seen them, I gave them to the soldiers I had sketched. They treasured them, partly I think because they realized that they might die at any moment. I felt great affection for them and they returned it many times over. From the commander down to the ordinary soldiers, everybody pampered me.

In one place, however, the commanders of the local guerrillas were surprised to learn there was an artist among the soldiers. They couldn't believe a painter had any value in war and they didn't try to hide their feeling that I was useless. So I lied and said I worked for a newspaper and had come to learn more about war scenes to make illustrations for my newspaper. But when I left that unit, the local soldiers wrote letters and asked me to come back. Then their commanders began to realize that an artist can be as important in war as a soldier.

When I was wounded in 1973, I was sent to Hanoi for medical treatment. There I never told anyone, even my closest friends and relatives, about my wartime experiences. I just didn't think they would ever understand. It's surprising and ironic that when I talk with American veterans I feel that we have more in common in some ways than I have with Vietnamese who were not in the South. Although we were on opposite sides, we shared the same battleground. When I talk about the red soil, they understand immediately. If I told my friends in the North about my war experiences they'd just think I wanted to brag. So I don't tell them anything.

There are too many sad memories, but the saddest thing was to see so many innocent civilians killed. Another thing that depressed me was not knowing when the war would end. It seemed endless. Year after year I thought it would end and it didn't. I worked in Phuoc Long, just a hundred and forty kilometers from Saigon, but they were as far apart as heaven and hell. Saigon always felt like home, even though I was away from 1954 to 1975. Not knowing when I could return to the city, maybe that was my most haunting thought in those years.

While we finish the prawns, he recalls how little food they had during the war. As an artist, his ration was a bit more generous than that provided to ordinary soldiers. For example, he often received a cube of salt with meals while the others went without. Even so, in some periods he survived almost entirely on cassava. "I'm still sick of cassava. I can't eat it."

NANCY SMOYER

"I can't believe the Donut Dollies got us to do that."

In 1967, she went to Vietnam as a "Donut Dollie." The nickname, dating from World War II, referred to women who worked in a Red Cross program called Supplemental Recreational Activities Overseas. In South Vietnam, Donut Dollies visited servicemen and engaged them in games intended to lift their morale. "We were a little bit older than most of the men and tended to see ourselves as older sisters. Their dream was to go back to 'the World' and drive cars and date girls and have fun. None of us knew that we weren't going to be kids anymore." She works now as a vet center counselor in Fairbanks, Alaska.

My first assignment was with the 1st Cav and they picked me up in Saigon in a chopper. The pilot tried to scare me by flying low, but I thought it was fabulous. One of the great things about being a Donut Dollie was getting to fly to remote firebases and LZs [landing zones]. We got farther forward than any other women except journalists.

Our programs were a cross between a TV quiz show and a board game like Monopoly. We would have a theme—like sports, or cars, or women, or movies. We'd make up a bunch of questions and have a board of some kind where they tried to get from A to Z or whatever. We'd divide the men into teams and stand up in front and ask them questions. In one game, we had them spell out their answers with children's A-B-C blocks. They really got into it. I would say to them afterwards, "Can you believe you guys just spent an hour playing with kids' blocks?" It was fun to tease them. They'd say "Oh, no! I can't believe the Donut Dollies got us to do that."

We wore baby-blue seersucker dresses. The guys all around us had flak jackets, helmets, and weapons and we were in our little blue dresses. The incongruity was amazing. We always tried to wear lipstick and perfume and look our best for the guys, but unlike being home, our looks weren't important. The guys were just so appreciative to see American girls. They never made me feel self-conscious even when I wore dorky glasses because the dust was so bad I had to stop wearing my contact lenses.

Sometimes they were just stunned into silence by seeing us unexpectedly, or they'd try to flirt with us but they were so out of practice they could barely do it, or else their rough language would get in the way and they'd embarrass themselves. They were like cute little boys who were surprised to see girls and didn't know how to act. Sometimes they'd say things like, "What are you doing here? What are you getting out of this?" It was just this intense feeling of wanting to protect them and do whatever was possible to make this miserable place a little more bearable.

One day I was with one of my favorite groups, a long-range reconnaissance unit, and they were just not interacting at all. We couldn't figure out what was going on. The game was about famous people. So finally, trying to engage them, I said, "Well, who is the most famous person in your unit?" They named somebody and I said, "I don't remember him. Who is he?" They said, "He was killed a few days ago." So we just sat down and talked to them for the rest of the time. We were so naive that a lot of the times we just didn't grasp what they had been through. All of us were so innocent. If I had known what I know now I couldn't have played games with them. I'd have probably been trying to warn them and warn myself.

Whenever we were in public we were always "on." We always had hundreds of eyes on us and we had to be smiling and pleasant. For the most part, that wasn't difficult. But if you had just been through a bad time, or you knew the men had, it was hard. It was a strange role to be sweetness and light in a war zone. And it's even more incongruous to think about it now because of all the changes in gender roles and also the fact that there are a lot more women in the military. It just wouldn't work today.

Unfortunately, we got a reputation for being in Vietnam only for the officers. Some of that stemmed from the fact that the Red Cross rules said we were only supposed to date officers. And sometimes we wanted to eat with the enlisted men and the officers insisted that we eat with them. We struggled with that because we really felt we were there to be with the enlisted men. It was a fine line we had to negotiate, but I know several Donut Dollies who married enlisted men they met in Vietnam.

It sounds strange to say, but it was exciting the whole time. It was a wonderful tour. The reason that it was so good is that you were in a war zone where there's such intensity and adrenaline. The little things don't mean a thing and the bonds you form are so strong. It gives a luster to war that's extremely seductive. But it's so costly. Somehow, even then, I knew it would be the high point of my life, and it was. And it's sort of sad to know that at age twenty-four it's as good as it's going to get.

Three months after I got back in 1968 my younger brother Billy went to Vietnam as a marine lieutenant and three weeks later he was killed in an ambush. It was a tremendous loss to my family and to his many friends and teachers. In 1965, when I was a senior in college, I remember thinking, thank goodness he's so young. The war will be over by the time he is old enough to go.

Since the Vietnam Veterans Memorial was built in 1982 she has worked countless days as a park service volunteer at the Wall. "I like talking to the veterans, asking how they're doing, and just being there. I remember a few years ago hearing a nurse say, 'I think about Vietnam every day.' I thought, of course you do. It never leaves."

VU HY THIEU

"Nothing was more essential than our sandals."

We sit in a hotel lobby in Hanoi, his daughter serving as interpreter. His face has refined, almost delicate features, but it's the dark, liquid eyes that are memorable. At one point they look down and away, and he falls silent. One of his hands swipes the air several times as if brushing away an insect. He's just mentioned a large U.S. bombing strike on the Ho Chi Minh Trail that caused hundreds of casualties. The silence lengthens, his chest shudders, and his daughter reaches over to touch his hand. "It's hard," she says.

After graduating from the School of Fine Arts in Hanoi, I was offered a chance to study in the Soviet Union, but I turned down the opportunity so I could go south. In times like that everybody wanted to do their best for the country. I had to apply repeatedly because only one artist was being selected from each province. The two main criteria were talent and political orthodoxy. They finally approved my petition.

In my group there were about ten artists and one hundred doctors and nurses. Our training was basically the same that regular soldiers underwent. We trained for three months in the Luong Son Mountains. Every day I had to climb a mountain carrying a pack filled with thirty-five kilograms of stones and sand. I weighed about fifty-two kilograms then.

We began the trip south in trucks. The only personal belongings I took were some family photos and a small notebook in which I had written the wishes of my family and friends. Basically, everyone gave me the same wish—be well and come back. I kept that notebook in a small pouch tied around my neck for good luck.

There were about ten of us in the back of every truck and they were all covered with tarps, so from the outside they just looked like ordinary supply vehicles. I vividly recall driving through Hanoi at 11 P.M. It was the end of November 1966. We couldn't resist taking a last look at the city, so we used our bayonets to cut small holes in the tarp. Only a few streetlights glimmered because electricity was strictly conserved. It was raining lightly. So many people had evacuated the city it looked deserted. There wasn't a soul to be seen and the city was wrapped in a veil of soft, yellow light and drizzle. It looked unspeakably sad.

Resting by day, we traveled at night in small convoys of two or three trucks so there'd be no big targets. We camouflaged the trucks with tree branches, which made it harder for the American bombers to detect us. In Thanh Hoa Province the road became so bumpy we had to stand up and hold onto the overhead rack. We weren't even permitted to talk because we might bite off our tongues. The bumps were that bad! We stood the whole night.

Past Nghe An Province the main road had been bombed so terribly we had to look for an alternate route and got hopelessly lost on back roads. After hours of fruitless searching we decided to continue on by foot. To lighten our loads we gave away clothes and extra food and transferred our medicine from boxes into plastic bags.

We walked for a week on relatively flat land until we reached the beginning of the Truong Son [the Ho Chi Minh Trail] on the western border of Quang Binh Province. We saw a lot of volunteers, mostly young girls, working on the trails. The guides were mostly boys. Each guide would take us to the next station where another guide would pick us up. Usually the distance between stations was about seven kilometers.

I remember one station that had been repeatedly bombed by B-52s. The trees were completely destroyed. It was like traveling through a desert. The earth was like powder. Every part of the trail had tons of mosquitoes and blood-sucking leeches. Ordinarily you pulled the leeches off with your hands, but when we weren't in a hurry we'd put some salt in a piece of cloth, dip it in water, and press it against the leech until it fell off.

We learned to cook without producing smoke. First we dug a big hole for the stove and then a long trench leading away from the hole. In the trench we put a pipe that carried the smoke away from the fire. If you covered the end of that pipe with leaves, the smoke would filter through it very slowly. This was called a Hoang Cam cooker and for all of us northern soldiers who had to carry parts of it, it was our closest companion.

You had to be extra careful about smoke because reconnaissance helicopters and airplanes hovered overhead day and night. A minor mistake like hanging your wet clothes in an exposed place or giving away your presence with just a wisp of smoke and five minutes later aircraft would be bombing you. Many people died because of such mistakes. I saw one convoy of four hundred people killed that way. [He pauses to collect his emotions.]

Another mistake was to scatter in all directions when the bombers came. If the pilots saw people running they'd call in helicopter gunships to go after people individually. So we were instructed to lie down and be still. You might be killed anyway, but there was less chance of their seeing you and calling in gunships.

For food we often bartered with the ethnic minority people who lived in the mountains. They had a strong fancy for our trousers, which we traded for chicken eggs, or we made necklaces and bracelets from the handles of pots and pans and exchanged them for food. Laotian women loved those things. For us, nothing was more essential than our sandals. We made them from tires. You simply could not walk in the Truong Son Mountains barefoot. If you lost your sandals it was a huge disaster. They were so valuable you could barter a pair of them for a whole pig. Some soldiers stole sandals to buy pigs, so at night we tied them around our bellies.

When we arrived in Quang Tri Province in the South the road had been almost totally destroyed by continuous air strikes and food was scarce because so many of our rice sheds had been blasted. What rice we did have was mostly stale or rotten thanks to the jungle dampness and humidity. The guides in that region suffered the most. Their bodies were swollen from beriberi and they looked like hell. Since we were on the move, we had a better chance to find food. Knowing their situation, we shared our meager supplies with them.

After five months we arrived in Tay Ninh, but my ordeal didn't end there. I had to travel to a military base in Binh Thuan Province on the coast. Two or three artists were assigned to each province. On arrival, my first job was to draw anatomical figures for a nurse training course. Fortunately, I had taken anatomy at the School of Fine Arts.

We bought our paper from people living in strategic hamlets. Every night we infiltrated those hamlets to buy supplies. The strategic hamlet program was designed to isolate the people from us and turn them against us. We had to explain to them why we opposed the program and the crimes of the enemy. Some of us would give political talks while others would buy supplies, and I would draw posters to inform people of the victories won by the Liberation Army or to mobilize people to rise up and overthrow the government. During the day I prepared everything for the night's work. To draw the posters, I'd hold a small flashlight in my mouth, leaving both hands free. Many young people turned out to help me. After I'd make a sketch, they'd fill in the color. But later those kids were arrested and tortured, so we decided not to let people help us that way any longer. We usually left the hamlets around three in the morning.

Sometimes, at sunset, near our jungle base, we'd move close to the edge of the rice fields to watch people working. We could do that safely because the puppet troops didn't dare stay in the fields after dark. We often played with the buffalo boys and they leaked tidbits of information about the puppet soldiers—how many were in a nearby outpost, the number of weapons they had, or when they moved to another outpost. Those buffalo boys basically functioned as our messengers.

We also taught children to rig booby traps and set land mines. They were responsible for letting the local people know where the explosives were hidden. In the evening, we'd unrig the traps for their safety. I was an expert on booby traps. They were a very effective weapon against government troops who stopped at nothing to destroy the revolutionary forces. Killing those thugs was like killing criminals. One time they decapitated, dismembered, and disemboweled one of our thirteen-year-old messenger boys. I used to rig booby traps above the posters I put up on walls at night. When some aggressive puppet soldier came to rip it down his head would be blown off. One time we inserted dynamite into a flagpole, tied it to the top of a tree, and flew the Liberation Army's flag. Not long after that an American chopper spotted the flag. It came in, hovered next to the tree, and a guy leaned out to pull down the flag. The flagpole exploded and he was killed instantly.

During the Tet Offensive of 1968 we attacked Phan Ri. The puppet troops were completely taken by surprise. We met with no significant resistance. After securing the city we gathered the people and I spoke to them. It was high time, I said, to overthrow the government and seize power. I appealed to them to join the revolutionary forces. "If you have children serving in the puppet army, ask them to come back to serve the revolution." But we only held the city for one night. The fact is, we had not been well prepared and were badly undersupplied with ammunition. We didn't even have enough rifles for everyone. The situation for the regular troops was bad enough, but the guerrilla forces had it worse. The enemy outnumbered us twenty to one and were strongly supported by aircraft and tanks. When they launched their counterattack the next morning half of our forces were decimated on the spot.

In 1965 and '66 my gut feeling was that victory was imminent. In those years, I didn't feel depressed. But fighting the American GIs was not an easy job—they had a lot of weapons. One time American tanks advanced on us while a swarm of choppers hovered overhead. There were only twenty of us at our base. Stay put and the tanks would run over us; run away and we'd be sitting ducks for the enemy choppers. I told my comrades, "Even if some of us are killed, let's cling to the ground." We covered ourselves with grass and tried to squeeze between the advancing tanks. We were nearly run over but we survived.

The American 199th Infantry Brigade were good jungle fighters. They came by chopper and then divided into small units, which were very mobile. They moved well in the jungle. Even when we heard them, we didn't know where they were. They were excellent pathfinders and good at spotting our old footprints. To avoid discovery when we cut through the grass, the last person in our unit used a stick to make the grass stand up again as if no one had passed through. But our most lethal opponents were Australian commandos. Some were aborigines who lived in the jungle like fish in water. They could sleep in the mud and sneak right up on us.

When the U.S. Army started their withdrawal we knew that victory was close. In 1974, I was sent to a liberated zone in Tay Ninh. For the first time in eight years, I was given a small salary. The first thing I bought was ice cream. Those of us from Hanoi love ice cream.

By March 1975 there was news of victory everywhere. Early in April we knew that we would win. I was ordered to prepare everything for the publication of a newspaper for Saigon. So we began to set up *Liberated Saigon (Sai Gon Giai Phong)*. I served as editor and also created the paper's design. Saigon people, unlike those of us from Hanoi, are very informal and easygoing, so I wanted to make the design of the newspaper simple, much like it had been before 1975. I put the word *Liberated (Giai Phong)* in small letters below a much bigger *Saigon* because my intention was to remove *Liberated* from the title a few months later. But people wanted to keep it and it's still there.

On April 25 we were ordered to move toward Saigon. On April 29 we spent the night in a rubber plantation fifteen miles from Saigon but no one could sleep. We just kept looking at our watches. Early the next morning we started for Saigon. On the way we saw lots of dead bodies beside the road and some trucks on fire with southern soldiers inside. In the city people crowded the streets to welcome us. They came close to touch our hands. At first, we had no idea where to go, so we pulled over in front of a movie theater and took a break. People brought us food and watched us while we ate. They even examined us to make sure we didn't have tails like monkeys. Mixing with the crowd were ARVN soldiers who had stripped off their uniforms and wore only shorts and T-shirts. I was deeply moved to see a patch of sun on a high wall. It had been nine years of jungle living since I had seen the sun rising over a city.

JOE MCDONALD

"I was president of my high school marching band."

Come on all of you big strong men,
Uncle Sam needs your help again;
He's got himself in a terrible jam
Way down yonder in Vietnam;
So put down your books and pick up a gun,
We're gonna have a whole lot of fun!

And it's one two three,
What are we fighting for?
Don't ask me, I don't give a damn,
Next stop is Vietnam.
And it's five six seven,
Open up the Pearly Gates;
There ain't no time to wonder why,
Whoopie—we're all gonna die!

It was one of the most dramatic moments of Woodstock, the 1969 music festival in Bethel, New York. In the middle of his "I-Feel-Like-I'm-Fixin'-to-Die-Rag," "Country" Joe McDonald paused to say: "Listen people, I don't know how you expect to ever stop the war if you can't sing any better than that. There's about three hundred thousand of you fuckers out there. I want you to start singing." By the end of the song, virtually the entire ocean of people had come to their feet to sing, clap, and cheer. The irreverent, provocative, black humor rag touched a nerve not only in the antiwar movement but more broadly in the culture, appealing and offending in ways not always predictable.

He grew up in El Monte, California, and joined the navy in 1959 at the age of seventeen.

I was wandering around downtown and saw a poster that made me want to wear the uniform. I thought if people saw me in that uniform I'd have a lot of girlfriends. Unconsciously, I believe I was trying to prove that my family was patriotic because my parents had been investigated by the FBI and the House Un-American Activities Committee for their left-wing activities.

My mother joined the Communist Party when she was sixteen years old. Her parents were Russian emigrants and her mother had participated in the

1905 revolution in Russia. My father grew up in Oklahoma and during the Depression he gravitated towards the Communist Party as many people did. In the forties, soon after my birth, they became dissatisfied with the party and left. They were ostracized forever by their former comrades. By the time they were investigated in the fifties they were just liberal Democrats. The shit hit the fan in 1954 when my father was "let go" from the Pacific Bell Telephone Company one year away from a vested retirement fund. But the FBI kept an active file on them for forty years.

I grew up with songs by Woody Guthrie, Pete Seeger, the Weavers. I took up the guitar at a very early age and had a band, but in school I played the trombone. I was president of my high school marching band, student conductor, the whole nine yards. When I was sixteen, I became very attracted to rhythm-and-blues and rock 'n' roll and started writing songs.

In the navy I was based in Japan but didn't know there were any kind of hostilities going on in Vietnam. After I got discharged in 1962, my mother began to work with a group called Women's Strike for Peace and my father began a job as the custodian for the 1st Unitarian Church in Los Angeles, whose minister was quite active in the antiwar movement. So I was aware of the Vietnam War but it wasn't a big part of my life yet. I was trying out being a student at Los Angeles State College. I was in the Folk [Music] Club and the civil rights movement was capturing my interest. I participated in some sit-ins around L.A. to try to integrate restaurants. That was the main concern in '63, '64, not the Vietnam War.

I rolled into Berkeley in the summer of 1965 at the end of the Free Speech Movement and the beginning of the really visible anti–Vietnam War movement. I fell into a very rich cultural and political scene, and began working on some songs for an anti–Vietnam War play by Nina Serrano. One day, I sat back, strummed a few things on my guitar, and this song just popped into my head really quickly.

I'd formed this skiffle band and a few months later in October of 1965 we recorded the "Fixin'-to-Die-Rag." My friend Ed Denson wanted to call the group "Country Mao and the Fish" after Mao's saying that revolutionaries move among the people like fish through the sea. I said that was a stupid name and so he said, "Well, let's call it 'Country Joe and the Fish' after Joseph Stalin." I said that at least Country Joe had a nice sound to it. Oddly enough, I learned later that I had been named after Stalin by my gung-ho Communist parents in 1942. We pressed a hundred of those discs and sold them for about fifty cents. I sold a few copies at the second Berkeley teach-in on the Vietnam War.

Vanguard Records signed us as a rock band and they didn't want the song on the first album, so it wasn't until 1968 that "Fixin'-to-Die-Rag" came out as a commercial release. It never was a commercial success like a Top 40 song. As I look at the lyrics now, I realize it had all the perspectives I developed being a red-diaper baby. I didn't like any organized political groups because I felt that they betrayed the rank-and-file. That included the Communist Party and the military. I saw military personnel as being working-class and generals and businessmen as the top brass who were just using the workers and soldiers and sailors. I grew up with a knowledge from my parents of how the Krupp family and the Rockefellers made fortunes off of war, so I had a lot of contempt for those people. I was very proud of my working-class roots and my song places no blame for war on soldiers.

Come on, Wall Street, don't be slow,
Why, man, this is war Au-go-go;
There's plenty good money to be made,
Supplying the army with tools of the trade;
Just hope and pray if they drop the Bomb,
They drop it on the Viet Cong!

You also have to remember that I was twenty-three years old and still had a young person's sarcastic sense of humor. I grew up with people like Woody Guthrie and Will Rogers and Langston Hughes who all had a very sophisticated sense of irony. And since I had been in the military as a teenager I knew that the civilian fantasy of "why don't you just put down your gun and go home" was nothing but a fantasy. I was well aware that you could be put in the brig or shot for treason. So although no one had expressed the sentiment, "Whoopie, we're all gonna die" before, I think it's a common feeling among people everywhere who are trapped in a situation against enormous odds and there's not much they can do about it except have a pretty good attitude.

"Fixin'-to-Die" offended the status quo on so many levels. It was also blasphemous because of my insistence on doing the "F-U-C-K" cheer before the song. It started as a "F-I-S-H" cheer—give me an "F," give me an "I." I got the idea from being president of the high school band and we always spelled out the name of the team. I thought let's do that for ourselves, which is a silly sort of thing, but one night the drummer got the idea to change it to the F-U-C-K cheer. It's the most taboo word. In today's climate it doesn't seem like much, but in 1969 some people were fired from the radio for playing the cheer. It managed to take the song out of the nicey protest area and put it in the unacceptable protest area because it starts off with everyone yelling "fuck."

"Fixin'-to-Die" was hated by the top brass and the prowar people who were safe. It was also hated by some of the rank-and-file, but as the years went on and the war went on, I don't think there were many military people from that era who disliked the song. I was surprised to find out that it was sung and played in Vietnam by American soldiers. And years later I also met Phil Butler, who was a POW in North Vietnam for seven years. He told me Hanoi Hannah [the English-speaking propaganda broadcaster for Radio Hanoi] used to pump the song into the Hanoi Hilton [Hoa Lo Prison]. The North Vietnamese thought it fit their party line. Phil told me when they played "Fixin'-to-Die-Rag" the prisoners would smile and hum along. It was a morale booster for the American prisoners. The Vietnamese never understood that. The French-educated Vietnamese who were running the Communist Party during the war thought that they understood Americans because they had studied Jeffersonian democracy, but the song contains something which I think is unique on this planet—an American sense of humor.

The song had elements which offended some left-wing leaders as well. They viewed it as facetious and sacrilegious. It didn't fit a party line. A lot of people in the peace movement saw the North Vietnamese leaders as being some kind of saints and saviors, but I didn't consider it impossible that the North Vietnamese Communists were mean motherfuckers.

Woodstock was, like the writing of the song, just a whimsical, fatelike thing. We got added onto the program very late. We weren't going to play until two days later but I got up very early on Friday and was just sitting onstage listening. That was how I intended to spend the whole day. When Richie Havens finished singing there was literally no one to put on the stage and he was too tired to play anymore. They came over and asked me if I would begin a solo career by entertaining the troops. I didn't have my guitar so they found one, tied a rope to it for a strap, and pushed me out there. I sang a mixed bag of stuff, maybe five songs, and no one paid any attention. I walked offstage and nobody even noticed I'd left the microphone. I asked someone on the production staff if he thought it would be okay if I sang "Fixin'-to-Die-Rag." We were planning to do it with the band on Sunday. He said, "Nobody's paying any attention to you so what difference will it make?" So I went back out there and that was the full-blown debut of "Fixin'-to-Die-Rag." It proved to be an incredible high point of the whole concert.

We became kind of like a USO show going around entertaining the troops. And then my wife, Robin Menkin, got involved with Jane Fonda putting together the FTA Show.* They asked me to come along and do my little shtick with them. By that time I had a couple of other songs from a military

*FTA was GI slang for "Fuck the Army" (or, more politely, "Free the Army"). The first FTA show in March 1971 near Fort Bragg drew five hundred GIs. The shows were conceived as antiwar challenges to the conventional entertainment provided by the military.

point of view like "Kiss My Ass" and "Tricky Dicky." Donald Sutherland [the actor] and Ben Vereen [the dancer] were also involved. They did these agitprop antiwar comedy skits. We went around to GI coffeehouses. They were off-base and run by various left-wing or religious groups. We would get a hundred or so GIs.

Then I got into a disagreement with Jane Fonda and left the tour. We were having a discussion about a new skit and I suggested that one of the women in the cast could play LBJ. Jane said that was too far out, that we couldn't have a woman play a man because the audience was made up of GIs who were working-class guys who didn't even know how to spell. Spelling has always been a problem for me my whole life and I was raised to be proud of being working class. Jane wanted very much to be in charge of our media image and wanted me to behave and I'd blurt out things at press conferences and was combative when I should have just let her talk because she was the superstar and I was just a guy in the show. I thought she was condescending so I just went home.

"'Fixin'-to-Die-Rag' was something that worked for and against me in many ways. Some people believed it was a made-up act, a kind of one-off thing that wasn't part of a body of work. What happened to me is very similar to what happens to lots of people in war. You do something that dominates your whole life and identity for the rest of your life. One day I sat down and wrote a song in twenty minutes and it's all people want to talk about or respond to and it eclipsed everything else I've ever done."

He continues to tour as a musician and political activist.

AIR WAR

The United States spent more than half of its $200 billion war chest on air operations in Vietnam. Every day for more than a decade the skies over Vietnam were filled with a myriad of lethal aircraft, from the AC-47 "Spooky" gunships that fired eighteen thousand machine gun rounds a minute, to the A-1 Skyraiders that swooped down to the treetops to release 150-gallon canisters of napalm, to the B-52 Stratofortresses that were each capable of dropping twenty-seven tons of bombs from six miles high. From 1962 through 1973 the United States struck Vietnam, Laos, and Cambodia with eight million tons of bombs, more than three times the amount it dropped in World War II. In addition, the U.S. sprayed about nineteen million gallons of defoliants on South Vietnam in an effort to deny Communist forces food and jungle hiding places.

At the heart of the air war was an American assumption that bombing would eventually cause enough pain and devastation to move the Vietnamese to quit. As General William DePuy, commander of the 1st Infantry Division, put it in 1966, "The solution in Vietnam is more bombs, more shells, more napalm . . . until the other side cracks and gives up." And even if bombing did not crush the enemy's will to fight, many policy makers clung to the hope that it would destroy their capacity to fight. Presumably, if you eliminated enough of their troops and supplies they could no longer field a sufficiently large force to challenge the United States and the South Vietnamese. However, with each escalation of the bombing it became apparent that the Vietnamese were still able to wage war at times and places and for durations largely of their own choosing. Privately, policy makers often conceded that the bombing was failing to discourage or defeat the enemy. Then they would insist that the bombing was still necessary because it demonstrated American toughness and resolve to both the enemy and the world, and it would improve the morale of our South Vietnamese allies.

A crucial fact of the war, unknown to many Americans, is that most of the U.S. bombing fell on *South* Vietnam. Almost 75 percent of all American sorties were flown in South Vietnam where four million tons of bombs were dropped, four times the amount dropped on North Vietnam. Much of it took the form of "close air support" for American and South Vietnamese ground forces. A firefight would begin and troops on the ground would call for helicopter gunships and planes to strafe, bomb, and napalm enemy positions. On a typical day in 1967 about eight hundred sorties were flown by fighter jets in support of U.S. and ARVN ground forces in the South. Since a substantial amount of combat occurred in or near hamlets and villages, this use of air power often resulted in civilian casualties. And even when civilians survived such bombings, much of their land and property was destroyed. South Vietnam eventually became the most heavily bombed country in the history of warfare.

The U.S. military designated many areas of South Vietnam as "free-fire zones." Deemed to be enemy strongholds, these zones were subjected to indiscriminate bombing and shelling while ground forces were given free rein to fire on anything that moved. "Arc Light" strikes consisting of six B-52s frequently carpet bombed free-fire zones, blanketing miles of countryside with hundreds of bombs, each one producing a massive crater.

The fear and suffering produced by U.S. bombing, far from crushing the Vietnamese will to fight, did as much as any single factor to generate anti-American hostility. When family members died in bombing strikes, Vietnamese did not need Communist propaganda to persuade them that the United States was a foreign aggressor. And in the South, villagers were often confronted with the contradiction that their land was being bombed by the very people who claimed to be protecting them from external Communist aggression.

The U.S. air war also failed because of the simple fact that Vietnam was not industrially developed enough to be paralyzed by bombing. Moreover, its human and industrial resources were so decentralized the destruction of any single target did not have a major impact on the whole society. And even when the United States wiped out most of North Vietnam's electrical capacity, Hanoi could rely on small generators and human labor to carry on the war effort.

Nor was the United States ever able to prevent the North from sending ample troops and supplies to the South. No matter how many roads or bridges were destroyed, the Vietnamese found alternate routes or quickly repaired those that were damaged. Consider the case of a target American commanders regarded as absolutely crucial to North Vietnam: the Thanh Hoa Bridge. Seventy miles south of Hanoi, it seemed a vital link in North Vietnam's supply line to the South. Completed in 1964, the fifty-six-foot-wide bridge was part of the only north-south railroad track and highway (Route 1) that ran the entire length of the divided country. It was known to the Vietnamese as Ham Rong—The Dragon's Jaw. Hundreds of missions were flown against it between 1965 and 1968, when U.S. bombing of the North was suspended. For all that, the United States was unable to destroy the bridge until President Nixon renewed massive bombing of North Vietnam in 1972 and it was hit with laser-guided bombs. Prior to that the Vietnamese had always repaired the bridge, causing only temporary delays. They also surrounded it with antiaircraft weapons and successfully shot down many U.S. planes. But the larger point is that no single bridge was ever essential to the Vietnamese capacity to continue waging war. Whenever one was damaged or destroyed, they built temporary pontoon bridges nearby.

As devastating as the bombing could be, it was hardly unopposed. In the South, Communist forces relied primarily on small-arms fire and antiaircraft artillery to defend themselves against U.S. and South Vietnamese helicopters and bombers. Some two thousand U.S. helicopters were destroyed by the Viet Cong and North Vietnamese in South Vietnam, and roughly twenty-five hundred were lost due to crashes, mechanical failures, or other nonhostile causes. Helicopter pilots and crewmen suffered the highest casualty rates of any contingent of U.S. forces in Vietnam. More than thirty-five hundred were killed.

In North Vietnam, U.S. pilots eventually faced one of the most sophisticated air defense systems in the world. Provided primarily by the Soviet Union and China, the heart of the system was comprised of antiaircraft artillery (AAA), surface-to-air missile sites (SAMS), and MiG jet fighters. During the initial U.S. bombing attacks on North Vietnam in 1964 and 1965 its air defense was still quite limited. However, by 1967 the North had seven thousand AAA guns, two hundred SAM sites, and more than a hundred MiGs. All told, the United States lost 8,588 aircraft in Vietnam, Cambodia, and Laos, about one-fifth in operations against North Vietnam.

JONATHAN SCHELL

"I had my notebook right there in the plane."

Rushing into the magazine's office, his cheeks flushed, he flops down on a couch looking impossibly burdened by the distractions of a journalist's life. The odds seem slim that much of value will be gained by dredging up a thirty-year-old topic. As soon as the subject is mentioned, however, the present evaporates. It's as if the middle-aged man has entered a time machine dated 1966. That was the year he went to Vietnam on a whim, at age twenty-three, hoping to write "something" about the war. On the basis of that trip, and another in 1967, he wrote two book-length articles for The

New Yorker *that were later published as* The Village of Ben Suc *and* The Military Half.

I wasn't very political in college but I do remember noticing that this Vietnam War seemed to be a sort of unsolvable problem. At the time, I didn't see how we could pull out and I suppose I bought into the domino theory. But I didn't see how we could win. It just looked bad. When I graduated from college in 1965, I went to Japan to study and spend a year abroad.

On the way back from Japan I had a round-the-world ticket that permitted me to stop anywhere I wanted. I had a certain ambition to be a writer of factual pieces so I decided I would go to Vietnam. I remember reading Bernard Fall's latest book on the plane, which was my little crash education. When I landed in Vietnam I was the very definition of a pest—a graduate student who had no knowledge and who vaguely thought he might like to write something. Somehow or other it occurred to me that Francois Sully might be in Vietnam working for *Newsweek.* He was a French reporter I'd met at Harvard when he was a Nieman Fellow so I called up the *Newsweek* office and, lo and behold, he was there and invited me over.

It was a loft-like office with a back room full of the pseudomilitary gear that journalists wore. When I greeted Sully I had Bernard Fall's book under my arm and mentioned that I had been reading it. There was another fellow at a desk who said, "Could I see the book?" So I went over and gave him the book. He opened it up and signed it. It was Bernard Fall!

So here were these two ebullient, life-loving Frenchmen, brave and brilliant journalists, both. And just out of sheer high spirits, they took me up—this nuisance, this pest, this ignorant graduate student. They used their connections to perform a kind of miracle. They persuaded the military to give me a press pass on the somewhat deceptive basis that I was there for the *Harvard Crimson.* I had actually written for the *Crimson,* and very possibly they would have wanted me reporting for them, but we made up that little tale.

Well, if you had a press pass in Vietnam, it was a free travel ticket all over the country. You could hitchhike rides on helicopters and transport planes, wherever you wanted. It was a meal ticket. It was a hotel reservation anywhere. It gave a fantastic freedom to see what you wanted to see. I think the reason was the cooperation between the press and the military during the Second World War, and the Korean War had carried over for a while to Vietnam.

So just a day or two later Fall and Sully called me up at my ratty hotel and said, "Something is going to happen. It's all secret, but you can go and see it if you want. Come over to such-and-such a place at four-thirty A.M. and there'll be a bus." These two wonderful journalists, both of whom later lost their lives in the war, gave me this one hundred and eighty degree life-changing gift, which set me on the journalistic path I've been on ever since.*

We got on a bus and were taken out to an airstrip where we were flown off in a C-5 to a big dusty field in the jungle. A spiffy major with an easel told us we were there for Operation Cedar Falls—the largest military operation of the war to that date. The idea was to clear out the infamous Iron Triangle [a forty-square-mile patch of jungle with its southernmost tip just a dozen miles north of Saigon], which had been the source of so much woe for the South Vietnamese army and a revolutionary stronghold since the war against the French. The American military wanted to clear it out once and for all. On the major's easel there was a great menu of things they were going to do. One of the items on the list was a helicopter attack on the village of Ben Suc. When we got to that item on the list, I asked, "What's going to happen to the village after it's attacked?"

The major said, "Well, we're going to destroy it and move the people out."

"Then what?" I said.

"Well, we're going to bulldoze it and bomb it."

So I thought, okay, I'll just follow that particular story from start to finish. It didn't feel like a singularly adventurous or bold thing to do. And I do recall one little act of cowardice. When they asked which of the sixty helicopters we wanted to go on, many of the journalists were clamoring to be on the first or second helicopter. I was delighted to be on helicopter number forty-seven.

You could say that the operation came off beautifully. It worked exactly as planned. The helicopters flew in, moved the people out, destroyed the village. Mission accomplished. But to what end? Most of the reporting about Operation Cedar Falls told you how many Viet Cong were captured or killed, and those may have been true facts. But they left out what I believed was fundamental—that we were destroying villages and throwing people off their land. The unmistakable fact was that the general population despised the United States and if they hadn't despised it before we arrived, they soon did after we destroyed their villages. Our whole goal was to build up a political system that would stand after we left, with a functioning government supported enough by its people so it could fight on its own. But our policies were destroying whatever support that government might ever have had, which was probably about zero to begin with. The more we'd win on the battlefield—and we did just about every day in just about every battle—the more we lost the political war. The more we "won," the more we lost. That was the paradox of Vietnam.

*Bernard Fall died in 1967 when he stepped on a land mine while covering a U.S. Marine operation. In 1971, Francois Sully leapt seventy-five feet from a burning helicopter and died several hours later. He left his life insurance to Vietnamese orphans.

American soldiers went over thinking they we were freeing an enslaved people from their oppressors. I do think the Communists were pretty oppressive. However, it just so happened that they were the representatives of national dignity and that seemed to trump whatever oppression they dealt out. Whatever the reason, the people by and large supported them and they were the de facto government of a very considerable part of South Vietnam. So the idea that the Viet Cong were a sort of mysterious band of people that could be rooted out and separated from the population at large just didn't have a basis in political reality.

One thing that struck me very powerfully was the capacity of both the officer corps and the press corps to see things in terms of a story they had brought with them to Vietnam and not to see what was actually going on under their noses. For example, when I came back to Vietnam in the summer of 1967 I went up to Quang Ngai Province and saw that the place was being leveled by American bombing. But when I got home, I remember reading a story in *The New York Times* about how the marines had built a hospital in this area. Apparently the Hiroshima-like devastation that was around that hospital was not visible to the reporters of *The New York Times* because they weren't telling about that.

And it wasn't a subtle thing. The fire and smoke was pouring up to the heavens. You didn't have to be a detective or do any investigative journalism. The flames were roaring around you. I mapped it all out and seventy, eighty percent of the villages were just dust—ashes and dust. But that was not the story. The story was still how we were going to help the South Vietnamese resist the attack from the North. In Vietnam I learned about the capacity of the human mind to build a model of experience that screens out even very dramatic and obvious realities.

When I first went back to Vietnam that summer I joined the journalistic pack, the "boys on the bus." What they were covering at the time was this fraudulent election, a completely farcical election. One day we were all taken to a village for a campaign rally, but the candidates somehow didn't make it. Apart from the journalists, the only person who showed up was an ancient guy going around with a bullhorn shouting that there was going to be an election rally. This was supposed to be democracy in action and we were the only people there.

To report on that as if it was something real would have been an absolutely absurd so I just took the next helicopter out and somehow decided to begin covering the air war in the South—the air slaughter, really. People had been writing about the bombing of North Vietnam, but the air war in the South was far more devastating and not getting much attention.

So in Quang Ngai I started going up in forward air control (FAC) planes—little Cessna two-seater spotter planes that would direct the pilots to their targets. These little planes were constantly turning and twisting, in part to avoid enemy ground fire. That and the overwhelming heat made me constantly nauseous. But I had my notebook right there in the plane and the setup was unbelievably perfect for reporting. It was as if it had been designed for reporting. It gave you this fantastic perch. You could sit over the scene of the action, witness it, and you were conveniently supplied with earphones in which you heard conversations among the pilots, the forward air controller, and the ground. The quotes were coming right into the earphones and I wrote them down as if it were a lecture at Harvard. It was an amazing stroke of journalistic luck.

The idea that the U.S. military was operating under constraints in South Vietnam is ridiculous. We pulverized villages from the air if we merely imagined that we received hostile fire. I witnessed it with my own eyes and I saw the leaflets we dropped which said, "If you fire on us, we will destroy your village," and then a follow-up leaflet that said, "You did fire on us, and we did destroy your village." And U.S. planes were actually bombing churches. They would see the church, target it, and blow it up. I saw that happen.

And sometimes they cracked jokes about it. They were trying to imagine that the war was something like World War II. When you were in the air you could try to forget about all the paradoxes of policy that made your very successes counterproductive. But I sensed a deep uneasiness and regret among the pilots. They sometimes sang rather brutal ditties that seemed to me like confessions in a way:

> *"Strafe the town and kill the people,*
> *Drop napalm in the square,*
> *Get out early every Sunday*
> *And catch them at their morning prayer."*

I wasn't inclined to blame the people doing it so much as the people ordering it. I got along well with the soldiers and their officers. I liked them very much. Maybe that was a defensive thing. It would have been very uncomfortable for me to be in a position of feeling fury at the people doing it. Those are deep questions. You know, just following orders is no excuse. These were atrocities—bombing villages from the air, just pulverizing houses, attacking people on the basis of little or no information. And there was this absurd supposition that if someone ran away from your attack, they automatically belonged to the Viet Cong.

It was a massacre from the air that was going on every day and I was a part of it in a way. I was kind of doing it. That was the feeling. The FACs were equipped with phosphorous rockets. They were used as markers for the bombers, but phosphorous rockets are particularly horrifying weapons—worse than napalm. It's something that burns that you can't put out. The rocket would blow up the house and then people would run out. I was witnessing from a distance, but I had a real feeling of complicity. I mean I didn't push the button, but I was there.

When I got back from Vietnam I met Jerry Wiesner, provost of MIT and a friend of my parents. He had been Kennedy's science adviser and knew Secretary of Defense McNamara. We had lunch and when I told him about what I'd seen in Vietnam he said, "Would you be willing to go and talk to McNamara about this?" I said, "Yeah, sure," and the meeting was arranged. So I went down to the Pentagon, where I'd never set foot, and was ushered into the secretary of defense's office. It's the size of a football field—a proper imperial size. And there was McNamara, all business as usual, with that slicked-back hair of steel. I began to tell my story and he said, "Come over to the map here and show me what you're talking about."

Well, I truly had my ducks in a row. I had overflown the entire province of Quang Ngai and half of Quang Tin. And so I really had chapter and verse. After a while he interrupted and asked, "Do you have anything in writing?" I said, "Yes, but it's all in longhand." So he said, "Well, I'll put you in General so-and-so's office—he's off in South America—and you can dictate it." And so for three days I sat in the general's office dictating my longhand, book-length *New Yorker* article on the air war in South Vietnam. Up from the bowels of the Pentagon would come typed copy. It was a dream for me, probably saving me a month's work because this was long before word processors.

Three days later, stinking to high heaven because I had no change of clothes, I reappeared in McNamara's office. I handed it to him, he took it, and that was the last I heard about it from him. But I learned later that a foreign service officer in Saigon was sent around Vietnam to retrace my steps and reinterview the pilots and the soldiers I had quoted. He even read back to the pilots the gruesome ditties they had sung for me at the bar. The foreign service officer had to admit that my book was accurate but he added, "What Schell doesn't realize is what terrible circumstances our troops are in. He doesn't realize that old ladies and children are throwing hand grenades because the people are against us." Hence, the Vietnam War makes sense because the South Vietnamese are against us!

So why couldn't we get out? When it became clear that the costs were so much greater than anything at stake on the ground in Vietnam itself, then why couldn't we just withdraw? None of the official war aims made much sense. It was hard to maintain that we were fighting for freedom or democracy in South Vietnam since the government we were defending was so obviously corrupt and dictatorial. Nor could we honestly claim to be preventing aggression when the only foreign combatants in Vietnam were Americans or soldiers paid for by the United States like the South Koreans. Even the domino theory seemed to fall apart in the face of intense nationalism, support for reunification throughout Vietnam, and the historical conflicts between Vietnam and China.

But the one justification that proved most durable was this idea of credibility. Fighting for American credibility was not a tangible goal; it was the defense of an image—an image of vast national strength and the will to use it. According to the doctrine of credibility, the United States was engaged in a global public-relations struggle in which a reverse in any part of the world, no matter how small, could undermine the whole structure of American power.

Part of the concern with maintaining credibility stemmed from a kind of psychological domino theory. In other words, policy makers worried that if the United States did not prevail in Vietnam, it would cast doubt on our determination to prevail anywhere. If the United States lost in Vietnam, then countries and revolutionaries all over the world would see that we were a paper tiger who couldn't win wars and they would be emboldened to resist our will. So what was at stake in Vietnam was the ability of the United States to maintain control all over the world on a psychological basis.

But there was another component of the doctrine of credibility that is in a way the most subtle and the least noticed, but I think the most important. It was nuclear policy. In nuclear strategy one of the crucial facts is that you can't actually fight a nuclear war. The moment that you fight the war you've lost it because everybody loses in a nuclear war. The purpose of deterrence is to prevent a nuclear war from happening. It depends entirely on producing a psychological impression in the mind of the enemy that you are a very tough guy—so tough you're ready to commit suicide and drag the enemy down with you.

Well that is a kind of crazy proposition. It doesn't have a lot of inherent credibility. Why would you commit suicide to defend yourself? So it's a real strain to keep producing an impression of toughness. All you could do in the arena of nuclear confrontation was build up your arms and talk tough. You couldn't prove your toughness by actually using the weapons. 'Round about the end of the 1950s there were a number of thinkers, including Henry Kissinger, who began to say, well, okay, we're paralyzed in the nuclear arena, but we can go out and win a few on the periphery. Here's a place where we can actually fight wars and show how tough we are. At the same time [Soviet Premier] Khrushchev began to talk about the necessity of fighting wars of national liberation in the Third World so the Soviets were making their own contribution to the rhetorical battle. Thus, the model for Vietnam was actually created before we ever went directly into that war. Because the so-called peripheral wars were supposedly winnable, and since they occurred in a context of a very shaky credibility based on nuclear weapons that you couldn't use, these limited wars came to bear an additional burden. It was as if World War III were being fought in Vietnam. In the nuclear age, the whole structure of credibility and deterrence seemed to depend on winning these wars out there on the periphery. This was the sort of theoretical trap that the policy makers found themselves in. They thought they were not only preventing the toppling of dominoes but total war itself. And if you believed the assumptions, then almost no cost was too high to pay in Vietnam.

Since the war he has written many books, including The Fate of the Earth, *his well-known jeremiad about the risks and consequences of nuclear war, but he has never gone back to Vietnam. "I have a mysterious resistance to it. There's a special psychology that was produced by the Vietnam War, which has elements of obsession and elements of avoidance. I think I have both. I feel very akin to the veterans. You somehow can't quite get rid of it but, on the other hand, you don't want to dwell on it and let it take over your life. In the first years after I came back from Vietnam I had dreams about it. There was one dream in which I was myself killing Vietnamese people with my bare hands. And children too. I was fighting with them in a ditch and trying to kill them. It was some kind of raw, elemental, purposeless fighting that was somehow going on. Yeah, they were attacking me or—and I was—I don't know. I don't know. I don't know."*

HARLAN S. PINKERTON JR.

"Good luck and good hunting."

Aside from the six years he served in the air force, he has lived his whole life in Sand Springs, Oklahoma. "My father and grandfather were members of the Sons of the American Revolution, my mother and grandmother were Daughters of the American Revolution, and as a child I was very active in the Children of the American Revolution. So I was patriotic before patriotism was cool."

From 1967 to 1968, he served with the 557th Tactical Air Squadron. Flying a Phantom F-4, most of his missions were over South Vietnam. He was based in Cam Ranh Bay, "where the sewer meets the sea. The only time the water dispensers were clear was when [President Lyndon] Johnson came to visit." He practices law and lives with his wife in the home his grandparents once owned.

There's nothing more gratifying than flying a jet plane and putting it through its maneuvers. When you light those burners and go screaming down the runway it's a tremendous sensation. You stroke those burners and feel fifty thousand pounds of thrust coming out the back end of that airplane. You've got that stick in your lap and you're just waiting for the nose to come up. Then you start playing with the back pressure on the stick and you're airborne. It's just a wonderful feeling.

After taking off, the most comforting thing we heard came from the Australians who had the radar site on top of the mountain out in Cam Ranh Bay. As they handed you off, the last thing they always said was, "Good luck and good hunting." Then, once you got to your target, you started trying to find your FAC [forward air controller]. Sometimes that was the hardest part because they flew little camouflaged Cessna 172s over heavily forested areas. Sometimes if you didn't see him he'd just shoot you a flare and say there it is. Basically you didn't know what you were doing. You were just dropping bombs on the flares. We'd roll in at a forty-five- to sixty-degree dive at four hundred and eighty knots and drop the bombs at about three thousand feet. You'd see the flare, but most of the time you couldn't see the ground.

One day we were scrambled off to some sort of army post that had a trench around the perimeter. The gooks were going through the trench and overrunning the place. So the lead plane would go by and put napalm in the trench. The ones that didn't get burned up would jump out and the number-two plane would come along and spray both sides of the trench with bullets. Then the enemy would jump back into the trench about the time the lead came around again with the napalm. We'd do that for four passes. Then we'd go off station and somebody else would come in behind us. I would like to tell you that I saw the enemy but I don't know that I did.

Daylight flights weren't usually in support of ground forces under attack. For example, you could be prepping a landing zone [bombing and strafing areas where ground troops would soon be inserted by helicopter]. But when you were scrambled at night, usually it was because ground troops were being overrun and you had to go out and drop your bombs to protect them. The greatest accomplishment was going from a sound sleep to being airborne at twenty thousand feet in fifteen minutes, going to your target, delivering your ordnance, and hoping that the ground troops were going to live one more day because of your ability to drop your bombs on your target.

On most days, you'd get up, go fly, come back, get debriefed, go back to the squadron to see if there was anything else you had to do, and then you were free to do whatever you wanted. You could chase Donut Dollies, you could sunbathe, you could go to the bar and start drinking, or you could go home and have a nap. At night you passed out after drinking so you took a nap in the afternoon when you were sober to make sure you could still go to sleep naturally. We called them "practice naps."

We had our own private clubs. The bar was a rectangular building in the middle of a courtyard with a red tile roof on it. There was a horseshoe bar inside with a big area to the side where you could dance or sit around and talk. It was a fully stocked bar but the only beer we could get was Carling Black Label and that's just like drinking tomcat piss.

We had this one colonel and every time he'd walk into the bar he said, "Anybody who can't tap dance is queer." So you'd see a whole bar of pilots get up and try to do the soft-shoe so they wouldn't be accused of being queer. We just got up and shuffled our feet, sat down, and went back to drinking.

The bar was open all night long. Then the wing commander got tired of pilots showing up hungover for the four A.M. flights and required all the bars to close at midnight. So at closing time we'd take four or five drinks with us out on the patio, put on an hour-and-a-half tape of music, and sit out on the patio to finish our drinks. We played the Doors, Gary Puckett and the Union Gap, Peter, Paul, and Mary, whatever the popular music was. Then we'd John Wayne our glasses off the red tile roof and listen to the glass sprinkle down on the patio. We had this banana tree in our courtyard and everybody'd stop on the way to their hootch and take a leak on the banana tree. You just hoped that thing never bore fruit. Then you'd stagger in and go to bed. You knew you had to be able to work the next day. You may have felt bad but you never canceled a flight unless you were sick from something other than alcohol.

We would get reports about the protests in the United States but it really didn't affect us. What we wanted to hear were the replays of the football games. Some guy's parents would tape-record the games and send them on a cassette. I remember I was disappointed that Oklahoma lost to Notre Dame while I was over there.

I never did sit around with my wife or friends and commiserate that we were going to war. To me, it was my responsibility as an American citizen. I didn't really question it. I had orders. My country had made the decision that we were going to take part in that conflict over there and it was my duty to my country to follow the orders. And if I was going to serve, I wanted to serve in a way I considered first-class. I wasn't gonna dig ditches. I wasn't gonna polish the brass on my uniform. And I can't complain about my orders. What more can you ask for? One, you're an officer and, two, you're a fighter pilot. You're a walking god. That was it.

When I went to Vietnam my uncle told me he wanted his name on a bomb, and so on Christmas Eve 1967, I went out with a stencil that said, "From Uncle Dave With Love." And then one of the backseaters came out with another stencil that said, "Merry Fucking Christmas." I had my picture made in front of that airplane with that bomb close up and sent it to him. He said it was one of the best Christmas presents he ever received. We still laugh about it.

"To this day I do not adhere to the idea that we lost the war. We withdrew and handed the reins over to the South Vietnamese. They're the ones that lost the war. They didn't have the stamina or the dedication to fight for their own country."

LUU HUY CHAO

"Before I trained as a pilot I had never been in an airplane."

An elfin man of sixty-seven with a strikingly dark bristle of hair, he flew a MiG-17 against American planes in the skies over North Vietnam. His entire chest is covered with decorations, including six highly coveted Ho Chi Minh medals, golden profiles of Ho on bright red fields. He received one for each American plane he shot down. Then there are more than a dozen silver and gold stars dangling from folded ribbons. As the former ace eagerly describes the tortuous path of his aircraft in battle, his medals clink and clack like wind chimes.

The first plane I ever saw close-up was a French aircraft shot down by the Viet Minh in the early 1950s when I was in my teens. I was so curious I walked more than fifteen kilometers to see it. It made me scared. I thought, I sure wouldn't want to end up like that pilot. He must have been a lot taller than I am and he still died. I'd rather be an infantryman. Near the end of the French War I was sent to Dien Bien Phu as a reinforcement, but the battle was already over by the time I arrived. A few years later the Vietnamese government was casting around for pilots and I was on their list. In 1957, I was accepted into the air force. In 1959, I went to China for six years of training.

Before I trained as a pilot I had never been in an airplane. I hadn't even been on a boat! The instructor put two of us in the back seat and took off. It felt so weird when he turned the plane and everything went upside down. I wasn't scared, just a little sick to my stomach. I had graduated from high school, but some of our best pilots only had elementary school educations. Like any discipline, some people are very good, some average, some not so good. I considered myself a little above average. The worst thing about the time in China was the weather. Every morning when we went to the airport, it was so cold my skin cracked.

When I got back to Vietnam in 1965, I immediately engaged in air combat with American pilots. The first time I shot an American plane was in February 1966 over the skies of my home province, Thanh Hoa. It wasn't a real battle because the enemy target was just a C-47 [cargo plane]. It was transporting some southern commandos who were going to parachute in to sabotage the area. As far as I know, Americans did not fly that plane. My formation consisted of four MiG-17s. When I saw the enemy plane, the squadron commander ordered me to attack. The C-47 pilot was smart. As soon as he saw us, he dropped his altitude and swiveled through the mountain range. He must have known that a MiG-17 can't fire effectively below six hundred meters. Since he was under me, I put on my brakes to tilt my guns at the right angle. The first shots went ahead of him. I shot again and it exploded. The following day people found eleven bodies at the crash site. They were all Vietnamese.

Once I had a brush with four F-105s in the sky above Nghia Lo. We were on a routine sortie and I discovered the F-105s at six kilometers altitude. I asked my number one for permission to engage them and he said, "Go ahead, I'll back you up." So we immediately rose up and the Americans saw us. Two of them dove down and two of them turned to attack us from behind. I did not hesitate for a moment because I realized I was in a very serious situation. I immediately turned around and fired at one of the two attacking F-105s. It immediately exploded. The other guy was busy looking at his friend and went too low. The F-105 has a kind of automatic pilot system that keeps it from dropping below fifteen hundred meters. But the mountains in that area are more than two thousand meters. He crashed into the mountains. The other two F-105s flew away. When I came back they said I shot down both planes, but I denied it. When the film from my plane was developed I said, "You see, I just shot down one of them."

I met President Ho Chi Minh on three occasions. The most memorable time was after I had shot down my fourth plane, and he invited some pilots to his office. He gave us candies and watched some movies with us and offered us words of encouragement. Basically he said, "This is the first time we have fought the enemy in our skies." Then he pointed a finger at each of us. "You have shot down two planes, you have shot down three planes, and you have shot down four planes. That's great. But don't be overconfident. You must be extra careful when you fight the Americans. They come from a very advanced country and their aircraft are much faster and more powerful. Even so, we can deal with them if we keep up our spirit and never lose our courage."

What President Ho said was true. The F-4, F-8, and F-105 flew so fast! Their maximum speed was two thousand five hundred and sixty kilometers an hour while the maximum speed of the MiG-17 was just a thousand and sixty kilometers an hour. And we never went the maximum because it could break our wings. The whole plane shook when you went too fast. Plus, we had to slow down to fire. All the MiG-17s we had were twenty years old. The mechanics were very simple. I had three buttons in front of me. If I wanted to use the two machine guns on the wings I pressed one button. If I wanted to use the cannon on the nose, I pressed another. And if I wanted to use all three, I pressed the third button.

Now that the war is over, I want to be completely honest. I had only three hundred .47-caliber bullets. In just a few seconds of air combat I would run out of bullets. But most of the time, when American pilots saw us they just flew away in a flash. I never caught any of them. We flew almost every day, but only rarely did I have a chance to fight. When I discovered American planes they were always above me and I rose up to meet them. Then, poof, they disappeared in an instant.

One time an F-4's rocket hit one of my wings. I heard a big explosion and passed out immediately. My plane fell into the clouds until I was only two kilometers from the ground. Ordinarily, when an American aircraft hits you with a rocket your time has come. Fortunately, I came to and managed to land. I went right to the air controller and said, "Why didn't you tell me there was an F-4 tailing me like that?"

Not counting the "Dien Bien Phu in the sky" [a common Vietnamese expression for Richard Nixon's "Christmas bombing" of Hanoi and Haiphong in 1972], the most violent period of the air war was probably April and May 1967. For example, on May 19, President Ho's birthday, the Americans launched a massive air attack over the skies of Hanoi. In response we sent up more than thirty MiGs. This period was so violent it was the first time our antiaircraft units accidentally shot down our own MiGs. Cases of friendly fire also took place among American pilots. We know that some American jets were shot down by air-to-air missiles, and since our MiGs didn't have missiles, they had to come from other American planes.

Once I had shot down an F-4, I was no longer scared of any type of American aircraft. The psychological factor is very important in any battle, especially in the air. The Americans shot down a lot of our planes, but part of my confidence came from knowing that if I had to bail out I would be landing in my own country. An American pilot in the same situation must have been very scared of the Vietnamese people waiting for him down below. Being bombed made them so enraged they were ready to kill him with anything they could lay their hands on.

Many times my comrades dove down to shoot at an American parachuting to the ground and I ordered them to stop. I would say, "He won't attack us again. Let him alone." One time when I tried my best to stop a man in my squadron from shooting, he said, "Why not? They do it to us." I said, "Well, we're different."

Once I had a chance to talk with a former American pilot and I told him, "We were only soldiers, we didn't cause the war." American pilots had to obey their commanders. That's a fact. The suffering caused by war is immeasurable. The dead are only a small part of the whole. A dead soldier causes suffering to so many other people—his father, his mother, his siblings, his relatives, his friends. It was such a tragic war and it caused serious consequences on both sides, especially ours. As a fighter pilot I'm not sorry to have shot down American jets, and American pilots shouldn't be sorry if they shot down Vietnamese aircraft. That's what we were supposed to do. Now my only wish is that there be no war.

NGUYEN QUANG SANG

"That was the first time I ever saw an American."

A well-known writer of short stories, novels, and screenplays, he still has the unaffected country accent of An Giang Province, about two hundred miles southwest of Saigon, where he grew up. In 1940, when he was eight, many of his neighbors joined the resistance against the French. One day, some of them were arrested. "They were tied together with a steel wire pierced through their palms and led away."

We meet at the Writers Association in Ho Chi Minh City on his sixty-seventh birthday. He is barely five feet tall, but his shoulders and arms are thick and powerful. During the American war he served in a Literature and Arts Section ("Van Nghe"), providing entertainment and inspiration for soldiers from the North and southern guerrillas.

When I fought against the French everyone saw me as a little kid, a young messenger boy. But when I fought against the Americans, I was the oldest guy in my unit. They saw me as a father figure and called me "Pop."

Most of the time I lived deep in the jungle and didn't do any fighting.

When everything was quiet I would lie in my hammock and write stories. We even had a publishing house in the jungle. We printed books, newspapers, and leaflets. The famous *Liberation (Giai Phong)* newspaper was printed in the jungle. A lot of young soldiers who wrote poetry and prose sent us their works. We published the ones we liked and returned the others with our comments on how they could be improved. After I finished writing one of my own short stories, I telegraphed it to Hanoi and the government would have it read over the radio on the "Evening Stories" program. It was broadcast all over Vietnam, even in the South. As long as you had the right frequency you could hear it. Every soldier knew my stories because there was no alternative entertainment.

In 1966, a bomb from a B-52 hit a house only thirty meters away. All five people in the house were killed. That was my first real taste of the American War. But I had a more nightmarish experience when I was transferred to Dong Thap Muoi near my hometown. There was no jungle there—only water below and the sky above—so it was much easier for the helicopters to spot you. Those of us in the Van Nghe section just carried pistols. Only regular soldiers were authorized to carry rifles and shoot at the helicopters. If we had tried and missed, we knew from experience that they would just call in a bunch of jets to drop bombs on our heads. So whenever helicopters attacked we tried our best to hide or keep still and hope they thought we were just common peasants.

One day in 1968 our unit was following a group of soldiers moving toward Saigon when a helicopter saw us and pinned us down. It was scarier than the B-52 attacks because those bombers flew so high they couldn't see you. They just dropped their bombs indiscriminately and flew off. If the bombs got you, you'd die instantly without even knowing you'd been hit. But when the helicopters spotted us, we had to run for our lives. It was terrifying. The area was completely open. There was only water, water everywhere. So when the helicopters approached I just dove into a canal. From eight to five I hid in that canal with a lot of other people. Helicopters came and went, hovering over us all day long. Often we had to hold our breath and dive as deep as possible. When the gunners stopped firing, we popped up for air. I saw many people killed around me, including the painter Hoang Anh. Once, when a helicopter dropped down especially close to the water, I even saw the face of the door gunner. That was the first time I ever saw an American. I'm still haunted by it in my nightmares. Whenever there's a change in the weather I have the same nightmare—a helicopter chases me and I have to hide in the water.

In 1980, he wrote the screenplay for a Vietnamese film called The Wasted Field. *"That movie was completely based on my experience of being chased by helicopters."*

FRED BRANFMAN

"What would it be like to hide in a cave day after day for five years?"

From 1967 to 1971 he lived in Laos. He was hard to miss. In addition to being six feet, three inches tall—the Laotians nicknamed him "Mountain"—he walked around wearing Viet Cong–style black pajamas, had long bushy hair, and wore an assortment of traditional string bracelets and Buddha necklaces.

He went to Laos for International Voluntary Services, a nonprofit organization devoted to education and economic development in Third World countries. After two years, having become fluent in Lao, he decided to stay on as a freelance interpreter and journalist. He was one of the first Westerners to expose the fact that the United States had been secretly bombing northern Laos since 1964. Many of the attacks focused on the Plain of Jars, a high plateau controlled by the Laotian Communists, the Pathet Lao. It had been populated by some fifty thousand Laotian peasants who lived among six-foot-tall vessels believed to have been ancient funeral urns—the famous jars of the plain. In September 1969, Branfman and British journalist T. D. Allman interviewed survivors of that bombing, some of the tens of thousands of refugees who had been moved from their villages to refugee camps by the Americans and their Royal Lao allies.

The first conversation changed my whole life. We just walked up and started talking to this peasant. We asked, "Why are you here?"

He said, "Well, the planes were bombing us."

"Really? How long have they been bombing you?"

"Five years." I'll always remember how he squatted down and drew an L in the ground. It was a picture of the cave they had hidden in during the day. They would go inside this cave to hide from the planes. What would it be like to hide in a cave day after day for five years, terrified of being killed?

Every single one of the refugees told the same basic story. The bombing started in May 1964, slowly accelerated, and got really bad in 1968. I later found out that when Johnson declared the bombing halt over North Vietnam just prior to the November '68 election they simply diverted all the planes into northern Laos. Then Nixon and Kissinger came in and leveled the entire Plain of Jars.

The refugees told us that the Pathet Lao soldiers were the last people to be hit. They moved through the forest and could protect themselves. Northern Laos is very heavily forested and the only clearings are the villages. The U.S. military would always define a village as a bivouac storage area or transshipment point, but they were nothing but villages of wooden huts that burned easily. There was no running water or electricity.

Many of the air strikes dropped "pineapple bombs"—antipersonnel bombs. They couldn't destroy trucks or antiaircraft emplacements. They were only meant to kill people. They'd shoot two hundred and fifty thousand pellets across an area the size of a football field. Then they refined them with these little fleshettes so they'd enter your body and were almost impossible to remove.

I felt three levels of horror. The first was just anger. I couldn't believe the American executive branch had been bombing this country without telling anyone. Nobody knew about it. Even Congress didn't know. It was incredible. The second level was seeing kids with missing legs and listening to some guy who's telling you about his grandmother being burned alive in front of his eyes. But the ultimate horror was realizing that the bombing was still continuing. From that day in September 1969 until the war ended, I worked twenty-four hours a day, seven days a week, to stop the bombing. Not that I thought I could, but all I knew is that I had to. I rarely discussed anything other than the war. It just transported me into a whole other state of consciousness. You had the United States, the most powerful people in the world, bombing the weakest people in the world.

One of the refugees I interviewed turned out to be a former Pathet Lao soldier named Ngeun. He was a fantastic character. His story was that the Pathet Lao had told him to come down with the refugees because he was too undisciplined to be a soldier, but he believed in them and made no bones about it. I loved the guy. He lived with me for six months and we talked about the Pathet Lao every night. I learned all sorts of things. For example, a basic guerrilla tactic is to attack fixed emplacements. The guy who goes first falls on the barbed wire and then the others climb on his body to get over. I'm thinking, Jesus, no one would want to do that, so I said, "It must have been tough to get guys to volunteer for that." He said, "No, no. You don't understand. Everybody volunteered. They killed my mother, I want to go first, I want to be the one." To this day, I believe he was telling me the truth.

Then one night before we went to bed I said, "Let me ask you a question. What exactly do you want out of all this?" He was very somber and serious and said, "Look, Fred, I've already almost died so many times I really don't expect to be alive when the Pathet Lao win, but I do hope that years from now when someone says, 'Hey, whatever happened to old Ngeun?' someone will say, 'Oh yeah, Ngeun. He loved the people.' "

In the late eighties, the Lao minister of culture was putting together a commemorative volume for Souphanouvong—who was sort of the Ho Chi Minh of Laos. I agreed to write a chapter called "The Sons and Daughters of Prince Souphanouvong." I told the story of Ngeun. I didn't know what had happened to him and had the idea he was dead. I ended by writing, "Ngeun, wherever you are, I just want you to know that somewhere, someplace, someone is saying, 'Ngeun, he loved the people.' "

In 1993, I went back to Laos and found out Ngeun was still alive. We went up to the Plain of Jars and spent a week together. But instead of being the young, strong guy I remembered, he's got a potbelly and looks like an alcoholic. His story is that when the Pathet Lao took over he was overjoyed. He got a really important job in charge of the books for the general who ruled Vientiane. For a year he's ecstatically happy and then one day the general comes to him and tells him to falsify the books 'cause he wants to steal some money. Ngeun refused and was thrown in prison for seven years without a trial. One night when we were up on the Plain of Jars we got drunk and he said, "I had to eat grass to survive, Fred, I had to eat grass." Seven years. That was enough to sour me on the Pathet Lao.

As I look back on it, I realize I was naive and wrong in my belief that if the North Vietnamese and Pathet Lao won it would usher in a better world. Communism is obviously no better than capitalism. But I certainly have no regrets that I tried to stop the bombing.

The most disturbing legacy of the war is that we don't teach our children that our country is capable of conducting mass murder of civilians. I agree with William Bennett and the right wing that there's been a coarsening of American life, a desensitization to the value of human life. But most of it began with our war in Indochina and conservatives bear most of the blame. People like Henry Kissinger never thought of the Indochinese as humans, as people who had as much right to live as we do.

At a very deep level we were betrayed by our elders. One of the most profound things that happened to this country was that an entire baby boom generation, at least on an unconscious level, knew that their parents were prepared to see them die for a cause they didn't believe in. This generational betrayal applies both to antiwar people like myself and Vietnam veterans. Many vets were the most angry. I think a lot of them know how they were sold out by their leaders who never really cared whether they lived or died.

We baby boomers grew up in the aftermath of the "Good War" and in the fifties we really believed in America. We had a coherent value system. Then along comes Vietnam and every ideal was totally destroyed. I think that shock threw an entire generation into a moral abyss and I don't think we've crawled out of it yet. We've lucked out through economic prosperity and no war, but we all know deep down inside that this place feels kind of empty.

In 1971, the Laos government expelled him from the country because of his persistent efforts to reveal the scope of America's secret bombing. He returned to the United States to form Project Air War and the Indochina Resource Center, both organizations devoted to ending the war. He also published a collection of short essays written by Laotian refugees called Voices from the Plain of Jars.

PRISONERS OF WAR (I)

When most Americans think of a Vietnam War POW they envision a gray-haired ex-fighter pilot who was shot down over North Vietnam and held captive in the "Hanoi Hilton." Traumatic as their experience was, it was not widely shared. Fewer Americans were captured and imprisoned in Vietnam than in any major war of the twentieth century. There were roughly 800 U.S. POWs in the Vietnam War, compared to more than 7,000 in the Korean War, and 130,000 in World War II. The Vietnam POWs comprised not only a small fraction of U.S. forces, but were also in many ways an unrepresentative sample. While the military as a whole was comprised primarily of young, racially diverse, working-class, high school graduates, the typical American POW was a thirty-year-old, middle-class, college-educated pilot.

American POWs were also a small minority of the total number of Vietnam War POWs. The overwhelming majority were Vietnamese. At the time of the Paris Peace Accords in 1973, the government of South Vietnam had more than forty thousand Viet Cong and North Vietnamese prisoners. If political prisoners are included in the total, the number may be three to five times as high, and vast numbers of South Vietnamese suspected of pro–Viet Cong activities were imprisoned briefly for interrogation and released. Many were imprisoned more than once. War-related captivity in South Vietnam affected hundreds of thousands of individuals and countless family members who tried to visit their relatives in prison, bring food and clothing, or, when possible, bribe officials to release them.

The Communist side took far fewer South Vietnamese prisoners during the war, in part because of the difficulty of holding them in jungle prison camps or transporting them to the North. Yet their numbers certainly exceeded those of American POWs. And after the war the Socialist Republic of Vietnam put approximately one million of its former enemies in "reeducation camps," a polite euphemism for prisons that subjected people to intense political indoctrination and forced labor.

Put another way, every Vietnamese directly involved in the war was vulnerable to imprisonment. For Americans, unless you flew on missions over North Vietnam, your odds of becoming a POW were slim.

PORTER HALYBURTON

"I don't see how you've got a worse place than this."

A professor of strategy, he is talking in his tidy, book-lined office at the Naval War College. A colleague interrupts to borrow a copy of Thucydides. The soft-spoken man from Davidson, North Carolina, picks up where he left off. He has the kind of calming voice you would gladly hear from the cockpit when the turbulence is bad. As the "backseater" in a two-man Navy F-4 Phantom, his responsibilities included radar, navigation, and radio communications. In October 1965, on his seventy-fifth mission, his plane was shot down over North Vietnam. He was imprisoned until 1973.

More than half the missions I flew were at night. As we flew over the ocean from our aircraft carrier—the *Independence*—you could see all these lights. But as soon as they heard us coming they would sound an alarm, so by the time we got over land just about all the lights in the whole country would go out. Most of the time we were out looking for truck convoys going from north to south to connect to the Ho Chi Minh Trail. We were not very good at it. The Vietnamese were masters at camouflage. They put fresh-cut greenery over the top of trucks. They'd hear you coming and pull off the side of the road where they just looked like a clump of bushes.

We'd go out there with four Phantoms—fifteen million dollars worth of airplanes—just looking for trucks on the road, and we weren't going to find them. So what do you do? You can't bring the bombs back, so you've got to find a place to get rid of them. Usually, you had to go to Tiger Island and just dump your bombs there. It was known to be heavily occupied by North Vietnamese troops and it was kind of a free-fire zone. I can't imagine how many tons and tons of ordnance we dropped on Tiger Island.

We were very frustrated that our targets were not very significant. If we bombed a bridge, three or four days later it was fixed, or they had constructed a ford. They also moved industries out into the jungles. And flying in the North, we were very, very constrained. In the South, the B-52s would lay down a string of thousand-pound bombs and just completely devastate the entire area. But in the North, President Johnson said, "You're not going to bomb an outhouse up there without my permission." The rules said we couldn't even attack a SAM [surface-to-air missile] site unless they launched a missile at us first. We had to send in somebody as bait to try to get them to fire a missile so we could attack the SAM sites. That kind of stuff really infuriated us.

Some places were very heavily defended. You just could not believe the barrage of antiaircraft fire. The day I got shot down, there were thirty-five airplanes in our flight. It was the largest strike of the war up until that time. Our target was a major bridge on the road that comes down from China to Hanoi. We were flying flak suppression. Our job was to use our rockets to fight it out with the antiaircraft sites and then the bombers were going to attack the bridge.

I saw the flak coming from the right. You don't hear anything, you just see the little black puffs. All of a sudden there was this thud. We took a hit right in the cockpit. The airplane was still flying level but I could see the pilot's helmet was gone. Papers were blowing all around the cockpit. I put my hand up to my oxygen mask and realized it was blown away. Then I looked down and saw a big piece of metal sticking out of my hand. I pulled that out and then pulled my ejection handle.

It happened so quickly. One minute you're sitting there and the next minute your parachute is opening. I could hear people shooting at me. I could hear bullets going through the canopy of the parachute. I landed pretty close to this village on the side of a little hill. There wasn't anyplace to hide. I tried to get away but I had a lot of gear on and my mouth just turned to cotton. I couldn't go full speed for long. When I had to stop and rest they pretty much surrounded me. They took my boots off and I had to walk barefoot to the village.

I have to tell a story about those boots. I went back to Vietnam last year and we went to the Army Museum. Inside this Plexiglas display case were these boots and you could see part of the name inside the boot. I leaned way over and there was my name! Those boots looked like they had been around. Somebody had obviously worn them for a while before they wound up in the museum.

Anyway, they took me back to the village, put me in a kind of animal shed, let me smoke cigarettes, brought me some water and a bowl of rice. After a couple of hours the army showed up in a jeep and we began our trip to Hanoi. They told me, "If you cooperate with us, and repent for your crimes, we will move you to a new camp, a really nice place. You'll be with all your friends. You'll have nice food and you can play games and write to your family. But if not, we'll move you to a worse place." Sure enough I was moved to the "Zoo."

I had nothing in there. It was completely dark. And yet at the top of the bricks there was a space of about three inches for ventilation that was covered with bars and shutters. One day I heard a noise up near the vent. I put my bed board up against the wall and climbed up to look. A tree had forced a leaf up between the shutters—a green leaf. I took that as a sign that no matter how isolated I was, God was somehow going to send me a sign.

But I wouldn't cooperate so they moved me to an even worse place—a coal storage area. Ants, rats, mosquitoes by the ton. They would put my shitty little bowl of rice outside the door and leave it there for hours. By the time they finally gave it to me, it was completely covered with ants. It was inedible. I had dysentery by then and was getting disheartened. I hadn't talked to an American in months. The constant interrogation and indoctrination were wearing me down. I was about at the end of my rope and they're telling me again, "If you don't cooperate, we're going to move you to a worse place."

I said, "I don't see how you've got a worse place than this." That's when they moved me in with Fred Cherry. They said, "You must care for him. You must be his servant." I think they thought that would be the worst thing they could do—order a white guy to be a servant to this black guy. They very definitely tried to pit the two of us against each other, but it didn't take us long to become friends. I lived with Fred for eight months. He went through an awful time.

Fred had punched out of an F-105 at about six hundred knots. His arm was just about ripped off and he had a broken foot. He couldn't do anything. They decided to operate on him and that's when his real troubles began. He was out of his mind with infection. Pus was dripping out of his cast. It was just horrible. He really couldn't do anything so I had to bathe him and feed him and help him go to the bucket. And I started really raising hell with the camp authorities to give him antibiotics.

Fred credits me with saving his life. I don't know about that, but I am certain that he turned my life around. When I moved in with him I said to myself, "God, this guy's in a lot worse shape than I am and he's not complaining." I had been out of touch with other people and was beginning to feel pretty sorry for myself. Taking care of Fred gave me a sense of purpose outside my own survival. It was very liberating. It was really the beginning of the idea that we were all in a brotherhood, all part of a big family. We would do anything for each other.

On June 29, 1966, the United States bombed a target in Hanoi, an oil and lubricant storage area. The Vietnamese claimed we'd bombed civilian targets and all that kind of crap, as they always did. They launched this big propaganda campaign, and on July 6 sixty of us were marched through Hanoi, handcuffed in pairs. They told us we had to endure the anger of the Vietnamese people and show that we were repentant and bow our heads. Every time we raised our head we'd get hit on the back of the head with a rifle. So we started marching down the middle of the street and we had armed guards on either side. The crowds were lined up on the curbs. You could hear the Vietnamese guards prompting the crowds to yell slogans and chants. "Yankee imperialists! Air pirates! Murderers!"

The crowds got out of control and we were hammered. They pressed in and we got hit with mud, shoes, spit. That was really the only time during my captivity that I thought I probably was not going to make it. Even the guards were in a panic. Fortunately, they opened the gates to a stadium and we all kind of pushed in there and left most of the crowd outside. Then we went back to the prison.

Right after that I was moved to a prison out in the country that was very primitive—"the Briarpatch"—and they began a systematic torture program to force us to write confessions. First, they just beat the crap out of you to soften you up. Or they made you sit on a little wooden stool for days. It became a gauge of your endurance. My limit was about three days before I collapsed from lack of sleep and food and water. We found out you could get a little water by faking sleep. They'd throw water on your face to wake you up and if you opened your mouth you could get a little swallow.

After that, the torture began. The method they used on me we called "max-cuffs." Your arms were pulled up behind your back and then they put these handcuffs on the upper part of your arm. Then they tied a rope on your wrists and pulled it up. I could actually see my fingertips over the top of my head when they did that. It pressed the nerves against the bone. It was like molten metal flowing through your veins—just indescribable pain.

They did that until they got the documents they wanted. One time it was for a confession, one time it was for biographical information, another time it was for a list of military missions. They did it repeatedly. It was much more difficult to refuse after you'd already given a certain kind of confession. The first time was the most devastating. I was in really bad shape. It was the middle of the night and if you wanted to speak to an interrogator or report anything you were supposed to say "*bao cao*" to the roving guard. It means "report." I was yelling "*bao cao, bao cao.*" I was really in bad shape.

Psychologically, I think this was more damaging than the physical torture because you felt like you had completely failed. You had given up. You had capitulated. You had violated the code of conduct. You'd let everybody down. It was very depressing. Eventually I found out that everybody else, including the people I respected the most—like Jim Stockdale and Jerry Denton and Robert Risner—had been through exactly the same thing and had reacted pretty much the same way I did.

At first we really tried to stick strictly to name, rank, service number, and date of birth. But it was a very unrealistic approach. You were taught that you should be willing to give up your life before saying anything more, but what if you can't kill yourself and they don't kill you? What if it's just continual, unbearable pain? We began to realize that nobody was successful in just saying no. Everybody had some physical limit. So it soon became an official policy among American prisoners that we all had permission to give up after we had been tortured. It almost sounds un-American but it was very practical. The ranking officers gave us guidance. You were to give up when you still had some mental acuity and could lie effectively. If you held out to the very end you'd have no mental skills at all. So you were supposed to accept some torture but it was okay to give up and make up some kind of cover story. We became adept at lying and covering up and using their ignorance of American customs and history and language and humor.

For example, the Vietnamese wanted to get evidence of war crimes to send to the Bertrand Russell war crimes tribunal in Stockholm. So they selected a navy F-4 crew to write a confession. They were tortured to do it and they wrote this confession. They had to confess to everything short of nuclear weapons—bombing schools, hospitals, civilians, dams, dikes, everything. And they had to give a list of people in their squadron. So they gave them the squadron roster and the Vietnamese took this off to Stockholm and read the list. The commander of the squadron was Dick Tracy and the other men included Clark Kent, and a whole bunch of other comic strip characters. This was an international embarrassment, because to force a POW to make a written statement is a war crime in itself, so they really indicted themselves. I think they finally figured out that we hated them enough that we would try to screw them at every opportunity.

By 1969 I was living in the Zoo Annex in a room with eight other men. Shortly after Ho Chi Minh died in September of that year we began to see changes. I think they realized that torture hadn't worked very well and took Ho's death as an opportunity to change their policy. They hadn't really converted anybody and couldn't trust the stuff they forced from us. Also, Americans were making a big deal about our treatment, wearing POW bracelets and sending letters by the truckload to the Vietnamese delegation in Paris. I think the Vietnamese worried that this outcry might jeopardize the antiwar support they had nurtured so carefully.

They stopped taking us out for interrogations as much and the food improved. They added a meal—breakfast—a piece of bread with some grease and sugar on it. The cigarette ration was upped from three to six a day and they let us outside a bit more. Then we got to write and receive letters. The letter from my wife in 1970 was the first one in five years. But the biggest change was they quit torturing people

They also built a special prison from the ground up that was to hold everybody. Compared to every other place it was pretty nice. There was even an area where they said they were going to put a Ping-Pong table and let us all out together during the daytime. But after we had been there a few months the Son Tay raid occurred.* After Son Tay they moved us all to the Hanoi Hilton [Hoa Lo Prison] and that ended a pretty good deal.

Security was tighter after Son Tay, but they didn't torture anyone on a regular basis, plus they kept us in big cells with forty or fifty people and we were so damn happy to be in a bigger group. During the years of solitary confinement we had communicated with other POWs using a tap code—tapping on the walls. During the time I was tortured I mainly tapped on the wall with Howie Dunn, a marine F-4 pilot. I poured out my heart to him. We talked about what the Vietnamese were doing to us, we talked about food, we talked about women, we talked about our past lives and what we wanted to do in the future. We tapped for hours. At one point I said, "Howie, what do you look like?" He tapped back and said, "Actually, I look a lot like John Wayne." We were moved away from each other and I didn't talk to him for about five years. Right before we were coming home the Vietnamese allowed us to all get out together in a big compound and "greet one another" as they said. So I'm standing there talking to some people and this guy walks up to me—he's short and bald and nondescript, a complete and absolute stranger. I had never laid eyes on him before. He sticks out his hand and says, "Hi, I'm Howie Dunn." In a flash, there he was, my best friend.

After the war, he began hearing claims that some U.S. POWs had not been released by the Vietnamese and were still being held captive. "That really concerned me because we had tried so hard to make sure that didn't happen. We had memorized the name of every American in the North Vietnamese prison system, plus his rank, service, type of airplane, and date of shoot-down. We thought we knew them all." Still, doubts nagged at him and in the early eighties he and some other ex-POWs pledged two million dollars to any Southeast Asian who brought out a genuine American POW. "News of this reward was disseminated over radio and by leaflet drops and plugged into every

*On November 21, 1970, army rangers attempted to rescue U.S. POWs at Son Tay prison camp, about twenty miles northwest of Hanoi. The plan failed because the prisoners had been moved to another compound several months earlier.

grapevine. Laos was filthy with people trying to sell phony bones and ID cards, but no one every produced a POW. That to me is as telling as anything that no POWs were left behind."

TRUONG MY HOA

"They tried to make us say, 'Down with President Ho!'"

She is the vice-chair of the Vietnamese National Assembly and a member of the Central Committee of the Communist Party. We sit at one end of an enormous meeting hall in Hanoi's National Assembly under a huge portrait of Ho Chi Minh. She is dressed in a formal, dark blue "ao dai"—a high-necked, long-sleeved tunic with split sides, worn over trousers—the traditional dress of Vietnamese women. An interpreter hunches over in his chair behind us and a handful of colleagues and assistants sit at a distance. A television cameraman videotapes the interview.

A southern revolutionary, she was admitted to the Communist Party in 1963 at the age of eighteen. She was imprisoned for eleven years by the American-backed government of South Vietnam. Her voice is barely louder than a whisper—a quiet voice in a large room.

I was born to a revolutionary family and inherited a revolutionary tradition. My hometown of Tien Giang was a revolutionary hotbed. My parents had taken part in the resistance war against the French for which both were arrested and imprisoned. My brothers and sisters and I were imprisoned during the American War. Altogether my family spent half a century in jail.

In 1954, my father regrouped to the North in compliance with the Geneva Accords. My mother remained in the South with the children and, like everybody else, she thought that general elections would be implemented two years later and the country, as well as all the families, would be reunited. However, the puppet government of Ngo Dinh Diem unilaterally carried out a bloody war, supported by American imperialists.

I began to participate in the revolution at age fifteen, in 1960, when the Saigon regime took its guillotine throughout the South to behead patriotic revolutionaries and even nonrevolutionary common people. I realized in my heart that we had no alternative but to struggle against the Diem government and its henchmen. That was the only way we could achieve peace, independence, and unification. Because of Diem's terror in the countryside, my mother took us to

Saigon. There, right in the gorge of the puppet regime, I became a revolutionary. I participated in propaganda aimed at mobilizing high school and college students. We urged them to resist military conscription and the invasion of our country by American imperialists.

I was arrested on April 15, 1964. The Saigon Military Tribunal accused me of disrupting order and political stability. I was officially sentenced to eighteen months of confinement, but they kept prolonging the sentence and held me in prison for eleven years. I was released on March 7, 1975. I experienced all kinds of imprisonment—Gia Dinh Police Headquarters, Thu Duc Prison, Chi Hoa Jail, Tan Hiep Jail, and twice I was imprisoned for one year in a tiger cage on Poulo Condore [Con Son Island].

A tiger cage was about one and a half meters wide and about two meters long. Inside they built a cement pillory used to shackle the feet of prisoners. Overhead were iron bars where they always had three things: a pail of powdered limestone, a can of water, and a set of rattan whips. The wardens walked on top of the cages and whenever they discovered us talking they poured powdered limestone down on us. We were so choked we couldn't even cry out in pain. The lime was burning hot and if they poured water into it the burns were even worse. The lime got caught in our hair so we sharpened the edge of a can and cut off our hair.

In the tiger cages we weren't allowed to take a shower for the whole year and we were given only one set of clothes. Five women were confined together in one cage—eating, urinating, and defecating in that tiny place. When we had our periods we had to tear our pants and sleeves into rags to use as sanitary napkins. By the end of the year we barely had anything left on our bodies and sometimes we were completely naked. I'm sorry to have to mention that, but I want to emphasize that Vietnamese women are very sensitive about exposing their bodies.

An American congressional delegation came on a fact-finding mission to Poulo Condore and saw with their own eyes what we had to endure. We told the delegation everything. Consequently, the world came to know about the existence of tiger cages in a regime backed up by American imperialists. The news came like a bombshell.*

One time the puppet government gave the death sentence to three Communists, one of whom was my brother-in-law, Le Minh Chau. But the Hanoi

*In July 1970, two congressmen and an aide (now Senator Thomas Harkin) were led to the tiger cages by Don Luce, who had spent more than a decade in Vietnam, much of it as director of the International Voluntary Services. Luce's efforts exposed the tiger cages to international attention. A year later he was expelled from the country by the South Vietnamese government.

government responded immediately by claiming that three American pilots would be executed in retaliation. One of the three pilots was John McCain. The American government had to intervene and ask the Saigon government to stop the execution to save the lives of their pilots.

Over the years I underwent a lot of interrogation and torture. I was beaten with a police bludgeon and an electric whip. My hands were put in an electric vise. My hands, legs, and fingertips were hammered with nails. We were spread-eagled on a long table and tied down. They poured soapy water into our noses and mouths. Sometimes they put a hose into our mouths and turned it on. They used to tie our hands to a beam and let us hang so that our feet did not touch the ground. Then they hit us back and forth as we swung between two men, each one taking turns hitting us. They called this "flying a plane." Many of my comrades died in prison and many were permanently disabled. Some women were blinded and some crippled. I fared better, but my body still suffers.

Always they asked if we were going to talk, or not, and they slandered our political loyalties. They tried to make us salute their flag and condemn Communism. They tried to make us say, "Down with President Ho!" And, of course, they wanted to know about our revolutionary organizations and bases. But we would rather die than bow to their will. They stopped at nothing to lure us into doing what they wanted. For example, if a prisoner was suffering from dysentery, a nurse would come with a syringe of medicine and ask if she agreed to salute the Saigon flag. If the prisoner refused, the nurse emptied the syringe on the ground and left. They said if we complied with their demands they would give us more food and our relatives would be permitted to visit us. They tried to use those who were submissive as bait to make the rest of us surrender. It was not easy to cope with these psychological tactics, but we were unyielding. The prison wardens called us tigresses because even the tiger cages could not tame and subdue us. Prison was primarily a struggle to protect our integrity. We learned by heart one of To Huu's poems in which there is a stanza that reads: "Becoming a revolutionary, I grow to understand / Means acceptance of prison and exile / Swords always close to the throat, guns to the head / I consider myself a half-dead person already." A revolutionary's integrity is sacred because it allows you to preserve your ideals. We always reminded ourselves that because the Vietnamese Revolution was a just cause, we could overcome any trial. Whenever possible, we organized classes to teach ourselves revolutionary ethics. We also taught each other songs and poems and tried to transform our prisons into schools.

The support of peace-loving people throughout the world, and especially from the American people, was a great source of strength and encouragement to us in our struggle. We knew we were not alone. For example, on November 2,

1965, we learned that [Norman] Morrison had immolated himself right in front of the Pentagon to demonstrate his opposition to the American war in Vietnam. We were deeply touched, so we dedicated a minute of silence in our cells to his sacrifice.

The memory of Norman Morrison brings tears to her eyes. Near the end of the interview, asked if she had any regrets that so many former enemies were imprisoned after the war, she answered, still in a quiet voice, but with an edge of anger, "Those who worked for the puppet government had to be imprisoned in reeducation camps because they were obviously guilty; they had a blood debt to the Vietnamese people. They killed our people, so they were guilty. They were the henchmen and lackeys who served the foreigners and betrayed their own people. They had to be punished for their crimes."

RANDY KEHLER

"Friction against the wheel."

A trim, middle-aged man, he was one of roughly five thousand Americans who went to prison for their resistance to the draft. Several times his memories seem to catch him by surprise, pulling up emotions that make his voice suddenly crack.

In the summer of 1963, after my freshman year at Harvard, a friend invited me to a jazz concert at Lewisohn Stadium in New York City. I took a train from Scarsdale to 125th Street in Harlem. I got to this street corner and there was a huge crowd listening to a speaker. Somebody had given me a tape of Malcolm X's speeches and even though I had a snotty, condescending attitude about protesters, I was completely fascinated. I thought maybe this was actually Malcolm X.

All of a sudden three black guys came up behind me and put their hands on my shoulders, gently but firmly. I turned around and I was freaked. They said, "You better get out of here, this is a very dangerous place for white people. We'll escort you out." It was very clear that they were sincerely trying to help and they whisked me into this doorway and up these stairs.

It turned out they were members of CORE—the Congress of Racial Equality—and this was their office. They were organizing for the 1963 March on Washington. I didn't even know there was going to be a march. I didn't know what CORE was. I had heard about the civil rights movement, but to tell you the truth, I remember feeling that people who protested were egotists seeking publicity, that they were just troublemakers who weren't really sincere or committed. I dismissed them. It was a typical Harvard, Exeter, Scarsdale attitude. Scarsdale, New York, where I grew up, was one of the most affluent suburbs in the United States. So I had the most elite upbringing you can imagine.

Anyway, there I was in the CORE office and they were putting out a mailing about the March on Washington and I offered to help. There were a lot of older women around and they were happy to have me. I just blew off the concert at Lewisohn Stadium and my poor friend didn't know what had happened. I ended up working all that summer as a volunteer for CORE, mostly raising money in Scarsdale to send buses from Harlem to Washington.

In late August, I went to Washington for the demonstration on a CORE bus. We left Harlem at midnight. When I got on the bus the only available seat was next to this very old white guy, the only other white person on the bus. The moment I sat down he handed me this booklet and quietly said, "Read this." It turned out to be the annual War Resisters League calendar. Every page had the biography of a long-time pacifist. This guy had it open to a page about someone named Max Sandin.

So I'm sitting there reading that Max Sandin was born in Russia in the late nineteenth century and refused to fight in the czar's army. He could have been executed, but he managed to escape and come to the United States, just in time to be drafted for World War I. He refused again. His mother had taught him that war was wrong, that's all there was to it. So he was imprisoned here in the U.S. After the war he refused to pay any taxes for war and was persecuted for that. Anyway, Max Sandin had led this completely consistent life of antiwar pacifism. So I gave the book back to the old guy and said, "That's an amazing story." He turned to me and said, "I'm Max Sandin."

I'd never met anyone who put their principles ahead of everything else—career, reputation, material well-being. It planted a seed, but I still had the notion that it would be totally dishonorable not to fight to defend your country. To me, everything was "defense." I had no idea that the United States might fight an offensive war.

When I was a sophomore I wanted to take a year out to teach in East Africa. You had to get permission from the draft board to leave the country. I was barely aware of this stuff going on in Vietnam and I was totally ready to go into the military service if called. Part of me liked the idea of going into the military. I had played war games and football. I was a Boy Scout. I really loved camping out, getting muddy and dirty, trudging up hills and pitching a tent—all that sort of stuff appealed to me.

When I went for my draft physical I had every intention of passing. But the night before the physical I had a bad nightmare about Africa. It was about a lion at the mouth of my tent and I jumped out of bed and smashed an overhead light with my pillow. The shards of this big porcelain lamp cut me all over my body. When I went to the physical, the army psychiatrist asked me about these wounds and after hearing that I had a history of nightmares and sleepwalking he said, "I'm sorry, we can't take you." So they gave me a I-Y, unfit for military service except in times of national emergency or a declaration of war. I was disappointed. I felt sort of ashamed.

On the bus going back to Cambridge all the working-class kids who had passed the physical were saying, "Dammit, how did you do it?" I was amazed how many of them did not want to go and had not eaten for a week or had faked psychiatric problems. The irony is, they all passed. They were razzing me, "Yeah, you Harvard guys are so smart, you know all the angles."

Going to Africa in 1964 sensitized me in a way that led straight into antiwar activity. Part of it was just living in a Third World country and realizing that this was pretty much the way the great majority of the world's population lived. And while I was there the United States was covertly involved in suppressing a rebellion in the Katanga province of the Congo. At one point there were Congolese refugees streaming into western Tanzania where I was teaching. They claimed their villages had been napalmed by unmarked U.S. planes.

One day I was playing goalie for a local soccer team and some of these Congolese refugees noticed that I had a knapsack that said "U.S. Army" on it. They mobbed me and started beating on me. They thought I was connected somehow to the same U.S. military that had just caused them to lose their villages. My own teammates, who were African, had to pull them off. It was a terrifying and eye-opening experience. I was completely naive. What? My country?

When I came back and started hearing that the United States was dropping napalm in Vietnam, another Third World country, I thought, I can't support this. In 1965, a classmate and I started this very mild-mannered thing called "Letters for Peace" to get people to just rain down letters of protest about the war on elected officials in Washington.

Then one day I was in the library with some serious studying to do, but I couldn't do it. The morning paper had a picture of a Vietnamese person who had been hit with napalm. I couldn't study. I was crying. I was just in tears and I remember circling the library, round and round, and thinking, what am I gonna do? How can I collaborate with this? I need to somehow make my opposition much more felt and known.

Shortly after that a "We Won't Go" petition was going around Harvard and I signed it. It was a public letter declaring our opposition to the war and to the draft, our refusal to be inducted if drafted, and our willingness to commit "conspiracy" to advocate that other young men also refuse to be inducted for military service in Vietnam. It was the first concrete action I took that I thought was likely to lead to arrest and imprisonment.

In Thoreau's essay on "Civil Disobedience" he talks about the difference between just removing oneself from some evil and taking the next step, letting your whole life be a "friction against the wheel." That's what I felt I had to do. But it's one thing to think theoretically about it and another thing when someone says, "Sign here." The moment your pen touches the paper you imagine that the hand of the law will grab you by the neck and fling you into prison for the rest of your life.

But there were no consequences immediately. I went off to graduate school at Stanford in education. I wanted to teach elementary school in the inner city. I got involved in antiwar demonstrations right away in the fall of 1967. I was taking a course at the Mid-Peninsula Free University on active nonviolence taught by some preeminent pacifists—Roy Keppler, Ira Sandperl, and Joan Baez. It was clear that this was going to be a hands-on course and one of the first projects was a big civil disobedience action at the Oakland Induction Center as part of Stop the Draft Week. The whole thing was pretty new to me and a little frightening, so I went thinking I would just observe. But it was so inspiring I decided to join hands with some people and sit down in the street. We were arrested for blocking a bus of kids being brought in for induction. All one hundred and twenty-five of us got ten-day sentences.

I was in prison not only with lots of student-age people but an amazing number of older people. I remember saying to myself, "You mean you can live your whole life being true to your convictions? It's not just something you do after college?" They would tell me stories about people refusing to fight in both world wars, and soon I realized that this tradition went back almost to the beginning of recorded wars. I just felt, oh my God, I'm in this long, long line of people. Max Sandin had planted that seed years before, but it had taken a while to germinate.

In jail, Roy Keppler said, "How'd you like to come to work for the War Resisters League?" I had been chomping at the bit for a couple of years to really throw myself fully into stopping the war, so he didn't have to ask me twice. I quit Stanford and spent the next two years working for them.

In December of 1967, three hundred of us blocked one of the entrances to the Oakland Induction Center. Those of us who were second-timers were sentenced to forty-five days and put with the regular prison population in these little cells. You couldn't see out of your cell, only up through the ceiling grates. The guards walked around on top. If they wanted to, they would knock the shit out of you with a high-powered water hose. I wasn't particularly mistreated, but I heard other people screaming bloody murder. It was just bedlam in there.

After getting out, I spent the next two years going up and down the Northern California coast trying to encourage draft resistance. We also worked a lot with military AWOLs and deserters. We did one sanctuary action in July 1968 called "Nine for Peace," where a bunch of us, including a lot of clergy, chained ourselves to nine AWOL men from all four branches of the service. They had all found their way to the War Resisters League, they had all gone AWOL, and they did not want to go to Vietnam. We issued a public statement saying that we were standing with these men because the war was immoral and that people of conscience should support them.

Probably less than a day later, the military police and regular police descended on this little church, cut the chains, and dragged people out. They didn't arrest anybody but these nine AWOL soldiers. It was awful. Naively, we thought the police wouldn't come into the church, that it would be too embarrassing for them. So it was devastating to see our friends dragged away knowing they were going to face terrible things.

What initiated my imprisonment for draft resistance was a demonstration in front of the Federal Building in San Francisco in July 1969. We were reading aloud a list of the war dead, name after name after name. These men who looked like reporters came up with notepads and said, "Are you Randy Kehler? Could we interview you?" I agreed and they said, "How about we go around the corner? It's a bit noisy here." So I went around the corner with them and they grabbed me and said, "You're under arrest." They were all FBI agents posing as reporters. I said, "What for?" They said, "You know."

Actually, there were so many things I could have been arrested for, I really *didn't* know. For example, I had helped military deserters get out of the country, which was highly illegal. They said, "Come with us." I said, "I'm not going anywhere until you tell me what I'm being arrested for." At that point I went limp and they pounced on me. My friends came around the corner and started trying to pull them off. One of the FBI guys was kicking my friend in the ribs so I yelled, "Stop, stop, I'll go."

So they walked me into the Federal Building, put me into a jail cell, and I was arraigned for refusing to cooperate with the draft. Though I had received a I-Y in 1964, the selective service had called me back for another physical in 1968 and I'd refused to go. There were thousands of men my age who were refusing to register or had refused a physical, but they were selectively prosecuting and I was very visible.

In February 1970, I had a jury trial and chose to defend myself. The first sentence out of my mouth was, "I did exactly what I'm charged with doing and I want to tell you why I think it's your duty to acquit me." I rested my argument on the theory of jury nullification, which I had researched. It goes all the way back to the Peter Zenger case in colonial times, when the jury refused to convict Zenger of treason. He was a printer in New York City and the jury thought that the law itself was unjust and what Zenger was printing was true.

The prosecutor asked me why I didn't apply for conscientious objector status. I said that even if I'd thought I could qualify, I felt it was just an easy way for them to take a whole group of people and give them a personal out that made it safe for them. I just felt it was a form of cooperation. I didn't look at it so much intellectually, I just knew in my gut that if they wanted to remove me, they would have to put me behind bars. I'm gonna keep organizing and protesting this war until I can't do it anymore and they will have to physically stop me. That's how I felt. So they did.

The jury didn't take long to convict me. In sentencing me, the judge said, "Well, if you had been inducted you would have had to serve two years, so I'm going to make you serve two years in prison."

At the time of the trial my father was retired. He had silver hair, wore a suit, very respectable looking. My father said to the judge, somewhat sternly, "Your honor, if you're determined to put someone in jail, you should put me in jail. After all, my son is only trying to live out the values that we taught him." [He fights back tears.] Actually, that wasn't quite true, but it was great of my father to say so.

I was sent to this place in southern Arizona called Safford, a minimum-custody prison camp out in the middle of the desert. I had just been married and my wife and I drove down and scoped out the place the night before. It was the eeriest thing you could imagine. Here were these barracks out in the middle of nowhere, all lit up with floodlights. It was an old air force base but it looked like a concentration camp on the moon. I was petrified.

I was fearful of being treated badly by fellow prisoners. I'd been warned that they would hate us for being yellow-bellied, Commie cowards. But there was virtually none of that. A lot of the rough characters that you met in prison actually had respect for us draft resisters. There were about one hundred of us out of about three hundred prisoners. By 1970, when I went in, there was a lot of disaffection with the government and the war, and the prevalent attitude expressed by other prisoners was a kind of macho antiauthoritarian, "Good for you, you told 'em to go fuck themselves. You got balls, man."

I remember this one tough old con named Earl who was a friend of David Harris, another draft resister at Safford who was married to Joan Baez. Earl had been to Alcatraz, all the big federal maximum pens. He said to me once, "I really think that David is right about all that nonviolence stuff. He's talked to me about it and he's got me convinced. But I'll tell ya one thing, if they ever put a hand on David, I'll kill 'em."

In prison, a lot of draft resisters talked about whether we should consider ourselves prisoners of war. We were wary of using the term publicly because we knew that whatever hardships we were going through, they didn't compare to what prisoners in war zones were suffering. But among ourselves, we felt we were, in a way, prisoners of war.

The guards and warden were always threatening to "send me out" to La Tuna, a medium-security prison. I was written up for so many petty little things I lost all my "good time" days. I was literally written up for "asking too many questions." Another time the charge was "having a bad attitude toward this prison and prisons in general." But the real reason they finally sent me out to La Tuna was that I organized a boycott of the dining hall in solidarity with prisoners at Leavenworth who were on strike. That was the last straw.

So after six months at Safford, I did sixteen months in La Tuna, outside of El Paso, Texas. At first I worked in the carpentry shop there and did some organizing to protest prison conditions, in particular to get the health situation cleaned up. But nothing happened and eventually I refused to go to work. So I was put in the hole for thirty days to see if they could get me to change my mind. It was a basement cell with no mattress, one blanket, very little light, and it was damp and cold and you heard people screaming. Then I spent nine months in a two-man cell that was nine-by-six. After that, I was ready to get out.

When I was released from prison, I was completely disoriented. Even riding in a car was a terrifying experience. I remember going to an antiwar protest just after I got out and feeling kind of lost. At one point the police got really rough and were dragging people around, throwing them down. This cop grabbed my friend Lee and flung him into the middle of the street. I was filled with instant rage. I was just seconds away from going out and jumping on this policeman. I felt a surge of violent anger and I thought, "Whoa, where did this come from?"

In the 1980s, he cofounded and led the Nuclear Weapons Freeze Campaign. Beginning in 1979, he and his wife, Betsy, stopped paying federal taxes. Instead, they have given all the money they owed in taxes to charity—one half to victims of U.S. war making abroad and the other half to local homeless shelters and food pantries. In 1989, the Internal Revenue Service seized the Kehlers' house and sold it at auction. Today he works with several organizations for the abolition of privately financed election campaigns.

CAMERAS, BOOKS, AND GUNS

For the Vietnamese it was total war, an upheaval of such magnitude it infused every aspect of their culture—work, family life, art, literature, photography, music, education, the entire fabric of daily life. In North Vietnam and Viet Cong–controlled areas of the South every organ of communication was marshaled to the cause. Public posters showed idealized guerrillas in heroic poses, radio news trumpeted expressions of support from around the world, and theatrical troupes celebrated the virtue and ultimate triumph of "people's war."

For Americans, the war was at once limited and limitless, remote and omnipresent. Lacking total mobilization or nationwide sacrifice, it was, for most Americans, a secondhand experience, yet one causing so much political and moral controversy it commanded years of national attention. The ambiguous nature of U.S. intervention in Vietnam—both partial and endless—generated a cultural response that reflected both conspicuous avoidance and intense preoccupation.

From 1965 to 1972 the Vietnam War was such a common feature of nightly television it became known as the "living room war." By 1968 there were about five hundred correspondents in Vietnam from all over the world, about two hundred of them American. The media had greater access to the fighting and less governmental censorship than in any war before or since.

Defenders of U.S. policy have often claimed that media coverage was hostile to the American cause and undermined public support; that, at the very least, daily exposure to gruesome images of war led many Americans to doubt the value of persisting. The most extreme versions of this argument blame the media for defeat itself. However, careful studies have demonstrated that the great majority of media reports from Vietnam were based primarily on official U.S. sources and were supportive of the American objectives. Indeed, according to William Hammond, a historian at the U.S. Army Center of Military History, "until at least 1968, television was lopsidedly favorable to U.S. policy." Nor was coverage filled with excessive blood and gore. Between 1965 and 1970, less than 5 percent of all film reports from Vietnam shown on the evening news included graphic images of violence, and the networks made an agreement with the U.S. command not to show American casualties (on the grounds that family members might otherwise view their wounded son on television prior to receiving official notification of his condition). Moreover, there was never live coverage of the war. Most film was several days old before it was edited and broadcast in the United States.

Beginning with the Tet Offensive of 1968, the media more frequently challenged official U.S. claims about the war, but it rarely raised questions not already broadly voiced throughout the nation. And while the media's skepticism increased along with the public's, coverage of Vietnam dropped off significantly from 1969 to 1975.

In fact, millions of Americans found the mainstream media far too limited and timid in its war reporting and turned to alternative sources of news. Young activists and writers generated an enormous body of politically radical and countercultural publications. Now largely forgotten, by the late sixties there were hundreds of "underground" newspapers that included wild graphic designs, subversive cartoons, audaciously subjective articles, and articles from media outlets such as the Liberation News Service and the Underground Press Syndicate. There were also scores of GI newspapers, many produced by active-duty soldiers and sailors, which challenged the prowar coverage of military papers like *Stars and Stripes*. GI papers like *The Fatigue Press* and *About Face*, along with underground papers like *The Great Speckled Bird* and *The Old Mole,* carried Vietnam stories that rarely appeared in the mainstream media—exposés of U.S. use of chemical and antipersonnel weapons, reports of atrocities (including graphic photographs of, for example, a GI holding a severed Vietnamese head), information about draft avoidance and resistance, and coverage of news releases from Hanoi and the NLF.

Yet there were important limitations on how much even the most curious Americans could learn about the war. No subject was more strikingly inaccessible than the experience of ordinary Vietnamese on all sides. Though the media did occasional reports about Vietnamese leaders (especially of the South Vietnamese government), there was little about combatants and civilians. Beginning with *The New York Times* reporter Harrison Salisbury in 1966, a small number of American journalists began to pay brief visits to North Vietnam to file stories. However, no U.S. reporters were allowed to report from behind enemy lines in South Vietnam until after the American withdrawal in 1973, and the U.S. media rarely used stories from foreign correspondents who could.

However much the war came to dominate American headlines and fill the streets with demonstrators, it was conspicuously absent from much of American popular culture—movies, novels, and television dramas. From 1964 to 1972, the years of most intense U.S. fighting in Vietnam, Hollywood released only one major film about the war, *The Green Berets* (1968). Starring John Wayne, it was based on the only wartime novel about Vietnam to become a best-seller. The appearance of this one pro–Vietnam War film stands in striking contrast to the scores of flag-waving war films produced by Hollywood during World War II. Equally noteworthy is its defensive tone. While World War II movies took it for granted that audiences accepted the underlying justice and necessity of the combat they dramatized, *The Green Berets* struggled awkwardly to answer the question of why the United States should be fighting in Vietnam.

Short on effective prowar films, Hollywood was no more able or willing to invest in explicitly anti–Vietnam War films. Films like *Little Big Man,* about white frontier atrocities against Native Americans, clearly drew on antiwar perspectives and the Vietnam War, but did not address the war directly. Nor did Hollywood risk making movies that focused on antiwar activists and their undeniably dramatic challenges to American policy. Even in the postwar years when Vietnam combat films became hits, peace activists were almost always missing from the story or treated unsympathetically.

Unlike Hollywood, publishers brought out a flood of wartime books about Vietnam, most of them nonfiction. With many previous wars, passionately antiwar books tended to appear only years after the conflict, but in the case of Vietnam the most severe critiques of American intervention were written during the war itself. The war writing of scholars like Noam Chomsky and Howard Zinn, for example, were crucial in shaping the intellectual underpinnings of the antiwar movement.

Since the 1970s, public memory of the Vietnam War has been deeply affected by Hollywood war films. From *Apocalypse Now* (1979) to *Platoon* (1986) to *We Were Soldiers* (2002), most of these movies dramatize the experience of American soldiers. That focus has also characterized the abundance of postwar Vietnam War novels and memoirs, a great many of them written by American veterans. No other war in our history has generated such a wealth of literature written by those who fought it.

PHILIP JONES GRIFFITHS (I)

"Go see what they did to those people with your money."

The burly Welshman leans over a table in his Manhattan apartment inspecting a photograph of a mud-caked Vietnamese woman edging past a column of U.S. troops in a bombed-out neighborhood of Saigon during the Tet Offensive. It was one of the thou-

sands of photographs he took during the war for Magnum, the famous cooperative photo agency. Now in his midsixties, he has lost count of all the faraway places he's been to take pictures. "I come from a little village. The only thing I've ever been afraid of is boredom." Many of his Vietnam War pictures were published around the world, yet relatively few appeared in U.S. newspapers and magazines. "I was told that my photographs were too harrowing for the American market." In 1971, after the publication of Vietnam, Inc., *a collection of his photographs, the South Vietnamese government banned him from reentering the country.*

Before I got to Vietnam I hadn't seen people blown apart and I wondered how I would react. I steeled myself to do the job. I always had in mind that I should emulate a doctor. A surgeon who faints at the sight of blood is useless. A photographer who starts to cry when he's supposed to take a picture is equally useless. I just channeled my emotions into the end of my index finger. Later, when I was back home, safely in the darkroom and looking through contact sheets, then it all came flooding back. That's when I found myself desolate and weeping. Then there was time to break down and it didn't do any harm. If you can't focus the enlarger, you simply wait until the tears dry, and then you focus the image.

The only time I almost passed out was not in the heat of battle but when I was doing a story about a hospital. The Americans had got something called an inflatable hospital—a small version of what they use now for urban tennis courts that could be erected close to the action. It was all pretty gruesome stuff. I just photographed what was there. When they were sawing the guy's leg off I took a picture. I found I was okay; I wasn't passing out. But then one night they brought in this soldier who was only semi out of it. They got out this huge drill and started making a hole in the guy's head. And then they put a finger in and started poking around. I was still okay until one doctor says, "Oh shit. It's the other guy that's got the head wound. This guy is a leg." Then I felt myself going over. I had to sit down and put my head between my knees.

I was very methodical about my work. I was the antithesis of the photographer who goes straight to the AP office and says, "Okay, where are crimes against humanity happening this afternoon?" I decided I would visit every province in South Vietnam and I did. I was just looking really, trying to get an overall view. If there were pictures to take, I'd take pictures. But I certainly never wanted to have anybody say, "This guy came with an agenda. He'd already made up his mind about the war." The truth is I hadn't. Of course, being ornery, when I read stuff in *Time* magazine I was inclined to believe the opposite. [Laughs.]

I have photographs that would make you throw up. But what's the point of that? Fortunately we're all equipped with safety mechanisms and when it all gets too much we close our eyes or turn the page. So you try to take pictures that captivate people. That means leaving out some pictures of horrendous things.

Many of my pictures are not gruesome. I took quite a few photographs confirming the spiritual bond between the Vietnamese and their rice, and their land, and their ancestral graves. I wanted to show that it was a society we should be emulating rather than destroying. I think that struck a chord in many people.

The closer you got to the war, if you had a functioning brain, the more you objected to what you saw. Eventually I believed what America was doing in Vietnam was genocide. There was no possible justification for what was going on and nothing to back up the righteousness of the American side.

There was a napalm ward in the provincial hospital in Quang Ngai where the people were so badly disfigured they could probably never go back into society. Many had been put in there to die. I was there once and saw this kid. He had his eyelids burned off, his nose burned off, and his lips burned off. He was halfway to becoming a skull, but he was still alive. I could hardly look at him—he was so ugly, so frightening, really, really frightening.

So I just glanced at him and turned around. I was photographing someone else and I felt somebody pulling at the back of my shirt. I turned around and it was the boy. He indicated with sign language that he wanted me to take his picture. As I took his picture, I remember thinking that it will never get published but it's something we should have for the war crimes trial. Of course that never happened.

When I came out of that ward there was an American journalist. She said, "I can't go in there, it's too horrible. Can you take my camera and take some pictures for me?" I said, "No, you go in there. Those people were burned with your taxpayer's money. Go see what they did to those people with your money."

But the most horrendous events are not necessarily what make the most lasting impression. I was with the First Cav up in Binh Dinh Province and they were interrogating a boy, a slightly overweight kid of about fourteen. He was absolutely shaking with fear, completely distraught. The American was yelling to the interpreter. "Tell him we're going to kill his father unless he tells us where the VC are hiding." And the kid was shouting, "I don't know, I don't know, don't do this to me, I don't know." They just kept pushing and pushing and finally the American said, "Okay, kill the father."

They dragged the father off to the side and they shot. The kid was totally shattered. Then the American said, "Okay, he doesn't know anything." So they brought the father back and this kid looked up and couldn't believe his father wasn't dead because he'd heard the shots. And then a soldier grabbed some cans of C rations and thrust them into this boy's hands and said, "Go home. Get out of here." Of course, this was a standard interrogation. They weren't doing anything they hadn't done many times before. But it was one of those little incidents that you never forget.

LARRY HEINEMANN

"We had this idea that we were king of the fucking hill."

A lifelong Chicagoan, he arrives at the coffee shop in jeans and a Jack Kerouac T-shirt, a spiral notebook under one arm. He is suffering from a hacking cough. "I've really got to quit smoking."

In Vietnam, he drove an armored personnel carrier in a mechanized battalion of the 25th Infantry Division from 1967 to 1968. In 1987, he won the National Book Award for Paco's Story, *a novel about the lone American survivor of a Vietnam firefight.*

We lost the war because the Vietnamese just flat out beat us. And we lost the war because we didn't understand that they were poets. That's true. In 1990, I went back to Vietnam for the first time. There was a literary conference in Hanoi. At one of the lunches I sat next to this little bitty guy who turned out to be a professor of American literature at Hanoi University—Professor Nguyen Lien.

I asked him what he did during the war and this is the story he told me. He said that his job was to go to Beijing and learn English and then go to Moscow University to read and study American literature. Then he went back to Hanoi and out to the Ho Chi Minh Trail and gave lectures on American literature to the troops traveling south. It was not like a six-week survey, just an afternoon, but he talked to them about Whitman, Jack London, Hemingway, Faulkner, Fitzgerald.

A lot of Vietnamese soldiers carried translations of American literature in their packs. Le Minh Khue [see pp. 508-11]—a young woman who worked on the Ho Chi Minh Trail disarming unexploded bombs—carried Ernest Hemingway. Professor Lien asked me this question, "Now what Vietnamese literature did the American military teach to you?" I laughed so hard I almost squirted beer up my nose. I told Professor Lien that I would have been surprised if the U.S. Army had given us classes in *American* literature.

I grew up in a house where there were no books and when you graduated high school you were told to get a job. I was the only one of four brothers who said, "Well, I'd really like to go to college." So I went to a small junior college in Evanston, right across the street from Northwestern, but I ran out of money and had to quit. That's when I got drafted. Nobody told me I could go to Canada. Nobody told me I could phony up the physical. The word in my house was, "Go into the army, it'll make a man of you."

When I got back from Vietnam I went to an arts college in Chicago—Columbia. It's this rinky-dink little ma-and-pa sort of hip pocket operation. All you needed was a high school diploma and a checkbook. I took a writing class because I thought it was going to be a snap "A" and I wasn't gonna have to work.

The first night of class I will never forget. We sat down and the teacher hauled out this crummy little old book, so old and beat up you couldn't see the title on the front. And he reads this story about these guys on a ship and all of a sudden they see this whale and everybody jumps into boats and they row out and a guy named Stubb kills the whale. It was a body-count story. He read this and I got up and I said, "What book is that?" He said, *"Moby Dick."* I thought, before I read anything else, I have to read *Moby Dick*. It's about a lot of things, but it's also about a shitty job. There's a reason why the passing of this kind of work is not mourned. This was butchery and these were huge animals and they fought back! That's where I got the idea of talking about war in terms of work.

In Vietnam I drove an APC, an armored personnel carrier, a "track." In the most perverse kind of American teenage way, the tracks were great fun. They were these huge, ugly, loud, nasty-looking things—thirteen tons and nobody fucked with us. We had this idea that we were king of the fucking hill. God, they were great fun to drive. Thirty miles an hour, top end, and we drove them top end, flat out, all the time.

There were only ten of them in our platoon but we sounded like a million. We never surprised anyone. You could hear these things coming all day. You're eighteen years old and you take a big loud machine, drive it to town, and park it anywhere you want. There isn't a Vietnamese cop within a thousand miles of you that's going to give you a ticket. And if an MP had tried, we would have beat him up. We ran people off the road. We boomed into back-country hamlets, pushing over trees as big around as you can reach. We felt invincible.

On my track some asshole had painted a bull's-eye right behind my seat. The track is made out of inch-and-a-quarter aluminum alloy armor plate. The

Vietnamese had this dynamite antitank weapon called an RPG [rocket-propelled grenade]. An RPG will go through inch-and-a-quarter armor plate like spit through a screen.

Our tracks were gasoline powered—ninety gallons of gasoline. A gallon of gasoline is equal to nineteen pounds of TNT and a gallon of gasoline has enough energy to lift one thousand pounds one thousand feet into the air instantly. Don't fuck with gasoline. You got ninety gallons here and if an RPG hits the bull's-eye you go up like the head of a match. And if there's a mine in the road, and the mine goes off right under you, the driver just gets popped right out of the hatch. The driver is in the track from the neck down. Everybody else is sitting up on top. If anything happens, the driver always dies. You're driving around with your asshole puckered the whole fucking time.

January 1, 1968, was the worst night of my life. We just worked all night. It was a place called Suoi Cut, about a quarter of a mile from the Cambodian border, straight north from Nui Ba Den [Black Virgin Mountain]. We were on the site of a village but there was nothing there and there hadn't been anything there for a long time.

This was the first time we'd fought NVA—actual North Vietnamese issue troops. These were not southern Viet Cong. These guys were coming out of the woods five, six, eight guys at a time, just running right into the teeth of this amazing firefight and it lasted all fucking night. They told us later it was the 272nd NVA regiment, which was about fifteen hundred guys, and we killed five hundred. It was ugly.

The thing I most remember was the morning. The sun came up and the smoke cleared and the dew burned away. There was meat everywhere and the wood line looked like ruined drapes. Everything was covered with dust and looked antique. Halfway through the morning someone came down and said we had to clean up because Westmoreland was coming out to inspect the thing. All we wanted to do was clean our guns, smoke some grass, and go take a nap. We had been up all night.

We had a bulldozer with us and this bulldozer digs a ditch. The guys from the line company start picking up the bodies and throwing them into the ditch. They did it like you do lasagna. There was a layer of bodies, and then a layer of quick lime, and then a layer of bodies, and then a layer of quick lime, and then a layer of bodies. Later in the morning, I remember the stretcher-bearers coming up the road from the south. They had been sent out to look for the guys from Bravo Company who had gone out the night before to set up an ambush. They all got killed. They came in on the stretchers with their arms sort of flopped over the side. These guys were stiff as a fucking board.

My youngest brother, Philip, and I were in Vietnam at the same time. My mother let him drop out of high school when he was seventeen and join the Marine Corps. There's a regulation that two brothers didn't have to serve at the same time in Vietnam, but he volunteered. In 1967 everyone in the Marine Corps volunteered or they'd beat the shit out of you until you did. He got wounded and I tried to go see him up in Danang. I put in for an emergency leave. I went to see the Red Cross guy and said, "I have this letter. My brother's wounded and I want to see him." This motherfucker knew that all it was gonna take was one phone call. He just dicked around for three weeks and when I finally got up to Danang, Philip had already gone home. Months later, during the Tet Offensive, the Red Cross guy got blown up by a mortar. Everybody but me was sad he died.

Philip and I were very close. I was closer to him than my other two brothers. When I got home I didn't know what to say. I came back without a scratch. He was deaf in one ear and his eye was all red and dripping this stuff. But he recovered enough to go back on active duty and they sent him back for a second tour.

When he got orders to go back, I went to a lawyer in Chicago. They knew who I was. My grandfather had been a lawyer on LaSalle Street and he'd only been dead a few years. I went into the office of an ex-Marine Corps colonel from the judge advocate general's office. I said, "Look, my brother's going back to Vietnam for the second time and I want to know who I have to pay and how much to get these orders changed and I don't want any Marine Corps bullshit. My brother's already been wounded, I've been there once, and enough is enough. I want to find out from you, in the name of my grandfather, what you can do for me." A couple weeks later he called back and said there was nothing he could do.

For some reason my mother told Philip that I had gone to a lawyer and he got really pissed off. That's why he and I never spoke for ten years. It was just like this *thing* between us. It was just like a corpse in the house. I could not bring myself to write my brother the whole time he was there. I did not want to see a letter come back with the big red stamp that says DECEASED. It's one of the serious regrets of my life that I didn't write him.

My brother came back from his second tour in 1970. He drove a bus. My dad was a bus driver and got him a job driving for the company. He got married and had two kids and then he got divorced and it's a long, dumb story but around 1980 he disappeared and no one has seen him since. It's not one of those things you like to dwell on. He was just not equipped to deal with this and took off. We tried to get the Salvation Army to locate him. They have a locator service, but the rule is they tell the person they're trying to locate that you are looking for them and it's their choice whether to get in touch with you. We did that twice. Both times they came back and said, we've located him but he doesn't want to be in contact.

Something happened to him in the war that he just can't get around. There are a lot of guys like Philip who just bumped up against the war like a fly on a screen. The war was devastatingly brutal. This happens after every war and it really does depend on every individual's inner resources. After living in this wallow, how do you come out and reconnect with your own humanity? Is it possible to love someone knowing that you have done all these things, and are capable of all these things, and have seen all these things?

These are the dark things on your heart. I asked a doctor once if there were actually dark places on your heart. He said that when you get a heart attack part of your heart muscle dies. It becomes like a bruise and turns dark. The dark places on my heart are not going away.

DUONG THANH PHONG

"We didn't need a darkroom."

Born in 1940, the combat photographer learned how to take pictures from his aunt when he was a young boy growing up in the town of Trang Bang in Tay Ninh Province, northwest of Saigon. His aunt owned a photo shop that doubled as a meeting place for revolutionaries fighting the French. In the late 1950s, as a teenager, he used his photographic skills to make fake IDs for underground operatives waging a new campaign against the American-backed regime of Ngo Dinh Diem.

In 1965, he went to the "R zone." R is short for rung, *the Vietnamese word for jungle. Among southerners, "going to the jungle" was a euphemism for joining the Viet Cong and going to the "R zone" meant going to a Communist-controlled area. For Phong it was only a short trip from home. He spent most of the American War photographing guerrilla operations in and around the tunnels of Cu Chi. His work includes photographs of the woman guerrilla fighter Tran Thi Gung (**see pp. 15–19**). "I knew Gung very well, so well a friend used to joke that before squeezing the shutter on my camera I would take her into the tunnels to push her buttons." [Laughs.]*

In 1965, the puppet army was going to draft me so I had to go the R zone to join the revolutionary forces. Since I was good at photography they assigned me to work as a combat photographer. My mission was to keep up the spirits of our troops and also to take pictures to send abroad for anti-American propaganda. Photography can be a political weapon. As soon as I developed my pictures we had public exhibits in the hamlets. When people saw themselves in the pictures they were so excited, it was no longer just political. They would say, "Look, there I am!" They liked knowing that what they had done on the battlefield had been documented and memorialized.

We got all the photographic supplies we needed in Saigon. Infrastructure operatives would buy the film and chemicals and carry them out to the jungle. And we didn't need a darkroom because the tunnels had the darkest rooms in the world. They were perfect.

At the beginning of the war, we didn't have much more than sharpened bamboo stakes to use against the puppet troops. We planted the stakes in pits and covered them up so the enemy might fall into them. Our tunnel system was left over from the French War. It was very simple and not very well developed, just ditches and foxholes that had been covered by bamboo and grass. So we began to develop the system by digging down two and a half meters before branching out horizontally.

My first encounter with the American enemy came when I was with a team of guerrilla fighters underground. Through a small hole in a bunker I could see the advancing American soldiers. I saw an American GI fall down in front of me and one of the guerrilla fighters used a stick to reach out and pull in his rifle. Then another GI came to take the body of that dead soldier. For the first time I witnessed an American crying and it occurred to me that the Americans are like the Vietnamese. I mean, when they embrace their dead comrades, their gestures and facial expressions are exactly like the Vietnamese. Suffering is universal. It was such a small hole only one person could see this at a time and we fought among ourselves to watch. That scene made a deep impression on me because when the Americans arrived we didn't know how powerful they were or even what they looked like. So when I saw an American fall down and another crying over his body, I realized that we could fight them. I realized they were human beings, not aliens, that they were like us.

In many of the tunnels we had three levels and were often safe. We stretched out on hammocks and when the bombs thundered over our heads the hammocks swung back and forth. Most of our casualties were caused when shells or mortars caught people out in the open. But we usually knew in advance when the big B-52 air strikes would come just by looking at the sky. When there were no reconnaissance planes or helicopters in the air we guessed a big attack was on the way. Since most of the area around Cu Chi was a free-fire zone there were always all kinds of helicopters and aircraft overhead. But the B-52s flew ten kilometers high and the skies below had to be empty or they might hit other American aircraft. When everything was very calm overhead we moved to the deepest parts of the tunnels.

Almost continuously we had to endure the sounds of bombing, choppers, and mortars. We fought against the Tropical Lightning Division [the 25th Infantry] around the clock. An armored unit from Tay Ninh also impressed us with its firepower and we received a lot of shelling from an American base at Ben Cat. Usually we slept in the tunnels by day and only went out at night.

I lived that way from about 1965 to 1972. The worst time for me was the dry season of late 1969. In 1968, we had mobilized all our forces for the Tet Offensive, but in 1969 the enemy launched a powerful counteroffensive. All our efforts were focused on survival as they tried to sweep us from our bases in Cu Chi. I was the leader of our photographic team. We had about fifteen members and seven were killed. Many times I was nearly killed. For example, one time during a mortar attack I was next to two bomb craters, either of which I could have jumped into. Just as I jumped into one, two mortar rounds dropped right into the other. Another time an F-105 jet fighter dropped a bomb straight into my tunnel. It went all the way down but didn't explode. I'm really a very lucky guy.

If people say they were never depressed during the war, it's not true. You know, a lot of our people were killed. But once you accepted your own self-sacrifice, your own death, you didn't feel fear anymore. And when I felt depressed the noble cause of the revolution and American cruelty forced me back to the front lines. The ultimate goal was always national liberation, so we just kept on. How could you allow yourself to be depressed when you saw people making their homes inside the hulk of a tank like this. [He points to one of his photographs of a Vietnamese family living inside the remains of a destroyed U.S. tank.] Looking at people like them, we knew our task wasn't finished. They were the real source of our psychological motivation.

In 1968, one of my friends introduced me to my future wife. She was also a revolutionary, working as a doctor's aide. We got married that same year. On my wedding day my friends went to the market and bought a pig's head. But on the way back they spotted a detachment of enemy commandos setting up an ambush. They had no choice but to go to another guerrilla base and wait. They boiled the pig's head to keep it from spoiling. Two days later, after the commandos had left, we had the wedding in the jungle with just a dozen guests. During the ceremony we all sat very close to a bomb crater in case of an air strike. My wife and I spent three days together and then we parted. Very rarely did we see each other again during the war. From 1968 to 1972 commandos were everywhere, making travel extremely dangerous. Sometimes I only saw her once a year even though she was just fifty kilometers away.

On the morning of April 30, 1975, I was on a truck traveling toward Saigon on Route 1. As we passed the Quang Trung Military Training Center of the puppet forces, the street was covered with boots and uniforms left by the southern troops. I didn't even get off the truck to take this picture. [One of his best-known photographs, taken on the last day of the war, it shows a highway littered with hundreds of boots.] It speaks volumes about our victory. I shot many pictures of the southern soldiers as they took off their uniforms and waved at us while we were moving into the city. But I didn't want to use those pictures and humiliate them, and anyway, I think this picture of just their boots tells more about the war. I was standing in the back of the truck shooting backwards as we headed into the city. We drove over the boots like a boat going over waves. It was fun bumping up and down like that.

JOAN HOLDEN

"The counterculture was visible everywhere."

In 1964, at age twenty-five, the ex-graduate student moved from California to Paris to become a writer. "I had a good time, but no adventures worth writing about." In Vietnam, however, the war was escalating and with it, in America, an antiwar movement. "I began to feel that I was on the wrong continent." She returned to the United States in 1966 and soon wrote an antiwar satire for the San Francisco Mime Troupe, a politically radical avant-garde theatrical group founded in 1959. "The first time I heard lines I had written make people laugh I was hooked. It's been my life ever since."

When I got back to Berkeley in 1966 it was like moving from black-and-white into Technicolor. It seemed to be a completely different world. Suddenly everybody was dressed like Indians. There was this whole new style that seemed to have burst out of nowhere—psychedelic posters and handbills, tie-dyed clothes, men with long hair, and people peddling underground newspapers. The counterculture was visible everywhere. It grew in the cracks, like dandelions pushing up through sidewalks. How could that have happened in two years?

It was amazing and wonderful, like arriving when the surf is high and just riding on it. There was so much to do—in art, music, theater, politics—it all merged together and it was all about asserting freedom in every medium and opening your mind to alternative possibilities. I never wanted to lead a "regular" life but till then I hadn't found a way out. At the same time, I've always been a puritan. I believe in doing socially useful work. The sixties showed me how to lead a life with purpose and joy; that you could do important work and have a great time doing it. All you had to do was wade in and be taken by this wave.

I never thought I'd hear myself say this, but drugs really played an important role, especially LSD. I never did much acid, but it didn't take much. It was an Alice in Wonderland experience—stepping through that little door—that gave you the sense you could cut loose from everything tying you down. Doing acid wasn't "self-medicating." It was about opening your mind, not dulling it. It was about tripping. That was a very important word.

When I got a chance to work for the San Francisco Mime Troupe it was a dream come true. It was come one, come all, join our carnival. But the carnival had a serious purpose. We wanted to create the best possible art about the most urgent issues, and blow people's minds by offering it to everyone, outdoors, for free.

In the forties and fifties we were raised to believe that there were no limits on what we could achieve in the future: a happy society, a fruitful land, technological paradise. In the sixties we translated those aspirations, but that feeling of immense and limitless possibility was the same. And the expanding economy made it possible to quit a job one week and get another the next when your money ran out. In 1967, I was living in North Beach in an apartment with a view of the bay for a hundred dollars a month. With roommates you could make it on twenty-five dollars a week. You didn't expect to make much money, but you could live really cheaply and do what needed to be done.

The right has successfully painted hippies as lazy. Actually, everybody worked like demons, just not nine to five. Theater is labor-intensive. At the Mime Troupe we worked ten to ten. We actually had to make a rule: "There shall be one day off a week."

We did three plays against the war between 1967 and 1971. Ronnie Davis, who founded the Troupe, was the director and he used to find old plays to adapt rather than waste time with inexperienced writers. My first show was an adaptation of an eighteenth-century Italian commedia dell'arte play by Goldoni, *L'Amant Militaire* [*The Soldier Lover*]. We used the French title—I don't know why. It's a typical plot about an old man wanting his daughter to marry for advantage and she wanting to marry for love. But it's set while the Spanish army is occupying Italy, two countries that could be taken for the U.S. and Vietnam. Into this play—this outrageous satire—we poured all of our energy and anger about the war. It was a very free adaptation. We pumped up all the values in the play and made the antiwar politics very clear. The captain became a general, the commander of the combined Spanish and Italian forces who was going to drive out the rebels with his next big offensive. He uses just the kind of twisted language we were hearing from Westmoreland and Johnson about Vietnam. He says things like, "The fundamental policy of the Spanish government is to pursue peace with every available weapon" and "The rebels are on the defensive, as is proved by the growing number of their attacks."

Somehow, the idea developed that 1967 would be the "summer of love" and people should converge on San Francisco. And they did. But the Mime Troupe was not into "love." We were on the political end of the hippie-political continuum. We wanted to satirize the naïveté of the flower children. The hippie idea was you change the world by changing yourself and the radicals said you do it by changing institutions. So in *L'Amant* the general's daughter becomes a flower child who's convinced she can persuade him to change his ways and give up his arms. It doesn't work and she and her friends all get arrested and are about to be shot, till the servant girl dresses up as the pope and stops the war by decree.

We did these plays outdoors in parks or on college campuses, sometimes in front of thousands of people. As it happened, *L'Amant* toured the Big Ten midwestern campuses neck and neck with the Dow Chemical [job] recruiters. Dow made the napalm that was defoliating Vietnam and burning Vietnamese kids, so everywhere its recruiters went they were faced with big demonstrations and sit-ins. As word got out that this antiwar play was coming, we got huge, enthusiastic crowds. The play itself would become a demonstration. There was a character who would get the audience chanting, "Hell no, we won't go." In the parks, when we passed the hat after the performance we occasionally got a draft card.

We were also banned and picketed in a number of places. The debate over the war was ferocious. As much as we thought we were going to change history, we were always aware of serious opposition out there.

The Mime Troupe marched in every demonstration. We had our own marching band and wore these kind of ragtag mummer costumes. I played the triangle and cymbals. We had quite a range of songs—"When the Saints Come Marching In," "Louie Louie," "the *Marseillaise,*" "The East Is Red," and "The Ballad of Ho Chi Minh."

[She sings]: "Ho Chi Minh was a deep sea sailor / Served his time out on the seven seas / Work and hardship were part of his early education / Exploitation his ABC's. Ho, Ho, Ho Chi Minh . . ."

Those of us on the political side of freakdom knew that the Vietnamese were waging a true national liberation struggle and we really believed they "stole neither a needle nor a piece of thread from the people"—Mao's phrase. Our faith in Third World movements crashed against a lot of things in the course of the seventies and eighties. In my mind, though, the sixties didn't really end until Reagan was elected in 1980. There were bumps on the road, but it remained an enormously optimistic time until the end of the seventies.

OLIVER STONE

"He lived to kill. He was like a real Ahab."

His movies often generate as much controversy as acclamation. Yet no other Hollywood director has attempted to address more fully the history of the Vietnam generation, from the assassination of JFK *to the presidency of* Nixon *to the world of* Wall Street *in the 1980s. He has also made three films about the Vietnam War. The first,* Platoon, *drew on his own experiences as an infantrymen in Vietnam. The second,* Born on the Fourth of July, *tells the story of Ron Kovic, a paraplegic Vietnam veteran who joined the antiwar movement. Finally,* Heaven and Earth *is based on the life of Le Ly Hayslip, a Vietnamese woman who experienced all sides of the Vietnam War before coming to the United States with her American husband.*

In 1965, at age nineteen, Stone dropped out of Yale and went to Vietnam to teach school. Then, after a short stint in the merchant marine and another try at Yale, he returned to Vietnam in 1967 as a soldier.

I was not a Yalie. I never felt comfortable. I felt like an outsider. My dad would have wanted me to go on to Wall Street and who knows where my life would have gone. I might have been like Charlie Sheen in *Wall Street*. I had a nervous breakdown or as close to it as I could get at that age. I felt really fragile—very much like Holden Caulfield.

Yale was a really white world and only boys. I didn't know black people until I got to Vietnam. I hadn't heard Sam Cooke and Otis Redding. I didn't even know who they fucking were. I wondered what the hell I was doing. That kind of privileged life didn't feel right.

I read *Lord Jim* and that really influenced me. I thought there was an exotic other world in Asia. Somebody suggested I get a job with the Free Pacific Institute. They would hire you to teach in Asia pretty much as long as you could get yourself there and you spoke English. I had hundreds of students and I worked like a dog. It was in Cholon, a wholly Chinese community in Saigon. I was probably the only white guy except for a few priests. Later I had the suspicion that the Institute was funded by the CIA. In a weird way I was sort of the

"Quiet American," the Audie Murphy guy out there in shirtsleeves teaching school the American way to our "little brown brothers."

Then, to make a long story short, I went to Yale again briefly, got fed up with the whole fucking thing, and decided I had to make a complete break and put my whole life on the fucking line. The Vietnam War was going to be over soon if you believed Henry Luce [the publisher of *Time* and *Life* magazines], so I asked for frontline combat infantry. I wasn't going to OCS [Officer Candidate School] and bullshit around. I wanted the worst. It was the one time I got what I asked for. I saw the war of my generation as close as I could get.

I was totally anonymous, just a guy who didn't talk too much and tried to learn things as fast as I could. They didn't know your fucking first name. I was just "Stone." They were pissed off, angry people. I tried to stay out of trouble cause it was pretty heavy and I was a rookie. You're a replacement troop in a demoralized unit and everybody's counting days to get back home. I tried not to get too noticed. Just did my job and shut up. Don't get picked on. I was pretty good at that because some of the other new guys were really irritating to them and believe me, when you were a new guy they'd kill you. They don't really care about you, because you're an FNG [fucking new guy]. They'd put you up on point all the time. If you don't know what you're doing you're dead. And if they really wanted to fuck with you, they'd put you on an LP [listening post], which is spooky as hell because you're only two people outside the perimeter.

The whole fucking thrust of the American media was I Corps—the marines, the Rockpile, the DMZ, Khe Sanh, all that glamour shit. You never heard about the 25th [Infantry Division] or the 1st [Infantry Division] down at the Cambodian border. I don't remember seeing one fucking journalist in the 25th Infantry, ever. It was such an unglamorous fucking job. III Corps, where I was, was supposed to be the second front, but it was the first front. I Corps—that's the jab. The real punch—the right hook—was coming from the Ho Chi Minh Trail to III Corps aimed at Saigon, which is the head. That's the knockout punch. You cut the fucking head, the snake dies. All their tunnels, all their complexes, all the spies, most everything they had that was heavyweight was based around Saigon.

They were a very capable enemy. Would not miss a detail. When they hit us on Firebase Burt on January 1, 1968,* we found on the dead bodies the next day exact drawings of our perimeter, the spaces between our foxholes, and practically every piece of equipment that we had. They knew what they were doing. They're like fucking warrior ants. The Firebase Burt firefight was the

*This battle is also described by Larry Heinemann on pp. 243–247.

one I put at the end of *Platoon*. They put RPGs [rocket-propelled grenades] all over us. The only thing that saved my ass is that my company started out on the inner perimeter. If I'd been in C company I'd probably be dead. They were completely overrun down there. They were fighting with entrenching tools. I got a beehive up my ass that night. Beehives [artillery rounds filled with hundreds of small metal darts] were wicked things. Our guys were firing them from howitzers on the tanks point blank across the perimeter at the gooks and they didn't care if you were in the way. The beehive lifted me up and carried me about thirty yards and put me down somewhere. I didn't know what happened for about an hour.

I got two wounds in the 25th, which meant I could take a noncombat assignment in the rear. So I went to Saigon with an auxiliary military police unit. It was the most boring fucking job, but you can't go to sleep or some sapper will come out on the fucking street and blow you away so it was really nerve-wracking. You go crazy after a while. Anyway, I got busted for the usual stuff. There was always fighting between the REMFs [rear-echelon motherfuckers] and the frontline troops because we'd come back and some asshole would always say, "Shine your shoes, blouse your pants, shave." My attitude was, kiss my ass. I had contempt for them because most of them had not been in the field. They were just cowards making money in the rear selling PX shit. I hated their fucking guts 'cause kids were dying out there.

They were going to file charges against me for insubordination so I made a deal. I said, "Send me back to a combat unit. You get rid of me and I'd rather be there than here anyway." They sent me to the long range recon patrol in the First Cav, but I ended up being busted out of the Lurps, too, and I went across the road to the 1st of the 9th where I spent the last four or five months doing infantry. That was the unit the "Barnes" character [from *Platoon*] was in. He was a hell of a sergeant. He could kill and he knew how to get them. I remember one time we snuck up on 'em as they were eating breakfast. It's rare to sneak up on the VC, but he smelled the fish heads. We got them at dawn. The guy just loved killing. He really hated them, hated their fucking guts. He had scars on his face and he lived to kill. He was like a real Ahab.

I was in the 1st of the 9th when I got a bronze star. It was a purely military action. I mean I don't think there was any doubt about what I did. It was a potentially disastrous situation. We were under fire, taking casualties, and there was a lot of confusion. People didn't know where they were going, units were crossing each other. It was just a jugfuck in a village about six klicks from the beach. We were on tracks that day and I remember the dog getting killed. Then the goddamn lieutenant and the sergeant got killed. A lot of snipers were popping up everywhere. So this one guy pops up in the middle of about fifty people and starts firing. He didn't hit anybody but you knew it was gonna happen. We were all spread out around his spider hole so there was no way you could shoot at this guy without hitting one of our own men. It was a complete fuck-up. I just reacted and my baseball arm came through. I got the grenade right in the hole, first throw. If I'd missed the hole the fucking grenade would have rolled into my own men. It was pretty dicey, but I felt good 'cause I saved some men, I think. I also saved men all along the line. I saved men from drowning. And I saved villagers from being killed when I could, or raped.

I don't like it when veterans say, "Well, it's a war, you can do anything you want. It's such a fuck-up you civilians would never understand it." I don't buy that bullshit for one fucking second. It's so tiring to hear these clunkheads say you can blow anybody away in a war. Even though war brings out the worst behavior in every man, there is a moral place. We were destined to lose because this war had no moral purpose and it was fought without any moral integrity.

NGUYEN DUY

"Whoever won, the people always lost."

He is one of the most highly regarded Vietnamese poets of his generation. Distant Road, *a selection of his poems, is offered by Curbstone Press, a leading English-language publisher of Vietnamese literature.*

When I was twenty years old, in 1968, I served in a communications unit. One of my jobs was to clean rifles. You know, we northern soldiers loved our AK-47s. They fold up really easily and they're extremely powerful. I cleaned them with genuine devotion and kept them in peak condition. They were always shining. One day while I was cleaning a rifle my regimental commander walked by. The colonel said, "A beautiful weapon, don't you think?" I said, "There's nothing beautiful about it—it's just an instrument of war and I don't think there's anything beautiful about war." The colonel stared at me. He admired my skill as a poet so he said, "Okay, but don't say that to anyone else."

I spent my childhood in the countryside where life was very peaceful. When I was a young boy I never imagined myself a soldier. I just wanted to lead an ordinary life like everybody else. We were poor, of course, but it didn't trouble us too much. During the time I was serving in the army, my only wish was to return to that poor but peaceful village. When I came back after the war, everything had turned upside down. That peaceful beauty had vanished.

War had radically changed the nature of our society. There is a line in one my poems that goes, "In the end, in every war, whoever won, the people always lost."

YUSEF KOMUNYAKAA

"Soul Brothers, what you dying for?"

Born in 1947 in Bogalusa, Louisiana, he was the eldest of six children, the son of a carpenter. His given name was James Brown, but as a teenager, a few years after his parents' separation, he decided to adopt the name of his maternal grandfather who slipped into Florida as a stowaway from Trinidad.

In 1969, he served in Vietnam as a reporter for The Southern Cross, *the newspaper of the Americal Division. After returning to the United States in 1970 he went to college at the University of Colorado. He published three books of poetry before writing explicitly about the Vietnam War in* Dien Cai Dau *(1988). In 1994, he won the Pulitzer Prize in poetry for* Neon Vernacular. *Today he teaches writing at Princeton University.*

I think changing my name had a lot to do with the fact that I was sort of dreaming myself away from Bogalusa, even when I was in the woods creating treehouses and learning the names of birds and trees. One time my mother purchased a round viewfinder which showed very bright images of Mexico, Japan, and Africa. Those images penetrated my psyche and facilitated my dreaming. I was making myself part of a larger landscape.

The Ku Klux Klan was deeply entrenched in Bogalusa. Around 1964 a black man named Sims was shot by the Klan while making a call at a public phone. That's really what instigated the formation of the Deacons for Defense, a group very few people have heard of. It was started by a Vietnam veteran in Jonesboro, Louisiana, to protect civil rights workers and the most active branch was in Bogalusa. They felt they were not going to let the Klan and other violent elements suppress the nonviolence of the civil rights movement. The Deacons for Defense actually intervened to break up Klan meetings. Eventually they forced the Klan underground and civil rights workers could carry on with their voter registration.

Black people had never had an armed presence in Bogalusa except in a few individual cases. For a black man to carry a gun was to invite death, if not from the Klan, at least from the police. But the Deacons for Defense held together through secrecy and codes of silence. In a way, those individuals were heroes to me. They emboldened the whole community. I would never have attempted to desegregate a movie theater without the presence of the Deacons for Defense.

There were two theaters on Columbia Street in Bogalusa—the Ritz and the State. Blacks always sat in the balcony and whites on the lower floor. Some friends and I decided to challenge it. We had it all planned out for a Sunday matinee. I brought Loraine, a friend who had been talking about civil rights, but when it was time for the show to begin no one else showed up. We decided to go in anyway. When we got to the ticket agents he said, "I suppose you want to sit downstairs." Somebody had obviously tipped them off that we were planning this. We said, "Yes," bought our tickets, and went through the downstairs. I didn't know what to expect. Right before the lights went out, I glanced in the back and there was a whole row of policemen. It was the first time in my life I really welcomed the sight of policemen. By sheer luck, nothing ocurred.

When I was drafted and went to Vietnam I didn't have a strong opinion about the war. It was a tug of war in my mind and body. I was there and would attempt to survive, but I also identified with the Vietnamese to an extent. I saw them as peasants and that's how I grew up. I had trusted the land I'd grown up in and I'm quite sure those people had a kinship to the land.

I was writing stories for the divisional newspaper. A lot of them were human interest stories. A private whose life had been saved because he had one of those little army-issued Bibles in his breast pocket and it stopped a bullet—stuff like that. But I also went out to a platoon that had refused to obey their lieutenant. They were fighting an NVA unit and were in a desperate situation. Half of them were wounded and they were afraid of being overrun. They had this gung-ho greenhorn ROTC platoon leader and nobody trusted his orders. It wasn't that they were refusing to fight, just to take orders from him. Eventually a PFC with more experience took over. The authority was given to him by the other men. I know that story didn't appear in *The Southern Cross.*

There was a whole racial divide in Vietnam that hasn't really been talked about that much. It was intense. At the clubs in the rear, once people started drinking, there was a lot of name-calling. And, of course, Hanoi Hannah [the English-language propaganda broadcaster on Radio Hanoi] would talk about race. It was as if she were talking directly to you. She'd say things like, "Soul Brothers, what you dying for?" It was like a knife in the gut. And she also had some idea of the popular culture of black Americans. Just the mention of a singer like Ray Charles or B. B. King sort of legitimized her voice. You felt a momentary hesitation. It stopped you in your tracks. And sometimes that's enough to get you killed—that moment of doubt. Most of us didn't have the privilege of doubt.

There was an individual in Vietnam whose code name was "Black Lang." No one knew his real name. He was from Senegal and he was the commander of the 5th Viet Cong regiment around Danang. He had come to Vietnam from Africa when he was very young, brought by the French to fight against the Vietnamese. He later crossed over and sided with the Vietnamese. Stories circulated about him. We heard that one of his psychological tactics was to hit U.S. units and spare the black GIs. There was also some indication that he could speak English and might be infiltrating our bases to talk to black GIs. He was definitely a figure who caused some pain and confusion in our psyche.

I don't know if we've grown in the United States to the extent that we can embrace the idea of black American war heroes. I don't think any of the Hollywood movies about the Vietnam War really do justice to the black presence. I particularly think of the black GIs who threw themselves on hand grenades to save the men around them. There were as many as fourteen or fifteen black servicemen who did that. You can't rehearse yourself for that kind of action. What is it in the psyche that would make one do that? One of those men was Milton Olive [a posthumous recipient of the Medal of Honor]. I have a photograph of him and it's haunting when you think about his demise.

H. D. S. GREENWAY

"We would write something and the magazine would ignore it if it wasn't upbeat."

He covered the war for Time *magazine and* The Washington Post *from 1967 to 1975. Neat and trim, he has the accent of a Boston Brahmin. His father had gone to Indochina in the twenties and thirties as a naturalist. "I'd seen some of the movies and pictures he'd taken. They had a funny old French car that had wheels up in front of the radiator so it could crawl over logs."*

Vietnam was enormously exhilarating. You tended to forget everything else and just concentrate on that one story. Years later when I was foreign editor for *The Boston Globe* I went down to see our man in El Salvador, and he said, "The difference is all you guys fell in love with Indochina and not too many of us fall in love with El Salvador."

I think we all had a sense that this was our generation's defining moment and a huge story, an historical event that you didn't want to miss. It would be impossible to deny that Ernest Hemingway had an influence. I recently found a dispatch Hemingway had done from the Florida Hotel in Madrid during the Spanish Civil War and I went back and looked up a file I'd done about the last days of Saigon when the shells were landing. I wouldn't be accused of plagiarism, but it had a lot of the same feeling.

After five or six months in the field, you began to see that everything the U.S. Mission was saying in Saigon was nonsense, that things weren't going as well as they were saying and they were deluding themselves and deluding their bosses back home and deluding the American people.

There was a terrific struggle going on for the soul of Time-Life. One faction thought we had to stand up to Communism and back our government. The other side felt the war could not be won at any cost that the United States would be willing to pay. Most of the journalists in the field, even if they began rather hawkish as I did, soon said, "Look, this isn't going well at all." And some people thought it was immoral.

Hedley Donovan was the editor-in-chief and a supporter of the war. When he would come out on state visits we'd all look forward to the dinner so we could try to change his mind. Time-Life is a big battleship to turn around, but eventually it did.

Dick Clurman was our immediate boss, our chief of correspondents. He had absolutely no physical fear, so he would go out on military operations and walk with the soldiers. I remember one time we were with the Americal Division. They had caught a prisoner and they had a dog, a German shepherd, and they were encouraging the dog to chew the prisoner. Dick was horrified. He said, "We've written all these stories that these are the clean-limbed, idealistic American youth, and this would never happen." And I said, "Well, it may have been that way in the very early days, but this is a big war now, and these are draftees coming out and the morale isn't terribly good. Now I'm not saying that this is typical, but this kind of thing happens a lot and I've seen it happen a lot."

Time-Life started to change its mind in late '67. They did a cover story on Con Thien [a marine outpost near the DMZ that was subjected to intense North Vietnamese artillery fire] and it cast some real doubts about the war—that it was just a kind of hopeless stalemate. By the time the Tet Offensive came, there was some real questioning. Before then it was very frustrating and very sad because we would write something and the magazine would ignore it if it wasn't upbeat.

I was in Hue during the Tet Offensive and there was street fighting going from house to house. We were at a ruined wall and this one marine looked through an opening and got shot through the throat. The corpsman was trying to carry him out and couldn't manage. So I helped carry him out. Then a mortar or a rocket came and hit a lot of us and killed the guy we were carrying. I got hit with shrapnel and they took me back to a field hospital, where they looked at Americans first and Vietnamese second. Some of the doctors were very angry about that. Even so, you had to lie out in the rain for a long time before they could get to you.

It wasn't a serious wound, but I started to feel like the man in H. G. Wells's *Time Machine* after the Morlocks have moved his time machine. I had had this attitude that I'm not going to get hurt because I'm from a different century, a different time and place. And yet all of a sudden maybe I can't leave. I can't find the time machine. I may be stuck here and I may never get out. And the time machine was everything that got you around. It was the helicopters and planes that would get you out while the Vietnamese couldn't. Within hours I could get from I Corps to a wonderful French meal and bath in Saigon. It would take a Vietnamese months to get to Saigon from Hue.

It's true that the Viet Cong took a terrible licking during Tet and the North Vietnamese had to take over the war. But the Communists could always retain the initiative. They could lick their wounds and come back and fight another day at their time and their place. They weren't fighting to win every battle, but to wear us down and outlast us. So to say that we killed all those people and they didn't kill so many of us misunderstands the whole Vietnam War. It was a victory for us only in the narrowest sense. It was always a political war. They weren't fighting so much for territory but to win a political war and to mount something as effective as the Tet Offensive showed that all the American ideas of progress were an illusion. In a few years they could do the same thing. And when you get rid of our commanding general [Westmoreland was replaced by Creighton Abrams soon after the Tet Offensive], and the president of the United States says he isn't going to run for reelection, and the United States sues for peace in Paris, well I think that pretty well loads the balance sheet as a victory for them.

ANTIWAR ESCALATIONS

The Vietnam War produced the largest antiwar movement in American history, yet it was built on a long tradition of peace activism. Even the most popular and celebrated of our wars have spawned dissent and resistance. During the American Revolution roughly a third of the colonists supported the British. A generation later, a defiant New England nearly seceded from the Union in opposition to the War of 1812. When the United States invaded Mexico in 1846 there were tremendous flag-waving demonstrations, but within two years a once prowar Indiana newspaper would reflect the growing antiwar sentiment by calling for the impeachment of President James Polk. In 1861, a critic of the Mexican War named Abraham Lincoln became president. The civil war he led provoked violent draft riots in cities of both the South and North, and more than 10 percent of the soldiers on both sides deserted. During the 1898 war against the Philippines, an Anti-Imperialist League attracted a half million members, including Mark Twain, Andrew Carnegie, and former presidents Grover Cleveland and Benjamin Harrison. With the entrance of the United States into World War I, Congress passed draconian laws designed to suppress every expression of antiwar sentiment. Even so, the government classified more than 330,000 men as draft evaders. World War II, the "Good War," was perhaps the most popular in our history and yet the government imprisoned six thousand conscientious objectors who refused to fight. The Korean War began at the height of McCarthyism in 1950, a time when public dissent was extremely dangerous, yet after just six months of fighting, polls indicated that only 40 percent of the public supported the war.

Today people often refer to Vietnam as an "unpopular" war, but it really only became that after four years of steady military buildup (1961–64), and three more of intense escalation and fighting. Like the war itself, the antiwar movement developed over many years. Even in the first days of 1968, 61 percent of Americans still identified themselves as "hawks," only 22 percent as "doves." Within a few months, doves would slightly outnumber hawks.

Against considerable odds, the antiwar movement began to grow in rough parallel to the war. In April 1965, twenty-five thousand demonstrators gathered in Washington for the first national protest, roughly equivalent to the number of U.S. troops then in South Vietnam. Four years later, on October 15, 1969, a nationwide antiwar Moratorium drew at least two million Americans into public protest (up to five million by some estimates), many times more than the half million American troops stationed in Vietnam.

Never a single, unified, or centrally organized cause, the antiwar movement was fed from a great variety of streams. Many came to it from other movements—civil rights, nuclear disarmament, economic justice, religious activism, or pacifism. For others, it was their first experience of political involvement beyond the voting booth. Over time it came to include representatives of every imaginable category of Americans—students, clergy, businessmen, homemakers, factory workers, Vietnam veterans, even the wives and children of a considerable number of American policy makers. By war's end there were more than one thousand antiwar groups.

The movement's actions were equally diverse. Participants collected signatures for antiwar petitions, wrote letters to editors and congressional representatives, conducted teach-ins to scrutinize Washington's claims about the war, stood in silent vigil, spoke to neighbors door-to-door, sat down on highways to block troop movements, worked for antiwar political candidates, burned draft cards, handed out leaflets, offered draft counseling, protested against companies that manufactured napalm, organized fasts, published antiwar books and newspapers, provided sanctuary to military deserters, and participated in mass demonstrations in countless cities and on virtually every college campus. As the years passed and all of these activities failed to bring an end to the war, some came to advocate more extreme actions—taking over offices of the powerful, burning down ROTC buildings, provoking violent confrontations, even going underground to plan for an overthrow of the government.

Presidents Johnson and Nixon publicly claimed that the antiwar movement had no impact on their war policies or their morale. Inside the White House, however, antiwar activities were a serious, sometimes obsessive, focus of concern. In late 1966, for example, as the military urged Johnson to bomb Hanoi and Haiphong, he wondered aloud how long it would take "five hundred thousand angry Americans to climb that White House wall . . . and lynch their president if he does something like that?" In response to protest, Washington concocted hundreds of plans to attack, spy on, infiltrate, sabotage, harass, imprison, smear, divide, and discredit the antiwar movement. This counteroffensive included the CIA's Operation CHAOS, an illegal domestic spying program that lasted from 1967 to 1974, while the FBI used hundreds of *agent provocateurs* to infiltrate the antiwar movement and encourage the kind of wild and violent actions that top FBI officials thought would tarnish the movement's reputation among the wider public.

The effectiveness of the government's assaults on the movement is hard to measure, but it is certainly true that antiwar demonstrations provoked fervent opposition. Many Americans saw the protests as one of many signs that the very structure of society was crumbling; that traditional authorities were losing control; and that overly permissive parents and institutions had encouraged a generation to flaunt its privilege. By the time polls showed that a majority of Americans opposed the war, they also showed that an even greater number opposed antiwar protesters.

The antiwar movement rarely received fair or full media coverage and in the postwar years it was characterized even more harshly. Of all the American wartime experiences, participation in the antiwar movement has perhaps been the most ignored and distorted. Antiwar figures have rarely appeared in American popular culture of the past two decades, and when they have, they are often portrayed as frivolous, spoiled, cowardly, self-absorbed draft-dodgers who liked nothing more than spitting upon returning Vietnam veterans.

This stereotype does not hold up to historical scrutiny any better than did the caricature of Vietnam veterans as drug-crazed killers that appeared in movies and TV shows of the early seventies. The great majority of men and women who participated in the antiwar movement volunteered their time and energy out of deep conviction and in spite of obvious risks to themselves and their futures. And while many were bitterly hostile to the military as an institution, there is no persuasive evidence that they were routinely hostile to individual soldiers.

While the antiwar movement sought to forge alliances with GIs and military veterans, those efforts were strained by class inequalities built into the draft system. The fact that class privilege enhanced the odds of avoiding Vietnam merely widened the gulf between those who went and those who didn't. Many soldiers were deeply angered by the antiwar movement, but not so much because the protesters opposed the war as the fact that many of them did not have to share the burden of fighting it. Those who fought in the war and those who fought against it shared the struggle of their times, and in that sense they had more in common with each other than they did with the millions of young people who quietly avoided the war.

TODD GITLIN

"A rather grandiose sense that we were the stars and spear-carriers of history."

A student political activist, in 1962 he chaired "Tocsin," a nuclear disarmament group named after a French alarm bell. A year later, at the age of twenty, the young college graduate became the president of Students for a Democratic Society (SDS), which by the late sixties became the largest radical student organization in the country. Founded in 1960, SDS introduced itself as a "new left," contrasting itself with a hidebound "old left" constrained by its affiliations with the American Communist Party and the government's efforts to attack it. The young radicals were committed to nothing less than the end of racism, imperialism, economic exploitation, and human alienation. Its 1962 manifesto, "The Port Huron Statement," remains an extraordinary testament of utopian idealism tempered by the terror of the nuclear age. "Our work is guided by the sense that we may be the last generation in the experiment with living."

In the 1970s, Gitlin went on to an academic career as a sociologist. A professor at Columbia University, he is the author of The Sixties: Years of Hope, Days of Rage.

The founders of SDS had an international perspective and were looking for an end to the Cold War, but the Cuban Missile Crisis of 1962 hit us in very complex ways. It was shocking, of course, and seemed to confirm all our trepidations about the possibilities for mass destruction built into the Cold War. But here's the strange thing. The fact that we'd survived it actually muffled the significance of foreign policy for us. There was a sense of relief that we could now focus on domestic matters. When I became president of SDS in 1963 it was not much concerned with anything outside our national boundaries. What we were mainly talking about then was organizing the black and white poor into a class-based alliance. We were completely absorbed in community organizing and setting up conferences on poverty.

In 1964, though, we raised some money from an eccentric Texan peacenik to set up an office in Ann Arbor, Michigan, to organize for world peace. We called it the Peace Research and Education Project and we decided on two projects—South Africa and Vietnam. At the time, I perceived South Africa as the more interesting issue and particularly wanted to point out the role of American corporations in shoring up the apartheid regime in South Africa.

But Paul Booth [another key figure in the early SDS] and I were also very aware that the war in Vietnam was growing and we wanted to jolt SDS into doing something. So we convinced Izzy Stone* to talk to our National Council Meeting in December 1964. He played an important part in galvanizing the organization into active opposition to the war. Somebody proposed that we organize a national demonstration against the war and there was a groundswell of support.

We scheduled the demonstration for April 17, 1965, in Washington, D.C., but nobody thought it would be very large. SDS was still a tiny organization with maybe two thousand members and Vietnam was not very much on anybody's horizon. But in February, Johnson began the steady, daily bombing of North Vietnam. That created a lot more campus interest in the demonstration. Even so, I remember feeling that all the glamour and pizzazz in SDS were still with the community organizers in ERAP [the Economic Research and Action Project]. That's where the sex was in SDS and I was feeling a bit envious.

So when I got on a bus in Ann Arbor on April 16, I felt I would be happy to see five thousand people. When we rolled into Washington I remember seeing great flocks of buses parked along the mall, scores of them. It was a sunrise experience and it was staggering. I thought, we're in business, we're rolling. The antiwar movement is going to be really substantial. It will be a real contest. We had maybe twenty-five thousand people and everything about it felt good.

It was a beautiful day and if you look at pictures of the crowd you'd probably be surprised by how straight everyone looks. People are sitting on the grass around the Washington Monument wearing sports jackets and dresses. It looked like a prom. We had music by Joan Baez, the Freedom Singers, and Phil Ochs. Most people thought the best speech was given by Paul Potter, then the president of SDS. His argument was that the brutality manifested in Vietnam was connected to the brutality of American society and that in order to stop the war we had to change the system. That was the key phrase. Some people thought it was a huge mistake, a radical deepening of what was at stake, but it was a momentous speech and what most resonated with people was the very clear call to fortitude and commitment.

One of the myths that circulates about the sixties is that what the antiwar movement did was easy because everybody was doing it. Bullshit. The war was very popular at first and remained popular by polling standards until after the Tet Offensive. That's something most younger people don't understand. People were actually beaten up on some campuses for carrying picket signs at peaceful antiwar demonstrations. It was not "the thing to do."

That fall, in October, somebody from the University of Tulsa asked SDS to

*Born in 1907, I. F. Stone was a radical journalist who wrote primarily for the *New York Post* and *The Nation* magazine before starting his own own four-page newsletter, *I. F. Stone's Weekly,* that ran from 1953 to 1971.

send an antiwar speaker. I volunteered to go. By the time I got there, the university administration had forbidden any on-campus speech, even a debate, so my talk was thrown off campus to a coffeehouse in downtown Tulsa. Only fifty people or so showed up but one guy was the editor of the student paper at Little Rock University in Arkansas. This guy had traveled several hours to go hear a talk against the Vietnam War. It was hard not to feel giddy. To me experiences like that were more powerful in some ways than seeing a big demonstration.

A few years later I found myself stranded in Lincoln, Nebraska, with no money and no place to stay when I saw this guy wearing a "Resist" button.* I just went up to him and introduced myself and ended up crashing in some vaguely communal place. It felt like you could be anywhere in America and find friends almost immediately. That was an extraordinary experience. There was also a delusional aspect to this. I think it led many of us to believe that we represented more of the country than we did, not just on the war, but on politics overall. As the movement took off in 1967 and '68 from Stop the Draft Week to the March on the Pentagon to the Columbia Strike to the Chicago Democratic Convention we had become a big story. We were now on the front page. Think how far we had come. In 1960, when I was seventeen, we put together a demonstration of forty students. In 1962, we got eight thousand people in Washington to protest nuclear testing and the fallout shelter movement. In 1965, we got twenty-five thousand people. By 1968, there were antiwar activities all over the country. Everything in our experience contributed to a rather grandiose sense that we were the stars and spear-carriers of history. That was the psychological underpinning of various severe misjudgments as to where we were in relation to the rest of the country. The delusional assumption was that we could do anything. We underestimated the forces of reaction. You don't have a reformation without a counterreformation.

At the same time that polls showed a majority had turned against the war in 1968, a survey asked people to rank by popularity a variety of national organizations or forces. The most unpopular entity in America was the antiwar movement. That to me encapsulates the fundamental tragedy. We were hated. We were seen, not inaccurately, as part of a radical ensemble that really wanted to turn a great deal upside down. Most of the country didn't want to have that much turned upside down.

*"Resist" was the slogan of the Resistance, a national network of draft resisters.

TOM ENGELHARDT

"It was like Vietnam had somehow come all the way into our living rooms."

He is a book editor and writer, author of The End of Victory Culture: Cold War America and the Disillusioning of a Generation. *In anticipation of the interview he's collected a folder of antiwar artifacts from the 1960s and early '70s—flyers, articles, photographs, and letters. Flipping through them at his kitchen table, he laughs at some of the old pictures, but it is clear that the long ago experience still moves him deeply, the emotion rising with his opening words. "The first thing I want to say is that the war ate us. That was the way it felt. The whole thing was so improbable—this little country that nobody had ever heard of convulsed a whole society." In 1969, he dropped out of a graduate school program in East Asian Studies to work full-time in the antiwar movement.*

Our image today is that there were two sides in the war—the warriors and the antiwarriors. But the most striking thing I remember is that there were at least two sides in everybody. There was a real military side in me. My dad had been in the Second World War and he took me to military parades all the time. We went up to West Point just to see the Long Gray Line march and it was thrilling. America in the fifties was a strangely militarized land. You read now about the guys who went to Vietnam talking about John Wayne, but John Wayne was in us too.

My dad didn't talk about his war at all. He was incredibly silent. There was none of this "greatest generation" stuff, but he didn't have to say anything because his war was everywhere. It was on screen and it was glorious. John Wayne made me weep with patriotic pride. You went to any park and all you needed were two sticks and you'd begin jumping into ditches and shooting. We were always mowing down the Germans and the Japs.

I was an only child and kind of a timid one at that, very alone in the middle of New York City. I had parents who were escaping their parents' Jewish pasts, so in a way I had no past except the American one and I grabbed it really hard. I was a Civil War nut in my teenage years. I read everything conceivable about the Civil War and World War II as well. I was so moved by General Wainwright's message to Roosevelt when he surrendered Corregidor to the Japanese that I memorized it. It began something like, "I go, Mr. President, in sadness but not in shame, to meet the Japanese commander." I was so American.

My dream was to be either a diplomat or a foreign correspondent, but the future seemed kind of set and there was nothing very exciting about it. My experience of the fifties was that nothing would ever happen to the end of time. The horizon was empty and yet beneath it all was an underworld of fear. We were in the middle of the Cold War. We did duck-and-cover nuclear drills the way kids did fire drills. I remember hearing Kennedy's Cuban Missile Crisis speech my freshmen year in college. I thought we were going to be toast tomorrow. As far as I knew, the president was talking about the end of the world.

But when the crisis was solved and nuclear testing went underground we all stopped thinking about the bomb for a few years. I really believe one thing that secretly sparked the antiwar movement was the ability to put aside the possibility that the world could end tomorrow. In a funny way the Vietnam era was the last moment when we almost got out from under the bomb. And part of leaving behind nuclear fear was that people were able to dream about another and better world. When you look at SANE, the 1950s antinuclear organization, by the time you get to the Vietnam era, nuclear war drops farther and farther down the agenda notes of their meetings and Vietnam rises and rises. That was really the story of the period. Fear of the end of the world dropped away but Vietnam rose and rose as in some horror movie until it engulfed everything.

The war just swallowed us all—those who were for it, against it, in-between. It just swept everybody up. Look at the beginning of Students for a Democratic Society. They weren't an antiwar movement. They were going out to start a movement for economic justice in poor communities. They didn't even want to lead the antiwar movement when it started. It's like that great scene in *Modern Times,* the old Charlie Chaplin movie. He's walking along the street when suddenly a truck whizzes by and a danger flag falls off the back. Chaplin picks it up and starts waving it to signal the truck. A parade of protesters sweeps around the corner and all of a sudden he's at the front of the protest waving this red flag. He's swept away and then, of course, the cops descend. The movement was a little bit like that for everybody.

You were also swept up in confusion. Life wasn't a straight line. In the summer of 1964, I hitchhiked around Europe with a friend and I can remember defending the American response to the Gulf of Tonkin incident to French kids. By 1965 and '66 I was starting to feel anger about the war, but it took so long. After all, the war had been going on for five, six years by then and I hadn't been in a hurry to protest. One of the things to remember about the fifties was the nervousness it created about involvement. My mother was a cartoonist for the liberal *New York Post* and she did some quite savage caricatures of Joe McCarthy, but one of the things she pounded into my head was, "It's the whale that spouts that gets caught." That was her phrase. You weren't supposed to sign petitions. I signed them anyway but they made me anxious straight on through the movement.

And even in 1967, after a year of graduate school in Asian Studies, I was against the war but not yet fully against the government. I was kind of bored with school and wanted to get into the world. So I applied to USAID [the United States Agency for International Development]. They didn't want me, so I turned to the USIA [the United States Information Agency]. Just a few months later I would have called it a propaganda agency. I went to Washington for an interview. Every agency had their own little security vetting service, a holdover from the McCarthy era, and some ex-marine took me into a little room and started plying me with stories about beautiful Soviet spies who seduced guys in Polish hotel rooms and asking me if I'd taken drugs and if anybody had anything bad to say about me. He scared the bejesus out of me. Even so, I still hoped to get the job. I just told them I didn't want to go to Saigon. Fat chance of that. I had studied French and Chinese. But it took them so long to vet me, by the time the job offer finally came, months had passed and by then it would have been inconceivable for me to accept it. It could take a long time to completely turn against your government, but when you flipped it happened with incredible power.

One of the things that drove a wedge deep into the society was, of course, the draft. People like me were not really in danger. I was being channeled into helpful work for the country. The China field was flooded with government money and considered a kind of national service. On the other hand, I felt, how come I was being saved if other guys were having to go? This feeling built up in me so that by the spring of '68 I felt I couldn't bear my own privilege anymore. I got involved in a draft resistance movement called the Resistance. I went with two friends to the Boston Common and we handed in our draft cards. There must have been hippies out there and people with long hair but I wore a jacket and tie. I wanted to look proper. I wanted to make a point that it wasn't a bunch of crazies doing this but normal people like me. We had to walk down an aisle to hand in the cards. It was like a religious experience. It was possibly the most exhilarating experience of my life. I felt like I was floating. I was so scared before I did it but in this picture of me after the ceremony I look as ebullient as I've ever looked.

Not long after that I got a letter from the government saying I had received a National Defense Foreign Language Fellowship. I wasn't sure what to do. I was still this kid who wanted to do very straight stuff and just wanted the war to end. But we really thought about things then. There was this roiling mass of people all yakking and passing papers back and forth and organizing and thinking. My friends even offered me arguments for why I should take the scholarship. But in the end I sat down and wrote a letter rejecting it. What moves me when I read that letter today is that it was very honest and not particularly strident. I actually apologize for having applied in the first place. Here at the end I say, "I cannot expect something of others if I am not willing to take a first minor and somewhat hesitant step toward it myself."

At the point I joined the Resistance I began working as a draft counselor, writing against the war, organizing, doing anything I could. Trying to stop the war was now my life. Then, somewhere in the midst of all this organizing I just burned out for a few weeks. It was like a collapse. For days I watched television. We had an old TV that didn't even have a dial. You had to use pliers to turn the channels. I lay there on my bed at all hours with the TV about ten inches away and those pliers in hand and what passed across the screen were all the old movies of my childhood—the cowboy movies and the war movies, the movies I had loved and which I still basically love. All of a sudden I looked at them in the light of the Vietnam War. I saw all those Indians and Japanese and Chinese dropping by the hundreds for every single white that went down and I went, Oh my God, it's Vietnam. I had watched this all my childhood and it had looked so wonderful. But what was I watching? I was watching slaughter. What kind of indoctrination did I go through? That was what I started asking myself. I had this feeling that outside my windows Vietnamese were dying and I couldn't stop it. It was like Vietnam had somehow come all the way into our living rooms. Those guerrillas had just fought so damn hard and long and finally they made it into our world and infiltrated our brains. They had fought year after year until we finally noticed them. And once we noticed them we noticed other things. I noticed my whole childhood. I thought, ah, that's what John Wayne was doing.

I want to emphasize what a timid guy I was. I did things that scared the hell out of me but I felt they had to be done. On the other hand, it was also thrilling. It wasn't all for other people. The sixties had the effect of lifting me out of a life I was bored with. The main thing is that the war built this anger to a point where you did things you previously couldn't have imagined doing.

Finally I was called up for my draft physical. I met a couple of people called up at the same time and we agreed to do some kind of demo at the draft center. There was just total fear but I had a friend take a magic marker and write on my chest, "Fuck the Draft." And on my back she wrote, "For Draft Information Call" and a couple of telephone numbers. So when I took my shirt off for the physical I was a walking billboard as well as a walking insult. I also had a doctor's letter and the military was happy to get rid of me. They classified me I-Y [a broadly phrased exemption that could be applied to just about anyone the army did not want, whether the reasons were mental, physical, psychological, or "administrative"].

But my draft board was very angry that I had turned in my draft card. They made me appear before them and said I was a delinquent I-A and they were going to call me up as soon as possible. At that point I went to Canada with a friend on a kind of reconnaissance trip. I didn't know what I was going to do. Canada felt like another land and I felt so deeply American I couldn't imagine going there. I knew two people who had gone to jail and I admired them, but wasn't sure I could do that either. Another alternative, or really just a fantasy, was to go in the army and try to organize against the war.

I can't fully explain what happened next, but one of the first women's groups called something like "Five Women Against Daddy Warbucks" broke into my draft board at Rockefeller Center, took the delinquent files, ripped them up, and threw them out the window. As far as I know they didn't have duplicates. Mine must have been one of them because I never heard again. That's what solved it for me.

There's this mythology that without the draft none of the people who were protesting would have done anything. It's true that the draft created a sense of danger, even for middle-class kids, that otherwise wouldn't have existed, but I knew relatively quickly that I wasn't going to be drafted and, if anything, my efforts against the war only increased and continued until it finally ended. I don't think that was atypical. And the draft certainly doesn't account for all the women in the antiwar movement or all the women who went to Canada.

By this time, 1969, I had dropped out of graduate school and was working for an underground print shop. We were completely aboveground but it was romantic to call it underground, like the "underground newspapers" which were totally open and aboveground. We printed strike posters and movement literature on these old inked presses.

At some point we got information that there were two guys who had deserted the military and I was asked if I would help get them to Canada. That was really illegal and I was still this kid who had grown up believing if you met a policeman you said, "Yes, sir." You just didn't cross authority. But I went with a very strong and impressive woman. We picked up these two guys who claimed to be ex-Green Berets. We're locked in this car with them driving north and they're starting to tell these incredible stories. They claimed to have been wandering around Laos at a time when it wasn't commonly known that we'd been in Laos. And basically they were saying that they had done war crimes, had just slaughtered people. One of them was sitting in the front seat and as we're going past suburbs he'd suddenly pretend to shoot out the window, going "Dat-dat-dat-dat-dat." I thought, Oh my God. They scared me, and that was before they pulled out the dope. I couldn't believe we were going across the border with dope in the car. I thought, I've just had it, I'm going to be in jail for life. But somehow we got them to Toronto and the overriding thought was, I'm taking somebody away from the war.

You know, one myth of the postwar years that drives me nuts is that we spit on returning vets, that the soldiers and protesters lived in two separate worlds and loathed each other. Yes, there was tension between us—mostly class tension—but in the years after I left campus my life was amazingly mixed up with soldiers and I don't think I was especially unusual.

For instance, in 1970, I was working as a printer in California and this guy I slightly knew approached me and asked me to write an article. He knew a medic at Travis Air Force Base who was pissed as hell with the war and wanted to sneak a journalist into the hospital to interview some of the wounded GIs. I wasn't actually a journalist and I wasn't eager to sneak onto a military base, but I'd done a fair amount of antiwar writing and was angry enough about the war to agree.

So the medic drove me onto the base—I don't even remember how we got past the guards—to a two-story, green building overlooking the flight line at Travis, and the next thing I knew there I was inside interviewing his fellow medics and the war-wounded. These guys, some of them lying in bed with stumps, were way angrier than I was and remarkably antiwar in all sorts of complicated ways. I became good friends with the medic who brought me in. He played a mean guitar and had written this enraged, ironic antiwar song. It was a mix of Country Joe's "One, two, three, what're we fightin' for," "Johnny Comes Marchin' Home Again," and his own experience. Look at this. [He hands me a copy of the lyrics]:

> *Well, it's one, two, three, look at that amputee*
> *At least it's below the knee,*
> *Could have been worse you see.*
> *Well it's true your kids look at you differently,*
> *But you came in an ambulance instead of a hearse,*
> *That's the phrase of the trade,*
> *It could have been worse.*

Anyway, I wrote a series of articles about these guys and took them to Pacific News Service, a new antiwar outlet. They sent them around the country to the mainstream press and asked me to join them as an editor. So the career that became my life really began in the antiwar movement.

Looking back, I have no regrets for what I did. I think the antiwar movement made a difference. It reined in our government in some ways. It reined in our military urge in the world for decades. But we couldn't stop the damn war. That's my real regret.

Whenever I visit the Vietnam Wall, all this emotion wells up in me, tears and feelings I can hardly describe, but also anger, because there were people in the antiwar movement who lost their lives and then, of course, there were those millions of Vietnamese, and all of us, our stories, are gone. All that's left of America's Vietnam are those fifty-eight thousand Americans who should never have lost their lives in Vietnam in the first place.

VIVIAN ROTHSTEIN

"What? Meet separately with women?"

In 1964, as a freshman at Berkeley, she joined the Free Speech Movement and was arrested in a protest against racial hiring discrimination at an automobile dealership in San Francisco. "I thought I'd done something great, but my family was horrified. My sister was sobbing in the back of the courtroom. She said, 'Now there's a jailbird in the family.'" In 1965, after a summer of civil rights work in Mississippi, she dropped out of school and moved to Chicago to be a community organizer.

In September 1967, she was asked to a conference in Bratislava, Czechoslovakia, for American peace activists and Vietnamese representatives from North Vietnam and the Viet Cong. From there she was invited to go to North Vietnam with a small delegation of Americans.

The focus of the Bratislava conference was on the South Vietnamese contingent from the National Liberation Front. They had formed the Provisional Revolutionary Government and this was their public introduction to the American peace movement. That was important because Washington's line was that the North Vietnamese were trying to take over South Vietnam and this was a way for the Vietnamese to show that there was an indigenous opposition movement in the South. We were much more drawn to the South Vietnamese representatives then the delegates from the North. They were younger, less established, and more approachable.

The Czechoslovakian Communist operatives who ran the whole thing were these old, gray, boring party functionaries. The Vietnamese couldn't stand them and neither could we. We met some young Czechs in Prague and were surprised to discover that they supported the United States in Vietnam. They distrusted their own government so much they figured that if the Czech government said the American war in Vietnam was bad, then it was probably good. But between the Americans and Vietnamese there was just this spark. Since our countries were at war it was an incredible thing to be meeting and opening up a line of communication. We were supposed to be sworn enemies yet we were desperate to connect.

The Vietnamese women in Bratislava wanted to have separate meetings for women. I thought, "What? Meet separately with women?" The whole concept was unfamiliar. I really had no feminist consciousness at all. But the Vietnamese felt there were special concerns women shared, things they cared about that no one else did, and it was very important to meet separately. Among other things, we learned that the Vietnamese had their own Women's Union with organizations in every village.

The Vietnamese made it clear that they saw us as critical to building the antiwar movement and that American women in general would understand why the war was so bad because they were mothers and sisters and wives. The Vietnamese women thought we had a special ability to communicate the horrors of war. I'd never thought about women being a powerful constituency on their own with special talents and sensitivities.

A South Vietnamese woman in Bratislava named Mrs. Van who spoke very good English made a tape for me speaking to American women about the ways the war was particularly hurting Vietnamese women. She described how American GIs brutalized women, raped them, put broken coke bottles up their vaginas—horrible things. She also talked about the way Vietnamese women were organizing, how they had a "long-haired army" of women who would beg American troops to leave their villages alone. I played her tape hundreds of times in the States.

I got invited to go with a small American delegation to North Vietnam directly from Bratislava. Frankly, the only reason two American women went to Hanoi was because the Vietnamese insisted that there be women in our delegation. I thought, my God, this is an amazing opportunity and I have a responsibility to do it, but I'm scared to death. I'd never been anywhere outside the U.S. before except Canada and now I was going to another Communist country, this one in the middle of a war with the United States. I was afraid of the bombing and afraid I might go to jail when I got home and afraid I would never be able to get a job. I was also very worried about what my mother would think. My parents were first-generation Americans and their citizenship was extremely important to them. I might be threatening my citizenship and was afraid my mother would be absolutely furious. I was twenty-one years old and had just gotten married. I was completely terrified.

We flew in and out of Hanoi on the International Control Commission* plane from Vientiane, Laos, through this air corridor that was marked by balloons in the air. That was the only air space the Americans agreed not to bomb. I felt like I had dropped off the edge of the world. As soon as we landed at the airport in Hanoi all the lights went out. The windows had paper cutouts pasted to the glass so if the airport were bombed the glass wouldn't turn into flying weapons. We got into three waiting Russian-made cars and the bridge into Hanoi had been bombed so we had to go over the river on pontoons. Since everybody traveled at night to avoid the daytime bombing there were hundreds and hundreds of people on the roads.

In Hanoi, we were treated like international ambassadors, like royalty really. In a weird way we were like an official delegation of nobodies. I mean the Vietnamese were putting their hope and trust in this group of young people to make a difference. They said to us, "You are the true sons and daughters of Washington and Jefferson." They invested tremendous importance in us to help save their lives and end the war. I think all of us were wondering how we could ever live up to that responsibility.

At first we spent most of our time in Hanoi going to museums and seeing cultural performances. We visited a museum of American weaponry and learned about napalm, and phosphorous bombs, and concussion bombs, and antipersonnel cluster bombs that had embedded in them plastic pellets which couldn't even be found in the body by X ray. We stayed at the Metropole hotel and in the middle of the day when the bombing was heaviest we had to go down into a bomb shelter. The Vietnamese were very concerned about our safety so we traveled mostly at night in camouflaged jeeps and were required to wear helmets. They were also very concerned about our feelings. We went to a performance of Vietnamese music and before hearing a traditional single-string instrument they said to me, "Would you like to leave?" I asked, "Why?" They said, "Well spouses who are separated have a very hard time listening to this instrument." I had just been married and they thought it would make me too upset.

When we complained about staying in during the days and not getting out of the city, they took us on some trips outside of Hanoi. The whole society in North Vietnam had been decentralized and moved out to the countryside to

*The ICC consisted of representatives of Canada, India, and Poland. It was established by the Geneva Accords of 1954 to oversee the terms of the agreement, but had no powers of enforcement. While it participated in some peace initiatives, it did not play a decisive role in the war.

lessen the impact of the bombing. All the children had been evacuated from Hanoi. We visited hospitals and schools and factories which had been relocated into existing thatch-roofed buildings in the country. After one bombing attack we went the next day to the site, a pile of rubble, where we spoke to children who had just lost their mothers. It was very painful. We visited hospitals and met people who were victims of American weapons. In one village we saw a "house of hatred" the villagers had built with pictures of people who had died in American bombing runs. It just got heavier and heavier emotionally.

We also had a meeting with American POWs and that was a very intense and difficult encounter. Most of the time we were taken around by the Vietnamese-American peace group and they were very understanding, but we saw the POWs with the North Vietnamese Army and that was tense. All of us were antimilitary so we didn't like their military any more than we liked our own.

We met with three POWs. The men in our delegation began bonding with the prisoners, talking about sports and things and the Vietnamese really did not like it. The Vietnamese general in charge was not happy with us. One of the POWs was in a cast and obviously had been seriously injured. The Vietnamese said he'd gotten excellent medical care. It seemed like it was so set up. They wanted us to go back and say the POWs were treated well, but I had no idea how the prisoners were treated so I felt sort of manipulated. And the POWs had no reason to trust us at all. They probably hated us and saw us as Communists who were part of the North Vietnamese support apparatus. I didn't feel comfortable being seen that way. I felt sorry for them but I also saw them as professional soldiers, as military officers who knew they were bombing villages so there was no way I could bond with them. The whole thing was confusing and very upsetting. I felt like I was on quicksand. There was nothing to hold on to that you were sure of and yet I really wanted to be helpful to the Vietnamese people.

We ended up staying in Vietnam five days longer than was planned because one of the two ICC planes got shot down while we were there and we couldn't fly out on schedule. When I found out about that plane we were sitting at breakfast and I started crying. I thought I'd never get out of North Vietnam. I really wanted to get home.

When I came back to the U.S. I helped start one of the first independent women's organizations called the Chicago Women's Liberation Union. For me, there was a direct relationship between the Vietnam War and the women's movement. This whole concept of building a political base with women as the constituency was something I brought back from Vietnam. I talked to my colleagues in Chicago about the Women's Union in Vietnam and how it had chapters in every little village and built institutions for women with political power. So we sort of modeled our organization along those lines. We had chapters and subchapters and some of them built alternative institutions like women's health clinics and an abortion counseling service.

I also did a lot of public speaking against the war. I had never done it before. I spoke to churches, high schools, community organizations. I would talk to anybody who would invite me. A male friend of mine from SDS went to one of my presentations and afterwards he said, "This trip has changed you so much. It's incredible how different you are." My husband said, "She's not different at all. You just never listened to her before."

Today Rothstein directs a living wage campaign for the hotel and restaurant workers union.

Of course women did not have to go to Vietnam to find the inspiration to initiate a movement on behalf of gender equality or to realize that men in the antiwar movement could be dismissive of women's full participation. The women's movement of the late sixties had many roots, but the civil rights and antiwar movements were among the most crucial. They gave thousands of women the experience, skill, and political self-awareness that would fuel their own movement, a movement that endured long after the war and created many lasting institutions.

"THEY SLEPT AT OUR HOUSE"

PAUL WARNKE

"We fought the war for a separate South Vietnam, but there wasn't any South."

In 1966, Robert McNamara asked him to be general counsel for the Department of Defense. "I said I'd love to but he had to realize that I did not think the war in Vietnam was a good idea. Somewhat to my surprise he said it doesn't make any difference." After six months as the Pentagon's chief lawyer he became an assistant secretary of defense. Journalist David Halberstam described him as "marvelously irreverent and iconoclastic toward all the myths of the period." In his late seventies, he sat behind big stacks of papers at his law office in Washington, D.C., where, he insisted, his work had "practically dried up. I never retired, but my clients did." He died in 2001.

I first went to Vietnam in the summer of 1967 after being named to succeed John McNaughton as assistant secretary of defense for international security affairs. I didn't yet have any official duties so I decided to see if I could just find out something for myself. I got on an Air America helicopter and went down to the Delta and did a tour of the countryside. The first house I went into had two pictures on the wall. One was of Jack Kennedy and the other was of Ho Chi Minh. I thought, we're in trouble. The people I talked to didn't seem to have any feeling about South Vietnam as a country. We fought the war for a separate South Vietnam, but there wasn't any South and there never was one. I think that was our big mistake. We used to talk about nation-building, but no outside force is going to build a nation. There just wasn't a government there in South Vietnam that had any popular support. We had great difficulty coming to that conclusion. So I had very serious doubts as to whether there was anything we could do effectively to bring about an independent, non-Communist South Vietnam.

Very few people realized that at one point Roosevelt was in favor of Ho

Chi Minh's getting independence for Vietnam. When the French moved back in after World War II, the Europeanists [in the State Department], who always tend to dominate American foreign policy, were of the opinion that if France lost its empire, the Communists would take over, not just in Indochina but in France itself.

So initially we thought of the Vietnam War as being part of the fight against worldwide Communism and drawing the line against China—all that stuff. The fact was, it was strictly an internal struggle. But some people never changed their minds. I know [Secretary of State] Dean Rusk went to his grave still thinking we had done exactly the right thing. I think he had been traumatized by the "loss of China" [to Mao Zedong's Communist forces in 1949]. See, he was in the State Department at that particular point. I remember one time a reporter asked Rusk, "Why are we still in the Vietnam War?" and Rusk said, "We're in it because of a billion Chinese armed with nuclear weapons." That's really the way he saw it. Another time he said, "It's not as though we're the French. We're the United States of America and when we push on something, it gives." He was pushing on his desk as he spoke and it didn't give an inch. [Laughs.] The people in favor of the war genuinely believed they were doing the right thing, that if there was a Communist takeover of South Vietnam the same thing would happen to other countries like Burma and even Thailand. The domino theory.

I remember the October 1967 demonstration at the Pentagon very well because my oldest daughter was at Radcliffe and she brought a number of friends down to Washington who were part of it. They slept at our house. I'd go into the Pentagon with all these demonstrators outside and there were troops to protect us. But there was really no danger. They weren't violent. Some of them would bring flowers to stick in the barrels of the guns. So I would go off to work in the morning, come back in the evening, and talk with my daughter and her friends. Our discussions weren't heated because I thought they were right. Most of them were calling for immediate withdrawal but I thought some kind of compromise solution was possible; that there was a chance of getting some kind of useful negotiations that would have allowed a more orderly kind of transition. I don't know whether the war was morally wrong, but it was killing so many people. There's no question about the fact that if you're engaged in that kind of activity in a civil war you have things like the My Lai massacre. And if you went there and saw what was happening to South Vietnam, you had the feeling that this is wrong.

In 1968, I believed that the policy was going to change and we were going to get someplace with the peace talks. If so, the war wouldn't have gone on for those additional four years with more and more people getting killed and more and more animosities being built up. But then the Nixon people basically torpedoed the talks. Have you heard the story about Anna Chennault?* She was asked by the Nixon people to go to Thieu and tell him to hang on because Nixon was probably going to win [the 1968 presidential election]. Don't agree to any [Democratic] settlement because Nixon's going to take a position that supports you. And then, much to my surprise, Henry Kissinger was instrumental in keeping the war going as long as it did. He had been very interested in working with us the previous summer to establish contacts with North Vietnam through a couple of Frenchmen. That's when we developed what came to be known as the "San Antonio formula," which was basically that we will stop bombing if that will lead promptly to constructive negotiations. Henry was very interested in conveying that message, so I was surprised by how dedicated he was to Nixon's policy. I really think he saw it as part of the overall contest between the United States and the Soviet Union.

I went to Vietnam with three different secretaries of defense—Bob McNamara, Clark Clifford, and then Melvin Laird. I had resigned by the time Laird was the secretary, but he asked if I would stay for a few months and one of his reasons was so I could go to Vietnam with him. He came in with a reputation of being a total hawk, but he wasn't. He could talk up a good hawkish game, but down deep he was quite sensible. When we were over there Laird made it quite clear to [U.S. ambassador to South Vietnam] Ellsworth Bunker and to [General] Creighton Abrams, who had taken over for Westmoreland, that he thought the entire thing was a disaster. And I remember that when we got back to Andrews Air Force base, there was a White House delegation waiting to make sure Laird didn't have a press conference. I would say all three secretaries of defense were very much against the war.

Nonetheless, it wasn't the military that pushed us into the war in the first place. It was a civilian misadventure rather than a military mistake. Of course, once the military got in, their reputations were at stake and they wanted to win. Westmoreland and Abrams were totally convinced of the correctness of the cause.

I don't think Americans today regard the Vietnam War as a terrible blow to American prestige. It wasn't. I think most of our friends have concluded it was a mistake and everybody makes mistakes. You certainly can't look back at the history of France and Great Britain and Germany and say they've been flawless in their conduct of foreign affairs.

*Born in China, and married to the World War II commander of the Flying Tigers, General Claire Chennault, Anna Chennault became a major Republican fund-raiser, a devout supporter of Taiwan and South Vietnam, and the chair of Republican Women for Nixon.

"My wife and I used to have debates about what would happen if our sons were of draft age. Fortunately, they were a little too young. She would have perhaps given them a ticket to Canada. I felt that they probably would go to Vietnam and I wouldn't tell them not to. I didn't think it was fair that people were able to get out of it. But, my God, it would have shattered me."

PART FOUR

THE TURNING POINT (1968–70)

TET

Tet, the lunar New Year, is the most important holiday on the Vietnamese calendar. In American terms, it's as if you combined Thanksgiving, Christmas, New Year's, and the Fourth of July—a time for family visits, spiritual renewal, gift-giving, patriotic celebrations, fireworks, and feasting. In the mid-1960s, U.S. and ARVN soldiers looked forward to Tet as a brief escape from the war, a short holiday cease-fire. For Hanoi, however, Tet was viewed as an appropriate moment to rekindle devotion to the struggle for national liberation by linking the sacred holiday to the sacred cause. There was historical precedent for such a linkage. On Tet in 1789, the Vietnamese hero Nguyen Hue led a surprise attack against the Chinese, successfully driving them from the country. Until his death in 1969, Ho Chi Minh annually dramatized the patriotic importance of Tet by composing a short holiday poem and reading it over Radio Hanoi at midnight on lunar New Year's eve. His poem for Tet 1968 had greater significance than usual:

Even more than the beauty of Spring,
News of triumph illuminates the land.
Northerners, Southerners facing the Americans, advance!
Victory is ours!

Advance they would. On January 31, more than eighty thousand Viet Cong and North Vietnamese troops launched a massive, coordinated, surprise attack on hundreds of targets all across South Vietnam. They struck five of the six largest cities, thirty-six out of forty-four provincial capitals, and dozens of airfields, military bases, and government installations. It was a shocking and unprecedented attack. Never before had Communist troops entered major urban centers in force to wage open warfare. Nor had they attempted a synchronized offensive throughout the country. It inaugurated the war's bloodiest, most widespread fighting, greatly escalated public debate about the value and efficacy of U.S. actions in Vietnam, and pushed American officials to think seriously about changing their policy in Vietnam.

Despite intelligence warnings, U.S. commanders simply did not believe the enemy had the will or capacity to wage such an all-out campaign. General William Westmoreland believed the primary danger was a more localized offensive in the northern provinces of South Vietnam. In the months prior to Tet, his attention was focused on a remote combat base near the village of Khe Sanh six miles from the Laotian border. The North Vietnamese had surrounded the base with at least twenty thousand troops and held six thousand U.S. Marines under siege. So worried was President Johnson that he forced his top generals to promise the siege would not culminate in another Dien Bien Phu.

In fact, Hanoi had moved large numbers of troops into remote border locations like Khe Sanh, Con Thien, and Dak To primarily to lure major U.S. forces away from the heavily populated targets they would hit during Tet. While Westmoreland sent more than half of his combat troops to the five northernmost provinces, the Communists quietly but steadily moved thousands of Viet Cong guerrillas into and around major towns and cities.

Hanoi's highest hope was to strike a devastating blow against South Vietnamese and American forces that would inspire a mass uprising of the urban population, toppling the Saigon government and forcing the United States to withdraw. According to Communist leaders like Vo Nguyen Giap, such a "General Offensive-General Uprising" would be the final stage of revolutionary struggle and should be launched when the enemy was most vulnerable. However, in 1968, Hanoi decided to go forward with a Tet offensive even though the odds of achieving a final victory were low. Whatever the results, they believed it essential to counter three years of massive American escalation with a direct and dramatic challenge. American intervention had forced millions of rural Vietnamese into the cities or into refugee camps near large military bases and away from the territories controlled by the Viet Cong. At the very least, the Hanoi leadership thought that taking the war to the cities would expose the fragility of U.S. control in South Vietnam, demonstrating that the enormous U.S. buildup was not offering Vietnamese civilians real security.

In the months preceding Tet, U.S. policy makers and military commanders had expressed more public optimism than ever before. American and South Vietnamese forces, they claimed, were steadily gaining the upper hand, military escalation had finally turned the tide, the enemy was faltering, the end was in sight. Tet presented a shocking contradiction to those claims. The Viet Cong had been able to penetrate every part of the country, even the grounds of the American Embassy in Saigon. In Hue, U.S. Marines fought house to house for almost a month to regain control of the old imperial city. The whole country seemed up for grabs.

Perhaps the most famous media image of Tet was a street-corner execution, graphic footage of South Vietnamese police chief General Nguyen Ngoc Loan firing his pistol point blank into the temple of a Viet Cong prisoner, the blood shooting in a stream from the other side of his head. To many, this single act symbolized the brutality of the government American forces were fighting to sustain. Then, in late February, Walter Cronkite, the CBS news anchor widely regarded as the most trustworthy man in America, arrived in Vietnam. In a prime-time special report, Cronkite acknowledged that the American and South Vietnamese troops had successfully beaten back the offensive, but concluded by saying, "It now seems more certain than ever that the bloody experience of Vietnam is to end in stalemate."

The U.S. and ARVN counteroffensive inflicted massive casualties on North Vietnamese and especially Viet Cong troops. Communist forces had roughly as many deaths during Tet as the United States had for the entire war, about fifty-eight thousand. The American military lost 3,895 during Tet, and the ARVN 4,954. Westmoreland based his claim of victory on the disparity in losses and on the fact that his forces had successfully regained military control of all major cities and provincial capitals. Yet to many Americans and South Vietnamese it did not feel like a victory, or at least not the kind that promised to lead to full and final control of the South. Indeed the U.S. counteroffensive raised as many questions as the Communist attacks. To push back the Viet Cong, the United States launched air strikes on many heavily populated areas. Countless homes were destroyed and more than fourteen thousand South Vietnamese civilians were killed. The most famous defense of the bombing was offered by an American major in Ben Tre who said, "It became necessary to destroy the town in order to save it." A growing number of critics took the statement as an epigram for the entire war.

Less clear to Americans was that the North Vietnamese and Viet Cong had slaughtered many civilians during the Tet Offensive, most notably in Hue. At the beginning and end of their monthlong occupation of the imperial city, Communist forces rounded up and executed South Vietnamese they had identified as supporters of the Saigon government. No precise count of this massacre exists, but perhaps two thousand to three thousand civilians were murdered. Many were later found in shallow graves with their hands tied behind their backs.

In Washington, Tet prompted an internal debate about the direction of the war. It led President Johnson to announce that he was bowing out of the 1968 presidential election, stopping the bombing of North Vietnam above the twentieth parallel, and seeking peace talks with Hanoi. He also rejected General Westmoreland's request for an additional 206,000 troops and soon replaced him with General Creighton Abrams. For the first time, U.S. policy makers began to believe they needed to find a way to deescalate their war in Vietnam.

TRAN VAN TAN

"He asked me for directions to the police station."

We meet at the newly built office of the Ho Chi Minh City Veterans Association. The wall behind us is decorated with four black lacquered panels inlaid with mother-of-pearl floral designs. Above that, a color print of Ho Chi Minh. On the table are mangos and oranges. A thin man with long fingers and prominent cheekbones, he is about five feet, nine inches, considerably taller than most Vietnamese. He was born in the countryside of Quang Nam Province near Danang. "My father took part in the revolution against the French colonialists and was shot dead in a French raid when I was four years old." In 1960, at seventeen, he moved to Saigon and soon became an underground agent for the National Liberation Front.

At the time of the Tet Offensive I was a textile worker. That was my legal cover, but my real work, day and night, was as a secret agent. I was a "one-line operative," so-called because you only answered to one man who knew your role. For your own protection, you weren't allowed to reveal your secret revolutionary activities to anyone else, even your own parents.

During the day, in the textile mill, I tried to recruit workers to join the revolution. But I had to be very careful and selective. Once I targeted a worker for recruitment, I first had to learn as much as I could about his family and social background. Only then would I begin to talk with him, little by little, about politics. Of course I never revealed that I was working for the revolution. It took a lot of patience and flexibility to get a feel for the target's political viewpoints, to make friends with him, and finally convert him to the cause.

Since everyone was being drafted by the Saigon military, one of my first goals was to persuade workers that fighting for the puppet government meant shooting and killing your own people. If I couldn't persuade them to work for the revolution, maybe I could at least convince them to dodge the draft. I had to avoid the draft myself. On three different occasions I had to get fake birth certificates showing that I was too young to be drafted. I have no idea how they made them. Some contacts in my home village in Quang Nam took care of everything.

My area of operation was Bay Hien intersection in the Tan Binh district of

Saigon. One-line operatives worked according to preestablished codes. If you were to receive a message or be assigned a task you had to arrive at a specific location at exactly the right time, know exactly what to wear, what to carry in your hand, what to say, and so on.

During the Tet Offensive I was one of the operatives who guided revolutionary troops to their targets in the city. On the second day of Tet, I went to a street corner to meet my contact. After we exchanged codes, he told me to stay put and wait for a specific directive. A few hours later a woman came by and told me I would soon be contacted by regular troops. At dawn the next day a knock at the door woke me up. It was a Liberation Army commander. He asked for a glass of water. That was the code of recognition. Then he asked me for directions to the Nguyen Van Cu police station and where I thought enemy units might be located. I told him everything I knew. Not too long after that, I heard the sound of American tanks coming into the area. People were fleeing the neighborhood and I saw a swarm of choppers circling overhead. I went to the Minh Phung rotary and stayed in the Hue Lam pagoda, mixing in with all the people who were evacuating the area. I thought I might pick up some information. Later I went to the scene of the battle and saw several burned-out American tanks. People there told me that the revolutionary forces had destroyed them with B-40 rockets.

So my role was not very significant. I didn't take part directly in the combat, I just provided a little information. I didn't even know in advance about the Tet Offensive. A few weeks later, I came under suspicion. Some government soldiers knocked on my door, accused me of being a VC, and hauled me away. But just as we got outside I saw Hai Than. He was a security officer I had befriended. I used to buy him drinks all the time. As a secret agent, it's crucial to make friends with people who can protect you. So Hai Than was on the other side of the street and I called out to him. He came over and said, "What's up?" I told him I had just been arrested as a VC suspect. He told the soldiers to let me go, that I was a close friend of his. After they released me Hai Thanh said, "If you actually are a VC, I'll kill your whole family, from your grandparents on down, with my own hands. Understand?"

When I told that story to my direct commander he decided the noose was getting too tight around me and it was time for me to move out to the Liberated Zone. So from then until Liberation in 1975 I served in Artillery Battalion 8. We fought in many places around Cu Chi and Ben Cat [northwest of Saigon]. After Liberation I came back to Bay Hien intersection leading a detachment of combatants. The people in the neighborhood were stunned to see that I was a revolutionary soldier. They said, "Wow. That guy used to hang around with security cops!"

BARRY ZORTHIAN

"Then—boom!—Tet comes along."

From 1964 to 1968 he was, in effect, the *official voice of America in Vietnam. As director of the Joint United States Public Affairs Office (JUSPAO), he was in charge of all media relations and served as the principal public relations adviser to the U.S. ambassador and the commander of U.S. forces. Every day at five o'clock he ran a press briefing in a two-hundred-seat auditorium at the JUSPAO building in downtown Saigon. Laden with statistics and routine claims of progress, the daily briefing was frequently so at odds with many reporters' experience of the war that by the midsixties they began to call it the "Five O'Clock Follies." As journalist Michael Herr wrote in* Dispatches, *"Cam Ranh Bay could have dropped into the South China Sea and they would have found some way to make it sound good."*

Zorthian concedes that U.S. officials "tended to see the glass half full," but believes many journalists were predisposed to look for negative news: "One of the problems is that the media had access to anyone and everyone and they had a tendency to find the critics. I've often said the media would give as much weight to the opinions and judgments of a private first class as they would to General Westmoreland. Well, that PFC may not have had the whole picture."

On the first night of the Tet Offensive I was having dinner in my residence when the noise of the attacks began. It didn't arouse much curiosity at first because we always heard distant shooting in Saigon. But it soon became clear that something unusual was going on. I got in touch with the Combat Operations Center [COC]. The first reports were very fragmentary, but it looked like the start of a wide-scale assault on Saigon itself. After midnight, I got word from COC that there was shooting at the embassy. I tried to call over there on a civilian phone, two military lines, and an emergency embassy radio net, but couldn't get through.

I finally thought of George Jacobson, who was special assistant to the ambassador and had a house on the embassy grounds. Eventually I got through to him. He was leaning out his second-story window. George said that VC sappers [commando infiltrators] had penetrated his house and he could hear people downstairs. There was shooting outside on his side of the compound, shadowy figures floating around, and occasional bursts of gunfire. As far as he could tell the embassy was still secure. He had a pistol and after we hung up he shot one of the sappers coming up the stairs.

The shooting at the embassy went on all through the night, but the marine guards held off the VC sappers and eventually everyone who penetrated the compound was killed. Maybe a few got away. There was a story later claiming the VC had penetrated the embassy building itself, but that wasn't the case. They may have entered the outer door but they never did get into the embassy proper.

The next morning shortly after dawn I went down there and met Westmoreland. I urged him to talk to the press and put the whole event in context. He was surrounded by VC dead and the marines who had fought through the night. He gave a very strong tribute to the bravery of the soldiers and their victory over the VC. He was heavily criticized for claiming success in repelling the VC at the embassy and saying everything was under control. But he was talking to his troops, not to the world. Unfortunately, with modern communications, his words and the footage circulated around the world. The media carried his words accurately, but when you heard them in the face of headlines about VC attacks in forty different places, penetrating the embassy compound, and fighting in the heart of Saigon, it almost sounded fatuous to be complimenting his troops on their victory.

Initially, the attack on the embassy got most of the media attention. Many journalists lived in the area and on January 31 they were awakened by combat literally around their residences. What do you write about in that situation? You write about what you see. They weren't getting reports from the field about all the attacks that were repulsed. The front page of *The Washington Post* showed a very vivid picture of dead Viet Cong on the embassy lawn. And CBS sent back raw footage of the fighting in the center of Saigon that was run unedited. Those kind of pictures had an enormous impact back in the U.S.

The second day [U.S. ambassador to South Vietnam Ellsworth] Bunker gave a briefing. I happened to write the briefing notes for him. He said that fighting was still going on in Saigon, Hue, and Bien Hoa, but that most of the attacks had been beaten back and that militarily the VC and the North Vietnamese had suffered a defeat. He said it was true that the offensive had had quite an impact psychologically, but that was the only lasting impact they might have. All that was lost in the coverage and his remarks were seen as more false optimism by the government. Tet was interpreted as a defeat for the U.S. and South Vietnamese forces. It wasn't until August that Charlie Mohr finally wrote a front-page story in *The New York Times* saying that in military terms Tet was a tremendous setback for the North Vietnamese and the VC.

The sudden shock of these attacks, and the fact that they hit so many places at the same time, was a tremendous blow to U.S. public thinking and particularly to government officials and Congress. Our credibility was very low of course. There was this picture that we didn't talk facts. The 1967 election of General Thieu as president of South Vietnam hadn't helped. LBJ had sent out a commission to monitor the election and they said it was "reasonably honest." Those claims were questioned and our credibility suffered. Obviously it wasn't the cleanest election. The government was pressing for a margin of victory and in many cases pressure was put on voters. But how do you expect the Vietnamese, who have not had a democratic election in a thousand years, to come out with that clean an election?

Another thing that hurt our credibility was the lack of visible military progress. Westy [General Westmoreland] would say, "Hell, we never lost a battle." But places that were not secure in 1965 were not secure in 1967. The nature of the war was that you didn't have territorial advances or cleared-out security. While progress was being claimed, with some reason, there seemed to be no movement, so a very skeptical media and others questioned the accuracy of those claims.

Then Westy gave that speech in Washington at the National Press Club [in November 1967] at the urging of President Johnson. Westy was under pressure from the president to put a positive spin on the war because Johnson didn't have anyone else with any credibility. LBJ was being attacked left and right and he said, all right, let's get our guy in uniform here. Westmoreland said, very cautiously, that the beginning of the end was in sight and that in the next two years we should be able to reduce our troops in South Vietnam. Well that was interpreted as claiming enormous progress. Then—boom!—Tet comes along after all those reassurances that things were improving and the impact of those multiattacks was devastating. If I were in Congress I'd feel the same thing—what the hell are you saying?

There was a *Life* picture of an armored personnel carrier in Hue with dead and wounded U.S. Marines stacked on top of it and that kind of thing had quite an impact. Then [South Vietnamese police chief] General [Nguyen Ngoc] Loan's outright shooting of a Viet Cong was captured on film and left an enormous impression.* Of course it was a horrible thing, but what that picture didn't provide were the circumstances and background. That particular VC had just killed a close friend of General Loan's, one of his police officials. Loan was a very volatile, emotional character to start with and in the heat of the moment he pulled that thing. But a picture can never give the background.

*The photograph of Loan's public execution of the Viet Cong prisoner by Eddie Adams for the Associated Press quickly became one of the most well-known images of the war. There was also film footage of the killing taken by NBC. General Loan came to the United States in 1975, operated a pizza shop in Virginia, and died in 1999.

When [CBS news anchor] Walter Cronkite came we briefed him fully on what most people have forgotten, which is that Westmoreland did predict that something would happen during the Tet period. Not chapter and verse, but Westy did have sufficient concern, based on intelligence reports, that something was underway. He persuaded Thieu to cut down the traditional all-hands-on-holiday during Tet to fifty percent. And the Americans troops were on full service. Walter was shown on a map how Westmoreland had positioned troops in anticipation of Tet. But I don't think Walter ran that story. Walter himself, it seems to me, was taken aback at the degree and scope of the Tet Offensive and he delivered that famous statement that the war is at a standstill and we're not going to win. It may be apocryphal, but LBJ supposedly saw that on television and said, "If I've lost Walter Cronkite, I've lost Middle America."

During Tet we had a blackout for quite a while. I remember riding through Saigon at night in a black embassy sedan with dim lights and going through military checkpoints. In April I had to go back to Washington. I went out to Tan Son Nhut airfield in the dark, got on a plane in the dark, and landed in Washington where there had just been riots after the Martin Luther King assassination. I rode to my hotel in the dark and there were military patrols in the streets. At that point I didn't see a helluva lot of difference between Saigon and Washington.

Despite the controversy over whether the Tet Offensive was anticipated or not, the fact that the VC were able to undertake such a major effort, even though they were beaten back, nevertheless indicated that they still had enormous strength and lasting power. Look, we lost the war on the ground, that's all. The idea that the press lost the war is bunk. We didn't appreciate the determination of the North. I think maybe with the right involvement and investment we might have won it on the ground, but what did that mean? A million American soldiers? Another billion dollars of aid? I don't know. I don't know if we had the commitment to stick with it.

When Washington asked us for our recommendations, my answer, in writing, was to go to the Vietnamese government on our side and say, "Look, you either get your act together and start performing better or our responsibilities to our citizens and our country require us to pull out." Corruption was endemic. Many senior people in the government and the military were involved. Some of the generals were charged with being involved in the drug trade. And, as a general statement, the wives of Vietnamese officials were awful. Women in Asia were much more active in business at that time than in the West and they used their power behind the scenes to enrich themselves.

Still, if the Tet Offensive did have a considerable impact on the South Vietnamese, at no point in Vietnam did whole units collapse or surrender or go over to the other side. When Chiang Kai-shek collapsed in China, whole divisions surrendered to the Communists. Now, in South Vietnam, there were individual defections certainly and battlefield losses, but the Vietnamese did fight during Tet. Maybe not as effectively as they could have, but there was no, "We give up, take us all prisoner."

Tet was a military victory in the conventional sense, but it didn't destroy the enemy. They came back and were able to force our withdrawal because of the casualties we were taking and then they devastated the South Vietnamese forces. We probably could have gotten the deal we ended up with in 1973 as early as 1969. And between 1969 and 1972 we almost doubled our losses. It's easy to second guess but I've never been convinced that those last twenty-five thousand casualties were justified.

I remain comfortable with my role in Vietnam because I tried to insist on realistic briefings and avoid undue claims of progress. I don't think we communicated as successfully as we might have, but I'd like to give us a B. A lot of the journalists would probably give us an F-minus. Of course there was some basis for skepticism. Very often the government was not as forthcoming as it should have been. I used to go out to the provinces on Saturday and Sunday. I think I visited Long An Province five times over the years for briefings by the province team. The fifth briefing was almost the same as the first. The same areas were being cleared and made secure and the same degree of progress was announced and yet the province still wasn't cleaned up. After that fifth trip I said, "That's it, I've had it. We just haven't made any progress."

I stayed on after Tet but I'd used up all my credit to both the government and the media. In a job like the one I had, you eventually get enough criticism of your performance that in due time you're persona non grata. My war was over.

PHILIP JONES GRIFFITHS (II)

"You're not safe in those cities."

During the Tet Offensive he took many photographs of Vietnamese civilians. Pointing to a picture, he says, "A lot of these people are running for their lives."

This is District Eight in Saigon. Many of the people in this area were middle-class Catholics who worked in the South Vietnamese government or owned businesses. That's why they had big backyards and nice carved chairs. The Viet

Cong were so incredibly clever. They sent a dozen guys into District Eight and got them to shoot a few policemen and fire a few rounds knowing that the Americans would overreact. And indeed, within an hour U.S. helicopters were killing everything that moved.

The Americans had always told the Vietnamese that they'd be safe in the cities. But what happened in '68 is that the Viet Cong said, "You're not safe in those cities." And that's when the big disillusionment set in. Everybody talks about how the Tet Offensive disillusioned the Americans, but it also disillusioned many Vietnamese who had been loyal to the government. If you looked at a map of Saigon in '68 and said, "Where is the highest concentration of pro-American Vietnamese?" it was District Eight. And that's the district that the Americans destroyed.

NGUYEN QUI DUC

"I was living a double life."

When the Tet Offensive began in 1968, he was a ten-year-old boy, the son of a South Vietnamese government official, deputy governor of the five northernmost provinces of South Vietnam. The family was staying at a government guest house in Hue as Communist troops advanced on the famous imperial city. His father was captured by North Vietnamese soldiers, marched to the North, and imprisoned for twelve years. With the fate of his father uncertain, Duc left Vietnam with an uncle in 1975 and came to the United States. In 1984, his parents received permission to emigrate to the United States. Today he is a journalist and writer who hosts a National Public Radio program called "Pacific Time" from KQED in San Francisco.

All night we heard explosions and kept thinking they were just New Year firecrackers. We could not believe that Communist soldiers were fighting in Hue itself. It didn't even enter our mind. Before that the war had been out in the fields and jungles. We'd had a very sheltered life. At one point my father looked out the window and saw people in uniform and thought they were the compound guards. He didn't know the guards had run away and northern soldiers had surrounded the building.

When the soldiers came into the house my mother screamed. We were completely terrified. It was the first time seeing the enemy. The most frightening and shocking thing was realizing that they were regular NVA soldiers who had come down the Ho Chi Minh Trail and spoke with very strong northern accents. They'd been described to us as atrocious, horrific people. We were herded into a little temple in the back of the house with about a hundred other people. My father took all his business cards and papers from his wallet and hid them under the mat. I remember my mother telling him, "Just say you are a teacher."

Then we were given a lecture by one of the soldiers. As scared as I was, I had the impression that he was a very persuasive and eloquent man. I don't remember his words, but there was passion in his speech and I was moved by the way he talked about the nation. I knew I wasn't supposed to feel admiration. I should be fearful of these people and feel hatred for them. I did have fear—I could feel it in my stomach—but also that surprising admiration.

Then the men were taken to the main house and the women and children were put in the basement. Early the next morning, about two A.M., everybody was sleeping and I saw my mother looking out a tiny window. She allowed me to climb up on a chair next to her. Between the bars of the window, I saw my father's silhouette. His arms were being tied behind his back and he was tied to other men in a file. You are a ten-year-old child so what are you going to do? Scream or cry? Run out and save him? I was fearful, but numb, watching in silence. It was like a silent movie with these dark silhouettes. Then I saw the file of men marched away. My mother and I shared this moment in this tiny window and we couldn't begin to talk to anybody about it. It was a private grief. There was such a magnitude of fear and finality.

About ten days later we were driven out of the compound by American soldiers and taken to the university, which had been turned into a refugee camp. On the way, we saw that the bridge over the Perfume River had been blown up by Communist soldiers. It was lying in the water. I was so shocked. That bridge was an incredibly graphic symbol of Hue, a symbol of the whole nation. It was the subject of many poems and songs. You expect war to have its casualties and for people to be killed, but even then I thought that if you go so far as to blow up that bridge, a bridge that had so much significance for so many Vietnamese, then you no longer have respect for history and culture. You no longer have respect for the nation.

When my father was taken away we refused to believe that he might have been killed, even after they discovered all these mass graves in Hue. My mom went out to look at one of the graves to see if he were there, but there were so many dead bodies and the stench was so bad she turned away. She was so horrified she never went to another one. She had a blind belief that he was alive somewhere, but it was terrifying. I would sometimes find her at a neighbor's house crying because she couldn't cry at home. She was hiding the news of my father's capture from his own parents.

When I was a kid in Vietnam I was living a double life. There were so many conflicting and contradictory influences. Outwardly I was part of the elite who believed in the cause of the South Vietnamese. I was friendly toward Western culture, went to a French school, and had contact with Americans. But inside I was struggling to understand why the enemy was fighting. Did they have a real reason? Even part of the Western influence raised contradictory questions. American youth culture was very catching to me and my friends. We wore peace symbols and went to the flea market and bought T-shirts with the names of American universities on them. We grew our hair long and listened to Jimi Hendrix and Neil Young and the Who. We wanted to be the cool kids in town. At some point my friends and I began to ask, how can a country that produced hippies and such cool people also fight a war and kill people and act cruelly? You would see American GMC trucks go by and soldiers reaching down to whack a girl riding a bicycle. They would yank at her hat and she would get thrown and she would die. You would see Americans do this and feel like they can do anything in our country. But then you'd take an English class with an American soldier from Ohio who seemed just as nice as anyone, yet he was a soldier too. And the Viet Cong would rocket the city and you'd hear about the terrors of the Communists. Among this ugliness and fear we listened to songs and loved. We learned to play songs by Santana and Creedence Clearwater Revival and then at a certain moment late at night you listened to the antiwar songs of Vietnamese like Trinh Cong Son. At that point you became an adult.

"I suffered the loss of my father for sixteen years and when people ask about my life they expect anger and hatred. But somehow I don't have hatred in my heart. I think what happened to my family, my friends, and the nation were the circumstances of birth and war in the context of history and ideology.

"My parents worried that we were all young birds that were forced to leave the nest when they weren't around to guide us. The comfort for them was that we turned out to be good people. My father passed away from cancer last year. Over the years we had seen him as a superhuman. He'd survived so much with sanity and dignity and a firm belief in his country. At the end he became human again. That was difficult and comforting.

"So much of my life has been colored by having to leave my homeland. When I go to Vietnam I am not seen as Vietnamese and it hurts. And I could never be what other people see as American. The older I grow the more I think I don't belong anywhere. Nomads in the old days traveled around looking for food, for shelter, for water; modern-day nomads, we travel around looking for ourselves."

BOB GABRIEL

"We buried our own men right there."

He's a tall man with a sense of wonder about all he's survived. He lives alone in rural southern Ohio and works as a carpenter. In Vietnam he was assigned to Bravo Company, 2nd Battalion of the 12th Cavalry, 1st Cavalry Division. One historian has described the 2nd of the 12th as the "lost battalion" because it was cut off from air support during the Tet Offensive of 1968.

I was born right down the road. My parents still live here. My father was in World War II and he stressed that if I was called upon I should go. I actually thought about going to Canada a few times, but I wanted to hold honor with my dad because I really respected him and still do. I was drafted and I had to go, so I went.

When I got to Fort Polk, Louisiana, this big drill sergeant said, "ninety-nine percent of you guys are going to Vietnam." Then somebody asked, "Well, what about the other one percent?" The drill sergeant said, "They're going AWOL." [Laughs.]

They sent me to the field on Christmas day 1967 to LZ [landing zone] Leslie. Two or three days after I got there we called a Mad Minute. That's when everybody would fire at the same time, as much as you could, for a minute. By chance the Vietnamese happened to be rushing our line just as the Mad Minute started. The gooks were coming in the wire and we just mowed them down. We had tracers in our guns so we could see the bullets hit them. It was intense. I thought, "God, man. I've only been in Vietnam a week, and here I am in this goddamn battle." When it was over there were like a hundred bodies laying around our perimeter.

On the morning of January 15, I think it was, Larry Herbert came to my hootch and he's kind of hysterical. He said, "I'm going to die today. I'm going to die today." I go, "No, Larry. Think positive." "No, man. I know I'm going to die today." He told me to write a letter to his girlfriend and all this stuff. We go all day long and every time we stop we dig a foxhole because it was so intense. That evening around six o'clock we walked up on this old landing zone where another company had been and had dug all the holes. We're like, "All right! No digging tonight," you know? We get a break. We're all running around saying, "This is my hole, this is my hole." Larry says, "This one is mine," and he jumped in. It was booby-trapped. It just killed him right in front of me.

From LZ Leslie we patrolled the Que Son Valley. God, it was just terrible.

We couldn't stay overnight there because they'd run us back out. Every day we had contact. We had orders to burn all the villages in the valley. We'd tell all the people to go to the little town of Que Son. We burned a lot of villages. We'd just go burn people's houses down. It was sad. I mean here's these people who live in poverty anyway, and then we'd just come in and wipe out everything they've had all their life, you know? A lot of them were holed up in bunkers and stuff and we'd tell them to come out, and they wouldn't come out and one thing leads to another and somebody will throw a hand grenade in there and people would get hurt.

I don't think we were there more than two or three weeks and we got moved to Camp Evans above Hue. Then the Tet Offensive started and Hue got overrun so we got orders to cut off the North Vietnamese supply lines so we could stop the siege of Hue. We ran into a lot of NVA regulars who were real tough fighters. The first day we started up this paved road and as we went across a bridge they opened up on us with a machine gun. A couple of guys got hit and I dove to the pavement. I don't know how they missed me, but I didn't get hit. So there's three of us on the road. Everybody else got off to the side in a ditch. There's a dead guy in front of me and the guy in back of me panicked and stood up. They shot him so I'm laying between two dead guys and every time I move they shoot.

Somehow the South Vietnamese got some artillery off down our way and these big pieces of shrapnel would come sliding down the blacktop—big, jagged strips. One stopped right beside me and it was still smoking. I thought, "Man, I've got to get off this road." I say, "I'm coming over to you guys." Somebody goes, "No, man. Don't do it. There's not enough room in here." Not enough room? I jump on top of somebody.

So then the battalion commander is flying around in a helicopter and he's going, "You have to charge that machine gun. Get some volunteers and charge that machine gun." The lieutenant looks at me, and he goes, "All right, you wanna go?" I go, "Hell, no, I was just laying out there in the road and nobody wanted to help me." I said, "I just need a little breather here." So he gets two guys to go with him, man, and as soon as they jumped out, all three of them got killed. Just that quick. [He snaps his fingers.] So everybody panics. Everybody's freaking out.

A sergeant E-5 takes over and we're like, "Goddamn, we're going to die here." The colonel keeps flying around saying, "Charge that machine gun!" I'm looking at him flying over, thinking, that son of a bitch. So I actually fired a couple rounds at his helicopter. He's like, "Hey, I'm getting in-coming, we gotta go." He flies off and I go, "Yeah, all right!"

But we still can't move. I go, "Hey, here's what we do. Let's just drop down in the river and go back. It's only knee deep with a four-foot-high bank. They say, "Great idea. Here's the machine gun. You wait here and hold them off. We'll get everybody out of here, go a little ways, and wait on you." So they dropped down the river and split. I mean they just took off. Left me there all by myself.

So here comes the Vietnamese. I'm shooting at them and they're shooting at me. I'd fire and run, fire and run. It seemed like it took forever. Finally an American comes toward me up the river and he goes. "You Gabriel?" I go, "Yeah." And he goes, "Well, all your guys are way back there. They sent us up to get you." So they kind of escorted me back.

Once the action starts something takes over and you do stuff you don't even realize you do until it's over with and they say, "Jesus Christ, man, you're a real hero. You exposed yourself to fire and saved our lives." I go, "I did?" All I was trying to do was stay alive. Killing somebody is never easy. Even though your life's in danger, still the stuff gets in your mind. You know, like, why them and not me? I never enjoyed it.

Then we got stuck at one place just outside of Hue for several days taking all kinds of fire. We had like fourteen guys shot in the head. We couldn't get any air support because the weather was bad and the clouds were real low. Finally we just figured we had to get the hell out of there. We had a bunch of wounded and dead and all their weapons. So we stacked all the weapons we couldn't carry in the middle of our perimeter and booby-trapped them. Then we buried the dead right there. We'd never done this before and never did it again—we buried our own men right there on the spot. It was unheard of, but we just couldn't get any helicopters in to get them out. It seemed like there was ten or fifteen bodies.*

So we started out. This guy named Commacho led us out of there. He was the point man. Everybody respected that dude. He was great. After all the troops left the perimeter we could hear the Vietnamese kind of running in there and somebody set off the big stack of ammunition. We walk and walk and walk all night long until almost daylight. We're so fucking glad to be out of there and we're kind of laying around on this big hill. Then they mortared us. Two or three more guys got killed and a bunch of guys got wounded. They're just kicking our ass so we get really low and go up to this old French compound which has these big concrete bunkers, so we're pretty safe there for a while. We stayed there a couple of days—tried to get our shit together. By

*The eleven bodies were later recovered by another American unit. See Charles Krohn, *The Lost Battalion* (Westport, Conn.: Praeger, 1993), p. 109.

that time my platoon was down to three guys. We'd lost so many men they replaced them with South Vietnamese soldiers, which was a definite mistake. They were just cowards. Every time we'd hit fire, they'd run backwards. It was terrible.

Then I got in-country R and R for killing the most gooks in a month. Everybody sort of kept track. I had like fifteen confirmed. So they gave me a three-day, in-country R and R at China Beach in Danang. I went with this cool lieutenant, a really great guy. Me and him were really good friends. We both got so fucking drunk. We ended up spending about a week and a half. [Laughs.]

In April they sent us up to Khe Sanh. They just kept running these helicopters all day long till we had it completely surrounded. It was the weirdest thing because Khe Sanh looked like the moon. And it was the first time I ever got fired at by enemy artillery. We'd been mortared but these were big guns. It was scary as hell. Shit was flying everywhere. Make your asshole pretty tight.

Sometime around then I shot my best friend in the foot to get him out of the field. Nam was so intense for him, you know. He just couldn't stand it. And he had some of the traits that Larry had—the guy that told me he was going to die. We'd been in a couple of skirmishes and we got shelled the night before and he was really worried. He'd say, "Gabe, I don't think I'm going to make it, man." And on and on and on.

So one morning, we got up and he was bent down, looking into his pack or something. I had an M-60 machine gun and just kind of pointed it at his foot. If you lift the feed tray up on it, it'll discharge because there's a round ready to go. I lifted that feed tray up and "pop"—just like that. The medic came down and morphined him up real quick. He was hurt pretty bad and I'm like, "Oh, I really fucked up." But they sent him right back to the States and his mom and dad sent me this thank-you letter. "Who knows what would have happened to Dwayne if you hadn't shot him in the foot." He's probably my best friend in the whole world. He thought it was an accident.

I never got a scratch on me during Tet. Not even a hangnail. It was the weirdest thing.

A few months later he was wounded by an enemy hand grenade. He spent four days in the hospital and then rejoined his unit. "They don't let you sit around very long." After a second wound he was given a desk job.

"I feel good about going and serving my country. I wouldn't take a million dollars for the experience I had. I think I learned a lot. But I definitely wouldn't want to do it again. I know a lot of people who have problems now did stuff over there that was inappropriate. Mutilation and raping women and just all kinds of stuff. Americans are

really mean, vicious people, given the chance. We all have it, but we just don't realize we have it. I never cut off any ears and never cut off any dicks. I just wasn't that kind of a person. So my conscience doesn't say, 'Well you killed somebody and you shouldn't have, or you raped somebody and you shouldn't have.' But I feel bad that so many people from my generation lost their lives for what I think was not a good cause. I mean when McNamara just come out and said it was a bullshit war and they were just doing it for political reasons—I'd like to strangle his ass. Like goddamn, man, you just threw us over there and let us die for what?"

TUAN VAN BAN

"Attack! Attack! Attack!"

A dapper man of sixty-one, he wears a gray cap and a bright blue sweater vest. In 1968, he was an infantry lieutenant who commanded a company in the 320th Division of the People's Army of Vietnam [North Vietnamese Army]. His first experience of combat came on the opening night of the Tet Offensive when his battalion attacked a U.S. Marine base near Cam Lo in Quang Tri Province.

Around midnight we moved as close as possible to the American perimeter. We just wore shorts and covered our bodies with dirt for camouflage. Uniforms can snag on barbed wire so we wore as little as possible. When everyone was in position we all dug foxholes and waited. Some guys were even able to sleep. However, many of the men in my company had, like me, just come from the North and had no combat experience. We were too excited to rest. Some guys were so eager they couldn't stop talking. At one point the deputy battalion commander came to me and whispered, "Damn it, get your troops to shut up. They're going to give away our position."

As we waited, small munitions teams crawled forward to place explosives under the barbed wire and other obstacles around the perimeter. One of my platoons was responsible for doing that in our area. A second platoon was prepared to attack the bunkers just inside the perimeter where the Americans were on guard. Then a third platoon would rush in and try to spread out deeper inside the base.

We did a lot of careful planning before the battle. Weeks before, as part of a small reconnaissance team, we had crawled and cut our way through the mines and barbed wire to get a close look at the base. We drew maps of the layout, including the positions of all the bunkers and buildings so our mortar men could preplan their targets. We were especially determined to hit the communications center. In preparing our troops, we made sure they understood the importance of fighting as close to the enemy as possible. As much as possible we wanted to take the battle right into the enemy bunkers and grab the Americans by the belt buckle. If we merely fired from a distance they could destroy us with artillery from Camp Carroll or from offshore destroyers.

We launched the attack at five A.M. First we fired a flare. That was the signal to detonate the dynamite that blasted holes in the perimeter. At the same time our mortar men and machine gunners began firing into the base at their preplanned targets. Within seconds we blew a bugle and whistles to signal our troops to advance. All four hundred of us moved forward screaming, "Attack! Attack! Attack!"

Just five minutes after we began to move, artillery fire started falling. Fortunately, by that time most of us had penetrated the perimeter and the shells landed behind us. With a few other men I raced through the opening and tried to make it to the communications center. It was very dark and incredibly chaotic. It was nearly impossible to see where you were going or what you were firing at. Bullets were flying in every direction.

We knew we couldn't maintain a dragged-out battle. Enemy forces throughout the area were very strong and that base itself had an enormous amount of firepower. So we just destroyed as much as we could and gave the signal to withdraw. We were in an out, all well before daybreak.

We had about seventy men wounded and twenty killed. I have no idea how many died on the other side. Most of our casualties were hit by artillery fire during our withdrawal. These great losses were always the hardest part of the war to endure and they still are. So many died without an opportunity to see their country reunited and at peace. My first battle, it turned out, was just one of hundreds of attacks that took place that morning all over the South. At the time, though, I had no idea of the scale of the Tet Offensive. People with much higher rank coordinated it all. For me it was only the first of many battles that would continue until 1975.

MEMORIAL DAY 1968

CLARK DOUGAN

"He Was Only 19—Did You Know Him?"

In the 1980s, he coauthored seven books for The Vietnam Experience, *a twenty-volume series published by Time-Life Books. Now an editor for a university press, we meet at a conference of the Organization of American Historians. He relishes conversation on any number of topics, so we talk late into the night, but this was the story he wanted most to tell.*

I went to Valley Forge High School in Parma Heights, Ohio—a big, working-class, white, ethnic neighborhood just outside Cleveland. We were the Valley Forge "Patriots." Something like thirty-five kids from Parma died in the war. The principal would come on the intercom periodically and say, "We've just received the very sad news that Terry Kilbane, a marine lance corporal, has been killed in Vietnam. Let's please observe a moment of silence."

I think we sensed that we were all pawns of forces much larger than we were, and over which we had no control. It all seemed somehow like a roll of the dice. Some would go, some wouldn't, and it depended on accident, on how well we did in school, on what our parents' expectations were for us, lots of factors—but none of us were really that different from one another.

There was this one guy who sat next to me in homeroom named Greg Fischer. I played basketball, he played hockey. We didn't know each other very well, but because my last name began with D and his with F, we were in the same homeroom for three years. Toward the end of our senior year I remember talking with him about our plans for the future.

I said, "Well, actually I'm going to college next year. I just went down to visit this place called Kenyon and it seemed kind of cool. What are you going to do?"

He said, "Ah, I don't think I'm going to go to college. I'm thinking about going into the marines."

"The marines? Really?"

"Yeah, I mean, I'm going to get drafted anyhow, so if I'm going to get drafted, why not the best, you know?"

When we heard those obituaries over the school intercom it was a reminder that the war was there, and it was real. But one of the ways we coped with it was through a sort of black humor. It was almost as if the humor was an effort to make it go away, to make it unreal. For example, a few months after my talk with Greg Fischer, all eight hundred and thirty-five of us marched into Cleveland Public Auditorium for commencement—the class of 1967. Suddenly some kid starts whistling the theme song to *The Bridge on the River Kwai*—the movie about British prisoners of war. And we all joined in! Believe me, it's not easy to whistle when you're laughing. This was followed by a very low, teenage, guttural version of "The Caissons Go Rolling Along." I'm not kidding. Meanwhile, in the background, the high school band is wailing away on "Pomp and Circumstance." You can just imagine all these guys in bright blue caps and gowns with the gold tassels, laughing away. It was fantastic.

So I go off to my first year in college and I'm really kind of oblivious of the war. The Tet Offensive is raging across South Vietnam and I'm trying to figure out what the hell *Paradise Lost* is all about. But I came home from college in late May.

On Memorial Day 1968, I opened up the *Cleveland Press* and there was an editorial on the front page with the title "He Was Only 19—Did You Know Him?" It turns out to be about Greg Fischer and how he died at Dong Ha up near the DMZ. It just hit me like a hammer. I remembered that conversation in homeroom and it suddenly had this profound significance. I had gone off to this cloistered college while he was going off to die in Vietnam.

Unlike some, I've never had any guilt for not going to Vietnam. But I understand how easily it could have been me. Like any kid who had grown up in the fifties there was a certain allure to the military. And especially the marines. But my parents hadn't been able to go to college and they were determined that I would.

The *Cleveland Press* article concluded by quoting a letter Greg had left in the drawer of his desk. On the envelope he had written, "Open this if I don't come back from Vietnam." The letter was about what to do with the ten thousand bucks his family would get from his military life insurance—the standard death benefit for an American KIA. Primarily he wanted the money to go to his sister so she could go to college. The letter ended with a P.S., "Don't forget to give Joey my hockey skates."

The editorial was really asking, how many more people like Greg are we willing to waste? This is just an ordinary kid we're talking about. He wasn't an Eagle Scout, or a class president, or an all-American athlete. He was a kid who had worked in the local pharmacy. We all know the high school kid who works in the pharmacy, even if we don't know his name.

I think that was the moment when "Middle America" really turned against the war. The *Cleveland Press* was part of the Scripps-Howard chain, a conservative syndicate that had strongly supported the war. So it was remarkable that this newspaper would run such an angry editorial about an American casualty. It reflected a feeling that was spreading all over working-class communities like Parma. I think a lot of World War II vets who had been sitting around their kitchen tables saying, "You've got to fight for your country," were starting to say, "Fuck this. It's not worth Greg Fischer's life or his buddy's life." Or maybe they weren't saying it, but they were starting to feel it.

In 1982, I went to Greg Fischer's grave. What struck me more than anything else was the simplicity of Greg's marker. There's just one small plaque on the ground surrounded by hundreds of marble headstones. It has his name, the dates of his life, and one word: "Vietnam." That's the only epitaph.

I felt good about having gone. And stood there. And remembered. The only tribute you could really pay, and I can still pay, is to remember. What else is there?

FROM JOHNSON TO NIXON

From the death of John Kennedy in 1963 to the throes of Watergate a decade later, the American home front was ruptured by repeated episodes of assassination, racial strife, political turmoil, mass protest, and civil upheaval. While the Vietnam War had not literally come home, it increasingly felt to many citizens as if the United States itself might be the "domino" most at risk of tumbling as a result of the carnage on the other side of the world. People still went to work, raised their children, had backyard barbecues, watched movies, and cared about the outcomes of baseball games. But events of historic magnitude kept impinging on the lives and consciousness of the whole society.

The year 1968, in particular, seemed to have the critical mass of an entire decade. Almost every week brought some new and unexpected calamity. On January 23, a week before the Tet Offensive, North Korean patrol boats seized an American intelligence-gathering ship, the USS *Pueblo,* with eighty-three crewmen aboard. In response, Lyndon Johnson called up fifteen thousand air reservists, the first mobilization of the reserves since the Cuban Missile Crisis. The *Pueblo* crisis was quickly dwarfed by the Tet Offensive, and when the crewmen were finally released almost a year later, their story had nearly been forgotten under the weight of other events. (A decade later when fifty-two American hostages were taken in Iran, it would be front-page news not for a few weeks, but for more than a year.)

The aftershocks of Tet were still rippling through the political culture when President Johnson's reelection was thrown into doubt by challengers within his own party. Senator Eugene McCarthy had been running against LBJ since the previous fall and Senator Robert Kennedy, the dead president's brother, announced his candidacy on March 16, both pledging to find a way out of Vietnam. Johnson, a landslide victor in 1964, felt so damaged politically by four years of escalation in Vietnam that he dropped out of the campaign before it was even fully joined.

Less than a week later, on April 4, Martin Luther King was assassinated in Memphis at the age of thirty-nine. Though King was the most prominent proponent of nonviolent resistance since Mohandas Gandhi, many took his murder as further proof that violence was too deeply entrenched in American culture to be overcome peacefully. The assassination sparked rioting in 120 American cities and on military bases at home and in Vietnam, resulting in at least forty-six deaths.

Antiwar protests continued to mount. On April 26, a million high school and college students participated in a one-day boycott of classes to demonstrate opposition to the war. That same week Columbia University students and activists occupied several campus buildings to protest the university's acceptance of military research contracts and its relationship to the neighboring black community. A thousand city police were called in to clear the occupied buildings. When some of the two thousand protesters resisted arrest, police attacked with nightsticks, and 148 people were injured.

While radicals had little faith that mainstream politics might end the war, many liberals found inspiration in the presidential campaigns of Robert Kennedy and Eugene McCarthy. With both of them winning primaries, hopes rose that one of them might be able to defeat LBJ's logical successor, Vice President Hubert Humphrey. On June 5, Kennedy scored an enormous victory in California attracting a broad coalition of workers, minorities, and middle-class liberals. Just a few minutes after giving his victory speech, he was assassinated. It was one more unspeakable convulsion of violence, further weakening the faith of many Americans that conventional politics would resolve the war in Vietnam.

Uprisings in the United States were not only inextricably connected to Vietnam, but seemed part of a nearly global challenge to authority in 1968. In France, for example, demonstrations and strikes by radical students and workers nearly toppled the government of Charles de Gaulle; in Mexico City, hundreds of students protesting their government's repression were killed by soldiers and police; and in Czechoslovakia, Soviet troops brutally attacked a powerful movement toward the democratization of the Communist government.

In late August attention shifted to Chicago, site of the Democratic National Convention. In anticipation of large planned protests, Chicago Mayor Richard Daley turned the city into a virtual armed camp, mobilizing the entire police department and the Illinois National Guard. With the threat of violence so omnipresent, the turnout of protesters was much smaller than expected. But the five thousand to ten thousand demonstrators who filled the streets and parks of Chicago were beaten and tear-gassed so intensely it looked to many as if civil war had truly begun. Journalist Stewart Alsop, a longtime defender of the Vietnam War, wrote, "In Chicago, for the first time in my life it began to seem possible that some form of American fascism may really happen here."

At the convention, Democratic delegates nominated Hubert Humphrey.

Though Humphrey had misgivings about the war, he offered no convincing evidence that he would chart a different course in Vietnam than his predecessor, even refusing to endorse a modest peace plank. Meanwhile, the Republicans nominated Richard Nixon, a man whose political career had seemed forever finished when he lost the presidential race to John Kennedy in 1960 and failed to win the California gubernatorial election just two years later. In 1968, however, Republicans championed a "new Nixon," claiming that he had successfully shed his prior reputation as a fierce and shady partisan ("Tricky Dick" as he was once dubbed), and become a more moderate and conciliatory statesman. Pledging to bring unity and order to a divided nation, Nixon also capitalized on the growing disenchantment over the war. "When the strongest nation in the world can be tied down for four years in a war in Vietnam with no end in sight," he said, "then it's time for new leadership for the United States of America." Without specifying how he intended to do it, Nixon promised "an honorable end" to the war, persuading many voters that he was more likely to bring peace than Hubert Humphrey.

Trailing badly in the polls, Humphrey began to take a more critical line on the Vietnam War. Then, just days before the election, Johnson announced that he was stopping all bombing of North Vietnam and that the South Vietnamese government had agreed to participate in the Paris peace negotiations. With this news, Humphrey rapidly closed the gap. His momentum was perhaps fatally blocked, however, when South Vietnamese President Nguyen Van Thieu denied any intention to negotiate with the Communists. Thieu was secretly encouraged in his stance by the Nixon campaign, which had dispatched an intermediary to Saigon to make sure he understood that his government would find more support in a Nixon administration. On election day, Nixon won by only a half million votes. The war would continue for six more years and kill another twenty-five thousand Americans, at least another million Vietnamese, and hundreds of thousands of Laotians and Cambodians.

JOHN GILLIGAN

"Our only shot was to help Humphrey break away from Johnson."

A Democrat from Cincinnati, he was elected to Congress in 1964 where he served a single term. In 1968, while running for the Senate, he proposed that the Democratic National Convention include a "peace plank" in its platform calling for an unconditional stop to all bombing of North Vietnam and a "swift conclusion" to the war.

Under pressure from President Johnson, Democratic presidential candidate Vice President Hubert Humphrey rejected the peace plank and it was defeated by a vote of 1,567 to 1,041. Hundreds of peace delegates tied black ribbons around their arms in protest. It was one of the most contentious political conventions in modern times, a fact easily forgotten given the violence raging in the streets outside.

Gilligan went on to become governor of Ohio, administrator of the Agency for International Development under President Jimmy Carter, and a Notre Dame professor. At age eighty, he is now a member of the Cincinnati Board of Education.

When I went to Congress I was still going along with the war. Then Speaker John McCormick put together a group of House members for a trip to Vietnam. We were all combat veterans from World War II. The first time I had a look at Cam Ranh Bay I was shocked. It made Pearl Harbor look like a used-car lot. It was vast. They were unloading stuff everywhere and had put in an airfield next to it. Clearly we had built this thing for a long stay.

Then we had a briefing one night by General Westmoreland. He said, "We have complete air superiority," which was hardly a surprise. I mean, the Viet Cong didn't have a box kite, never mind an airplane. Then he said, "And we can do anything we want anywhere we want. We can put our people in and out of any place in the country. It's just a question of how much punishment the enemy wants to take." Well, in the years that followed it turned out that they were willing to take a lot more punishment than we were.

I remember another little incident from that trip. While we were in Saigon two American aircraft got shot down trying to take out a bridge up near Hanoi. The same day some guy on a bicycle with six pounds of plastique took out a bridge down in the Mekong Delta. We lost two planes and two pilots and failed and the Viet Cong with a bicycle took out a bridge. I began to think, jeez, this ain't the kind of war we're used to. Of the dozen of us on that trip, about nine came home opposed to the war.

When we got back to Washington we were taken directly to the Cabinet Room at the White House where Lyndon Johnson said to us, "Well, you've been there and you're all combat veterans, what do you think?" So we went around the table. The wording was different from each individual, but most of us said, "We're in a helluva mess over there and we gotta get out." Johnson blew his stack. He said that was a lot of goddamn defeatism and we've got to tough it out.

In 1968, I won the Democratic nomination for the Senate in a primary against Frank Lausche, a five-time governor and twice-elected incumbent senator. He was Republican in all but name, so I agreed to take a run at him and we got people out on the peace issue and I had strong support from labor. But every time I walked out of the house I was bedeviled by the question of whether I was for Humphrey, Kennedy, or McCarthy. I couldn't say anything without losing two-thirds of my group so I said, "Well, I'm just proud to be part of a party that has three great candidates." But I really supported Bobby Kennedy. I had become firmly convinced that he was the only guy who could win. And if he did, we'd be out of the war and have a different kind of country. We'd also have been spared six years of Richard Nixon. Bobby was unique in his ability to attract enormous support from both the black community and white blue-collar workers. Both groups were fundamental to the Democratic base but they had been badly split. Kennedy was the only one who could bring them together and inspire them. He lit them up. They idolized him.

Right after I won the primary he came out to Ohio. I went out to the airport and rode into Columbus with him and Ethel and Bill Barry, his security guy. It was an open car and instead of going down Broad Street they turned off and went through the heart of the city to a black neighborhood. The crowds came out in the street and were so thick they stopped the motorcade. We couldn't move. Kennedy stood up on the trunk of the car, reaching out and shaking hands with people. The crowd was friendly but it was just craziness. Bill Barry was kneeling on the back seat with his arms wrapped around Kennedy's waist. After getting Ethel up in the front seat—she was about six months pregnant—I grabbed Bill's belt trying to hold him in. Eventually somebody in the crowd got hold of Kennedy's arm and pulled him off the car. Have you seen crowds in football stadiums where they pick up a kid and pass him up over their heads? That's what was happening. Bill and I dove into the crowd. I thought, my God, we're gonna have the guy killed in front of our eyes. We managed to get hold of Kennedy and dragged him back into the car. By the time he got to the hotel his shirt was in tatters, his cufflinks were gone, and he looked like he'd just gone through ten rounds. That was the kind of excitement he was capable of generating. Three weeks later he was dead.

After Kennedy's death it was between Humphrey and McCarthy. I went around to see McCarthy at his office and said, "The Democrats have problems with you and with Hubert."

He said, "What are the problems with Hubert?"

"Well, they think he's tied too closely to Johnson—that he can't get rid of this war and it's gonna take him down."

"Well, what's the problem with me?"

I said, "They don't really think you want to be president, that you aren't serious."

He said, "What the hell do you think I've been doing out there in the snows of New Hampshire and everything?"

"Oh, you want to win the debate, but do you really want to sit in that office and play with those awful knobs and levers of power?"

McCarthy said, "Well if that's what the job requires, that's what I'll do."

"Good," I said. "Pick up the phone right now and call [Chicago Mayor] Dick Daley and ask for his support."

He said, "Oh, I'm not gonna talk to Dick Daley."

"Then you aren't serious about this job," I said. After that I was convinced our only shot was to help Humphrey break away from Johnson. Hubert was operating under wraps and he couldn't be candid about the issues without getting himself in trouble with Johnson.

So with a small group of six or seven people at lunch in Washington about six weeks before the Democratic Convention I proposed the idea that we help Hubert by adopting a peace plank in the Democratic platform. Twenty years earlier, when Harry Truman was facing what was thought to be certain defeat, a young mayor from Minneapolis named Hubert Humphrey went to the Democratic Convention and introduced a civil rights plank and a tough one. Truman didn't want it and he did everything he could to get away from it, but when Humphrey and others got it passed, he accepted the nomination and embraced their platform. I think it got him elected. Well, I said to Hubert, we're trying to do for you what you did for Harry Truman in 1948. We're not asking you to endorse this thing, we're just asking you to get out of the way. And then if we get it passed you can do what Harry did—stand up, accept the nomination, and embrace the platform you've been handed.

While the peace plank was being debated in the platform committee we had lengthy conversations with David Ginsburg, one of Hubert's top people. He finally said there wasn't a dime's worth of difference between our position and the vice president's. So we thought it might go through. But then Johnson sent [Louisiana congressman] Hale Boggs out from Washington to take over the convention and knock people into line. They allowed about three hours for a debate of the peace plank. We were hopeful right down to the end that it would pass, but many of its opponents called it abject surrender. They said it was a betrayal of our boys in the field. A lot of wild stuff was said. What had been a pretty narrow disagreement over the language in the platform turned into a wide-open debate between hawks and doves. I really think it was the first time that the American people ever saw the issue debated in public by reputable political figures in any party.

I remember saying to someone that if we could just get this damn thing through, Gene McCarthy would be compelled to stand up and endorse Humphrey and support him in the campaign. Instead he went off and sulked for eight weeks and his young supporters never rallied behind Humphrey.

PETER KUZNICK

"Political conversion was the greatest aphrodisiac."

As a college student at Rutgers University, he hitchhiked all over the country organizing for the antiwar movement. "You could travel anywhere in the United States during those years and be immediately embraced by a whole community simply based upon the way you looked and dressed. There was always a safe haven for radicals and activists." He teaches history at American University.

I was attracted to Rutgers by a magazine article that described it as the Berkeley of the East. In 1965, at a Rutgers teach-in, an English professor said we were fighting in Vietnam to preserve civilization. My future mentor Warren Susman started pounding the podium saying, "How do you define civilization? How do you define civilization?" He pounded so hard his watch exploded and the springs and mechanisms went flying all over the audience. [Laughs.]

As a freshman in 1966, I supported SDS, but thought it was necessary to reach out to a much broader student body. SDS was too radical for students who were just beginning to question the war. They weren't ready to join an organization that was already talking about revolution. I defined my role as creating a bridge between leftist and more moderate students.

In the spring of 1968, it looked like Chicago was going to be the focus of national efforts so I decided to attend. I certainly didn't go to Chicago looking for violence, but I knew it was a real likelihood based on all the advance word that had come out of Chicago. A lot of people decided not to go because they feared it was going to be a bloodbath. The Daley Machine and the Chicago Police had given sufficient indication that the last thing they had any respect for was the first amendment right to gather and protest in public. And during the uprisings in Chicago after Martin Luther King was assassinated in April, [Mayor] Daley had issued a shoot-to-kill order to the police. So the turnout from around the country was not nearly what people had hoped. The original estimates of a hundred thousand quickly dwindled to five to ten thousand.

The number of people being killed on a daily basis in Vietnam made this a serious enough situation that most of us were willing to put our bodies on the line. We didn't at all feel that our decision to avoid going to Vietnam was based on fear or cowardice. We weren't afraid to risk bodily harm and even our lives. Our commitment to ending the war was certainly as great as the government's commitment to prosecuting it.

A lot of our time in Chicago was divided between Lincoln Park where there was an ongoing "be-in" and Grant Park where there was an ongoing political demonstration. Lincoln Park was supposedly our turf but the police had made it clear that they were going to throw people out by eleven o'clock at night. Had people tried to hold the park, it really would have gotten ugly. It became clear very quickly that this was not your friendly local police force. Their hatred toward the demonstrators was palpable and they were just itching for an excuse to atttack. Fortunately, the leaders didn't really encourage people to hold the park overnight. There was some of that revolutionary, adventurist machismo, but it wasn't the dominant riff.

There was a lot of music and dope smoking, talking and mingling, chanting and singing, and getting to know each other. There were all kinds of demonstrations. The Yippies held a rally to announce the candidacy of a pig for president— "Pigasus." The police broke it up and impounded the pig. The next day a story circulated—it might be apocryphal—that the Yippies brought out another pig and said it was their new candidate for president. One of the reporters asked how they could support a new pig since they had just endorsed "Pigasus." Either Jerry Rubin or Abbie Hoffman said, "Well, we run on the same principle as the Democrats and Republicans, that one pig is as good as another."

My goal in Chicago was not only to protest against the war but to try to radicalize some of the moderate and liberal students who were attending the convention as delegates for Eugene McCarthy and George McGovern. I tried to show them the limitations and contradictions of the way they were viewing things and to marshal enough evidence to show them that the war was not an aberration but part of a long-standing pattern. A big part of our analysis was that this was the liberals' war and students who were embracing liberal capitalism as a solution seemed to be blind to many of the lessons of history. Meeting young women who were McCarthy delegates could have personal as well as political consequences. Henry Kissinger once said "power is the greatest aphrodisiac." I always thought that political conversion was the greatest aphrodisiac. The sexual side of the movement was almost as present as the political and it was certainly part of what was going on in Chicago. That reminds me that the first or second night we were told to buddy up with someone else for protection and I was coupled with Ed Sanders of the rock group the Fuggs. Their music was a combination of revolutionary politics and sexual iconoclasm, songs like "Kill for Peace" and "Wet Dream Over You." The connections between politics, culture, and sex were really a lot deeper than many histories of the period suggest.

It seems like there was an ongoing fight from the time we got to Chicago. You were either confronting violence or the threat of violence throughout the several days. At times it was chaotic and just a question of luck as to who was going to get his or her head cracked open. The police would charge in waves and most people would try to scatter. I was clubbed like everybody else but not seriously injured. They'd usually be coming at you from behind because we'd be running. Sometimes there was no place to go. People would get trapped between buildings and the oncoming police. That's why so many people were pushed through the plate-glass windows at the Hilton Hotel. Once the police got people down they would club them mercilessly. They were totally unrestrained. It often looked like the Rodney King video. The degree of their hatred was stunning. They particularly liked to get women and men with long hair, and they seemed to have a penchant for attacking journalists. Part of the reason why the coverage was so honest was that many of the reporters and cameramen were clubbed gratuitously. It was happening all over. It gave you a sense of what a police state would be like.

I'm sure some kids were taunting the police. People called them "pigs" and there were chants like, "Pigs Eat Shit." But more of the chants were "U.S. Out of Vietnam," "End the War," and "The Whole World Is Watching." We thought that the last one was especially effective until we saw the public opinion polls afterwards and realized that the whole world may have been watching but the American public, at least, wasn't sympathizing with us. There was much more sympathy for the police than for the victims of the police. That was quite a sobering realization for many of us. We thought that unarmed demonstrators fighting to end an unpopular war would be received more sympathetically by the public than policemen who were trampling on civil liberties.

For all our bravado, I certainly didn't feel we could fight the police. They were armed to the teeth. They had layers and layers of jackets and shields and sometimes wore gas masks. They had clubs and used them freely and many had removed their badges so they couldn't be identified. And the national guardsmen were there with bayonets drawn. We had nothing to protect ourselves with. It was a scary scene and it didn't make me want to become a violent revolutionary. The disparity in force was clear. You know, we could take over the ROTC building at Rutgers and negotiate with the police so they wouldn't come in and break heads. Most campuses were somewhat safe havens compared to Chicago.

There was a macho cult of violence developing in the New Left that led to the approach taken by the Weathermen shortly thereafter.* It was ludicrous to think that anything could be achieved by the use of violence. But I agreed that a confrontational politics could unmask the violent nature of the American state by showing that the same wrath and ruthlessness it used to kill millions of Vietnamese would also be turned against Americans who challenged its power.

The next to last night there was a big rally in Grant Park across from the Hilton Hotel. There were thousands of us there with some singing and a few planned talks. By this point, there had been brutal beatings by the police, the violence was pervasive, and the antiwar plank [at the Democratic Convention] had been defeated overwhelmingly by the Humphrey delegates. All these Democratic delegates were hanging out in their hotel rooms watching us down below. I remember very clearly that Mary Travers, from "Peter, Paul, and Mary," started addressing the delegates up in their hotel rooms. She said, "Now that all you peace delegates have been defeated, you'll be with us in spirit." So she urged them to show their support by flashing their lights on and off. Well that got to me and I fought my way through the crowd to get to the microphone. The organizers were very hesitant to let me have it. But they did and I said that given the seriousness of the situation we were confronting, flashing lights on and off in a hotel room was simply a hollow, self-gratifying gesture. If these people were serious about supporting the cause, they had to be out there in the streets with us challenging the authorities.

"Chicago had a radicalizing effect on campuses. It was a real dividing line. In the spring of '68 I felt that on most campuses antiwar students were a distinct minority. But that fall the movement mushroomed and there was a pervasive radicalization."

J. SHAEFFER

"The palace guard."

During the Democratic Convention of 1968 he was a rookie cop. After two days of riot duty with the Chicago police, he spent several more days in the streets with his National Guard unit. "The crowd is yelling at us, 'You guys are killing people in Vietnam. Don't you guys understand what you're doing?' And I'm thinking to myself, jeez, just two days ago I was catching hell because I was a 'pig.' "

*The Weathermen, later Weatherpeople, was an SDS splinter group founded in 1969 that formed underground cells to plan, and sometimes execute, acts of revolutionary violence.

I grew up in middle-class neighborhoods of Chicago, first on the old West Side and then, after 1956, on the North Side. It was a rough time for kids of that age group because of the draft. There were no clear choices unless you had an "A" average and money behind you. If you were eligible for the draft, people didn't want to hire you. And if you were in school, you had to maintain a certain grade average to maintain your deferment. There was a lot of anxiety.

In my world we were the ones supplying the military. I was eventually going to be drafted, so I wound up enlisting in the Illinois National Guard. I went on active duty in the middle of 1967. I had also applied for the police department. Both things happened just about simultaneously. So in the late sixties I did dual service. I was in blue and I was in green. And I was involved in just about every situation dealing with domestic civil disobedience that I'd ever want to dream of. It was constant. A lot of times we'd be out for twenty-four, forty-eight, seventy-two hours. I can remember even sleeping in parks. During the 1968 convention I'll bet you it was close to a week that I was away from home before it was all over with. It must have been pretty rough on my wife.

In those days the rank-and-file of the police department—the blue shirts, the patrolmen, the guys that really did the job—we had no contractual agreements with the city, no union. They could deploy you and tell you what to do. You had no recourse. We couldn't say, "We only should work eight hours." When you joined up they called it a semimilitary organization. It was actually more than semimilitary. It was the palace guard.

We used to make jokes about it, referring to ourselves as the palace guard. This is the revolution and we're surrounding the palace. They want to tear down the flag, tear down the castle. We're protecting the establishment. It was kind of like the same situation that was going on in other countries. I never in my life had ever envisioned seeing army tanks rolling through the streets of my home town. I used to tell people, "Hey, I wasn't born in this uniform." You're taking orders from the establishment, but it's a public service job. You're there to serve the laws and the people.

In 1968, I would say a great percentage of the police department, probably as high as eighty-five percent, was World War II and Korean War veterans. Some guys were even Vietnam veterans. They served their community with respect and honor. Most people from my background supported the police so you didn't feel that this dissident movement really had any strength. But they were getting support and money from somewhere. I think the incident that really sparked this whole thing was when they took the flag down off the flagpole in Grant Park. Most of the guys have always remembered the Iwo Jima flag-raising during World War II, where marines were killed just to raise the American flag. And here they're taking it down.

Michigan Avenue was the main focus because that was where the convention headquarters was. I don't think anybody anticipated what would happen. We were very regimented. We were told when we started, "You're going to obey the Constitution and you are going to enforce the laws." But on the other side of the coin, it was just the total opposite. They were considered to be rabble. Here's people that are desecrating the flag. I don't think there could have been any other way of controlling the situation. I'm thinking to myself, they're against the war in Vietnam. Why are these people taking it out on us? What are they really trying to get at? I realized later that we are the only entity of government that people can get to. They can't get to the mayor or the political establishments.

Even a lot of police-oriented people at that time started to see that the Vietnam War was a big mistake and that it was causing a lot of problems here. But I thought the protesters were just a bunch of spoiled kids. Maybe a lot of them didn't believe in the republic of the United States. They had some other agenda. They're Socialists, Communists, and they're trying to overthrow what we've always known all our lives as America.

I've always been a fair-minded person. Even now, when I look back, I think some of them were just drawn into this. But a lot of them were there to aggravate you, to incite something. Here we are, we're being held on line and we're getting shit thrown at us and jeers and name-calling and all this stuff. And your training was to take orders and not break ranks. But in the back of your mind you're thinking, hey, wait a minute, we're not supposed to take this crap. Our job is to keep the streets in order. When a policeman tells you something, you obey it. Just like we all had to obey orders. Everybody has to take orders from somebody.

I always remember this one incident. The police shot tear gas in there after things really started to heat up. But I'll tell you the truth. It was like a Vietnam thing really because you never knew who was who. I mean *they* could have been throwing tear gas. Who knows who started some of this stuff?

So everybody starts running. When I say everybody I mean the police as well as the—I'm not going to call them rioters—the dissidents. I wind up running from this tear gas for about half a block, choking and gagging. I run around the corner and go into a doorway. I can't even see, my eyes are burning so bad. When I am finally able to see, I'm in this doorway with two of these hippies. [Laughs.] Here we are. We're taking shelter together. I mean can you imagine what a picture this would have been? And believe me when I tell you, I did not have the slightest thought to arrest them or do anything. So we're just standing there saying, you know, "Son of a bitch," swearing and choking. You feel like you can't breathe.

So I just walked away thinking, what the hell is this insanity? In fact, you know what? I think we were all victims together in this whole business, this whole thing.

SAMUEL HUNTINGTON

"You had to be pretty stupid to stay out in the countryside."

Meeting the mild-mannered political scientist in his Harvard office, it is hard to recover the intense visceral anger his work once generated among antiwar activists who knew about his role as a consultant to the Johnson adminstration on "nation-building" in Vietnam. In a controversial 1968 article in Foreign Affairs, *Huntington estimated that the urban population of South Vietnam had moved from 15 percent in the early sixties to roughly 50 percent in 1968 and that this "urban revolution" would undermine the rural revolution of the Communists. By driving peasants off the land and into the cities, U.S. policy, he concluded, was depriving the Viet Cong of its support in the countryside.*

My home was attacked at one point. Somebody came by and painted in big, black letters on our yellow door, "A War Criminal Lives Here." It was done at night. I remember our five-year-old son brought in the newspapers and said, "There's writing on the door." And so our ten-year-old son went out and saw this. He came back with this awful look on his face and said, "Daddy, I think you better look."

Some people picked up on a phrase I used in an article in *Foreign Affairs*—"forced draft urbanization." I said rapid urbanization was happening in Vietnam as a result of the war and our bombing and so forth. It was descriptive. I wasn't advocating it. They said, "Hey, he's in favor of forced draft urbanization." All I was saying was, if we're bringing more and more of the people of South Vietnam under government control, it's not because we're expanding our control in the countryside and appealing to the peasants there; it's because the peasants are being driven into the cities. That was precisely what was happening.

I went out to Vietnam in the summer of 1967 and spent most of the summer there traveling around. It was a fascinating experience. I had been in Saigon briefly back in 1962. Five years earlier it had struck me as an Oriental version of a small French provincial town—very quiet, peaceful, nice. When I went back in 1967 it had just exploded. There was construction all over the place, fantastic traffic jams, mobs and mobs of people. It was an entirely different city. At that point everybody said South Vietnam was eighty percent rural, but as I traveled around it was clear to me that that was just way off. I came to the conclusion that at least fifty percent, if not more, was urban.

People were moving into the cities for two reasons. First, the countryside was dangerous. There was bombing and free-fire zones and so forth. Second, by South Vietnamese standards, you could very easily become incredibly well off in the cities. There were all these wonderful jobs that had been produced by this overpowering American presence. So you had to be pretty stupid to stay out in the countryside and not move in to the cities.

I didn't advocate increasing urbanization, but I said it was a fact we ought to come to terms with. You ought to focus on the problems in the cities. I remember there was a big debate when I was out there on the problem of garbage collection in Saigon. The Vietnamese obviously should be collecting the garbage and disposing of it. Our government was continually torn between trying to get something done and delegating it to the Vietnamese on the theory that we want to transfer responsibility. But half the time nothing much would happen. So do we do it ourselves and get it done more quickly? I think eventually the U.S. Army began cleaning up the garbage in Saigon.

But I didn't really focus on how the war was being fought—free-fire zones and whatnot. I really didn't deal with that. Clearly on the military side, we didn't fight it in the most effective way. We fought as if we were fighting a major conventional war, and by the time it became a major conventional war with North Vietnamese mechanized divisions rolling into South Vietnam, we had pulled out.

My view on the war shifted as a result of being out there. It just seemed to me we weren't going to win it. By 1967, it seemed to me that the need for us to be that much concerned with Vietnam had declined considerably because the Southeast Asian economies were beginning the process of development in Thailand, Malaysia, and, to some extent in Indonesia. The Communist efforts at insurrection in these other countries had not succeeded and hence the danger of South Vietnam being the domino that would bring others down was greatly reduced.

During the 1968 presidential campaign I was actively involved in Hubert Humphrey's campaign and was chairman of his task force on Vietnam. We came up with a proposal to suspend the bombing of North Vietnam. But President Johnson beat up on him and Humphrey retreated and didn't issue the statement. Later, on September 30, he delivered the speech in Salt Lake City, which did call for a suspension of the bombing. But by then he'd had the disastrous convention in Chicago. I remember Humphrey came to Boston a year or two later and said to me, "If I'd only issued that statement that you people drafted before the convention I could have been elected president."

I think Humphrey would have done pretty much what Nixon did, but he would have faced the problem of all the Republicans saying, "You're selling out." Nixon could get away with reducing our involvement because he was Nixon. But I think Humphrey would have moved pretty much along those lines.

DOUGLAS KINNARD

"While we had the power, it turned out they had the will."

His divorcing parents put him in an orphanage at age four. "I was never adopted, but after seven months in the orphanage, I was placed with an Irish Catholic family and raised by them." An ambitious boy, he became an Eagle Scout and won a coveted congressional appointment to West Point. He graduated on D-Day, June 6, 1944, and was sent to the European front as a forward observer with an artillery unit. At twenty-three, he made captain.

He was the third member of his West Point class to become a general. "I was told I was a cinch for three stars." But in 1970, at age forty-eight, after two tours in Vietnam, the one-star general retired from the military and went to Princeton to pursue a Ph.D. in political science.

"I wasn't disillusioned with the military, I was disillusioned with the nature of the war and what it was doing to our country. I was disgusted with the whole thing. I'd had enough." In his new life as a scholar, he wrote a book called The War Managers, *based on a 1974 questionnaire he sent to all 173 army generals who served as combat commanders in Vietnam.*

I had no idea what kind of response I was going to get, but two-thirds sent back completed questionnaires. I was astonished by that, and by the critical nature of their responses.

Probably the most startling thing to me was that almost seventy percent said they really didn't understand the war's objectives. They knew their own goals—for example, one mission of the 25th Division was to clear the VC out of War Zone C. But when they thought about the overall objective, they said, "Why were we doing this? What was the overall purpose?"

[He picks up one of the old, yellowing questionnaires.]

This general wrote: "I'm not sure why the U.S. made such a tremendous effort. The announced reasons by President Johnson didn't wash. What were we really trying to do, whose bacon were we really trying to save? I keep asking myself." Every time I received one of those responses my reaction was, that makes two of us.

But critical as the generals were of the political leadership and the lack of a coherent strategy, they were even more upset by the media. That surprised me. Around ninety percent had a negative view of the media. They felt the media was undercutting them and looking for ways to degrade home-front support—that these guys were running around Vietnam without inhibitions, that they didn't really understand the war, and that they were reporting things just to get headlines.

The media got bad grades, but I think a lot of it was undeserved to be honest. I think after the Tet Offensive the American people very rightfully saw the fruitlessness of the whole thing. And while the media did become more critical after Tet, early on much of the media had supported the war and even later you had some press guys who thought everything was going great.

This was not always their fault. For example, in 1969 *Newsweek* carried an article by Stewart Alsop in which he waxed enthusiastic about an unescorted automobile tour he took with [CIA director of rural pacification] William Colby from Ca Mau to Can Tho in the Delta. The fact that they could drive safely in this area was billed as an example of the impressive gains in pacification. What Alsop didn't know is that they actually had a large military escort. Armed teams and helicopter gunships preceded and followed the car just out of sight.

My first tour in 1966–67 I was chief of operations analysis. I volunteered for that tour and I was gung ho when I arrived. We used to brief Westmoreland once a month with the Measurement of Progress Report. Since the war had no front line in the conventional sense, you could not easily tell who was winning or losing based on territory held. So we had something like sixty-two statistical indicators to judge progress. One was the "body count" and another was the "kill ratio"—how many enemy we killed for every one of our men who got killed.

What it basically came down to was attrition. I think we were always working under the assumption that if you just kept hitting the enemy hard enough he would quit. Everything was based on that assumption. But the assumption was totally wrong. The enemy was not going to quit, no matter how good our statistics looked. We had made it a war of wills, rather than a war of power. The problem was, while we had the power, it turned out they had the will.

By the end of my first tour, the summer of 1967, I think I'd decided that the war was a losing proposition, that it could go on forever. I was glad to go home and be disassociated with it. I didn't think I'd be involved with it again. By the fall of 1968 I decided to apply to Princeton in political science. But in March 1969, just before I was accepted at Princeton, I was alerted to return to Vietnam as commanding general of Two Force Artillery.

So in May 1969 I returned to Vietnam. Princeton allowed me to defer admission for a year. I think I was the only commanding general in Vietnam on a leave of absence from a graduate school. [Laughs.] Of course I couldn't tell anybody over there. I had eight thousand troops to command. I had to put all of that behind me until I got home.

The boss of Two Field Force when I arrived was Julian Ewell. He had been the commander of the 9th Infantry Division where he was known as "the Butcher of the Delta." The body count was a big deal with him. I went to my first briefing and Christ, the first seven charts were on body count—-this year versus that year, this unit versus that unit. The body count went on for about twenty minutes. He'd say things like, "We're going to screw them into the ground." This was a very intense guy.

The pressure to increase the body count worked its way right down from the top. One time, standing in line for refreshments after a change-of-command ceremony, I overheard a senior general talking to a colonel, an up-and-coming brigade commander. They were discussing the body count and the colonel said to the general, "Well, the VC are getting harder to find." And the general said, "Well, brigade commanders aren't." What he meant, of course, was—you better get off your ass and get some kills or you might be replaced. Well, it may have been absolute coincidence, but a day or two later the young brigade commander was out supervising a squad-level action, going for kills, and he was killed himself. Jesus Christ, the guy had a wife at home and a lot of children.

I think one of the great failures of the war among senior general officers was not in the field but in Washington. There were many occasions when senior military should have faced up and told McNamara and Johnson—"Look, this is a lousy strategy. It isn't going to work. You've got to call up the reserves in order to mobilize the home front. If you can't do that, you won't have their support and we should just get the hell out and avoid needless casualties."

The Joint Chiefs did, in fact, recommend mobilization of the reserves, but when Johnson said he wasn't going to do it, they backed down. In July 1965, Chairman Earl Wheeler agreed that it would be all right not to. In this instance, he was a wimp in his dealing with LBJ and McNamara. He wasn't doing his job. It's wrong to advise a senior civilian guy that it's all right when it isn't, especially on something so vital to the outcome of the war.

A lot of the senior leadership didn't stand up and be counted. Harold Johnson was the army chief of staff during the buildup period. After the war he told me that when Johnson refused to call up the reserves he intended to resign.

I said, "Well, why didn't you?"

He said, "What difference would it have made?"

At the end of his second tour, in the spring of 1970, General Kinnard's job was to plan the U.S. invasion of Cambodia. He discovered there were no decent maps of Cambodia, so he asked MACV (Military Assistance Command, Vietnam) to provide some aerial photographs. There was a big delay, but after applying some pressure, he finally got the pictures. "Then I realized why MACV had been so reluctant to release them. They showed thousands of B-52 craters on Cambodian territory. We had been secretly bombing Cambodia for a year and only a handful of American officers had been told. I had no idea we were doing that."

When he began graduate school at Princeton in the fall of 1970, he was not going to say anything about his Vietnam experience. "Given the antimilitary situation on campus at the time, I had intended to go underground about that." But after the first class, one of his young classmates asked: "Doug, were you here during the riots this spring over the Cambodian invasion?" The former general could not resist the "punch line of a lifetime." "Well no," he said. "Actually, I was in *Cambodia."*

"A THREE-SQUARE-MILE PIECE OF THE UNITED STATES"

TOM O'HARA

"It was like being in a minimum-security prison."

Like many men of his generation, he joined the National Guard to reduce the risk of being sent to Vietnam. It was a well-known safe haven because at the outset of major U.S. escalation in 1965 President Johnson had decided against mobilizing the National Guard and military reserves out of concern that it would ignite greater antiwar protest.

As the draft calls expanded, so, too, did the waiting lists at virtually every nonregular military unit. Sons of wealth and power had the easiest time jumping to the top of those lists. Professional athletes were also notoriously welcome. At the height of the Vietnam War, the Dallas Cowboys had ten players in the National Guard. All told, fewer than 2 percent of the reserves were African American and the percentage of college graduates was three times greater than in the regular army.

There were, however, no guarantees. Some guardsmen and reservists found themselves mobilized to suppress urban and campus uprisings, avoiding the war abroad only to find themselves fighting the war at home. And in 1968, roughly fifteen thousand guardsmen and reservists were actually sent to Vietnam. Tom O'Hara was among them. He heard the news while reading a geology textbook at Rutgers University. Today he is managing editor of the Palm Beach Post.

I was a life support specialist in the 177th Tactical Fighter Group. We took care of the pilots' parachutes and oxygen masks and helmets. We would drive the pilots out to the flight line, drop them off at their planes, pick them up at the debriefing shack when they were done with the flight, drive them back to their air-conditioned trailers, keep the squadron refrigerator full of soda and beer, and make sure there was coffee when they came in for the five A.M. preflight briefings. And whenever I had a chance, I played Ping-Pong in the squadron building.

The pilots were not going to share their innermost feelings with a twenty-one-year-old jerk like me. If they had doubts or questions about the war they certainly weren't going to express them around me. All I ever heard was that these guys loved to fly those jets. I mean it was macho-fighter-pilot, Tom Cruise stuff. If I'd been one of them, I suspect I'd have been the same way.

It seemed like ninety percent of the time the pilots would go out and "drop 'em in the trees." That was always their comment. I would pick them up in this van—I called it the bread truck—and they would sit in the back pissin' and moanin' because they had just "dropped 'em in the trees." But every once in a while you'd pick up a group that had actually dropped bombs on real people and they were so excited. They were so excited to have targets out in the open and see the bombs hit them and blow up. And I thought, "God, have I gone to a mental institution or what?"

This was at Phu Cat Air Force Base near Qui Nhon. It was on the "coastal bend," about equidistant between Danang and Saigon. They made it sound like a tourist destination—"the coastal bend." It was like being in a minimum-security prison. I didn't want to be there, but it was a completely mindless routine that I was capable of coping with. My strategy was to sleep ten to twelve hours a day. Figured I was cutting my time in half.

The first two weeks I was on edge, but then I relaxed because it was a very safe place. Only twice during the entire year I was there did the Viet Cong ever penetrate the perimeter. You wouldn't even hear about it until the next morning. Somebody would say, "Oh, they killed six Viet Cong last night." And the grotesque thing is I remember guys running down to the Military Police compound because they heard the bodies were out front. They all took their new Nikon cameras that they bought at the PX and ran down to take pictures of these poor bastards who had broken through the perimeter, thrown a couple of hand grenades on the flight line, and got mowed down.

A lot of people tried to hype what they were doing but basically everybody on that base was just doing a low-class, blue-collar job to keep the planes flying. You did it six days a week and you put in twelve-hour shifts. Every once in a while you got on a bus to Qui Nhon like a Boy Scout outing. You get there at eleven in the morning, put on a bathing suit, and go out to the beach. Then you go into the bars and these really unattractive Vietnamese girls come up and sit in your lap. I just found it all unseemly and offensive so I think I only went to town once.

There just wasn't much opportunity to dramatize what we were doing because we were in a three-square-mile piece of the United States of America. America had come over, slapped down asphalt, put down runways, built buildings, and put a fence around it. The officers all had TVs in their air-conditioned trailers and we had one in the barracks. The reception was pretty lame, but you could sit around and watch American TV shows. The entire year there I never established a relationship with a Vietnamese.

Maybe I was just depressed and pissed off, but when I was in Vietnam, I generally didn't like any of the people. The officers were arrogant pricks and the enlisted people were dull and uninteresting.

I didn't want to go to Vietnam but I didn't have tremendous philosophical opinions about it. I remember going back to school at Rutgers and I saw these assholes out there protesting against the war like they had a great moral position. I felt like going up and throttling them. You know what I mean? Why don't you just stand up and say, "I don't want to spend two years having some asshole berate me and go over and get shot at." That makes sense. But don't couch it in all this moral shit. So I was pissed off coming and going.

When you say "Vietnam vet" the public sees a balding guy, with stringy hair, with his hat on, and his fatigues, and his little fucking medals, weeping somewhere. But the veterans who dress up in their flak jackets and go weep at the Vietnam Memorial Wall are a tiny portion. They're the ones who just aren't giving it up.

Maybe some percentage of those people have legitimate post-traumatic stress syndrome and are legitimate Vietnam victims, but the rest, in my opinion, would be sitting somewhere weeping about something even if they had not gone to Vietnam. I have low tolerance for Vietnam vets who blame everything that's happened to them in the last thirty years on the twelve months they spent over there. The fact of the matter is that ninety-five percent of vets are normal, functioning, completely well-adjusted people just like everybody else. The vast majority of vets just put the war behind them and moved on.

I don't think my life is much different from what it would have been without the war. I got a nice job, a nice family. In the newspaper business you read these wire stories—a guy mows down people and he's a Vietnam vet. I've actually said to the staff: "If somebody's done something fucked up and they're a Vietnam vet, what has that got to do with what this person has done? We shouldn't even mention it unless he's up there with a flak jacket and a helmet yelling, 'I'm gonna kill the gooks.' " So when I read these things it just irritates the shit out of me because it fosters the notion that somehow this war has traumatized a generation of American men. I'm sorry, but it hasn't.

FAMILIES AT WAR

JOHN DOUGLAS MARSHALL

"You will not be welcome here again."

He adored his grandfather. He knew "Poppy" was famous, that he appeared on TV, that he wrote newspaper articles, that he was a brigadier general in the army reserves, that he was the author of war books, including Pork Chop Hill, *the one they made into a Korean War movie starring Gregory Peck. But mostly Poppy was just the life-loving, cigar-smoking grandfather who lived a few miles away—the man who played catch and participated in a family club with its own emblems and funny rituals. "Growing up, I thought more about making my grandfather proud than my own father."*

The grandfather was S. L. A. Marshall. In the 1960s, "SLAM" Marshall was one of the staunchest defenders of American policy in Vietnam. He championed the cause in a syndicated column and several books. In 1967, the grandson was a sophomore at the University of Virginia when he received his grandfather's Battles in the Monsoon *with this inscription: "To John Marshall goes this first copy of the new book—and Johnny, I hope you like it."*

But the grandson did not like the Vietnam War. In 1969, he completed ROTC simply because "it was expected" by his family and then trained as an infantry officer at Fort Benning. His doubts about the war escalated during his first year of service. Awaiting the all-but-certain assignment to Vietnam, he immersed himself in the literature of pacifism and nonviolence—Gandhi, Martin Luther King, Thoreau.

Concluding that all war was wrong, he applied to leave the army as a conscientious objector. On his application he wrote: "I can no longer deny the calling of my conscience . . . regardless of my family heritage . . . I can no longer hide my true beliefs beneath my uniform." Twenty-seven people wrote letters testifying to the sincerity of his convictions. The application was approved and he received an honorable discharge.

In 1969, my grandfather gave the commissioning speech at Virginia for the ROTC graduates. After the speech, each new officer came up, saluted him, and he handed them their commissioning certificate. This was on the great lawn that Thomas Jefferson had designed, as hundreds of people watched. Finally my name was called and I walked up to my grandfather and raised my arm, but he said, "Don't you dare salute me." Then he grabbed me and gave me a big bear hug in front of this crowd. Everybody was kind of shocked at first and then they started to applaud. That was the last close moment the two of us ever shared.

Once my application for conscientious objector discharge was approved, I wrote my family and my grandfather saying what I had done and why I'd done it. I didn't hear from my father for over a year. But I soon got a letter back from my grandfather. When I saw that it began "Dear Mr. Marshall," I knew what would follow would not be pleasant. But it was far worse than I imagined:

> "That the Army seemingly prefers to give you an honorable separation means nothing to this part of what was once your family. . . . We know why you quit. It wasn't conscience. You simply chickened out. You didn't have the guts it takes. Vietnam or any point of danger was unacceptable to you. You may fool the Army but you cannot fool and fail your family at the same time. No male among us has ever been like that and the women, too, thank heaven, are stronger. That means you don't belong. So go on the course that you have chosen for yourself, that of comfort and convenience, all sweetness, love and lollipops. . . . You will not be welcome here again and you are herewith constrained not to use our name as family in any connection. Truly, S. L. A. Marshall."

I was staggered. It was a huge blow. I never saw him again. We never reconciled while he was alive. He died in 1977 and I did not attend his funeral. I figured I wasn't welcome there either.

Our relationship was another casualty of the Vietnam War. I think his letter shows what the war did to many American families. Somehow, in the passing years, it seems to have escaped notice that the war caused bitter splits along generational lines within families. The war was divisive to the country, but it was also incredibly divisive in families—much like the Civil War.

Years later, however, John achieved a kind of reconciliation with his late grandfather. In 1989, an American Heritage *article accused S. L. A. Marshall of lying about his life and fabricating some of the research for his books. The grandson decided to investigate the charges, traveling twelve thousand miles around the country.*

"I just wanted to see what the truth was. The report card turned out to be kind of

*mixed, like the report card on most of us would be." Writing a book about the investigation—*Reconciliation Road*—John came to know his grandfather far better and forgave his rejection. In 1990, when his daughter was born, she was named Samantha in honor of her great-grandfather.*

HUYNH PHUONG DONG

"Receiving a letter was a mixed blessing."

While her husband talked, she offered tea, spring rolls, and fruit. When asked for her own story, she did not hesitate, but her words were few. Like her husband, she was born in the South and moved to the North after the French War. They met in Hanoi, married in 1956, and had two children. Her husband went south with the People's Army in 1963 and she would not see him again for a decade. She worked as a nurse, then a doctor's aide, and by 1972, as a full-fledged physician.

During the American War I worked as a doctor's aide in Phu Tho Province [northwest of Hanoi]. When the Americans started bombing the North in 1964 we moved most of our patients out of the city hospital into the countryside where they would be safer. But many patients needed operations or serious treatment, which they could only get at the hospital with its modern facilities. So we were constantly moving patients back and forth between the countryside and the city. At first the Americans bombed mostly at day so we moved patients into the city at night. But after a few years there was no predicting when the bombs would fall.

If we were performing an operation we had to carry on even in the midst of bombing strikes. We were under explicit orders not to abandon our patients. They were not to die alone. That's why, whenever possible, we did our operations in underground bunkers that had been built during the French War.

In those days everybody hated the Americans. We could accept that the Americans would attack military bases for military purposes, but they even attacked hospitals, civilian centers, and dikes. There were a lot of civilian casualties, so naturally we were full of anger. But Uncle Ho taught us to make a clear distinction between peace-loving Americans and warmongers. The evil ones were hawkish imperialists who wanted to continue the war, while good Americans supported our struggle for independence. Many Americans objected to the war and refused to fight. And Mr. Morrison even immolated himself as a protest against the war. We also made a distinction between the ordinary soldiers who carried out orders and the policy makers who initiated the war.

Of course I was scared, but like everybody else I just blocked it out for the sake of the patients. The biggest problem for me was the separation from my family. My husband was in the South while I worked in the North. My kids were in the North but they were evacuated to a safer place so I rarely saw them. One of the ways to lessen my loneliness was to devote all my free time to medical studies. But I always worried. Letters from the South took at least three months and sometimes as much as a year to arrive. When you did receive a letter it just meant that your loved one was alive and well on the day he wrote, but there was no way to know if he was still alive. In many cases people received letters saying everything was okay when, in fact, the writer had already been killed. So receiving a letter was a mixed blessing. At first you were so happy, but then you looked at the date it was written and started to worry all over again. I was separated from my husband for ten years and he was separated from our two children for thirteen.

In 1973, I went to the jungle of Tay Ninh Province in the South to work in the department of public health. It took me three months and eleven days to walk the Ho Chi Minh Trail. When I arrived, people told me my husband was in Binh Long Province so I had to wait one more month to see him. Even then, Tay Ninh was not completely liberated so it was very dangerous for him to visit. Finally, one night at one or two A.M., someone knocked on my door and said my husband was outside. I remember the moment so clearly. The news sent a shiver down my spine. I opened the door and saw him sitting on a bench. He looked at me and said simply, "You're just as I remembered you."

"After the war Americans came to Vietnam to look for the remains of their GIs and they gave us a lot of headaches about that. They didn't understand that we couldn't even recover the remains of our own soldiers. Many thousands of Vietnamese mothers still mourn the fact that the remains of their children are unrecovered. If American mothers understood this, they would not complain about the slow process of finding their missing. We care more about peace than hard feelings, but forgiveness doesn't mean we should forget the past. The [Communist] party says we should leave the past behind us, look to the future, and build friendly relations with the Americans. But the wounds of the past are not easy to forget."

RICHARD HOUSER

"They told me I needed to choose between my country and my brother."

While he went to Vietnam, his older brother, Nathan, went to Canada. "Nathan and I are as close as any two brothers you'll find." They grew up in Butler, Indiana, a town of sixteen hundred people. Today, after a career in banking, Richard runs a refractory company in Fort Wayne. "We make the material that keeps metal furnaces from melting."

We didn't have a damn dime growing up. We grew our own food, Mom canned, we hunted, we fished. Dad was a factory worker making ninety to a hundred dollars a week. He was an ardent Democrat and a union man. He raised a little hell, womanized a little bit, gambled, smoked, and stopped for a drink after work. My mother was a very devout religious evangelical in a church where smoking was bad, dancing was bad, cards were bad, poolrooms were bad, never mind drinking. So we were exposed to opposite ends of the spectrum. But they did a good job of sticking together as far as the kids were concerned. I think their differences were instrumental in teaching us to make decisions on our own.

Dad was from the old school—either follow my rules or get out and do it yourself. Nathan and I always knew we would leave and we left early on. I was sixteen when Nathan and I took an apartment in Fort Wayne, about thirty-five miles from Butler. That was 1964 and it was a time to do everything yourself anyway—that's the generation we were. Nathan had just been elected president of his class at Taylor University, a religious school, when he decided that he didn't want to go there anymore. So he dropped out and we both got jobs.

There was a small coffee shop in Fort Wayne called the Fourth Shadow where people gathered to play chess, to talk about all the world's problems, and listen to some folk music. When it closed, if we still had some talking to do we went over to the Java Shop in the Van Orman Hotel. We got thrown out of there two or three times for drinking coffee with blacks. The manager would call the police. One night the police were having an altercation over nothing with one of our friends who happened to be black. I said something and one of the police hit me upside the head with a flashlight. The next thing I knew, Nathan was getting me from the hospital with a bunch of stitches.

When we discussed the Vietnam War there were times when neither one of us was going, there were times when both of us were going, there were times when Nathan was going and I wasn't, and there were times when I was going and he wasn't. The question we were wrestling with was, what do you owe your country? I finally came to the conclusion that even if the war wasn't the best thing to be doing, which we kind of thought it wasn't, as long as I was going to live in the States, I needed to serve. It wasn't anything noble, or honorable, from my vantage point. Part of it was I probably didn't want to embarrass Dad. Anyway, I decided if I wasn't ready to leave the country and they were going to be in this damn thing, I might as well get it over with. I've never been good at waiting for things to happen. And if I'm going to do it, I thought I might as well go with what we thought was the toughest branch and join the Marine Corps.

I had no question I was going to Vietnam. I volunteered. I also volunteered for a seven-month extension in Vietnam after my first tour. I got in-country in 1966 and left in 1968. I was in avionics with the 56th Marine Air Wing. We kept all the radios, radar, and electrical equipment for the aircraft in working order. I also volunteered as a crew member on helicopters. But the worst memory for me didn't have anything to do with war. On Christmas Eve 1966, a Flying Tiger aircraft crashed into a small village right outside Danang. There was only a crew and one other person on the plane but the village was devastated. I spent Christmas Eve and most of Christmas morning picking up arms and legs and throwing them in the back of a truck. A lot of them were kids. I think a hundred and twelve people died. There was never anything more gruesome. We put field lights out to be able to see it. I went back to the hut, got myself a bottle of Jack [Daniels], and missed the rest of Christmas.

One of the scariest situations in Vietnam also didn't have a damn thing to do with the Viet Cong—it was when Martin Luther King was assassinated. When the news was received over Armed Forces Radio, it was as explosive a situation as you could possibly have. There were major fisticuffs that night. I'd just come in from flying and was going down to the shower. I walked out the back of our hut and right into the middle of a melee. It was a fairly major brawl, probably twenty guys. I hit two or three people and realized I wasn't getting hit. I turned around and a good friend of mine named Laney—a black guy big enough to play pro football—was throwing guys off me who were trying to hit me from the back. I got the hell out of there as soon as I could. Officers took control of the situation so it wasn't an all-out war of Americans against Americans, but it came very damn close to boiling over. You had racists on either side and some of them died during that time.

Even when I was in Vietnam, Nathan and I stayed close. In 1967, he and Suzie were getting married and needed some money. I had made a little money playing cards, so I sent him about three hundred dollars. I also managed to get a ham radio hookup so I could call him. One time a kid named Yogi overheard one of my calls to Canada and started in on the damn draft dodgers. He indicated that my brother was a lily-livered chickenshit who just didn't have the balls to come to Vietnam. After I stuck his head in the urinal and explained the facts of life to him we became very good friends.

The FBI had a major file on my brother and when they found out I had called him a number of times they thought there had to be something terrible going on. I got questioned a few times in Vietnam by intelligence agents. They couldn't understand how I could be doing one thing and Nathan another and us be as close as we were—there had to be some sinister action somewhere. It's understandable that there would be questions. I'm trying to be fair. I was working with some sensitive equipment and I'm sure they needed to know who I was. But it was Joe McCarthyism in another form. They went too far. They thought Nathan was a horrible person who was part of a group that was putting together a stockpile of weapons to overthrow the government. They said my brother was obviously a Communist, a traitor to the United States, and a coward—a lot of nasty words. They thought I was part of the conspiracy, that I was undercover in Vietnam stealing weapons and giving away war secrets. I told them I must be awfully brave to be willing to put up with shells and rockets just to try to steal weapons. At one point they told me I needed to choose between my country and my brother. I told them to stick it up their rear end. I was loyal to both and would remain loyal to both and they could do what they wanted to do with their families.

Once home from Vietnam, he visited Nathan many times. "Once I smuggled Suzie and Nathan back home to see the parents and a policeman stopped us at a speed trap. Here I am in the United States Marine Corps with a criminal draft evader. They could have charged me with treason at that point." The FBI continued periodic questioning of Richard even after the war had ended. "One time they came right into the bank where I was working and tried to cost me my job. Of course I was still smuggling my brother into the country when I wanted to, so I wasn't blameless in the eyes of the law."

NATHAN HOUSER

"A sign this country has grown up will be when there is a memorial erected to the war resisters."

Richard Houser's older brother, he was among the more than fifty thousand Americans who sought exile in Canada as a direct result of the Vietnam War. They included draft dodgers, draft resisters, military deserters, and various other people who wanted to separate themselves from their nation and its war. Canada was by far the most common destination, though Sweden also received at least a thousand Americans. Both countries offered liberal emigration laws, work permits, and full legal status. The Vietnam-era exodus was the largest war-related out-migration from the United States since ten thousand Tories fled the United States during the Revolutionary War.

Nathan Houser was the president of Youth for Christ in Butler, Indiana. "I learned from very early on that my relationship to things divine had to be worked out through my own rational processes using what I believed was the word of God." In the midsixties he lost his faith in God and in the war his nation was waging in Vietnam. Unwilling to fight a war that contradicted his understanding of what was right, he and his wife, Suzie, went to Canada. He lived there for fifteen years, returning in 1983 to take a job on the philosophy faculty at Indiana University where he now teaches.

I grew up believing that America was God's chosen country and that the American way of life was the right one and the just one. This was preached to us in the Cold War period. I fully shared a typical midwestern attitude that somehow war was glorious and being a soldier was the pinnacle of bravery. I was very comfortable with guns and shooting and would get up before dawn and go into the woods with a rifle to go hunting. I'm saying this because later on when I became opposed to Vietnam it had nothing at all to do with some unfamiliarity or discomfort with the idea of war.

I didn't get seriously interested in politics until Kennedy's assassination, but in 1956 our seventh-grade class took a vote on election day. Adlai Stevenson got one vote and that was mine. My father was a union rep for his factory and when I told him, he said, "Well, I'm probably the only other person in town who voted for him." I remember very well that Stevenson was criticized for something that even in those days I understood to be a good thing. Whenever an issue arose, he could see two sides to the question. That was put forward as something negative, while the media praised Eisenhower because he could make a decision instantly.

Around that same time a teacher went off on a tear about the evils of Communism. Of course I was opposed to Communism, but I was trying to imagine what it would be like to live as a Communist so I asked, "Don't you think a Communist mother feels about her children a lot like our mothers feel about us?" My teacher wouldn't take a minute to think about this. She just told me not to bother.

I never had the fear of or antipathy to Communism that I guess most of my peers and neighbors had. That was also partly due to my religion because frankly, I thought a lot about my religion and Socialism is quite compatible with Christianity. But I was very patriotic. When a new post office opened in Butler, I was selected to read the "Ode to the American Flag." And when I graduated from high school in 1962, I was given the American Legion citizenship award.

I went to Taylor University, a religious school in Upland, Indiana. Not long after I got there, the Cuban Missile Crisis happened. We thought war might be coming and all the young men on campus were caught up in the fervor. At some point we all picked up broom handles or anything that was long and gun-like, slung them over our shoulders, and marched around the campus in file demonstrating our support for this great nation in crisis.

Kennedy's assassination had an enormous impact on me. In addition to the shock of it, two things really struck me. I heard that the Secret Service had spirited off the Kennedy children to a safe hiding place because they thought it possible that a coup was in progress. It had simply never occurred to me that there could be a coup in the United States. The mere fact that the Secret Service thought it was possible put things in a strange light. I also heard a radio interview with the Dallas chief of police who said, "Oh yeah, I know this man Oswald [the suspected assassin]. He's done some work for the FBI." That's the last I ever heard of that chief of police and I immediately distrusted the official stories coming out about what happened. That's when I began taking a critical stance toward our government.

I was a fundamentalist when I arrived at Taylor but I began to have a sense that something was seriously wrong. The school was filled with Christians of slightly differing perspectives, minor differences that presumably could lead to eternal salvation or eternal damnation. The prayer meetings began to seem very odd and cultish. I was still saying my morning and evening prayers but at a certain point I started to pray, "Dear God, if you exist . . ." And then one day I just ceased to believe. It just was finished.

The summer of '64, I went to Washington as a political intern for Senator Vance Hartke. That was another turning point because I still aspired to maybe become a politician. But the workings of politics just floored me. So much of it seemed artificial and self-serving. That was also the time when things were beginning to happen in Vietnam and I began to learn some of the war's history. It troubled me that the United States had been opposed to the 1956 elections in Vietnam called for by the Geneva Accords. Our reason was just straightforwardly that we knew Ho Chi Minh would win. It was pretty clear that we weren't really interested in democracy for Vietnam. I began to feel there was a whole lot of duplicity and lying going on.

When I got back to Taylor I was still the president of my class but felt I was in the wrong place. So I dropped out with a friend of mine and hitchhiked to California. But we couldn't find work and my brother Richard had dropped out of high school and I was worried about him. So I moved to Fort Wayne, lived with Richard, got a job in a General Electric factory, and enrolled at Indiana University.

There was a strong youth movement developing and in Fort Wayne it was especially exciting because it crossed many boundaries. A lot of people had this feeling of a rising counterculture and it brought together people in the arts, dancers, intellectuals, college teachers, students, factory workers, people from all walks of life. Richard and I would go to a coffeehouse called the Fourth Shadow and after it closed people would come to our apartment. Sometimes I'd wake up and there would be six or seven people lying around the apartment.

I remember a fellow at the university who passed out a magazine called *Viet Report.* I read these regularly and they were quite critical about what was going on in Vietnam—you couldn't find much criticism in the Fort Wayne *News Sentinel* or the *Journal-Gazette.* But I was still thinking on both sides of the subject. I still had this general idea of war as something kind of glorious. The Green Berets were the glory of glories. At the very same time I was growing more critical of what we were actually doing in Vietnam, I called a Special Forces recruiter to talk about my options. I didn't join up but I was looking at that possibility.

By the fall of '65 I was burned out from working all the time to keep the apartment scene going and the money I was making was really going to support a whole lot of fun for other people. So I decided to transfer to New York University. But I didn't have enough money to start in the fall so I began working for a trucking company. In the meantime, I lost my student deferment and was classified 1-A. I had to go back to school in Indiana to keep my deferment.

By this time Richard had joined the marines. I didn't know he was going to do that and I was sort of surprised, but it hadn't been too long since I myself had talked to a recruiter. It was during that year, 1966, when my thinking got very resolved against the war. When you mixed together concerns like mine about the way the war was being conducted, the veil of secrecy that the media cloaked itself in, and the music of Bob Dylan and Joan Baez, there began to be a real dichotomy between the so-called establishment and this youthful protest movement that was growing. I was getting settled in on the side of the dissenters.

What I was going to do after graduating in 1967 started to become a real concern. I decided I wasn't going to fight in Vietnam. I felt it was wrong. It was clear to me that we weren't fighting for democracy. I was completely willing to do something that I thought was good for the country, but I just couldn't accept that I was going to be forced to do something I thought was bad. It really boiled down to that.

I still felt patriotic and decided I would go join the Peace Corps. I was accepted and waiting for an assignment to South America when I got a letter saying that Peace Corps volunteers could no longer discuss foreign policy while abroad. It was abundantly clear that the Peace Corps had become a supporting branch of United States foreign policy and I didn't want to go under those circumstances.

I pretty much decided to go to jail or go underground to resist the war. I thought that was the right thing to do and maybe braver than leaving the country, which I regarded, to a certain extent, as a possibly cowardly thing. But by the fall of '67 I had met Suzie, developed a relationship, and we got married. She didn't think it was particularly interesting to start a marriage with me in jail or underground so we began to think about going to Canada. We made contact with the Toronto Anti-Draft Program, learned a bit about the whole process, and in March we left.

We didn't know what we were getting into. We didn't have jobs and didn't know where we were going to live. The drama of that experience had a lot more to do with heading into the unknown than worrying about what was being closed off.

I got a job with a bookstore chain. Very quickly I became the manager of one of those stores and then the supervisor of the chain, so I was responsible for hiring a lot of people. It didn't take very long before I was the first stop for many of the Americans coming in. They would go to the Anti-Draft office and be told, "Go talk to Houser and see if he's got a job for you." In order to get landed [become a legal resident], having a job offer gave you a lot of extra points. So I wrote scores of letters offering employment to guys coming in. For a time I'd say more than half of the people working for the Toronto book stores were draft resisters.

There was a great variety of people and they had as many reasons for coming to Canada as people had for going into the service. Some people were afraid to serve, just as there were probably a lot of people who were afraid not to serve because of social sanctions. Maybe some people were swept up in antiwar feeling and rhetoric not so different from the people who went into the service swept up with war rhetoric. And there were people who did it simply because they didn't want to have their life trajectory disrupted. But a lot of people—and I put myself in this class—had serious philosophical or moral reasons.

There were times when Richard called me from Danang and those were poignant moments. We always felt really connected. I didn't politically agree with the stance he was taking, but I didn't begrudge him having made his own decision. My concern was more at the level of governmental policy than individual decision making. I think his contact with me caused him some grief with military intelligence. The fact that I was involved with giving so many jobs to draft evaders probably made me seem more pivotal to the antiwar movement than I was.

My parents didn't support what I was doing but they were probably more worried than upset. They obviously felt more comfortable with my brother being in Danang than with me being in Toronto. My mother gave the FBI my address because she thought that was the right thing to do. It wasn't a big deal. It just meant that the RCMP [Royal Canadian Mounted Police] came around to tell me I'd been indicted. But my parents certainly didn't shut me out. In fact, at a certain point they came up to visit me.

And I came home a number of times. That was a little frightening, because this was small-town America and people didn't like what I had done. If certain people had seen me I suppose that would have been it. When I came home, first with Suzie but more often with my second wife, Aleta, we'd trade cars with a friend along the way so we wouldn't have Canadian plates. When we'd get to the edge of town we'd call my father so he'd have the garage door open. I'd get down on the floor in the back seat and Suzie or Aleta would drive into town and into the open garage and my father would close the door. I didn't go out of the house except a few times when I'd put on a black trench coat and take a little walk after dark. According to my father, two hours after I left one time to come back to Canada the chief of police stopped by and said, "Listen, you better tell him not to come again because if he does I'm gonna have to pick him up." So somehow they knew I was there. It was always a little scary.

When Richard got back from Vietnam he would sometimes come up and visit and he was always well accepted among the draft resisters. I know there was animosity from soldiers toward protesters, but there wasn't much the other way around. People opposing the war generally assumed that the solders were not particularly culpable. I think there was a certain sympathy for them.

Vietnam for me represents an incredible discontinuity in the course of my life. Taking this stand resulted in an awful lot of life interruption. For the five years I worked for the bookstore I was just trying to make a living and get my life together. There were five or six pretty wasted years and when I look at my own accomplishments relative to other professors my age, I can see that there was a loss. But I met people I liked, especially my present wife, Aleta, who came up with another draft resister. I gave her first husband a job in one of the bookstores.

America should recognize that many resisters of the Vietnam War acted entirely patriotically. A sign this country has grown up will be when there is a memorial erected to the war resisters. Until that happens I would say we're still in our cultural and intellectual infancy.

SUZIE SCOTT

"This nice young man from the FBI was here."

On a Saturday morning she's painting her Toronto home. Pulling a drop cloth off a chair, she sits down, lights a cigarette, and talks about her experiences as one of the approximately twenty-five thousand American women who sought exile in Canada during the Vietnam War. Not well known is the fact that roughly half of the American wartime exiles were women. A considerable number emigrated on their own, but the great majority came with husbands or boyfriends who were evading the draft or deserting the military. Raised in Bluffton, Indiana, she married Nathan Houser in 1967. After three years together in Toronto they separated. Today she is a Canadian labor lawyer.

We arrived in Toronto on March 17, 1968—St. Patrick's Day. Meanwhile, back in the States, the FBI was visiting Nathan's parents. His mother is a born-again Christian and all her letters started with six pages of Bible quotes. The real news was written around the edge of the last page. In one letter she wrote, "This nice young man from the FBI was here and he says he understands your position perfectly. He'd like to talk it over with you, and if you come back, he can arrange something." She just didn't get it. Nathan would have been arrested instantly. This guy must have visited her three or four times—thought he had a live one, I guess.

Nathan was the American Legion scholar in high school—the finest his town had to offer the world. Everybody was so proud of him. His younger brother, Richard, became a marine. They really liked each other, but here's one signing up for the marines, and here's the other one coming to Canada, evading the draft.

When he got back from Vietnam, Richard came up to visit us and we drove back to Indiana with him. You know what the border is like—it's easy—no problems there. But they lived in a very small community where everybody knows him, so we sneaked in from the garage under the cover of darkness. The last day of our visit, Nathan's father was pulled over by the local sheriff, who said, "Frank, I know your boy Nathan is in town. Get him out of here so I don't have to do anything."

My political views really didn't develop until I got to Canada. Before that it was just, you know, "Hey, yeah, let's go." I knew things were going from bad to worse in Vietnam but nothing more than that. I'm sure there were some teenagers in New York who knew all about it, but you didn't know it if you lived on a farm in Indiana.

When we first got to Toronto I hated it. I was really homesick. I remember seeing *The Graduate* when it came out and there's a scene where a big American flag is flying behind Dustin Hoffman. I remember saying, "That flag means something. There is a star for every state, a stripe for every original colony, the blue stands for loyalty, and the red is for the blood shed defending it. But this Canadian flag—a maple leaf—what's that stand for?"

It took several years of being here to realize how much propaganda I had been fed all my life—in every school, church, everywhere. I mean, if you're my age, you were told from the day you're born that if you're white, twenty-one, and an American, you've got the world on a string. People in Fort Wayne were saying, "How could you trade being an American for going to Canada? Canada is just a podunk country. I guess if you want to live in a really small place you can go to Toronto." What? Now I love Canada and I doubt I'll ever move back to the States.

LAM VAN LICH

"I was away from home for twenty-nine years."

Raised in Ca Mau, the southernmost tip of Vietnam, he left home at fifteen in 1946 to fight the French. "We had no food, no clothes, no education. National liberation was synonymous with self-liberation." In 1954, he "regrouped" to the North and was trained as a pilot.

The war caused a lot of casualties and pain. Just take my family for instance. When I returned to the South in 1975 I found that many of my own family members had been killed. The pain of those deaths was greater than the sadness I felt for participating in the killing. I was away from home for twenty-nine years. I gave my family a few days' advance notice that I was coming, but when I entered the house I saw my older sister and mistook her for my mother. And when my mother came in she didn't recognize me. Even after I introduced myself she kept saying, "Lich? Lich?" She didn't believe it. She insisted on examining my head. When she finally found a familiar mole, she cried out, "It's you!" Even though we were fully prepared for the reunion, we cried our hearts out. During the war my mother was arrested many times. All her sons where engaged in revolutionary activities so the local government frequently took her in for questioning. For the protection of the family she didn't tell the younger members of the family about me. When I returned in 1975, many of my nieces and nephews didn't even know I existed.

MY LAI

On December 5, 1969, *Life* magazine ran a cover story on African wildlife featuring a remarkably beautiful variety of antelope. Tucked inside the same issue was a set of obscene color photographs: a trench full of bodies, obviously dead; a close-up of a baby, smeared with its own wet blood; a group of women and children huddled together in panic and disbelief. A caption says they, too, will soon be killed. You are looking at the final seconds of their lives.

The pictures had been taken by military cameraman Ron Haeberle on March 16, 1968, the day U.S. infantrymen from Charlie Company, 1st Battalion, 20th Infantry, 11th Light Infantry Brigade of the 23d Americal Division killed some five hundred Vietnamese civilians in My Lai-4, a subhamlet of Son My village in Quang Ngai Province. The carnage was not a spontaneous convulsion of violence, but an almost leisurely slaughter that lasted for several hours, so long that many of the GIs took breaks to eat C rations and smoke cigarettes. They never received a single round of hostile fire. However, American commanders summarized the event in their "after-action report" as a successful firefight in which 128 "Viet Cong" had been killed in action. Relying exclusively on U.S. military accounts, *The New York Times* reported on page one: "American troops caught a North Vietnamese force in a pincer movement on the central coastal plain yesterday, killing 128 enemy soldiers in day-long fighting." The army's lie successfully covered up the atrocity for a year and a half.

Many Americans, especially since the war, believe the media had an antiwar bias and eagerly looked for stories that might cast U.S. policy in a negative light. Yet, the mainstream media played no role in the initial uncovering of the My Lai massacre. It might never have surfaced without the persistence of a Vietnam veteran named Ron Ridenhour. Though not present at My Lai, he had heard details of the massacre from five eyewitnesses. Upon returning to the United States, he summarized what he had heard in a letter he sent to the Pentagon, the State Department, the Joint Chiefs of Staff, and congressional leaders. Only then was the military pressured to begin an investigation that led, in 1969, to the arrest of Lieutenant William Calley, a platoon leader at My Lai, for the premeditated murder of 109 Vietnamese civilians. News of Calley's arrest was ignored in the press for months and stories by freelance journalist Seymour Hersh were initially rejected by major publications, including *Life.* Finally, Hersh sent his investigative work to Dispatch News Service, one of several small, alternative media outlets that blossomed in the 1960s in opposition to the major media's tendency to focus primarily on officially approved subjects and sources. Through Dispatch, the story finally exploded into national and global consciousness.

Many Americans reacted with a kind of desperate denial. Some insisted the story was a hoax, that the photographs had been fabricated, or that the Communists had actually done the killing. Others struggled to justify the massacre. "It sounds terrible to say that we ought to kill kids," one woman conceded, "but many of our boys being killed over there are just kids, too." One poll found that 65 percent of Americans claimed they were not upset by the massacre.

For all the denials and evasions, My Lai eventually brought a turning point in American attitudes almost as significant as the Tet Offensive. Millions who had believed the war a misguided policy or a tragic mistake began to consider the possibility that it was fundamentally unjust and immoral. That claim had long been a staple of speeches at antiwar rallies and articles in underground newspapers, but now it was debated for the first time in small-town coffee shops, executive offices, and mass-circulation magazines.

No American atrocity in Vietnam of such dimensions had ever come to light before (or has since) but accounts of smaller-scale acts of mutilation, torture, rape, and murder began increasingly to surface. When they did, many concluded that My Lai was not an isolated event, but an extreme yet logical outgrowth of a military strategy that sent young men on "search-and-destroy" missions into rural villages under extreme pressure to locate an enemy largely indistinguishable from civilians and measured success by the number of dead bodies produced. The "body count," after all, was not a dirty little secret of the war, but a daily feature of military briefings that made its way onto virtually every nightly news broadcast, a standard scorecard for how well the United States was doing. While many Americans may have become inured to the human significance of those routine tallies, the My Lai massacre made graphically clear that not all the people listed as "enemy KIA" had been killed in combat.

As attention shifted from My Lai to a broader scrutiny of the war, Americans learned that many parts of South Vietnam had been designated "free-fire zones" in which anything that moved was deemed a legitimate target of American ground fire and bombing. Free-fire zones were routinely and randomly shelled with "harassment and interdiction" fire. The military insisted that the villagers in those areas had been warned to leave, or physically removed to refugee camps, but that in itself raised troubling questions. Was the uprooting and displacement of peasants (five million by the most conservative estimate) justified in any war?

Americans also learned of the "Phoenix Program," a CIA-run campaign to destroy the Viet Cong "infrastructure" that assassinated many thousands of Vietnamese believed to be guerrilla agents. Then there were reports about the "tiger cages" into which the South Vietnamese government threw political prisoners who were then subjected to unimaginably brutal treatment. Finally, in the early seventies groups of antiwar Vietnam veterans began to testify about their own participation in, and observation of, acts they explicitly labeled war crimes—including cutting ears off enemy dead, torturing prisoners with electric shocks from field radios, poisoning wells and food supplies, and systematically burning down villages.

Defenders of American policy argued that the Communists had committed atrocities as bad or worse than these, including mass executions in the old imperial capital of Hue during the Tet Offensive. Yet the "everybody does it" argument was of little consolation to Americans raised to believe that the United States had a higher regard for human life than our adversaries and abided by a higher standard of civilized behavior.

Journalists and scholars like *New York Times* reporter Neil Sheehan and former Nuremburg war crimes prosecutor Telford Taylor began to write that legal action for war crimes in Vietnam was warranted not only against low-ranking military personnel like Calley, but against the highest civilian and military leadership who established atrocity-producing policies. This incendiary idea flourished briefly but quickly fell out of mainstream discussions of the war. In the years since, even the My Lai massacre is largely unknown to younger generations. Reminders occasionally surface, as in 2001 when it was revealed that former Nebraska senator Bob Kerrey had commanded a SEAL team that killed some twenty civilians in a small Vietnamese hamlet (whether they did it accidentally or intentionally remains in dispute). However, in the brief storm of media attention that followed, few questioned whether anyone above Kerrey's rank of lieutenant should be held culpable for such killings.

The evidence from My Lai indicated that at least fifty American officers, up to and including generals, had significant knowledge of the massacre, either through firsthand observation or eyewitness reports, and all had supported the cover-up either by suppressing the truth or refusing to act upon the information they received. Yet there was no mass tribunal with dockets full of high-ranking officers. Criminal charges were eventually brought against eighteen officers, but every one except Lieutenant Calley was acquitted or had his charges dismissed without a trial. Calley was convicted of killing twenty-two civilians and sentenced to life imprisonment. However, through President Nixon's intervention, he was released after three and a half years under house arrest.

LARRY COLBURN

"They were butchering people."

After a long day, the salesman sits in a bar booth sipping a Coke. Once again, he's asked to recall the events of March 16, 1968, when he was a helicopter door-gunner who helped to stop some of the killing at My Lai. His pilot, Hugh Thompson, landed their observation chopper in the midst of the ongoing massacre to protect a group of villagers threatened by GIs. Thompson and his two crewmen were prepared to shoot any Americans who tried to harm the Vietnamese. Thirty years later, the U.S. Army awarded the Soldier's Medal for Gallantry to Thompson, Colburn, and Glenn Andreotta (who died in combat a few weeks after the My Lai massacre).

We weren't pacifists. We did our job and when we had to kill people we did. But we didn't do it for sport. We didn't randomly shoot people. In our gun company it was very important to capture weapons, not just to legitimize your kill, but psychologically it was easier when you could say, "If I didn't do that, he was going to shoot me."

We flew an OH-23—a little gasoline-engine bubble helicopter. We were aerial scouts—a new concept. Instead of just sending assault helicopters they'd use our small aircraft as bait and have a couple gunships cover us. Basically we'd go out and try to get into trouble. We'd fly real low and if we encountered anything we'd mark it with smoke, return fire, and let the gunships work out. We also went on "snatch missions," kidnapping draft-age males to take back for interrogation. We did that a lot in 1968.

On March 16, we came on station a little after seven A.M. The only briefing I got was that they were going to put a company on the ground to sweep through this village. Normally we'd go in beforehand to see if we could find enemy positions or entice people to shoot at us. It was clear and warm and the fog was lifting off the rice paddies. On our first pass we saw a man in uniform carrying a carbine and a pack coming out of a tree line. Thompson said, "Who wants him?" I said, "I'll take him." So he aimed the aircraft at him and got it down low and started toward the suspect. He was obviously Viet Cong. He was armed, evading, and headed for the next tree line. I couldn't hit him to save my life. We worked that area a little more but that was the only armed Vietnamese I saw that day.

After that we just started working the perimeter of My Lai-4, -5, and -6 and I remember seeing the American troops come in on slicks [helicopters].* We got ahead of them to see if they were going to encounter anything and we still didn't receive any fire. It was market day and we saw a lot of women and children leaving the hamlet. They were moving down the road carrying empty baskets. As we went further around the perimeter we saw a few wounded women in the rice fields south of My Lai-4. We marked their bodies with smoke grenades expecting that medics would give them medical assistance.

When we came back to the road we started seeing bodies, the same people that were walking to the market. They hadn't even gotten off the road. They were in piles, dead. We started going through all the scenarios of what might have happened. Was it artillery? Gunships? Viet Cong? The American soldiers on the ground were just walking around in a real nonchalant sweep. No one was crouching, ducking, or hiding.

Then we saw a young girl about twenty years old lying in the grass. We could see that she was unarmed and wounded in the chest. We marked her with smoke because we saw a squad not too far away. The smoke was green meaning it's safe to approach. Red would have meant the opposite. We were hovering six feet off the ground not more than twenty feet away when Captain Medina came over, kicked her, stepped back, and finished her off. He did it right in front of us. When we saw Medina do that, it all clicked. It was our guys doing the killing.

The bodies we marked with smoke—you find yourself feeling that you indirectly killed them. I'll never forget one lady who was hiding in the grass. She was crouched in a fetal position. I motioned to her—stay down, be quiet, stay there. We flew off on more reconnaissance. We came back later and she was in the same position, right where I'd told her to stay. But someone had come up behind her and literally blew her brains out. I'll never forget that look of bewilderment on her face.

Around ten A.M. Thompson spotted a group of women and children running toward a bunker northeast of My Lai-4 followed by a group of U.S. soldiers. When we got overhead, Andreotta spotted some faces peeking out of an earthen bunker. Thompson knew that in a matter of seconds they were going to die so he landed the aircraft in between the advancing American troops and

*My Lai-4, the scene of the massacre, was one of six subhamlets identified as My Lai (1–6) on U.S. Army maps. All were part of the village of Song My. Vietnamese residents of My Lai-4 called their subhamlet Xom Lang.

the bunker. He went over and talked to a Lieutenant Brooks. Thompson said, "These are civilians. How do we get them out of the bunker?" Brooks said, "I'll get them out with hand grenades." The veins were sticking out on Thompson's neck and I thought they were actually going to fight. Thompson came back and said to Andreotta and me, "If they open up on these people when I'm getting them out of the bunker, shoot 'em." Then he walked away leaving us standing there looking at each other. Thompson went over to the bunker and motioned for the people to come out. There were nine or ten of them.

We had a staredown going with the American soldiers. About half of them were sitting down, smoking and joking. I remember looking at one fellow and waving. He waved back and that's when I knew we were okay, that these guys weren't going to do anything to us. No one pointed weapons at us and we didn't point any weapons at them.

Thompson called Dan Millians, a gunship pilot friend of his, and said, "Danny, I've got a little problem down here, can you help out?" Millians said sure and did something unheard of. You don't land a gunship to use it as a medevac, but he did. He got those people a couple miles away and let 'em go. I think he had to make two trips.

We flew over the ditch where more than a hundred Vietnamese had been killed. Andreotta saw movement so Thompson landed again. Andreotta went directly into that ditch. He literally had to wade waist deep through people to get to a little child. I stood there in the open. Glenn came over and handed me the child, but the ditch was so full of bodies and blood he couldn't get out. I gave him the butt of my rifle and pulled him out. We took the little one to an orphanage. We didn't know if he was a little boy or little girl. Just a cute little child. I felt for broken bones or bullet holes and he appeared to be fine. He wasn't crying, but he had this blank stare on his face and he was covered with blood.

The only thing I remember feeling back then was that these guys were really out for revenge. They'd lost men to booby traps and snipers and they were ready to engage. They were briefed the night before and I've heard it said that they were going in there to waste everything. They didn't capture any weapons. They didn't kill any draft-age males. I've seen the list of dead and there were a hundred and twenty some humans under the age of five. It's something I've struggled with my whole life, how people can do that. I know what it's like to seek revenge, but we would look for a worthy opponent. These were elders, mothers, children, and babies. The fact that VC camped out there at night is no justification for killing everyone in the hamlet.

Compare it to a little town in the United States. We're at war with someone on our own soil. They come into a town and rape the women, kill the babies, kill everyone. How would we feel? And it wasn't just murdering civilians. They were butchering people. The only thing they didn't do is cook 'em and eat 'em. How do you get that far over the edge?

At the end of the day, he went to see Colonel Oran Henderson, the commander of Task Force Barker, who was flying in a command and control helicopter at fifteen hundred feet over My Lai throughout the massacre. "I told him there was needless killing of civilians going on that day, blatant killing of lots of civilians. He took some notes on a legal pad and said, 'Okay.' Didn't hear anything more about it until the trials of Calley, Medina, and Henderson. F. Lee Bailey cross-examined me about the woman we saw Medina kill. He said, 'Mr. Colburn, you said that this woman was moving her arm?' I said, 'Yes, like she was gesturing for help.' He established in front of the jury that she made this quick move and because of Medina's keen combat edge he just turned and fired. Malarkey. I think that's when I realized that there would be no justice for those people who died."

In 2001, Colburn went back to Vietnam to participate in the opening of a My Lai Peace Park and the dedication of a new elementary school in the village—both projects initiated and largely financed by American veterans of the war. While in My Lai, he was reunited with the boy he saved from the ditch, now a man of forty-one named Do Hao. "I have worried about Do Hao for thirty-three years. All these years I've prayed he was four or five years old and had no memory of it, that the horror would be erased. Turns out he was eight. He remembers everything."

MICHAEL BERNHARDT

"The portable free-fire zone."

He fondly recalls his boyhood in suburban Long Island, New York. Neighbors were always helping each other build garages or add breezeways on their small Cape Cod houses. "It was way different back then. We all got together and did things. There was a sense of community. By the time I left, everybody had their own private castle and you could be living right next door to someone and maybe not know 'em."

He prides himself on the military training he received. After becoming an army paratrooper he trained for a Long Range Reconnaissance Patrol (LURP). But just before leaving for Vietnam the elite unit was broken up and sent to ordinary infantry companies. Bernhardt was assigned to the company that committed the My Lai mas-

sacre. On the day of the atrocity, however, he did not fire his weapon. Ordered to stay near the command post, by the time he arrived in the hamlet, most of the killing had already taken place. Afterward, he refused to participate in the cover-up.

When I was assigned to Charlie Company I knew there was something wrong. You could see it and smell it. These guys were all individuals. None of them thought they belonged to anything. There was no sense of community, no sense of duty or responsibility, no sense of pride. Whenever there was anything to be done, people would just disappear and the officers didn't have the slightest idea how to run an organization. Captain Medina did not maintain control and Calley—how on earth did Calley get through Officer Candidate School? Anybody who says these guys were typical just doesn't know what they're talking about. They could not possibly have had the same training and indoctrination that I had. This was the worst bunch of crap I had ever seen.

A lot of people think My Lai happened because there was too much military discipline, too much indoctrination. Not so. It was the exact opposite. There was way too little in that company. They were just like a bunch of street thugs doing whatever they wanted to do. It was a group that was leaderless, directionless, armed to the teeth, and making up their own rules out there, deciding that the epitome of courage and manhood was going out and killing a bunch of people.

I think something like My Lai probably had happened many times before. It was just a matter of scale. Here's the thing. The whole war effort was built on three pillars—the free-fire zone, the search-and-destroy mission, and the body count. The free-fire zone means shoot anybody that moves. The search-and-destroy mission is just another way to shoot anything that moves. I call it the portable free-fire zone—you tote it around anywhere you go. And the body count is the tool for measuring the success or failure of whatever you're doing. When you've got those three things it doesn't take a genius to figure out how it's going to end up. I would bet my house against anything right now that it had happened before and even after.

A few months before My Lai, they sat the whole company down on a hillside to watch a firepower demonstration by a helicopter gunship just to show us how the stuff works. There was a village down in the valley and we watched as the gunship pilot strafed the village with rockets and miniguns. There were people running everywhere. I'm thinking, what the hell is this all about? Did I miss something? Nobody said there was any threat down there or any reason to strafe that village. These guys don't seem to care who the heck they shot. I don't know if the company took the message, but I'm still not surprised at how it turned out in My Lai because of the way I saw things being conducted.

A few weeks before My Lai we were moving through some unknown territory and we came to a big, open rice paddy. We had three volunteers—myself and two other guys—go across the paddy to the other side. We got halfway across and the gunfire started coming in. How the hell they missed me, I don't know. So we all hauled ass back to the safe line with the bullets following us the whole way. We called in some air support and everything kind of calmed down again so we picked up and went across the paddy. When we got to the other side there was a village full of people. Underneath their homes they had little bomb shelters and we were searching those out. I went down into one of them and there was an old woman down there hiding. I said, okay, fine, hide. I went back up and when I came out there was Calley, his drawers down to his ankles, and he had a woman kneeling in front of him and he's got a .45 there in his hand that he's pointing at her head. I really, really wanted to kill that guy but there were just too many guys around. I saw him as pure evil. I missed an opportunity to snuff Calley and I guess maybe I should have. He was rotten to the core. I think if he'd been replaced by another officer of a different stripe, the whole damn thing wouldn't have happened. These guys were not difficult-to-manage people. They were kind of waiting for someone to tell them what the hell to do, to make some kind of moral judgment for them.

The night before the massacre there was a combination briefing and memorial service for the guys we'd lost. Medina made reference to the fact that My Lai was held by the enemy, that they supported the enemy, that we could expect to find them there, and more or less catch them flat-footed. He also said this was payback time, that we were going to get our revenge for the terrible things they were doing to us and the people they had taken out on our side. It was a pep talk that was inflammatory and had a kind of hidden message that it would be alright if you went ahead and shot somebody you weren't supposed to shoot.

Almost as soon as we hit the ground the next morning and started moving forward they called me back because they had found a large ammo box. I had a rope and they wanted me to tie it around the thing and yank it to make sure it wasn't booby-trapped. We opened it up very carefully and found a few medical supplies but no ammunition. Meanwhile, I could hear a lot of firing up in front. I was very anxious to get up there where I was supposed to be but it was very difficult to do because we were separated and I was stuck near the command post. It sounded like all the fire was coming from our weapons with nothing coming backward. You can hear the difference between an AK-47 and an M-16. By the time I got into the village there were bodies everywhere—children, infants, women, old people laying around in various places. They must have just opened up on everything that was there. There was livestock and chickens and dogs and pigs all just laying in a mingle with the humans. I was trying to get to where I could intervene or do something but it seemed like every time I got somewhere it was too late. I didn't encounter anyone that I could have passed a word with. I just saw several Americans at a distance throwing hand grenades and setting fire to things and firing into hootches. I really felt like somehow this was my fault.

I was the designated pain-in-the-ass of the company. I had spent a lot of my time up until that point getting between American soldiers and Vietnamese civilians and it somehow deflected many of these things. Unfortunately, on March 16 I utterly failed to do what I had been able to successfully do many times before. But I had no authority. I was a private.

The other guys in the company knew that if this ever got out we could all be in some deep shit and they all knew I was the weak link. So it was me they were all looking at. I stayed awake for three nights after this thing happened.

When we returned to Duc Pho I got summoned to Medina's bunker. There were five of us altogether and Medina was asking me things like, "Well, what's your take on this?" I said, "What we did was completely wrong. It made no military sense. It made no sense of any kind. What the hell do you think we accomplished by doing this? Did we get anything done? Did we in any way hurt the enemy? Did we advance our own position here somehow? Did we take some ground? We got nothing out of this and we just killed a whole bunch of people for nothing." That was my appeal to him—that it didn't make any sense. Never mind the humanity of it. They were beyond that. Then they appealed to me to just bury it and forget it.

For the rest of my tour I was just trying to stay alive, get the hell out of there, and get home. When you get two weeks away from the end of your tour you shouldn't be in the field. You're supposed to be out of there. But I was still in the damn mud. I guess they were holding out hope that maybe I wouldn't make it. So I was over there twelve and a half months, maybe longer.

I was in pretty bad shape. I had gone through a bout of dysentery and I hadn't gotten any help from anybody except a Vietnamese guy who got me up and going again. I also had immersion foot—this rot that was up past my boots. I couldn't dry my feet out and I didn't know what the hell it was. It was getting worse and worse to where there wasn't any skin left on my feet and they were still not bringing me in. Finally one of the medics said, "Look, the next time a helicopter lands, when it takes off, you be on it. I'll cover for you." As luck would have it, the very next day somebody got shot and I was with the bunch of guys that was putting him in the helicopter. I threw myself on and away it went. When we got to the evac hospital they weighed me and I was a hundred and five pounds. I wasn't in the hospital more than a day before Ron Ridenhour found out where I was and came around. We had trained together as LURPS, but he had found some way to get the hell out of Charlie Company. He couldn't believe the way I looked. He looks at this mess and says, "How long were you out there like this?" I said, "I can't remember."

Apparently Ron had found out about My Lai from some of the other guys. They said, "We told you, but that's it. If you say anything to anybody, we'll deny it." They just did not want any part of it. But they told him that I would talk. I always looked up to Ron and I knew he would know what to do.

"YOU LOOK LIKE A GOOK"

In World War II movies of the 1950s combat units were meant to represent the best of American democracy. Hollywood's melting-pot platoons always included a smattering of ethnic and regional types—a midwestern farm boy, a Boston Italian, a Brooklyn Jew, a southerner, an Irishman. When African Americans were sometimes included (usually as cooks), there was rarely a hint that the military which defeated fascism had itself been segregated. The overarching theme was that a mélange of citizen soldiers had rallied to the flag in a virtuous, victorious cause and, as the government's wartime posters proudly insisted, they were "Americans All."

Many youthful movie-goers of the fifties would feel betrayed, a decade later, by the contrast between the glorious images of the "good war" they had grown up with and the harrowing actualities of Vietnam. However, the movie imagery of the military as an ethnic cross-section of America became ever more the reality of the postwar armed forces. After all, President Truman desegregated the military in 1948, at least two decades before many school systems, North and South, were forced to do the same. By the 1960s, many believed the military, for all its hierarchies and its obvious authoritarianism, was functionally the most democratic major institution in the United States. That it was the only reliable employer for many young, disadvantaged men, and the only one to conscript its workers, did not change the fact that it was one place in America where you could find whites, blacks, Latinos, Asians, and Native Americans all living and working together.

While World War II had made military service virtually universal, most men of the Vietnam generation were never in uniform. For every draft-age man sent to Vietnam, three served in the military elsewhere and six remained civilians. And for every American combat soldier in Vietnam, at least five others served there as clerks, cooks, truck drivers, mechanics, and in other rear-echelon assignments. Fewer than 2 percent of draft-age men were sent on combat missions in Vietnam.

For Americans, then, Vietnam was truly a minority experience, but what sort of minority was it? Despite its racial and ethnic diversity, the U.S. military in Vietnam was hardly representative of the larger society in terms of class. Men from privileged and prosperous families were far less likely to enlist than those from lower economic classes and they had many more resources to take advantage of the draft system's multiple exemptions, deferments, and loopholes. Of the roughly two and a half million enlisted men who served in Vietnam, about 80 percent were from working-class and poor families.

In the early years of U.S. escalation, 1965–66, African Americans comprised more than 20 percent of U.S. casualties, about twice their portion of the U.S. population (11 percent) and also more than twice their portion of the entire military (10 percent), indicating that blacks were much more likely than whites to be sent to Vietnam and assigned to combat units. Civil rights leaders like Martin Luther King drew attention to this striking racial disproportion in sacrifice, and in response to that criticism Pentagon officials ordered a cutback in the number of African Americans in combat positions. Accordingly, the percentage of black casualties steadily declined until, by war's end, African Americans represented 12.6 percent of all U.S. fatalities in Vietnam. While some anecdotal evidence suggests that Latinos and Native Americans also served disproportionately in frontline units, the military did not keep separate figures for those groups, making it very difficult to test the claim.

Among the war's many complexities, U.S. forces sent to Vietnam carried with them all the attributes of a nation divided by increasing racial turmoil. In the war zone, that stew of racial animosities, racial liberations, and racial confusions melded with an older American tradition of war-fueled racism that went back to the Indian wars of the nineteenth century and before. Not surprisingly for a generation raised on movie Westerns, GIs sometimes referred to enemy-occupied areas of Vietnam as "Indian country." Americans in Vietnam also drew, at least unconsciously, on a long tradition of "yellow peril" imagery honed in the three wars the United States had already fought in Asia—in the Philippines at the turn of the century, against the Japanese in the Pacific in the 1940s, and against Koreans and Chinese in Korea in the early 1950s. In fact, the most common derogatory term for the Vietnamese, "gooks," may have derived from a song popular among American troops during the counterinsurgency war in the Philippines that referred to Filipino "goo-goo eyes."

As in these three prior wars, American soldiers of all races found themselves fighting Asian enemies in Vietnam who were physically indistinguishable from the civilians who were said to be allies. From basic training on, American soldiers were encouraged to demonize the Viet Cong and North Vietnamese enemy in unambiguously racist terms as "gooks," "dinks," "slopes," "gooners," and "zipperheads" who did not place a high value on life. What remained maddeningly ambiguous in the field, however, was how to differentiate between "gooks" and South Vietnamese civilians.

On the ground in Vietnam, Americans soldiers learned that many of their commanders were, in fact, not overly concerned about making fine distinctions between friends and foes. Under pressure to produce high body counts on search-and-destroy missions, GIs learned that the rule of thumb in the field was, "If it's dead and it's Vietnamese, it's VC." The rage and violence that attends all wars, coupled with the intense confusion and frustration of fighting a counterguerrilla war, created an atmosphere in which racism toward a whole society's people could flourish.

Ironically, American troops were in many ways more admiring of their enemy, whose skill and commitment were everywhere evident, than they were of their Vietnamese allies. With a measure of respect, GIs sometimes called the Viet Cong "Mr. Charles" (derived from Victor Charlie, the phonetic alphabetization of VC). It is still not uncommon to hear veterans say they wished they had had the Viet Cong, not the ARVN, on their side.

Though racism was a pervasive underpinning of the U.S. intervention, many American veterans of all races recall an extraordinary unity in combat that encompassed all racial and ethnic differences, a harmony that transcended anything they had experienced before or since the war. It is a remarkable claim, especially given the enormous strains on unit solidarity created by the constant influx of new men rotating in and out of the war on one-year tours and by the absence of a truly unifying cause.

As the war went on, however, American forces became increasingly divided along every fault line. Disillusioned by an apparently endless war without a promising end in sight beyond personal survival, GI morale fell dramatically and tensions mounted between races, between officers and enlisted men, between combat and rear-area soldiers, and even between "juicers"—those who liked to drink—and "heads"—those who preferred to smoke marijuana.

Racial tensions were especially acute in rear areas where the unifying threat of enemy fire was less imminent. Soldiers of color became more acutely conscious that they were fighting a nonwhite enemy for a nation that had not accorded them full equality at home. They knew that they, too, were regarded as "gooks" or some equivalent by at least some of their fellow soldiers and officers. And by the late sixties, many soldiers were aware of, or had participated in, home-front movements of racial solidarity that identified the enemy not as Vietnamese, but as a "white racist establishment."

Thus, Vietnam proved not only a foreign war, but in certain ways an internal one as well in which America's most tortured racial struggles were played out by young armed men in an environment permeated by violence. From 1968 on, racial brawls and full-scale riots between GIs broke out on many bases in South Vietnam. Some officers spent as much time responding to divisiveness among their troops as they did fighting the enemy.

VINCENT OKAMOTO

"Damn, I'm a gook."

Now a Los Angeles attorney, in 1968 he was a lieutenant with the 25th Infantry Division. He received the Distinguished Service Cross, the second highest award conferred by the U.S. Army.

Like many Japanese Americans who fought in Vietnam, he was born in a concentration camp during World War II. His family was among the 110,000 Japanese Americans interned by the U.S. government after Pearl Harbor. "Everything they had worked for all their life—all their property, all their jobs—was taken away, and they were stuck in an unknown place for an undisclosed amount of time with no charge or trial."

I am the last of ten children, the seventh son of Japanese immigrants. I was born in Poston Relocation Camp in Arizona. In World War II, two of my older brothers served with the 442nd Regimental Combat Team.* My whole life I grew up on the tradition of the 442nd. I was convinced that one of the reasons we were allowed to get out of the camps and accepted in American society to the degree that we were, was the blood shed by the 442nd. So growing up, I thought military service was an inevitable rite of passage. All six of my older brothers had served in the military. I could hardly wait for my turn.

At UCLA I was in ROTC. I took a regular army commission in the infantry, went to jump school and ranger school at Fort Benning, recon commando training at Fort Bragg, and I volunteered for Vietnam in April 1968.

My parents often used the Japanese term *shi kata ga nai,* meaning "it can't be helped." If something is *shi kata ga nai,* it's inevitable, so you just accept it and go on with your life. Once I got to Vietnam that type of philosophy was an immeasurable help because you can't quit. You just try to do the job as best you

*The 442nd was a regiment of Japanese Americans sent to fight in Europe. Volunteers were recruited from the camps and from the noninterned in Hawaii. When volunteerism dropped off, the army drafted young men from the camps. The 442nd was the most highly decorated American unit of World War II.

can. My mom and dad would write, "Do your best. Do your duty." At first that was very comforting because I thought I was doing the right thing. But after six or seven weeks in Vietnam and you've seen a couple of napalmed villages and civilians blasted to hell—your mom and dad don't know anything about that. That was not what I joined up to do.

When I got there my guys were talking about gooks, and zipperheads, and slants and I said to myself, "Damn, I'm a gook, I'm a zipperhead, I'm a slant." But it didn't take too long before my mentality became just like theirs. I should have known better, yet within a relatively short time we were all thinking alike. If it became a question of maximizing protection for your men or giving some Vietnamese civilian the benefit of the doubt, after a while there was no choice on my part. I just went with protecting my people. Even so, I was nearly killed by Americans who mistook me for a Vietnamese.

One night an artillery fire support base was damn near overrun so they flew my company in to reinforce them. It was already dark when the choppers took us in. I fed my people into the perimeter and started to check the bunker line—a bunch of grunts who had never seen me. I'm bopping down the line saying, "Everything okay? You guys squared away?"

All of a sudden I heard this voice with a distinct southern drawl say: "Halt! What's the password?" Well, I gave him the password. When I moved forward he pulled off a round. He missed me from fifteen feet. Finally, the artillery lieutenant shows up and says, "What the hell's going on?"

I tell him and that lieutenant said, "Well, you look like a gook. If I was you and it gets dark, I'd dye my hair blond and whistle 'Dixie.' "

I got hit on June 9, 1968, in an ambush. I was in the hospital for several days and they gave me light duty for three or four days to let the wounds dry out. I returned to the field June 16. That night we got hit by a human wave attack on the Cambodian border and I was back at the 12th Evac hospital the morning of the seventeenth. In most divisions in Vietnam, once you got your second Purple Heart they'd give you a noncombat job in the rear. But after Tet 1968, so many people were getting wounded or killed, they changed it to three Purple Hearts.

So I went back to my platoon. The next time I got nailed was August 24. It was the single worst night of my life. A reinforced battalion of the 9th NVA Division—about eight hundred guys—started dropping mortars on us at ten o'clock. We were only about a company and a half—maybe one hundred and fifty of us. The initial assault was so intense they blasted a hole in the perimeter at my platoon sector, knocked out two bunkers, and wasted three armored personnel carriers with rocket-propelled grenades.

I saw the break in the wire and knew we had to plug it back up. So five of us got over to a bunker and just started spraying out fire. But the volume of fire from the bad guys was so intense our suppressive fire was ineffective. We couldn't aim. We were just holding M-16s over our heads and firing blind. We're yelling, "Here they come, here they come." But everybody had their own little war in their own little bunkers and what was happening in our sector was of no great moment to them, so there was no outpouring of support from the other positions.

It really was a slugfest. All these eighteen- and nineteen-year-old high school dropouts, these kids were magnificent. They really were. There was no political issue, they were just fighting for their lives. They didn't have a whole lot of investment in America, but they were sure fighting their ass off.

After the NVA killed my two radio operators I ran over to one of the armored personnel carriers. An RPG had blasted the hell out of it, but the main turret with the fifty-caliber machine gun had not been touched. I had to push the dead machine gunner down into the APC to get at the gun. I fired until it ran out of ammo and ran to another partially destroyed APC. I fired that one until it malfunctioned.

There was one more APC. I climbed on board and fired up the last of its ammunition. Right about then everybody was shooting off star clusters and flares and helicopter gunships were circling and artillery was falling. Through it all I could see a group of NVA setting up a mortar. I'm afraid of mortars so I went down into the APC to look for more fifty-caliber ammo. I couldn't find any, but there was a case of hand grenades. I figured if I crawled along the flank I might be able to get close to that mortar team. And I did. I threw three frags and turned them into long-division problems. But I wasn't quite as slick as I thought because a concussion grenade landed in the little depression I was in. I tried to jump out, but I wasn't quick enough so I got injured from the waist down.

I hobbled back to the perimeter and got back on the horn. With that radio I was like God. I could call down from the heavens destruction on a massive scale. The radio connects you to eighteen howitzers that can fire shells from seven miles away. You got helicopter gunships with miniguns that could fire six thousand rounds per minute. And you got these goddamn crazy air force fighter bombers who break in on the net and go, "Bravo Six, I'm at your location and I've got eighteen thousand rounds of twenty-millimeter cannon and four five-hundred pound bombs. Where do you want 'em, over?"

For a twenty-four-year-old lieutenant, it was really incredible. You are desperate. I was practically deaf from all the noise. You're literally screaming into the radio and they're screaming back at you. It's really hard to capture the chaos. I still have nightmares about it. You see your guys' bunkers being blown up with satchel charges. Four hundred NVA coming out of the woods with fixed bayonets on their AK-47s. It's almost surreal.

My emotion was not so much fear as anger. I lost just about everybody in my platoon, the company lost maybe thirty percent, and I'm bleeding from about four or five different spots. It wasn't really until later in the hospital that I started trembling and shaking uncontrollably.

When I got hit that third time, I was recommended for the Distinguished Service Cross. I don't know how much my decoration was for bravery or how much was politically motivated. They needed a hero because they caught us napping. I mean, we should have had observation posts further out. When you get your butts kicked they want to compensate. I think that was part of it. It's kind of like corporate America. The management doesn't want to say bad things are happening.

Anyway, I thought, "Hey, three Purple Hearts, I'm out of here. From now on its air-conditioning and cold beer." But then they said you not only needed three Purple Hearts to get a rear job, you had to have at least seven days of hospitalization each time. So they sent me back out to the weeds for three more months until my Distinguished Service Cross was finally approved. When you got that award you could pretty much pick your own assignment and that's when I got out of the infantry.

When they sent me back to the weeds after that third wound, I was a very unhappy person. I was so gun-shy, we'd take maybe a single sniper round and I'd hit the deck. When I hit the deck the radio operators expected me to exercise leadership. They're saying, "Here's the handset sir." And I'd say, "Get the hell away from me." The radios are the keys to the kingdom of firepower, so the enemy was always trying to knock them out. Plus, they had these six-foot whip antennas to aim at.

On one occasion during this period I remember a platoon leader calling me up on the radio saying, "Bravo Six, Bravo Six, we're taking fire, what do we do?" I said, "I don't know about you, you son-of-a-bitch, but I'm hiding behind this tree." I wasn't a very good officer after August 24.

It reached a point where I couldn't function. The battalion medics had access to a pharmaceutical store that would warm the hearts of the biggest drug dealers on Earth. So we would be getting Benzedrine to maintain what they called "foxhole strength." I'd say, "Hey Doc, I'm really pooped, I need something," and he'd give you a roll of Benzedrine—we called them "whites." But then you do that for a couple of weeks and you're wired like no tomorrow and you can't sleep.

In my case, it reached a point where I was taking downers when the sun went down and uppers when the sun came up. I knew that was crazy but the only alternative was to go to the battalion commander and say, "I want to be relieved. I don't have what it takes." I didn't have the guts to do that.

For a while they made me an intelligence liaison officer with the Special Forces. At first I was happy because we worked out of a camp where there were refrigerators and cold beer and hootch girls. That was wonderful because nothing was more wretched than being a grunt—nothing. But it turned out I was assigned to the Phoenix Program.* I had never heard of it until they told me I was part of it. I did it for two months and didn't like it at all.

You know, Vietnam was so totally fucked up nothing surprised you after a while. The avowed purpose of the Phoenix Program was to eliminate the Viet Cong infrastructure. The theory was that the North Vietnamese units were strangers in South Vietnam. They could speak the language and had the same culture, but when they took the Tay Ninh off-ramp from the Ho Chi Minh Trail they needed the local population to meet them, guide them around American ambushes, and take them to base camps where they could launch their attacks. The goal of the Phoenix Program was to wipe out these local supporters.

So the CIA and the boys in Saigon would feed information into computers and come up with a blacklist of Vietnamese who were aiding the enemy. The blacklist would say, Nguyen so-and-so lives in Bao Trai village and he is an agitprop officer, or he is a tax collector, or he is a cell leader whose people guide North Vietnamese units from the border area to safe havens in the Iron Triangle—something like that. The problem was, how do you find the people on the blacklist? It's not like you had their address and telephone number. The normal procedure would be to go into a village and just grab someone and say, "Where's Nguyen so-and-so?" Half the time the people were so afraid they would say anything. Then a Phoenix team would take the informant, put a sandbag over his head, poke out two holes so he could see, put commo wire around his neck like a long leash, and walk him through the village and say, "When we go by Nguyen's house scratch your head."

Then that night Phoenix would come back, knock on the door, and say, "April Fool, motherfucker." Whoever answered the door would get wasted. As far as they were concerned whoever answered was a Communist, including family members. Sometimes they'd come back to camp with ears to prove that they killed people. This was uncontrolled violence and at times I think it be-

*Introduced in 1968, the Phoenix Program was designed to eliminate the Viet Cong "infrastructure" (VCI)—its network of local agents and supporters. Run by the CIA under William Colby, by 1972 Phoenix claimed to have "neutralized" some eighty thousand VCI, killing more than twenty-six thousand. While defenders believe it was one of the most effective U.S. pacification programs of the war, it clearly relied on assassination as one of its principal methods and therefore, critics argue, was a war crime by definition, regardless of debates about whether its victims were accurately targeted or not.

came just wholesale killing. And think of the consequences. If Phoenix goes in and murders someone who was not a Viet Cong, and they abuse the mother and the sister, well anybody in the family who survives is going to be a card-carrying Viet Cong by the next afternoon.

A few years later, while going to law school, he was watching television. There on the screen was William Colby, the director of the CIA, the man who ran the Phoenix Program. Colby was answering questions before a congressional committee. "Goddamn William Colby said that Phoenix was a 'civil action program.' Well, Phoenix did not dig wells, improve hygiene, conduct classes, and distribute chewing gum."

WAYNE SMITH

"I was thanking God they didn't have air support."

People would sometimes tell him, "You look just like Jackie Robinson." The second of eleven children, he grew up in Providence, Rhode Island. When he was ten years old his father died as a result of trying to put out a fire in the basement of their home, a tragedy that forced the family into public housing and poverty. Wayne Smith, the oldest son, served in Vietnam as a combat medic in the 9th Infantry Division from May 1969 to November 1970.

Before being assigned to an infantry unit I was working at an aid station in Tan An [in the Mekong Delta]. One day I had to go out back to a steel supply shed and I came across several body bags. For some reason, I wanted to take my first look at death in Vietnam so I unzipped one of the bags. I just remember this white brother's hand. There was mud on his fingers and he was wearing a peace ring. I was stunned. Somehow my mind took me back to the States where his family was probably eating dinner and didn't even know their son was dead.

I was very naive. I thought we were going to help free the Vietnamese from Communist aggression. I volunteered. I believed in it. My family was *proud* of me. The African American community was very divided about the war. There were some certainly who came out against the war like Dr. King, but there was also still a belief that we should go into the military to show the nation that African Americans could make an equal contribution to the cause of freedom and equality.

My older sister was aggressively opposed to the war and to my going. But I thought, what does she know? And even Muhammad Ali. I thought, okay, he's a good boxer, but what did he know about it? The Muslims were always a little strange to me anyway. I wanted to fight for this country, and believe in it, and have hope in it, and contribute to it. But I knew somewhere in my heart and soul that if our foreign policy was just a little different, we could be fighting this kind of war in Africa.

My first experience with combat happened at night. We were moving out to set up an ambush and we walked into an ambush they had set. It was fucking chaos. The Vietnamese opened up on us and guys were screaming and yelling and shooting in every direction. I was as afraid of getting hit by our own guys as I was of enemy fire. It was like, pow, pow, pow, "Medic! Medic!" I thought, "Oh, fuck." It seemed like it took me a long time to move toward the first wounded man. The difficult part was just getting him to quiet down. He was in a lot of pain. Four of our guys got wounded that night and some of them may have been hit by friendly fire. We pulled back and the Vietnamese broke contact. But we couldn't get a medevac in until the next morning. To tell you the truth, I think we were lost and didn't know the coordinates. The wounded were crying most of the night.

Combat was horrible, but there was a beautiful side as well—the brotherhood between black soldiers and white soldiers and Hispanics and Native Americans. When we were in combat all that mattered was trying to survive together. I never imagined I could be so close to men. I can honestly say I felt closer to some of the people I served with in combat—of all races—than my own family. Unfortunately, it is very hard to hang on to that communion off the battlefield. It's like what you experience during blizzards and floods when people come out and work together digging out or filling sandbags. But when it's over they retreat back to their burbs or inner cities or barrios.

There were very definitely some racial problems. There were guys who really did hate the other race. Some brothers just didn't want to be around white guys. And in war zones people's anger gets magnified. At times it was just guys who wanted to punch people out, but there were some who wanted to kill people and they had guns! Even though I felt a powerful communion with my African American brothers, I had grown up in an integrated community and my best friends were Italian and Irish so when the lines were drawn, I could sort of see both sides. Some brothers didn't even know that Rhode Island was a state. They'd call me "Long Island," or "New York." Or, if they knew, they'd tease me. "You mean there are black people in Rhode Island?" So I had to fire back, "Hey man, I'm as militant as you are." I remember feeling jammed up in the middle.

It was a time when James Brown had come out with, "Say it loud—I'm black and I'm proud," and the young soul brothers had a real sense of communion. We would tap each other on the forehead like we were giving knowledge. And you couldn't walk down the street without putting your hand in the air and showing a closed fist, showing power. That was like saying, "Hi."

And we always gave up the "dap." The dap was a very elaborate hand shake. Two guys would tap each other on the hands and arms and chest. It took maybe a half minute to get through the whole thing. We would go through so many fucking gyrations it almost makes me blush to remember it now, but we were so serious. I think we got the word *dap* from the Vietnamese word *dep,* which means beautiful. Some white soldiers got into it, but some were intimidated and I'm sure some got frustrated standing in chow lines behind a group of soul brothers who were giving up the dap and bullshitting and causing delays, like, "What the fuck are they doing?" It must have seemed like some kind of secret society, like we've got our own "Skull and Bones" society or our own Masons, and that could provoke anger. But I also think some white brothers may have been envious of our willingness to show affection.

In combat all that matters is: are you going to do your duty and cover my ass when I get hit? I was a good medic and my men trusted me. It was kind of thrilling, almost intoxicating. I was eighteen and knew a little about how to save lives and people confided things in me. I did some risky things to get to the men who were wounded and after one of those times they nicknamed me "Captain Trip." We were in a place called the Plain of Reeds down near the western border of Vietnam that abutted Cambodia. It was rather exquisite country—flat and swampy and absolutely vivid. You could see for what seemed like miles. We were up to our knees in water and up to our chests in reeds. This was in early 1970, just before the invasion of Cambodia. We were part of a big operation and some guys hit a booby trap that had been strung across some posts just above the waterline, hidden by the reeds. It was called a daisy chain. When the wire was tripped several grenades went off. So as I ran over there, some of my men yelled, "Doc, don't run." It was pretty stupid to run through an area that's been booby-trapped, but I got to the wouned. One fellow had a throat wound and couldn't breathe. So I did a tracheotomy on him and he survived. I had a scalpel in my bag and a little tube to stick in the hole I cut. Another fellow had a punctured lung, a sucking chest wound. The chest cavity was punctured and air was escaping directly out of the lung. It's a dreaded wound because if your lung collapses you can die pretty quick. I was able to contain this one. The training really worked. We were given these crumpled up pieces of gauze coated with Vaseline. You put it on the wound and it prevents the air from escaping. If you don't panic it's not hard, but you always have that fear of fucking up and causing someone to die. There's nothing worse than that for a medic.

I wanted to be a medic to save lives and I didn't know if I could kill. I wasn't raised to kill. But when I was in combat I was tainted by this blood lust and I, too, became a combat soldier. There was blood on my hands. I wanted to kill the enemy and I even wanted to lie and exaggerate my desire to kill the enemy. I never participated in any mutilation, but I did violate one line. All through training, and even my first six or seven months in Vietnam, I never called the Vietnamese gooks because I knew intuitively that it would be the same as saying nigger. And it was. Yet in combat I began to call them gooks.

I did not believe my country was capable of going in and killing people and counting their bodies and claiming a victory because we killed more of them than they did of us. But there was a real incentivizing of death and it just fucked with our value system. In our unit guys who got confirmed kills would get a three-day in-country R and R. Those guys got sent to the beach at Vung Tau. At the time I would have said, "Yeah, I can't wait to get to Vung Tau." But now I'm proud to say I never went. I never got a confirmed kill. I did try—with malice—but me and twenty other guys were trying, so I never knew. And the easiest way to confirm a kill was to cut off an ear or a thumb. One month in the fall of 1969 the 3rd Brigade, 9th Infantry, got a Presidential Unit Citation because we had the most confirmed kills.

I hated my association with all the lies. For example, if we came across four different body parts we called in four kills. But even with the inflated numbers we killed a lot of people. Aside from the promise of an R and R, I think the kills mattered more to the officers than to us. It was a way for them to get their ticket punched to get promoted. We had a captain who really pushed us hard for body counts and that pressure came right down the food chain. They always wanted us to get out there and "make contact" so they could kill the enemy. Ultimately this captain was awarded a silver star based on gallantry in the face of enemy fire. It was really for putting his men at unnecessary risk and exaggerating the number of people we killed.

In the Delta we did not have large-scale firefights. They typically lasted only five or ten minutes and then they pulled back to avoid the air strikes. You really have to salute the enemy. They fought a war based on economy, not on how big the weapons were or how much ammo could be fired. We felt very grateful when we had artillery and airpower. We just wanted them to rain on Charlie. We would cheer when it came. Just hearing the jets and helicopter gunships coming was exhilarating. And when the air force dropped napalm it was one of those bizarre feelings. I don't like to admit to it, but I felt very glad those sons of bitches were going to get killed. At the same time I was thanking God *they* didn't have air support, which was something I didn't know when I first went over to Vietnam.

When we were back in the rear, I treated a lot of guys for venereal disease. Right at 9th Infantry Headquarters in Tan An, there was a "steam bath." It was a whorehouse, in effect. These pretty young Vietnamese teenagers were being fucked by American soldiers. At the time I rationalized it by thinking, well, once we kill off the enemy, the Vietnamese will be able to be fully free and there won't be any more prostitution. But this was clearly just exploitation.

When I reupped for another six months I got rotated out of combat and spent all my time going to the villages and treating the Vietnamese. I was proud of some of the work I did. Instead of forcing them into this war and telling them where to live and giving them weapons to kill off other Vietnamese, that was legitimate medicine.

When I came home to Rhode Island it was like another fucking planet, like an episode out of *The Twilight Zone.* All these people had changed. All these sons of bitches cared about was going to the beach or who was dating who. I had just left people who were fighting and dying. It was unbelievable. I hated America. I hated our materialistic superficiality and our indifference. To make matters worse, my mom was really proud of me. I had gotten a couple stripes and medals and she wanted me to go to the church I was raised in with my uniform on. I went for her but really resented it. All these people came up to me and said, "Oh, Wayne, you look so good."

And then some of my friends had a surprise party for me when I came home. It was really a disaster. There were lots of friends and good music but after a couple minutes I made my way to the bathroom and I couldn't come out. I couldn't wait to go back to Vietnam. I could not explain what I was feeling. I was in deep pain. I don't mean to sound pure—I'm far from pure—but what we were doing in Vietnam was completely unlike what I was raised to do.

CHARLEY TRUJILLO

"It sure as hell wasn't 'English only' in Vietnam."

Born in 1949, he grew up in Corcoran, a cotton town in California's San Joaquin Valley. "I started picking cotton when I was six. We also used to go to Oregon to pick strawberries, San Jose to pick prunes, Sacramento to pick tomatoes. We'd sleep right there in the field. No tents, no nothing. As soon as it was first light you'd be right back to work. We'd make something like eighteen dollars a day, all five of us." He was an infantryman with the Americal Division in 1970. He lost an eye in combat.

All the Chicanos lived on one side of the town and the whites called us greasers. We were ashamed of taking our tacos and beans to school because that was "beaner" food. So we'd hide behind the backstop where the whites wouldn't see us eating. I don't think our generation of Chicanos has gotten over that. From about the fourth grade to eighth grade I really wanted to assimilate into white society. I couldn't afford all the nice tennis shoes, but I tried to dress like the white kids and hang out with them, even joined the Boy Scouts. I really wanted to be white bad, man.

I was gonna get drafted so I went ahead and volunteered. It was part of trying to be an American and patriotic and the whole romantic notion of war. When we got to Vietnam, we wanted to prove that we really were Americans. Even now I think we Chicano guys want to prove how patriotic we were.

Out in the bush I've never felt such affinity and togetherness with men of other cultures and races as I did in Vietnam. But as soon as we got back to rear areas everything changed again. The blacks and some whites used to call us "chingos," I guess because Mexicans use that word a lot. *No me chingo* means "don't fuck with me." I used to say "*chingo* your mama," and that used to piss them off. We called the whites *gabachos* and *bolillos*—little white rolls. We called the blacks names too, like *mayates*—which are June bugs—and *chanates*—black crows.

They brought three Puerto Ricans from the 1st Infantry Division into my platoon and those guys didn't speak a lick of English. They were from the island. So I was their interpreter. I'd have to defend them because people would try to fuck them over with more duty. One time a bunch of us were speaking Spanish and this guy said, "You shouldn't be talking like that cause when I first got here some guys heard it through the bushes and thought it was Vietnamese and killed 'em." When I went to school they didn't allow you to speak Spanish. It was all "English only." But it sure as hell wasn't "English only" in Vietnam.

One firefight really sticks in my mind. We were on the second day of an operation and stopped to eat. I was sharing some C rations with this Italian guy from Lynn, Massachusetts. That guy was always really melancholy. He was pretty nice but he just had a thing against blacks. Back in the rear he used to say stuff like, "I hate niggers." But there was a lot of stress with everybody. Even the nonviolent guys turned hostile. So we're eating and he started singing "And When I Die" by Blood, Sweat, and Tears.

Pretty soon we moved out. We didn't get more than thirty yards and we got hit. The guy from Massachusetts got shot in the chest. A black medic jumped on him and started giving him mouth-to-mouth resuscitation. Then the medic got hit in the head from really close range. The rounds of the AK went clean through his helmet, little red holes. When we got up to them the medic was laid out right on top of the Italian guy. They were both dead. I kept thinking, here's this guy who said he hates niggers and this black guy died giving him mouth-to-mouth. We used to call it "kissing the dead."

Our glory-seeking CO ordered us to continue the direct assault and we took some more casualties. All of this was done by just four North Vietnamese who were dug in right in front of us. We finally blew them up with hand grenades. On the way back to the village we were operating out of, we took some sniper fire. The North Vietnamese just didn't know when to quit. At some point a few guys dropped their rifles and ran. I felt really angry. Some of the other guys thought I was too gung ho and I was always walking point, but it was just that I felt I had to do my best.

When we got back to the village the South Vietnamese Popular Forces were playing volleyball and having a grand old time drinking Cokes. They were supposed to be on our side and helping to fight. Meanwhile, the North Vietnamese were kicking our asses. Then some of the black soldiers started saying, "This ain't our war. Our war's at home. This is a white man's war." It made me start to think.

They told us we were going back out in the morning and some of us said we weren't going to do it. Then they brought in a new company commander and he gave us a really good pep talk. It was like halftime at a football game. It was almost the same shit, man. You would never think you would see that in the military—this guy trying to talk the men into going into battle. You'd think he'd just give an order, right? But he looked like a really nice and sincere guy and I think that really pulled it. We argued about it all night and the majority were still against going. But the next morning a few guys moved out and the rest of us felt obligated to go with 'em.

After that, though, my whole idea of the war started to change. The few times we got together with Vietnamese they'd point to my skin and say, "same-same." And some of the guys in my unit would say, "Hey, man, you better watch out because from behind you look like a gook." Then one time we went into this village—it was maybe six or seven Montagnard hootches. The indigenous Vietnamese. They kinda looked like Asian Indians. It looked like they could identify with me. Those poor people were almost like Stone Age people. Very primitive, man. But technology-wise, not as human beings. We were gonna take them out of the area the next day. I felt bad because what am I doing taking these people from their home? That wasn't right.

I was very naive. I got my idea of war from movies where the good guys don't get killed. We were taking a lot of casualties and then I started thinking, are we really the good guys? What am I doing fighting these guys? This is a gringo army and when I get home I'm just gonna be another Mexican, so fuck these people. I even thought that maybe I should join the enemy, they seem to have the better fight. I thought, those motherfuckers have a lot of balls, man, and they're kicking ass. One time we saw some Vietnamese out of our range and called in an air strike on them. The jets came in and those guys popped out of their holes with their AKs and duked it out with the jets. I said, wow man, what makes people do that?

Then I said, no, no, I can't be a traitor. And what makes me think I'm so good that they're gonna accept me on the other side? They're just gonna kill my ass and I'd never see my family again. But I thought about it. Some other Chicanos got pissed with me for talking that way, man. They accused me of being a no-good traitor, but at the same time they could see my logic.

Anyway, I decided I wasn't gonna walk point anymore. I'll just walk in the middle and try to keep alive. At that point we practiced search-and-avoid. They'd tell us the enemy was coming from one direction and we'd say, "Roger that" and go in the other direction. But that's dangerous 'cause you can get caught with your own artillery if you're not where they think you are. They were still pushing for body counts, but a lot of our fearless leaders wouldn't lead us. One time the colonel landed his helicopter near the end of a firefight. He just came by and sniffed the bodies a little bit and as soon as he heard a shot he got back on his helicopter.

About the time I'd decided to be more careful we had all new guys in our platoon with a new lieutenant who didn't know anything. I decided that if I didn't walk point I was gonna get killed for sure. There was no doubt in my mind. So I decided to take charge. They took us out about six in the evening, July 21, 1970. I led 'em up a mountain and we got to a trail. I saw these Vietnamese guys coming toward us and I thought, man, should I tell everybody really quick? No, I got greedy. I wanted to be John Wayne again. I wanted to say I killed those suckers. So I started firing. I'm not sure what hit me but it was like somebody put a hot ice pick in my eye. I went down and didn't feel anything. It just went black, but my mind was going and I started praying. I said, "God, if you let me live, I promise I'll pick cotton free the rest of my life." I actually saw myself picking cotton. Then I started thinking about Mom and home and the medic kept talking to me.

We were out there all night. That was the lowest part. I slept about an hour and when I woke up it was predawn. When we moved out I didn't feel my eye anymore. They brought me to an open place and put me in a jacket with a cable on it—a jungle penetrator—and pulled me up. The machine jammed and

I was just hanging from the helicopter. Good thing I only weighed about a hundred and thirty 'cause they started pulling me up by hand. They took me to the hospital and I knew I'd made it. I gave a power salute to the black guys and a peace sign to the whites.

"One of the few things I got out of Vietnam was that I said, hey man, I'm not inferior to anybody. Not that I'm superior either, but I was the de facto platoon sergeant by the time I left and there were mostly white soldiers and a few blacks in my platoon. They were following me. You make the wrong decision, people get killed. Now that's pressure. That helped give me a lot of confidence. Nothing else is that serious."

In 1990 he founded Chusma House Publications, a company specializing in Chicano literature. He wrote an oral history of Chicano soldiers from his hometown, called Soldados.

"AN ACUTE LACK OF FORGETFULNESS"

GLORIA EMERSON

"Before the war, I was Miss Mary Poppins."

The author of Winners and Losers, *one of the classic books on the war, she does not want to talk. "I can't remember a thing. It would be like talking to someone with aphasia." Her rebuffs multiply as the requests continue: "Don't interview old journalists! We have nothing more to say. We're all lacquered over." In truth, she remembers far too much and there isn't enough lacquer in the world to seal her passion.*

"I had a certain urgency about what I would do with my life. I could get married or I could try for the real world. After two marriages, I took the leap and tried for the real world." She went to Vietnam for The New York Times *from 1970 to 1972, but long before that she had covered international crises.*

My life at *The New York Times* was quite peculiar. Women were extremely restricted and there were no jobs open except on the woman's page. In the Paris bureau I was obliged to cover the French haute couture collections twice a year. They were far more important then than they are now. The garment industry looked to Paris for trends. But in between the collections I had unusual freedom. One year I covered the civil war in Nigeria when Biafra seceded, a horrendous conflict. I reported from Northern Ireland when the "troubles" were heating up very fiercely. So I wasn't a sheltered raw reporter when I finally got to Vietnam, but nothing could get you ready for that.

I was staunch. Young men who went to Vietnam as war correspondents had to prove something, had to prove how fearless and unflinching they were because they weren't much older than the draftees. But I didn't have to prove anything. I knew who I was—the bravest woman in the whole world. That was the lie I told myself.

I realized it was a lie about the second week I was there. I was riding in a dustoff [medevac helicopter] and trying to hold the hand of a badly wounded soldier. But I was getting in the way of the medic and so I let go. He died and I thought it was because I let go of his hand. It's not good to think that way. You're taking on a delusion that will kill you. Holding the hand of a wounded soldier is not what's going to keep him alive. He didn't even know I was holding his hand.

I went to Vietnam to write about the Vietnamese. They had been totally ignored. I hired Mr. [Nguyen Ngoc] Luong as an interpreter. He was a genius in the way he could dance from Vietnamese into English and back. He was fascinated by Americans. He was just thunderstruck by them—their size, their manner, their way of walking, all the food they ate. He would always ask, "Is my back wet?" American soldiers always had these great circles of perspiration on their backs. Mr. Luong wanted to have a wet back. He wanted that big, dark circle. And whenever we checked in for a ride on an army helicopter they would ask you your weight. I was dropping down to one twenty-eight and Luong weighed one twenty-five. But he would always exaggerate his weight because we were surrounded by Americans with these massive bone structures. They were huge.

The memories are mercifully dimmer now, but I can still conjure the badly burned Vietnamese woman who said she was once pretty. She dreamed she was on the beach in her yellow bathing suit, normal again. And there was a young soldier from the North who walked down the Ho Chi Minh Trail. He remembered a favorite dream that let him be a child again, at home in his village, close to his mother.

And then the two young Vietnamese women, handcuffed like criminals, arms behind their backs, waiting for a helicopter to take them to official headquarters where they would be interrogated and have a very bad time of it. They were suspects. I remember the soldiers had to adjust the plastic handcuffs because their wrists were so small. I stood behind them, desperate to pull off a rescue. The two women were terrified and somehow, despite the handcuffs, they managed to hold hands. The chopper came for them with that terrible wind and they were lifted up and sent to their doom. A thousand times they have come back to me.

Mr. Luong and I must have plunged into many hundreds of lives with our endless questions, but because of him, no one refused to talk unless they were under arrest. People must have known we couldn't help them, or make their lives easier, but there were Vietnamese who had urgent things to say and needed to speak. In Phu Yen Province, Mr. Luong took me to meet two men who had once fought the French in the war for independence. They were fighters—*chien si*—with the Viet Minh, forces considered by the West to be a Communist movement because that was a convenient label. But neither man knew what a Communist really was and said so. It was their honor to fight. Men with their history were not held in high esteem. The government and local officials saw them as dangerous or subversive. The war stories they told that day were unlike any I was ever to hear. One of the men was issued a long knife and four grenades—that was all. They admired the National Liberation fighters facing American firepower. The younger man had a paralyzed left hand. He said, "If I were with the Front now I don't think I could stand it. The younger generation is more courageous—look what they have to face!"

It was their pride that made them memorable men.

All sorts of memories make disorderly and capricious claims. There was the laundry boy who worked for Americans and was ashamed to reveal that he ate the leftovers from their breakfasts. There were the two Catholic priests sentenced to prison for writing critically of the government and the war, and no one who could protect them. And always, the twelve-year-old boy in a detention center in Danang where police poured water up his nose and used electric shock to make him talk. He and a little girl were believed to have lived with Viet Cong cadre. The head of the Special Police Branch told us, "We use little fish to catch big fish." The boy, who spoke in a soft croak, said he did not want to be alone anymore and asked for money to buy a can of fish.

Before the war, I was Miss Mary Poppins. Red, white, and blue forever. I was profoundly ignorant and believed in the Americans tidying up the world. When I came back from Vietnam someone asked me what I wore to officers' dances. Or people would say that it was good a woman had been there. And then I would say something despicable like, "Oh, you mean instead of a nineteen-year-old boy from Kansas who had his leg blown off?" It made me very hateful for a long time. I ended one magazine article with the sentence: "Perfectly nice people said that Vietnam had been good for my career and thought I was smiling at them."

I looked at my stories after the war and thought they all were like ice cubes. There were no nails there. I was horrified, so I threw them all out. They weren't nearly good enough. Not strong enough, not bold enough. I thought they were at the time.

I didn't know how to climb out of the war. It was like being on the bottom of a crater and I kept slipping as I tried to get up the sides. After the war, Mr. Luong knew what my trouble was. In one letter he wrote, "You suffer from an acute lack of forgetfulness." A few years ago, he wrote saying that he did not want to talk about the war anymore. And neither do I, so I'll stop now.

NGUYEN NGOC LUONG

"To get their ID cards, the girls had to go to bed with the police."

"English is very easy because I'm not shy. I shout out all the time." Drafted by the South Vietnamese army in 1962, he was trained as an interpreter. At night he worked for the Saigon Daily News, *an English-language newspaper. From 1969 to 1975 he did translations and research for* New York Times *reporters such as Gloria Emerson. Eventually the* Times *also ran some of his stories and photographs.*

He grew up in a small village in the North. In 1954, at age eighteen, he moved to the South where he has lived ever since. "I just wanted to see the country, so I took advantage of the cease-fire in 1954 to receive a free air ticket to Saigon."

I saw too much. I saw too much even when I was a young boy. In 1945, two million people died because of a famine caused by the Japanese. When you opened the door in the morning the bodies were lying along the road. They were people who left their villages because there was nothing to eat and they thought they would go to Hanoi as beggars. On the way they died. As a nine-year-old boy I helped the grown-ups put the bodies in the ox-cart and followed the cart to the mass grave. It lasted for many days and many months.

From 1954 to 1960 I worked in the [southern] countryside as a social worker. In the late fifties I became the director of social welfare for Kien Giang Province. We went to the hamlets and looked with our own eyes at what the people needed. We were very successful. The local Viet Cong were doing the same thing as us—exactly the same thing. Many of them were my friends. The party secretary of the district even came to say hello and have a drink. We just had different bosses, that's all.

But I became very angry with the Diem government. The big, beautiful speeches we heard every day were quite different from what was happening in the countryside. The money never got down to the village or the hamlet. We had proof that one district chief was very corrupt and when I took it to Saigon nothing happened. And everybody in the area was ordered to the police department to get an identification card. They gave all the beautiful young girls appointments at nine and ten o'clock in the evening. To get their ID cards, the girls had to go to bed with the police. Can you believe it? How could they refuse? The government had all kinds of power. The families were so ashamed they arranged for their daughters to move to Saigon to start a new life. So many beautiful young ladies disappeared from the hamlets where I worked.

Without American intervention there would have been no war. Reunification one way or the other would have happened in 1956. So all the people in

Vietnam thought the war was caused by the Americans. And most of the South Vietnamese soldiers knew that some members of their family were on the other side. When you shoot into an area, maybe your own blood brother is there. And fighting against Communism, what is that? Nobody understood. They knew they were fighting against other Vietnamese and the other Vietnamese were fighting against foreigners. So in our heart we had sympathy with the other side.

When I came to *The New York Times* I told them, "Don't ever force me to meet the VIPs. No ministers, no generals—I hate them. If I see them I am not myself." I did not work for the Americans in a political sense. I was there to make money and to be a witness. To see with my own eyes.

I spent a lot of time going to bars near my home. That was the way to get to know American soldiers and Vietnamese bar girls. Most of the bar girls were from the countryside. Because of the fighting there they had to run away to the city. They couldn't find anything to do, so step-by-step they became bar girls. They didn't understand anything about the war. They thought, we don't know why we are punished this way. We didn't do anything wrong. Maybe our ancestors did something wrong so now we are punished. It was confusing for all of us, not just for the bar girls. The GIs didn't understand anything at all about Vietnam. They always talked about being here for just one year. Look at their calendars—XXX every day. Everywhere GIs lived they had their calendars, marking off every day, counting the days. By the time they had some understanding, it was time to leave.

I don't think many bar girls became prostitutes in a strict sense, but most of them had a small room somewhere nearby where everything was paid for by one specific GI. They had a GI boyfriend and when he died or went home they would have another. They liked the GIs very much. Most American soldiers were very good with girls. Very amiable. You'd have to be there to see it. The girls behaved very warmly with the GIs and the GIs were like children with them. Like babies. The girls took care of them.

The GIs bought a lot of things from the PX and brought them to the girls and their families. One GI I met rented a small house and the bar girl's whole family moved in. He supplied everything—food, school fees for all the children, clothes, perfume for the lady, everything. But one soldier told me, "Don't think that I can spend money like this in America." What he meant was that he could live well as a soldier in Vietnam, but in America he was poor.

Many Americans tried to marry their girlfriends and take them home. I still remember one story written by Gloria [Emerson] about that. Gloria and I went to the consulate general's office where they took care of all the marriage applications. It was very busy and noisy. There were all these GIs with their girlfriends. There was a lot of red tape, but there were more marriages between GIs and Vietnamese during the war than between Americans and Japanese [during the U.S. post–World War II occupation of Japan].

As individuals, the American soldiers were very gentle and very polite. But as a unit, they were very cruel. When the My Lai story broke in the United States we did not know anything here. The Vietnamese press could not publish the story. The censorship at that time prevented it. The man in charge of the Vietnamese press here said, "Don't even mention it." But I went to My Lai many times. I went with Gloria and sometimes I went alone. We forget the names from so many years ago, but there is still one I remember—Mrs. Thieu, exactly the same name as the former president of South Vietnam. She lived in My Lai. On the day of the massacre her house was burned and she ran away with her children. But she was thrown in with a group of old people and babies and they were all shoved and kicked into a ditch. The Americans kept on shooting and she tried to pretend that she died. She was facedown in the ditch. Then, because the blood of other bodies began to rise up and up and up she had to turn her face to breathe. She was afraid if she made any kind of movement the soldiers would shoot her, but she turned her head very slowly so her nose would be out of the blood to breathe.

All my life I've been obsessed with things like that. The young people now have no idea about the war. They are too busy studying and trying to get a job to help the family. But the old people are still obsessed with it. We don't care about the present and the future; we are obsessed with the past. I spend almost all my time with the past. But I keep it to myself.

At the end of the war, The New York Times *offered to take his family to the United States. He refused. Twenty-six years later, in spite of a postwar life of hardship and stunted opportunity, he does not regret his decision. "Personal pride explains why I am here. And pride in Vietnam. So many people were nervous about getting out, getting out, getting out. But in my case, it is a question of feeling. It's very simple. This is my country, so I stayed in my country. And many of us were ready to live in hardship because of our pride in Vietnam. Three countries in the world were cut in two—Korea, Germany, and Vietnam. Vietnam was the first to be reunified. Reunification in Vietnam is very important—it's deep in our heart. And peace. There are many people like me, but we just keep quiet and accept life as it is."*

FROM CAMBODIA TO KENT STATE

When Richard Nixon assumed the presidency in January 1969, he knew Congress and the public were unlikely to tolerate additional deployments of U.S. combat troops to South Vietnam. There were already more than 525,000 American servicemen in the war zone, and in 1968 alone more than 14,000 were killed, a degree of sacrifice that was politically unsustainable. However, neither Nixon nor his national security adviser Henry Kissinger were willing to withdraw from Vietnam without securing a non-Communist state in the South. Their goal was to achieve that end while simultaneously reducing American casualties and troop levels.

But how could you deescalate the American ground war *and* force the North Vietnamese to accept a settlement they considered tantamount to surrender? Nixon insisted that for complete U.S. withdrawal Hanoi would have to remove its troops from the South and recognize the legitimacy of the American-backed government in Saigon. Why would the North accept the very terms it had rejected through a decade of American escalation, especially once they realized that the United States intended to diminish its own participation in combat?

Nixon and Kissinger believed they could resolve the dilemma with a two-tiered strategy. On the one hand, they would lower American casualties by slowly removing U.S. ground forces—hoping this would demobilize the antiwar movement as well—while building up the South Vietnamese military. On the other hand, they would increase the military pressure on North Vietnam by escalating the bombing, expanding the war into Cambodia where the Viet Cong and North Vietnamese had sanctuaries, and threatening even more brutal actions in the future.

Thus, in the spring of 1969, Nixon initiated a program called "Vietnamization." It was, in a sense, an effort to make real what American policy makers had always claimed in theory—that the Vietnamese themselves would ultimately have to be responsible for determining their own fate. Since 1954, however, the Saigon regime had essentially been a proxy state so dependent on U.S. intervention that collapse was always likely if its powerful benefactor pulled out. The challenge of Vietnamization was to expand and improve the South Vietnamese military to such a degree that America's direct military role might eventually be relinquished to Saigon. Nixon calculated that if Americans believed their own war in Vietnam was winding down, however slowly, domestic pressure for immediate withdrawal would abate.

Meanwhile, in secret, he expanded and escalated the air war. On March 18, 1969, just two months after taking office, Nixon ordered B-52 bombing strikes on Cambodia. Called Operation Menu, the bombing was so secret that even many high-ranking government officials and military commanders were not informed. The strikes were launched at night, bomb release coordinates were programmed from the ground, and false flight records were submitted to preserve the fiction that the Cambodian targets were actually in South Vietnam.

In part, the attacks were designed to destroy enemy staging areas in Cambodia. Nixon's primary aim, however, was to prove to Hanoi and Moscow that he was tougher and more ruthless than his predecessor, that he was prepared to take every measure necessary to achieve his ends. He described his approach to aide Bob Haldeman as the "madman theory." "I want the North Vietnamese to believe I've reached the point where I might do anything to stop the war. We'll just slip the word to them that, 'For God's sake, you know Nixon is obsessed about Communists. We can't restrain him when he's angry—and he has his hand on the nuclear button'—and Ho Chi Minh himself will be in Paris in two days begging for peace." It is not clear how seriously Nixon considered actually pushing that button, but he certainly entertained the idea of nuclear attacks in his discussions with Kissinger.

U.S. bombing of Cambodia, which continued until Congress cut it off in the summer of 1973, was no more successful than any other American air campaign in breaking Hanoi's will to continue fighting or moving the Communist leadership to "beg for peace." Its primary impact was to drive Communist forces deeper into Cambodia and to antagonize Cambodian civilians who survived the bombing, a growing number of whom joined the Khmer Rouge, a fledgling Communist movement that had few supporters prior to the attacks. However, Nixon did manage to cover up this dramatic expansion of the war. The few news reports about the airstrikes were officially denied. Three years later, when the Watergate scandal broke and the bombing of Cambodia was proposed as an article of impeachment, it was still a part of the war's history unknown to most Americans.

In the summer of 1969, as the secret bombing continued and Nixon announced the first reductions in American troop levels, Henry Kissinger was working on plans for Operation Duck Hook, a "go-for-broke" attack on North Vietnam. This "savage, decisive blow," as Kissinger called it, was to be used as a threat against the Communists unless they agreed to significant concessions in peace talks prior to November 1, 1969. If the ultimatum failed, the Duck Hook plan called for massive bombing of major North Vietnamese cities and dike systems, the mining of harbors and rivers, and possible use of tactical nuclear weapons on the Ho Chi Minh Trail or rail lines connecting Vietnam and China.

As the ultimatum's deadline approached without a change in Hanoi's position, Nixon decided not to go forward with Duck Hook. According to his memoirs, he was inhibited by concerns that "after all the [antiwar] protests . . . American public opinion would be seriously divided by any military escalation of the war." With major new antiwar demonstrations already planned for November, Nixon delayed further escalation.

However, he was far from abandoning his faith that force could prevail. Embarrassed by his decision to back away from the fall ultimatum, the following spring Nixon launched a ground invasion of Cambodia despite the opposition of his secretaries of state and defense and knowing full well that it would have a "shattering effect" on his already tenuous domestic support. In a television address on April 30, 1970, he described the "incursion" as an effort to attack North Vietnamese troops in their Cambodian "sanctuaries." He further intended to find and destroy the "military headquarters" for all North Vietnamese operations in South Vietnam, thereby providing time and security for American troop withdrawals and Vietnamization to go on apace. As with the bombing, however, his larger aim was simply to demonstrate his willingness to widen the war until Hanoi backed down at the bargaining table.

The invasion included eighty thousand American and South Vietnamese troops. While many weapons were captured, no significant military headquarters could be found (Communist command centers were always small and mobile), and North Vietnamese troops generally avoided combat. At best, the invasion temporarily interrupted Hanoi's war-making capabilities. It did, however, enlarge the U.S. commitment to the support of Cambodia's Lon Nol, a general who had recently overthrown the neutralist government of Norodom Sihanuouk. Sihanouk had allowed the North Vietnamese to use eastern Cambodia for operations in South Vietnam, but he had nonetheless managed to keep Cambodia out of the Vietnam War and under his rule the North Vietnamese gave little support to the Khmer Rouge. With Lon Nol in power, Hanoi offered substantial help to the Cambodian Communists. The Lon Nol regime relied on massive U.S. aid and was even more vulnerable than Nguyen Van Thieu's in South Vietnam.

In the United States, the Cambodian invasion caused an enormous furor. Student strikes erupted on more than a hundred college campuses and some turned violent. About thirty ROTC (Reserve Officers' Training Corps) buildings were burned or bombed. Nixon added fuel to the fire by referring to campus protesters as "bums." National Guard units were sent to twenty-one campuses. On May 4, 1970, at Kent State University, guardsmen fired on demonstrators, killing four and wounding nine. That spurred still further protests. Eventually students at more than seven hundred colleges and universities declared strikes and many campuses were effectively shut down for the remainder of the semester.

Dissent was expressed from every quarter. Two hundred and fifty State Department employees signed a letter of protest and several of Kissinger's top aides resigned in opposition to the policy. In Congress, the Senate voted to cut off funds for U.S. forces in Cambodia. Though the measure died in a House-Senate conference, it was clear that support for Nixon's escalations of the war was shrinking by the day. Nixon promised to remove U.S. troops from Cambodia by the end of June (though ARVN forces remained longer).

The month before winning the presidency Richard Nixon told *The New York Times,* "We can't have a foreign policy with Vietnam hanging around our necks. I will deal with it within six months." A year and a half later he embarked on a policy that made the war even larger and apparently left it as irresolvable as ever. It was now "Nixon's War" and he felt it more and more as a personal crisis. The White House increasingly adopted a siege mentality, dividing the world between "us" and "them" and introducing new measures to spy on and punish those regarded as political enemies.

ANTHONY LAKE

"Quitting wasn't heroic."

He went to Vietnam as a young foreign service officer from 1963 to 1965. In 1969, he became special assistant to National Security Adviser Henry Kissinger and accompanied him to Paris for secret negotiations with North Vietnamese representatives. "At that time we were negotiating with Xuan Thuy [Hanoi's chief delegate to the Paris peace talks from 1968 to 1970]. Because I was suggesting a more flexible position than Kissinger, one of his aides started referring to me as Xuan Lake, which sounds like Swan Lake."

On April 29, 1970, one day before the invasion of Cambodia, Lake and Roger Morris, another top Kissinger assistant, submitted their resignations in opposition to U.S. policy. Shortly thereafter, Nixon had the FBI wiretap Lake's phones, a step he had already taken against a handful of other aides. As the White House became ever more secretive, suspicious, and authoritarian, Kissinger readily supported Nixon's efforts to root out dissenters.

In 1993, after years of teaching international relations at Mount Holyoke College, Lake became President Bill Clinton's national security adviser.

A week before the Cambodian invasion Kissinger called a few of us into his office saying he wanted to meet with his "bleeding hearts." He told us they were planning an incursion by South Vietnamese forces with some American forward air controllers and asked what we thought of it.* We argued that it wouldn't work from a tactical point of view and that politically all hell would break loose. At the end he said, "Well, Tony, I knew what you were going to say." I remember thinking to myself, "If you knew what I was going to say then there isn't much point in my saying it anymore." I had become so predictable I had lost my effectiveness. I didn't have to be there.

I spoke at Amherst College about six months after I resigned and somebody asked me how I felt about it. He expected me to say I felt proud or heroic. I said what first came into my mind, that I felt guilty about leaving. The reason I felt guilty was that I knew I had more of an opportunity to argue about the conduct of the war and how to end it by being in the White House than I did by becoming a citizen again. I still believe that.

Guilt may be too strong a word, though, because I certainly did not think it was right to work in a White House in which I had to write speeches attacking people I agreed with. I just wasn't going to do it. But quitting wasn't heroic. Maybe we should have gone out with a great public flourish, but we wanted to have an impact on Kissinger's thinking and show him that we were quitting because we were very serious, not for the sake of personal fame. In retrospect, I know it didn't have much impact on anybody's thinking within the White House, so perhaps we should have tried to have more public impact. But if we had resigned dramatically it would have been a one-day story.

During the sixties, all of us on the inside who were becoming increasingly opposed to the war never said, "The war is wrong, just stop it" because nobody would listen to you. So you would argue it issue by issue. For example, you would argue for a more flexible negotiating position. I can remember how angry I was at some distant relatives who would send me letters in effect accusing me of being a war criminal at the very time I was really getting drilled inside for doing whatever I could to try to bring an end to a war that I thought

*Kissinger had privately told some of his aides the truth, that American troops would also be used in the invasion, but those who knew kept it confidential in the meeting.

was wrong. I resented friends on the outside with whom I agreed hurling abuse at the government officials who were closest to their own views. When you do that you simply piss the officials off and it generally has the effect of stiffening them rather than moving them. They should have been yelling at the hard-liners. I found this all very painful.

A. J. LANGGUTH

"I think they pictured it as a kind of huge bamboo Pentagon."

He covered the war for The New York Times *in the midsixties, returning on assignment in 1968 and 1970. In recent years, as a professor of journalism at the University of Southern California, he wrote a long history of the war called* Our Vietnam. *He has the wry smile and droll wit of an old journalistic pro.*

When I went back to Vietnam in 1968 the Tet experience had really shaken the military, but a lot of officers still thought maybe we could pull it out. By 1970, hopelessness and despair was commonplace. Nobody wanted to be the last person killed in Vietnam. GIs had peace signs on their helmets and smoked pot quite overtly.

I was really annoyed by the very idea of Vietnamization. By that time well over a hundred thousand South Vietnamese soldiers were dead, crops destroyed, cities in ruins, and we're talking about Vietnamization as though the Vietnamese weren't already bearing the brunt of the war. It was one of those words that gave a reassuring ring in Washington, but it was really insulting.

The idea of pulling out U.S. ground troops and replacing them with ARVN soldiers was just at its beginning in 1970 when Nixon announced a new escalation of the war—the invasion of Cambodia. His rationale was that COSVN [Central Office for South Vietnam]—the command headquarters for the Communists—was operating out of Cambodia and that Cambodia was a protected sanctuary for Communist troops because Johnson had prevented the military from going over the border. The military told Nixon and Kissinger that they had finally located COSVN and if the wraps were taken off, they could go into Cambodia and put an end to this whole network.

A mythology had grown up about COSVN in the minds of American policy makers. I think they pictured it as a kind of huge bamboo Pentagon. Though they had some relatively sophisticated communications tools, COSVN was really just a collection of small jungle outposts that could be abandoned at a moment's notice. The idea that somehow you were going to go in and wipe out the source of the infection once and for all was preposterous. But that was the argument.

The invasion set off a great outcry in the United States and around the world. It caused campus protest that was far worse than anything Johnson had seen. To stem the damage, Nixon made an arbitrary announcement that American troops would be pulled out of Cambodia within two months, by the end of June. But the South Vietnamese army was still going over the border throughout the summer. In August, I decided to see how Vietnamization was actually working by going out to spend time with an ARVN unit in Cambodia.

My friend Neil Davis, the cameraman who was later killed in Bangkok, knew the South Vietnamese army better than any Western journalist and he told me to go out with General Tran Ba Di, the commander of the 9th Division. He said he was their most skilled and honest general. But the ARVN just weren't up to the job. Part of it was that by 1970 their equipment was wearing out and they didn't have what they needed, or what they felt they needed, to win battles. Just getting to their divisional command post a few miles away on a South Vietnamese truck, we broke down several times. The driver got out, lifted the hood, and started blowing on wires. When I arrived they were just finishing an operation sixty miles inside Cambodia and the Vietnamese Air Force could only give them about three or four air strikes a day.

In 1970, the U.S. army had thirty-five hundred helicopters in Vietnam, but they had supplied the Vietnamese with only slightly more than a hundred. An American officer told me that the Vietnamese didn't have the same need for helicopters because they were used to walking and didn't expect hot meals like our troops. The helicopters were not only crucial for logistics but for medical evacuations. I met an ARVN doctor who said his unit had lost thirty men in Cambodia because they didn't have helicopters to medevac them out; that if they'd been allowed to use American helicopters they would only have lost ten men. Some of the wounded had to wait more than twenty-four hours to get to a hospital and many died before they could get treatment.

General Di was a professional soldier and one of those people who believed in the cause and was going to fight as best he could. He introduced me to a young aspirant—a candidate for lieutenant—who told me he only earned six thousand piasters a month, about eighteen dollars. All his friends in the unit said they were broke. I was curious about looting because there had been reports in Saigon about quite massive looting by ARVN troops in Cambodia. These troops had been accused of it as well and when I asked General Di he admitted that it had happened. He said it had been a failure of leadership, including his own. He said, "The soldiers are very poor. That's no excuse, but they come into a Cambodian town and to them it looks very rich." Also the Vietnamese felt very superior to Cambodians and were quite arrogant and disagreeable toward them. But while I was with them I didn't see any real abuses.

Some of the young ARVN officers felt the Cambodian campaign had taken pressure off their outposts in South Vietnam, but to keep the pressure off they would have to continue attacking the Communists in Cambodia. They felt they just didn't have the strength to do that. They were not hopeful. General Di had a shrewd sense of the political mood in the United States and knew he was eventually going to have to get along alone. We'd already begun our withdrawal and they knew it was inevitable. The ARVN were terribly apprehensive about what was going to happen. In their one major battle during the Cambodian invasion they outnumbered the Communist troops two to one, but most of the VC escaped. The ARVN just didn't pursue the enemy after making contact.

General Di was losing an awful lot of people by desertion and it was getting worse as more and more Vietnamese were being drafted against their will. Back in 1967 and '68 a lot of wealthy boys from Saigon would be hanging around the cafes. It used to infuriate our people who saw them lounging about. By 1970, many of these kids had been pressed into service. But as soon as the troops got back to their bases a considerable number would take off.

The South Vietnamese draftees were young kids and none of them were gung-ho. Most of them wanted the war over. They didn't want to fight. That was the problem from the very beginning, going back to the early sixties. And by 1970 the American GIs were no more keen to fight than they were.

TOM GRACE

"As much as we hated the war on April 29, we hated it more on April 30."

He was a sophomore at Kent State University when President Nixon announced the invasion of Cambodia on April 30, 1970. Along with hundreds of thousands of students on virtually every American campus, he demonstrated against Nixon's expansion of the war. This nationwide outcry was dramatic evidence that antiwar convictions were not confined to elite campuses like Harvard or Berkeley, but had permeated the American heartland.

In response to the Kent State protests, which included the burning of a ROTC building, Ohio Governor James A. Rhodes ordered twelve hundred national guardsmen onto the campus. On May 3, the governor made a speech in which he described the an-

tiwar protesters as "worse than the [Nazi] brownshirts and the Communist element and the night riders and the vigilantes. They are the worst type of people that we harbor in America." A day later, on May 4, a crowd of students gathered for a noontime rally. A contingent of national guardsmen huddled near a football practice field. Then they marched to a hilltop near a campus sculpture known as the Pagoda. From that vantage point, they turned in unison more than halfway to their right, raised their M-1 rifles, and fired into the crowd. They killed four students and wounded nine. Tom Grace was among the wounded. A bullet shattered his left foot.

Today he is a social worker and the president of his union in Buffalo, New York. A passionate baseball fan, he suggests we go to a Toronto Blue Jays game. Only later that night do we talk about May 4. "I'm basically a fairly introverted person," he warns. "Besides, getting shot wasn't an accomplishment. It's something that happened to me. I don't like to see myself as a victim."

My friend Alan Canfora was carrying a black flag that had "KENT" spray-painted on it. Alan was shot through the wrist and dropped the flag as he fled the area. One of my other roommates, Aquinas, picked up the flag. Everyone called him Aquinas because he was from a religious family and was so nice. He had some saintly qualities about him. Aquinas picked up the flag and went over to where Jeff Miller had been killed. Miller was the student in the famous photograph where the girl is kneeling over his lifeless body with her arms outstretched and that awful look of anguish in her face.

This is a bit difficult to talk about. I had already been removed from the area but friends told me that there was a huge puddle of blood after Miller's body had been taken away. Aquinas took the black flag and dipped it in the blood, really saturated it, and began jumping up and down in the blood. After that he proceeded to whip this flag around as quickly as he could, spraying blood everywhere.

He was never really the same after that. He had always been so angelic, just so peaceful. I don't think he had ever hurt anyone before in his life. But a few weeks after the shootings, he and some friends were down on a little island in the Cuyahoga River. They came upon a bird's nest and Aquinas took a tree limb and just started smashing the bird's nest. It was pointless, mindless.

When my parents visited me in the hospital, I felt I'd really let them down. They sent me out there to go to school and here I am shot. I didn't feel like I'd done a good job by them but they were quite supportive. My father was a New Deal Democrat and he absolutely detested Richard Nixon. What really influenced his politics was the Depression experience. There were a lot of times when they just couldn't make the rent and were evicted. Once, when I was about fourteen, he drove me all around the South Side of Syracuse, New York.

He showed me eleven addresses they had to move out of. My views are further left than my father's, but in all other respects I'm a fairly conventional person. I'm a church-goer and try to instill those values in my children.

I was almost like a circuit rider in terms of my participation in antiwar demonstrations. The year or so before the shootings at Kent State I had been involved in no less than fifteen demonstrations—in Chicago, Washington, Cleveland, as well as Kent. On Thursday evening, April 30, Nixon announced the invasion of Cambodia, which he repeatedly referred to as an "incursion" rather than an invasion. There were demonstrations all weekend.

My girlfriend, Nancy, and I spent Sunday evening studying for a history examination scheduled for the next morning. We showed up for class at nine A.M. and Professor William Kenney announced that because of the magnitude of the disorders and how distracting they were, if anyone felt unprepared to take the examination that morning they could consider themselves excused. History was one of Nancy's weaker areas so she decided to make her exit. But I was fully prepared and, in fact, eager to take the exam. So we agreed to meet back at her apartment about twelve o'clock.

She was worried about me and she made me promise that I would not go to any demonstrations that day. Her brother Donny had been killed in Vietnam in 1967 so the war had already touched her family very deeply. She was opposed to the war but she was very uncomfortable at demonstrations. We had been together at an antiwar protest in Cleveland on April 15 that had some touch-and-go moments. The police came in on horseback and were clubbing people and she just seemed to be in over her head.

So I assured Nancy that I wouldn't go to any demonstrations on May 4. It was a genuine, sincere commitment on my part. I felt I had given my word to my friend and when you give your word to someone you keep your word. That's how I was raised. But after my morning classes I was reminded that there would be a rally at noon on the commons. So I had to sit there and wrestle with this momentous decision. And I do recall that it felt momentous. I wanted to keep my word to Nancy, but that was in conflict with another value I had which was to do everything that we could to stop the war. We hated that war, and as much as we hated the war on April 29, we hated it more on April 30.

Something else was operating on me at the time. My friend Alan's best friend from boyhood had been run over by one of our own tanks on the Cambodian border in mid-April. We found out about it just before a demonstration in Kent on April 14 and we had been to his funeral less than a week before the events of May 4. His name was Bill Caldwell.

But my feelings went beyond the war. By that point I was totally opposed to the American political and economic system. The event that put me over the edge was the murder of the Black Panther Fred Hampton in December 1969. When the Chicago police assassinated Hampton in his bed I remember seeing a picture of the cops carrying out his body. They were grinning from ear to ear. I was absolutely incensed when I saw that and I thought, if this is the kind of country where these things happen, I don't want any part of it. So I had all these things operating on me and I decided to break my word to Nancy and go to the rally on the commons.

It was a short walk from my class to the commons. There were a few hundred students chanting, "One, Two, Three, Four, We Don't Want Your Fucking War" and "Pigs Off Campus, Pigs Off Campus." At least another thousand people had gathered nearby to observe. At this point, a campus policeman in a National Guard jeep ordered the crowd to disperse, which did nothing but whip the crowd into a further frenzy. We felt that this was our campus, that we were doing nothing wrong, and that they had no right to order us to disperse. If anyone ought to leave, it was them, not us.

I was standing there yelling and screaming along with everyone else, and then someone flung either a rock or a bottle at the jeep, which bounced off a tire. The jeep drove back to the National Guard lines on the other side of the commons. Then the guardsmen leveled their bayonets at us and started to march across the commons in our direction, shooting tear gas as they came. I was tear-gassed along with perhaps a thousand other people. Unlike some of the students, who stayed to throw rocks or tear-gas canisters back in the direction of the National Guard, I chose to leave the area. I retreated to a girls' dormitory where students were passing out moistened paper towels so people could relieve the effects of the tear gas.

In the meantime, one troop of the National Guard advanced downhill onto a practice football field where they were ringed by students. After cleansing my eyes I cautiously moved a little closer and watched. Some students were throwing rocks at the National Guard and some of the guardsmen were throwing them back at the students.

Then the guard troop seemed to get into a little huddle before leaving the practice field. When they reformed their lines and proceeded back up the hill, the students just moved to one side or the other to let the guardsmen pass, because no one in their right mind would have stood there as bayonets were coming. A lot of people were screaming at the guardsmen. But, oddly enough, in the midst of all this, some students were still wandering through the area with their textbooks, as if they were completely unaware of all that was taking place.

When the guardsmen got to the top of the hill, all of a sudden there was just a quick movement and then a crack or two of rifle fire, and I thought, 'Oh, my God!' I turned and started running as fast as I could. I don't think I got more than a step or two and I was on the ground. The bullet had entered my left heel and literally knocked me off my feet.

At first I thought it had blown my foot off. It did blow off my boot. Later I saw a photograph of it on a sidewalk next to a pool of blood. I tried to get up and someone yelled "Stay down, stay down!" So I lay as prone as possible although, like most people, I was right in the open. There was no cover. It seemed like the bullets were going by within inches of my head. We know today that it only lasted thirteen seconds, but it seemed like it kept going and going and going.

After the shooting stopped, a guy I didn't know named Harold Bluestein tried to pick me up. I'm only five foot, six and a half inches and I weighed a hundred and forty pounds, but Harold was three inches shorter than I am and probably weighed a hundred and fifteen drenching wet. So he was not much help. All of a sudden another stranger—a husky football player named Mike Brock—picked me up like a sack of potatoes and threw me over his shoulder. He carried me into a girls' dormitory. The female students were screaming as I was carried in and placed on a couch. They knew something terrible had happened outside but some of them still weren't sure what it was. I was losing a lot of blood. It was an ugly wound. There was a bone sticking through my green sock and it looked like somebody had put my foot through a meat grinder. Fortunately, a young woman announced that she was a nursing student and knew what to do. She told everyone to clear away while she put a tourniquet on my leg.

When the ambulances arrived and I was carried outside, there were hundreds of people standing around. I remember putting my fist into the air. It wasn't pride, it was just raw anger. The worst thing that can happen to you is to be in a situation where you're being fired upon and not have any way of returning the fire. We had no way of stopping them from doing what they were doing. If I'd had a gun, I definitely would have fired back. Without question. For me, it just would have been self-defense and survival. Of course that would just have unleashed more killing.

They put me into the top tier of the ambulance. As they slid me in, my foot hit something and that triggered the most intense pain I've ever experienced in my life. As the ambulance left campus I looked down and saw Sandy Scheuer on the stretcher below me. I had met her very briefly about a week before. She had a gaping bullet wound in the neck and the attendants were tearing away the top of her blouse and doing a heart massage. Then I heard them say, "It's no use, she's dead." They just pulled the sheet over her head.

I honestly can't say that the Kent State shootings altered my political perspective. But it did reinforce an existing one and the anger I felt about it was my political fuel. It really kept me going. It also gave me a lot more visibility. I didn't welcome it, but I became something of a symbol. Prior to the shooting I had never passed out a flyer. I had never run a meeting. I'd never written a handbill. I'd gone to a lot of demonstrations, but I didn't make speeches. So these were all things I had to learn how to do. I became involved in the McGovern campaign in 1972, became a Democratic committeeman in 1984, ran Jesse Jackson's campaign in my congressional district in 1988. And I have been involved in the union movement since the midseventies.

The first time I heard "Ohio" by Crosby, Stills, Nash, and Young was July of 1970 and I had just gotten out of the hospital. Aquinas was visiting me in Syracuse and he couldn't believe I hadn't heard it yet, so he insisted on trying to find a copy. He walked about two miles barefooted to a shopping center. He took a shortcut through a cemetery and cut his foot going over a fence. His foot was still bleeding, but he made it back with the record.

Tin soldiers and Nixon's coming,
We're finally on our own.
This summer I hear the drumming
Four dead in Ohio.
Four dead in Ohio.
Four dead in Ohio.
How many more?
Four dead in Ohio.

PART FIVE

ENDINGS (1970–75)

THE END OF THE TUNNEL

At every stage in the war, American policy makers and generals assured the public that their goals in Vietnam were being achieved, that progress was steady, that "the end" was in sight. What the end would look like was never entirely clear. In the early years, officials pledged to achieve a victory against Communism that would produce an "independent" South Vietnam. After the Tet Offensive, U.S. leaders dropped virtually all talk of "victory" in favor of such vague formulations as Nixon's "peace with honor." Some defenders of American policy simply relied on the era's most memorable promise of a long-awaited happy ending: "There's a light at the end of the tunnel." As the tunnel proved ever longer and darker, some critics began to claim that the only light at the end would come from an onrushing train.

By 1971, fully 71 percent of Americans told pollsters they believed intervention in Vietnam had been a "mistake" and, remarkably, 58 percent regarded the war as "immoral." A clear majority believed all U.S. troops should be removed by year's end, though that would not happen until January 1973. Nixon sought to mollify his domestic opponents with slow but significant reductions in troop levels. By the end of 1970, 335,000 American servicemen remained in Vietnam, down from a peak of 543,000 in the spring of 1969. By the end of 1971, the number was 185,000.

In light of that deescalation, Nixon and Kissinger once again felt compelled to find some dramatic way to demonstrate America's will to prevent a Communist takeover in the south. Consideration was given to an invasion of North Vietnam or another move into Cambodia. Creighton Abrams, commander of U.S. forces in Vietnam, successfully convinced Nixon to invade neighboring Laos in an effort to sever the Ho Chi Minh Trail and so block northern troops and supplies pouring into the South. In anticipation of congressional and public criticism, the administration decided to rely on South Vietnamese combat troops with Americans restricted to flying air support. It would be the first major test of Vietnamization.

In February 1971, fifteen thousand ARVN troops invaded Laos in Operation Lam Son 719. Supported by U.S. artillery, helicopters, fighter-bombers, and B-52s, the South Vietnamese advanced a dozen miles into Laos without significant opposition. At that point ARVN forces were met by five divisions of North Vietnamese troops in a massive counteroffensive. What had been intended as a three-month operation became, within weeks, a rout. South Vietnamese troops abandoned 150 tanks as they fled back to the Vietnamese border. Some ARVN soldiers were so desperate to escape that they clung to the skids of overpacked evacuation helicopters. Though thousands of North Vietnamese were killed by air strikes and artillery, the South Vietnamese suffered more than eight thousand casualties, many from the most elite units. Despite the debacle, Nixon went on television in early April to announce that "Vietnamization has succeeded."

In reality, demoralization within the South Vietnamese and American militaries was becoming endemic. Between 1966 and 1971, desertion rates among U.S. forces quadrupled to more than seventy soldiers out of every thousand, several times higher than the worst rates of the Korean War. The South Vietnamese military had the war's highest desertion rates, losing some 120,000 servicemen annually. Communist forces were also affected by war weariness and disillusionment (as dramatized in Bao Ninh's brilliant postwar novel *The Sorrow of War*). Some twenty thousand Viet Cong and North Vietnamese army troops defected to the U.S. and South Vietnamese side every year.

Communist forces, however, never suffered a major collapse of their will to fight. That could not be said of the U.S. side. By 1969, many small units were already covertly avoiding combat by "sandbagging" some of their missions; that is, by finding relatively safe hiding places and calling in fabricated reports to headquarters. Instances of outright mutiny became more common in the final years of the war. The Senate Armed Forces Committee counted thirty-five cases of "combat refusal" in the 1st Cavalry Division alone in 1970. Many acts of disobedience among GIs went unrecorded and unpunished because officers knew their careers would be tarnished by any admission that they could no longer control their troops. Moreover, a growing number of officers were themselves less willing to pursue aggressive tactics in a war that seemed ever more likely to end in stalemate or defeat.

Nothing more dramatizes the decline in morale among GIs than the rising number of "fraggings," the violent assaults by enlisted men against their officers. Named after *frag*mentation grenades, fraggings were most often carried out with these weapons because they "left no fingerprints." Officers who insisted that their men search dangerous tunnels or walk down easily ambushed trails were typical targets. The army reported 126 fraggings in 1969, 271 in 1970, and 333 in 1971, especially steep increases given the drop in troop levels during those years. As with combat refusals, the number of actual fraggings surely exceeded the reported incidents, in part because those occurring out in the field could, in many instances, be attributed to accidental "friendly fire" or combat.

The erosion of military discipline and morale was also marked by a startling rise in drug use among GIs. A wide variety of potent drugs were readily and inexpensively available in every South Vietnamese city and near major American bases nationwide. Most of the heroin came from the "Golden Triangle" border areas of Laos, Burma, and Thailand, a trade which profited the Laotian commanders and Hmong tribal leaders who were fighting a CIA-sponsored secret war against the Laotian Communists, the Pathet Lao. Marijuana, sometimes laced with opium, was particularly available to GIs, and by 1969 surveys found at least a quarter of them were using it. That same year the military launched a crackdown on marijuana, arresting as many as a thousand soldiers per week. The arrests inadvertently created a market for heroin, which was much easier to conceal than the pungent marijuana. GIs could purchase pure heroin for as little as two dollars a vial. A 1974 study of the White House Office for Drug Abuse Prevention found that at the peak of the epidemic in the early 1970s, 34 percent of U.S. troops had "commonly used" heroin in Vietnam.

Commenting in 1971 on the general collapse of the American military, General Creighton Abrams said, "I've got white shirts all over the place—psychologists, drug counselors, detox specialists, rehab people. . . . Is this a goddamned army or a mental hospital? Officers are afraid to lead their men into battle, and the men won't follow. Jesus Christ! What happened?"

One thing that happened was that American soldiers were becoming increasingly opposed to the war they had been sent to fight. By the early seventies, Vietnam veterans had moved to the forefront of the antiwar movement, providing a powerful infusion of energy and passion to a cause afflicted by burnout, frustration, and sectarian factionalism. In 1967, six veterans formed Vietnam Veterans Against the War (VVAW), a group that had twenty thousand members by 1971. Their graphic denunciations of American policy included personal testimonies about witnessing or participating in war crimes ranging from the mutilation of enemy corpses to the torture of prisoners, from the burning of villages to the beating and shooting of civilians. The VVAW held public hearings on the war, performed "guerrilla theater" in American streets, and sponsored many antiwar demonstrations, the most famous of which occurred in May 1971 on the steps of the nation's Capitol when some seven hundred veterans threw away the medals they had been awarded in Vietnam.

In 1972, Nixon embarked on his surprising and widely heralded trip to Communist China to meet its leader, Mao Zedong. This was part of a long-planned effort to enhance U.S. power by improving relations with each of the major Communist powers, China and the Soviet Union, while promoting tensions between the two of them. The president hoped, as well, to persuade each to pressure the Communist leadership in Hanoi to reach an accommodation with the United States. The strategy was bold, but in the end it only reinforced Hanoi's determination to achieve its objectives. Only a month after Nixon's trip to China, the North Vietnamese launched a major offensive. With two hundred Soviet tanks, thirty thousand NVA troops crossed the Demilitarized Zone into Quang Tri Province. The "Eastertide Offensive" successfully gained control of most of the province, including the provincial capital. Another seventy thousand northern troops attacked Dak To in the Central Highlands and An Loc just northwest of Saigon.

While American forces were by then few in number and restricted almost wholly to noncombat duties, U.S. airpower was still enormous. With air strikes hammering NVA positions throughout South Vietnam, the offensive was successfully blocked, preventing what might have been a complete collapse of the Thieu regime. Nixon also responded by launching Operation Linebacker, which included the first sustained and massive air strikes of North Vietnam since 1968, and the mining of northern ports and rivers.

In the fall of 1972, after four years of fruitless diplomatic meetings in Paris, Hanoi and the United States finally agreed to terms by which American forces would withdraw from Vietnam. However, South Vietnamese President Nguyen Van Thieu, angered that the settlement would allow North Vietnamese forces to remain in the South, refused to cooperate. Unable to gain Thieu's support for the agreement, Kissinger presented the North Vietnamese diplomats with a new list of conditions. With that, the North Vietnamese delegation issued its own counterdemands, suspended talks, and returned to Hanoi.

Without a public explanation Nixon then unleashed a ten-day series of B-52 strikes on Hanoi and Haiphong. Beginning on December 18, with a day off for Christmas, the United States dropped thirty-six thousand tons of bombs on factories, railroad yards, bus stations, and radio broadcasting stations. Although the attacks included new laser-guided "smart bombs," the "Christmas bombing" hit Hanoi's largest hospital, Bac Mai, and the residential neighborhood of Kham Thien. The civilian death toll of 2,196 might have been far greater if authorities had not already evacuated more than half of the city's population. After the bombing, both sides returned to the negotiating table and agreed to virtually the same cease-fire terms that had been worked out in October. The end of the tunnel, at least for the United States, had finally been reached.

ALEXANDER M. HAIG JR.

"Even the tough guys . . . caved in."

No other American served at a higher level during the Vietnam War as both a military officer and a political adviser. In 1966–67, he was a battalion and brigade commander in Vietnam with the 1st Infantry Division. Two years later, Henry Kissinger appointed him to the National Security Council where he soon impressed President Nixon. In 1972, Nixon made Haig vice chief of staff of the army and promoted him to the rank of four-star general, bypassing 240 higher-ranking generals.

Nixon had always kept extremely tight control of executive decision making, especially on matters of foreign policy. Even his secretary of state, William Rogers, was frequently disregarded. As the Watergate scandal began to unfold and Nixon became even more secretive and authoritarian, he turned increasingly to Haig for support, appointing the general to be his chief of staff in 1973.

After discussing his career, I asked him what war-related contribution made him proudest. "I think it was supporting the Christmas bombing" of 1972.

I've always said, if you don't go in to win, don't go in at all. And to win you frequently have to break a lot of china. Either you conduct the conflict with all the assets the United States has at its disposal to bring about a quick and successful outcome or you stay out. We didn't do either in Vietnam.

The source of the war in Vietnam was Moscow, just like the source of the war in Korea was Moscow. And as I was wont to say at the time I was secretary of state, "You have to go to the source." Moscow and Hanoi had to know we were serious and they would pay a very serious price for what they were doing. What was necessary was to send a message to Moscow that we were going to win that war by taking it to Hanoi while giving an ultimatum to Moscow that we were going to take every step necessary to promptly bring this conflict to a conclusion. I don't think Vietnam was anything more to them than a target of opportunity. They had bigger fish to fry. All Moscow would have to say to Hanoi is, "We're not going to support you anymore." They were the logisticians and were even manning their air defenses. Their ships were coming to Haiphong—two, three, four a day. Hanoi couldn't have done it without them. The war wasn't a struggle for hearts and minds; rather it was an externally supported aggression through the utilization of proxies.

The main problem in Vietnam for the U.S. was what I call incrementalism. As a lieutenant colonel in 1964, I was working as deputy special assistant to Secretary of Defense McNamara and I wrote a memo back before the Gulf of Tonkin and said we're going to lose this conflict because of incremental escalation. Incremental escalation started before Vietnam. It reflected the transition from massive retaliation in the Eisenhower years to flexible response written about by General Maxwell Taylor.* It was part of the contingency planning for the defense of West Berlin. It was a tit-for-tat strategy that assumed the enemy would be stopped at the lowest level of combat intensity. For example, if the Russians used a platoon to block a road, we would counter with a platoon to open the road, and then, if necessary, a company, and then a reinforced battalion. No one seemed to recognize that this kind of incrementalism usually invites rather than discourages escalation. At the Army War College in 1965 I gave a paper attacking the irrationality of incrementalism. Max Taylor was sitting in the front row as I condemned a policy he was part of. He got up and stormed out. [Laughs.] I thought, well here's the finish of a great career.

Following the Gulf of Tonkin incident—which proved to be a pretext rather than a fact—General Harold Johnson, the army's chief of staff, asked me and another young army officer to give him a list of recommendations on what we should do in Vietnam. We gave him a list of over thirty measures. It included full mobilization of the United States military and ultimatums to both Hanoi and Moscow. It was my conviction at the time, and I still hold that conviction, that had we done that, Moscow would have told Hanoi to back off. Any American who was really thinking strategically concluded that we could do this by just demonstrating the fact that we weren't going to tolerate the overthrow of a friendly regime in the South by a Soviet proxy and that we were going to take every step necessary to promptly bring this conflict to a conclusion.

Now I happen to have been very close to the deliberations at the outbreak of the Korean War and witnessed the launching of limited war and incrementalism. Later, when President Truman left office, Eisenhower came in with an entirely different approach. Using massive retaliation as the basis of national strategy, he conveyed to Beijing and to Moscow that if we didn't achieve a truce and a negotiated conclusion in Korea, all of the stops would be taken off the kind of weaponry the United States might use. That was a veiled threat to resort to nuclear weapons. And that began the peace talks that finally ended the Korean War in 1953.

But in 1965, just before our overt entry into Vietnam, General Johnson submitted his final list of recommendations to President Johnson and he eliminated over half the measures we had proposed. It was just the minimum stuff and excluded all the more vigorous actions. He may have thought it was all the traffic would bear, or what was politically acceptable. But generals have an obli-

*General Maxwell D. Taylor was chairman of the Joint Chiefs of Staff (1962–64) and ambassador to South Vietnam (1964–65).

gation to follow their own consciences when they speak to political leaders, not to do what's expedient. There's a lot of blame to go around, but you've got to understand that all of these things that happened in Vietnam were contributed to by uniformed top leaders who didn't have the strength of their own convictions and declined to stand up and say this is not the way to do it.

In 1966, I volunteered to go to Vietnam to see the war firsthand. By 1967, I was a battalion commander of the 1st Battalion, 26th Infantry, during the culmination of the "main force" battle period. I won the Distinguished Service Cross as a result of action in War Zone C in the Battle of Ap Gu. It was probably the largest battalion-size operation of the war. We were put in as bait very close to what was confirmed to be COSVN [Communist Office of South Vietnam] headquarters. It was guarded by a North Vietnamese regiment—the 271 Regiment—as well as elements of the 272 Regiment and the Capital Guards Division. After landing the battalion in a heliborne assault, we established a perimeter. I then deployed the reconnnaissance platoon to probe north of the perimeter when suddenly it was ambushed and pinned down. We then deployed B Company and it, too, got pinned down. That gave us an indication of the size of the force we were confronting. During the ensuing and heated firefight, I went airborne in a small two-seater helicopter so as to be able to more accurately direct air and artillery against the enemy force. My helicopter was shot down and crash-landed in the midst of attacking enemy force. We successfully disengaged, spending all night digging in and preparing our positions. I had no doubt the enemy was going to hit us en masse. The defenses we constructed had interlocking bands of fire and overhead cover. That really saved the battalion and resulted in hundreds and hundreds of enemy deaths. As expected, before sunlight the next morning the enemy hit our perimeter with multiple human wave attacks. C Company was penetrated so I was forced to leave my bunker and accompany what was left of our reconnaissance platoon in an effort to block the developing C Company gap. I went with them because the day before we had lost the platoon leader. To contain the multiple assaults we had to bring napalm right into our positions. Some of it splashed on our bunkers. I tell you, when napalm is two or three hundred yards from you it feels like your shoes are curling. I don't want to suggest that I was sitting in one of those bunkers—I was fifty or a hundred yards away—but close enough. Luckily, as the last major wave attack came we hit it with CBUs [cluster bombs] and the assault was crushed. Our losses were minimal. In the entire battle I think we had nine men killed. Enemy losses were confirmed at six hundred and nine bodies with countless more dragged away. There was no doubt in my mind, as a commander on the ground, that almost without exception every battle that we fought in Vietnam we won decisively. There were, of course, rare exceptions.

The war was not lost on the battlefield in any sense of the word. It was lost in Washington. My first lengthy conversation with Henry Kissinger on the war convinced me that he was hawkish—no doubt about that—as was I. But the composition of the National Security Council staff was a product of Henry's own experience. A lot of them were students who worked with him at Harvard. They were all bright and talented people, but they were ideologically at odds with the president they were serving.

I was very instrumental in the so-called secret bombing of Cambodia. To claim that it was done without legislative knowledge is hogwash. Dr. Kissinger and I briefed the leaders of the House Foreign Affairs Committee, the Senate Foreign Relations Committee, and both Defense Committees on precisely what the B-52 strikes were all about and what their objective was. The bombing was asked for by the constituted leader of Cambodia and there was nothing illegal about it. Never in the history of our country have we sat by and let an enemy attack us from sanctuary and failed to conclude that we had the right to strike him in those sanctuaries. That was a period when everybody with authority was being threatened with criminal trials. Later, when we went into Cambodia with ground incursions, it was also at the request of the legitimate Cambodian government. Again the incursion was treated as some kind of criminal act. Actually, we found vast amounts of enemy supplies and arms even though we pulled out much too soon.

The Paris Peace Accords were a direct product of doing exactly what we should have done in the first place—the so-called Christmas bombing and the mining of Haiphong. Remember, we started the Christmas bombing during the [congressional] Christmas recess and the only people that supported it in the cabinet and staff were myself, Dr. Kissinger, and John Connolly. Everybody else seemed opposed. Nixon was a lonely president with only three supporters. When, as a result of the bombing, Hanoi came back and said they were ready to resume the talks, I said to the president, "Keep up the bombing and demand that the enemy get out of the South." This time I was all alone. Even the tough guys around the president like John Connolly and Henry Kissinger caved in. They feared Nixon's impeachment and told the president he'd have to take Hanoi's offer.

I told President Nixon to keep bombing and he confimed it would mean impeachment. I am still convinced that if he had risked impeachment then and continued the bombing of Hanoi we could have negotiated far more favorable terms. It would have taken maybe two months or less. Had it been properly implemented it would probably have brought about a successful outcome and there would still be a sovereign South Vietnam today. I think we could have done it, but it was very late in the game and the American people had lost their stomach for the war. There was also massive opposition in the Congress. I can't overstate how strong it was. The legislature was radicalized during that period and legislative discipline totally collapsed. The more outrageous you were, the more notice you got in the press. There wasn't party or structural discipline in the committees. It used to be all you had to do in the executive branch was get the leaders over, reach a consensus, and the leaders would deliver. Actually, Congress began to strangle the South Vietnamese military structure—cut, cut, cut, cut, over an extended period, so when that final battle took place Hanoi was so cocky they sent fifteen divisions to Saigon and there was very little to throw back at them.

It's absolutely untrue that the Christmas bombing was designed to just get Thieu to accept the agreement worked out between Washington and Hanoi. Precisely the opposite was the case. What really happened was the North Vietnamese put their finger in Kissinger's eye after he thought he had "peace at hand." Then when the negotiations resumed the president sent me over to sit in with Kissinger in the last sessions. It wasn't necessary, however, because Henry was as angry at the North's duplicity as I was. The Vietnamese withdrew every single concession they had made so there was no agreement. The North Vietnamese broke off negotiations and we were forced to begin the so-called Christmas bombing, this time with most of the wraps taken off. The bombing began in order to get the negotiations started up again. There was no alternative other than surrender.

You know, President Thieu wouldn't pass the litmus test of a Wilsonian democrat, not by a long shot, but I think he was a realistic patriot who truly believed that the peace settlement that was imposed on him by Washington was flawed because it permitted a major North Vietnamese presence in the South and was dependent on sanctions that he began to question knowing the body politic in Washington. But there wasn't anybody, from the president to Kissinger to anybody else, that intentionally double-crossed Saigon. Don't buy that line. I think Nixon and Kissinger both felt they got the best deal they could get. Had the American Congress taken a responsible position, had we applied sanctions in the face of clearly apparent North Vietnamese violations of the Accords, and had we continued to support South Vietnam with supplies and equipment, it would have been sufficient to hold those accords together.

But that wasn't to be. Even Nixon's secretary of state and secretary of defense were vehemently opposed to the war. Years later President Nixon said, "Al, you think Watergate was my greatest mistake." And I said, "Well, I might think that." [Laughs.] He said, "It wasn't. My greatest mistake was the failure to win that war in Vietnam and end it in the first six months of my presidency. You told me at the time I had the opportunity to do that when the EC-131

[U.S. intelligence plane] was shot down off North Korea." My recommendation then was to react very strongly with air strikes against North Korea and then go to Moscow and tell them we're now going to bring the battle to Hanoi unless we have a settlement that returns South Vietnam to sovereign control of the southern people. But the president decided to turn the other cheek because the secretaries of defense and state and many of his advisers were vehemently opposed. Nixon told me that his failure to act then was his greatest mistake. Watergate drew most of its venom from that failure. The president had enough sense to know that both of these problems had merged. Some of the atrocities of Watergate were a direct product of the failures of Vietnam. The so-called plumbers were established by the president through John Ehrlichman without the knowledge of Henry Kissinger or myself. That was a product of presidential paranoia justified by a measure of disarray in the body politic. Watergate and Vietnam blended and one drew great strength from the other. Certain elements of Watergate—like the Pentagon Papers leakage—led Nixon to undertake protective measures which, when added to the break-in of the Democractic Campaign Headquarters in 1972, really proved to be fatal in the long run.

When asked for his comments about the revelation in 2001 that former senator and Medal of Honor recipient Bob Kerrey had, while a SEAL officer in Vietnam, commanded a unit that killed nineteen Vietnamese civilians, Haig said: "It's inconceivable to me that a guy worth his salt would have stooped to tactics which resulted in the deaths of innocent people. I cannot believe Bob Kerrey would have willingly done so. You know, I can remember when I was the G-3 in the 1st Infanty Division. I was there when some staffers recommended dropping dead North Vietnamese soldiers from helicopters on top of North Vietnamese troops simply for the psychology of it. I said, 'If that happens I'm resigning right here and now.' And it didn't happen. The general overruled the proposal but I think he might have done it if no one had objected. That kind of behavior is not my idea of the American military way. I know there were some military people carrying around ears of the dead enemy and mock-tough things of that kind, but if that had ever happened in my unit I'd have fired 'em all."

MORTON HALPERIN

"Kissinger did not trust anybody fully."

As deputy assistant secretary of defense in the final years of the Johnson administration, he headed a Vietnam Task Force that undertook a major review of war policy. The review convinced Clark Clifford, the secretary of defense who replaced Robert McNamara in 1968, that the war was unwinnable.

When Nixon came into office, Halperin was hired by Henry Kissinger to be a senior official in the National Security Council. Halperin had been a junior colleague of Kissinger's in the Government Department at Harvard. Two months after the United States began the secret bombing of Cambodia in March 1969, Kissinger had Halperin's phones wiretapped to test his loyalty to the administration. The taps continued for two years. Disturbed by Nixon's handling of the war and his own exclusion from policy debates, Halperin resigned in September 1969, the first of several Kissinger aides who would resign over the coming year.

At the time of our interview he was President Clinton's director of policy planning at the State Department.

I signed a prowar ad that appeared in *The New York Times* in 1965 and one of my last acts at Harvard was a debate on the Vietnam War between me and Norman Thomas [an antiwar activist and frequent Socialist candidate for president]. You can guess which side Norman Thomas was on and that'll tell you what side I was on. So I started out being supportive of the war. But by the time I got involved in the government in the spring of '67, I had concluded that we could not win and should get out.

Many things troubled me. When we were bombing the North, it wasn't doing any good and was probably interfering with efforts to stop the war. And we did not understand the depth of corruption of the South Vietnamese government and the fact that it had no credibility in its own society, that it was comprised of people who had fought on the French side and worked with the Japanese. Nor did we understand the degree of its penetration by the Viet Cong. I was also troubled by the fact that we were fighting the war in a totally mindless way. American casualties were much higher than they had to be, in part because of the system of one-year tours, with only six months of combat for commissioned officers. The data was very clear that you could drastically cut American casualties by having two-year combat tours because the critical factor in U.S. casualties was how long the commissioned officer had been in command of the unit. There was no interest in fixing any of that stuff.

By the way, I refused to have a map of Vietnam in my office until the Tet Offensive. I just had the big wall map of the world you see in many Pentagon offices. People would come in and they'd start to tell me something about the Mekong Delta or the Ho Chi Minh Trail and they would say, "Where's your map of Vietnam?" I'd say, "Use that map." Half of them couldn't find Vietnam on the world map and the other half would say, "Vietnam is too small on this map to show you what I want to show you." I would look at them and say, "That's the point!"

I also had an imaginary chart in my office. I would describe it to people who came in saying we should get out of the war. I would say, "Column one is reasons why we have to get out of Vietnam. It's a very long list and we pay nothing for additions to it. Column two is ways to get out of Vietnam. We have one or two ideas, of which Vietnamization—or de-Americanization—is the most promising. Column three is how to persuade Lyndon Johnson we should get out. That column is empty." I always believed that what it came down to was his belief that if he got out, Bobby [Kennedy] would run against him and accuse him of selling out and doing what his brother John would never have done. I think Johnson believed that to his core. If you listen to the recently released tapes of LBJ talking about Bobby, it's clear that the paranoia was very strong.

I was deeply involved in the March '68 review of Vietnam policy. The whole focus was to ask the Joint Chiefs how many forces and how many years they would need to assure victory. [Secretary of Defense Clark] Clifford thought that was a perfectly reasonable question. And the chiefs said, "No matter how we answer that question, we cannot guarantee victory." The military gave him an honest answer and it had a profound effect on Clifford. We thought Clifford was for the war. He was Lyndon Johnson's best friend and Johnson had picked him to make sure he didn't again have a secretary of defense who was going around town making clear that he didn't agree with what Johnson was trying to do in the war. It turned out that Clifford had been more skeptical of the war than we thought. He had made a trip through Southeast Asia and discovered to his amazement that none of the countries in the region shared our view about the dominos—that the dominos didn't believe in the domino effect.

Until that review, except for some McNamara memos to the president which, as far as I know, went over there and disappeared, there really was no raising of fundamental questions. What was extraordinary about the March '68 review is that suddenly you could put all the choices on the table and begin arguing about the real issues. Before that I'd sit in meetings and there were people in the room with profoundly different views about what was going on and what to do about it but we never talked about it. Everybody was very polite and the discussion was all about immediate, operational issues, not fundamental questions.

I also concluded that the Nixon administration was planning to escalate rather than get out and I thought that was profoundly wrong. When Nixon said he had a secret plan to end the war it really was a repeat of what he thought Eisenhower had done—that he had threatened the North Koreans with nuclear weapons through the Chinese and that's why they agreed to a settlement. A major flaw in that reasoning is that Eisenhower accepted the deal that Truman had refused to accept so the war ended because we switched our position, not because the North Koreans switched. But it became clear that Nixon was going to threaten escalation, including threats of nuclear escalation, to try to get the Russians or the Chinese to put sufficient pressure on North Vietnam to force them to end the conflict.

Once the strategy was set in place, Kissinger carried it out in great secrecy, even from his own staff. But it was clear that his strategy was to bring the casualties down and then to combine that with escalation and threats of escalation to eventually wear the North down, or at least to get into a state that was sustainable indefinitely.

It was a very hard place to work because Kissinger did not trust anybody fully and he'd set one staff off against another. I picked up the paper one morning and discovered that Nixon had written Ho Chi Minh a letter. I walked into Kissinger's office and said, "Henry, I don't want to work on Vietnam unless I know everything that's going on. If you don't want to tell me everything I'm happy to work on other subjects." So he says, "Well, this is an exception. The president told me not to tell. But you know everything else." I walked out of the office—a true story—and did what we all did on that staff, I stopped at Al Haig's desk and read upside down the pieces of paper on his desk. And there's a memo to the president on Vietnam that Kissinger had sent an hour before which I knew nothing about. So I picked up the memo, walked back into Kissinger's office, and said, "Henry, what's this?" "This is another exception," he said.

I think Kissinger had a real impact on the president because he very quickly understood that the way you influenced Nixon was not to go in there and push him. If you pushed, Nixon would agree with you and then call up [his chief of staff H. R.] Haldeman and say, "I just promised Secretary so-and-so x, y, or z. He's not to have it and I never want to see him again." The way to deal with Nixon was to talk around your idea until he picked it up. And then, if he liked it, he would make it his idea. Then you could agree with it. And if he got it slightly wrong, you'd sort of talk around until he figured out the right version of it.

Something I persuaded Kissinger and then Nixon to do was to go to a population control strategy. There was no point in chasing the Viet Cong around the countryside, because they controlled the level of casualties. Encounters occurred because they attacked, not because we attacked. Therefore this crazy theory that we could reach a crossover point where we were killing more of them than they could replace was totally nuts because they could control the level of casualties. Therefore we should switch to a strategy of protecting the villages. We had maps showing that about eighty-five percent of the people lived in about fifteen percent of the area, so they were easily protectable.

Nixon and Kissinger believed that they could take all our troops out as long as we continued military assistance to the South Vietnamese and there was a credible threat that we would resume the bombing if North Vietnam launched an offensive. Kissinger still believes that it was only the decision of Congress to cut off military aid and prohibit the resumption of the bombing that enabled Hanoi to launch the final offensive and win the war. And but for Watergate, I think it is clear that Nixon would have been strong enough to veto legislation cutting off the bombing and that he would have done so. And I think he also would have been strong enough to get at least some military aid for South Vietnam. It is possible that, had we renewed the bombing in 1975, there might have been another [antiwar] eruption in the United States forcing them to stop it, but the Kissinger-Nixon view was that the opposition to the war was fueled by the draft and that once you took the draft away and once you took the casualties away, you could have resumed the bombing. The question that's unresolved is, would the South have collapsed even with massive U.S. bombing and continued massive U.S. military aid in the absence of U.S. ground forces?

I always thought the antiwar movement was totally irresponsible because of the assumption a lot of people had that you could negotiate this magic thing called a neutral, democratic, independent South Vietnam. I didn't think there was such a thing. The North believed that Vietnam was one country and they were going to fight until they got it. And they had a totalitarian government. They weren't interested in democracy. So you had to just say that the U.S. is powerful enough to survive in a world in which not only China and North Vietnam are Communist, but also this one more tiny sliver of the Asian mainland.

"I had no idea I was being wiretapped. Kissinger says now that he warned me I was being watched and I should have understood that I was being wiretapped." For twenty years Halperin pressed a damage suit against Kissinger and Attorney General John Mitchell arguing that the wiretaps were placed without a warrant and therefore violated federal law. "It went on forever and ever. It went up to the Supreme Court once—they split four-four, and it went back down. Finally we negotiated a settlement with Kissinger and I got a written apology so we dismissed the suit."

JUDITH COBURN

"Vietnamization wasn't working any better than Americanization."

She reported on the wars in Vietnam and Cambodia for the Village Voice, Pacifica Radio, *and the* Far Eastern Economic Review. *In 1979, she was one of the first Western journalists to visit Cambodia after the Khmer Rouge massacred more than a million of their own people.*

We talk in her small Berkeley home on a sunny California day with a cool breeze blowing through the window.

One of my father's closest friends was Clark Clifford, who became secretary of defense in 1968 during Lyndon Johnson's last year in the White House. For many years my family went to the Clifford's house in the Washington, D.C., suburbs for Thanksgiving. This one Thanksgiving, in 1967, Clifford also invited Stuart Symington, the senator from Missouri. Symington had a big role in the war because he was the only senator on both the Arms Services and Foreign Relations Committees. And he had just come back from a fact-finding trip to Vietnam.

So we're all at Thanksgiving dinner in this beautiful house. Black servants, silver trays, all the amenities. When dinner was over, Symington, Clifford, and my father moved down to one end of the table and started smoking their cigars and drinking their brandy. The women and children got up to leave, but I stayed at the other end pretending I wasn't there—like, don't mind me, I'm just twenty-three and a girl. Pretty soon Clifford says, "Well, Stu, tell us what you really saw over there."

He said, "Well, you know, it's the usual dog-and-pony show. I went to MACV and they said we're winning the war and so on. I saw this person and that person, but I'll tell you the one thing that made a deep impression on me. I went up to Danang and they gave me another dog-and-pony show but I know this fellow up there—a bird colonel—and he's got men out there in the field. So I went to see him late one night and we had a couple of drinks. I said, 'So, what's really going on out there, Colonel?' You know what this guy said to me? He says, 'Well, Senator, I'll tell you, mainly I have the feeling that one day soon if I lead my men into battle I might turn around and they won't be there.' "

I could see how much that shook these guys. You have to remember that they were World War II people. My father had been the military governor of Saipan and Clifford had been Truman's naval aide. For these guys, the questioning of American policy in Vietnam was a completely foreign experience.

When I got to Vietnam in 1970, I was reminded of Symington's story about the colonel's fear of mutiny, because by then some troops really were openly refusing to carry out orders. Tet '68 had broken the morale of the American war effort. Peace talks were going on, and nobody wanted to be the last guy to die in Vietnam. They'd drop a group of guys into the jungle and they'd just sit there for a couple of days calling in fake coordinates, smoke a little weed, and wait to get picked up. Of course there were other missions where people were greatly heroic, but it was pretty obvious that the military was gradually losing control of its own men.

In 1971, there were dozens of guys in the Americal Division at Chu Lai who were completely antiwar and they planned an antiwar demonstration for the Fourth of July. They put up posters announcing an "Independence Day Peace Rally" and calling for "an immediate and total American troop withdrawal." The MPs would no sooner tear them down than new ones would reappear. The division commander made every man sign some kind of pledge that he would not participate in the rally. But that was really unenforceable because there was a USO party already planned at the beach and so when July Fourth rolled around something like fifteen hundred guys showed up. They didn't want to provoke a crackdown, so nobody carried any antiwar banners or started a march, but I interviewed a lot of guys and it was hard to find anyone on that beach who did not favor immediate withdrawal. It looked like a "be-in" at Golden Gate Park. Guys were wearing peace symbols and beads and smoking pot. All the military authorities did was take a few pictures. After all, what were they going to do, bust them all? When I hear people say we could have won the war, I always think: where were you going to get the soldiers?

Then there was the famous Henry Rollins case. Rollins was stationed at Long Binh, this huge American supply base right outside Saigon. It was the biggest base in Vietnam, something like twenty thousand guys. Long Binh was also the site of the most famous stockade in Vietnam—Long Binh Jail—which everybody called "LBJ." Basically black guys ran the base—all these enlisted black guys. By 1970, they had pretty much taken over. And Spec 4 Henry Rollins, at twenty-four, was one of the main leaders. He controlled something like fifteen Quonset huts with thousands of dollars of stereo equipment and black panther posters all over the walls. It was like a liberated zone.

The military had pretty much given up on policing regulations regarding hair and uniforms and most of the black guys, like Rollins, were sporting big Afros which exploded out beneath their hats. One day Rollins was accosted by a white, southern sergeant major who said, "Soldier, where's your hat?" Rollins took one look at him and knocked him down. So he got court-martialed and it looked like he was going to do a lot of time. But there was a group of activist civilian lawyers in Saigon who offered free legal services to GIs and Rollins got one of them, Joe Remcho, to represent him. Well somehow Remcho, who went to Harvard Law School, convinced the commander of LBJ to let Rollins be tried by a jury of his peers. Ordinarily court-martial panels are made up entirely of officers. This may have been the first time in American military history that a GI was tried by his peers. So I walk into this court-martial hearing and I look over at the panel and it's all these black dudes with Afros which, at Long Binh at that time, was truly a jury of peers. So the white sergeant major gets on the stand and says, "I told Rollins that he was out of uniform and he should have his hat on. He knocked me down and that's an outrage to the military system of discipline." So then Henry got on the stand and said, "Well, he's a racist motherfucker and I popped him one." The verdict? Innocent!

The corruption and war profiteering were just incredible. There were countless scams. I knew one guy who ran a string of hookers connected to a USO show. It was a Vietnamese theatrical road show and the hookers were also the entertainers. By the early seventies there wasn't anything you couldn't buy. If you had enough money and some good contacts you probably could have bought an F-4 Phantom jet! But mostly it was just layers and layers of low-level corruption. For example, we used to eat at a restaurant in Saigon where all they served were T-bone steaks that were somehow ripped off from the officers' messes on navy ships.

The early seventies was also the period of "Vietnamization," when American troops were being withdrawn and the South Vietnamese Army was supposedly doing a larger and larger share of the fighting. You hear some American vets say that all the South Vietnamese troops were cowards and all the officers were corrupt. I don't subscribe to that. There were some very competent South Vietnamese officers and some serious fighting units. But for the most part it is true that the Vietnamese Army was a paper tiger. They were not loyal to the government—which they knew was corrupt and installed by the U.S.—and most ARVN grunts were there simply because they got drafted and would go to prison if they didn't fight. Out in the countryside you'd see the police arrive and round up every male between the ages of fifteen and forty and off they'd go in trucks to the army.

When the South Vietnamese army invaded Laos in 1971 on operation Lam Son 719 it was a debacle. The North Vietnamese routed them. The ARVN abandoned something like a hundred armored personnel carriers and were clinging to the skids of helicopters to get out of there. It was pretty clear that Vietnamization wasn't working any better than Americanization.

On the night before the invasion I was with a unit of South Vietnamese soldiers on the Vietnam-Laos border along with the photographer Larry Burrows and the reporters John Saar from *Life* and David Burnett from *Time*. We were all standing there watching this gorgeous sunset at that magic moment before it goes dark. Suddenly, this American jet came diving toward us and bombed the shit out of our position with cluster bombs. The pilot must have thought we were the bad guys on the Ho Chi Minh Trail just across the border. We all would have been dead if there hadn't been a gully right next to us. We just dove right in. By the time we looked out, it was pitch black.

I'll never forget Larry Burrows. His head went up first and he said, "Come on. There are people up there who are hurt." Once he got up, the rest of us did. Larry runs up this hill and—ever the photographer—he's taking pictures as he runs. But the minute we got to the top where all the wounded were, he said, "Let's get these guys down to someplace where we can get a chopper." There were bodies everywhere. Maybe a dozen people were killed and fifty or sixty wounded. So we started taking the bodies down the hill. You'd try to pick up some of these people and their bodies just fell apart.

A few days later, there were hordes of journalists jockeying to get on choppers into Laos. It was very hard to get on these choppers. I'd been waiting for three days. Finally, I got into a chopper and it was totally loaded with people. At the last moment, just before it was going to take off, Larry Burrows shows up and says, "Can't you take one more?"

The chopper pilot said no. So the other journalists and photographers rose up as one and told me to get off the chopper. They didn't say why, but it was obvious. I was, after all, only writing for the *Village Voice* and I was a girl and the great Larry Burrows was there. Of course, I thought he was great too, so I got off. The helicopter flew into Laos and crashed. They all died. It was so shocking I can't even remember now who else was on that chopper.

A year later I got kicked out of Vietnam. During the Easter Offensive of 1972, I went up to Quang Tri Province. The North Vietnamese were taking over the whole province and in Saigon the daily press briefings said that the Communist troops had dug in on either side of Route 1 and were killing civilian refugees who were moving south. There were thousands of people on the road.

I got on a motorbike with a Vietnamese journalist and we started up Route 1. We discovered that the Communists were, in fact, doing some shooting into the mass of refugees. South Vietnamese soldiers were deserting, shedding their uniforms, and mixing into the refugee crowds for protection. Every time these little pockets of North Vietnamese soldiers thought they saw South Vietnamese soldiers they would shoot. But, as it turned out, most of the civilians were being killed by artillery fire from American navy ships offshore. They had Route 1 zeroed in and fired barrage after barrage. They may have been hoping to hit North Vietnamese Army units but the civilian carnage was just incredible.

So I went back to Hue and filed a bunch of radio reports for *Pacifica* and a piece for the *Village Voice*. I said that MACV in Saigon was completely misrepresenting the situation and I described the American shelling. It was very rare in a refugee situation to see people abandon their children but in this case the artillery was killing so many people and everyone was so panicked I saw lots of abandoned toddlers as people fled down the road.

That went on for a couple weeks and then I went to Hong Kong to get my visa renewed. Many journalists in Vietnam only had thirty-day visas. So you had to leave every month and go to some other country to get your visa renewed and come back. I had gotten about twenty of them renewed in Hong Kong. It was routine—you just drop off the application and pick it up three days later. But this time, when I went back they didn't have my visa. I said "Why not?" They said, "We don't know." So that was it. I never could get back into Vietnam. I tried many, many times. I tried from Thailand, Vientiane, and Singapore. It was obvious that Saigon or American officials had not liked my reports and decided to expel me. Until 1972, very few journalists were thrown out by South Vietnam because the Americans told them it would be bad public relations and possibly hurt congressional funding. But by 1972, things were so rocky with Congress threatening to cut off funds for the war that the Saigon government no longer cared much about offending Congress and a number or journalists were kicked out or refused entry.

In December of 1979, I returned to Vietnam for the first time since '72. I had not been able to get in as a journalist so I went with a group of women antiwar activists. We were given an audience with Foreign Minister Nguyen Cao Thach and he asked if there was anything he could do for us. I knew this was just a courtesy, but I said, "Well, there is one thing. We should go to Cambodia. People should see what happened there." Surprisingly enough, he got us three-day visas to Cambodia and we were the first Americans to go in after Vietnam had overthrown the Khmer Rouge.

I spent the whole three days trying to get my visa extended and finally succeeded. So I found a Cambodian woman to be my guide and translator and we spent the next six weeks driving around the country. We drove from village to village and we never saw another car or truck the entire time. The Khmer Rouge had dug deep trenches in the road everywhere to stop the Vietnamese tanks. It took hours to go a few miles. Everyplace we went people would run out on the road when they saw our car. Nobody had seen a Westerner in years. People would stop us and say things like, "Have you seen my sister?" or, "If you see my sister, please give her this note." Of course you're thinking, "That's ridiculous, we'll never see your sister—there are millions of people in Cambodia and she's probably dead." But you couldn't say that. So we took all these notes from people. We had bushels of them.

When we arrived in a village everyone came rushing out. There would be these huge welcomes and almost as soon as we got out of the car they would take us to the mass grave where their friends and family who had been slaughtered by the Khmer Rouge were buried. Everybody had to tell their story. I think they saw me as the person from the outside who was going to tell the world what they had suffered. People said, "Five people in my family died." And then they gave you their names. It was very important to them that I took notes. I had nothing else to offer them. I have whole notebooks with just these lists of names. We'd go from village to village looking at mass graves. Then we'd stand around and cry. Then they'd scrape up the entire food stock of the village—a few handfuls of rice or roots—and try to feed us. No one had any dishes. At one place they made a big ceremony of bringing us some coconut milk to drink and it became clear that they were serving us with the only glass left in the whole village.

I'm telling you we'd go to village after village, day after day, and every one had a mass grave. I just remember being like a zombie the whole time. I was often desperate to escape, to go home, but I didn't want them to think I didn't care about them. So I felt like I had to put on a performance. My interpreter and I would lie in the fields at night and just cry until we fell asleep.

At one point she confessed to me that one of the reasons she wanted to go on this car trip was to get to Pailin. It was the Cambodian town closest to Thailand and she'd heard that they actually had colorful sarongs for sale that had been smuggled across the border. Under the Khmer Rouge people could only wear black clothing. Finally we got to Pailin and sure enough there were all these gorgeous, brightly colored sarongs. My interpreter went into a complete frenzy. We loaded up the back of our destroyed car with piles of sarongs. I gave her every bit of money I had left. It was bizarre but it pulled us out of some kind of psychological hole. On the way back we still stopped at every village and saw every mass grave, but in between I would think about her trying on all those sarongs and giving them to her friends. I thought about how beautiful Cambodia is and started to fantasize that none of the killing had ever happened.

"WE REALLY BELIEVED . . ."

BEVERLY GOLOGORSKY

"God forbid my boss finds out I'm here."

Her political activism was all-consuming. "The movement was so profound, and so intense, and so twenty-five-hours-a-day you didn't have time to analyze your emotions. For nine years I did not allow myself to have a child because I wouldn't have time. I mean I never slept. In 1973, the war was coming to an end so I could finally have a child."

She gave her daughter the middle name "Binh," in honor of Madame Nguyen Thi Binh, the wartime foreign minister for Vietnam's National Liberation Front.

"We really believed we were going to change everything."

I came out of a different background than many people in the movement. I was born and brought up in the South Bronx—very poor. My father cut leather in a factory for many years. When the kids were a little older, they bought a pretty horrible little candy store and worked there fifteen hours a day. We never had books in the house. When I was eight or nine I would sneak into the adult section of the library and grab whatever books I could. I was just starving. I quit high school because I was bored out of my mind and they were tracking me into stenography.

In 1964, I was working as a typist at a nursing magazine. One of the young women there asked me to go to lunch. We had a bag lunch in Central Park. She was starting a magazine with a bunch of people and they needed someone to do office work. She asked me how I felt about the war and I said, "I don't like the war at all." She said, "Well, why don't you come over to the office tonight and type some subscription cards?"

So I went to the office and there were Carol Brightman, Straughton Lynd, Tom Hayden, Carol Cina, and a couple of other people. The magazine was called *Viet Report* and they were just getting out the second issue. All these people were talking about how they were going to stop the war. They had no doubt. A lot of them were enabled by their backgrounds to believe that they could change the world. It was amazing. Their optimism, their assurance, their sense of entitlement—I was just charmed. I fell in love. Here were people who felt they had the power to do right. I hated injustice and so it was such a great feeling to be in the room with those kinds of sentiments. And they weren't waffling.

At times, though, my background would clash with other activists. For example, we organized a huge demonstration around the Pentagon. Thousands of people were coming in buses from all over the place and we had to get houses for people to sleep in. I was in one house with maybe twenty people. There were three beds and the rest was floor space. So all of them wanted the floor. I said, "Why? I would love a bed." And they said, "That's too bourgeois." And I said, "Hey, wait a second. We're in this so that everybody has a bed. That's what we're about." Or I'd be in jail with a bunch of people and I'd say, "I've got to get out. I want to go home." And they were happy to stay for a few days. They could afford to stay in jail, but I thought, "God forbid my boss finds out I'm here."

I never told anybody the truth about my background because I was ashamed of it. And since I was a leader in Students for a Democratic Society, most people in the movement assumed I, too, was from the middle class. I was part of the Columbia strike because I lived in the neighborhood, so they assumed I was a student there. I never corrected anybody. I actually liked it. It was a great feeling. I once told some guy who was very well known in the movement that I had not gone to university. And he said to me, "Come off it."

In 1969, some of us opened a coffee shop outside of Fort Dix, an army base in New Jersey. The idea was to organize the soldiers who were being trained for Vietnam. It was an uphill battle, but we did get guys who came in. Most of them had never really gotten any information that challenged Washington's view of the war. I especially remember this one guy from Nebraska. He was so tall he had to duck when he walked through the door. He'd only been outside the base a few times. I poured him a mug of coffee and we went over to a small table to talk. He was very shy and kept looking around at my friends who were behind the counter laughing at something they were reading. I asked nonstop questions about his home and family. After a while I asked if he was afraid of the war. He said he was and that he didn't look forward to what they said he would have to do there. He didn't elaborate. I wanted to protect him. I wanted to keep him hidden in the back room. He never came to the coffeehouse again and I have no idea whether he made it back from Vietnam.

That same year a bunch of us women walked out of Students for a Democratic Society and had an all-women's conference. We remained very antiwar and antiracism, but we were adding antisexism to our vernacular. We wanted to organize around all three. We started something called the Madame Binh Brigade. We decided that CBS News was not telling the truth about the war so we planned a sit-in at the news station. Two women managed to get job interviews for the day of the sit-in so they could open locked doors for us.

There were about twenty-five of us. We all dressed up so nobody would guess we were demonstrators. We wandered around the building until the right time. As soon as the door was opened we just smashed right into the newsroom and sat down. We wouldn't leave until we got what we wanted. We had written something about Madame Binh and what was happening with the peace talks and we wanted them to read this thing on the radio. And they did. It was a wonderful action.

Out of that we organized the Women's Union. We wanted something that would live beyond the war. One of our projects was to get child care in New York. Taxes went to the Pentagon and the war and we wanted spending for children. So one morning we had hundreds of women bring child care into the streets of Columbus Avenue on the Upper West Side. We barricaded the street and stopped traffic. We actually had child care in the street and we said we would have child care in the street every single day unless the city gave us child care in a storefront. And they did. We set up five or six child-care centers that the city helped to subsidize. And we still have them.

I don't think we ever lost hope or determination. But because the war was around for so many years the frustration was high and we ran out of what to do next. I mean first you have a picnic type of peace demonstration in the park, then you take it to Washington, or you have five demonstrations in five key cities. But that's not working. They're not paying attention. They don't care if you have a peaceful demonstration. It doesn't take any toll on the establishment. They can still pursue the war. There's no price they have to pay. They don't care if we don't go to school. They don't care if we're out of our jobs and running around Washington or staying up all night. They don't care.

I mean the state seemed to do whatever it wanted with impunity. It would decide, "Oh, well, we'll bomb Cambodia today," or, "Oh, we'll send people into Laos." We couldn't stop them. And there didn't seem to be anyone who said, "If you do that, then you're going to have to worry about going into your office." It seemed the war would just go on and on if the state was not made to pay a toll for what it was doing. That was the impulse that drove some people toward violence and the underground.

And the state had a lot to do with pushing people toward militancy. I have a girlfriend who was beaten by the cops at a demonstration. She was more stunned than hurt. "How could they do this to me?" You know, like "I'm this privileged white girl. My father runs a hospital." When you were gassed and hit you suddenly realized that whatever privilege you might have was not going to protect you.

I had never seen such hatred on faces as I saw on the police in Chicago. Also in New York. They really hated us. I mean they hated us in a way that was beyond politics. Many of them were our age. We had put them in a position of being the state and they hated us for that. And they hated us because if they came over to our side of the barricade their lives would be over—they would lose their jobs, perhaps lose their place in the community. They had so much to lose.

I have two friends who were so severely beaten in New York at an anti-Nixon demonstration that they had several operations. They were taken by the police and we couldn't find them for nearly three days. The cops wanted one of them to say, "Bobby Seale [a leader of the Black Panthers] is a fuck-face." And he wouldn't say it. They beat the shit out of him. He said that if he said what they wanted, something in him would have broken down.

On April 10, 1971, we had a Women's March Against the Pentagon. It was a great thrill to see those buses arrive from across the country. At one point I nearly fainted with happiness at the thousands and thousands who turned out. We had worked for five months organizing the demonstration, but we really didn't know what to expect. In those days it was harder for women to disentangle themselves from their lives and come to Washington. Many had never left home to go to an all-women's function. And these women weren't primarily students. Many were leaving behind husbands, and jobs, and children. There was a great mixture of ages and classes. We really felt our Cheerios. Many of us knew what it felt like to be *part* of a movement, but that march was the first time I truly felt how strong women together might be, and how much strength we could give each other—the kind of strength we couldn't give to each other when men were in the same room. And that made us feel not only strong but free, and at the center of a movement that would go on way beyond that day and beyond the war. It was one of the highest moments in my entire life.

Our march got some coverage, but the media really got reinterested in the antiwar movement because of the Vietnam veterans who came to Washington a month later in May. Their presence was a gift to the antiwar movement. These were young men who had been there, seen it all, and now wanted to do something to help end the war and repudiate their own participation in it.

There they were for the world to see—a long, long line of guys in army jackets and other military apparel snaking past the Capitol, throwing away their

Purple Hearts and other medals they'd received. Many of them stood before a microphone and made brief statements about why they hated the war so much they could no longer bear to keep what the military had awarded them.

I can remember standing there sobbing as the vets were throwing their medals into this trash bin at the Capitol in Washington. I mean sobbing. We were watching this heroic act by these guys and I could cry thinking of it now. Their faces were very powerful. Most people in a lifetime don't have a chance to begin again and that was what we felt was happening. They threw away those damn things and it was like opening a door to a new life.

I remember just one face in particular. He was trying not to cry. That's the only way I could interpret it. But it got harder and harder and he couldn't stop himself. Having thrown the medals away he started to walk off and collapsed on somebody's shoulder. The hardness went out of him. Everything just went soft. And this guy was waiting with his arms out and just put his arms around him and collected him. We cheered and we cried. We cheered and we cried.

She doesn't want "closure" on the Vietnam War. It might be important for people who fought in the war or who lost loved ones, "but there shouldn't be closure for the country, because if there's closure, there's just a chance it could happen again. I think 'remember Vietnam' is a good thing." Not accepting closure for herself, she wrote a novel about the wives and girlfriends of Vietnam veterans called The Things We Do to Make It Home *(1999). "My hatred of that war and the intensity of the movement were so profound it took me twenty years to mull it over and refract it into a novel."*

NGUYEN NGOC BICH

"Why should my son die for your country?"

In the late 1960s and early '70s, the peak years of campus protest, he visited dozens of American colleges to speak in defense of the South Vietnamese government and its U.S.-backed war against Communism. He often confronted audiences of antiwar students, some of them loud and hostile. An unenviable task, one might think, but for him the memories elicit whimsy, thoughtfulness, and pride. "I must have done a pretty good job because in 1973 I picked up an issue of Playboy *and the lead article referred to this gutsy little South Vietnamese diplomat who spoke at the University of Connecticut in spite of a bomb threat."*

He was born in Hanoi in 1937, the ninth of ten children. In 1946, several older brothers were imprisoned by the Viet Minh for their activities with the Vietnamese

Nationalist Party, a political rival. One of the brothers moved south to escape further Communist reprisals and Bich soon joined him.

In 1956, he attended Princeton University and went on to graduate work in Asian history and literature first at Columbia and then at Kyoto University in Japan. From 1967 to 1971, he was the director of information at the South Vietnamese embassy in Washington, D.C.

I was at Columbia University when the first antiwar sit-ins took place in 1965 and rather dumbly my wife and I thought people were against the war just because they were afraid to go into the army or because they were isolationists who didn't want to help a country like Vietnam. We thought the policy makers would have the final say and the protests wouldn't last. To our amazement we saw them spread from campus to campus.

At first, I spoke at universities thinking America was our ally and was surprised by all the hostile questions. Obviously I got a few bruises. A lot of the questioners were very critical of South Vietnam. The misinformation was so bad that at one point there was an idea floating around that South Vietnam had two hundred thousand war orphans, two hundred thousand prostitutes, two hundred thousand paraplegics, two hundred thousand political prisoners, two hundred thousand everything! One time when they threw those figures at me I said, "Look, use your brain. Don't you think this two hundred thousand figure is kind of funny? Are we so standardized that even the victims of war all have the same number? It tells you something is not quite right." They said, "But we saw it in *The New York Times.*" I said, "What tells you *The New York Times* gives you the right figures?"

In 1969, I went to give a speech at Purdue University in Lafayette, Indiana. At that time there was a whole rash of kidnappings of American diplomats and ambassadors in Latin America. When I arrived the police said, "We've had some calls that they might try to kidnap you. Do you want to cancel?" I said, "Well, since I'm here, why don't I go talk." The first two rows had about sixty kids all dressed like flower children of the sixties and full of revolutionary emblems. I was the only speaker. They just sat there staring at me. I said, "Ladies and gentlemen," and immediately the students stood up, pulled out their NLF flags, and chanted, "HO HO HO CHI MINH, THE NLF IS GOING TO WIN!" After a while they stopped, but as soon as I tried to open my mouth the whole thing started up again. It went on for about five minutes so finally I said to myself, I'm not going to be able to get rid of this group unless I do something really dramatic. There was a table in front of me so I just climbed up, lay down, and made believe I had gone to sleep. They must have thought, this is a strange animal here.

In the meantime, there were some old women in the back knitting. They started waving their knitting needles, especially at the girls, and yelling, "LET HIM TALK, LET HIM TALK." So then the kids started chanting, "TALK, TALK, TALK." I just kept snoring away. "TALK, TALK, TALK." I kept snoring away. The tension in the room was palpable. Only the first rows were antiwar people. The rest were local citizens. Finally the students didn't know what to do so they decided to troop out. I stood up and said, "I'm really sorry for what happened. I didn't know I had to teach these people manners." Then I gave my talk. The protesters had left, but there were still some very hostile questions. One man in the back said, "Well, how come South Vietnam cheated and didn't carry out the elections they were supposed to have in July 1956?"

I said, "Sir, where did you get your information?" He said, "It's right in George Kahin's *The United States in Vietnam*." I said, "May I ask for a volunteer?" A few hands went up. "Could one of you please go get me that book in the library?" So I took a few more questions until someone came back with the book. I said, please turn to such and such a page and read it for everybody. It says that the final declaration at Geneva calling for nationwide elections in 1956 was never signed. There was only an oral agreement. Absolutely nobody signed. Not even the North Vietnamese, the Russians, or the Chinese. Actually, it was supposed to be signed by most countries, with the exception of South Vietnam and the United States, but at the last minute King Sihanouk raised a big ado about the arrangement for Cambodia. People were so tired and anxious to get an agreement they said, okay, let's not worry about signatures. So I tried to demonstrate my arguments in a very rational manner.

Of course, most Vietnamese up to this day believe in one Vietnam, even after the Communist takeover, which was certainly a bitter disappointment to many of us. We also believed in one Vietnam, but the question is, how would reunification come about. There was every reason to believe that if we had an election with the Communists in 1956 they would not allow it to be free and fair.

At the end of that talk at Purdue, the antiwar group trooped back into the hall. I said to the leader, "You didn't succeed earlier, what do you want to do now?" He said, "I have this for you," and he pulled a grenade out of his pocket and threw it on the floor between us. I did some quick thinking. If this is real, he's going to get it as much as I do so there's no point running. It turned out to be tear gas. The police rushed in and the guy who did it got thrown out of school. Some of the other students rushed up to see if I was okay. Then one of them said, "Mr. Bich, can we talk to you?"

I said, "Sure. If you're game, join me at my hotel." A group came and we talked until three in the morning. Finally they left and some of them had tears in their eyes. One of them said, "You know, this is the first time I've had a real talk about the Vietnam War with anyone."

When I went to the South and the Midwest, people tended to be more supportive of the war. They generally accepted the idea that the United States had to go to war to support a country that was the victim of aggression. On the other hand, they could ask some very blunt questions. For example, in Nebraska one man stood up and said, "I hear what you're saying, but why should my son die for your country?" I really got choked up. I said, "Well, sir, of course I cannot presume to make policy for the United States. Only the president of the United States and Congress have the right to send American citizens to war. We are very grateful to the American people for their help, but we have no right to demand it. We only have the right to yell out for help when our country is being attacked." But I felt so bad. How can you not feel for someone like that? When I gave my answer I knew immediately that I did not satisfy him. It was almost a cop-out to put the responsibility on somebody else. In situations like that you feel very strongly that arguments are only so many words. It was not a hostile question, just a very basic concern.

I usually felt I had better answers to questions that were clearly antiwar rather than human questions that went beyond intellectual deliberations. In fact, anything that was quantifiable or where you could call on clauses and conditions was relatively easy to answer because you could prove your point, but that man's question hit me very hard.

My faith in the war was quite solid. On a personal level I didn't have much doubt about the merits of the war and the sacrifices it called for. I thought we had no choice. But that's answering from the point of view of a South Vietnamese who had a lot at stake. And, to be honest, I was trained to respond to antiwar arguments. But I also had arguments with the American side about how the war was being fought. During McNamara's time as secretary of defense there was the famous "body count." McNamara and some in the military believed that if you keep pounding on someone's head there will come a point when he just has to crack. They called it the "threshold of pain." They said, even if the Vietnamese can take more pain than the Americans, we can multiply the threshold of pain and eventually they'll quit. I thought that was pretty heartless.

It led me to write a series of articles explaining that the North Vietnamese had enough children and food to go on for a long, long time; that even at the current rate the U.S. was killing them, it would not offset their capacity to maintain themselves. So some of my American friends were not too happy with me. The American idea was to draw the Communist side into large battles so they could kill a lot of people. I thought those things were not only murderous but almost meaningless, because the enemy could still infiltrate the cities and do a lot of havoc and aim at the civilian population with terrorism. We should have countered with the kind of thing the marines tried with their civic action among the population. Instead of fighting the big battles and having lots of statistics I thought a lower intensity approach would probably work better.

The hardest questions that came up when I gave speeches were those having to do with My Lai and Lieutenant Calley because in some places, especially southern states, many people were very solidly behind Calley and I had to stand there and say, "Yes, war is murderous and barbaric. Nonetheless, there are rules of war and no one should tolerate the deliberate killing of civilians. The only thing Lieutenant Calley is entitled to is a fair trial, but if he's found to be guilty, he should be punished." A lot of people just thought, America right or wrong.

I'd say that draft dodgers played a very minor role in the antiwar movement. There was a general feeling that there was something dishonorable about that. Many who were antiwar were misinformed about what was going on in Vietnam, but they were really very serious and had legitimate concerns as to why the U.S. should be involved. If you somehow managed to reason it out with them, they might not come over to your side, but at least they gave you some respect. Most people were antiwar by conviction. So despite all the dangers of those years, it was very moving to me to have people in the movement come to at least understand my position. And if you had the chance to talk with them you'd see they were still open-minded and willing to listen to a good argument. I believed in their good faith. That remains with me to this day.

In 1971, Bich returned to Saigon to found Mekong University. On April 19, 1975, less than two weeks before the end of the war, he was one of two men sent to Washington by President Nguyen Van Thieu in a last-ditch effort to gain additional American support. They walked the halls of Congress. "It was totally hopeless. Most doors were closed on us. The few doors that were opened revealed people with blank stares."

He returned to Vietnam on April 26. "I told a few intimate friends about the situation so they could make up their minds quickly and flee. And my wife gathered twenty-six people who came out with us. First we went down to an island in the Gulf of Siam. From there we went to sea and were picked up by a ship called the American Challenger. *We were told the capacity was one thousand and eighty people. Eventually seven thousand people packed that boat. It was night and you had this big American steel ship and all these tiny, tiny little fishing boats coming out to it with lanterns by the hundreds. Cecil B. DeMille would have made a wonderful picture of that. Ropes were handed down and women who were nine months pregnant had to climb up. Some people fell and a few people actually died. Amid the tragedy there were some very funny scenes. A rather stocky man climbed up and yelled, 'I still have something down there.' An American marine said, 'What is it?' thinking it was a baby. He said, 'My dentist chair.'*

" 'What do you need a dentist chair for?'

" 'How can I practice when I go abroad?' Well, now he's practicing in Santa Ana, California, and we became very good friends."

Today Bich is the director of the Vietnamese Service of Radio Free Asia.

CHALMERS JOHNSON

"The campus was turning into a celebration of Maoism."

As chairman of the Center for Chinese Studies at the University of California, Berkeley, from 1967 to 1972 he supported the American war in Vietnam. In those same years he was a consultant to the CIA's Office of National Estimates and was given the government's highest security clearances. "I remember having wonderful evenings at [the CIA's] Camp Perry on the York River in Virginia. You wanted to be goddamn careful not to walk off the paths because the place was thoroughly mined. Every once in a while we'd have venison with our martinis and we knew what had happened."

In the 1990s, however, he changed his mind about the Vietnam War. As we sit down to dinner with his wife in their home near San Diego, he says, somewhat whimsically, "You know, Sheila, maybe we're being too defensive. After all, we were on the wrong side."

My original position on Vietnam was that it was obviously a civil war and we shouldn't get involved. But having gotten involved, I increasingly took the view that we couldn't afford to lose. The menace of the Soviet Union was genuine and something needed to be done to counter it. I believed Vietnam was a legitimate front in the Cold War and accepted the proposition that if the Cold War was global, then we had to confront the Soviet Union and the forces of international Communism wherever we met them. Moreover, the idea that so-called people's wars, or wars of national liberation, were exportable was in the wind and, like many people at that time, I was very concerned about it.

I also had a strong trust in government and was mesmerized by the aura of Washington coming out of the Kennedy years. I was unbelievably excited by John Kennedy. I recall thinking what a genius McNamara must be simply because Kennedy had appointed him. Now it seems like such a sham as you discover what lying went on in the highest reaches of our government, but at the time I think the propaganda worked. Maybe I was a gullible citizen. I suppose I was also motivated by careerism. I was in my thirties, quite successful, and didn't have the nerve, or didn't think it was worth it, to challenge the whole apparatus.

I still believe the antiwar movement was naive and ill-informed. I just didn't think these kids knew anything about Soviet, Chinese, and Vietnamese Communism. I used to argue that what's wrong with them is that we've instilled in them the single most corrosive of all emotions, namely guilt. They knew that so long as they were in a university they were exempt from serving in the armed forces and that much of their acting out was a reaction to that guilt.

My irritation at the antiwar movement also had an element of class in it. I came from a relatively poor background in Buckeye, Arizona, and my mother insisted on moving the family to California so I could go to the University of California. I enrolled in the fall of 1949 when tuition was thirty-nine dollars a semester and I lived at home. I was enormously proud of Berkeley. I had come as Joe Freshman and ended up chairman of my department. I thought the students were crazy to be attacking the university. This was sacred territory from which you might examine the social ills of race relations and things of this sort, so it got on my nerves when students trashed the place. I had the feeling that they had no loyalty to the university and that they were self-indulgent brats who were sort of acting out at a YMCA camp. My attitude was that these were rich kids irritated at the way life actually works and they don't know what they're talking about in terms of the war. I was much more sympathetic to the black protest and worked closely with black students in the courses I taught.

My wife and I were supporters of Lyndon Johnson because of the war on poverty and the civil rights acts. On March 31, 1968, we were listening to Johnson's speech when he said he wasn't going to run again for president. We were really shocked and livid. We said, "The sons of bitches got him." Politically, I was then inclined to be sympathetic to Nixon.

I took up Vietnam as a puzzle. How could we win once it was determined that we should? But for me Vietnam was a bit of a sideshow. In the Office of National Estimates we thought the most important event in the world was the Sino-Soviet dispute, which was built into the nature of the Chinese Revolution but came into the open only in the 1960s. I kept thinking that the Vietnamese couldn't win without a re-creation of Communist solidarity behind them and that wasn't happening. That was the hardest thing to explain. I mean if Russian bombers had appeared over Paris, the NATO alliance would have instantly united. But we put American bombers over Hanoi and it seemed to be driving the Chinese and Russians further apart. It didn't honestly make sense.

By the early seventies what was of much greater concern to me than the Vietnam War was the Cultural Revolution in China. It was an unmitigated disaster. They were eating each other alive. Perhaps thirty million lives were lost. One of the reasons I accepted the CIA offer was precisely because the campus was turning into a celebration of Maoism and I was convinced that the Chinese revolution had turned into a horror show. Mao and Che Guevara were tremendous symbols on campus. If you were a teacher in those days you'd walk into class and every student would look like Che. They were all dressed in little berets with little droopy mustaches and little droopy Vandykes.

I think I was also misled by the doctrine of counterinsurgency, which really began with the Kennedy administration. We were infatuated by it. It was a subject a lot of people were writing about and I was Berkeley's person on that subject. My Ph.D. dissertation was on Japanese pacification warfare in North China after 1937. I was working at the Japanese Defense Agency in 1961 and '62 just as the war was getting started in Vietnam. Retired Japanese military officers were more than willing to talk with a foreigner about Guadalcanal or Singapore, but they did not want to talk about China. One colonel said, "You must understand that we've been accused of war crimes, of behaving like beasts." Years later, after the Vietnam War began to crack wide open, he wrote me a letter saying, "Now maybe you understand that we were not beasts, we were just as stupid as you people are. We were caught up in a guerrilla insurrection in which the population was being used as a massive intelligence net with everyone mobilized. You can't tell a villager from a guerrilla. Mao said the relationship of the guerrilla to the people is like the fish to the water. We called our operations in North China 'draining the water'; you call yours 'free-fire zones.' We killed indiscriminately and committed war crimes, no question about it, but were we really so different from you?"

In retrospect, I should have supported the antiwar movement. I'd have to say I wasn't sensitive enough to the moral implications of the Vietnam War. I'm still not certain the antiwar protesters knew what they were talking about in terms of the war and I'm certain they were ill-informed about Communism. But they grasped something essential about the nature of America's imperial role in the world that I had failed to perceive. For all their naïveté and unruliness, the protesters were right and American policy was wrong. I wish I had stood with them.

STEVE SHERLOCK

"Steve Sherlock, bronze star with a V."

It's morning in Hanoi. A short, bald American is hunched over his bowl of pho, *the traditional Vietnamese breakfast soup. He stops to chat for a few minutes with a waiter, practicing the Vietnamese he's been studying for three hours every day. He grew up in Lafayette, Indiana, the son of a Ralston Purina maintenance worker. In 1968, he went to Vietnam as a lieutenant in the 101st Airborne. His growing objections to the war drew him to the antiwar movement in 1970. In 1991 he founded Aid to Southeast Asia, a nonprofit humanitarian organization that donates medical supplies and equipment to hospitals in Vietnam.*

When I joined the army in 1966 I was a super war supporter. I believed we were fighting Communists in Vietnam so we wouldn't have to fight them on the shores of the United States. I thought we were fighting the equivalent of the Nazis and that it was a noble cause similar to World War II except in a contained area.

I think my doubts started in April 1968, before going over to Vietnam. When Martin Luther King got killed, I was sent down to Washington, D.C., with the 82nd Airborne for riot control. We got on the trucks and you could see the city in flames across the river. We waited until morning to go in, set up a perimeter around a liquor store, and basically said, "Don't fuck with us." About three-quarters of my platoon were black or Hispanic and they'd all just come back from Vietnam. We had no trouble but it was clear that I was already in the middle of a kind of war. It just didn't feel right to be there and Vietnam was somehow connected to it.

By the time I actually went to Vietnam in October 1968, I was in a state of confused neutrality. Within a few months, without understanding the political details of the war, I had the sense that we didn't have any business being in Vietnam and that if it was wrong for us to be there, then it was wrong for us to be killing people there.

Around December some guy at Camp Eagle put a petition up that just said, "Fuck War," and I signed it. This guy from intelligence came down to interview me and was fucking outraged that an officer had "betrayed his duty" by signing an antiwar petition. He was livid. But the mood was still not that confrontational. I suggested they send me somewhere else so they gave me an infantry platoon with the 2nd of the 327th at a village called Nguoc Ngot. It means sweet water. It's about twenty kilometers north of the Hai Van pass [near Danang].

The first night the captain wanted me to set up an ambush at the end of the village. It was rainy and dark. One of my squad leaders heard something and fired on a house. As soon as he opened up all shit broke loose. There was actually an NVA platoon around the house and they all started firing back. We had this long firefight and finally most of the NVA withdrew. The captain was on the radio saying he wanted an accurate body count so we had to sweep the area and bring all the pieces in. This one guy had literally been decapitated by our fire, so we had to carry in his head with everything else. We had killed seven and had three prisoners. One of the dead was a woman. We found out later she was a schoolteacher from the next village who was probably a Viet Cong local guide.

The next morning the colonel and the assistant division commander flew down and they had this medal ceremony. Two guys got silver stars and I got a bronze star. This other lieutenant said to me, "Man, you're really lucky. I walked the bush for a month and never had one contact. You got it on the first day in the unit."

A few weeks later the captain wanted to go with me on a patrol. He was a real rah-rah jerk. We got in a small fight and killed two or three people. We were looking at the bodies and this one guy had the usual stuff in his pockets, like a picture of his wife or girlfriend. But he also had a rosary on him. The captain said, "Oh my God, how can this guy be a Communist and a Catholic?" I said, "Who knows if he's a Communist or a Catholic? Or if he's both, so what?" I just didn't want to let it go so I added, "I hope the rest of them got away. I'd like it even better if they didn't run into us and we didn't have any more fights." He really went berserk. "Your job is to destroy the Communists." I said, "No, they're just people like us." He said, "They are not people. They're the enemy and you're the reason we're losing this war. You're a coward and a traitor."

A few days later I had just come in from a night ambush without any sleep and the colonel was waiting for me. He said, "I'll give you one chance to retract your statements about the Vietnamese." I said, "You mean that they're people?" He said, "Yes." I said, "I can't do that." There was no discussion. He just said, "You're relieved. Get in the jeep." I asked if I could say good-bye to the platoon and he said, "No. You can't have any more contact with them. You're a disgrace and a bad influence."

It wasn't an intellectual protest, just a gut feeling from what I was seeing and hearing. It seemed so ludicrous to claim that these Vietnamese weren't people. When I got back to Camp Eagle I had to write a response to being relieved of command. One of the charges was that I had taken evasive action. That simply wasn't true. I was willing to fight, I just always hoped we didn't have to. A sympathetic colonel finally offered me a position in civil affairs running the "Kit Carson" scout program.*

When I went back to Purdue at the beginning of 1970 I ran into an ex-marine and we talked about opening a chapter of Vietnam Veterans Against the War [VVAW]. But the place was so right wing we decided it would be better to call it Veterans for Peace. I think we had a maximum membership of seven. Because the antiwar movement at Purdue was very small I found it easy to be involved. They weren't judgmental about my having been a combatant. For me it was a very good experience. People were supportive. They understood the value of veterans speaking against the war, that our having served in it gave us some credibility and moral authority.

In May of 1970, I was asked to come to an antiwar rally in Kokomo [Indiana]. I went alone on my motorcycle and when I got there the school was surrounded by this huge crowd of rednecks, some of them carrying ax handles. There were cars cruising the area with big signs that said things like, "Communists Get Off the Streets." Kokomo was a very old [Ku Klux] Klan stronghold. Only about forty of us were gathered on the lawn for the demonstration. At twenty-three, I was probably the oldest protester and these students were looking to me. I could see we were outnumbered about ten to one so I took the bullhorn and was going to tell them that we should probably cancel the meeting. Before I could get anything out this whole crush of people started rushing me and knocked me down. They were screaming things like, "What do you think about burning the flag?" Then one of the counterprotesters stepped in and said that as long as these people don't say anything and go on their way, there's no need for violence. So people started dispersing and I got on my motorcycle and rode out of town.

In 1971, I got a call from my old high school friend Jim Pechin, who had started a chapter of VVAW at Indiana State in Terre Haute. He said the VVAW was having a demonstration the following week in Washington, D.C. I wasn't sure I could afford to go. I was married with two kids and we were living on a very tight budget. But Pechin said the national VVAW could provide enough money to cover gas. So he sent me thirty bucks or something. The idea of a strictly veteran protest seemed like a good chance to get national attention and credibility for the peace perspective. Part of the plan was to turn in our Vietnam medals as a strong symbolic statement that they couldn't buy our silence with decorations. The purpose was to focus public attention on the fact that veterans who actually fought in Vietnam, and had been decorated for it, were

*Kit Carson scouts were Viet Cong defectors who served in American units primarily as guides, interpreters, and intelligence agents.

opposed to the war and that it wasn't unpatriotic to be fighting against a wrong and harmful policy.

I went with one other vet I didn't know very well and at first I wasn't really thinking about the demonstration emotionally. It just seemed like a good political tactic. But when we pulled into Washington and drove down to the Mall it was overwhelming. There was this huge encampment of vets. I was used to seeing a couple of token vets in a crowd at a peace demonstration, but here the whole Mall was full of hundreds and hundreds of veterans. They were setting up food lines, throwing up makeshift lean-tos, laying out sleeping bags, and building little fires. Most were wearing at least the tops of their old jungle fatigues with all the unit patches, insignia, name tags, and rank. Some were wearing their medals. A lot of guys had grown their hair, not outrageously long in most cases, but over their ears and down their necks. A lot of us had beards. It looked like a shaggy, ragtag, casual military.

There were police ringing the encampment all the time but it was pretty open during the day. It was primarily VVAW people but there were also girlfriends, groupies, politicians, and supporters. We mixed around and talked. Some conversations were very mundane, the kind veterans anywhere might have—where were you in Vietnam, and when, and did you know anybody in that unit.

But when it got dark they seemed to tighten the security and it became a kind of sealed circle of vets. It was a very eerie thing. Even though we were in the middle of a city it definitely felt like a military encampment. At night in Vietnam we never built fires, but this still had a very strong feeling of mixing the present and the past. There was an incredible camaraderie and exhilaration. We were all together again but this time it was a peace army. It really did seem like a noble cause.

That night before the medal turn-in was when it got very emotional. That's when we talked about trying to end the war and bring people home. Everybody I talked to felt this wasn't just another protest, because we were people who had already served with no danger of being drafted or being sent back to the war, who knew the war firsthand from experience, who had demonstrated our patriotism. And many had been wounded—there were guys with crutches and in wheelchairs.

I'd never worn my medal. I just kept it in a box. When I went to Washington I took it and the citation and put them in my pocket. Except in a few cases, I felt the medals were pretty random. In any firefight there were always things going on that could get someone a decoration. There were thousands of medals awarded for routine combat actions. Only a few guys dragged ten people out of a firefight. In my case, the bronze star with a V [for Valor] was sort of a generic award and the citation just said stuff like "moving among his men directing fire with disregard for his own safety." There was always a feeling that everybody was doing that.

I felt the war was entirely wrong at a political and moral level, and in that sense you could argue that all the symbols of it, including the medals, were meaningless. Some of the other veterans at the demonstration saw their medals as badges of dishonor, but that wasn't my feeling. For me, there was a certain pride in having been recognized with the medal for doing a good job. So I wouldn't say it felt good to throw it away. It was a mixed feeling. I felt the contradiction between doing your best and hating the war, between having the brotherhood of the unit in the field yet knowing that the war was wrong. The medal was like that. Some veterans never got beyond that contradiction. They may have felt the war wasn't right, but they knew that the people they were with were good and they couldn't reconcile that. Most of them didn't become huge war supporters but they couldn't deal with opposing the war either.

I didn't take my medal out until we lined up in front of the Capitol steps. Each veteran went up to the microphone, said their name, maybe their unit, what medals they had, and some said a few words about the war. But there was such a long procession that most of the time I was too far back to really hear what was being said. Then people threw their medals over this wire barricade that had been put up across the steps of the Capitol. I don't know why they bothered with the barricade. It wasn't as though we intended to storm the building.

It was a high-energy emotional thing. I remember being sort of overwhelmed and a little bit shy, not knowing what to do and feeling like, God, what do I say? I was still sort of unsophisticated. The crowds were very supportive. There were young people and parents of veterans and "gold star mothers" who had had kids killed in Vietnam. It was like being in a sea of emotion. A lot of people were crying.

When I finally got up there it was incredibly quick. I had wrapped my medal inside the paper citation and crumbled it into a ball. I think I just stepped up and said, "Steve Sherlock, bronze star with a V." Then I threw it over the barricade and stepped away.

WATERGATE

Richard Nixon's administration collapsed under the weight of "Watergate," a long train of criminal activities that finally forced the president to resign in August 1974 and led to the convictions of more than forty government officials. Though Watergate encompassed scores of illegal acts, many initiated in the first months of the Nixon presidency, our memory often reduces it to the Nixon White House's 1972 election-year schemes to sabotage Democratic Party opponents. That narrow view stems, in part, from the fact that Watergate derives its name from a single crime—the June 17, 1972, break-in at the Democratic National Committee headquarters located in Washington's Watergate office complex. Over the next two years investigators discovered that the burglary had been authorized by President Nixon's reelection committee, that the president himself had ordered hush money to be paid to the burglars, and that he used federal agencies to help cover up White House responsibility for the crime.

It has never been widely understood that Watergate had its origins not in the 1972 presidential campaign, but in the Vietnam War. From his first days in office, Nixon took extreme measures, including illegal ones, to attack those who opposed the war or might expose his secret plans to expand and prolong it. He and his aides compiled an "enemies list" of some two hundred politicians, journalists, celebrities, and activists, most of whom had been outspoken in their criticism of the Vietnam War. Nixon then used the FBI, CIA, IRS, and other government agencies to spy on, harass, and defame his "enemies." In May 1969, when an article appeared in *The New York Times* alleging that the United States had begun to bomb Cambodia without congressional approval or public awareness, Nixon authorized illegal wiretaps to be placed on the phones of government officials and journalists suspected of leaking information about the covert escalation and expansion of the war.

Two years later, in 1971, Daniel Ellsberg, a former Defense Department official, made public the Pentagon Papers, a top-secret collection of documents on the history of the war from its origins through the Johnson administration. National Security Adviser Henry Kissinger helped persuade Nixon that Ellsberg posed a dire threat to national security, not so much because he released materials that exposed evidence of war-related lies told by prior administrations, but because he might also reveal information about Nixon's secret war plans. Nixon ordered White House counsel John Ehrlichman to do "whatever has to be done" to prevent Ellsberg or anyone else from leaking government secrets. Ehrlichman then set up a Special Investigations Unit with a broad mandate to pursue people the administration deemed a threat to national security.

This unit of covert operatives, dubbed "the Plumbers," broke into Ellsberg's psychiatrist's office in search of documents that might be used against him. Many of the Plumbers were then hired by the Committee for the Reelection of the President (CREEP), headed by Attorney General John Mitchell. CREEP engaged in numerous operations, illegal as well as merely sordid, to discredit potential Democratic presidential candidates, focusing on those, like Senator Edmund Muskie, who they believed had the best chance to defeat Nixon in 1972. When the Democratic Party nominated Senator George McGovern, the most liberal of the candidates, CREEP celebrated the outcome. Even so, taking no chances with the whims of democracy, they launched additional operations to tarnish McGovern. In the fall of 1972, Watergate was still a minor story that did little to lower Nixon's political standing. Buoyed by his historic diplomatic breakthrough with China and news of progress in negotiations to bring an end to U.S. involvement in Vietnam, he defeated McGovern in a landslide.

Beginning in 1973, however, the Nixon administration found itself under ever more intense legal and congressional investigation. Gradually, one crime after another was exposed. With each new revelation, Nixon proclaimed his personal innocence. Clinging to power, he fired several of his indicted top aides, including Bob Haldeman, his chief of staff, and John Ehrlichman. When it was discovered that Nixon had tape-recorded many of his most private conversations, crucial evidence in establishing the president's guilt or innocence, he refused to turn the tapes over to Senate investigators. Ultimately the Supreme Court had to order the president to release all the subpoenaed tapes.

As Nixon's guilt became steadily more obvious, the House Judiciary Committee launched impeachment proceedings and in July 1974 it voted for three articles of impeachment. Although none of them were directly related to Nixon's conduct of the Vietnam War (the committee rejected an article accusing the president of violating Congress's war-making powers by bombing Cambodia), his insistence on prolonging the war without open debate and his efforts to silence dissent led to many of the abuses of power that finally destroyed his presidency.

DANIEL ELLSBERG

"We're eating our young."

In 1971, the White House regarded him as a defector and a traitor. Kissinger described him to Nixon as "the most dangerous man in America," a "hawk turned peacenik" who "must be stopped at all costs." Ellsberg, a former Defense Department official, had just released the Pentagon Papers, seven thousand pages of secret documents about the history of U.S. decision making in Vietnam from 1945 to 1968. A White House Special Investigations Unit known as "the Plumbers" was assigned the task of digging up whatever damning information they could find about him.

Ellsberg had indeed been a fervent cold warrior. After graduation from Harvard in the early 1950s, he joined the marines. One night, as a marine lieutenant on leave in Italy, he went to a restaurant and noticed John Wayne eating at another table. "I asked the waiter to send him a bottle of champagne." The star of Sands of Iwo Jima *later invited the young officer to join him. "That was not like meeting a celebrity, that was like meeting Moses. He recruited us all."*

In 1959, Ellsberg was hired by Rand, the California think thank, to study nuclear defense policy. Equipped with a brilliant analytical mind and great ambition, he quickly rose within the world of top-secret military planning and Pentagon consulting. In 1964, he was hired by the Department of Defense and began working almost entirely on Vietnam. Though he had doubts about the effectiveness of bombing and conventional military methods, he volunteered to go to Vietnam and worked there with counterinsurgency expert Edward Lansdale.

Returning from Vietnam in 1967, Ellsberg was part of the team that compiled the Pentagon Papers, a project initiated by Robert McNamara in his last year as secretary of defense. Ellsberg was one of the few people who bothered to read the entire study and it "stripped away all legitimate rationales for what we were doing" in Vietnam. Increasingly opposed to further American involvement in Vietnam, by 1969 he began to photocopy the massive set of classified documents. At first he tried to get antiwar congressmen to conduct hearings based on the papers. When none of them were willing, he leaked a copy to The New York Times, *which began to publish excerpts of it in June 1971.*

The Nixon administration issued injunctions to stop The New York Times *and then other newspapers from publishing the documents, but the Supreme Court ruled in favor of the press. Ellsberg was charged with theft, conspiracy, and violations of the Espionage Act. Eventually the presiding judge dismissed the case when evidence surfaced that the Nixon administration had illegally wiretapped Ellsberg and the Plumbers had broken into his psychiatrist's office.*

People wonder how such smart men could have been so wrong about what they thought they could achieve in Vietnam. How could they be so misguidedly optimistic? But the Pentagon Papers showed that American policy makers were often quite pessimistic and knew their policies were failing. They were being told that the prospects of success were very low. They weren't wild optimists or gamblers, but they went ahead anyway, prolonging and expanding the war, despite their pessimism. And they had to be secret about it because the public wouldn't have accepted it without much better prospects than our intelligence agencies were providing. This happened with four presidents. They were quite different in personality and party, but they all behaved very similarly.

Vietnam showed that American leaders were psychologically unwilling to negotiate a solution that would be called a defeat by some people, even if the American people could have lived with it very well. There is simply no evidence that the public would have voted against a president for getting out of Vietnam. I think they prolonged an unwinnable stalemate not just because they cared about getting reelected, but because they cared about what they were called. They were willing to send men and women to death to avoid being called losers. They would rather keep going, no matter how many people died, to save face. In Vietnam the crucial thing was, don't lose. Nixon's mother said to him, "You're not defeated until you say you're defeated." He got it.

Many of them felt terrible about sending men to die in what they saw as a hopeless venture, but they couldn't bring themselves to get out. Each of the Joint Chiefs was being driven mad by the thought that they were responsible for the deaths of all these men in what they thought was a feckless, hopeless operation. Harold Johnson, the army chief of staff, said at the beginning of the war that he was going to write the parent of every American killed. He did for a while. He was writing hundreds and hundreds of letters and finally had to stop, not just because it was too many, but because it was driving him insane. Yet even generals who believed the president wasn't doing what they regarded as necessary to win did not quit in protest. For all of them, the generals as well as the policy makers, quitting or withdrawing posed questions about their masculinity and courage.

In August 1969, I went to a conference of the War Resisters League. I met a young man named Randy Kehler, a Harvard graduate who had gone on to Stanford but then stopped his studies to work for the War Resisters League.* He gave a talk announcing that he was on his way to prison for refusal to cooperate with the draft. This came as a total shock. It was the first time I had come

*For Randy Kehler's account see pp. 231–37.

face-to-face with Americans willing to go to prison for refusing to collaborate in an unjust war. I thought, we're eating our young. We're relying on them to fight the war and to end it. I went to the men's room, sat on the floor, and cried. I was thirty-eight at the time and thought it was up to older people to end the war. I asked myself, what can I do if I don't worry about what will happen to me, if I really discard any consideration of its effects on my career? I had unconsciously rejected any actions that might make me unemployable by a president. I had thought serving the president was the highest calling, a knightly calling. Was I willing to forfeit that? Was I willing to go to prison?

I was led to my final decision about a month later when I read about a Special Forces team that was on trial for having killed one of their own Vietnamese agents. They suspected he was a Viet Cong double agent so they took him out over the South China Sea, shot him, and dumped him over the side weighed down with chains. Most Americans thought, why are we putting these brave men on trial for doing what they thought was right? There was such a public outcry the men were taken out of confinement. Then the trial was dropped. It was clearly a White House decision but the secretary of the army said it was his decision. There were lies at every level of command, from sergeants all the way up to the commander in chief, all to cover up a murder. At that point I decided I just wasn't going to be part of this lying and murder anymore. To me it wasn't just the lying, but that it had been lying in the service of an unjust war, and killing in an unjust war is unjustified homicide, mass murder.

I was willing to do anything that was nonviolent and truthful. I realized that one thing I could do was copy the study I had on the origins of the war. I had seven thousand pages of top-secret documents in my safe [at the Rand Corporation], evidence of a quarter century of aggression, broken treaties, deceptions, stolen elections, lies, and murder—I had proof of it all. It wasn't clear how much good it would do to bring it out because it only went up to 1968. It didn't deal with Nixon. If I had documents to prove what I'd been told about Nixon's plans to expand the war, I would have put those out instead. That would have been much more relevant.

Nixon wasn't worried about the actual release of the Pentagon Papers. They weren't embarrassing to him. They mainly made Johnson and Kennedy look bad. The reason he was so preoccupied with me had entirely to do with his fears that I would release information about *his* plans to escalate the war. He thought I knew his plans and might be able to prove it, so he had to shut me up. That's what led Nixon to take criminal action against me and finally made him vulnerable.

My motivation was entirely to change Nixon's ongoing policy. Based on information I had from people who worked for Nixon he expected to threaten his way to something close to victory or, if necessary, to bomb his way to it. I thought Nixon was likely to carry out major bombing escalation possibly leading to the use of nuclear weapons. The nuclear threats may or may not have been bluffs. The public understood him to be promising to get out, but his strategy was to carry on with quite ambitious goals. Unfortunately, I didn't have documents to prove it. But since I did have the Pentagon Papers I took them first to Congress hoping they would move them to hold hearings and subpoena witnesses that could expose Nixon's strategy. But no one in Congress was willing to do it. That's when I decided to give the Papers to the newspapers.

There wasn't much reason to believe it would have a big effect unless Nixon overreacted to it. Which is exactly what he did. If Nixon hadn't issued injunctions against the newspapers it would have sunk like a sub. Nobody would have read them. The first day they started coming out in *The New York Times* it didn't even make the TV news. It didn't become big news until it became a court case. Then I was underground. There was a big manhunt for me. They said it was the biggest one since the Lindbergh kidnapping [when the famous aviator's child was abducted in 1933]. Each time the White House ordered an injunction against a newspaper I'd give documents to another one. It's always said that *The New York Times* and *The Washington Post* were so brave, but fifteen other papers published documents from the Pentagon Papers before the Supreme Court decision ruled on its legality. There's never been an episode like that in U.S. history, where one newspaper after another absolutely defied the government's judgment. The government was saying the Papers were damaging national security in wartime and the newspapers were saying to Nixon, in effect, "Fuck you."

In those years I had been thinking a lot about an idea I called "revolutionary judo." It came from my understanding of Viet Cong tactics in Vietnam. The Viet Cong would initiate some fire from a village and the American side would bomb the village. Two-thirds of the survivors would go into refugee camps and the remaining third would join the Viet Cong. The Viet Cong were deliberately getting us to call fire down on the villages and it was a very good operation for them. By provoking abuse of the people they generated recruits and support. If you don't have the resources to persuade people that the government is bad, let the government persuade people that they're bad. The Pentagon Papers were a kind of revolutionary judo against Nixon. I didn't have the power to persuade people just how bad he was, but by overreacting he did the job himself.

To this day the actual break-in at the Watergate can't be traced to Nixon. So if he had not gone after me, there would have been no Nixon component to Watergate. Without the Plumbers, Nixon would have had no personal need to involve himself in the cover-up. He wasn't interested in covering up to protect [Attorney General John] Mitchell or [Chief of Staff Bob] Haldeman. Nixon bribed the Plumbers not so much to keep them from talking about the break-in at Watergate but to keep them from talking about their actions against me and others they viewed as antiwar opponents. So Nixon's effort to get me was the foundation of Watergate.

And without Watergate I think Nixon might have been able to keep up the bombing of Vietnam indefinitely. I think Watergate shortened the war by at least a couple of years and possibly much longer. Apart from its connection to Watergate, the Pentagon Papers definitely contributed to a delegitimation of the war, an impatience with its continuation, and a sense that it was wrong. They made people understand that presidents lie all the time, not just occasionally, but all the time. Not everything they say is a lie, but anything they say could be a lie.

Since releasing the Pentagon Papers, Ellsberg has never been offered another position at a think tank or in government.

EGIL "BUD" KROGH

"Let's circle the wagons."

In 1969, the twenty-nine-year-old lawyer went to the White House to work for John Ehrlichman, a senior Nixon aide. A devout Christian Scientist, Krogh soon earned a reputation as a tireless and fervent defender of the administration.

The zealous staffer might have been forgotten to history had his boss not ordered him to form a Special Investigations Unit to track down damaging information about Daniel Ellsberg, who had just released the Pentagon Papers to The New York Times. *The new group called themselves the "the Plumbers" because their general purpose was to plug leaks of classified government information. Their first major operation, which preceded the more famous break-in of Democratic National Headquarters by a year, was to break into the office of Daniel Ellsberg's psychiatrist, Dr. Lewis Fielding. Conducted by former FBI man G. Gordon Liddy and former CIA operative Howard Hunt, it was one of the earliest criminal precursors of Watergate. In late 1973, Krogh pleaded guilty to violating Fielding's civil rights. He served four and a half months in prison and was disbarred for five years.*

My first job in the White House was to coordinate our response to antiwar demonstrations in the District of Columbia. In 1970, Nixon's Cambodia incursion came as a shock, even to some of us on the White House staff. We had communicated a gradual deescalation of direct U.S. activity in the war and there was no way to construe this as anything other than an escalation. It provoked an immediate and strong reaction that extended beyond the antiwar movement. A lot of people were very upset and started to move almost immediately to Washington, D.C., to protest. It just spread like wildfire and we had to move quickly to protect the White House. I remember the meeting at the Justice Department when I said, "Well, John Wayne had it right. Let's circle the wagons. We ought to just go out and get a bunch of buses and put them around the White House chockablock." If you line up police with clubs and masks it's almost an invitation to attack, but it's really hard to get exercised about a bus. So that's what we did. We also moved military units into the old Executive Office Building.

I was basically living in a command post under the White House tracking everything that was going on. I had radio and telephone contact with the police, the Secret Service, and the military. We also had a sophisticated television system so you could see the streets. About four-thirty in the morning [on May 9], with demonstrators descending on Washington from all over the country, a message came over the loudspeaker saying, "Searchlight is on the lawn." Searchlight was the president's Secret Service code name. I called Ehrlichman immediately and he just said, "Go render assistance right now." I rushed through the West Wing and got outside just in time to see Nixon's limousine driving out. I commandeered a White House car to follow him and when I finally caught up he was at the top of the steps of the Lincoln Memorial in the middle of a little circle of students. I ran up the steps and stood at the back. The students looked like they were in a state of utter disbelief. I mean, was this Rich Little pretending to be Richard Nixon? They were all tired having driven all night to come to protest and all of a sudden they're meeting the president of the United States at the Lincoln Memorial. The students would say things like, "We feel very strongly about the war. You ought to withdraw." And then he would say, "I understand how you feel." He said that when he was a young person he had been very idealistic and very supportive of Neville Chamberlain's effort at Munich [in 1938] to reach an agreement with Hitler so they wouldn't have to go to war. He had been wrong, he said, but it had taken a long time to sink in. Then he talked about a lot of things—the value of traveling and seeing the world, a sort of meandering conversation.

Then he got into his limousine. I'm thinking we're going back to the White House but we roared right up to Capitol Hill and that was one of the eeriest hours I've ever had. Nixon had his valet with him, Manolo Sanchez. They go into the House Chamber and the president asked Manolo to give a speech. Manolo was very embarrassed and the president said, "No, no, go ahead, give a speech." So he started to speak and the president clapped. It was bizarre. This just did not strike me as supremely rational. Finally the posse arrived in the form of Bob Haldeman and the first-string handling group so I thought I could go home. But we all got into the president's limousine and Nixon said, "I don't want to go back now. Let's go to the Mayflower Hotel for breakfast." I think it was the first time he'd eaten outside the White House since he'd been president and it was in the middle of an unscripted antiwar demonstration. People were pouring into the city. As we drove along the Mall you could see a lot of people in sleeping bags. After breakfast the president said, "I'm gonna walk back to the White House." I started walking next to him. The limousine was just moving gradually along the street and Haldeman said, "Stop him." It's one of the hardest things I ever did. I had to put my hand in his arm and say, "Mr. President, you can't walk back, we can't get in by walking." He pulled his arm away and swore, but he got in the car.

I spent most of the next year on the drug problem in the military. You couldn't get current information from the Defense Department. Reports from the field got tinkered with and tweaked all the way up to the point where a senior officer told me the number of heroin addicts in the military was about a hundred. I said, "How did you come up with that number?" He said, "Well that's how many people we've been able to prosecute and convict." I realized I couldn't get accurate information working through channels so I went over to Vietnam. I started out at Charlie 2, a firebase just south of the DMZ. I just went out, wandered around, and found a group of guys sitting around smoking marijuana. I said, "Hi, I'm Bud Krogh from the White House." They just looked at me and one of them said, "Yeah, man, and I'm from Mars." I said, "Look, nobody's gonna get punished, but I just want to get an idea of the availability of drugs over here." He said, "Well what kind of shit do you want?"

That was replicated in more or less the same vein on firebases all over the country. I reported to the president in San Clemente and told him, "You don't have a drug problem, you have a drug condition. It's available everywhere, it's cheap, and you got guys who are sick and tired and bored and unhappy and scared and they're going to make use of these substances.

I was in Vietnam when the Pentagon Papers were released. When I got back Ehrlichman said he wanted me to set up a unit to investigate all aspects of it and why it happened. It was presented to me as a very serious national security crisis, a traitorous act done by an enemy of the United States. It's difficult to describe the intensity of feeling we had about Ellsberg. The order was to leave no stone unturned. Who's behind it? Is there espionage involved? Did Ellsberg work alone? The Pentagon Papers stopped before Nixon and there was nothing in them that could possibly have embarrassed him, but they wanted to know the likelihood that Ellsberg might release other documents that could be dangerous to us. Ehrlichman said, "The president feels very strongly about this, as does Henry [Kissinger]." Kissinger may have been concerned that Ellsberg had access to recent information about some of his own internal planning on Vietnam.

Nixon indicated that Ellsberg might be working for the Russians. Lurking in the back of his mind was Alger Hiss.* The president told me to read the chapter on Hiss in his book *Six Crises,* just as I was getting under way with the Plumbers. I think he was equating Daniel Ellsberg with Alger Hiss—a guy who might have had an illustrious record working for the U.S. government but had been "turned" [by Communist agents]. Exposing Hiss was one of Nixon's great triumphs early in his career and he wanted to go back to it. Every president is paranoid about losing power, but Richard Nixon's paranoia was at a fever pitch.

So I put together a team of Gordon Liddy and Howard Hunt. There was no explicit direction from the White House to go after Ellsberg's psychiatrist. It was either Liddy or Hunt who said, "Let's go see if we can look at Fielding's files on Ellsberg because sometimes people disclose things to a psychiatrist they won't disclose elsewhere." The break-in wouldn't have happened if I hadn't sent a memorandum to John Ehrlichman to go forward with the operation. I take full responsibility for it.

I got a call from Liddy right after the break in saying they hadn't found any files on Ellsberg. I was disappointed they had failed in the objective but relieved that they were able to get away without anything traceable to the White House. When they came back with photographs of what they had done I was horrified. They'd smashed up the office to make it look like there was some kind of a break-in for drugs. That was far beyond what I had thought a "covert" operation would mean so I showed the pictures to Ehrlichman and he said to shut down the operation immediately. Hunt and Liddy wanted to go back to California and break into Dr. Fielding's residence. The White House Plumbers was not the most rational group of people.

Somehow we were able to justify all of that conduct under a national security theory. My conscience was not engaged sufficiently. I didn't ask the question "Is it right?" I viewed it as basically just a busted operation conducted under the president's national security authority, not a crime or a constitutional

*In 1948, Hiss, a former State Department official, was investigated by the House Committee on Un-American Activities about charges that he had given classified government documents to the Soviet Union in the late 1930s. Richard Nixon, then a congressman, spearheaded the probe. When the case went to trial in 1950, Hiss was convicted of perjury.

violation. I assumed we were doing the right thing. Our actions were driven by zeal, anger, and fear.

One thing that started to change my thought was the Watergate break-in. I had moved on to the Department of Transportation but when I read the names of the men who were caught I thought, "I know all those people. They worked for me." I began to realize that if we hadn't carried out the break-in of Dr. Fielding, if we had just said, "This White House will not accept that kind of activity," then Watergate might not have happened. But once it did, I could have done everybody a whole world of good if I'd just said, yeah, here's what happened. Instead, when asked questions about it I perjured myself until 1973. Oddly enough, it was a feeling of patriotism that led me to perjure myself.

Finally, in May 1973, when Daniel Ellsberg was being tried for espionage and larceny, I wrote an affidavit, point by point, about what had happened in 1971 and sent it to the judge. Because of our misconduct, the charges against Ellsberg were dismissed within forty-eight hours. In the months that followed it became clear to me that I could no longer defend the right of government to strip away another citizen's constitutional rights. The only course of action was to plead guilty. It was like this huge burden dropped off my shoulders.

In hindsight, I'd say what Ellsberg did was extraordinarily courageous and I think he was following his highest sense of right. At the time I felt that it was a treacherous act of a traitor, but I've come to see it differently. I came to appreciate that Ellsberg was a patriot.

"THE WORLD WAS COMING TO AN END"

FRANK MAGUIRE

"The whole attitude was, stand back little brother, I'll take care of it."

"I went to Vietnam because it was there. I was thirty-five, a bachelor, and an officer. I don't think I had a choice." He served three tours in Vietnam as an adviser to the Vietnamese, first in Quang Ngai (1965–66), then An Khe (1967–69), and finally in the Mekong Delta (1970–71). "It was a very sad experience, but for me it was wonderful. I sometimes get a guilty conscience because I enjoyed it so much. People laugh when I say I kept going back because of the girls and the food, but that's not too much of a lie."

The first year was the best. I was a district adviser to the 2nd ARVN Division and I thought we were doing well for the people. There was a sense of progress and security. You weren't looking over your shoulder all the time. The guys in the 2nd Division were getting more confidence in their own infantry and we were involved with a lot of civic action, reconstruction, and local security. I liked my Vietnamese counterpart—he was a good man. We cut ribbons together on several schools and dispensaries. The whole thing started with such high hopes. When I went home in '66, I remember making speeches and telling people we weren't just running around killing people, that we were building and trying to improve people's lives. I felt so good about it and so did the country.

When I went back to Vietnam in '67 I worked in the An Khe district. I lived in what had been a Protestant mission that had Western-style plumbing and a generator. It was a soft life, but I was discouraged. There was nothing for me to do. The 1st Cav took over all the civil operations. If the Vietnamese wanted a road built, they didn't get Vietnamese out there with shovels to do it. They got the 1st Cav engineer detachment to come out with all their graders and bulldozers to put it in. The Americans did things I tried to talk them out of. One American general looked around and said, "They need a high school." I said, "They do, but they don't have any teachers for this area." Nobody paid attention. They built this beautiful two-story concrete high school and the Vietnamese said, "Thank you, but where are the books and the teachers?" Of course the Americans thought the Vietnamese were ungrateful bastards. The whole attitude was, stand back little brother, I'll take care of it. The Vietnamese weren't developing their own resources.

Shortly after Tet, I heard the word *Vietnamization* for the first time. Of course, it was always supposed to be their war, but it was lip service because all the Americans wanted to get in and win it by themselves. The Vietnamese just stayed in the background. We felt that by giving them new weapons somehow they were going to be inspired soldiers and they weren't. They kept looking over their shoulders. Where are the Americans? As things went on it got worse.

Another indication of where the war was going was the Hamlet Evaluation System (HES). One day I saw my radio operator, Foley, with this huge print-out—the HES report. I said, "Let me see that." They had all sorts of questions as to the attitudes, intentions, political leanings of every hamlet in our district. I said, "Foley, where do you get the information to answer all these questions?"

He said, "Oh, I just fill it in." I looked at it and said, "You say everything in the district is fine."

"Yeah, I always do." Then I said, "Foley, you say here there's no VC within two hours of this location."

He said, "Yeah?"

"Foley, there's no place in this whole damn country where there isn't a VC within two hours. When you go out the gate and into An Khe town, do you take a .45 with you?"

He said, "Do you think I'm crazy? Of course I do." So I changed the report and within seventy-two hours I was on my way to Saigon explaining why I had downgraded the evaluations. I met the youngest full colonel I'd ever seen. He was a computer nerd and it was his absolute conviction that when he finished his plan he would be able to predict what was going to happen anywhere in Vietnam at any time. I said, "But Colonel, what you're dealing with are my guesses. My guesses become your facts." He said, "Well, we have a factor built in to take care of that."

One of my jobs was taking the figures from the HES reports and turning them into briefing charts. I remember the time a colonel and I sat up one whole night with a bottle of Scotch, not changing the figures but moving them around and labeling them so it would turn out that we were winning. And in those days after Tet it looked like we were. Tet was a disaster for Charlie. I never did see another VC. They were all blown away. Anybody we killed after that was North Vietnamese. I could drive from Qui Nhon to Pleiku and back.

It was a weird existence because it was war, yet you were often divorced from war. Every Sunday they had a meeting of all the district advisers in Qui Nhon. I drove down and after the meeting we'd all get on a PT boat with some New Zealand nurses and female doctors and a fifty-five-gallon drum full of beer and go cruising out in the islands and take a swim. There were some fabulous beaches there. And when I got promoted to lieutenant colonel they pulled me into Qui Nhon and my quarters were located right on the beach. I could stand on the balcony and look out at a white beach, a big moon, and mountains rising up above the lagoon. I thought, all I need is Dorothy Lamour.

When I came home I was assigned as an adviser to the Indiana National Guard. It was a kind of preretirement position. Unfortunately, with that job I automatically became the area notification officer. If a soldier or marine in the area was killed in action I had to deliver the news. And if the body came home you stayed with it until it was buried. I had one case where the mother wanted to look at the body and the undertaker said, "If the colonel and I look and say it's him, will you accept our word?" She said yes. So we opened up the casket and there was an army green uniform, complete with necktie and ribbons. Buttoned up inside the blouse was a plastic garbage bag. That was him. A helicopter crash. It exploded and burned and that was all that was left. We lied like troupers to the mother. That's when I asked to be sent back to Vietnam.

When I got back to Saigon in 1970, the city was dead. It was like a bad movie set with papers blowing in the street. There was a lot of frenetic gaiety. I felt defeat and loss everywhere. Friends tried to talk me out of it, but nobody ever did. The world was coming to an end. The VNAF [Vietnam Air Force] officers club outside of Tan Son Nhut had great Chinese food. The whole thing was organized for the American trade. They had girls available and people were banging them under the tables at lunch. Another Vietnamese club was always full of American State Department people and this very senior guy was playing the piano like mad and everybody was getting laid and drunk. It was like dancing on the end of the inferno. And the State Department ran a hotel that came completely equipped with girls for every room. My last assignment was for JUSPAO [Joint United States Public Affairs Office] down in the Delta. Since JUSPAO was a State Department operation, whenever I came to Saigon they put me up in their hotel and the same girl would hop into my bed. It was sanctioned by the State Department!

Everybody was on the make. There was a fat guy out of an old Warner Brothers movie who asked me if I could figure out where he could sell three

P51 Mustangs with ammunition. There was a young Englishman who arrived without a penny in his pocket, bought a barge on spec, and one night with a bottle of cognac I helped him name the twelve tugboats he'd just purchased. Even my Mafia friends in Brooklyn were kind of aghast at all this wheeling and dealing and end-of-the-world activities.

When I was in the Delta, I wrote a report and said that the local Vietnamese troops had picked up all of the nasty habits of unemployed mercenaries of the Thirty Years War. Somebody flew down from Saigon and walked me around for a couple of hours trying to explain that it wasn't really like that. One of the things we did was to support the Phoenix Program. I personally thought it was a good idea but I didn't think it was working. I came to the conclusion that any Vietnamese civilian killed on an operation who couldn't be identified was scratched off the wanted list of the Phoenix Program. We supported the program by producing the "Wanted" posters—photographs, descriptions, and offering rewards.

Some of our young officers and troops didn't identify the Vietnamese as people. It wasn't so much a question of skin color, it had to do with the fact that they didn't have American houses, they didn't have television, their clothes were different, and they ate funny. As some wise guy said, "What can you do with a people that use two sticks to pick up one grain of rice and one stick to carry two buckets of shit?" I remember a helicopter pilot in the Delta who said, "I must've shot up fifteen, twenty sampans and you shoulda seen those little mothers jump in the water. I got most of them." I said, "Were they VC?" He said, "Who the fuck cares?"

When I first got to Vietnam the American province chief gave a tour of the provincial hospital. You took a look at the kids and civilians and he said, "When you call for artillery, remember who's on the other end. We're not here to mutilate or kill these people." Somewhere along the line that kind of attitude got lost. I saw a GI truck driver barrel-assing down a road in Binh Dinh and he sideswiped a little Vietnamese minibus with about ten people on it. He scattered them and their stuff all over the road. Thank God he didn't hurt any of them. They were just shook up and badly bruised. But he never even slowed down. I pulled him over and he said, "What did I do?" Another time in An Khe I was crossing the road and said hello to one of the girls from Sin City. An American tractor trailer went by and brushed her. She just quivered and stiffened up. She was dead. The driver didn't even know it.

I think if we really thought about it, we had no business being there. But by the time I got there, so many Vietnamese people had made a commitment to that government and to us that we owed it to them. We shouldn't have been there in the first place, but hundreds of thousands of people believed what we told them. The sad thing is, there was a guy named Charlie Holland from Brooklyn. I met him once and we got terribly drunk together. Charlie had been in OSS in World War II and worked with Ho Chi Minh. He and Ho Chi Minh composed a letter to President Truman with an outline of the government they wanted to organize. They never got an answer. If we'd done the right thing, I'd never have made major, but we would have saved a lot of people.

I think it's a national trait that we always feel we know what's better for everybody. It was an attitude of misguided benevolence—that we know what's good for them and they don't really understand what's happening. We really wanted to win their hearts and minds, except we could never find one or the other.

CHARLES COOPER (II)

"All this area was Indian country."

As a major in 1965, he had been "an easel with ears," a witness to President Lyndon Johnson's tirade against the Joint Chiefs of Staff (see pp. 121–23). Five years later he went to Vietnam as a battalion commander. By 1970 he felt "things were going to hell in a handbasket." American troops realized the United States was beginning to pull out of the war while the other side seemed as committed as ever. "We used to say, 'Their guys just care more.' Whatever motivates 'em, or whatever they feed 'em, or whatever they believe in, whether its getting rid of the Europeans or all this Communist pap, they believe it. They were totally unselfish."

This was late in the war and the quality of people in the Marine Corps, and even more so in the army, had really gone down. Thanks to Project 100,000 they were just flooding us with morons and imbeciles.* It doesn't mean they couldn't eat and talk and move around, but they couldn't learn well and they'd get frustrated and become aggressive.

It was also a period when we really had some race problems. I was as concerned about race relations as I was about the enemy. I really didn't know what I was in for. Just a few days after I took over the battalion I'm trying to pick up

*Project 100,000 (1966–71) was launched by the Johnson administration as a program of social uplift. Each year a hundred thousand young men who scored at the bottom of military aptitude tests were to be inducted and provided with special training. In fact, most received little if any remedial education and many went to Vietnam. The military had already significantly dropped its admissions standards before Project 100,000 began, but the program contributed to the social and economic inequities of military service during the Vietnam War.

the pieces and get the outfit back in combat-ready status after they'd just had their butt kicked in a sapper attack. In the middle of that a bunch of guys came to see me saying they wanted to have black studies and black clubs. And then I learned that there was a secret underground society of blacks called the Mau Maus. It went back to the Kenyan story where the Mau Maus rose up and murdered all of the English settlers. At any rate, they were pro–Viet Cong. I don't know if they had contacts with the enemy, but they were very much against any kind of American victory over there.

So the first thing I did when I took over was to close down any access to alcohol. I just turned it all off. I wanted everybody to be a twenty-four-hour fighting marine. That helped a little but then I allowed myself to be talked into allowing a limited amount of beer and we had a Mexican standoff. A white staff sergeant and a few of his buddies went to the enlisted club and got to drinking. A staff sergeant should not even have been in there. Anyway, there were some racial slurs and some fisticuffs. There were no weapons allowed in the club so after the fight they all went back to their hootches and got their weapons and came right back. You had all whites on one side and all blacks on the other and they all had loaded weapons pointing at each other. Fortunately, this motor transport officer appeared on the scene, pulled out his .45, got everybody's attention, and somehow managed to calm everyone down. This guy was just an absolute hero.

Not too long after that one of my rifle companies was involved in a major battle in the Que Son Valley west of Fire Support Base Ross. They ran into a classic ambush and lost about thirteen men, some of their finest people. I was very concerned about this company. They had been under a lot of stress. I flew out and walked back in with them, about four miles, just to see how they were doing. They sounded pretty damn good. They were saying, "Well, sir, sometimes things just turn to shit and you just got to police it up and keep going." So I brought them in that night and let them get a night of sleep without having to be on watch. But we couldn't stop the war, so I had to put them out in the field the next day.

A day or two later they had a couple more men killed. This time it was done by a small child. This kid had waved to the marines while they were on patrol and signaled them to come over. As they closed in on him he reached down and pulled up an AK-47 and started shooting. Two guys were killed and a few more wounded and this kid capered off toward the village of Son Thang.

So this company was doubly depressed. They'd had their butt kicked in an ambush and they were just getting back into the field when they were made to look like a sucker by a little kid. The next night the lieutenant called me asking for permission to send out four or five guys on an ambush. They called it a "killer team." These teams would put camouflage paint on their faces and do all these little professional things designed to set up an effective ambush. So that night, as usual, I went to sleep in the command center with a radio in each ear. This B company called in and said their killer team had sprung an ambush of about twenty VC and had an estimated kill of four or five. There was just something about it that sounded a little fishy. Five men taking on twenty and not having any casualties of their own just sounded a little too perfunctory. So I got on the net and asked to speak to the company commander. I said, "Ron, this doesn't sound right. Did they capture any weapons?"

He said, "Wait one," and came back on and said, "They got one—an SKS. I asked for the serial number and it turned out to be one they had captured a couple days before. The next morning I sent Lieutenant Grant, my intelligence officer, to check out the site of this alleged fight. He didn't find anything at the supposed ambush spot so he went into the little village of Son Thang—the same one where the little kid had gone a few days before. He comes back up on the line and said he found twenty bodies, all women and children. He said, "This village got blown away and it looks like our troops did it. There are shell casings here." I said, "Oh shit." I called my regimental commander and said "Colonel, we got a real problem and I've got to come see you personally."

The year before I went to Vietnam, I wrote my thesis in the Army War College on the role of the media in Vietnam. Basically it says, be professional but be candid and tell the truth. Don't cover up, ever. That's the bottom line. So the next morning we had all the TV networks and major newspapers out for a briefing. I told 'em basically what I had found and briefed them on the fog of battle up there. I told them this company was probably my most aggressive and proudest unit and they had suffered a lot lately and were bitter. They had been involved in combat with women and children who had killed marines and that all this area was Indian country and a free-fire zone. We routinely fired artillery and mortars and ran air strikes into this area because it had supposedly been cleaned out of all the civilian population. All these people were VC families. But it's a little hard for lawyers to accept the fact that a VC family is part of the enemy.

The first guy that got up was from *The New York Times* and he says, "Well now, colonel, you told us about your mini My Lai." I just blew up. I said, "Look, come on. This happened a little over twenty-four hours ago. We discovered it. We don't know whether these men are guilty of anything or not, but we're telling you now that we think we have a problem and we're going to solve it and if somebody's done something wrong they'll be punished. But we're not hiding anything. We're fighting a war and the fog of battle up here is so thick you can't cut it. I've just spent thirty minutes explaining to you how difficult it is for these young men to understand who is the enemy and who isn't. We know that the VC live out here and we know their families live in that hamlet, so I resent the hell out of your calling it a My Lai." And the guy apologized. But from that point on, my entire time in Vietnam I had at least one or two reporters with my battalion every day.

One of the problems was we were getting kids who had fought with the 3rd Marine Division up near the DMZ and they were in a blow-away mode. They were at the height of bitterness and they wanted to kill somebody. That was like World War II up there. Everything that moved, you blew away. There wasn't any civilian population to hide the enemy. But the 1st Division was farther south and the rules of engagement were totally different. We were loaded with civilians. When the killer team went out that night they were all hit on the back by lieutenants and sergeants who said, "Get some." That's a marine expression for "kill some of the enemy." Well, they went out to what they thought was the enemy and killed 'em. They went into that village and cleaned it out with hand grenades and M-79 grenade launchers.

For all the media scrutiny, I actually got along very well with the press and came to respect many of them. The day I got on the airplane to come home, out came a media delegation—about twelve guys and one woman. They put a lei around my neck. This lei was made of six canteens tied together with bandoleers and each canteen had a different kind of booze—bourbon, scotch, gin, vodka. They all gave me a hug and a handshake and said, "You know, we've come to love you. Your a pro and you're one of the good things in this crummy war." It was against the law to serve booze to troops going home but I got the airline's okay and I passed out my canteens. When we got into Travis Air Force Base we were singing.

Four men were court-martialed for the killings at Son Thang. Two of the defendants were acquitted, including the patrol leader who admitted to ordering the shooting and himself firing an M-79. General Cooper testified at their court-martial trials. "I know my testimony was pivotal. I said to the jury, 'I think many of you have never experienced the fog of battle like these young men did.' I'm not trying to excuse the fact that they killed noncombatants, but who in the hell was a noncombatant?"

The other two defendents were convicted of unpremeditated murder and given five-year terms that were later reduced. One of them, Sam Green, an inner-city African American who participated in the killings on his eleventh day in Vietnam, committed suicide in 1975.

GEORGE EVANS

"I didn't know there was a bad war."

In the 1950s, when television sitcoms first began to make it look as if all Americans owned refrigerators, his father was a Pittsburgh iceman. "He carried hundred-pound blocks of ice up to third-floor apartments." Beginning at age six, the son worked for him every day, before and after school. "He was my hero and I loved him, but he was hard as nails and basically owned me." The father's domination became intolerable and when he was twelve, the son started running away from home, often sleeping in parks or living with friends, and was soon on his own. By 1969, he was a medic at an air force hospital in Cam Ranh Bay, Republic of Vietnam.

In the mornings my father and I would go down to the icehouse and load up the truck. It was dark and dangerous and wonderful. I ran around loose, which was absolutely against the rules, but the men in the icehouse let me have free rein because they knew my father was a very hard taskmaster. I amused myself by dodging the gigantic blocks of ice as they came down the chutes.

I was raised in a family and neighborhood of extreme patriots. My father was the commander of his VFW post and I got to go to the club and hang out with the veterans. I was their little mascot. All the men had been in World War II, and most of the women in the Women's Auxiliary had worked in factories during the war. Some of my earliest memories are associated with Flag Day, June 14, when we decorated the graves of veterans. I always looked forward to it. My father and his friends took it upon themselves to find the grave of every veteran. They had plotted out all the graveyards in that part of Pittsburgh and every year they split up the work. My father remembered an incredible number of names. He'd say, "Go see if so-and-so has a marker." He could tell me exactly where to go in the huge graveyards. I was a spotter. I would run around and shout we need this over here, that over there, and the veterans would tell me stories about the men whose graves we were decorating. You'd think it was mournful duty, but it was really fun. It was a living history lesson. After I spotted the graves, we put up bronze markers. They were heavy as hell for a skinny little kid. Behind the shield were two rings and you put the flag in the rings. The markers might say, "Grand Army of the Republic," "Spanish American Expeditionary Force," or "Filipino Expeditionary Force." There was one for every U.S. war.

Sometimes it took us two or three days, but by Flag Day the graves were all decorated. Imagine how beautiful it looked to a kid to see hundreds of graves in a geometric pattern, all with shining bronze plates and flags waving in the wind. At the end of every decoration day there was a big picnic in the graveyard. All the veterans would gather under some trees and set up a table. It was the best part of the day. They would sit around and drink beer and eat sandwiches and tell stories.

Whenever I was with the vets I never had any problems with my father. But eventually I sensed that something was not right with them. For all their patriotic talk and all their war stories, I could tell their lives had somehow disappointed them. At some level, I honestly wondered why they lived so much in the past. If things were so great, why were they hanging out in bars telling the same old stories? For a lot of them there was a deep sadness beneath everything. I mean, they were often incredibly generous and wonderful with me, but I knew they were hiding a lot of grief. Quite honestly, I think one of the reasons my father was so hard on me was that he knew I could see through a lot of their bullshit, that I could sense things they would never admit to each other.

But you just can't exaggerate the pull of the military on kids from neighborhoods like mine. Everything you'd seen and heard your whole life made it feel inevitable and right that you would do your time in the service. And if you didn't feel it yourself, there was always the presence of the draft. So I didn't really question it, even after my best friend warned me against it.

His name was Billy Dick, my best friend since kindergarten. We were like brothers. He was a great kid—truly intelligent and athletic. His father was not at home, and his sisters and mother doted on him. He had managed to transfer from our horrible school to a much better high school. He kept coming back to me saying, "You have to go to this school." So I put in the papers and somehow I was also permitted to transfer. I would jump on the boxcars and go across town in the morning and I liked it. It was not the world I knew. These were kids who were actually going to go to college and things were going to happen to them. That's what Billy wanted too. He really wanted to be somebody. But I drifted away and lost interest in school. I had this other life in the streets and he got involved with a girl from the suburbs so after a while we rarely saw each other.

But one day he showed up and said, "I'm about to be drafted, but I'm not going to Vietnam. It's a bad war." I didn't know there *was* a bad war. He said, "This is a bad thing and we shouldn't get involved." He had a plan to avoid the draft and the war, he thought, and wanted me in on it. There was an air force "Buddy Program," which meant you could enlist with a friend and be stationed together for four years, a clever enlistment device. Assuming it would be easier duty, with no Vietnam in the picture, Billy convinced me to join up with him. I was bound for the service anyway, so we did it. Unfortunately, he failed the physical, and I wound up going alone. He probably saved my life by doing that, sparing me from the marines or army. But then Billy did something truly incredible. He became a conscientious objector. I had never heard of anyone from the North Side of Pittsburgh doing such a thing. It was like becoming a Communist traitor. I was both appalled and thrilled. But the pressures brought to bear on him in the neighborhood were too severe. He was accused of being a Communist, a homosexual, a coward. I'd become a medic and was stationed in North Africa when I got a letter from him saying he was giving up. You could go into the service as a medic and still keep your conscientious objector status, so that's what he did. He was off to Vietnam in a matter of months.

When I got back from Africa I was assigned to a dispensary at McGuire Air Force Base, determined to go to Vietnam. I wrote to Billy telling him I had volunteered. He'd been in Vietnam four or five months. He wrote back and said, "I don't care what you do with your life, but do not come here. Stay out of this war. Just forget it. This is the most awful place on earth. There's nothing heroic about it. It's worse than I thought." Of course I didn't listen. I just thought, well that's his point of view. I liked being a medic and didn't hesitate.

About a month after he wrote, I got a letter from my mother saying, "I'm sorry to tell you this, but Billy Dick has died." The story I heard was he was traveling out to some village in a jeep and they ran over a mine. I went back to Pittsburgh for the funeral but I couldn't go. I couldn't handle it. I was devastated. Not long after that I went to Vietnam, really wanting to know what the hell was going on there.

When I got to Vietnam I was a spit-and-polish airman, a crack military cat. I'd been a street kid most of my life and knew that was my way out so I took my job very, very seriously. I did everything I could to learn how to be a good corpsman. I soon became staff sergeant and the crew chief of the night shift. At the same time my background made me question things. My father was a Teamster, so I grew up around politicized union people. I knew who Joe Hill was. The Wobblies were my heroes. That should have made me question going to Vietnam, but it didn't. Once I was there, though, it didn't take long to see how screwed up things were.

I had certain expectations of my government but they were exploded almost immediately upon entering the hospital in Cam Ranh Bay. When I walked in, I realized that the country I was from was not the country I thought it was. There was so much needless pain and suffering. Very early in my tour a staff sergeant lifer called me into the emergency room. He was probably around forty years old and a complete jackass. He pointed to some curtains and I think he said something like, "Go clean up the gook." I opened the curtain and there was this Vietnamese boy stretched out on the table. He was about eight or nine years old and he was dead. It was an amazing thing to walk in and see this beautiful child dead. There was not a bruise on his body. Someone had already cut his clothing off and I had to wash him. At some point I discovered that on the other side of the curtain was another gurney with his brother who had also died. I was in shock, but started cleaning his body. I had a pan of soapy water and was washing his feet, his limbs, and putting gauze in his rectum. Then the curtain flew open and it was a Vietnamese woman who worked in surgery sterilizing instruments. She became completely hysterical, screaming and shaking with emotion. I think the boys were hers but I don't know for sure. She scared the hell out of me. I'll never forget her face. I can see her still. I remember her hitting me on the chest, grabbing me, spraying me in the face with spit as she screamed. Then she was running back and forth between the two bodies, from child to child. She was lost. She didn't know what to do. She was not to be consoled. There were the children and she had the same question I had: what happened to them? They were like little dolls lying there.

I found out they'd been hit by an American military truck and that there was this kind of game going on in which, supposedly, guys were driving through town gambling over who could hit a kid. They had some disgusting name for it, something like "gook hockey." I think they were driving deuce-and-a-halfs—big-ass trucks. The NCO who ordered me to clean the bodies could have cared less. He was an awful person. He was completely different from the veterans I knew growing up, completely contrary to what I thought I knew about men in war and what I expected of them.

I still took my job seriously, but realized that the war was not a good thing. I felt betrayed and really angry. One day, about six months into my tour, I decided, fuck it, I'm going to quit cutting my hair, I'm going to quit shaving every day, I'm going to quit shining my shoes, and I'm going to quit looking like a soldier. I'll just do it and see what they do about it. I also started to make little posters against the war and put them on the bulletin board. They said things like, "Stop Being Just a Soldier," and "Fuck the War," and "Don't Do What They Tell You, Tell What They Do." At the time I thought my small defiance was islolated. I didn't realize that it was a tiny splinter in the midst of a sort of uprising among soldiers.

I had about three months left in my tour when a new company commander took over who was determined to make his mark by enforcing petty regulations. He called me into his office and told me I was setting a bad example. I didn't take him seriously but he was serious and he wanted my ass. He had no complaints about my job whatsoever but he knew I was speaking out against the war and refusing to look like a soldier.

One morning at dawn near the end of my shift I was out in our ambulance—the crackerbox—doing something on base. When I got back to the hospital, the entire unit was lined up on the helicopter pad, spit-and-polished. The new captain had called a major military inspection at seven A.M. I was exhausted and thought, fuck that, I'm not going. I started walking back to my hootch thinking the captain would never even see me, but suddenly I heard a shout: "You there, get over in this formation!" I shook my head and kept walking. He yelled, "I'm giving you a direct order." So I walked over and he said, "Look at you, you're a disgrace. You're out of uniform." There was mud on my fatigue pants and boots and I was wearing a marine cap that a wounded marine had given me the first week I was in Vietnam. I liked it better than the air force hat. I'd worn it the entire time I was there and nobody ever said anything. I'd even had somebody sew a green patch over the Marine Corps insignia.

Then he said, "What have you got to say for yourself?" I can't remember what I said but it made everyone laugh. It might have been something like, "Yeah, I'm a disgrace, but I'm a really good fucking disgrace." Anyway, everybody was laughing and he turned purple. He went really crazy. Finally he ordered me to fall into the formation and I refused. I said, "I worked all night and I'm going back to my hootch and go to sleep." He said, "If you leave, I'm gonna have you arrested." I used that now clichéd joke, "Well go ahead. What are they gonna do, send me to Vietnam?" That pissed him off even worse. It was as if I'd become a different person. I was saying all these things I never would have said before. Something in my head said I was done with the military and sick of the war and I wasn't going to put up with some twerp. I also thought it was fucking stupid to have everyone out in the open on a helicopter pad in broad daylight in a war zone.

So I ignored him and went back to my hootch. Suddenly the formation was over and my friends came back and said the captain had ordered a shakedown of the whole unit. People were throwing shit under the hootches, digging holes in the sand to hide things, it was unbelievable. This captain was bound and determined to get people in trouble. Later that day I was told to report to the captain's office, still exhausted. I looked around the office and all the contraband they had confiscated from the troops was piled up on tables. There was every fucking thing you can imagine—dope, knives, guns, pistols, brass knuckles, clubs, firecrackers, dynamite, hand grenades, and every medical instrument known to man except an iron lung.

I walked in and he said, "You're in big fucking trouble. I could put you in the stockade for what you did. But I'm going to give you an Article 15 [a nonjudicial punishment]. Sign this paper admitting your guilt or I'll have you up on court-martial charges." I said, "Do your worst, man, because I'm not signing anything." He said, "Who the fuck do you think you are? I looked at your records and you're just some high school dropout." We went back and forth, and that night I was ordered to report to the colonel. It was just a more polite version of the same conversation. He said, "Take the Article 15 and the whole thing will go away." I said, "If I sign that paper it means I agree with you, and I don't." Finally he said, "The only alternative is a court-martial." I insisted upon it, which was my right as a non-commissioned officer. To me, it was a further, more serious form of protest.

The two charges they came up with were absurd. [He picks up his old court-martial records and reads]: "Staff Sergeant George Evans, having knowledge of a lawful order issued by Captain X, that he was to wear only the authorized hat, an order which it was his duty to obey, did at Cam Ranh Air Base, Republic of Vietnam, fail to obey the same." And then charge two says, "Without authority he failed to go at the time prescribed to his appointed place of duty, to wit, a squadron formation between the hospital and medical squadron living area."

I wanted my day in court. That to me was the all-American thing to do. I thought, they can't possibly find me guilty, because once they hear my story they're gonna know this is ridiculous. They assigned a lawyer to me and he said, "You're fucked, man. You have no defense, you're gonna lose." He told me I could go to jail and be dishonorably discharged. Then I found out he was the roommate of the captain. They lived in the same fucking trailer.

I requested another lawyer, but I also began to think about deserting. I hadn't taken my R and R yet, which was owed to me, so I got myself set up to go to Sydney, Australia, before the trial began. It was one of the great weeks of my life and it changed me. That's where I discovered hippies. *Hair* was playing at King's Cross and I'll never forget it. I fell in with this beautiful hippie girl and she introduced me to some American deserters, a whole subculture of GIs who weren't going back to Vietnam. She also took me to a university garden party where I met professors and artists and other people who were part of the subculture. I saw the way they lived and liked it. I also found out it was possible for me to go to Sweden if I wanted to. There was a sort of underground that existed to support GIs who wanted to desert. I really wrestled with myself about what I should do. Near the end of my week I decided I would go back to Vietnam and face the court-martial.

I was found guilty of being out of uniform and fined seventy-five bucks. That's it. There was no reduction in rank, no dishonorable discharge, nothing. It was all theater. On my last day of duty I was called into the captain's office and he said, "If you want to clear your record I'll give you one last chance. If you'll confess guilt to these charges I'll get the court-martial thrown out."

I said, "I think you're out of your fucking mind," and then I went back to Pittsburgh.

George Evans lives in San Francisco where he writes and teaches. He has published five books of poetry. In the 1990s he ran a public art project called Streetfare Journal *that placed works of art and poetry on buses in cities throughout the United States.*

"EVERYBODY THOUGHT WE'D WON THE WAR"

CHARLES HILL

"Reporters just kept writing as if it were Tet '68."

From 1966 to 1969, he was a "China watcher" for the State Department stationed in Hong Kong. One of his major assignments was to evaluate the possibility that China might send combat troops into Vietnam just as it had intervened in the Korean War. "It was never more than a nightmarish conjecture. We saw no signs of any such movement."

In early 1969, he made a fact-finding trip to Vietnam. "I felt the whole effort was not working and morale was not good." He returned to the states for a year of graduate study at Harvard and found himself immersed in a campus culture dominated by the antiwar movement. Then, in late 1970, the State Department sent him to a very different sort of campus—the U.S. Embassy in Saigon—where he worked for the American ambassador to South Vietnam, Ellsworth Bunker, first as deputy mission coordinator and then as Bunker's chief aide. He was in his midthirties.

We talk in his office at Yale University, where he teaches International Relations. His manner is measured and his voice even-tempered.

When I got to Harvard in 1969, I was thrown immediately into an antiwar movement. That's what people talked about all the time, and everywhere you went that's what confronted you. In the course of any day at Harvard you'd go through about seven or eight gates and there would be people handing out leaflets against the war. I got caught up in this and I began to be quite persuaded that the war really had to be brought to an end somehow. I wasn't an activist, but I was certainly on the dove side.

By the spring of 1970 the university came to a halt. It was a kind of French Revolution scene with people holding mass meetings for this and that. Professors were being "struggled" with in the Red Guard sense—pressured into coming before the student body and accounting for their crimes. I was mostly with graduate students and I think everybody was a Maoist in some form. Everybody thought that the West was a vicious, war-mongering, racist, doomed entity, and that the only way to go forward in the future would be through some kind of movement toward Socialism and eventually Communism that would undermine the entire commercial structure of the United States.

Everywhere you looked, the intellectual heroes were on the side of a cleansing violence. No construction until destruction took place. In this reading, there was no other choice because the very essence of Western society was violent. The essence of American democracy was a kind of concealed fascism and racist and violent by its very nature. Therefore, there was no way to deal with it except by violence. And once that violence had taken place, then the revolution could proceed to consolidate and build an ideal society.

The first thing that struck me when I got to Vietnam at the very end of 1970 was how changed it was from early 1969. It was far more stable, sort of buoyant. People's attitudes were very positive and security really was not a problem. Of course there was still lots of concertina wire around and you'd still go up to the roof of the Bachelor Officer Quarters [the Rex Hotel] and see signs of a firefight out in the countryside. But it was almost a case in which the Americans there liked to exaggerate the insecurity just because they were supposed to be in an insecure place and people back home thought that was really cool, and they were really brave. Actually, they were sort of making up the dangers because it wasn't the way it was before.

Back at Harvard they had a picture of the war that was essentially Tet '68. Everything they heard was Tet '68, year after year. In a way that's what the activists wanted, because in order to stop the war, you wanted to hear the worst possible news. So it became institutionalized. The trend on the ground in Vietnam was toward more peace, but reporters just kept writing as if it were Tet '68. Books do the same thing. Until the last year or so it was impossible to find books that don't essentially stop at Tet '68 or '69.

I had been there about five or six months when a couple of other foreign service officers wanted to go to Dalat and I said, "Sure, let's go for a weekend." So we took one of these jeepster-style sedans and drove to Dalat. We just drove overland. Nothing ever got in our way and nobody said, "Don't go down that road—there was an ambush there two days ago." We just went there happily and came back.

I billeted with a real operator. He negotiated that we would move into what was by then a famous villa in Saigon, a place where there were lots of parties and where many young foreign service officers had lived—47 Phan Thanh Gian. It was quite grand, a really beautiful building with teak woodwork inside and marble staircases. We had been told that it had been built by Bao Dai [the figurehead emperor under French rule] for one of his mistresses. We had a cook, a gardener, and a watchman. Once a year we let the younger crowd run an annual party that had begun back about 1968 and become quite famous—the "light at the end of the tunnel" party.

Ambassador Bunker was extremely focused on the American role and American casualties. We spent a lot of time on that. But otherwise it was a regular embassy. There really weren't great problems because the war was being won by [General Creighton] Abrams and Bunker was running a winning program on the civilian side. Bunker just adored Abrams and Abrams really respected Bunker. They were the closest possible people.

Bunker was immediately my hero. When you looked at him, he appeared to be austere and distant, but you automatically knew that this was a kind man and someone who had a constant sense of humor. He came from a different world. He may have been the last of the antique WASP establishment of people who had a different way of acting, a different way of thinking, who had a kind of natural presence that just caused reverence in people. I've read about George Washington or George Marshall. When Marshall walked in the room, everyone just said, "That is a great and honest man and I must do whatever he says." And Bunker was that way as well. We became very friendly because I became the aide who briefed him the most. He and I shared an interest in Ivy League football so we had this rivalry between Brown and Yale. I rowed [crew] at Brown and Bunker had rowed at Yale, so we talked about that a lot too.

He was very interested in land reform. He considered himself a farmer, a dairy farmer from Vermont, and he was very concerned about the Vietnamese farmer and the security of the population. That was the key to winning the war and is the reason that we did win the war on the ground. A lot of people came into the cities, as is natural in a developing country, but that was accelerated by the fact that things were better. There was more economy there. It wasn't a real economy, but it was moving in that direction and Bunker was constantly talking to [South Vietnamese President Nguyen Van] Thieu about making the people's lives better.

Bunker also understood that the situation was upside down from what many American commentators were presenting it to be, those who said that the U.S. was destroying Vietnam, destroying its village culture, destroying its traditional culture; that America was big and mechanized, heartless and heedless, while those on the other side were traditional, village-loving peasant people who had their roots in ancient Vietnam. It was exactly the opposite. The North, and those in the South following them and supported by them, were the modern people. I mean, they had their traditional culture really wiped out by Communism in every regard and they were mobilized. How do you tell a modernized society? It's where people show up on time when they're told to show up on time. In the North they'd show up on time and in the South they didn't. We were very sensitive anthropologically, so much so that it did great damage to our progress. When there were traditional holidays we didn't say, "No, you've got to be here." And if somebody came in late and said, "I was home because my mother was sick," everything was fine.

The press would say that a large percentage of ARVN troops had deserted. And yet when you were out there on the ground, you realized that much of this was not desertion but troops fighting a war in an old-fashioned way, almost the way Europeans had fought the Thirty Years War [in the seventeenth century]. They would fight, then go home for a while, and then go back to the war. For example, I knew a Vietnamese woman who asked me if I could get a bottle of scotch for her brother. He was an ARVN grunt with a stomach wound and he left his unit to come home with his commander's knowledge. He was essentially going to the hospital, but the hospital was his home. And when he had recovered, he got his stuff together and went back to his unit. But he's counted as a deserter. Of course, the commander was taking the soldier's pay when he was home. The commander was corrupt, but that's the way it worked. The soldier says, "You get my pay, but I want to go home. My family will take care of me and I'll be back."

When I got to Saigon in 1970 the people in the press despised the officials and the officials had nothing to do with the press because you couldn't trust them. You couldn't tell them anything without it being manipulated in some way. By this time the people in the press were not the old hands. They were radicalized people who were politicized against the war, resenting and antagonistic toward anyone with any kind of government connection.

Back in 1969 you would have two hundred and ten firefights in the country in one day and the news in the evening would show you a firefight. And when I left in 1973 you'd have maybe two firefights, but the news would still show you a firefight. So if you were watching this you would see no change whatsoever. There was a kind of self-deception among a lot of the reporters. They would talk to Ambassador Bunker and he would say, "I was just up in Phu Bai, or wherever, and here's what's going on." And they would say, "Fine," and write down what he said. They'd have a drink, have some jokes. And then they'd go out and write a story about how terrible everything is and say, "Bunker claims that things are going good," making him look like an idiot. But there really wasn't any antagonism from him toward the press because he was too much of a nice guy and a gentleman.

When the Paris Agreement was announced by Nixon in January 1973, it was broadcast over Armed Forces Radio, Vietnam. We were all sitting with

Bunker in the Mission Council Room listening. Everybody was shocked to hear that the North did not have to remove their troops from the South. Everybody thought we'd won the war. How can they leave their troops here, when we won the war? But even with that, if we'd kept the basic flow of munitions going to the ARVN and if we'd guaranteed them that we'd continue to give them the same air support that we'd given them during the Easter Offensive of 1972, then I think Vietnam would have been okay. The North would have screamed bloody murder, but it would be a war of words. The North would have been like China, and the South like Taiwan. The North was in very bad shape. I mean good God, today in the North just going overland from Haiphong to Hanoi you'd think you were in the twelfth century.

PARIS

In the end, the war was settled with guns, not talk. By the time the Paris Peace Accords of 1973 marked the official exit of the United States from the war, there were fewer than twenty thousand Americans in South Vietnam compared to 150,000 North Vietnamese. The United States got back its POWs, the Thieu regime remained nominally in place, and the North Vietnamese were allowed to leave their troops in the South as part of a standstill cease-fire. To no one's surprise, both Saigon and Hanoi broke the agreement almost immediately, moving to improve their military and political positions in preparation for a virtually inevitable renewal of hostilities. Two years later, Communist forces launched their Final Offensive and achieved victory by taking Saigon on April 30, 1975.

There were always fundamental obstacles to a negotiated settlement. The North Vietnamese and their NLF allies were steadfast in seeking eventual control of a unified Vietnam while the United States insisted on the necessity of maintaining a permanent non-Communist South Vietnam. In addition, both sides were deeply skeptical of diplomacy, Hanoi because of its bitter memories of how the Geneva Accords of 1954 failed to bring national unification, and Washington because of its Cold War assumption that Communists could not be trusted to honor any agreement.

From 1964 to 1967, there had been hundreds of peace initiatives sponsored by private individuals, world leaders, and third countries, including efforts by French president Charles de Gaulle, U.N. Secretary General U Thant, Pope Paul VI, and the governments of Hungary, Canada, Poland, Britain, Romania, and Sweden. There were also a handful of initiatives put forward through foreign intermediaries by the Johnson administration. Several of the most promising were abandoned because U.S. air strikes were launched just as diplomats were about to meet. Former Secretary of Defense Robert McNamara now argues that a negotiated settlement averting the loss of millions of lives might have been achieved with better communications between the warring parties. His claim rests on the assumption that he could have persuaded Johnson to accept a coalition government in South Vietnam had Hanoi simply made clear that it was not a pawn of the Soviet Union or China and that it, too, was willing to honor such a government, at least temporarily. During the war, however, as McNamara concedes, Washington viewed Hanoi's call for a neutral government in South Vietnam as "pure propaganda."

The formal peace talks that began in Paris in the spring of 1968 were not negotiations so much as alternating exchanges of prepared speeches. Just before the 1968 presidential election there was a small breakthrough when Washington and Hanoi agreed to have representatives from Saigon and the National Liberation Front participate in the talks. But it then took months simply to agree on the shape of the table they would use and where everyone would sit. By the time that was settled Richard Nixon was president.

Nixon and Kissinger had little faith that progress could be made at the formal talks, but did believe it possible to achieve their objectives through intensified warfare (including the bombing of Cambodia), military threats, and secret diplomacy. In August 1969, Kissinger began meeting secretly in Paris with foreign minister Xuan Thuy, who was soon replaced as North Vietnam's principal negotiator by Le Duc Tho, a leading figure of the Communist Party politburo. After more than a year of fruitless meetings, Kissinger suggested a crucial adjustment in Washington's formal position. In exchange for the release of U.S. prisoners of war, the United States was now willing to set a date for the withdrawal of all American troops in return for a promise that the North would not send more troops into the South. Even more significantly, Kissinger, for the first time, did not demand that Hanoi remove its troops already in the South.

Hanoi regarded this as an important concession but continued to insist that the United States withdraw its support for the government of Nguyen Van Thieu in Saigon. Negotiations then stalled for another year and a half. In the fall of 1972, both sides made further concessions. Hanoi agreed to drop its demand that Thieu be ousted and the United States agreed to a three-nation Council of Reconciliation and Concord to administer elections in South Vietnam after the cease-fire. In October, they were so close to agreement that Kissinger announced, "Peace is at hand," and made plans to fly to Hanoi to initial the treaty.

Thieu, however, raised a storm of protest, arguing that any agreement allowing the North to keep troops in the South was utter capitulation to the Communists. Nixon agreed to impose new conditions on some sixty points. Outraged by Washington's last-minute reversals, Hanoi walked away from the negotiations. In response, Nixon ordered the "Christmas bombing," eleven days of the war's most intensive attacks on Hanoi and Haiphong.

Nixon and Kissinger later insisted that the bombing had forced the Communists back to the negotiating table with vital concessions. In fact, the treaty signed on January 27, 1973, was essentially the same as the draft agreement of the previous October. The Christmas bombing served merely to bolster Thieu's confidence that Washington's support for him remained firm. New promises of military aid (including a secret promise to intervene "with full force" should North Vietnam violate the treaty), induced Thieu to sign.

The Paris Peace Accords of 1973 proved to be a hollow shell, guaranteeing little more than that the United States would withdraw its ground troops and have its prisoners released. That the war would continue was a likelihood anticipated by all sides.

DANIEL DAVIDSON

"I wouldn't buy a used car from that man."

On March 31, 1968, President Lyndon Johnson famously announced that he would not run for reelection. Less remembered was his invitation to North Vietnam to begin "serious talks on the substance of peace." To the surprise of many U.S. officials, the Vietnamese agreed to begin peace talks in Paris on May 13, 1968. The United States sent a delegation under the leadership of Averell Harriman, perhaps the most senior figure in the Democratic Party foreign policy establishment. Daniel Davidson was a member of the American delegation.

The public meetings in Paris were complete farces. They would read their propaganda and we would read our propaganda back at them. There was double interpretation. They would speak in Vietnamese and translate it into French and then we would go from French to English. It made it particularly tedious and I don't know how we explained some things without sounding insulting. For example, one day the Vietnamese wanted to know what President Johnson had meant in one of his speeches when he told American troops that he wanted them to "bring the coonskin back and nail it on the wall." I don't know how they explained it.

On at least one occasion their French was superior to that of our interpreters. The North Vietnamese referred to General Westmoreland as "Limoges." It was just after Westmoreland was replaced by General Abrams and Westmoreland had been made chief of staff. It took a little asking around to find out what this very unusual expression meant. It turned out that Limoges was a city in the center of France where they assigned military commanders who had failed. In France, if you wanted to put a commander out of play you made him commander of the garrison at Limoges—a city equidistant from the French frontiers and therefore unlikely to involve him in further fighting. So it was a very sophisticated analysis of what had happened to Westmoreland.

In retrospect, it's hard to see what there was to negotiate about. The battle between Johnson administration hawks and doves was shadowboxing. One wanted to win through military pressure, the other through diplomacy. Neither hawks nor doves wanted to give up and North Vietnam was determined to win. So I don't see how our being more dovish would have made any difference unless we were prepared to give up. Nobody that I can think of in government was willing to say, "We've lost, let's just get out."

The only things of interest happened at tea breaks when we would always pair off with the same guy. My counterpart was a very impressive man. Before the presidential election of 1968 I was explaining to him why it was really in their interest to get something done to help Humphrey become president. I didn't use those words but I was going over his record favorably and then I said, "I don't have to tell you Nixon's record—I'm sure you know it." And he looked at me and said, using English for the first and last time, "I wouldn't buy a used car from that man."

It took us months to decide on the shape of the table and that reflected fundamental debates over how many legitimate sides there were in the war. The South Vietnamese preference, and ours, was something called Our Side–Your Side. Basically the United States and the North Vietnamese would be separated by a long rectangular table with either part being free to bring anyone it wanted to its side of the table. The North Vietnamese wanted a square table, with one side for each of the four parties to the negotiations—the North Vietnamese, the National Liberation Front, the United States, and the South Vietnamese. The South Vietnamese government thought it was vital that the National Liberation Front not be recognized as a separate negotiating party, which it would be if the talks were among four parties. The ultimate compromise was a round table with two side tables for support staff separated from the round table. When that idea came up we still had to determine how far the two side tables should stand from the round table. At that point a Soviet diplomat who was attending as an observer said, "How about my girth?" He was not a thin man.

With Nixon's election, Davidson was hired by Henry Kissinger to serve on the National Security Council. He was one of the handful of aides that Kissinger had wiretapped. "I didn't suspect that I was one of the people wiretapped. My [English] wife was suspicious because she heard clicks. She once wrote an op-ed piece with the headline 'Don't Be Silly,' My Husband Said, 'We Don't Do These Things in America.' "

"To me the unforgivable part of policy under Nixon and Kissinger was the

Christmas bombing of Hanoi, from which we got nothing. The agreement we had with the North Vietnamese before the Christmas bombing was the same agreement we got after the Christmas bombing and it is reasonably clear that the only purpose was to bring the South Vietnamese government on board. So we were killing people to bring our ally on board."

NGUYEN THI BINH

"The longest peace talks in history."

"Ho Ho Ho Chi Minh, the NLF is going to Win." So went one of the chants sometimes heard at American antiwar demonstrations in the late sixties. By 1969, another version surfaced: "Ho Ho Ho Chi Minh—the NLF and Madame Binh." To peace activists around the world, Nguyen Thi Binh became one of the most familiar and popular figures of the Vietnamese war against the United States. A founder of the National Liberation Front, she came to international attention as the NLF's foreign minister. During the Paris peace talks she was the chief delegate of the Front's Provisional Revolutionary Government. Forty-one and elegantly dressed, her presence was a striking contrast to the aging men who headed the other delegations.

After the Communist victory in 1975 she served as minister of education and as a member of the National Assembly. Today, at seventy-four, she is the vice president of Vietnam. We meet in a reception room on the first floor of the Presidential Palace in Hanoi. Her manner is cordial, but formal.

My grandfather was one of the great Vietnamese patriots, Phan Chu Trinh. For opposing French colonialism, he was imprisoned and sentenced to death. But thanks to the protests of French progressives, his sentence was reduced and he was deported to France. Unfortunately he died rather young, in 1926, just before I was born. But I inherited his patriotic spirit. I joined the youth and student movements in Saigon during the August Revolution in 1945.

Bear in mind that we didn't seek war with the United States. But after World War II, the United States intervened to give political and military support to France. As early as March 19, 1950, I clearly remember participating in a big rally to protest the arrival of two American warships in the port of Saigon. There were so many demonstrators the police were stunned and didn't know how to break us up. We marched through the streets burning all the French flags that flew in front of the colonial offices and then we headed for the American embassy to continue our protest.

Because of my anticolonial activism the French arrested me in 1951 and I was imprisoned for three years. When the Geneva Accords were signed in 1954 we understood very quickly that the Saigon regime was not going to implement the agreement. Instead, they began a great crackdown against all political dissent that forced many of us to go underground to continue our political opposition. In 1960, we realized that we had to begin a resistance war against the Americans so we formed the National Liberation Front.

In 1962, we opened a diplomatic front to work in concert with our political and military efforts. As a diplomat for the NLF, I went to many international conferences to mobilize support for our struggle. The foreign media helped us a great deal. Wherever we went, the people already knew quite a bit about the war. They understood the obvious fact that the United States was fighting ten thousand miles from its borders to make war against us. And they knew that Vietnam was a small, poor country fighting against the big, powerful United States. They could see that it was an unequal fight. So when we talked about our struggles, we received great sympathy. The Americans and the South Vietnamese regime nicknamed us "Viet Cong," a pejorative term, but many foreign activists came to hold up the name as a symbol of bravery worthy of emulation.

Equal rights for men and women was not our main aim at that time. Matters of life and death came first. But the international community took note of the fact that many of our representatives were women and that women played a significant role in the war. Our diplomatic mission was not only headed by a woman, but many of the delegates were also women. I met women peace activists from the United States in Jakarta, Bratislava, and France. Those American women truly loved peace so when we met we quickly felt mutual sympathy. I still remember many of them.

The Paris negotiations were among the longest peace talks in history. We started in November of 1968 and ended on the twenty-seventh of January, 1973. All of the four negotiating teams were quite different. The Americans changed the head of their delegation five times. The NLF had only one head from beginning to end so the media said that with our patience we'd win. Every Thursday during those four years we had a meeting of the four delegations. Each side would give their opinions and we had formal discussions. The American team did not recognize the Provisional Revolutionary Government, so we did not have direct contact with them. In the formal discussions we had, the American diplomats were very cold.

The only personal contact I had with Kissinger was the toast we made after the Paris Agreement was signed. And then after the signing there was a party held by Secretary of State Rogers and there I realized that other members of the American delegation were more open and congenial. Of course we always hoped to cut down the negotiating time but we understood that the situation on the battlefield would determine the results of the negotiations and the fighting remained quite serious until 1973. Also, I don't think the American government was willing at any point to accept a coalition government in the South of Vietnam. They understood that the NLF had greater support among the southern people and if there were to be any coalition government, it would have to accept our basic guidelines.

Unfortunately the Paris Agreement was not implemented. If the agreement had been honored, history would basically have turned out the same, but the losses and damages would have been lessened. The most important thing was the overwhelming desire of the people, North and South, for freedom, independence, and unification. During the war separations were not only geographic but emotional. In many families one spouse was in the South while the other was in the North. Many of the couples that reunited in 1975 had been separated when they were newlyweds. By the time they were together again, they were middle-aged.

Throughout the war my husband was in the army in the North while I was in the NLF in the South. I had to send my two children to the North to stay with one of my sisters. In my extended family, more than ten people died in the war. Most died in Quang Nam, my home province, which the Americans had largely turned into a free-fire zone. It had among the highest casualty rates of all the provinces. Some of my relatives were simply peasants who did not fight in the war but were killed because they lived in free-fire zones.

If I could make a comment to the overseas Vietnamese, including those in the United States, I would like to have their understanding that it was American policy that destroyed our nation and caused the separations of our people. Now the war is over and Vietnam is the country of all Vietnamese people. For the nation's interest and a brighter future, I hope we can heal the wounds of war. Vietnam has a glorious history and every Vietnamese can be proud of it.

NGUYEN KHAC HUYNH

"It wasn't a mistake, it was an inexplicable crime."

The intense, sinewy man wears a crisp white shirt and tie. All business, he glances often at his watch and apologizes for needing to return to his work as senior researcher at Hanoi's Institute for International Relations. A career diplomat, he began working for the Ministry of Foreign Affairs in 1954. He was part of the North Vietnamese delegation at the Paris peace talks from 1968 to 1973. He is seventy-seven.

After five years of formal talks that were mere shadowboxing, real discussions began in the summer of 1972. The famous draft agreement of October 8, 1972, finally broke the deadlock and within four days we reached a basic understanding. I was extremely excited. President Nixon and Premier Pham Van Dong exchanged diplomatic messages and President Nixon sent us a letter to praise the successful conclusion of the agreement. Every member of our delegation believed peace was near at hand. We'd had enough of hostilities and enough of negotiations. We were more than ready for peace. But only a few days later we had a shocking disappointment. The American side wanted to reopen talks after we had already reached an agreement. What was the point of reopening talks?

What the Americans did next was not only disappointing but enraging. They suddenly renewed their bombing in December. It happened thirty years ago but it's still fresh in my memory. It still doesn't make any sense to me. The Americans made many mistakes, but this was the biggest mistake they ever made. No, it wasn't a mistake, it was an inexplicable crime. After the agreement had been concluded, why did they bomb us and kill civilians? Nixon could have forced Thieu to accept the agreement without having done that.

Even when we once again reached an agreement in January 1973 it wasn't that simple. Outsiders might easily assume that when an agreement is reached, nothing is easier than signing it. But there were four parties involved—the U.S. and the Saigon government, the Hanoi government, and the Provisional Revolutionary Government—and the Saigon government still refused to sign the agreement. They said they did not recognize the existence of the "so-called" Provisional Revolutionary Government. This gave us all a huge headache. So after a number of discussions we agreed to have two different pages of signatures. On the first page there would be a line for all four signatures with each party clearly identified. Saigon would not have to sign that page since they refused to appear on the same page with the Provisional Revolutionary Government. On the last page we simply had a place for four signatures with no party identifications. Everyone signed that page. This illustrates the complexity involved in the whole process of negotiation.

In recent years, at conferences with Mr. McNamara and American scholars, McNamara has said that both sides missed opportunities to make peace earlier. I replied that we are not afraid of exposing our own mistakes, but we don't think we missed any chance to make peace. We were fighting in our own country with casualties much greater than those of the Americans. Why would we miss a chance for peace? When McNamara says both sides missed opportunities he wants to distribute the blame for the war equally on the shoulders of both parties and mitigate American responsibility for the war.

PRISONERS OF WAR (II)

Although the vast majority of POWs were Vietnamese, all but a few American media stories on the subject focused on the plight of our own nation's prisoners. From Washington's perspective, these reports were not initially welcome. For President Lyndon Johnson, who wanted to obscure the massive escalation of American military intervention, the less said about POWs the better. Under Richard Nixon, however, American POWs were deliberately brought to the center of American consciousness. In part, it helped deflect attention from Vietnamese suffering at the hands of the United States and the Saigon regime. That was a particular concern after the 1969 exposure of the My Lai massacre and the revelations that the South Vietnamese government had locked up tens of thousands of political prisoners and subjected many of them to torture and brutality, most notoriously in the "tiger cages" of Con Son Island. Nixon also drew attention to American POWs to bolster sagging support for the war's continuation. His administration courted and financed POW advocacy groups hoping they would remain staunch, reliable supporters of its war policy. And by 1972, Nixon sometimes made it sound as if the United States were fighting in Vietnam simply to get back its POWs, perhaps the only war aim that had not lost credibility with the public.

For Hanoi, American POWs served even more obvious political purposes. U.S. "air pirates" could be displayed not only to dramatize the brutality of U.S. bombing, but to celebrate Vietnam's capacity to shoot down the most advanced aircraft of its superpower enemy. The confessions of American prisoners, most of them compelled by torture, were a staple of Hanoi's propaganda. Communist leaders also sought to demonstrate compassion by occasionally releasing small numbers of POWs to delegations of U.S. peace activists visiting Hanoi.

In the postwar years, U.S. public concern about its wartime POWs evolved into a widespread belief that Vietnam continued to hold "live American POWs." Beginning in the 1980s, American popular culture was inundated with dozens of films and novels about the rescue of imaginary handfuls of emaciated U.S. POWs pulled away from their savage, but now slaughtered, Vietnamese captors. Central to virtually all these stories was the vivid insistence that the

U.S. government was part of a gigantic conspiracy to cover up the existence of these American victims. Though many doctored photographs and other phony evidence fed the faith, there has never been any proof that Vietnam failed to release all its American POWs. Nonetheless, as late as the 1990s, polls showed that two-thirds of Americans believed some of their countrymen were still captive in Vietnam.

Preoccupied by phantom U.S. POWs, Americans have known little or nothing about the actual prisoners held in postwar Vietnam. In the years after its 1975 victory, the Communist government imprisoned hundreds of thousands of its countrymen in "reeducation camps." Tens of thousands were subjected to at least three years of forced labor and political indoctrination. While most were former South Vietnamese military officers, officials of the Saigon government, and people who collaborated with U.S. intelligence agencies, anyone convicted of antigovernment activity in the postwar years was a prime candidate for the same treatment. In the years since 1986, when Hanoi introduced a series of reforms called Doi Moi, or "Renovation," the number of political prisoners has dropped, but overt criticism of the one-party state remains dangerous to Vietnamese citizens.

JAY SCARBOROUGH

"I read Anthony Adverse *about four times."*

Wearing a nondescript business suit, the tall, slightly overweight lawyer sits in one of the many leather chairs that surround a long conference table in a corporate office building. It's difficult to imagine him thirty years ago in peasant-style pajamas and rubber sandals. After graduating from Cornell in 1967, he went to Vietnam to work for International Voluntary Services and stayed six years, most of that time teaching English in a Cham village near Phan Rang. The Cham are descendants of the oldest known inhabitants of southern Vietnam and one of the nation's fifty-three ethnic minorities. "They have the driest land in Vietnam. The dominant vegetation is cactus."

During all those years in a country at war, the fighting rarely came close. "The Cham had an exemption from military service. I think their basic feeling about the war was, 'a pox on both your houses.'" He came to love the Cham. "They are very poor yet there's no complaining about it. There are many elements in their way of life worth adopting. They are intensely warm people. I'm a white Anglo-Saxon—affection is not considered one of the virtues."

Many of his Cham friends had rare, handwritten manuscripts about their history, culture, and literature. In early 1975, he returned to Vietnam to make a systematic photographic record of those manuscripts and suddenly found himself trapped in the perilous heart of North Vietnam's Final Offensive. He was captured by the North Vietnamese Army in March along with eleven other foreigners, most of them American missionaries. Though the war ended on April 30, 1975, the "Banmethuot 12" were held in captivity until October 1975. They were the last foreign prisoners released from the American war.

Just before I returned to Vietnam, the Communists took over Phuoc Long Province, not very far from Saigon. They had never held an entire province before and I probably should have been more concerned, but I wasn't frightened. I didn't know the North Vietnamese had built an oil pipeline down into the Central Highlands.

By the beginning of March, I had taken about five hundred rolls of film of Cham documents in Binh Thuan Province, south of Cam Ranh Bay. One of my bags was stolen on a bus and I lost my film loader. I had to order a new one and it was going to take a week to arrive so I decided to visit some former students who were attending a teacher training school up in Ban Me Thuot in the Central Highlands. I flew up on March 8.

When I got to the airport there was an enormous crowd in the ticket office trying desperately to get out. The road to the sea had been cut. The road north to Pleiku was always unsafe. My friend said, "The Viet Cong are one and a half kilometers from the town." I said, "How can that be possible?"

I spent the night at a technical high school immediately adjacent to the headquarters of the ARVN 23rd Division. My heart's already starting to thump when I remember that night. The attack started at three A.M. and it went on for four hours. Artillery shells were coming right into the 23rd Division—probably six hundred of them. It was very, very close. They say you shake with fear uncontrollably? That happened to me. I was that scared.

About seven o'clock a bunch of workers were coming to the school as if nothing had happened. Life seemed to be returning to normal and I thought it was over and I would catch my plane out at three o'clock. Then someone told me the NVA were in the city with tanks. I asked to go to the offices of the International Control Commission, but no one knew where it was, so I went to the American adviser's house. By the time I got there a group of missionaries and other foreigners had already arrived. That's where we spent the next two days.

The compound had a big wall around it and metal gates. Eventually we heard a banging on the gate. Since I was the most fluent Vietnamese speaker, I went out with the American adviser to open it. The young North Vietnamese soldier was surprised and asked how many people were in the house. He said, "Make very certain you tell me the right number." I did.

So I ended up as a prisoner with a bunch of missionaries. I was also thrown in later with hundreds of ARVN soldiers and officers, a group I had never had much contact with. And, of course, I had never had any contact with the North Vietnamese. So everything about that eight months was different from the Vietnam I had experienced before.

We had no inkling how long we would be held. That was the worst part of it. We thought we would be released soon after April 30 when the war ended. When Saigon fell we were in Duc Co, an old Special Forces camp near the Cambodian border. I remember the music coming from the radio—it was the Liberation Front song, which we had all been obligated to learn and which I can still sing word-for-word. They were playing this one passage very slowly over and over. [He sings it in Vietnamese.] It means "Arise, heroic people of Vietnam. Arise and pass through the storm."

We weren't released for another six months. I don't think it was anything deliberate. I think they just didn't pay attention to us. I mean we were absolutely the least of their problems. And frankly, I don't think the American government was very interested in us either.

Oh, I'm sure the Vietnamese had some suspicions of us. First of all, most of our group were missionaries and they didn't approve of missionaries at all. Look at Vietnamese history. They believe the French missionaries paved the way for the French conquest. Also, the missionaries were working with minority groups, which might awaken an anti-Vietnamese consciousness. During the Tet Offensive in 1968 some missionaries in Ban Me Thuot were shot in cold blood. But now that the war was over we were treated far less harshly than the U.S. pilots were and even among the pilots I think you find that those who were shot down late in the war were not treated as harshly as those captured before 1970.

They interrogated us at every camp. We had to write down our life history—everywhere you went, what you did, who you met. They weren't really very serious with me, but God, I could have been the most suspicious one of all. After all, I had no visible affiliation and spoke fluent Vietnamese. I was asked for the names of everyone I knew in Vietnam. I remembered hundreds of names, so I gave them a list of every student I taught. They asked me, "Who are your best friends? Who are you closest to?" I said, "Oh, I was a teacher. I couldn't distinguish between students." Fortunately, I didn't have to single out any individuals and all my students were part of the public record.

We were basically held in four different camps, part of the time with about one thousand ARVN soldiers. These Vietnamese prisoners had had their footwear taken away and were running around in bare feet. They only got a bowl and a half of rice a day, which is practically a starvation diet, whereas we were given all the rice we could eat. We were taking rice back to the kitchen and here were these people right next to us in great hunger. Plus they didn't know what was going to happen to them. We didn't know either, but we had a powerful government behind us. They didn't have anything anymore. Most of the Vietnamese prisoners were pretty decent guys, but one was an especially bad moocher and I just couldn't believe how upset the missionaries got about it. They were all basically good people, but I got really angry at them and went off by myself. I said to myself, "I don't want to be with these people. I can associate with the Vietnamese prisoners." One of the missionaries came over later and she said, "We're sorry but you shouldn't feel this way. We're under a lot of tension."

Just before we were captured I had grabbed a book from the house—the thickest one I saw. It was a historical novel called *Anthony Adverse*. That was our only reading material other than the missionaries' Bibles. We had a lot of time on our hands so I read *Anthony Adverse* about four times. And then we ran out of whatever we were using for toilet paper. So one of the missionaries said, "Well, *Anthony's* got to go." There were only a few of us who weren't missionaries. One of them, who didn't think too much of organized religion, said: "We have eight Bibles among us, and one *Anthony*. I suggest we use one of the Bibles." Well! He could not have offended them more. Needless to say, we used *Anthony*.

I got sick a number of different times. I'd get sick for a week and then be okay for a couple of weeks, but it was debilitating. I had gone from being overweight like I am now to one hundred and sixty pounds. And then, because of a gallstone, eating became extremely painful and all I could eat was sugar water. By the time we were released, I was down to one hundred and fifteen.

At the end of August we were trucked to Son Tay, a camp where American pilots had previously been held. Our living conditions improved dramatically. We had access to rudimentary medical care and they made a real effort to give us good food. We even had some decent books to read and two days of sightseeing in Hanoi. But mostly we were bored. Release finally came on October 30 when we were flown to Bangkok, Thailand, by the United Nations High Commission for Refugees.

I was very unhappy about leaving Vietnam. I cried when we left. I didn't know when I'd see Vietnam again. By the time they released us, if they had asked if I wanted to stay, I would have. And if any one of those missionaries had been told that they could go back and work with the Bru or the Hmong, I don't think they would have hesitated a minute. I mean, that was their life's work.

So it was tough. And then I had no news from most of my friends. When I got back to the States almost all communication had been cut off. I was very, very concerned about what was happening with the Cham. I might have been terribly naive, but I did not see that country becoming Communist and even when it did I thought I could live with it. As it turns out, I probably couldn't have. It was very repressive.

He has returned to Vietnam almost every year since 1988 for brief visits with his friends. His photographs of the Cham manuscripts have not been recovered.

TRAN NGOC CHAU

"The curriculum was designed to 'detoxicate' us."

A granddaughter runs in and out of the small study in his California home where he reflects on a long and complicated history. In the forties he fought for the Viet Minh against the French, rising to battalion commander. After four years he abandoned the revolution and eventually joined the French forces. With the nation divided in 1954, he joined the South Vietnamese military and rose to the rank of lieutenant colonel. In 1962, he was appointed province chief of Kien Hoa. For several years in the mid-1960s he ran a pacification program that was hailed by mavericks in the CIA and U.S. State Department as a brilliant counter to Viet Cong recruitment in the countryside. It became a model for the Phoenix Program, though he eventually criticized that program's ruthless and often indiscriminate violence.

In 1966, Chau left the military and won a seat in the National Assembly, rising to secretary-general of the Lower House. By 1969 he became convinced that the war against the Communists was unwinnable and began to advocate a negotiated settlement. He also began to criticize his former friend, President Nguyen Van Thieu.

Thieu was determined to destroy Chau and regain control of the National Assembly. First he launched a propaganda campaign accusing Chau of being a Communist agent. Then he put out a warrant for his arrest. Chau moved into the National Assembly building, hoping that parliamentary immunity would keep Thieu from arresting him there. It did not. Nor did Chau's American backers in the CIA prevent the government from trying Chau in absentia and sentencing him to twenty years. "They charged me with having relations with persons harmful to the national security." When the verdict came down, Thieu's police stormed the National Assembly and hauled Chau to prison where he remained for five years.

When the Communists took power in 1975, they, too, regarded Chau as a dangerous man. Because he had served in the South Vietnamese military and government, he was once again taken off to prison. He would spend three years in reeducation.

Years before my arrest in 1970, when I was just a lieutenant, President Ngo Dinh Diem had awarded me South Vietnam's highest military medal of honor. When we heard that the police were coming to arrest me at the National Assembly a friend of mine pinned the medal of honor on my chest. There was a law that police could not handcuff anyone wearing that medal. They were supposed to salute you and invite you to go with them. But when the police ignored parliamentary immunity and rushed into the National Assembly, they ripped the medal off, knocked me to the floor, and carried me away through the back gate so the crowd out front would not see me.

At first they put me in a cell with about forty common prisoners. But when I got there everybody stood up and applauded and treated me like a hero. They gave me food and took care of me. After a few days the officials decided to isolate me from the other prisoners and put me in a small room in part of the prison hospital. I was actually treated with special consideration. I don't think Thieu ordered it, but I was almost totally free in prison. Such treatment was accorded only to a very small group of people. I got newspapers, books—I even had a radio and television in my room so I followed all the news. And I spent a lot of time studying. One of the subjects I studied was Chinese, knowledge which would later save my life.

In 1975, a few weeks after the Communists took over South Vietnam, I was arrested and sent to a reeducation center twenty miles north of Saigon. Our barracks had nothing but iron sheets for roofs, corrugated sheets for walls, and bare cement for floors. The compound was surrounded by high rows of concertina wire. It was in the middle of this barren and deserted land.

The elite of the South Vietnamese anti-Communists were imprisoned there. Many of us had chosen to stay in Vietnam after the war, but most had been left behind by the Americans. Among the prisoners were the chief justice of the Supreme Court, Tran Minh Tiet, and hundreds of other senior judges, cabinet members, senators, congressmen, provincial governors, district chiefs, heads of various administrative departments, doctors, and professors. There were also about two thousand former police officers in our camp.

Our "guardian-teachers" were all North Vietnamese. Some of them had been senior military officers. We very rarely caught them smiling. After spending three months building our camp, we spent the next six months listening all day to long lectures, taking notes, discussing the lectures, and writing reports. The curriculum was designed to "detoxicate" us from our American and Western ideas, to enable us to recognize the crimes we had committed against the people and the revolution and to teach us Vietnamese revolutionary ideology so that we could contribute to a new Vietnam under Communist leadership.

Most of the prisoners regarded the lectures merely as punishment they had to endure. But I was curious. During my five years of fighting against the French in the 1940s I knew many Communists and learned some important things. One was self-criticism and group-criticism. It may seem like a small thing but it was very important. Whenever we came back from an ambush, for example, we would get together and criticize our performance. We liked the system because it helped us not only in the fighting but in teaching us how to be close to the people and each other. Although I am from the privileged class I felt guilty and ashamed and had great compassion for less privileged people. In the Viet Minh we were so close—like brothers. That was a big thing because we didn't get any material benefits. In my first two or three years with the Viet Minh we got no pay. The people fed us. Only in late 1947 did they begin to give us uniforms, sandals, and enough money for one bowl of soup every day.

But what I admired about the Communists also turned me against them. At the time, I had nothing against Communism but when they tried to recruit me to the party I knew I could not make the sacrifices they required. For example, one of my best friends was engaged to a beautiful teacher but he broke off the relationship because the girl, like him, was from a mandarin family. He knew that the party had already been generous to admit him from a reactionary family and the political commissar told him that he should stop seeing her because they needed to investigate her more fully. So when they asked me to join the party I said, "There's no way I can act like you guys." After 1975 they were corrupted, but when I fought with them I thought the party members were excellent. In reeducation camp I was still curious about what motivated them so I listened to their lectures very closely. I think they believed firmly in their teachings even when they didn't know what they were talking about.

After about six months of this indoctrination we returned to manual labor from five A.M. to five P.M. with political discussions only in the evening from seven to ten. We worked in the fields around the camp under heavy guard. Some prisoners went crazy. There were frequent suicides and deaths. Early one morning I woke up to see the man who slept by my side had died from an overdose of sleeping pills. We wrapped his corpse in a blanket and buried him near our barracks. His family was notified about three months later.

In the fourteenth month of our captivity the lectures and discussions ended and we were rewarded with visits from our immediate families. The day of the family visit we were assembled in a large conference hall under police surveillance. I waited almost half the day for my turn. When my wife and children were finally allowed to visit they did not recognize me at first because I had lost forty pounds. My wife told me that some twenty-five members of my family who had been with the Communists throughout the two wars had sent a petition to the Communist hierarchy seeking clemency for me. She also told me that my son who had been admitted to the National Conservatory of Music had been called in by the new Communist director and asked to withdraw.

Around Christmas 1977, on a rainy night, about one hundred and fifty of us were ordered to gather our belongings. We were moved to Thu Duc prison in Saigon. The Communists used the facility as a transit center where they gathered people they regarded as their worst criminals and sent them north. They put me into a small, dark cell. I was prepared to die before a firing squad for "the crimes" I had committed as an "American puppet" while exercising my duties as provincial governor of Kien Hoa—the cradle of the Communist revolution.

Instead they ordered me to write my biography. They put me in a room about three times bigger than my cell with a desk and a thick pad of paper. For exactly fifty-eight days, ten to fifteen hours a day, I wrote an eight-hundred-page document. The work was easy because two or three times during the first two years of captivity I had been ordered to write a similar biography. I wrote in a manner I knew the Communists would agree with—showing my prosecution of all the crimes I had committed.

Two weeks after submitting my biography I was led to a meeting. A political officer said they wanted specific answers as to why I had fought against the Communist Party. The Communists had never openly admitted that Vietnamese might become anti-Communist by reason of ideology. They had always insisted that anti-Communists were simply motivated by self-interest—by jobs, privileges, and other benefits generated by U.S. assistance. But gradually they began to acknowledge that some people opposed them because of "ideological intoxication."

They were especially interested in me because I was the only prominent South Vietnamese who had openly advocated a peaceful settlement between Vietnamese at the time Richard Nixon became president. The Communists wanted to know about my connections with everyone who opposed Thieu and the American establishment. They focused their interest on Buddhist leaders and my other former political supporters, several of whom had been "invited" by the Communists to join them after Saigon's collapse.

It was clear that the Communists were now less worried about the kind of anti-Communists represented by former South Vietnamese president Nguyen Van Thieu. To them, Thieu's brand of anti-Communism ceased to exist the day Americans stopped providing subsidies. They were easily unmasked as American mercenaries and they either ran away or were completely disarmed, materially and mentally. But the anti-Communists who opposed Thieu represented a greater potential threat to the Communists. They believed such people would mask their antirevolutionary efforts under the labels of nationalism and religious traditionalism. The Communists therefore began to target the Buddhist leaders and other nationalists whose anti-Communism was rooted in ideology and philosophy.

Most of the Buddhist leaders whom Thieu and the Americans had once suspected and condemned as Communist agents were put in jail, isolated, or killed after the Communists came to power. Venerable Thich Thien Minh, the powerful deputy chairman of the Vietnamese Buddhist Unified Church, who had been jailed by Thieu in 1967 for pro-Communist activities, was beaten to death in a Communist prison in 1979.

One morning, the guards took me to meet a stranger, presumably a senior Communist official from the North. He behaved strangely—he was friendly. He said I was the victim of a false illusion, but I was nonetheless an anti-Communist by conviction. As such, the party perceived me as a greater threat to the revolution than people who opposed Communism only out of self-interest. He focused particularly on my initial creation of the Phoenix Program. Suddenly he stared at me and said, "The Americans considered people like you consumable products. But the revolution is different. We believe people like you are still potentially useful to the country. The revolution has decided to set you free and ask for your contribution to the building and consolidation of the Socialist Republic of Vietnam." Then he asked if I would write a letter of appreciation to the government. I said I was so moved by the revolution's decision that I needed a few days to think about what I should do.

I wrote the letter, thanking them for my release and promising to do my best to serve the country. For the first three weeks after I got out, I stayed at home and avoided seeing anyone outside the family. Then one day the Communist who had interviewed me came to see me again. He inquired about my health and expressed his desire to see me return to "normal life." He wanted me to go out, renew my friendships, especially with my former political colleagues and religious leaders, a good number of whom had been working voluntarily for the Communists since the liberation. A few weeks later I was "invited" to join the Social Sciences Institute by members of the Central Secretariat of the Communist Party. I was assigned to do a study of the former leaders of South Vietnam. They said they wanted to know more about their

Vietnamese adversaries. At first, I was able to support my arguments by using the names of people who had already left the country. But when they kept asking me to inform on my friends in Vietnam, I knew I had to leave.

I stalled for time, saying it took time to rebuild trust before my former associates would tell me anything serious about their beliefs and actions. This provided my wife more time to prepare our escape. At that time the Vietnamese chased all the ethnic Chinese out of the country and my wife made an arrangement with one of them to let us mix in with them to get out of the country. Because I had learned Chinese while a prisoner under Thieu I was able to pass as Chinese. We landed in Malaysia. They kept us there for a month and then they took us out to the open sea and left us there. Again we landed in Malaysia and again they took us out to the open sea. The next time we landed on a remote island in Indonesia. We lived there for a few months. I had a small radio and at night I listened to the BBC. One evening I heard a report from an old American friend of mine, the journalist Keyes Beech. The Indonesians had sent a squad of police to guard us and I bribed one of them to send a telegram to Beech asking him to do whatever he could to help. I had little hope it would work, but about a month later a man in a helicopter came in and rescued the seven members of my family.

In the United States, Chau took minimum-wage jobs and went to computer school at night. Eventually he became a programmer and sent his children to college.

JOHN MCCAIN

"Americans like conspiracies."

On October 26, 1967, McCain flew his twenty-third bombing run over North Vietnam, his first against Hanoi. The target was a thermal power plant near a small lake in downtown Hanoi. The city was surrounded by three rings of Russian-built surface-to-air missile sites. Those SAM sites, combined with hundreds of antiaircraft artillery batteries scattered throughout the city, gave Hanoi the most formidable air defense system in the history of modern warfare. Approaching his target, McCain saw "thick black clouds of antiaircraft flak." Then the plane's radar indicated that a SAM missile was coming right at him, a "flying telephone pole." He dropped the bombs and just as he pulled back on his stick to climb to safer altitudes, the missile blew off a wing.

Ejecting from the airplane, he broke both arms and his right knee. His parachute opened mere seconds before he fell into Truc Bach Lake. When dragged ashore, an angry crowd beat him and broke his shoulder with a rifle butt. A woman finally persuaded the crowd to stop and an army truck arrived to take him off to Hoa Lo Prison, the "Hanoi Hilton." Few, if any, prisoners arrived in worse shape. "About the third or fourth day a guard came in and pulled the blanket off my knee. It was about the size, shape, and color of a football."

When taken prisoner, McCain was an unknown navy pilot. His father, however, was a four-star admiral who soon became the commander of all U.S. forces in the Pacific. The Vietnamese discovered their captive's pedigree and began calling him "the crown prince." Apparently hoping for a propaganda coup, they offered him freedom. McCain refused, honoring the code of honor that requires prisoners of war to accept release only in the order in which they were captured.

McCain has been a U.S. senator from Arizona since 1986 and came to national prominence during his presidential bid of 2000 when he was runner-up to George W. Bush for the Republican nomination.

When I was a little kid there was no doubt I was going into the navy. In the fifties, kids didn't have a choice. Sixties kids made a choice. Since my father and grandfather had both been naval officers I really never had a choice. That's one of the reasons why I was so rebellious at the Naval Academy. But I didn't resent my father or grandfather so much as I resented just being in the academy. I could never understand why a guy who'd been there a year longer than me should have all that power over me because so many of them were nerds and jerks. [Laughs gleefully.]

In prison it was important to have some spiritual faith and you had to have faith that your country wanted to bring you home. The Vietnamese always told us the opposite, that our country had abandoned us. You also had to have faith in your fellow prisoners, that when they did weaken and make a [propaganda] tape or sign a confession they had resisted to the best of their ability. Those were all-important factors in our survival, and another was a sense of humor. Our senior ranking officer, Bud Day, made me the room chaplain and the entertainment officer. I used to tell movies two or three nights a week. If I sat down for several hours to think about a film, I could recall incredible details. So everybody would come and I might take a full hour describing a movie. I told about a hundred movies while I was in prison. And some of them I'd never seen.

We also made fun of the guards. If you don't look out your captors become bigger than life because they have so much control over you. So we'd make fun of them and bring them back to reality. We called the camp commander

"Slopehead," and I pretended I had fallen in love with one of the Vietnamese women in the camp. I'd laugh at most everything I could because, you know, they're Communists, they're ill-educated, and they said stupid and amusing things.

Probably my worst time in prison was after I refused to be released and they subjected me to a long period of severe treatment. For about two weeks after my decision nothing happened. Then they took me out one night and that began about a month of pretty hard treatment. When one of the guys was knocking me around I fell and broke my arm. So that was really my lowest point, and they wrung a confession out of me and that was terrible—made me confess to war crimes, bombing villages and children and women, that sort of thing. I don't think I ever had any moments that low again. I had lots of beatings and ropes and that kind of stuff, but I never felt as low. I failed. I didn't live up to the standards that I think were expected. Others were stronger than I was. Some guys were a lot tougher. I just wish I could have done better.

One of the great surprises when I got home was learning about the depth of the antiwar movement because we never believed the bullshit the Vietnamese put out about it. And when I was shot down, the antiwar movement was nothing, so I never really believed it was significant until I came home. I was surprised at first, then a little angry, but after a while I decided people were doing what I was fighting for the Vietnamese to be able to do. I've never had a lot of resentment or anger toward the antiwar movement. I have resentment toward the excesses—like Jane Fonda visiting a North Vietnamese antiaircraft site or the guys that threw their medals on the steps of the Capitol. But an average American who thought the war was wrong and wanted to walk down the street with a sign—that's what America is supposed to be all about. I can't begrudge them that.

It took a long time before America became united again. There was a lot of anger, a lot of hatred. Probably the greatest tragedy of the Vietnam War was all those who could never really come back. There are vet centers that still have people who come for counseling and haven't been able to get all the way back. As a nation I would say that maybe the overall impact was beneficial. Perhaps we couldn't have won the Cold War if we hadn't lost the Vietnam War. It showed us what our limitations are and what our capabilities are. I think it also probably caused us to elect Ronald Reagan who presented strong leadership and a very clear vision of what our obligations are.

I still get a lot of mail attacking me for supporting the normalization of relations with Vietnam. These wacko people call me "the Manchurian candidate."* They've got a Web site. I'm evil incarnate. I cooperated with the Vietnamese. I'm a Vietnamese agent. Any moment I expect Angela Lansbury to come in and turn over the Red Queen. The vitriol and hatred these people display toward me is really staggering. But the concern of the POW activists is understandable. The government didn't do a very good job accounting for a lot of our missing. The war was over and everybody wanted to forget about it, including the Pentagon. Plus, Americans like conspiracies. The only POW activists I resent, and I resent them enormously, are the professionals who made money off the grief and sorrow of family members. And the ones who manufactured bogus pictures of supposed POWs—there's a special ring in hell for them.

At the last hearing we had in the POW/MIA committee in the Senate a woman came up to me at the end and said, "My husband was declared killed in action and I remarried. Years later a man came to my home with a picture of my first husband. I got a divorce, took all my money, and went to Thailand to track down my husband. Then I found out it was a manufactured picture. Tell me, what do I do with my life now?"

PATTY AND EARL HOPPER SR.

"What mushroom do they think we were hatched under last week?"

A veteran of three wars, Earl Hopper Sr. is a retired army colonel. In 1962, long before Americans had come to regard Vietnam as a synonym for war, he was an adviser to a South Vietnamese army brigade. In 1968, his son, Earl Jr., an air force pilot, was declared missing in action, his plane shot down during a mission over North Vietnam.

After the Paris Peace Accords of 1973, 591 POWs were returned to the United States, but Colonel Hopper was convinced that not all American prisoners had been released. He became a founding member of The National League of Families of Prisoners and Missing in Action, which he chaired for six years. Through that work he met his second wife, Patty. "What got me involved," she says, "was a classmate who was shot down in '72 and reported missing in action. I started asking questions and one thing led to another." From their home in Phoenix, Arizona, they run their own

**The Manchurian Candidate* is a 1964 movie about an American soldier who was brainwashed by the Communists during the Korean War and sent back to the United States to assassinate a presidential candidate. Angela Lansbury, who plays the veteran's mother, proves to be a Communist agent herself. She can control her son's actions by showing him the queen of hearts from a deck of cards.

POW/MIA organization, Task Force Omega, Inc. Both fervently believe that the Communist government of Vietnam continues to hold Americans in captivity.

Colonel Hopper begins: "Earl was on his thirty-seventh mission when he was shot down. He was the back-seater in an F-4D Phantom jet." His voice is so mellow and avuncular you might mistake him for a history buff warming to a favorite subject rather than a father reminded of a lost son. Before long, Mrs. Hopper jumps in, clarifying details and opening new avenues of analysis with unflagging urgency and conviction. "Let me explain one thing," she interrupts. "The F-4D is the only model of the F-4 that carries two qualified pilots. It can be flown from either the front seat or the back." She needs us to remember this detail, and many others, because it helps to explain one of her theories about Earl Jr.—that he might have been able to land his damaged Phantom from the back seat safely enough to survive the crash.

COLONEL HOPPER

I was having dinner at my brother's house when the phone call came. They notified me that Earl was missing in action. That was it, that was all I had to go on. I guess I got a little emotional because my son Mike said, "That's the first time I ever saw Dad cry." And we had just had my dad's funeral the day before.

When Earl was shot down the front-seater was Captain Keith Hall. It was the first time they had flown together. I talked with Keith after the war. It was a surface-to-air missile that got them. It exploded about a hundred feet below the right of their aircraft. The missile did some damage to the fuel and hydraulic system. They climbed up to eighteen thousand feet and turned toward Laos in an attempt to get back to where it was safer but the aircraft was catching on fire. Keith Hall told Earl to eject. Earl said, "It won't go, boss." Keith told him to try the alternate system and then Keith went ahead and bailed out himself. He was captured about twenty minutes after he hit the ground.

Evidently, Earl's backup ejection system didn't work either because he flew the plane for another six to eight minutes. Three other aircraft came into position—one on his right flank, one on his left flank, and one behind and above. Because one engine had cut out, Earl's aircraft started crabbing—turning a little sideways—and it was going down fairly slowly. Just as he was going into a five-thousand-foot cloud, the other pilots saw two objects leave the plane. They never could positively identify what the objects were, but they thought one was Earl's canopy and possibly the other was the seat with Earl in it. They never saw a parachute. The weather was bad and they lost sight of the plane. They weren't even sure where the plane went down because no one saw it after he went into the clouds.

About a week later we got a letter from Earl's squadron commander.

According to him, Earl's emergency beeper was picked up after the aircraft went down. So there is strong evidence that he got out of the aircraft or survived the crash.

PATTY HOPPER

On the second day another plane picked up the beeper, gave Earl's authenticator code, and said, "Hopper, if that's you, come back at fifteen-second intervals." Meaning, you transmit for fifteen seconds and go off the air for fifteen seconds. And Earl responded. He gave several sets. Now, things to keep in mind. This was a very rugged, isolated area close to the Vietnam-Laos border. The closest village in any direction was a Montagnard village about eight miles away. They wouldn't have any clue how to operate the beeper. They don't have that kind of sophistication. His beeper was tracked for three consecutive days.

COLONEL HOPPER

There were just over five hundred and fifty military men who were missing or prisoners in Laos. Of that entire group, we got eight back. Now common sense will tell you that all five hundred and fifty could not have died in Laos, yet that is what the government is claiming.

PATTY HOPPER

Let's get back to Earl for a minute. When Keith Hall came home he reported that in August 1970, better than two and a half years after the shoot-down, he was pulled out of his cell and interrogated about Earl Jr. All the Vietnamese wanted was personal information—was he married, did he have any children, where did he go to school, what were his hobbies. Keith's response was, "I don't know," which was true because they had only flown together that one time and didn't run in the same circles. When the interrogator got up to leave, Keith said, "Does that mean that Earl Hopper's here too?" The guy looked at him very sarcastically and said, "I don't know." But the point is, if they did not have Earl, they would not be asking this type of question better than two and a half years after the loss.

Now, in 1981, just after Reagan came into office, the Vietnamese offered to sell back fifty-seven POWs for four billion dollars. They sent communiqués through the Canadian and Chinese governments. At the bottom of the communiqué Reagan wrote, in his own hand, "No, we will not pay for POWs. RR." We are told that the communiqué is in the computer in the basement of the White House and inaccessible. They've not made it available to us, but government officials have testified to all of this under oath.

So Reagan nixed the ransom, but he did set up an intelligence operation to find information on live POWs in Southeast Asia—the Special Forces Detachment Korea (SFDK). Between 1981 and 1984 the SFDK collected information on roughly twenty-six prisoners of war by name and prison camp location in Laos. When SFDK was given this mission they set up an agent net throughout Southeast Asia. It included Thai Special Forces, Thai intelligence people, gunrunners, gold smugglers, drug-runners, common farmers, ethnic people, Montagnards, just a wide variety of people. This agent net went to work finding prisoners of war. They would talk with the POWs surreptitiously and bring that information back. Earl was one of the men they collected information on. In Earl's case, the first time his name came out, it came out garbled. It came out Hepper or Hopler. But they took the agent, told him they wanted the exact spelling, and sent him back in. Six weeks later the agent came back to report and he had the exact name, Hopper.

COLONEL HOPPER

Here's some more information I'm going to give you. I cannot prove if it's true or not, but there could be some logic to it. I had two reports during the eighties that Earl was in the hands of the Russians. This information came to me from some people who used to be active in the CIA. One bit of information was that Earl was in the hands of the Russians at Tchepone, Laos, and that he had been taken to Cam Ranh Bay for medical treatment for anemia and malaria. Later I received information from a different source, but also CIA connected, that the Russians were running a study of selected American POW pilots. They were very concerned about why the Americans pilots almost always won when they came up against Russian pilots or Russian allied pilots. They wanted to find out the differences between the typical American pilot and the typical Russian pilot. Earl was supposed to be used in that study. That would be logical because in the Air Force Academy, Earl took Russian and was very fluent in it.

PATTY HOPPER

In the last several years the government has identified three separate crash sites as Earl Jr's. They have been to the last site five times and excavated it. The only thing that IDs this aircraft is the engine plate from the left engine that was found on the surface of the ground in pristine condition, twenty-seven years later. We have seen it, we have held it. It looks like it has been either cut off or torn off. These things do not just come off of an engine. It is made of aluminum and is not corroded at all. Normal erosion would have taken this plate at least three centimeters underground. It's very, very suspect.

There was also some ammunition at the site. Now we have a report in our possession from the people at the Life Science Lab in Texas. It's a very, very good report and it shows that the ammunition included three Soviet-manufactured 7.62-millimeter shell casings that had been fired. When you look at the head cap you can see where the firing pin hit the primer. What's important here is that this lends credence to Earl riding the aircraft in and either walking away from it or crawling away from it. The only Asians that were allowed to have Russian armaments were military personnel or district-level Communist officials or higher. John Q. Peasant did not have access to Russian armaments. If they were ever caught with them they would have been murdered. And remember, the closest village was Montagnard—ethnic tribal people. The other thing is that the North Vietnamese Army and the Pathet Lao did not have ammunition to waste. They did not just cook off a round for the hell of it—they had to have a good target. There were no battles fought in this area. Earl was the only man down in this area and the only target that would have warranted them shooting. So if this was Earl's crash site—and we're not convinced it was—then the ammunition proves that Communist troops or officials were there and there is a very real possibility that Earl was captured.

Out of that crash site have also come five teeth or parts of teeth, and twenty-three small, unidentifiable bone fragments. The only two whole teeth are the number eleven upper right eyetooth and the number twenty-nine lower left premolar. There is only the front facing from the center right upper tooth, the number eight tooth. Then they have what they're calling the eighteen and nineteen molars and both have very little root structure.

The teeth are his—they match up to Earl's dental records. But the question is, how did they get to the site? They could have been knocked out in a beating by whoever captured him. I would have been a whole lot happier if one or more of these teeth were in part of a jaw bone. The last time we saw any of these guys from CILHI [the Central Identification Laboratory–Hawaii] we said, "Teeth don't mean anything." Their claim is that if the two molars had been knocked out he would have bled to death. We said, "You're telling us that an Air Force Academy graduate isn't smart enough to so much as stick his finger in his mouth and apply pressure to stop the bleeding?" And their response was, "The teeth are his, therefore he's dead, and these are his mortal remains." What mushroom do they think we were hatched under last week?

We have talked to several dentists, including board-certified odentologists, and all of them tell us the same thing—these teeth do not prove that he's dead. All they prove is that they came out of his mouth. There is no way to tell whether they came out while he was still breathing or if he was dead.

CILHI also has twenty-three small bone fragments, twelve of which they have glued together to form what they are calling a four-inch section of femur. Now all of these "human remains" fit literally in the palm of my hand. If these bones are his, then it doesn't necessarily mean that he died, because he could live without these bones. There are no ribs, no vertebrae, no parts of a skull, no pelvic, there is nothing that says that this man is dead. The bone fragments are crap. They might not even be human.

And the question is, how did the teeth and bones get to the site? We asked for a crash site schematic and when you look at that—where the bone fragments were found, where the teeth were found, where the life-support equipment and engines and the afterburners and everything was found—it doesn't make sense. It's like somebody went there and just tossed stuff out. And nothing is below eight inches. Nothing. They had sterile soil at eight inches. It begs the question of this possibly being a salted site. We think the remains were probably taken back and placed there. We have no idea how long ago or by whom.

The question is not, *are* there live POWs in Southeast Asia today? The question is, how many? Who? Where are they? And, what is it going to take to get them out? The greatest fear of all the past administrations, both major political parties, is that a returned POW, any long-held POW, will walk up to a sitting president and say, "What took you so long? John Doe died five years ago. Harry Smith died a year ago. Somebody else died a month ago. What took you so long?"

The type and breadth and quality and quantity of POW information is staggering. Live sightings are continuing to come in. Firsthand live sightings. There is satellite imagery of authenticator codes that have proven to belong to specific men. Names have been picked up by satellite. The initials USA. There's another one that is XMAS and the only people on the face of this earth that abbreviate Christmas as XMAS are Americans.

COLONEL HOPPER

The names of three POWs were stomped out in grass or formed by rocks on the ground. One sign came out that was on the top of a building in a POW camp.

PATTY HOPPER

If we get Earl's real remains, not just a handful of broken teeth, then we will cry, we will bury him, and we will fight like hell for the rest of them. It's just that simple. If Earl is dead we can deal with that. Getting real answers is what this issue is all about. Is he alive today? I don't know. I can tell you this. I am very confident that he was alive through the spring of 1984. You see, the hardest thing in this entire issue is to come to grips with the fact that somebody was alive years after the end of the war. The easiest thing is to think of them as dead, being at peace with their God and not suffering.

COLONEL HOPPER

I feel the same way. We have been lied to and deceived too many times by officials of the U.S. government and military services. If they can give me some evidence that is logical and in my own mind I settle it that Earl is dead, then yes, I'll go along with it. But in the meantime, we're going to fight this thing as long as we can.

GLORIA COPPIN

"The government wanted to control the POW/MIA movement."

A daughter of privilege, her father founded the Hydro-Mill Corporation, an aerospace manufacturer in California. At a dinner party in 1966 she met some UCLA students "who said they were having problems with antiwar demonstrators—that campus unrest was a distraction from their education. I said I would help." They founded the Victory in Vietnam Association (VIVA), an organization she chaired until 1974. "We first made national news at Los Angeles City College when VIVA students returned furniture that antiwar demonstrators had used to create barricades, reopened the school, and ended the violence that had hospitalized many."

In 1968, Bob Dornan, host of a television talk show who later became a congressman, introduced her to three women whose husbands were missing in Vietnam. "I recognized how torturous it was for them not to know if their husbands were even alive. I pledged to them that I would devote the entire efforts of VIVA to alert every American to the plight of POW/MIAs and their families." With this new focus, VIVA changed its name to Voices in Vital America.

People sometimes ask why I was so active in VIVA when I had no family member in Vietnam. I think it's because I can't conceive of how anyone has the courage to face war and guns. I would do whatever I could to support them. I'm a product of World War II when everyone worked for the effort. I was frustrated that I wasn't old enough to drive a Red Cross truck. I could only raise a Victory Garden. The war movies left such a deep impression, particularly one called *The Purple Heart.* Dana Andrews led a bomber crew that had a phony trial in Japan. They were convicted to die and went to their deaths whistling the Army Air Corps song. I just cried buckets.

In 1967, I gave the first annual "Salute to the Armed Forces" dinner. A major purpose was to entertain a hundred enlisted men, most of whom had recently come back from Vietnam. We underwrote the dinner by charging corporate sponsors to attend a VIP cocktail party with the the governor, senators, congressmen, and top Pentagon brass. A friend steered me to Leroy Prinz, the choreographer of fantastic musicals in the early forties. He did a grand entrance of the admirals and generals with lights low and trumpets blaring. It was just awe inspiring. It was heartrending to see enlisted men with tears running down their cheeks saying, "We didn't realize anyone cared."

In 1969, Bob Dornan dropped by and showed me an elephant-hair bracelet he had received from a Montagnard chief during a trip to Vietnam. He said that it reminded him that no matter how tired he got, the Montagnards were suffering more than he was. I started to think how wonderful it would be if everyone had a bracelet to remind them of the suffering of POWs. So I found a very caring man with a small metal-working shop in Santa Monica who made the first bracelets on consignment. They were polished nickel-plated bands engraved with the name of a POW or MIA and the date he was lost. We put them in plastic bags with a card asking that it be worn until the man on their bracelet either returned home from prison or had been accounted for.

We introduced the bracelet at the 1970 Salute to the Armed Forces Dinner and it soon got to be a major thing. People took this so seriously. The bracelets were worn by all the top movie stars and some had to have their costumes redesigned because they refused to take them off. We had letters from parents asking if we could give special permission to their children so they could remove their bracelets for surgery.

They cost us about fifty cents and we charged two and a half dollars. The demand grew to the point that we opened sixty-eight offices across the country staffed with thousands of volunteers along with about one hundred staff on the payroll. By 1973, VIVA was bringing in more than seven million dollars a year. We put all the profits back into the POW/MIA cause. We bought brochures, buttons, bumper stickers, billboards, and match covers, which we gave to the National League of Families of American Prisoners and Missing in Southeast Asia to distribute. There wasn't a day that there weren't three or four POW/MIA events going on somewhere in the nation.

During my last five and a half years with VIVA I never had more than two hours sleep a night. In 1974, I was hospitalized for five days and diagnosed as manic-depressive and told I needed complete rest. That's when I resigned from VIVA. When I left we had more than five million dollars in the bank. Six months later, VIVA's doors were closed and I still don't know what happened to the money.

I felt I had failed everyone—the MIA families, the many who had contributed to our efforts, but most of all my own family. I had neglected my husband and children. My husband had sat alone drinking saying, "I can't live with you and I can't live without you." The guilt increased as I eventually lost both of my sons, one to drinking and drugs, the other to suicide. I can't help but ask myself how great a part my lack of attention played in their deaths. I had always told my husband, "I can't abandon twelve hundred families that need help," but soon I wondered how I could have abandoned the most precious family of all. My daughter turned out fine but she only recently forgave me.

The government wanted to control the POW/MIA movement. I was called to the White House one time and told by two men, "You do what we tell you to do." I said, "This is a nonpolitical issue and, besides, I'm a registered Republican. Why should you worry about me?" I said, "Nobody's going to control me," and I left. A few days later we were kicked out of our office in Washington that had been donated by the Red Cross. After the peace treaty, the Defense Department's director of public information was sent to California to damn me on talk shows. He said I was in it for the money, when he knew I never took a dime from VIVA or anyone else. There was a concerted effort by the White House to attack any of us who were bringing to light that Nixon's promises had not been kept and the issue had not been resolved.

I finally wondered if Nixon had used this whole cause to prolong the war. The antiwar movement was gaining momentum when the prisoner-of-war issue came along. As soon as it became a major issue Nixon was constantly on the tube saying he wanted to end the war but had to get a full accounting of all prisoners first. Yet the truth is that he and Kissinger signed a peace treaty that left fifty-five men who had been known to be prisoners totally unaccounted for. Someone had to know what happened to them but their families never will. Nixon left hundreds of family members in torture to this day.

The fact that my efforts may have contributed to more deaths than the number it may have helped will always haunt me. The only thing that makes me feel a little better about the whole situation is that by drawing the attention of the world to the issue, I think it led Hanoi to treat the prisoners better. The greatest reward I could have ever dreamed of was when Captain Harry Jenkins, a prisoner for many years, said, "I wouldn't be here if it weren't for you." Nevertheless, our efforts to gain closure for these many families failed, and when you go to Washington you may still see some people selling POW/MIA bracelets. It makes your heart break.

COLLAPSE

By the early spring of 1973 it seemed to most Americans as if the war was finally over. The last U.S. servicemen had come home from Vietnam, most notably the POWs who returned to well-orchestrated fanfare, including a White House dinner where Richard Nixon joked about the pleasure of addressing a "captive audience." Yet the national mood was far from celebratory. Most Americans simply wanted to forget the whole, long ordeal. News organizations quickly closed or downsized their Saigon offices and Vietnam fell off the front pages of newspapers and off the TV screen. College campuses grew quiet and the country turned inward, riveted by ever more Watergate revelations and the slow-motion collapse of the Nixon presidency.

The war, of course, was hardly over. The Paris Peace Accords had called for a cease-fire but each side almost immediately renewed hostilities. In just the first three months after the treaty was signed, ARVN forces suffered six thousand deaths while trying to extend South Vietnamese control in the countryside. Hanoi was determined to achieve its ultimate goal of national unification, but in no rush to launch a military offensive. North Vietnamese forces needed time to rebuild, regroup, and replenish themselves. Communist leaders were also concerned about provoking a U.S. reentry to the war if they should too flagrantly violate the Paris Accords. They focused on consolidating their regions of control and modernizing the Ho Chi Minh Trail with surfaced roads and an oil pipeline. The Soviet Union and China continued to provide more than a billion dollars in annual military aid.

Nixon was not at all resigned to defeat, either his own or South Vietnam's. He once again encouraged Hanoi to believe he might do anything to defend the Saigon regime. While U.S. military personnel were officially withdrawn from Vietnam, Nixon left behind nine thousand civilians. Many of them were discharged servicemen hired by the South Vietnamese to continue advising ARVN forces. Nixon ordered reconnaissance flights to be resumed over North Vietnam and hinted that he might also resume bombing. Unknown to most Americans, the bombing of Cambodia, begun in 1969, continued long past the Paris Accords. Whatever message that bombing may have been intended to send Hanoi, its primary effect was to drive a flood of Cambodian refugees into the capital of Phnom Penh and give the ruthless Khmer Rouge Communists greater control in the countryside.

However, Nixon's ability to pursue aggressive action in Southeast Asia was curtailed by an increasingly resistant Congress. In the summer of 1973, as the Watergate investigations began to damage Nixon more directly, Congress finally voted to end all U.S. military activities anywhere in Vietnam, Cambodia, or Laos. Although Nixon vetoed the bill, he agreed to stop the Cambodian bombing and other military operations in the region by August 15, 1973. In November, Congress overturned a Nixon veto and passed the War Powers Act, a measure that limited the time a president could deploy U.S. troops abroad without congressional approval.

In the final three years of the war, with broad public support, Congress also forced the White House to reduce annual U.S. aid to South Vietnam from $3.2 billion to $700 million. The South Vietnamese economy, long dependent on massive infusions of U.S. aid, spun out of control, bringing severe inflation and massive urban unemployment. Thieu's popular support, never widespread, declined further and his rule became even more authoritarian.

With Nixon's resignation in August 1974, North Vietnam began to accelerate its planning for a final offensive. In January 1975, after Communist forces took the province of Phuoc Long, just fifty miles northwest of Saigon, Hanoi was confident that victory was near. In March, its troops moved on the Central Highlands and the provinces south of the DMZ. ARVN forces collapsed. A panicky retreat quickly turned into a rout. Yet neither the American ambassador, Graham Martin, nor President Thieu acknowledged the inevitability of total defeat. To defend Saigon, Thieu pulled his most elite troops away from the front, causing further panic, while Martin continued to argue that complete surrender could be averted. Even as fourteen North Vietnamese divisions moved on Saigon, Martin refused to initiate an evacuation. Worried about Communist reprisals, many Vietnamese tried to find their own way out, some fifty thousand of them evacuating in the final weeks. Several days before the end, Thieu fled the country, leaving his regime in the hands of General Duong Van Minh, who had led the coup against Ngo Dinh Diem in 1963. On June 29, Ambassador Martin finally ordered an evacuation of Saigon. Within twenty-four hours some seven thousand people were lifted by helicopter from the city to offshore ships.

On the morning of the thirtieth, North Vietnamese tanks broke through the gates of the Presidential Palace. General Minh greeted a North Vietnamese officer by saying, "We have been waiting for you so that we could turn over the government." The officer replied, "You have nothing left to turn over."

Nearby, the North Vietnamese commander who had led the Final Offensive, General Van Tien Dung, phoned Hanoi to announce that the flag of the Provisional Revolutionary Government was now flying over the Presidential Palace. In the background he could hear the sound of fireworks going off and crowds of people singing in the streets of Hanoi. "I choked with emotion," he recalled. "The suffering of our separation had ended."

Communist victory did not bring the "bloodbath" that Nixon and other American and South Vietnamese officials had long predicted. However, it did subject hundreds of thousands of former ARVN veterans, government employees, and Vietnamese who had worked closely with or been in the pay of the Americans to years of imprisonment and "reeducation." Over the next fifteen years more than a million Vietnamese fled the country. Many escaped on small, crowded boats. Tens of thousands of these "boat people" died at sea of exposure, dehydration, drowning, and murder when their vessels were subjected to mechanical failure, storms, pirate attacks, and abandonment by foreign ships. Those who survived often had to endure years of hardship in refugee camps before gaining permission to resettle permanently in another country.

The specter of a Communist bloodbath was made real in Cambodia when the Khmer Rouge toppled the American-backed government of Lon Nol. U.S. policy in Cambodia from 1969 to 1973 had played a crucial, if unintended, role in building support for the Cambodian Communists. A once insignificant rebel group, the Khmer Rouge did not gain strength until the United States began secretly bombing Cambodia and giving massive military support to General Lon Nol, who overthrew the government of Norodom Sihanouk in 1970. While Sihanouk had managed to maintain a precarious independence from the fighting that engulfed Vietnam, Lon Nol fully allied his country's fate to the United States. As his regime became increasingly dependent on American aid, the Khmer Rouge received military support from North Vietnam and expanded their rural base of power by opposing the unpopular Lon Nol.

When the Khmer Rouge entered the capital of Phnom Penh on April 17, 1975, they renamed the country Democratic Kampuchea, established a new calendar (Year Zero), drove everyone out of the cities, and began systematically executing government officials, military officers, doctors, teachers, engineers, anyone who gave any hint of formal education or Western influence. The rest were assigned to labor camps where many died of overwork, starvation, or disease. Within three years the Khmer Rouge had killed at least a million Cambodians, one-seventh of the population, among the worst genocides of the twentieth century. Their reign of terror ended only when the Vietnamese invaded in 1979, defeated the Khmer Rouge, and installed a government that would rule for the next decade.

In the United States the fall of Saigon and Phnom Penh brought the nearly forgotten war roaring back into the news and American consciousness with graphic scenes of defeat—crowds of frightened refugees trying to climb the fence at the U.S. Embassy, North Vietnamese tanks rumbling unopposed into the capital of South Vietnam, American servicemen pushing helicopters off the decks of aircraft carriers to make room for further evacuations. Though the humiliating collapse seemed to sum up the worst of everything four American presidents had sought to avoid, the end of the war was followed by an eerie silence. The superpower that had experienced its first defeat quickly averted its eyes from the disaster. With its own land bearing no physical scars of war, few Americans were eager to reflect on the wreckage they had left behind.

In the land of victory, however, the devastation of war was everywhere evident and unavoidable. Nearly two-thirds of the southern hamlets were in ruins and twelve million acres of forests had been destroyed, much of it by nineteen million gallons of chemical defoliants sprayed by the United States. There were more than two million widows, orphans, and disabled people. Tons of unexploded ordnance and land mines still riddled the land. The Vietnamese leaders retained hope that the United States would deliver the $4.75 billion dollars in reconstruction aid that Nixon had pledged in a secret protocol to the Paris Peace Accords. The United States not only refused to provide any part of that aid, but also extended the wartime economic embargo it had imposed on North Vietnam to the entire country. For the next two decades Washington refused to establish diplomatic relations with Vietnam, insisting that their former enemy had failed to provide a "full accounting" of Americans missing in action. Postwar hostility between the two governments lasted as long as the war itself.

FRANK SNEPP

"There was classified confetti all over the trees."

For many years he had nightmares about the Vietnamese voices that came in over the CIA radio pleading to be evacuated from Saigon in the final days of the war. "I'm Mr. Han, the translator. I'm Loc, the Nung guard. I'm Tran, the driver. Please do not forget me!"

He went to Vietnam in 1969 for the CIA as both an intelligence analyst and an operative responsible for interrogations and agent debriefings. In April 1975, with Communist forces closing in on Saigon, he pushed American authorities to begin evac-

uating the Vietnamese who had worked for the United States. After Saigon's collapse, when the CIA refused to conduct an internal review of the evacuation, he resigned and wrote Decent Interval, *a best-selling critique of U.S. actions in the final months of the war. In response, the CIA launched a successful legal campaign to seize his royalties and require that all his future writing be cleared by the agency, a restriction he is still bound to honor. His speech, however, is not subject to review and his memories of the war's end pour out, almost without interruption.*

The incredible thing was that our intelligence was impeccable. Because we had an agent inside the Communist command we had almost real-time fixes on changes in Communist planning. When Watergate had removed Richard Nixon in August 1974 we began to pick up intelligence reports that Hanoi was beginning to discuss the possibility that a military victory was in the offing. They thought Nixon was the craziest man around and might reenter the war at any point. But with him gone they began to think that the road to Saigon might be open.

Ambassador Graham Martin and CIA station chief Thomas Polgar had convinced themselves that the South Vietnamese army was in pretty good shape and could hold the line. Some of us in the embassy thought the ARVN was in serious trouble. Morale was terrible and corruption in the regime and army were endemic. Martin and Polgar thought these alarms were overdrawn and if only Congress would vote one more dollop of aid, that would solve things at least for the short term. I believed the South Vietnamese had plenty of materiel on the ground to hold the line but their commanders were stashing it away in the rear to sell for their own profit.

Throughout the fall of '74, the North Vietnamese were trying to find soft spots in the South Vietnamese defense lines, pushing and shoving, trying to determine if the South Vietnamese were ripe for the killing. They wanted to see if the United States in the wake of Nixon's resignation would send aircraft in response to provocation. In early 1975, they captured the provincial capital of Phuoc Long, not far from Saigon. The United States didn't respond with B-52s and that deeply impressed the Politburo.

We soon began to get intelligence that they were going to go for some real gains—not yet the capture of Saigon, but a major offensive. In March, they struck hard in the highlands at Ban Me Thuot and in MR-1 [the five northernmost provinces of South Vietnam]. That's when Thieu really began to trim his defenses, something he should have done much sooner but Ambassador Martin had led him to believe that the U.S. might intervene in a crisis, despite the War Powers Act and congressional opposition. Thieu's strategy was called "light at the top, heavy at the bottom," in other words, to lighten up on the defenses in the northern provinces and make them heavier around Saigon. But he didn't tell the United States Embassy what he was doing because he had come to distrust the Americans. He was also deeply concerned about the prospects of a coup. So instead of making rational decisions about which forces he should leave in the front lines, he decided to put his best units around Saigon to serve as sort of personal bodyguards. He pulled the airborne out of the North just as the Communists hit north of Hue.

Also, to maintain morale among front line forces, Thieu allowed them to keep their families with them very close to the fighting. So when the Communists struck and the ARVN began retreating they stumbled back upon their own families and you can imagine what that meant. Soldiers spent more time worrying about getting their families out of harm's way than trying to establish fallback defenses. In literally two weeks, half of the South Vietnamese army collapsed without putting up any major resistance.

I flew over MR-1 in the last days of March and saw General Truong's army literally racing into the surf off Danang. They were throwing their arms away and swimming for safety. It was total, utter panic. I've never seen anything like it. Thousands of soldiers were in the surf. They were retreating in the face of the North Vietnamese onslaught. In the Highlands the Communists began pushing very rapidly toward the coast from Ban Me Thuot as the South Vietnamese army retreated. Within a matter of three or four days the North Vietnamese were able to slice the country in two just north of Nha Trang.

At the time, Ambassador Martin was back in the United States having dental surgery and trying to persuade Congress that additional aid would save the Saigon regime. He arrived back in Saigon at the end of March just as the worst was coming to a head. I was his principal military briefer so I went into his office and said, "Mr. Ambassador, I just came back from flying over MR-1 and I've seen the South Vietnamese army retreating into the sea." He said, "I don't believe you. Your intelligence must be mistaken."

Let's pause for a moment to consider the ambassador. Martin had been sent to Vietnam because a lot of his critics and admirers thought he was the next best thing to a B-52. He was headstrong and absolutely impervious to persuasion. It was thought in Washington that Martin was exactly what was needed to hold the line. He was there to give the appearance of American stalwartness and commitment. He had also lost his adopted son in Vietnam, a combat soldier who was killed by enemy fire. Given all that, Martin was the last guy who was gonna concede that country to the Communists. Just to give you an idea of how strange his perspective was, after half of South Vietnam had been routed with virtually no resistance, Martin cabled Washington proposing a five-year economic plan for South Vietnam. He had drifted into a complete dream world.

Now we're in the first week of April and much to their own surprise the North Vietnamese have scored an amazing victory. The Politburo met and decided they were going to achieve total victory by Ho Chi Minh's birthday in May. Polgar became convinced that the situation was desperate but he had some secret feelers with Polish and Hungarian diplomats who persuaded him there was a chance for a negotiated settlement. At the same time the French ambassador began pouring the same message into Ambassador Martin's cup. So just as all this intelligence came in saying there was no chance of a political settlement, that the Communists were bent on total military victory, and just at the very moment when we should have been planning for an evacuation, Polgar and Martin were perusing the will-o'-the-wisp of a negotiated settlement.

Polgar did have me write an estimate of how many Vietnamese we would need to pull out in the event of an evacuation. At the very least, I thought we'd be facing the burden of getting out a million Vietnamese who had worked for the CIA, the embassy, and the U.S. military. But Polgar let our evacuation planning idle along and Martin was doing his best to ensure that no one planned for evacuation.

The only evacuation Martin embraced before the very end of April was Operation Baby-lift. The idea came to him as a result of the efforts of Ed Daly, the owner of World Airways. Daly had been instrumental in evacuating Danang and was trying to organize an airlift of Vietnamese orphans to the United States. Martin heard about it and urged the White House to organize a similar airlift. He hoped the spectacle of hundreds of Vietnamese babies being taken under the American wing would generate sympathy for the South Vietnamese cause and perhaps loosen some last-minute aid from Congress. He also may have felt it would help placate those pushing for immediate evacuation.

In many ways Operation Baby-lift was a fraud. Few of the children were actual war refugees. Many had been in Saigon orphanages for months or years and were in no immediate danger from the Communist offensive. But at the time I applauded the enterprise as a first step in the right direction. During the morning of April 4 an air force C-5A Galaxy jet landed with a huge load of new war materiel for the South Vietnamese army. It was the largest air transport plane in the world. As soon as the plane was unloaded they filled it with two hundred and forty-three orphans. Thirty minutes out of Saigon there was a mechanical failure. It turned around to come back, but crashed on its approach. It was heartbreaking. More than two hundred of the children were killed.

Hundreds of orphans were eventually evacuated but the ambassador continued to oppose any other efforts to help Vietnamese leave. In defiance of orders, young embassy officers began to sneak more and more Vietnamese onto outbound aircraft. And in Washington young officers at the State Department began to push Kissinger to get Martin focused on evacuation planning. But all of this was taking place with no formula or coordination. And no one was putting pressure on the Immigration and Naturalization Service to lift their ceilings to allow for more Vietnamese émigrés and to streamline their processing. Martin would later use this as his alibi for not evacuating large numbers of Vietnamese before the end.

By mid-April I became so concerned I decided to call our best agent in out of the field again to double check his earlier report. He came in disguise and I met him in Saigon. I always gave him a Budweiser and Salem cigarettes. They were Ho Chi Minh's favorites so he went for those. He confirmed that the Communists were going for broke. I raced back to the embassy and to my horror Polgar wouldn't let me send that report out through a top-priority channel.

Martin was still hoping to stabilize defenses north of Saigon at Xuan Loc and find a political settlement. He wanted somebody in the saddle he thought could deal with Hanoi so by April 23 he decided it was time to get rid of Nguyen Van Thieu. He persuaded Thieu to step aside and to make sure that Thieu didn't pull any funny stuff, Martin decided to get him out of the country. I'll never forget Polgar calling me to say, "I've got a very special job for you—you're gonna get Thieu to the airport tonight." I was assigned to drive the limousine to carry Thieu in total anonymity and blacked-out conditions to a rendezvous point at Tan Son Nhut air base, which was equally blacked out, to be picked up by a blacked-out CIA flight out of the country. When I arrived, Thieu came out with General Charles Timmes, a CIA operative. As they climbed into the back of the car some of Thieu's aides threw suitcases in the trunk. They tinkled like metal. Thieu had already moved most of his gold out of the country, so I think this was just his stash. The city was in chaos. One hundred and forty thousand North Vietnamese troops were within an hour or so of downtown Saigon. The defenses north of the city at Xuan Loc were collapsing. It was terrifying. There was great concern that Air Marshall Nguyen Cao Ky would step in to kill Thieu and take over by force so we were heavily armed. Thieu was crying all the way to the airport. At one point he was talking about the artworks he'd gotten out to Taipei and Hong Kong. We passed the sign outside Tan Son Nhut, a tribute to American dead that said something like, "The noble allied sacrifice will never be forgotten." Thieu sort of whimpered as we passed that.

The CIA plane was waiting in total blackness. As I swept across the runway toward what I hoped was the aircraft I nearly ran over Polgar. We pulled up at the waiting aircraft and the engines were going. It was right out of *Casablanca,* except Bogart and Bergman weren't there. Who was there was the ambassador. As Thieu got out of the car he leaned over and grabbed my hand and said, in his French accented English, "Thank you, thank you for everything." It went through my mind, thank you for what? I mean, we've lost fifty-eight thousand boys here, is that what he's thankful for? Or simply his own escape?

Thieu raced for the aircraft and Martin literally helped him by the elbow up the stairs. Then Martin leapt down and began dragging away the stairway as if he were trying to rip away the umbilical of the American commitment to Vietnam. I ran up to him and said, "Mr. Ambassador, can I help, can I help you?" He just stood there in panic saying, "No, no, it's done, it's done."

Thieu's departure didn't settle anything. Martin still believed there would be some kind of negotiated settlement and refused to plan for a last-ditch withdrawal. We hadn't even begun to destroy all of our classified files. So all during those final days and nights the embassy shook in a constant tremor as we tried desperately to rev up the incinerators on the roof near the helipad to burn our documents. At one point Martin walked out to the parking lot and there was incinerator dust all over his limousine and he began desperately wiping it off. He said, "We can't have this. It's a sign of flagging American will." He was becoming increasingly unhinged. About that time we asked him if we could chop down this great tamarind tree that overshadowed the parking lot so there would be room if we had to land choppers there to evacuate people. He refused. He said, "No, no, you can't take that tree down. It's a symbol of the American resolve and you would telegraph the wrong message."

There was not even a master list in the embassy of the Vietnamese we should be most concerned about. There was no attempt to prioritize who needed to get out. The ones who got out first tended to be the most corrupt and highest ranking members of the former Thieu regime. Several days before the end they were all happily waving good-bye and hopping into choppers in civilian clothes. It was every man for himself. Lots of Americans were cramming Vietnamese friends onto aircraft. They were lovers, housemaids, and friends but not necessarily the people in the greatest danger. The Vietnamese intelligence agents were getting no priority whatsoever. Many of them were still out in the boonies manning radios or translating documents.

On the morning of the twenty-ninth the Communists began shelling the edges of Saigon, just as our intelligence had predicted. Massive shelling. It blew me out of bed. I had hardly slept for fourteen days and had just gotten to sleep. I stumbled, pushed, and shoved my way through thousands and thousands of Vietnamese gathered outside the walls of the embassy.

We were getting information that the drive on Saigon was under way and that the Communists would not only hit the air base with artillery but would, at six o'clock on the twenty-ninth, begin bombarding the center of Saigon, the embassy, and the South Vietnamese presidential palace. We had no orderly airlift. The evacuation fleet had arrived offshore but because of a glitch in planning they had somehow screwed up Saigon time for Greenwich mean time. They had meant to have the big CH-47 choppers—the Jolly Green Giants—in Saigon first thing in the morning but we didn't see any of them until early afternoon.

In the meantime, the ambassador, still convinced there was a chance for a fixed-wing airlift, insisted on driving out to Tan Son Nhut through the chaos of the city to see the airstrip. When he got there, just as the defense attaché had told him, it was impassable. So he came back to the embassy and said, "Okay, it's time for stage four of 'Frequent Wind.'" That was the code name for the helicopter airlift. Americans and Vietnamese dependents in Saigon had been told to listen to the American Radio Service for notification that the evacuation was beginning. The signal was playing the song "White Christmas" followed by the statement "The temperature in Saigon is one hundred five degrees and rising."

I'm in the CIA operations room. We're hearing messages from abandoned Vietnamese agents screaming and pleading, "Please come get us, we're gonna die, we're gonna die." So I began helping Air America contract flyers move around the city in these small choppers to pick up Vietnamese and Americans at various makeshift rooftop pads. Nobody was telling me what to do. At one point a CIA guy raced in and said all our translators were still out there. We had about seventy of them and as the day wore on I discovered that the CIA agent assigned to make sure they were evacuated had evacuated himself and left them all at the CIA hotel. After the Communists took over they machine gunned most of the Vietnamese in that hotel.

Finally around two P.M. the big choppers began dropping in and moving people off the blasted runway at Tan Son Nhut and off the roof and parking lot of the U.S. Embassy. The incinerators on the roof were still going full blast, but they couldn't be worked fast enough to eat up all the material. There was dust all over the trees and at one point we took bags of half-shredded secrets down to the embassy courtyard and when the choppers began landing they blew open all of these bags. There was classified confetti all over the trees.

We began to move Vietnamese into the embassy itself to be pulled off the roof. There were people in the halls with farm animals, weeping children, and almost no water. The air-conditioning and the elevators broke down and it became a scene from Dante's *Inferno*. There was a terrible fear that the Vietnamese might riot if they believed they were being left behind. And there were all sorts of weapons around the embassy that Americans had discarded when they left.

At one point I went down to the ambassador's office. He was on his hands and knees shredding his own most classified files by hand. Around six o'clock we got word that the Communists had called off their bombardment because they believed the Americans were all leaving. By nine-thirty there were only seventeen CIA officers in the embassy. Polgar told me he wanted me to leave. He stayed to come out with the ambassador. I walked into this jammed hallway and the marine guards began beating the Vietnamese out of the way so that the seventeen of us could get to the roof of the embassy. I couldn't look in their eyes as I was making my way to the roof. When I got to the top I could see the headlights of the North Vietnamese Army on the edge of the city—pearls of light as the entire one hundred and forty thousand troops that had marshaled around Saigon moved in. They were within a half hour of downtown. They were so brazen they hadn't even extinguished their lights. Tracers were going out all along the horizon and the ammo dumps at Bien Hoa air base were going up in massive explosions. There were occasional American jets on the horizon putting down suppressing fire. This is not very well known since Americans were supposed to be out of Vietnam, but they were brought in because the situation had become so desperate. Over the edge of the helipad I saw thousands of Vietnamese in the streets. They were desperate but they weren't screaming. They were oddly silent. Everyone was looking towards the embassy for a rescue that would not come, but they were terrified that if they created any disruption they wouldn't get out. As the chopper made its way toward the coast we began taking massive ground fire. We gained altitude and got out but I kept thinking how ridiculous it would be to be shot down on the way out.

In many ways the war ended just as it had been conducted by the Americans, with an often total disregard for the lives at stake. And there was a personal aspect to it all. About forty-eight hours before the end I got a call from a Vietnamese woman I had had an on-and-off relationship with since my first year in Vietnam. She had disappeared from the city in 1973. Near the end of 1974 she showed up at my door with a year-old baby boy. I believe it was my own child. So just before the collapse she called and said, "You've got to evacuate me because the Communists will kill me for running around with an American and having an American child." I was working on another report for the ambassador so I said, "Look Mai Ly, call me back in an hour. I'll do what I can to get you out of the country." She said, "You better because if you don't I'm going to kill myself and this child." She called back in an hour or so and I was briefing the ambassador and missed the call. On the last day I saw a policeman who knew her and asked him to go find out where she was. He sent word back to me that she had killed herself and the kid. I've never been able to verify it, but as I came off the roof of the embassy I was overwhelmed with this numbing guilt. I was focused on trying to persuade a recalcitrant ambassador to pull the plug on the American commitment and I, too, had forgotten that lives were at stake. I should have been out there getting this woman and child out of the country. I had basically become what so many Americans became in Vietnam—all there to do the job but forgetting the human stakes.

TRUONG TRAN

"We could either lose or tie, but not win."

We live in the same Massachusetts town and have sons who went to high school together. He stops by one Sunday afternoon to talk about his life in Vietnam. Born in 1947, he was drafted into the South Vietnamese military and served from 1964 to 1969, rising to the rank of staff sergeant. During the final years of the war he was a rural development specialist for the U.S. State Department. He left Vietnam with his family in 1975.

I often think about why we lost the war. We received assistance from the most powerful country in the world, yet we lost. When the United States decided to land foot soldiers in Vietnam, with all good will, it put the South Vietnamese at a political disadvantage. The North was able to mobilize southerners as well as northerners to fight what they called the American invasion. All of our history has taught children that you have to be courageous enough to fight foreign aggressors. We could not tell our brothers and sisters that we were fighting for ourselves as long as American soldiers were in the country fighting for us. We said we were fighting to save the country from Communism, but that was too abstract and people could say that at least the Communists were Vietnamese.

I came from a very poor farming family in Vietnam. My mother died when I was five and my father died when I was sixteen. When the war broke out I lived with my old grandfather and my five half brothers and sisters. The Americans used defoliants to clear the jungle and it killed my grandfather's coconut plantation. I still remember when he showed me the dead trees. He said, "This is my only source of income for my old age, but now it's all gone." Then he cried.

We lived in Binh Dinh, a coastal province where there was fierce fighting. In our province, if you followed the Communists you became a very committed Communist, and if you followed the nationalists you became an ultranationalist. When we clashed there was no tolerance. It was either you die or

I die. There were even family divisions, with brothers fighting against one another.

When I was drafted into the armed forces in 1964, I decided to join the regional forces as a private so I could stay near home and watch after my grandfather and my younger brothers and sisters. As it turned out, I was assigned two districts away so I only saw my family about once a year.

Our company provided security for three villages. Our commander was highly respected because he went out with us on patrols and ambushes while most of our leaders stayed in secure areas when their soldiers were killed. He said our main objective was to stay alive, not to win promotions. We moved around all the time so the other side couldn't figure out our habits. Our tactics created a lot of problems for the local Communist infrastructure. While most other units just went out for a few hours and then home to sleep, our commander waited until one or two in the morning to send us out on ambushes. That's when the guerrillas came to the villages to visit the people and receive supplies. We waited for them to leave the villages and ambushed them.

Our commander was very strict about how we dealt with the local people. He severely punished anyone who was arrogant or stole property because even stealing a chicken or some vegetables could create negative political repercussions. Anyone caught doing something like that was thrown in a tiger cage for seven days. But most of the men in our unit were well behaved and we developed a good relationship with the people.

One morning in 1967 we went out on patrol and were ordered from one little subhamlet to another across a wide open field. We got ambushed and four of us were wounded. Two died almost immediately. I was wounded in my arm and stomach and stayed in the hospital for eight months. When I got out I couldn't use my hand for two or three years. Because my English was better than most, they transferred me to a noncombat unit to work as a translator for American military advisers.

When I got out I worked for an American nonprofit organization called Save the Children in Qui Nhon. That was the happiest time of my life because I could see the results of my work and we were very effective. We worked with local hamlets to select poor families who needed economic assistance. We wrote case histories and matched families to sponsoring families in the United States. The money was given to the family as an interest-free loan to finance economic projects with a timetable of repayment. They repaid it to a community development account and that money funded projects controlled by an elected committee of people in their own hamlet. We were trying to bring democracy to the lowest level of society in the South. The Communists hated us. They denounced us as tools of the CIA and one of our team leaders was executed.

Then, in 1971, I worked for the U.S. State Department as a community development specialist for Civil Operations and Revolutionary Development Support [CORDS]. I worked with some very nice and knowledgeable Americans, but corruption was a very serious problem. When a province chief received a million piasters from CORDS for village development he would take a hundred thousand for himself. The rest would go to the district chiefs and they could take a portion. Then it went to the village chiefs who might take a piece of it as well. By the time it got to the village it was about fifty percent of what it started as.

Having U.S. soldiers in Vietnam not only destroyed our political cause, it also destroyed our economy and social fabric. Ninety percent of the population had relied on the land, but during the war people could not grow crops and had to move to the cities. Some people were lucky enough to get jobs with the U.S. military, but many had to become menial laborers or even prostitutes. And the prostitutes lived better than high-ranking South Vietnamese officials. Most government officials had a salary of less than twenty dollars a month, while prostitutes made five hundred or even a thousand. To support their families many people abused their power to make more money. Of course there was corruption, but how could you live on twenty dollars and maintain the will to fight?

We also lost because we agreed to fight a war that we could either lose or tie, but not win. The best we could ever do is keep half the country. On the other side, the Communists could either win or tie, but not lose. Since we were never able to fight in the North, the worst they could do is keep half the country. And since all Vietnamese hoped for eventual unification of the country, once again the North had a more persuasive goal. People might not want Communism, but the Communists could at least promise national unification.

As the Communists mounted their final offensive, Truong faced enormous obstacles simply getting his family from Qui Nhon, where he was working, to Saigon. First he discovered that the United States would not evacuate his much younger brothers and sisters. "I had promised my father I would take care of them regardless of what happened. How could I leave them behind?" So he took his chances at the airport. "When the first plane arrived, South Vietnamese soldiers beat away the civilians and hijacked the plane for themselves and their families." As other planes arrived Truong managed to get his wife and children aboard. Getting his two brothers on required a last-minute idea. "I knew they had to push the rolling stairs out to the plane so as soon as the plane landed I went out to the American with the stairs and said, 'Can I help you, sir?' I pushed next to him and as soon as we got to the plane I pushed my brother up the stairs. I used the same trick with my other brother and it worked again though he had his arm broken by a soldier."

In Saigon the family reunited and Truong roamed the city looking for an opportunity to evacuate the country. On the final day of the war, he went to the U.S. Embassy, his last resort. By a stroke of luck, he happened to know one of the security guards who let his family past the barbed wire into an area just in front of the embassy. Then a marine guard checked Truong's ID and let the whole family into the compound.

"We got in line. First the Americans had to get out. Then the Filipinos and Koreans. We were last." Once again he managed to get his whole family on choppers one by one. When he finally had only himself to worry about the choppers stopped coming. "It was around one A.M. on the thirtieth. Those of us still in the compound began a demonstration. We were locked behind a fence and started shaking it, chanting 'Help us, help us, help us!' Finally a Marine Corps lieutenant colonel came out. I served as translator for the group. He assured us we would be picked up. Everyone said we shouldn't take his word for it, so I said we wanted to talk to the ambassador. About two-thirty or three in the morning Ambassador Martin came out. Very brave. He said, 'I'm on the phone with Washington negotiating to get some more choppers. I assure you I won't leave without picking you up.' About four A.M. the next chopper came and as soon as it landed I ran to it. Sitting in that Chinook was very emotional. I left my country in a shameful way, but history left me with no other choice. Flying away, I was already thinking of how I could return to Vietnam. After twenty-six years I still haven't gone home."

"THE MERRIMENT WAS SHORT-LIVED"

LE MINH KHUE

"The letters remain, but the senders are gone forever."

She smiles readily, but a sadness does not seem to leave her eyes. In all likelihood, her parents were the victims of the Communist land reforms of the mid-1950s. With both parents dead, Khue was raised by pro-Communist relatives and, in 1965, at age sixteen, she joined the Volunteer Youth Corps. In the final years of the American War she worked as a journalist. Today, she is one of Vietnam's most distinguished writers of fiction. A collection of her short stories has been translated into English and is called The Stars, The Earth, The River.

My father died in 1953, my mother in '57. One of the main reasons for their early deaths was the land reform. It was one of the biggest crises of our history. They got caught in those drastic changes and couldn't survive. You might say they had a middle-class lifestyle, but they were just ordinary teachers. Perhaps my father came under suspicion because my grandfather was a mandarin at the Hue Court. His family had been well-to-do, but by the time he died we could hardly make both ends meet. I was still very young then and they made my mother send me away to be raised in another home. When she died four years later I didn't know why and I still don't. Land reform claimed a lot of innocent victims. My parents were among them.

My mother's sister brought me up. She was a Communist Party member. People told her that if she broke off ties with my family she would be given a good job. I don't know for sure if that's true. Her husband was also wholeheartedly devoted to the Communist cause. Both were determined to cut off all relations with the past and embrace the revolutionary life. They were good people though, very sincere and honest. Maybe they were just a little naive.

I was strongly influenced by my aunt and uncle. They had pure motives and loved the revolution. Their fervor was almost childlike. The good education I received from them taught me to love our country. But our generation has a different understanding. We learned to distinguish truth from falsehood, rectitude from corruption. My foster parents could not make those distinctions. In spite of the fact that their own families were broken up, they still believed that no policy promulgated by the party could be a mistake. Sometimes when we argue with them, they get very upset by our views. Thanks to their purity of motive and their zeal they survived the war and even won a victory. That's good, but don't forget that there is still some dishonesty and crookedness lurking below the surface of everyday life. The older patriots are too pure to acknowledge that.

To be honest, we, too, never lost our faith in the cause. It was really a good and beautiful time, a romantic time. Perhaps I joined the Volunteer Youth Brigade for romantic reasons. In those days our whole generation suffered from romanticism I think. I went to war without any understanding. I was very young—just starting high school. The Vietnamese have a proverb: "Deaf people are not scared of guns." I was like that. I didn't know what war was like. I lied about my age to get in. We must admit that our propaganda machine worked very effectively then. It lured all the people to the front. Those not accepted for military service were very disappointed.

Before I joined the Youth Brigade I lived with my foster parents in a village in Sam Son [south of Hanoi]. Close to the village was a military camp. In the first days of the war the Americans tried to bomb that camp but the bombs hit the village. On that day we had left school early to go on a field trip. When we came back there was the most horrible scene I ever witnessed. Since it was one of the earliest days of the war no one had dug bomb shelters. They hid under trees holding their babies tightly to their chests and a lot of people were killed still holding their children tight. Some people tried to hide in a pond and died there. Bodies were piled everywhere. That's the first time I saw a lot of people killed. I helped carry the dead to the village road where the bodies were placed for people to identify. It looked so scary. The next day another bomb killed my favorite teacher, a very nice man from Hanoi named Tiep. His head was blown apart. Those were the two most horrible days of my life. I don't think people can imagine how ferocious the war was. It makes my spine shiver whenever I think of it.

I don't know how I survived. For a long time my volunteer unit worked close to Route 1. Every night we had to go down to a canal with a detection device to find and remove mines so our boats wouldn't explode. Sometimes bombs fell nearby and we couldn't see anything except smoke and fire.

There's one day that's always on my mind. I was carrying a box of ammunition over a bridge when I was caught in an American air strike. During the day we regularly removed almost all the planks from the bridge to reduce the damage that might be caused by bombs. We left just one plank on either side. At night we put them back so the trucks could cross. I was a small girl on a single plank and that box of ammo was just so heavy. I was halfway across when an American plane fired a rocket at me. I just stood there paralyzed. I couldn't move. I thought I was going to fall and die whether the rocket hit me or not. A young man came back and helped me cross. Even now when it comes to mind, I'm overcome by fear.

Every day we looked for mines and unexploded bombs, filled up bomb craters, tried to grow food, and helped transport the wounded. That was the daily routine. In some places the air carried such a horrible stench you knew many people had died. But even death becomes routine and we had to live—so even during air strikes we chitchatted. Now, whenever there's a thunderstorm it brings back the memories of bombing. I'm so scared of thunder and lightning a friend has to sit beside me to calm me down.

Even in such chaotic times we enjoyed moments of peace and beauty. You know, the jungle was so beautiful. There were about one hundred boys in my unit and fifty girls. We were like classmates. From the ages of fifteen to eighteen we stayed in the same unit, but when the boys turned eighteen they had to go to the front. I was too young for love, but when there was no bombing we enjoyed some very romantic moments. It was natural that we girls would have feelings for the soldiers. We saw regular troops all the time. They were young, healthy, muscular, and they looked cute in their uniforms. No girl failed to be impressed. But they never came back. Quang Tri Province was a meat grinder that let no one escape. So relations in wartime were always temporary. Soldiers passed through your life and sometimes sent back letters. I received quite a few and they were a great pleasure to read. The letters remain, but the senders are gone forever.

I didn't believe in anything. I just hoped for the war to end. When I was a kid I saw a lot of Russian movies with reunion scenes—tears and flowers and everything. So I always looked forward to that day for our soldiers.

As a war correspondent, if I saw something heroic, I would write about it. I was always crazy about heroes. I love anything extraordinary. I even got a crush on the driver I traveled with. He wore a steel helmet and a bulletproof jacket and he maneuvered a big truck so well during air raids. Sitting beside him, I was so impressed. When I look back on that period, sometimes I can't help laughing at myself. I think everybody misses the feeling of unity. Men were so good then—so nice and so good. I often slept in a hammock among tough truck drivers for weeks at a time and nothing happened to me. They were pure of heart. You can hardly find men like them now.

In 1975, I was among the first to witness the liberation of Danang. I entered the city on a military truck. As we approached, southern soldiers were fleeing the city in their shorts and undershirts. They had stripped off their uniforms. I wondered why they didn't attack us or try to retake the city, but they didn't make any effort to resist. They waved to us. It meant the war was over. What an unbelievable feeling. Those first days were so much fun. Students came forward to welcome us and children came to see us and learn some of our songs.

But the merriment was short-lived. I was soon overwhelmed by feelings of disappointment. People in the North always thought the cities in the South must be big and well equipped and luxurious, but when I walked around Danang I soon realized it was merely a consumer city. It lived on goods, so when the products were gone, it was just another impoverished city. There was plastic stuff everywhere—even the roofs were made of plastic—but there were no big factories, nothing.

I felt so bored. My only entertainment was reading. I found copies of books by Erich Remarque [author of *All Quiet on the Western Front*]. We were very fond of his work, maybe because he wrote about situations we had experienced. I stayed in my room and devoured all his books while everybody else went shopping. I don't know why, but I hated their desire to buy things. They all thought I was a crazy girl. Then everybody in my unit wanted to go to Saigon, but I refused. I had a premonition that something bad would happen so I returned to the North. By the time I got back to Hanoi, Saigon had been liberated for one month and I discovered Hanoi, too, had changed dramatically. People just talked about buying and selling things and going south. You can't imagine how crazy people were after the liberation. Their craving was so strong, it disgusted me. And the ten years after the liberation were a nightmare. Something had broken down; something had fallen apart. People had no money, but money was the master. We lacked everything, even soap and rice. It was terrible.

PART SIX

LEGACIES (1975–)

MISSING IN ACTION

TRAN VAN BAN

"We saw so many parents crying for their lost children."

He fought against the Americans from 1967 until 1972 when he was seriously wounded. After the war he went to medical school. Beginning in 1977, he has spent countless weekends trying to recover the remains of Vietnamese killed during the American War. There are, by most estimates, several hundred thousand Vietnamese missing in action. Most of his recovery efforts have focused on the "Iron Triangle," a region northwest of Saigon that was the site of innumerable firefights and massive U.S. bombing. "If you have time I can take you to the Iron Triangle where we cannot find dirt enough to fill up all the bomb craters."

During wartime I witnessed a lot of American deaths, but most of their bodies were recovered. The Americans cared deeply about their dead and were very successful recovering their casualties. Of course, in some cases their soldiers were killed alone in isolated places, especially pilots who crashed in the jungle or at sea and it was almost impossible to reclaim their bodies. However, during the war whenever we found Americans who had been killed, we buried them properly. After the war I showed the American MIA teams these burial sites so they could repatriate the remains.

Let me say why I did it. Many times I witnessed wounded American soldiers screaming and crying for their parents. That was our experience as well. And when we came home after the war we saw many parents crying for their lost children. We realized American parents also grieved for their children. Although we hated our enemy during the war, we now want to heal the wounds.

As for Vietnamese missing in action, it's hard to give a good estimate of their number. We didn't have a precise system for keeping track of all our forces. The American system was very clear—they had records for everyone who enlisted and where they served, so after each battle they knew immediately how many were killed, or wounded, or missing. But our forces were so diverse it was impossible to keep track of everyone. In addition to the regular troops from the North, we had volunteer youth, local militias, and southern guerrillas.

Even when we find the remains of our dead, it's often difficult to identify them. The Vietnamese didn't carry identification like the GIs with their dog tags. When we could bury our comrades after battles, we wrote their names on very small pieces of paper and covered the slips of paper with wax to keep them from getting wet. Then we rolled them up, inserted them into pens, and buried them with the dead, or sometimes we put the person's name inside a small empty medicine bottle and put it in his mouth. So if we find these burial sites we can often identify the bodies.

But despite our best efforts, these sites are extremely difficult to locate. When we withdrew from the battlefield, American tanks sometimes rolled through and flattened the markers we had left. And the U.S. bombed so much they left many of our battlegrounds completely unrecognizable. The landscape has changed so dramatically that even if we know there are bodies in a general area, we have no idea where to begin looking. And many bodies were blasted to shreds by the bombs and will never be found. Others have almost totally decomposed.

Also, many times we had to withdraw so quickly we couldn't recover our dead and the Americans buried them in mass graves. We are very thankful to the American veterans who've come back to Vietnam to show us the whereabouts of some of those burial sites. Unfortunately, when we do find mass gravesites we rarely identify anyone. Looking at those bodies and not knowing who they are or where they're from is really a tragic sight. We know they were our friends, but we have no names for them. We sometimes find personal belongings like hats, sandals, and pens. Seeing such things compounds our sadness.

We always wash the bones we find. Then we wrap them in a white cloth and put them inside a plastic bag along with whatever information, if any, we might have about the person. We never seek perfection. Even when we find only a piece of bone we consider that good enough and treat it as if it were the full remains of one of our comrades. If we don't know the identity we still have a solemn memorial service. We devote a lot of attention to the funeral oration in which we enumerate the achievements and sacrifices of the fallen soldiers and express our gratitude for their contribution. We must always urge the living to remember those who died for them.

TOM COREY

"Why do you hate the Vietnamese?"

In 1999, we meet at a Hotel in Hue, the old imperial city of central Vietnam, where he is leading a delegation from Vietnam Veterans of America (VVA). They have been coming to Vietnam to share information with the Vietnamese about missing in action on both sides. Originally from Detroit, the second oldest of ten children, he served in Vietnam with the First Cavalry Division. On the second day of the Tet Offensive in 1968, near the DMZ, he was shot in the neck and paralyzed from the shoulders down, later recovering only partial use of his arms. Despite the many discomforts of travel, he has been to Vietnam seven times over the past five years.

In 1993, VVA was part of a presidential delegation traveling to Vietnam to discuss American POW/MIAs. During the meeting the Vietnamese said, "You only come here to ask about missing Americans. Well, what about the missing Vietnamese? We have over three hundred thousand missing. Are you going to help us find them?" So we went home and started the Veterans Initiative. We sent out a letter to our membership requesting that they turn over any personal items they may have taken off Vietnamese bodies during the war—photos, letters, anything that might help identify someone. They were just souvenirs to Americans, but they're very important to the Vietnamese. We also asked our members for information about the locations of grave sites where they had buried Vietnamese bodies. We've received many maps that guys drew from memory. On our first trip back we brought a map of Tay Ninh Province and it led us right on top of a grave site at what had once been LZ [Landing Zone] Grant. So far we've returned information on over eight thousand Vietnamese MIAs and they've used it to recover the remains of over eight hundred people.

When we bring documents to Vietnam we always carry them in a briefcase. We treat them with great respect, as if they were people, and precious, not just a bunch of papers to be thrown in an envelope. In 1994, the first time we brought back information on missing Vietnamese, we met with General Vo Thu, the president of the Veterans Association in Danang. When we handed him a briefcase, he clutched it with both hands and walked back to his seat. He couldn't speak. Then he started weeping. When he began talking he was so quiet the interpreter had to lean over to hear. He told us that his brother was among the missing and that it was his great hope to have his remains discovered so they could be buried properly. On our next trip General Vo Thu was so happy to see us. He said, "I've got good news. We found my brother's remains. Only relatives of the missing can understand what that's like."

Our work has strengthened their commitment to help us find Americans. Just recently a Vietnamese veteran from Quang Tri Province came forward. It turns out that in 1966 he found the body of an American pilot washed up on shore and buried him. He never reported it until he read about what we were doing. So he went to the local veterans association and told them where he buried the body. That led to the recovery of remains. There are many examples like this one.

When American remains are repatriated in Hanoi they are returned to the Central Identification Laboratory in Hawaii. Once they make a positive identification they notify the family. There are some cases when families won't believe, or accept, the evidence provided. They say, that's not my husband's remains, or my father's, or my son's. They still believe he's alive so they keep pushing for more information, sometimes denying what's given. It's a very emotional issue.

One of the reasons many Americans believe prisoners are still being held in Vietnam is that the Vietnamese say they never tortured any prisoners. They say, "It was our policy not to torture. Ho Chi Minh made a clear statement that we didn't." I respond, "I understand those were Ho Chi Minh's words, but it happened and you know it happened. Don't sit here and tell me it didn't. That's what's hurting you. If you say you didn't torture, how will people believe you when you say you don't have live American POWs?"

There are a lot of Americans who still have anger toward the Vietnamese. That may never change for some. My brother-in-law hates the Vietnamese. He was a marine door-gunner and lost a lot of good friends. He always says to me, "Tom, do me a favor. When you're leaving, nuke the place." I say, "Why do you hate the Vietnamese? Did they ask you to come to their country and destroy it and kill their people? They were defending their country the same as we would if it was reversed." It was a bad situation for all of us. I mean, put the blame where it should go. Who sent us here? Who lied to us?

In Vietnam after the war, their veterans were welcomed back home. We weren't welcomed home, and we had to fight with Congress to address the needs of veterans suffering from post-traumatic stress disorder, from the effects of Agent Orange, and with health-care needs in many areas. The Vietnamese have had a lot easier time getting on with their lives. We've learned a lot by meeting the former enemy under different conditions. We're helping each other, veteran to veteran, to resolve issues from the war.

During our first trips here we had meetings with Vietnamese when some anger was expressed. I can understand why. We came here and bombed the shit out of them. I'm sure I would feel the same way. But they don't really take it out on us. They understand we were doing our job as soldiers, the job our country had called on us to do. My anger toward the Vietnamese was mostly in the heat of battle. My anger has been more in dealing with my disability, confined to a wheelchair, and about what our government did to us. I also had a lot of anger toward the protesters. I was in favor of what the war was supposed to accomplish. I supported it. I remember lying in a hospital bed watching the protesters on TV—even the Vietnam Veterans Against the War. I was angry because I still had friends fighting. I think they had a right to protest, but I don't think they knew what they were doing to the morale of our soldiers. Some protesters had nothing else to do with their lives. It was an excuse to stay high, carry flowers, and hang out at airports calling us baby-killers. There were other people who protested who understood more than I did at the time. But many didn't have to go to Vietnam. I didn't think it was fair that others had to go and those who knew someone didn't.

On my return to the States I was sent to Fitzsimons Army Hospital. I was totally paralyzed. I mentioned that my neck was hurting really bad so they decided to drill holes in my skull and put in these weighted tongs to sort of stretch it. I was on this electric bed that turns you in circles and they didn't strap me in good so I slid down with the weights in my head while still turning. I thought, get me out of this world. I was next transferred to the Memphis VA. I was in a room with three other guys from Vietnam with spinal cord injuries. We became best friends. Two of them committed suicide. I tried to figure out ways to commit suicide but I couldn't do it.

My father was very angry. He wasn't as much against the war before I went, but then he saw what was going on and realized that things weren't right in Vietnam. He came to hate the war and he hated Nixon. He still has a hard time looking at me like this in a wheelchair. I can see the pain in his eyes to this day.

When I come back to Vietnam I sit here on the balcony hearing the children playing and the birds chirping. There's a calmness in the air. It's so peaceful now.

He travels with a nurse, Janet Alheit. "My first time here with Tom, I was afraid. I thought the Vietnamese were going to be angry, but everyone was so kind. The irony is that this is where veterans heal. It's a very calming, subtle healing. It's amazing they had to come to Vietnam to get it. They got the welcome-home in Vietnam that they never received in the States."

WAR-ZONE CHILDHOODS

TRAN LUONG

"I never got there in time to capture an American pilot."

Like most Hanoi children during the American War, he was evacuated to the countryside. Born in 1960, from 1966 to 1972 he lived in eight different peasant villages. In the 1980s, he was a member of the "Gang of Five," a group of young, avant-garde Hanoi artists. In those years the Communist government forbade artists from exhibiting and selling abstract art because it fell outside the narrow strictures of Socialist realism, the state-mandated "people's art." In response, the maverick artists met privately every month to show each other their outlawed paintings. In 1990, the government loosened its artistic regulations and the "Gang of Five" had its first public exhibit. Much of his art is inspired by the many childhood hours he spent watching the "water life" in rural ponds and streams.

When the American bombing started we had to hide in the countryside. The government sent most of the rice to the troops so we ate everything we could find. The villagers taught me how to catch animals underwater by hand—shrimp, crabs, even fish. They showed me how to spot a fish underwater, how to keep very still, and then how to be . . . *very fast.* [Swiping the air with a hand, he laughs.] I could never do that now.

There was no real school. The older people just taught us informally at night underground by the light of a small oil lamp. A few times, for short periods, I went to school with other children, but we never gathered in large groups during the day. If you did, bombs would start falling in about fifteen minutes, and in the countryside there were no sirens to warn you of air strikes. We just ran as soon as we heard the airplanes. Sometimes the bombs fell just as people were starting to scatter for shelter. And if you were walking near a factory or the highway you always had to wear a long straw shield over your head and back to protect you from shrapnel. After bombing strikes we used to collect those little pieces of metal. They were still hot.

For many years I had a lot of nightmares, but they've disappeared. The most beautiful things still stay in my memory. You know, children always look for something mystical or romantic. I'm very thankful I had a chance to live in the countryside. The peasants were extremely kind and honest. They taught me a lot about Buddhism and traditional Vietnamese culture. If I'd grown up entirely in the city, I would have missed a priceless experience.

Vietnamese culture is largely based on water. Our words for country and water are exactly the same—*nuoc*. We've always depended on water to grow rice, for all our food really, and it's also what holds villages together since irrigation requires so much cooperation among neighbors. *Nuoc* has dozens of usages in Vietnamese and stirs deep feelings. It's not too much to say that it's synonymous with life itself. I spent a lot of time alone sitting quietly by a pond looking at the water life. I watched how a fish or a frog moved and even water grass kept me amused. There were no children's toys and no electric power and the real world I was living in was shot through with deprivation and suffering, but in the water I saw a peaceful and beautiful world that contrasted with the violent world of adults. It helped me maintain my love of life.

For all the pain I saw in the countryside, I wasn't terribly frightened. Adults were worried and scared, but for children wartime could be fun. When we saw American pilots floating down from the sky, we ran after their colored parachutes. We could recognize how high they were from the way the light changed as it shone through the parachute. I don't remember exactly how we did it, but we could say, "Ah, that man is very high." But the wind usually carried the parachutes far away. I ran and ran but I never got there in time to capture an American pilot.

Children hated American pilots because we could see the destruction they rained down on our country. In the fall of 1972 we returned to Hanoi. Everybody thought that peace was approaching. There had been no bombing for quite a while so the Christmas bombing caught us completely by surprise. Kham Thien Street in the busiest part of the city was destroyed by American bombs. Even the French embassy was not spared. The French ambassador and his wife were killed. The morning after the bombing I went to Kham Thien Street with some older children. I saw pieces of hair and scalp hanging on trees. It was an indelible sight.

BONG MACDORAN

"It's not worth my energy to lay blame on anybody."

"When I was young people would say, 'Oh, were you in a car accident?' I'd say, 'No, actually I was in the Vietnam War.' That usually sufficed. Most people didn't want to go any further and I didn't have any more information." She was born in a village south of Danang in 1965 or '66. She doesn't know the exact date. For many years, all she knew with certainty was that in 1968 she had been horribly wounded. Bullets had hit an arm, shoulder, and ankle, while an explosion of shrapnel ripped into her face. She was brought to the United States in July 1968 by the Committee of Responsibility to Save War-Burned and War-Injured Children (COR). Founded by American doctors and antiwar activists, COR provided medical treatment in the United States for about eighty Vietnamese children. Helping even that many was a huge effort given the red tape imposed by the American and South Vietnamese governments, each reluctant to support a project that drew graphic attention to Vietnamese civilian casualties caused, in many cases, by the American side.

Bong was one of the handful of COR patients who did not return to Vietnam. Since 1968 she has undergone fifty operations, some of them lasting almost fourteen hours. "I'm getting too old to do that anymore. I need one of those medical bracelets that tells everyone where my arteries have been moved." While part of her face remains scarred, she is an attractive, friendly banking consultant who lives in northern California. In the mid-1990s she began a concerted effort to learn about her history in Vietnam.

I've been slowly putting the pieces together. I was adopted when I was five, which is why I have this funny Scottish last name. I had five foster families between 1968 and 1971 before I got to the MacDorans. That was because my medical visa was renewed every six months. The Committee of Responsibility would tell people, "She just needs a home for six months and then we're sending her home." They were bound by their charter to return all of us to our Vietnamese families. My doctors would have huge debates about when I should go home because my surgeries were more complicated than a lot of the other kids'.

Even after I got to the MacDorans I was in limbo for a few years about whether I was going back to Vietnam. I took Vietnamese lessons and I hated them. I was an extremely obedient child and I'd do almost everything you could ever want me to do except learn Vietnamese. I rebelled against it. As a child I just wanted to melt into the background. I really wanted to be like all my friends who were Caucasian and normal middle-class Americans. I knew my mother was dead and after a while my Vietnamese father wasn't heard from again. Nobody could find him so the MacDorans decided they could adopt me.

I had no idea what happened to me in Vietnam but according to my American father I had a memory of losing my teeth and having a lot of blood in my mouth. When I was a little girl I had eating problems because I didn't have many front teeth. My father said, "One night at dinner you told us about spitting your teeth out. It grossed your mother out so much she told you to stop talking. I was really upset at her because you stopped and I wanted you to keep talking."

When I was in high school my father got a call from the girlfriend of my first foster father. That family had sent me away because they were having their own child. The girlfriend had found all the paperwork they had kept about me. It included these heart-wrenching letters from my Vietnamese father.

[From an album of documents she removes a letter dated April 10, 1972, addressed to the Committee of Responsibility. Only an English translation survives. It reads, in part:]

> I am the father of Nguyen Thi Bong. . . . I would like to send my thanks and best regards to COR and all people who have treated Bong through almost five years. The tasks that COR and everybody have done for Bong are as tremendous as the sky and as deep as the sea.
>
> However, it has been so long that I haven't seen her so I wish to receive her back soon. I am very grateful for your consideration and good-will.
>
> Sincerely,
> Nguyen Choung

When I first read this letter as a teenager I still wasn't prepared to think much about my past. I tried really hard not to be political, not to have an opinion. I knew the war was a huge issue for a lot of people as far back as I can remember. People were always trying to draw me into political discussions even at a pretty young age. I decided it was better to be ignorant than have to sidestep people's questions. It was a defense mechanism to be unknowledgeable about the whole subject.

In 1994, I was finally ready to find out about my Vietnamese heritage. I had a Vietnamese friend who was going back to Vietnam for a year so I gave him the one picture of my father I had and his last known address. My friend came back in 1995 and said, "I think I found your family." They had an exact copy of my father's picture so I was pretty sure we had the right people. It turned out I had a sister, a half sister, and two half brothers. I went back to Vietnam in 1996.

The hardest part about going back was learning that my father did not die in the early seventies as we believed. I asked, "Why did he stop writing?" The villagers said he went a little crazy, that even they couldn't find him for a number of years. He just wandered the countryside in a daze eking out some sort of existence and trying to find some meaning for his life. He'd lost his wife and half his children and his youngest daughter was in the United States. They said it tore him up inside to know I was alive but he couldn't see me. I heard over and over that he waited his whole life to see me again. They told me that one day a helicopter was circling over the village and my father ran out to greet it. He thought I was in the helicopter. Of course I wasn't. That was in 1990. The next day he died. If I had known he was still alive I would've jumped on the first plane to look for him. I would have gone back in a second.

Of course I also needed to know exactly what happened on the day I was injured. My village, Dien Ban, was attacked on January 26, 1968. I was told that the Viet Cong had control of the village at night, and the South Koreans had control during the day. When I heard them say South Koreans I thought I must have misunderstood. I didn't know South Koreans were involved in the war; I didn't even know what side they were on. Someone said they were sort of mercenaries for the Americans and some were horribly cruel. The South Koreans would torture villagers by locking them in a bomb shelter for days at a time with no water.*

On the morning of the twenty-sixth, the South Koreans grouped everyone together depending on where they lived. In one section of the village they burned everything and shot everyone. In another part they just shot everyone in sight but didn't burn the houses. In my part of the village I'm told they herded us all into a bomb shelter. I don't know how many people were in it, but when the villagers showed me the area in 1996 and judging by their hand movements, it appeared to be about twenty feet long and maybe eight or ten feet wide. The adults tried to cover the children with their bodies when the South Koreans started shooting everyone in the bunker. As they were walking away, I started crying. They came back, realizing not everybody was dead, and

*Through his "Many Flags" program, President Lyndon Johnson asked allies to offer military support to South Vietnam. Four nations sent combat forces—Australia, New Zealand, Thailand, and the Republic of Korea (South Korea). South Korea's participation was the greatest. Beginning in 1965, several hundred thousand Korean troops fought in Vietnam, with a maximum deployment by 1969 of about fifty thousand. Korean intervention was entirely financed by the United States and Korean troops were paid far more than their fellow soldiers at home.

threw a hand grenade into the shelter. That's what hit my face. My mother died and so did a brother and a sister. My older sister appears to have escaped without a single scratch. She and I were among the thirteen survivors. My father wasn't in the village that day.

The survivors telling me the story understood that I was a child and had no control over my crying. The nice way for me to think about it is that some action of mine actually put me where I am today because I truly believe if I hadn't been hurt by the grenade, the Committee of Responsibility would not have done anything for me.

The other really sad story that came out is about my oldest brother. I guess he was my favorite sibling. He had been gone a few days before the attack and I cried for him to come back. He came back the day before the massacre. As this story was translated to me it was sort of like hearing, "Your brother died because of you." When I kept hearing stories, it got to the point when I felt that I'd had enough gory details and didn't want any more.

I was the youngest child of the kids sent over by COR. They often used me as the poster child for a lot of their literature to tug at people's hearts. One reason they used my image was because I was so young nobody could blame me for possibly working on the "wrong" side. Some of the older kids had a hard time because some people would say, "How come you're helping them? They might have helped the Viet Cong."

Many people say the Viet Cong were this horrible enemy. When I found out they had saved me I was very confused. Five Viet Cong soldiers had been hiding in the jungle nearby and about six o'clock in the evening they came out and rescued the survivors. I have no idea how they got me to a hospital in Danang. I met two of these men when I was in Vietnam. It was nice to be able to look at those two Viet Cong veterans and thank them for saving my life. My ideas of who was bad and who was good got turned around. But there's really no bad or good. It's just people doing what they believe or what somebody else has told them to do. It's not worth my energy to lay blame on anybody.

The village was rebuilt near the old site. Where the village used to be is now a huge empty field. The South Koreans plowed under the whole village with bulldozers. In the middle of this empty field the villagers built a makeshift memorial for the victims of the attack. It's just a pile of dirt and rocks because they had no remains to bury. After it rains they pile more dirt on it.

My older sister still lives in Dien Ban. She grows rice and sweet potatoes and has twin girls whom she is raising by herself. When I saw how she lives I know I have a better life in the U.S. than I would have if I hadn't been injured. For that I am grateful. I acted very stoically when I was in Vietnam, but I was pretty overwhelmed. Between being horrified by the poverty, sad about my father, and thankful for my life in the U.S., I didn't have a lot of room for other emotions.

LOUNG UNG

"People just disappeared and you didn't say anything."

She was just five years old, one of seven children from a prosperous Phnom Penh family. Her father had been a captain in the military police under Lon Nol, the American-backed general who overthrew the neutralist regime of Prince Sihanouk in 1970 and who was himself driven from power five years later by the Khmer Rouge, the Cambodian Communists. "My father was powerful, my mother was beautiful, and I lived a charmed life. We had homes in different provinces and live-in servants. All that changed in 1975 when the Khmer Rouge took over Cambodia."

Like all the residents of Phnom Penh, her family was forced into the countryside. Over the next three years she lost both her parents and two sisters, victims of genocidal Khmer Rouge policies that resulted in the deaths of about a million and a half Cambodians, more than one-fifth of the population. In 1979, after the Vietnamese invaded to defeat their former Communist allies, she fled Cambodia by boat with her twenty-four-year-old brother and his wife. They spent several months in a Thai refugee camp before resettling in Vermont.

"The fact that the Khmer Rouge were able to commit one of the worst atrocities on earth is the fault of many countries, but without the U.S. carpet-bombing of Cambodia from 1969 to 1973, I don't think the Khmer Rouge would have come to power. Before the bombing the Khmer Rouge was a small guerrilla army with very little support from the peasants. The bombing gave the Khmer Rouge the propaganda they needed to recruit villagers."

I was playing hopscotch on the street when all these trucks roared into the city, every one of them filled with soldiers. I ran upstairs and asked my father who they were. He said they were Khmer Rouge and that they were destroyers. But why was everybody cheering and giving them food and flowers? He said it was just that everyone was happy the war was over. I started cheering with everybody else. The soldiers were so elated. When I came back upstairs my father and mother were packing up the house.

Everybody had to evacuate Phnom Penh—two million people. The Khmer Rouge soldiers weren't happy anymore. They were scowling and shooting in the air and screaming into their bullhorns for us to get out. They said, "You can come back in three days, but you've got to leave now because the U.S. is going to bomb." I remember sitting in the back of a truck. When it ran out of gas we walked. I had to carry a rice pot and it kept banging my shins. I was crying the whole time and kept asking my father when we were going home. Finally, he got down to my level, looked me in the eyes, and told me we weren't going back, that the Khmer Rouge had lied and I had to stop thinking about it.

We just kept walking and walking. At a military base the Khmer Rouge separated people into two lines. In one line they called for all the former Lon Nol soldiers, civil servants, and professionals. They said they needed all those people to help rebuild the country. But when people started to move into that line my father gathered the family around and quietly said with such urgency that he was going to tell them he was just a porter and that my mother had sold old clothes in the market. We were never to talk about our family or say anything that would permit people to know we were from the city. I was really confused but there was no time to explain. So we got in the line with all the poor people. The next day my brother said the people who went in the other line had all been killed.

I have a very sharp memory of arriving in a village and someone spitting at my father. I was so angry—I idolized my father—but he said nothing and told me to keep quiet. There were probably three or four hundred people in the town square who had just arrived. The soldiers started taking people's bags and emptying the clothes into a pile. Then they started preaching about how bad it was to have colorful clothing—how it was vain and Western and from now on everybody would wear the same black clothes, the same shoes, the same haircut, and eat the same amount of rice. When they got to our family, a soldier reached into my mother's bag and pulled out a little fluffy red dress my mother had made for me. The soldier threw it in the pile. Then he took out a match and burned everything.

Eventually they separated the children from their parents to allow the soldiers more control over us. I worked at a child labor camp in the fields every day from sunrise to sunset. They told us we were the saviors of society because we were pure. Unlike the adults, we had not been tainted by foreign powers, greed, and capitalism. Every day in the camps they taught us how to use guns or knives or sticks. We were encouraged to be the eyes and ears of the Khmer Rouge. We were told to look for traitors and inform on anybody who looked, acted, or spoke against the Khmer Rouge whether they were older, younger, neighbors, aunts, fathers, or mothers. It was like a witch-hunt spread over the whole country. When you pointed your finger at someone it didn't matter if the allegations were true. If the soldiers believed them, the person was shot or bludgeoned to death.

Many executions were done out of sight. People just disappeared and you didn't say anything. You didn't know if they had died or were killed or working somewhere else. Disappearance mixed hope with horror. It was psychologically unbearable.

I was so afraid the Khmer Rouge would find out I was from the urban elite I just stopped talking. I always knew if they found out more about me they would kill me, so I really never believed their propaganda. But there were many children who did and some were more brutal than the soldiers. My survival really depended on a lot of luck. There were millions of land mines underground and every time I went looking for berries or animals I could have stepped on one. I was also very resourceful. I knew where to find food, how to keep secrets, and I was a good thief.

We were living in complete terror every day. Hunger and sadness were all around. My fourteen-year-old sister died from starvation. You rarely saw people smile. Laughter was so uncommon, if you heard it you would be shocked.

When I was about thirteen and going to school in Vermont I always had nightmares about being chased by people trying to kill me. Once I told some classmates about a dream in which I was having trouble cutting the throat of a man who was chasing me because I only had a butter knife and the edge wasn't sharp enough. They all stared at me and their jaws completely dropped open. That's when I realized they didn't have dreams like mine.

Today she is the spokesperson for the Campaign for a Landmine Free World, a program of the Vietnam Veterans of America Foundation (VVAF). VVAF cofounded the International Campaign to Ban Landmines, the recipient of the 1997 Nobel Peace Prize.

SILENCES

TOSHIO WHELCHEL

"I didn't want her to worry, so I lied."

His mother was Japanese and his father American. He was born in Japan in 1954.

My older brother was born in 1947. He's my half brother. He's full Japanese from my mother's first marriage. We moved from Japan in 1962 to Southern California. My brother dropped out of high school and was working in a Japanese restaurant in San Diego when he was drafted. I remember seeing him after basic training with his olive green uniform and shaved head. After a week or two at home, we drove him to the airport. Then he was gone for a year and a half. We didn't see him again until he was out of the service. That entire time he told us he was stationed at Fort Sill, Oklahoma, as a truck driver.

Well, about six years ago I began research on Japanese Americans who served in the Vietnam War. I knew that many of my brother's friends had been in the army so I called him up and said, "Look, I'm doing this reserach. It's really important. Who do you know who went to Vietnam?"

Out of nowhere he said, "Well, I went to Vietnam."

I said, "No you didn't. You didn't go to Vietnam. You were at Fort Sill."

He said, "No, I made that up."

I was floored. "What? We all believed you were at Fort Sill."

He said, "Well, Mom was alone. I didn't want her to worry, so I lied."

My initial reaction was, "You're bullshitting me."

He goes, "No, I was at Tan Son Nhut. I was involved in microwave radio interceptions."

I said, "Well, we have to talk. You have to tell me the story! I have to know. I need to know. You're my brother."

And he said, "No. I can't talk to you about it. I don't want to talk about it."

And that was it. Nothing more. He shut down. I know nothing about his time in Vietnam.

R. HUYNH

"Your real self was only for you."

A child during the French Indochina War, she was an adolescent during the American escalation. In 1968, at age nineteen, she moved to Paris where she still lives, a single woman with a warm smile framed by short, slightly graying hair. We meet when she is in the United States on business for her biotech company. Though quite outgoing herself, she offers some general advice to foreigners who want to learn about Vietnamese history and culture. "Vietnamese may look like they are not paying attention, may even appear cold, but they are very sentimental. Vietnamese express themselves more in words and poetry and metaphors than by physical gestures."

I lived in Saigon, so I was an urban girl. I went to French schools. We learned French geography and French history. We didn't learn anything about Vietnam. When I went home I used to look at myself in the mirror and cry because I was taking the history book and trying to identify myself with the French heroes. There was no resemblance at all.

What I found very disturbing is that Vietnamese people had this sense of inferiority. Maybe unconsciously many people thought that what the white people were bringing to Vietnam was better than what we had. As a child I was very unhappy when we switched from traditional kitchen utensils like brass wash basins to plastic stuff. And when the Americans came everyone wanted to taste what they had brought to Vietnam. We had the most tasteful coffee in the world and people were buying Nescafé on the black market. And it was expensive. I admit that I, too, was attracted to some American products, especially television. I enjoyed *Star Trek*, *The Addams Family*, and *Wild, Wild West*.

Our house was in a little street in the center of the city near an American headquarters. The Americans just blocked off our street on both sides with barbed wire. To get to our house we were searched by military police. It was like we were no longer in our street. It was their street. I remember one time I had a brown bag with oranges. Unfortunately the bag broke and the oranges fell out. All the Americans soldiers dropped to the ground because they thought the oranges were grenades.

There were always Vietnamese kids hanging out in front of the U.S. headquarters. Of course it was surrounded by barbed wire. Young American soldiers would be sitting behind the barbed wire eating hamburgers and ice cream. I still remember this man who tried to attract the kids with his hamburger. The kids were trying to reach over the fence. And when they were nearly about to grasp the food he would just snatch it away and laugh. The kids were all cut on the barbed wire. For me it was not fun.

But I don't want to generalize either because I had some very good American friends. From the age of fifteen to eighteen I had long discussions with Americans who were thirty or forty years old. I think they honestly did believe they were coming to save our country. I think they believed in the mission. But some did not have the faintest clue about Vietnam. I have always considered Americans very naive. I'm sorry to say that, but it is true. What they think they see is what they think it is. If they have been trained day and night to look at a picture and they are told that it is a cat, even if it does not really look like a cat, eventually they believe that it is a cat.

In those days you couldn't say much because it was too dangerous. So your real self was only for you. Your real feelings, your real understanding of what was going on, you kept to yourself. For me, it was the feeling that maybe it was not a good thing that the Americans were in my country. But you don't share it—it's too dangerous. You would not share it with anyone.

In the 1980s, when I was in my thirties, I met a Vietnamese lady in France with two children—a girl who was about twelve and a young boy. I would stay weekends with them because they were alone. One night I heard crying so I went to the living room and I saw the little girl.

I said, "Why are you crying?"

She said, "Because my mother and brother are asleep. They won't hear me. Now I can cry and they won't be sad. I must give courage to my mother and be an example to my little brother so I can't show my distress."

So I said, "But why are you crying?"

She said, "I miss my father." I asked more and learned that they had fled Vietnam by boat. They were attacked by pirates and her father was thrown into the sea. He swam for eight hours trying to catch up to the boat. Eventually he drowned. Her mother was raped by the pirates. The little girl watched all that.

In France, they managed to have a normal life. She knew where she stood, but she was not thinking of herself. She was thinking of her mother and her brother and she would be herself only in the night. So many years have gone by and I still remember that night. But they would never tell you. There are things that we keep for ourselves.

JAYNE STANCAVAGE

"I just want to know what happened."

She was born in 1969, the third of seven children, from Mount Carmel, Pennsylvania. Her father was a career navy enlisted man who was in and around Vietnam for so long his family doesn't know how many tours he served. He died in 1984 at age forty-eight. A Veterans Administration doctor told the family—"off the record"—that exposure to the chemical defoliant Agent Orange was a factor in Mr. Stancavage's death. The family took part in the class-action suit against Dow Chemical and other manufacturers of Agent Orange. The case was settled out of court in 1984 for $180 million and each family received an average of one thousand dollars.

"It's been fifteen years since my dad died and I still think of him every day. There's a very thin scab over the wound and if I poke at it, it's just going to completely consume me."

After my father died we got his military records and almost everything from 1965 to 1973 is missing or blacked out. All I know is that he was a radioman on a C-121 and part of what he did was called Project Jenny. Apparently they flew propaganda missions up North. He never really talked to my mom about Vietnam. He told her, "There are some things you're not supposed to know."

I was always happiest with my dad. Wherever he was, I wanted to be. When I was eight and going through First Holy Communion he left. He just left—took the car and left. This was a pattern that went on for four or five years. He would come back for a little bit and go immediately. From the time I was eight until he died he was haunted. There's no other way to explain it.

So my mom had to go to work in a shirt factory a few towns away. There were eight of us living on a single income. I remember being in sixth grade and going to student-teacher conferences for my brothers and sisters because my mother had to work.

The hardest part was just waiting for my dad to come back. He would be gone for months and then he would call to say, "I'll be home next week." And from the time he called, every night I would fall asleep in the parlor. And by the time he was due back I would sleep right in front of the door so he would have to pick me up when he came in. The second he came through the door, I wanted to be there. I didn't want to miss a minute.

He tried to stay, but he would just hide on the back porch because he was afraid that they were going to get him. He never explained who "they" were. He said once, "the little people." I'd never seen him afraid of anything before. He was just a shadow of himself. It was as though someone else had replaced my dad, as though a cog wasn't catching right in a chain, just slipping and slipping. It was a mental thing but eventually it got to be physical. He had several massive coronaries and the cancer started spreading. At one point when he was in the vets' hospital his doctor was a Vietnamese American. My dad was just terrified by this. He would mutter things like, "They're coming to get me, they're here, they're here." He tried to get out of the bed to hide.

I just want to know what happened, what really happened, and feel like it isn't going to happen again so blindly. The government figures their responsibility ends when they hand you the folded-up flag.

SOUVENIRS

HOANG VAN THIET

"They bought Zippos as a kind of birth certificate."

You can buy souvenirs of the American War in most Vietnamese cities, especially in the South. There are GI dog tags, unit patches, medals, compasses, and, above all, Zippo lighters. Virtually all of these souvenirs have been manufactured since the war and many are artificially aged to look authentic. Vietnamese entrepreneurs have been turning out thousands of Zippo replicas complete with some of the wartime aphorisms GIs had engraved on their lighters. A sample: "Yeah though I walk through the valley of death, I fear no evil because I'm the meanest motherfucker in the valley"; "When I die I know I'm going to heaven because I have spent my time in hell"; "For those who fought for it, freedom has a taste the protected will never know"; "We are the unwilling led by the unqualified doing the unnecessary for the ungrateful"; "The object of war is not to give your life for your country but to make the other bastard give his."

On Le Cong Kieu Street in Ho Chi Minh City, Thiet does a small business in Zippos, but prefers to sell ceramics. During the war he was a drill instructor in the South Vietnamese army. He is fifty-seven.

I sell Zippos mostly to American tourists, but the Australians, French, and Japanese also like them a lot. There's a big market for these souvenirs. Of course, if they were all authentic there would be none to sell! After all, the war's been over for nearly thirty years. Think about it. How could we find so many real ones now? It's impossible. Actually, there are still a few original Zippos but they're so beaten up they have to be completely reconditioned. The best imitations are close enough to the original that only a professional can see the difference. Most tourists can't possibly tell the difference.

Look here. This one's a fake, this one's a fake—these are all fakes. Here's one I've had since 1976. It's a fake, too, but there are very few fakes as good as this one. For the best ones you can charge fifteen or twenty dollars. I can get most of them for less than a dollar. Here, look. You see this Zippo logo on the bottom? It's too gaudy. The original was very simple. Now, look at this one. I've kept this one since 1968. You see the difference in the hinges? You have to pay attention to what the original Zippo looked like. The engraving is irrelevant. It's easy to copy and even some of the originals had spelling mistakes.

Of course, right after the war there wasn't much of a market for Zippos. If you threw them out in the street people might not pick them up. Some of the first customers were children of American GIs and Vietnamese women. Most of them didn't know their father's name and had no documents so they bought Zippos as a kind of birth certificate. They would say it came from their father, and hoped that would be evidence enough to help them leave.

In the last decade it has become a very big business with tourists and it's very competitive. There are many workshops making them. I could get you as many as you want—fifty, a hundred, whatever. Some foreigners are buying up large quantities and reselling them in France and the United States. I think some of them were people who bought them as souvenirs and eventually realized that they were all fake, but came back to buy more believing they could sell them in their own countries as real. I have no idea why people buy them.

TAPS

> "Multiply the above by scores, aye hundreds . . . light it with every lurid passion . . . the lion's lapping thirst for blood—the passionate, boiling volcanoes of human revenge for comrades, brothers slain—with the light of burning farms, and heaps of smutting, smoldering black embers—and in the human heart everywhere black, worse embers—and you have an inkling of this war."
>
> Walt Whitman, *Specimen Days*

Almost three decades separate us from the day the last helicopter rose from the roof of the U.S. Embassy in Saigon. Inside, an ambassador sat with a folded flag, looking down on the land where U.S. military aircraft had been as common a sight as native birds. The American presence in Vietnam, once so colossal, had dwindled to a single spot in the morning sky. "The memories are mercifully dimmer now," journalist Gloria Emerson commented. Yet, as I listened to the people who told me the stories that are this book, I often felt as if their histories were just outside, pounding on the door, pouring through every crack, as vivid and present as ever. If these were the faded memories, we can only imagine what they might have been when fresh. Some had perhaps been literally unspeakable, requiring decades to form words the rest of us might hope to grasp. Some had simply been there all along, lying dormant, waiting for a moment when they could be shared. Countless others are lost forever.

These voices have called forth a time when millions of people in several countries felt war had become a near-permanent condition; when every day, for more than a decade, parents said good-bye to children who would never return; when teenagers learned to kill as a patriotic duty; when people of all ages crouched in holes and tunnels as bombs and artillery exploded above or around them; when soldiers drenched in sweat and beyond exhaustion searched for an enemy, families argued about the nature of the war and how to respond to it, toxic chemicals fell like rain from the skies, peasants saw their homes go up in flames, citizens stood in defiant opposition to their government, prisoners endured unimaginable forms of interrogation and torture, commanders moved troops on military maps, doctors and nurses treated bodies full of metal, leaders insisted the fighting must continue, and reporters filed dispatches about battles no one would remember but the survivors.

In the United States over the past quarter century only a surprisingly narrow range of Vietnam War experiences have gained widespread attention. American popular culture offers us an oddly diminished view of a vast history. A war that might have inspired epic films and novels with scores of characters from all sides and ranks, spanning decades and continents, has typically been reduced to stories about small units of American infantrymen fighting a silent, nearly invisible enemy at a single moment in time. Not only are the Vietnamese routinely left out, but most of the Americans who made Vietnam the contentious experience it was are also missing. We rarely encounter compelling representations of presidents making war policy, of antiwar activists challenging official claims, of generals in their command posts, of ordinary citizens drawn into wrenching debates about the war. Even the Vietnam Wall, our most moving and well-known symbol of the war, does not evoke the full range and dimension of the war's costs and consequences.

Why is so much omitted from our most familiar Vietnam war stories? The very size, length, and complexity of the war's history is a partial explanation, but the harder truth is that we have simply avoided a full public reckoning, the kind that would invariably confront us with unwelcome questions about American intervention in Vietnam—why it happened, why it was so vehemently opposed, what it did to the Vietnamese, Laotians, and Cambodians, what it actually did to us, and who was responsible. Instead we prefer stories that make us feel better about our nation and ourselves. Even when we believe we have confronted the war's most horrible realities, we often have been doing little more than licking our own wounds. For example, we tend to speak mournfully of the war as an "American tragedy," as if it were a fated imposition beyond our control that afflicted only us.

In Vietnam public memory has its own set of omissions and evasions. Officially, the war is memorialized as the culmination of a historic mission for national independence and unification. Yet the bitter internal divisions that were so much a part of those years, and still remain, are often dismissed as minor or irrelevant. Nor has there been a full acknowledgment of the widespread disillusionment with the victorious postwar government.

It may be a tribute to human nature that we seek some redemption from the past, that we look for meaning and hope amid the "black embers" of even the longest and costliest of wars. It is not a tribute, however, when the impulse leads us to avert our eyes from the war's destruction or to evade its most troubling moral and political implications. Remarkably, most of the people interviewed for this book struggled not only to describe their experiences candidly and directly but also to engage the ethical dilemmas the war brought into their lives.

Among the most heartening of these accounts are those offered by people who have sought to bridge the gulf separating former adversaries, not to deny the bitter history that divided our nations so deeply, but to establish a basis for a more complete understanding of our common past and the possibility of genuine reconciliation. They offer us no easy endings or simple sets of lessons learned, but rather unflinching visions of how entwined our histories have been and how dependent we are on each other if we truly care to explore them further.

LEROY V. QUINTANA

"Old geezers . . . playing taps on a tape recorder."

The tall, bearded, barrel-chested man grew up in Raton, a small town in northern New Mexico. "In the 1950s older veterans in the neighborhood were heroes. Every time they passed by, people called out their names."

In Vietnam he was a member of a Long-Range Reconnaissance Patrol in the 101st Airborne. They went into the jungle in small teams of five or six men. Their job was to report on enemy troop movements, not to initiate firefights. He takes off his glasses and rubs his eyes.

We would go for days without talking. Just signs and signals. If you pretended to break a stick that meant you wanted to take a break. If you pulled your eyes into slants it meant you had seen some Viet Cong. You lived in constant nervousness. At least in a regular line company you could fight back. It was scary because it was real quiet and all of a sudden something would pop out. One day we were sitting around and all of a sudden there was a great crashing and thrashing in the trees. I thought, Lord, Almighty. It was this big troop of baboons—huge baboons—going through the trees with their babies. It was beautiful to see, but so damn frightening.

Another time, during a monsoon, we'd been out for a week and it was just raining and raining and raining. Finally the rain let up and I got careless. I stood up and stretched. I turned my head and there was a file of Viet Cong coming toward us. I hit the deck. Everybody covered up in the brush. I was shivering in the mud and this is how bad it was: I wanted my mom. I really did.

It was so frightening. They kept filing by and filing by. My teeth were chattering. When it's really, really down, everything becomes very primal. When the choppers came for us some guys were crying just out of relief that we had gotten out of that situation.

It was scary, but I think recon saved my life in some ways. I didn't have to burn hootches or do away with villagers. Our mission was totally different. So I don't have to live with that guilt. I just met a guy who was in the infantry. He shot some people in the dark and they turned out to be children. He's been carrying that for thirty years. Even his wife doesn't know. How do you live with those kinds of secrets?

I haven't really talked that much to my wife about Vietnam. But a strange thing happened the other day. We were watching a report on television about how there aren't enough funds to provide for proper military burials anymore. Instead of a military honor guard, you have these old geezers from the American Legion going out there and playing taps on a tape recorder. I started crying, man. It might not mean anything to somebody else. So what if you don't get a military burial? But when my wife saw my reaction it was like something changed inside of her. I think she really began to understand.

In the years since Vietnam, he has published five books of poetry, including The History of Home, *which won the American Book Award.*

WILLIAM WESTMORELAND

"I was leading an unpopular war."

He was the commander of U.S. forces in Vietnam from 1964 to 1968. Today many young people do not recognize his name, but in the mid-1960s perhaps only President Johnson and Robert McNamara were more fully identified with the war by the American public.

He lives with his wife, Kitsy, in a retirement community in Charleston, South Carolina. Even at eighty-five, in casual civilian clothes, he is instantly recognizable—still that upright carriage, that strong jaw, that attention to grooming. He concedes, however, that his mind and memory have declined. These are, perhaps, his final public reflections on the war.

We sit in the corner of the living room around a small table designed for some kind of game neither of us can identify.

In my mind, Vietnam is ancient history and I've kind of divorced myself from it over the years. It was only one chapter in my history. See, I fought three wars. I'm an elderly man and I've lived all over the world. I've had some very interesting experiences. But I'm out to pasture now and I do what I damn please. I don't report to anybody except my wife.

It was a difficult situation. The Vietnamese leadership was weak. But I didn't make national policy, I carried it out. I was a professional soldier. I was quite aware that Vietnam was not necessarily a popular war because our national interest was not at stake. When we started taking casualties, which was inevitable, the American people began to wonder if it was worth the effort.

I got a lot of abuse on campuses and it never bothered me. But it's been tough on the family, particularly when I was leading an unpopular war, the most unpopular war we've ever gotten involved in. There was a bit of abuse of my children by antiwar groups on campus. It concerned me, but they adjusted themselves very nicely. I'm proud of the way they handled themselves. They were always loyal to me.

I fought in three wars. I played a role in history, as many others did in the military service. Being a soldier is a tough life, and it's a dangerous life. But after it's all over with, I think there's a certain amount of pride and satisfaction that you served your country. We didn't make the policies, we carried them out.

Of course the Vietnam War was a controversial war. Many in the American public thought that our participation was idealistic, but not necessarily in the national interest. I think there's some merit to that. It became very unpopular on the campuses of the country. Our national security was not in jeopardy and therefore the American public was not totally with it as they were in World War II. So it was somewhat difficult.

THAI DAO

"The first time I ever encountered the Vietnam War was in Hollywood movies."

He left Vietnam as a baby in 1975. Now he lives with his grandmother and divorced father in Westminster, California—"Little Saigon"—while finishing a degree at Irvine Valley College. In the summer of 1999, within a mile or two of his house, the Vietnamese owner of a video store displayed a portrait of Ho Chi Minh and the flag of the Socialist Republic of Vietnam. Many Vietnamese Americans were appalled by this public reminder, and apparent celebration, of the Communist government they had fought. For weeks, thousands gathered in the street outside the video store to protest.

I was pretty angry about the whole thing. I thought everyone was wrong. The guy who hung up the Ho Chi Minh picture is an idiot. To do something like that in a highly patriotic Vietnamese community is just asking for trouble. Of course it's going to cause outrage. But the Vietnamese community's reaction—well, they don't understand that this is America, it's a free country. That guy can be a total idiot, but he has the right to do what he wants. I heard Vietnamese people call up radio shows and demand that the police come and take down the portrait and the flag. The police can't do that. The protests got a little extreme and in some cases violence did break out.

But the American reaction was wrong as well. They lumped everyone into a single category, saying things like, "I just can't understand why 'these people' are protesting and causing so much trouble." The feelings of the demonstrators weren't getting any support from the American community and they had just as much right to protest as that guy had a right to hang Ho Chi Minh's picture. I may not agree with their views, but I can totally understand them because if I walk outside just about anyone older than me can name off family members or friends who died in the Vietnam War. And that's aside from the fact that they had to move from their home country to here, which is traumatic enough.

The only good thing about the whole video store event was the way it came to an end. The police couldn't nail the guy for putting up a picture, but they had to do something to resolve the issue because there was a risk of violence. What they ended up getting him for was video piracy. They couldn't get him head-on so, in the American way, they got him through a technicality. It's actually a good representation of how the American system can work.

The first time I ever encountered the Vietnam War was in Hollywood movies—*Platoon, Apocalypse Now, Hamburger Hill.* It was kind of a sad way for me to get a perspective of my own heritage. Hollywood always portrays the war as an American-Vietnamese War, so at a small age I wondered, was I the enemy? You would never know from those movies that there was a civil war between Vietnamese.

I was embarrassed by the Vietnamese images they portrayed. I mean, if you're going to show the hardship of the war why not show a Vietnamese family whose youngest son got blown away for the same reasons that American GIs did? And show how Vietnamese families were broken up, and how Vietnamese fought against each other. Show pictures of people begging for refuge away from the war.

They never showed that. When I was a kid there was this whole pro-American thing, like, "Yeah, remember Nam, remember Nam," and that whole army attitude of, "Let's kill 'em all and let God sort 'em out later." That's what I think sprang out of all the Hollywood portrayals of Vietnam.

When I think about Ho Chi Minh or Communism I don't look at them with any hate. Communism is just a different political ideal. I think both sides were fighting for what they perceived as the betterment of the country. But man takes those ideals and either distorts them or becomes blind to them and the only thing left is just shooting the person in front of you.

With that, Thai's grandmother comes into the room and says, "Excuse me, if you want to know about the Vietnam War you are asking the wrong person. He left Vietnam when he was one year old. He doesn't know anything. All my family was in the army. One of my sons was missing in action and my husband was killed by the Communists. He died when he was forty-two in 1960."

Thai pats the seat next to him. "Come sit here, Grandma. You have a lot to say." She smiles, but continues standing in the doorway. Addressing her grandson, she continues, "What you say is not right because you are here. You have enough food. You have a car. You've never lost anything. If you were in my country now you would sweep the street. Children of Communists go to university, but you could not." She leaves the room and Thai says: "As you can see, with my grandmother it's a very passionate topic. We totally disagree. My grandmother's feeling is that the Communists have almost succeeded with our generation because people like me no longer hate Communists. In her life they were surrounded by what they perceived as the evils perpetrated by the Communists. My grandmother's husband was bludgeoned right in front of her. And one of her sons was lost. It's all perceived as the fault of the Communists. To me, it's not Communism that was the root of all evil. It was the war."

TIM O'BRIEN

"You can't talk with people you demonize."

After graduating from college in 1968, he was drafted and sent to Vietnam as an infantryman in the Americal Division. His company often patrolled the coastal lowlands of Quang Ngai Province south of Danang where, a year earlier, the My Lai massacre had occurred. In Vietnam he wrote a few short pieces about his experience that became the basis of his first book, If I Die in a Combat Zone, Box Me Up and Ship Me Home *(1973). Perhaps the most acclaimed American writer of Vietnam War–related fiction, he has also written* Going After Cacciato *(1978),* The Things They Carried *(1990), and* In the Lake of the Woods *(1994). He speaks softly, in a deliberate and unassuming cadence that hints at the small Minnesota town where he grew up.*

I've never thought of myself as a war writer. Ultimately I'm trying to speak to everybody about the heart under pressure, the incredible spiritual pressure of seeking the right thing to do under difficult circumstances. I don't write about maneuvers and bombing and how guns work. I don't explain the mechanics of ambushes and patrols. These things bore me. They bored me even in Vietnam. I was too overwhelmed by the feeling of doing something really wrong and evil to be interested in the military nuts and bolts of it all. I was also too terrified.

It was just a blur of going from village to village through paddies with no sense of destination, or mission, or purpose. You'd just wake up and go to a village, search it, and leave. Somebody might die or not, and you'd come back a month later to the same damn village and do it again. It was like going in circles and not really achieving anything. You weren't winning hearts and minds and you weren't winning ground. You didn't know who to shoot unless they were shooting at you. The enemy seemed to be everywhere and nowhere.

The fundamental experience was like being in Wonderland. The old anchors of reality were gone. I've just finished something I've never written about before. A guy had been shot, a dying American guy, and he kept mumbling the same word over and over. Most often people would say stuff like "Momma" or "Daddy." They'd go way back into primitive childhood stuff. This guy kept saying the word *ever* over and over. Why that word? Maybe I just didn't hear him right. Maybe it was *never.* But it sounded like *ever* and he kept saying it over and over. Those are the kind of memories you're never going to wholly understand. We knew very few answers to anything in Vietnam and thirty years later you find the ambiguities waking you up in the middle of the night. You see that guy's chest bubbling and blood coming out of his mouth and hear that word *ever* just over and over.

I was in Quang Ngai Province, out in the middle of this bombed-out mess. The whole province was wasted. The My Lai massacre was just part of it. By the time I got there in 1969 our bombing and artillery fire had destroyed basically ninety percent of the dwellings. The villages were sometimes almost deserted. There had been a pacification program in which people had been moved out of their hamlets into refugee camps. Many villages only had about twenty or thirty people still there, mostly old people and VC. We were really hated. It was just so patent. You could see the hostility in everybody's eyes.

The My Lai story broke when I was over there. I just remember everybody saying, "Ah, number one, it didn't happen, it couldn't have happened, and number two, even if it did happen they deserved it. They're all the enemy. You know, babies and old women, they're all VC and deserve to die." It disgusted me back then and it still makes me angry and very, very sad. Maybe it's a universal trait to look away from your own ugliness. We Americans find it easy to be self-congratulatory about our country, but there's not a lot to congratulate ourselves about with regard to Vietnam.

Almost everybody I know who got out of the war somehow and stayed in the country says the same thing, almost to a man. They say, "Oh my God, I missed the great experience of my generation." They don't talk much about having done the right or wrong thing, they just seem to feel they missed out on something. I always say, "Well, you missed out on having your legs blown off and you missed out on having nightmares the rest of your life. You missed out on horror." They nod, but I can see they're thinking something else to themselves. They have a hard time articulating what it is they missed but it has to do with the American idea of manhood, with adventure, and with a gnawing sense of guilt. There's a guilt that not just Vietnam veterans, but the whole country carries around. I certainly don't relieve them of their guilt. I've got my own.

I've gone to Canada for readings and met people who left the country during the war. A lot of these guys are embarrassed by it. They're asking the question today that they asked back then—did I do this because I was opposed to the war or because I didn't want to die? Was it cowardice or conscience? And that plagues all of us—those who went to Vietnam and those who went to Canada and those who just got out of it through legal means. It plagues everyone because no one wants to die, even in a right war. But there were a lot of us in Vietnam who didn't want to be there and many of us didn't have the courage to do what the resisters did. It took a lot of courage to cross the border and leave behind your family and your hometown and your girlfriend. What looked like an act of cowardice to the Reagan-Dole Republicans took a lot more courage than I had. Even though I was opposed to the war, I still couldn't find the courage to walk away. When I was at Fort Lewis before going to Vietnam I planned to go to Vancouver. I came as close as you can come without actually doing it. I ended up going to Vietnam just to protect my reputation and sense of self-esteem, but the guys who went to Canada somehow were able to find the moral courage to make a choice they knew was gonna dog them the rest of their lives.

It stuns me how ignorant younger people are about the war, not just in high school, but college. They kind of know the music and they've seen *Apocalypse Now* or one of the other movies, but the actual issues that were at stake back then and remain at stake now, they know very little about. I don't think it's their fault so much as the teachers' or the curriculum. It's said to me all the time that school terms run out and they teach Vietnam in a day. And it's a lengthy, complex history! You have to go way back to really understand it.

I've had kids say to me, "*The Things They Carried* is the only book I've ever read." I say, "You mean about Vietnam?" And they say, "No, I mean the first book I've read all the way through." It makes me feel pretty shitty because to understand my books you do have to know at least some of the history. Otherwise, what's all this doubt about that these characters have and what are they running away from and why do they think this is so horrible? Similarly, *The Red Badge of Courage* would not be as rich and comprehensible if a reader knew nothing about the Civil War. I just took it as a given in writing these books that people would know something of the history.

"The few times I've spoken since September 11 I've really pissed people off. In many ways, the events subsequent to September 11 remind me of the early stages of the Vietnam War. If you spoke up against our military response in Afghanistan, you were a Commie and a peacenik and a fag and that's a little how I felt after September 11. It's just so hard to speak up now. I'll give all the disclaimers, that I'm not for a moment condoning the attack on the World Trade Center and how it was obviously an evil act, but I also talk about how we always demonize our enemies as barbarians and madmen, as evil, pure and simple. Watching bin Laden and Bush is like watching two six-year-olds. One says you're an infidel, the other says you're evil. But that's not gonna get you anywhere. It forecloses the possibility of discussion. You can't talk with people you demonize. I say that and they're all over me."

HUU NGOC

"We no longer hate the Americans."

At eighty-one, he easily climbs two flights of stairs to a meeting room at the offices of The Gioi publishers in Hanoi. As a young assistant serves green tea, the elderly writer leans forward with his hands on his knees. His eyesight is failing, but not his mind. An interpreter is unnecessary since English is among the five languages he speaks fluently. "In Vietnam I am nicknamed the 'importer-exporter of culture' because I write books to present Vietnamese culture abroad and to introduce foreign cultures to Vietnam."

At the end of the Second World War, we had much sympathy for America and our dream was that the United States would recognize Vietnamese independence. But our sympathy disappeared day after day when the U.S. helped the

French retake Indochina. We began to learn to hate the Americans, particularly after 1954 when they supported Ngo Dinh Diem.

During the American bombing in the 1960s my three children were evacuated to a village across the Red River about thirty kilometers from Hanoi. My eldest child, a daughter, was twelve years old when she was evacuated. In one letter she wrote something like, "The Americans bombed a neighboring village. We saw fire and thought they had bombed Hanoi. We all wondered if our parents had been hit or not. Did you live or not? We hate the Americans."

As a journalist I could sometimes travel from Hanoi to the village where my children were living. It was harder for my wife who was in the jungle studying to become a doctor. But one day we were both able to meet the children in their village and have a family reunion. Since we had so little to eat during the war, I brought a rice cake as a special treat. It was no bigger than this. [He makes a fist.] I handed the cake to my wife. She passed it on to my daughter. My daughter gave it to her younger brother. The elder brother gave it to the youngest. Finally, the youngest gave it back to me. We were all very hungry, but no one wanted to take the first bite. The war had cemented us together. Even children of twelve, ten, and eight years old refused to think of themselves first.

Now I think the ditch between the Vietnamese and the Americans is filling up. The feeling of hatred is weaker and weaker. One reason is that throughout history the Vietnamese have learned to survive living with a giant neighbor, China. The first Vietnamese state was conquered by China in the second century before Christ, and they dominated us for the next twelve hundred years. Every time we repelled the Chinese invaders we immediately tried to shake hands with them. We gave them gold and sometimes land. At the same time we tried to learn from them what might enrich our own culture. So there was always a double movement of repulsion and attraction. If you want to learn something from your former enemies you can't hate them. That is the policy of the weak.

Another reason we no longer hate the Americans is due to Ho Chi Minh's teaching. By distinguishing between the people of the United States and those responsible for the war, Ho prevented us from becoming chauvinists—ultranationalists. Of course the Vietnamese suffered, of course they wept for their dead, but in general they made a distinction between the common American soldiers and their commanders.

For most Americans I'm afraid Vietnam still has the face of war. To build a cultural bridge we must show them the spirit and soul of Vietnam, the face of peace. I think the strength of Vietnamese culture is that we stress the spiritual side of life and live for other people. But that's also our weakness. If you are too collectivist-minded you can't develop your individuality. In America, the materialistic side of life tends to prevail and people are governed by individualism. So we have to marry the best of both cultures. By chance I have just read this. [He holds up a copy of *Tuesdays with Morrie,* the best-selling book about the visits of a former student with his dying professor.] In this book the author stresses the importance of compassion, of giving more than receiving. It's a book that a Vietnamese would have been proud to write.

WAYNE KARLIN

"The roof that hasn't been built."

A novelist and teacher, he is also the coeditor of The Other Side of Heaven, *an anthology that brings together the writing of veterans from all sides of the war. In 1966 and '67 he flew as a marine helicopter crewman in Quang Tri and Quang Nam Provinces. He returned to Vietnam for the first time in 1994.*

There's a town called Hong Gai on Ha Long Bay. On Christmas Eve 1994, I went there and met a bunch of Vietnamese writers, all veterans. We introduced ourselves by asking, "Where were you in the war and when were you there?" It was as if we were trying to find out if we had ever tried to kill each other. We started a kind of drinking game, going around a circle and each vet had to drain a glass of beer. I was sitting next to a guy who had been a mortarman in Quang Tri. We'd gone around a few times and when it was his turn again he appeared really upset. He couldn't speak any English so he just looked at me, tapped his head, pointed at the beer, and said, "Quang Tri, Quang Tri." I understood immediately why he couldn't drink any more. It was awakening stuff he just didn't want to wake. So I took the beer and drank it for him. It was like sharing whatever he was feeling, taking it into myself for him. That was the unspoken power of the moment for both of us.

Eventually one of them said, "Okay, we're going up to the cathedral." There's a Catholic cathedral on top of a nearby mountain that was bombed in the war. It's nothing but a shell. On Christmas Eve everybody in town has this procession up to the cathedral even though very few are Christian. They shoot off firecrackers and at the top they light candles and place them on an altar.

I was fairly drunk. There were firecrackers going off all over the place. We're in this huge crowd. It's very dark and I start feeling all these people pressing in on me. I'm the only Westerner there. Running through my mind are these old images of American POWs being marched through Hanoi during the war and crowds of people screaming at them. I really start to lose it. Suddenly the guy from Quang Tri and a vet on my other side just grab my arms and hold onto my hands. The others form a protective circle around me. They can see what's going on, they've been in the war too. So we just go up that hill arm-in-arm.

I was remembering a story one of them had told earlier about being on an antiaircraft crew that shot down an American plane. Maybe that's why that POW image came to mind. He'd been in the party that went out in a boat to pull the pilot out of the water when people in the area just wanted to kill him. That's what it felt like—like they were pulling me out of the water.

The cathedral was completely wrecked. Its whole roof was missing. It seemed like a physical representation of everything about the war that hasn't been finished yet. There are so many things that aren't finished, the hard truths and damage that need to be faced and acknowledged, the humanity we couldn't see and still need to see. That's the roof that hasn't been built. On the other hand, being with those guys who just pulled me up the hill, I felt like that's what it takes to start.

DUONG TUONG

"Because love is stronger than enmity."

"I am no good at answering questions." He is a writer, translator, and critic. During the American War he worked for the Vietnam News Agency and the Commission to Investigate U.S. War Crimes. His responses are brief and epigrammatic. Asked for his feelings about Ho Chi Minh, he says, "They are not very different from any Vietnamese I think—love and respect." This is followed by almost an entire minute of silence. "I think in his late years he lost control of things. I think we missed some opportunities to make peace." He does not elaborate.

As for his former enemy, "I think the United States was supporting a regime they thought was better than Communism. But, in fact, it was a rotten one. The American soldiers who were sent to Vietnam were victims too. The American government lied to them. They didn't know what they were fighting for."

In 1995, he visited the United States and went to the Vietnam Veterans Memorial. He sat down, wrote a poem in English, and left it at the base of the Wall.

At the Vietnam Wall

because i never knew you
nor did you me
i come

because you left behind mother, father,
and betrothed
and i wife and children
i come

because love is stronger than enmity
and can bridge oceans
i come

because you never return
and i do
i come

ACKNOWLEDGMENTS

All writers need help, but oral historians accumulate truly staggering debts. I depended on the generosity of hundreds of people, beginning with those who agreed to be interviewed. Working with so many fascinating collaborators was a privilege and a pleasure. They taught me much more than I could ever hope to include in a single book. Among my hardest tasks was cutting almost two-thirds of the 350 interviews I conducted. Many accounts were excluded simply to keep the book at a readable length, not because I regarded them as any less valuable than those included. All who talked with me about their lives have my deepest gratitude.

On my first of four trips to Vietnam, I had the great fortune to travel with David Thomas, a Vietnam War veteran who founded and directs the Indochina Arts Partnership. A gifted and generous cultural ambassador, David offered me invaluable introductions and advice based on fifteen years of work in Vietnam. I also received vital help from Lady Borton. Lady has devoted much of her life to service in Vietnam, first in 1969 as a volunteer for the American Friends Service Committee and more recently as director of Quaker Field Services in Hanoi. She gave me much sage counsel and facilitated my relationship with the Vietnam-America Friendship Association (Viet-My), the organization that sponsored my work in Vietnam.

Viet-My arranged dozens of interviews, provided translators, hotels, and transportation, and in many other ways made my time in Vietnam productive and enjoyable. I am especially indebted to Hoang Cong Thuy and Nguyen Van Huynh, stimulating colleagues, congenial hosts, and now friends. Thuy did most of the translating I required in Vietnam along with Dao Ngoc Ninh, whose interest in Vietnamese military history was a great help in many interviews. I also received valuable assistance from Viet-My's Phan Thi Quynh, Luu Van Minh, Ha Van An, and Nguyen Thi My Hoa. For their companionship and support, thanks go as well to Vietnamese friends Ho Le Dzung, Ho Anh Thai, Nguyen Thi Phuong Duyen, Nguyen Tran Ha, and Le Tuan Tien.

In the United States, Dung Ngoc Duong, a superb linguist and scholar, did the final, written translations of my Vietnamese interviews. His insight and wit during the many days we worked together were a constant source of revelation and delight.

At the William Joiner Center for the Study of War and Social Consequences at the University of Massachusetts, Boston, director Kevin Bowen and his colleague, Nguyen Ba Chung, patiently responded to many inquiries and were always supportive. Chung also graciously served as translator for a key last-minute interview.

Jim Blight of Brown University extended a remarkably generous invitation to attend a conference on the war at the White Oak Conference Center in 1999 where participants included Robert McNamara and former Vietnamese diplomats.

My travels required many nights in hotel rooms, but along the way I received food, housing, and encouragement from many friends and relatives, including Bert Allen, Steve Baumann, Amy Bloom, Alex Bloom, Kevin and Moira Craw, Mike and Sharon Craw, George Evans, Steve Foell, Nancy Garrity, Allison Kempe, Peter Kuznick, Steve and Anne Lynch, Dugan Mahoney, Martha Martin, Martha Newcomb, De Pham, and Peter Vu.

Virtually everyone I talked with made valuable suggestions of people to interview. Particular thanks to a few important intermediaries—David Addlestone, Paul Baumann, Kevin Buckley, Greg Burham, Susan Faludi, Jim Fisher, Joe Galloway, Tom Geoghegan, Mark Godfrey, Bill Grace, Wayne Karlin, Jack Langguth, Nguyen Qui Duc, Jim Peck, Tran Tuong Nhu, Bob Whitt, Elizabeth Wood, and Jack Wright.

I am deeply indebted to the many scholars, journalists, novelists, and poets who have created such a rich literature of the war. Several of their personal accounts are included in this book. I cannot list all the other writers who have informed my work, but various works by the following have been especially important in the preparation of this book: Bao Ninh, Elizabeth Becker, Larry Berman, Kai Bird, Lady Borton, Robert Brigham, Robert Olen Butler, Noam Chomsky, William Duiker, Duong Van Mai Elliott, Larry Engelmann, Duong Thu Huong, Paul Hendrickson, Bernard Fall, Frances Fitzgerald, Bruce Franklin, Lloyd Gardner, James William Gibson, Graham Greene, David Halberstam, Daniel Hallin, Le Ly Hayslip, Michael Herr, George Herring, Seymour Hersh, David Hunt, Arnold Isaacs, George Kahin, Stanley Karnow, Jeffrey Kimball, Le Luu, Fredrik Logevall, David Marr, Bobbie Ann Mason, Edwin Moise, Andrew Lam, John Prados, William Prochnau, Neil Sheehan, Ronald Spector, Sandra Taylor, Karen Turner, William Turley, Roger Warner, Bruce Weigl, and Marilyn Young.

Kana Dower expertly transcribed scores of interviews, saving me countless hours and allowing me the freedom to continue interviewing. Toward the end, Nick Turse came to my aid with some timely fact checking.

My agent, Flip Brophy, knew better than I how massive this project would become and made it possible for me to complete it without facing financial disaster.

From the outset, I had extraordinary editors. It was Wendy Wolf, executive editor at Viking, who initially proposed the idea of writing a comprehensive oral history of the Vietnam War and I am forever grateful to her for believing that I could produce a work worthy of her vision. Without her inspiration, and wise, keen-eyed editorial advice, this book simply would not exist. My thanks also go to Viking copy editor Faren Bachelis and production editor Sharon L. Gonzalez for ably transforming the manuscript into a finished book, and to Jeffrey Ward for designing the maps.

Tom Engelhardt, my primary editor and good friend, fully deserves his reputation as one of the world's great editors. In the presence of his demanding generosity, probing intellect, and painstaking attention to questions large and small, I could not help doing other than my best. Above all, Tom has the rare ability to immerse himself in an author's work without striving to make it his own.

A few close friends warrant special thanks: Barry O'Connell, my greatest teacher, who is still a mainspring of inspiration for all my work; Clark Dougan, my closest colleague, whose acute judgment I have relied upon for this and many other projects; Fred Marchant, longtime confidant, whose insight and support I have never adequately acknowledged; Gloria Emerson, the godmother of this book, who tells me what to do and finds a way to love me when I don't; and Alex Green, John Foran, and Chris Keller, old friends who were there at the beginning and remain with me always.

My final and most important acknowledgments are to my family. Meri, my wife, has endured repeated absences, some of them during the most trying times, while carrying on with her own demanding career in fire safety education. Through it all, she sustained me with her love and steadfast belief in the importance of this book. Our children, Nathan and Henry, tolerated it all with their usual good cheer and, in the interim, developed into strong and loving young men. All three fueled my efforts more than they know or I can express.

Karen Baumann, my sister and first literary adviser, was, as always, an important provider of encouragement and welcome comic relief. Our father, a marine dive bomber in World War II, rarely talked about his war, but made clear long before his death in 1990 that curiosity about other lives could be the basis of a worthy career. My mother has always been endlessly supportive, but I am only now, in middle age, fully aware of just how much her love and artistry have inspired my own work. I dedicate this book to her.

INDEX